T0190329

Lecture Notes in Computer Science　　10902

Commenced Publication in 1973
Founding and Former Series Editors:
Gerhard Goos, Juris Hartmanis, and Jan van Leeuwen

More information about this series at http://www.springer.com/series/7409

Masaaki Kurosu (Ed.)

Human-Computer Interaction

Interaction in Context

20th International Conference, HCI International 2018
Las Vegas, NV, USA, July 15–20, 2018
Proceedings, Part II

 Springer

Editor
Masaaki Kurosu
The Open University of Japan
Chiba
Japan

ISSN 0302-9743   ISSN 1611-3349   (electronic)
Lecture Notes in Computer Science
ISBN 978-3-319-91243-1   ISBN 978-3-319-91244-8   (eBook)
https://doi.org/10.1007/978-3-319-91244-8

Library of Congress Control Number: 2018942338

LNCS Sublibrary: SL3 – Information Systems and Applications, incl. Internet/Web, and HCI

Printed on acid-free paper

This Springer imprint is published by the registered company Springer International Publishing AG
part of Springer Nature
The registered company address is: Gewerbestrasse 11, 6330 Cham, Switzerland

Foreword

The 20th International Conference on Human-Computer Interaction, HCI International 2018, was held in Las Vegas, NV, USA, during July 15–20, 2018. The event incorporated the 14 conferences/thematic areas listed on the following page.

A total of 4,373 individuals from academia, research institutes, industry, and governmental agencies from 76 countries submitted contributions, and 1,170 papers and 195 posters have been included in the proceedings. These contributions address the latest research and development efforts and highlight the human aspects of design and use of computing systems. The contributions thoroughly cover the entire field of human-computer interaction, addressing major advances in knowledge and effective use of computers in a variety of application areas. The volumes constituting the full set of the conference proceedings are listed in the following pages.

I would like to thank the program board chairs and the members of the program boards of all thematic areas and affiliated conferences for their contribution to the highest scientific quality and the overall success of the HCI International 2018 conference.

This conference would not have been possible without the continuous and unwavering support and advice of the founder, Conference General Chair Emeritus and Conference Scientific Advisor Prof. Gavriel Salvendy. For his outstanding efforts, I would like to express my appreciation to the communications chair and editor of *HCI International News*, Dr. Abbas Moallem.

July 2018   Constantine Stephanidis

HCI International 2018 Thematic Areas and Affiliated Conferences

Thematic areas:

- Human-Computer Interaction (HCI 2018)
- Human Interface and the Management of Information (HIMI 2018)

Affiliated conferences:

- 15th International Conference on Engineering Psychology and Cognitive Ergonomics (EPCE 2018)
- 12th International Conference on Universal Access in Human-Computer Interaction (UAHCI 2018)
- 10th International Conference on Virtual, Augmented, and Mixed Reality (VAMR 2018)
- 10th International Conference on Cross-Cultural Design (CCD 2018)
- 10th International Conference on Social Computing and Social Media (SCSM 2018)
- 12th International Conference on Augmented Cognition (AC 2018)
- 9th International Conference on Digital Human Modeling and Applications in Health, Safety, Ergonomics, and Risk Management (DHM 2018)
- 7th International Conference on Design, User Experience, and Usability (DUXU 2018)
- 6th International Conference on Distributed, Ambient, and Pervasive Interactions (DAPI 2018)
- 5th International Conference on HCI in Business, Government, and Organizations (HCIBGO)
- 5th International Conference on Learning and Collaboration Technologies (LCT 2018)
- 4th International Conference on Human Aspects of IT for the Aged Population (ITAP 2018)

Conference Proceedings Volumes Full List

1. LNCS 10901, Human-Computer Interaction: Theories, Methods, and Human Issues (Part I), edited by Masaaki Kurosu
2. LNCS 10902, Human-Computer Interaction: Interaction in Context (Part II), edited by Masaaki Kurosu
3. LNCS 10903, Human-Computer Interaction: Interaction Technologies (Part III), edited by Masaaki Kurosu
4. LNCS 10904, Human Interface and the Management of Information: Interaction, Visualization, and Analytics (Part I), edited by Sakae Yamamoto and Hirohiko Mori
5. LNCS 10905, Human Interface and the Management of Information: Information in Applications and Services (Part II), edited by Sakae Yamamoto and Hirohiko Mori
6. LNAI 10906, Engineering Psychology and Cognitive Ergonomics, edited by Don Harris
7. LNCS 10907, Universal Access in Human-Computer Interaction: Methods, Technologies, and Users (Part I), edited by Margherita Antona and Constantine Stephanidis
8. LNCS 10908, Universal Access in Human-Computer Interaction: Virtual, Augmented, and Intelligent Environments (Part II), edited by Margherita Antona and Constantine Stephanidis
9. LNCS 10909, Virtual, Augmented and Mixed Reality: Interaction, Navigation, Visualization, Embodiment, and Simulation (Part I), edited by Jessie Y. C. Chen and Gino Fragomeni
10. LNCS 10910, Virtual, Augmented and Mixed Reality: Applications in Health, Cultural Heritage, and Industry (Part II), edited by Jessie Y. C. Chen and Gino Fragomeni
11. LNCS 10911, Cross-Cultural Design: Methods, Tools, and Users (Part I), edited by Pei-Luen Patrick Rau
12. LNCS 10912, Cross-Cultural Design: Applications in Cultural Heritage, Creativity, and Social Development (Part II), edited by Pei-Luen Patrick Rau
13. LNCS 10913, Social Computing and Social Media: User Experience and Behavior (Part I), edited by Gabriele Meiselwitz
14. LNCS 10914, Social Computing and Social Media: Technologies and Analytics (Part II), edited by Gabriele Meiselwitz
15. LNAI 10915, Augmented Cognition: Intelligent Technologies (Part I), edited by Dylan D. Schmorrow and Cali M. Fidopiastis
16. LNAI 10916, Augmented Cognition: Users and Contexts (Part II), edited by Dylan D. Schmorrow and Cali M. Fidopiastis
17. LNCS 10917, Digital Human Modeling and Applications in Health, Safety, Ergonomics, and Risk Management, edited by Vincent G. Duffy
18. LNCS 10918, Design, User Experience, and Usability: Theory and Practice (Part I), edited by Aaron Marcus and Wentao Wang

19. LNCS 10919, Design, User Experience, and Usability: Designing Interactions (Part II), edited by Aaron Marcus and Wentao Wang
20. LNCS 10920, Design, User Experience, and Usability: Users, Contexts, and Case Studies (Part III), edited by Aaron Marcus and Wentao Wang
21. LNCS 10921, Distributed, Ambient, and Pervasive Interactions: Understanding Humans (Part I), edited by Norbert Streitz and Shin'ichi Konomi
22. LNCS 10922, Distributed, Ambient, and Pervasive Interactions: Technologies and Contexts (Part II), edited by Norbert Streitz and Shin'ichi Konomi
23. LNCS 10923, HCI in Business, Government, and Organizations, edited by Fiona Fui-Hoon Nah and Bo Sophia Xiao
24. LNCS 10924, Learning and Collaboration Technologies: Design, Development and Technological Innovation (Part I), edited by Panayiotis Zaphiris and Andri Ioannou
25. LNCS 10925, Learning and Collaboration Technologies: Learning and Teaching (Part II), edited by Panayiotis Zaphiris and Andri Ioannou
26. LNCS 10926, Human Aspects of IT for the Aged Population: Acceptance, Communication, and Participation (Part I), edited by Jia Zhou and Gavriel Salvendy
27. LNCS 10927, Human Aspects of IT for the Aged Population: Applications in Health, Assistance, and Entertainment (Part II), edited by Jia Zhou and Gavriel Salvendy
28. CCIS 850, HCI International 2018 Posters Extended Abstracts (Part I), edited by Constantine Stephanidis
29. CCIS 851, HCI International 2018 Posters Extended Abstracts (Part II), edited by Constantine Stephanidis
30. CCIS 852, HCI International 2018 Posters Extended Abstracts (Part III), edited by Constantine Stephanidis

http://2018.hci.international/proceedings

Human-Computer Interaction

Program Board Chair: **Masaaki Kurosu,** *Japan*

- Jose Abdelnour-Nocera, UK
- Mark Apperley, New Zealand
- Sebastiano Bagnara, Italy
- Kaveh Bazargan, Iran
- Nigel Bevan, UK
- Michael Craven, UK
- Achim Ebert, Germany
- Xiaowen Fang, USA
- Carla Faria Leitão, Brazil
- Stefano Federici, Italy
- Isabela Gasparini, Brazil
- Ayako Hashizume, Japan
- Wonil Hwang, South Korea
- Mitsuhiko Karashima, Japan

- Heidi Krömker, Germany
- Kun-Pyo Lee, South Korea
- Cristiano Maciel, Brazil
- Paulo Melo, Brazil
- Naoko Okuizumi, Japan
- Katsuhiko Onishi, Japan
- Philippe Palanque, France
- Roberto Pereira, Brazil
- Denise Pilar, Brazil
- Alberto Raposo, Brazil
- Guangfeng Song, USA
- Hiroshi Ujita, Japan
- Michiya Yamamoto, Japan
- Fan Zhao, USA

The full list with the Program Board Chairs and the members of the Program Boards of all thematic areas and affiliated conferences is available online at:

http://www.hci.international/board-members-2018.php

HCI International 2019

The 21st International Conference on Human-Computer Interaction, HCI International 2019, will be held jointly with the affiliated conferences in Orlando, FL, USA, at Walt Disney World Swan and Dolphin Resort, July 26–31, 2019. It will cover a broad spectrum of themes related to Human-Computer Interaction, including theoretical issues, methods, tools, processes, and case studies in HCI design, as well as novel interaction techniques, interfaces, and applications. The proceedings will be published by Springer. More information will be available on the conference website: http://2019.hci.international/.

General Chair
Prof. Constantine Stephanidis
University of Crete and ICS-FORTH
Heraklion, Crete, Greece
E-mail: general_chair@hcii2019.org

http://2019.hci.international/

Contents – Part II

HCI for Health and Wellbeing

HCI in Cultural Heritage

HCI in Complex Environments

Mobile and Wearable HCI

HCI in Medicine

Usability Evaluation of Origin of Replication Finding Tools

Isra Al-Turaiki$^{(\boxtimes)}$, Maryam Aloumi, Nour Aloumi, Noorah Almanyi, Khulood Alghamdi, and Sarah Almuqhim

College of Computer and Information Sciences, King Saud University, Riyadh, Kingdom of Saudi Arabia
ialturaiki@ksu.edu.sa, maryaloumi@gmail.com, nouraloumi@gmail.com, noorah556@gmail.com, khulood.alghamdi@gmail.com, s.almoqhim@hotmail.com

Abstract. Nowadays, there is a significant increase in the number of Bioinformatics tools and databases. Researchers from various interdisciplinary fields need to use these tools. Usability is an important quality of software in general, and bioinformatics tools in particular. Improving the usability of bioinformatics tools allows users to use the tool to its fullest potential. In this paper, we evaluate the usability of two online bioinformatics tools *Ori-Finder 1* and *Ori-Finder 2* in terms of efficiency, effectiveness, and satisfaction. The evaluation focuses on investigating how easily and successfully can users use Ori-Finder1 and Ori-Finder 2 to find the origin of replication in Bacterial and Archaeal genomes. To the best of our knowledge, the usability of these two tools has not been studied before. Twelve participants were recruited from four user groups. The average tasks completion times were compared. Many usability issues were identified by users of bioinformatics tools. Based on our results, we list recommendations for better design of bioinformatics tools.

Keywords: Origin of replication · Bioinformatics
Usability evaluation · oriC

1 Introduction

DNA replication is the process of copying a DNA molecule in order to produce two identical replica. This is a key step for the reproduction of living cells. It is initiated at a specific region in the DNA called the *origin of replication* (oriC). The whole process is regulated by a mechanism that recognizes both, the locations of oriC and the ideal time to start replication. In bacterial and archaeal genomes, there is usually a single oriC [13]. With the development of high-throughput sequencing technologies, there has been a rapid increase in the release of bioinformatics databases and tools. Ori-Finder 1 [9] and Ori-Finder 2 [14] are two web-based bioinformatics tools designed for predicting the location of oriC in bacterial and archaeal genomes, respectively. The two tools have been widely adopted by researchers for the identification and analysis of oriC.

© Springer International Publishing AG, part of Springer Nature 2018
M. Kurosu (Ed.): HCI 2018, LNCS 10902, pp. 3–13, 2018.
https://doi.org/10.1007/978-3-319-91244-8_1

Developers of bioinformatics software usually focus on validating the biological hypothesis. However, one feature that receives little attention is the usability of the bioinformatics tool itself. According to [5], the ISO 92491 defines usability as *"the extent to which a product can be used by specified users to achieve specified goals with effectiveness, efficiency and satisfaction in a specified context of use"*. This feature is very important quality of interactive bioinformatics tools. Failing to achieve a certain level of usability may result in many bioinformatics tools being unused. For this reason, evaluating the effectiveness and usability of bioinformatics tools is increasingly getting attention.

In this study, we investigate the usability of Ori-Finder 1 and Ori-Finder 2. To the best of our knowledge, the usability of these two tools has not been previously studied. Our goal is to highlight the main usability problems and to provide recommendations for better design. The rest of the paper is organized as follows: in Sect. 2 we discuss similar work for the evaluation of bioinformatics tools. Section 3 describes the two bioinformatics tools evaluated in this study. In Sect. 4, we discuss our methodology and the details of data collection. Results and design recommendations are discussed in Sects. 5 and 6. Finally, the paper is concludes in Sect. 7.

2 Related Work

The number of bioinformatics tools and users increase is growing. There is a need to ensure that the highest standards of usability are being met. Usability is an important aspect for the survival of software and bioinformatics tools are no exception. In this section, we discuss the literature of usability studies performed on bioinformatics tools and databases.

Mirel and Wright [15] highlighted the need to consider *usability* as a main goal when designing software for the scientific community. The authors focused on bioimaging software, proposing several criteria to be met, including: user and developer friendliness, interoperability, modularity, and results validation.

Bolchini et al. [5] conducted two usability studies in order to identify some critical usability problems in bioinformatics web-based databases. In the first study, a usability inspection using MILE+ protocol [6] was carried out to analyze the navigation and information architecture design of CATH database. CATH (http://www.cathdb.info/wiki) is a browsing-oriented protein classification database. Usability issues were identified in the navigation of different subsystems each with many releases. The authors showed that the user may be led to an old release of a subsystem. In addition, there were limited access paths available for content navigation. In the second study, user testing was conducted on three search-oriented databases: BioCarta (www.biocarta.com), Swiss Prot (www.expasy.ch/sprot), and NCBI (www.ncbi.nlm.nih.gov). Users had issues in search query formulation and in interpreting search results.

Mullany et al. [16] evaluated the effectiveness and usability of six existing bioinformatics databases. The authors used thirteen criteria, for each, a set of yes/no question were posed. The answers were coded with 1 for yes, −1 for no, and 0 for unknown. This enabled the calculation of a total score summarizing the effectiveness and usability of a database. Many limitations were identified across multiple databases, including: poor documentation, lack of pathway output, lack of database updates, and inconsistencies in nomenclature.

Al-Ageel et al. [2] evaluated the usability of four web-based bioinformatics tools for structure and sequence motif finding. MEME [4], FIMO [10], RNAMST [7], and RNAPromo [17] were inspected using a list of heuristics proposed by [15]. Several usability issues were identified in the inspected tools, such as: too much detailed results, poor user interface designs, and lack of tools for powerful interactions. However, strength points were also identified in their study. MEME and FIMO provide adequate documentation and examples that help users search for information about the tool and find steps required to perform a given task. The study also showed that FIMO had the most usability issues while MEME had least usability issues.

3   oriC Finiding Tools

We conduct a usability study for two well-known web-based tools for finding oriC. Here, we give a brief description of each tool.

3.1   Ori-Finder 1

Ori-Finder 1 [9] is a web server for predicting oriCs in bacterial genomes. Locating oriCs using Ori-Finder is based on an algorithm incorporating base composition analysis using Z-curve method, distribution of DnaA boxes, and the frequency of genes near oriCs. The server accepts sequences in FASTA format as an input. In addition, other parameters need to be set, such as: species-specific DnaA boxes, protein table, and display parameters. The output page shows the predicted region of oriC along with detailed information, including: oriC length, genome length, and DnaA box distribution.

3.2   Ori-Finder 2

The Ori-Finder 2 [14] is also a web-based tool for the prediction and analysis of oriCs, but in archaeal genomes. For annotated genomes, the tool accepts a sequence file in GenBank format or in FASTA format with corresponding protein table file. Ori-Finder 2 can analyze unannotated genomes by utilizing ZCURVE1.02 [11], Glimmer3 [8], and BLAST [3]. The workflow of Ori-Finder 2 is composed of FIMO and REPuter [12] for searching motifs and repeats, respectively.

4   Methodology

4.1   User Groups

For the usability test of the two bioinformatics tools we recruited participants from King Saud University, Riyadh, Saudi Arabia. Four of them were postgraduate students in the *microorganisms biology* department with no previous experience in using bioinformatics tools. Three our participants were HCI experts who previously taught HCI courses in the *Information Technology* department. One of them had knowledge in both HCI and usability. Our study also included four beginners in bioinformatics. They were postgraduate students in *Information Technology* who took one course in bioinformatics. Finally, one bioinformatics expert was invited to participate. In total, there were twelve female participants between the age of 18–40 years. The usability test session took about two weeks.

4.2   Test Scenario and Goals

For this usability evaluation, a scenario similar to a real application was designed. The scenario describes a situation where there is a need to locate origin of replication in Bacterial and Archaeal genomes using Ori-finder 1 and Ori-finder 2, respectively. Here, we describe the scenario, goals and tasks.

Scenario: *You are a member of a group of researchers looking for a treatment for a disease caused by Bacteria (or Archaea). The process of genome replication is one of the most important tasks carried out in the cell. One way that can help in treatment is targeting the origin of replication of the Bacteria (or Archaea) in order to inhibit its replication. Therefore, you will use Ori-Finder1 or (Ori-Finder 2) web-based systems designed to predict the origins of replication in Bacteria (or Archaea).*

Goal 1: Predict the oriC in a Bacterial genome and interpret the results.

– Task 1: *Now, you want to try to use Ori-Finder 1 web-based system at* http://www.tubic.tju.edu.cn *using the sequence example provided by the tool for Escherichia coli. The mismatches between the DnaA boxes are allowed to be two mismatches as you have decided with your colleagues.*
This task was further divided into the following three subtasks: Task 1.1: Use the example provided to upload a complete genome sequence in FASTA format. Task 1.2: Set the mismatch site to 2. Task 1.3: Submit sequence form.
– Task 2: *Now, you are about to inform your colleagues about the results you found using Ori-Finder 1. You want to report interesting information about the number of DnaA boxes, the location of the oriC region, the DnaA boxes identified in the sequence, as well as show them some relative Z-curves.*
This task was further divided into the following subtasks: Task 2.1: Find the number of DnaA box. Task 2.2: Find the location of oriC region. Task 2.3: Find The sequence of oriC. Task 2.4: Review the results in the form of a curve.

Goal 2: Predict the oriC in an Archaeal genome and interpret the results.

– Task1: *Now, its time to try to use the Ori-Finder 2 web-based system and run the tool on an annotated archaeal genome. You are going to do the experiment for Pyrococcus abyssi GE5 species which is a sequenced and annotated*

archaeal genome from NCBI genome database. Based to your colleague's decision, your are going to use Thermococcaceae for the motif taxonomy.
Task 1.1 Select a sequenced and annotated archaeal genome from NCBI genome database. Task 1.2 Select the Motifs taxonomy to Thermococcaceae. Task 1.3 Submitting sequence form.
– Task 2: *Now, its time to inform your colleagues about the results you found. You will report interesting information about the location of the oriCs with ORB sequence and the DnaA boxes identified in the sequence.*
Task 2.1 Find the location of oriCs with ORB sequence. Task 2.2 Find The sequence of oriC (i.e. the DnaA boxes identified in the sequence).

4.3 Pre-test and Post-test Questionnaires

Participants were asked to take a pre-session questionnaire. The purpose of the pre-session questionnaire was to gather information about: demographics, experience and frequency of using Bioinformatics tools, and their expectations about utilizing Bioinformatics tools compared to manual analysis. The questionnaire included both open-ended, closed-ended, and scale questions. After the participants completed the usability test for each tool, we asked them to take a post-session questionnaire. The questions were related to participants' impression of the tool after performing the tasks. The questions were related to issues that affect the usability of the system.

Our goal was to find out if the tools met the users expectation. We were interested in knowing whether they have experienced any problems with the design, layout, navigation, or output of each tool. Questions had a rating scale to assess the participant's overall reaction to the tools usability and satisfaction level. We also asked them whether they would use the tool in the future and whether they would recommend it to a friend. Finally, we asked them to provide their suggestions to improve these tools.

To get the participants overall impression, we finalized the usability test with a short interview with the following questions:

1. How was your experience?
2. What did you like and did not like while using the systems?
3. What is your overall impression?

Most of the participants appreciated the availability of such tools to facilitate the work in bioinformatics research. However, they pointed out the need to enhance user interfaces for more clarity and better understandability. This will help users better utilize such tool to their full potential.

4.4 Usability and Testing Session

The observation usability evaluation method was used during for the test sessions. This involved watching the participants while they interact with the web-based tools, taking notes, and asking questions. The testing environment setting was an electronic observation room setup. In this setting, there are two rooms. The first room is for the test moderator and the participant. The test moderator sits close to the participant having an excellent view of what is going on with the participant, while making her feel comfortable. The observers are in the second room. They are physically separated from the testing activity.

The test takes about 20 to 30 min for each participant, depending on their experience.

The collected data from the test sessions were classified into: performance and preference data. The performance data included: task completion time, completion status (completed successfully, completed with difficulty, failure). We calculated the average value per user group. In terms of preference data, we have the participants' opinions, expectation, and experience from pre-session and post-session questionnaires. All data were collected, summarized, and recorded in a spreadsheet for easy processing.

5   Results

The average time of task completion was compared to the expected completion time in order to measure efficiency. Participant's opinions from pre-session and post-session questionnaires were used as a measure of satisfaction. Usability testing data, including questionnaires, were automatically collected using *Morea software* [1]. In this section, we summarize the main results obtained from our testing sessions.

5.1   Ori-Finder 1

Goal 1, Task1: Figure 2 shows the average task competition time for all subtasks across the four participant groups. As shown in the figure, all participant groups took longer time in performing subtask 1. Three user groups struggled in finding the example of the genome sequence. This implies that there would be an issue with the example provided within the tool. When a participant clicks on the example, a new page appears with the example sequence. The user is expected to copy and paste the sequence in the textbox.

The least time for all subtasks was taken by the bioinformatics expert. This was expected as she is familiar with similar bioinformatics tools. The group of postgraduate students in biology took longer time in performing all subtasks. Overall, participants spent more time performing the first subtask. In addition, we found that two user groups struggled in setting the mismatch site to 2, subtask 1.2. This option was not clear in the form. Issues regarding subtasks 1.1 and 1.2 are shown in Fig. 1. All user groups were able to submit the sequence form (subtask 1.3) easily. For subtask 1.1, 58% of participants were exceed the task expected time. However, 58% and 75% were able to complete subtasks 1.2 and 1.3, respectively, within the expected time.

Goal 1, Task2: Figure 3 shows the average task competition time for all subtasks across the four participant groups. As shown in the figure, surprisingly the

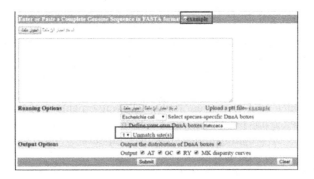

Fig. 1. Issues found for subtasks 1.1 and 1.2.

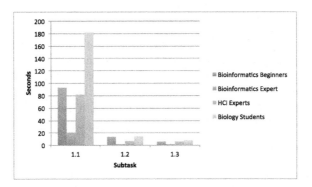

Fig. 2. Average task completion time for Ori-finder 1 task 1 in seconds.

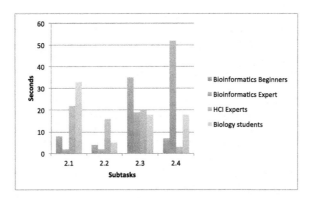

Fig. 3. Average task completion time for Ori-finder 1 task 2 in seconds.

bioinformatics expert took the longest time in identifying the oriC from the a Z-curve (subtask 2.4). Beginners in bioinformatics took the longest time to identify the sequence of oriC (subask 2.3). All groups found the location of oriC region easily. Subtask 2.1, 2.2, 2.3, and 2.4 were performed within the expected time by 75%, 83%, 58%, and 83%, of all participants, respectively.

5.2   Ori-Finder 2

Goal 2, Task1: Figure 4 shows the average task competition time for all subtasks across the four participant groups. We observed that two user groups had difficulty in selecting a sequenced and annotated Archaeal genome from the NCBI genome database (subtask 2.1). HCI experts and biology students took longer time since no action occurs when clicking on this choice to tell the user that the sequence has been selected. Users expected the sequence to be pasted in the textbox or a conformance message appears. Issue regarding subtasks 2.1 are highlighted in Fig. 5.

We also observed that all user groups had difficulty in submitting the sequence form (subtask 2.3). As shown in Fig. 6, the submit button is surrounded by other buttons and it does not appear at the end of the page as users expected. Overall, 75%, 66%, and 58% of all participants were able to complete task 1.1, task 1.2, and 1.3 within the expected time, respectively.

Goal 2, Task2: Figure 7 shows the average task competition time for all subtasks across the four participant groups. We observed that three user groups faced a problem with finding the sequence of oriC. As shown in Fig. 8, the DnaA boxes place was not clear and nothing is written to point to the place. Overall, 92% of all participants were able to complete task 1.1 within the expected time, respectively. However, 25% of all participants failed in completing task 2.3.

Fig. 4. Average task completion time for Ori-finder 2 task 1 in seconds.

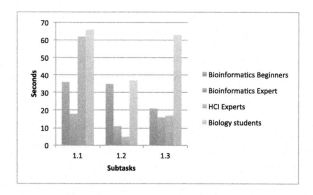

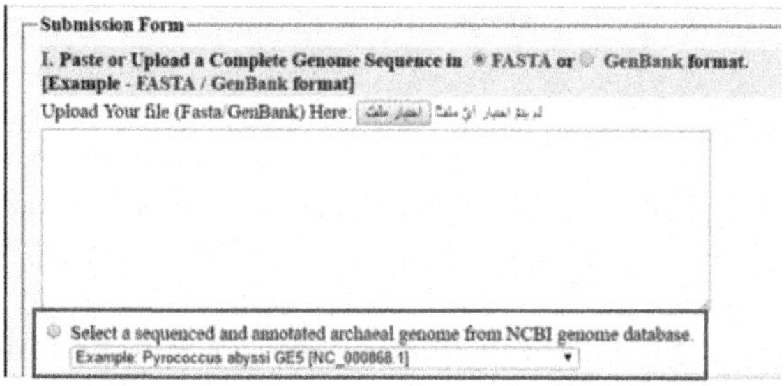

Fig. 5. Issues found for subtask 2.1.

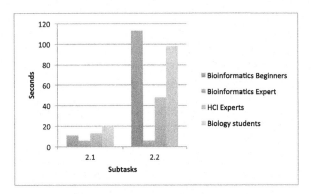

Fig. 6. Issues found for subtask 2.3.

Fig. 7. Average task completion time for Ori-finder 2 task 2 in seconds.

Fig. 8. Issues found for subtask 2.2.

6   Recommendations

Considering all the usability issues identified in this usability evaluation of the
two bioinformatics tools, we recommend the following improvements:

1. Enhancing colour scheme contrast between the text colour and the background.
2. Automatic load of sequence examples into textbox.
3. It is recommend to have a progress bar or a display of percentage of page
   loading in order to let the use know how long she needs to wait.
4. Provide messages and assistance to guide the user.

5. Provide explanations of technical words or use familiar icons in order to ensure that a non-expert can be conformable using the tool.
6. Improving the way of displaying the result of DNA boxes (the case of Ori-Finder 2).

7   Conclusion

Ori-Finder 1 and Ori-Finder are two popular bioinformatics tools for finding the origin of replication. In this study, the usability of these tools has been evaluated. Twelve participants were recruited from four user groups. The average tasks completion times were compared. Many usability issues were identified by users of bioinformatics tools. Based on our results, we discussed some recommendations for better design of bioinformatics tools. We hope that usability issues found in present versions of Ori-Finder 1 and Ori-Finder 2 can be addressed in future releases. We believe that research in bioinformatics usability is still in its infancy. There is a lot of room for improvement.

Aknowledgement. The authors would like to thank the participants who generously shared their time and experience for the purposes of this study.

References

1. Usability Testing | Morae | TechSmith. https://www.techsmith.com/morae.html
2. Al-Ageel, N., Al-Wabil, A., Badr, G., AlOmar, N.: Human factors in the design and evaluation of bioinformatics tools. Procedia Manuf. **3**, 2003–2010 (2015)
3. Altschul, S.F., Gish, W., Miller, W., Myers, E.W., Lipman, D.J.: Basic local alignment search tool. J. Mol. Biol. **215**(3), 403–410 (1990)
4. Bailey, T.L., Boden, M., Buske, F.A., Frith, M., Grant, C.E., Clementi, L., Ren, J., Li, W.W., Noble, W.S.: MEME Suite: tools for motif discovery and searching. Nucleic Acids Res. **37**(suppl-2), W202–W208 (2009)
5. Bolchini, D., Finkelstein, A., Perrone, V., Nagl, S.: Better bioinformatics through usability analysis. Bioinformatics **25**(3), 406–412 (2009)
6. Bolchini, D., Garzotto, F.: Quality of web usability evaluation methods: an empirical study on MiLE+. In: Weske, M., Hacid, M.-S., Godart, C. (eds.) WISE 2007. LNCS, vol. 4832, pp. 481–492. Springer, Heidelberg (2007). https://doi.org/10.1007/978-3-540-77010-7_47
7. Chang, T.H., Huang, H.D., Chuang, T.N., Shien, D.M., Horng, J.T.: RNAMST: efficient and flexible approach for identifying RNA structural homologs. Nucleic Acids Res. **34**(Suppl-2), W423–W428 (2006)
8. Delcher, A.L., Bratke, K.A., Powers, E.C., Salzberg, S.L.: Identifying bacterial genes and endosymbiont DNA with Glimmer. Bioinformatics **23**(6), 673–679 (2007)
9. Gao, F., Zhang, C.T.: Ori-Finder: a web-based system for finding oriC s in unannotated bacterial genomes. BMC Bioinformatics **9**, 79 (2008)
10. Grant, C.E., Bailey, T.L., Noble, W.S.: FIMO: scanning for occurrences of a given motif. Bioinformatics **27**(7), 1017–1018 (2011)
11. Guo, F.B., Ou, H.Y., Zhang, C.T.: ZCURVE: a new system for recognizing protein-coding genes in bacterial and archaeal genomes. Nucleic Acids Res. **31**(6), 1780–1789 (2003)

12. Kurtz, S., Choudhuri, J.V., Ohlebusch, E., Schleiermacher, C., Stoye, J., Giegerich, R.: REPuter: the manifold applications of repeat analysis on a genomic scale. Nucleic Acids Res. **29**(22), 4633–4642 (2001)
13. Leonard, A.C., Mechali, M.: DNA replication origins. Cold Spring Harb. Perspect. Biol. **5**(10), a010116 (2013)
14. Luo, H., Zhang, C.T., Gao, F.: Ori-Finder 2, an integrated tool to predict replication origins in the archaeal genomes. Front. Microbiol. **5**, 482 (2014)
15. Mirel, B., Wright, Z.: Heuristic evaluations of bioinformatics tools: a development case. In: Jacko, J.A. (ed.) HCI 2009. LNCS, vol. 5610, pp. 329–338. Springer, Heidelberg (2009). https://doi.org/10.1007/978-3-642-02574-7_37
16. Mullany, L.E., Wolff, R.K., Slattery, M.L.: Effectiveness and usability of bioinformatics tools to analyze pathways associated with miRNA expression. Cancer Inform. **14**, 121–130 (2015)
17. Rabani, M., Kertesz, M., Segal, E.: Computational prediction of RNA structural motifs involved in posttranscriptional regulatory processes. Proc. Natl. Acad. Sci. **105**(39), 14885–14890 (2008)

Development of Wireless Surgical Knife Attachment with Proximity Indicators Using ArUco Marker

Masanao Koeda[✉], Daiki Yano, Naoki Shintaku, Katsuhiko Onishi,
and Hiroshi Noborio

Osaka Electro-Communication University,
Kiyotaki 1130-70, Shijonawate, Osaka, Japan
koeda@osakac.ac.jp

Abstract. We have been developing a liver surgical support system. By matching the depth images of the real liver and the 3D liver model during surgery, the position of the liver, invisible blood vessels and tumors is estimated. The tip position of the surgical knife is measured by single point measurements camera using specific markers. By merging all information, the distance between the knife tip and the target parts such as vessels or tumors is calculated and the proximity of the knife to the target parts is determined. To indicate the proximity, we have been developing a surgical knife attachment with light emitting diodes (LEDs). When the knife approaches to the target parts, the LEDs on the attachment gradually turn on the light. The newly developed attachment becomes compact and lightweight than the previous one. It uses a wireless controller and ArUco markers which can be tracked by an inexpensive USB camera. We conducted experiments to check the performance of ArUco markers and the navigation of the operator using the new attachment. The results showed the new attachment had comparable navigation accuracy to the previous one.

Keywords: Laparotomy · Liver · Knife attachment · Proximity
ArUco marker

1 Introduction

The liver has several blood vessels such as arteries, veins, portals, etc. and these are not externally visible. By using X-ray imaging, computed tomography (CT) or magnetic resonance imaging (MRI) etc., the position of these vessels in the liver is checked preoperatively. During surgery, surgeons touch the incision part of the liver using their fingers, feel for a pulse-beat, and perceive the proximity of the vessels. However, this method is dangerous and can injury to the blood vessels and result in bleeding.

Surgical support systems for orthopedic, dental, or brain surgery are developed [1–3]. These systems determine the position of the surgical tools, synchronize with the tomographic images and navigate the tool to the target position. The target body parts of these support systems are rigid and exhibit negligible deformation during surgery.

However, the liver is soft and changes it shape during operation and the existing support systems cannot be applied to the liver surgery. Research targeted on the

© Springer International Publishing AG, part of Springer Nature 2018
M. Kurosu (Ed.): HCI 2018, LNCS 10902, pp. 14–26, 2018.
https://doi.org/10.1007/978-3-319-91244-8_2

surgical support systems for soft organs has been limited, and no effective system have been developed yet. We have been developing a liver surgery support system.

In this paper, the detail of our liver surgery support system and newly developed wireless knife attachment are described. It can alert the proximity of the target parts by lighting LEDs.

2   Our Liver Surgical Support System

The detail of our liver surgical support system was described in [4]. It uses two depth cameras with different characteristics. The first camera is lower precision, but a wide measurement range used for determining the shape of the liver during surgery. Kinect for Windows v2 developed by Microsoft is currently used. Three-dimensional (3D) polyhedron model is generated from tomographic images preoperatively. The 3D model contains the shape of the liver, inner blood vessels, and tumors. By matching the depth images from the depth camera and Z-buffer of the 3D polyhedron model during surgery, the positions of the liver is determined using simulated annealing algorithm and the location of the inner blood vessels and the tumors are estimated [5–8]. The second camera is higher precision and performs single point measurements using single markers [9] to determine the tip position of the surgical knife. MicronTraker3 (type H3-60) by ClaroNav is currently used. By merging all information, the distance between the knife tip and the vessels or tumors is calculated [10] and the proximity of the knife to the target parts is determined. To indicate the proximity, the LEDs on our surgical knife attachment are gradually illuminated (Fig. 1).

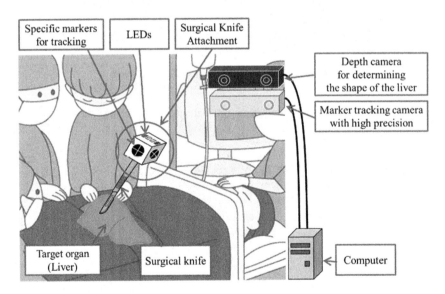

Fig. 1. Overview of our liver surgical support system

3 Conventional Surgical Knife Attachment

The conventional surgical knife attachment was presented in [4]. The size and weight of the attachment are approximately $70 \times 70 \times 70$ mm and 261 g respectively. The size of marker for MicronTracker3 is 30×40 mm. An LED bar module (OSX10201-GYR1) [11] and a piezoelectric speaker are mounted in the attachment and a micro-computer (Arduino Nano) controls them. The LED module has 10 LEDs (five greens, three yellows and two reds). The attachment has no internal power source. The electric power and control commands are externally supplied from the main PC through USB cable (Fig. 2). Specification details are listed in Table 1.

Fig. 2. Conventional surgical knife attachment

Table 1. Specification of conventional surgical knife attachment

Size	$70 \times 70 \times 70$ mm
Weight	261 g
Marker size	30×40 mm
Camera system	MicronTracker3
Microcomputer	Arduino Nano
LED	OSX10201-GYR1
Speaker	Piezoelectric speaker
Power source	DC 5 V, externally supplied

4 Wireless Surgical Knife Attachment with Proximity Indicators Using ArUco Marker

In the new attachment, the case was made smaller and lighter, and a microcomputer with a Wi-Fi module and a rechargeable battery were built in the case and controlled wirelessly (Fig. 3). We confirmed that this battery drive for more than 6 h. For the knife position measurement system, ArUco [12] was used. ArUco is a marker recognition library for AR which can estimate postures of cameras and markers. ArUco is built in the OpenCV library, it can be easily used with an inexpensive USB camera. ArUco uses black and white square markers (ArUco marker, Fig. 4). Specification details are listed in Table 2. The circuit diagram of the attachment is illustrated in Fig. 5.

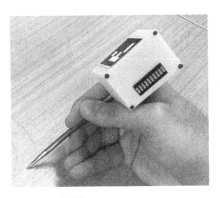
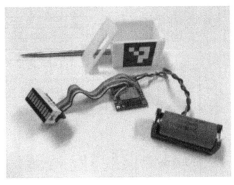

(a) Outer appearance   (b) Inner structure

Fig. 3. Tool for navigation experiment

Fig. 4. Sample of ArUco marker (DICT_4X4, ID0)

Table 2. Specification of new surgical knife attachment

Size	49 × 32 × 35 mm
Weight	46 g
Marker size	30 × 30 mm, ArUco marker
Camera system	Any camera usable on OpenCV
Microcomputer	ESPr Developer (ESP-WROOM-02)
LED	OSX10201-GYR1
Speaker	Not included
Power source	Lithium-ion rechargeable battery CR123A, 3.7 V, 1000 mAh

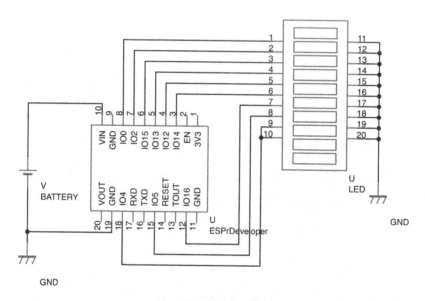

Fig. 5. Circuit diagram

5   Knife Tip Position Calibration

To measure the relative vector from the marker on the attachment to the knife tip, the calibration procedure described in [4] was basically used. Camera and knife coordinate systems are defined as $\sum_c$ and $\sum_k$ respectively. The knife attached marker and the table fixed marker are represented as M_{knife} and M_{table} respectively.

To acquire a relative vector from M_{knife} to the knife tip, the knife tip is placed at the origin point p_{table}^c of M_{table}, and the position and orientation of each marker are measured in $\sum_c$ coordinates (Fig. 6). The position and orientation of M_{knife} measured in

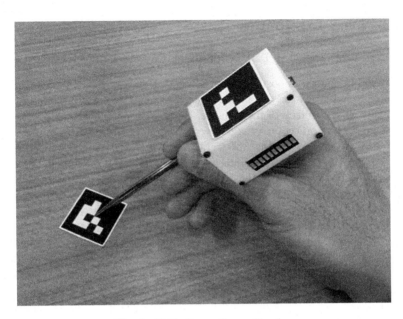

Fig. 6. Knife tip position calibration

$\sum_c$ coordinates are defined P^c_{knife} and R^c_{knife} respectively. The relative vector P^c_{rel} is calculated by the following equation. P^k_{rel}

$$P^c_{rel} = P^c_{table} - P^c_{knife}$$

To convert P^c_{rel} in $\sum_k$ coordinates, the following is used.

$$P^k_{rel} = \left(R^c_{knife} \right)^{-1} \cdot P^c_{rel}$$

Finally, the knife tip position P^c_{tip} in $\sum_c$ coordinates is estimated as follows.

$$P^c_{tip} = R^c_{knife} \cdot P^k_{rel} + P^c_{knife}$$

Note that the OpenCV returns the orientation of the ArUco marker as 3×1 rotation vector with reference to the marker coordinate system. In this rotation vector, the direction of the vector shows the rotation axis and the norm of the vector shows the rotation angle. To convert the rotation vector into a rotation matrix in the camera coordinate system, the Rodrigues' rotation formula was used.

6 Preliminary Experiments

6.1 Positional Precision in Distance Between Camera and Marker

We verify the difference in position measurement of the ArUco marker depending on the distance between the ArUco marker and the camera. Since it is quite difficult to verify the absolute accuracy of the distance, we will examine the repetitive accuracy.

The experimental procedure is as follows. 30 × 30 mm sized ArUco marker (ID 0 of DICT_4 × 4) was set on the horizontal table. A USB camera (Logicool C615, resolution 1600 × 896 pixels) was attached to a tripod and placed above the marker. By capturing ArUco marker from the camera, the position of the marker was measured. The distance between the marker and the camera was set to about 500, 600, 700 mm (Fig. 7), and the position of the marker was measured 100 times respectively.

The measurement result of the marker position is shown in Fig. 8. The positive direction of the x, y and z coordinate axis is the right, the downward and the backward direction with the camera position as the origin respectively. You can see that the measurement distance is almost correct from the graph. The standard deviation of the measurement distance of each axis is shown in Fig. 9. The standard deviation in the z direction is larger than in the x and y directions in all measurement distances. However, all standard deviations are less than 1 mm. From this result, it was found that the ArUco has a high repetitive accuracy of distance and the accuracy is not much different with the distance of the camera under 700 mm.

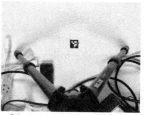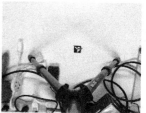

(a) Approx. 500mm aboove   (b) Approx. 600mm above   (c) Approx. 700mm above

Fig. 7. Captured camera images of ArUco marker set on the flat table

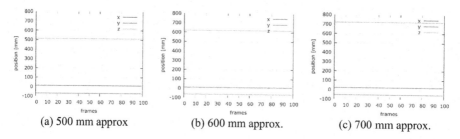

(a) 500 mm approx   (b) 600 mm approx.   (c) 700 mm approx.

Fig. 8. Measurement result of ArUco marker position for 100 times in the distance between the marker and camera of 500, 600 and 700 mm approx.

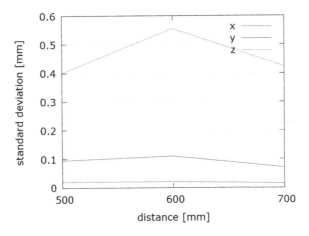

Fig. 9. Standard deviation of marker position in x, y and z axis

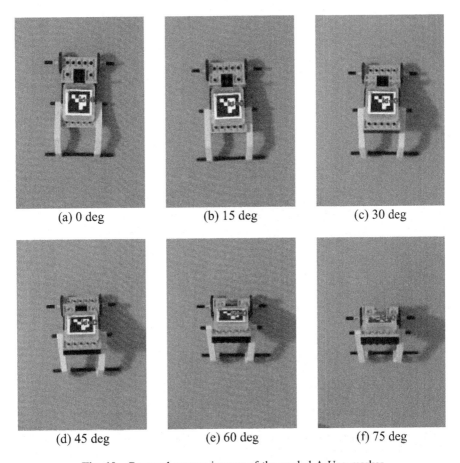

| (a) 0 deg | (b) 15 deg | (c) 30 deg |
| (d) 45 deg | (e) 60 deg | (f) 75 deg |

Fig. 10. Captured camera images of the angled ArUco marker

6.2   Positional Precision in Changing Angle of Marker

We verify changes in marker positional precision due to camera and marker angle. As the method in the previous section, the position of the ArUco marker was measured by the camera above the ArUco marker. The marker was tilted to 0, 15, 30, 45, 60 and 75° around x axis (Fig. 10), and 100 times of the marker position were measured for each.

The measurement result of the marker position is shown in Fig. 11. You can see that the measurement distance is almost correct from the graph. The standard deviation of the measurement distance of each axis is shown in Fig. 12. As the marker angle increased, the standard deviation of the Z axis tends to decrease. On the other hand, the marker detection rate tends to decrease as the marker angle increased (Fig. 13). Summarize these results, it is better to use ArUco markers at around 60°.

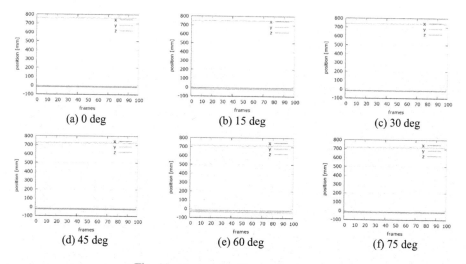

Fig. 11. Captured ArUco maker images

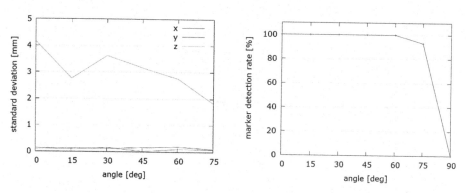

Fig. 12. Standard deviation of angled ArUco marker position in x, y and z axis

Fig. 13. Marker detection ratio

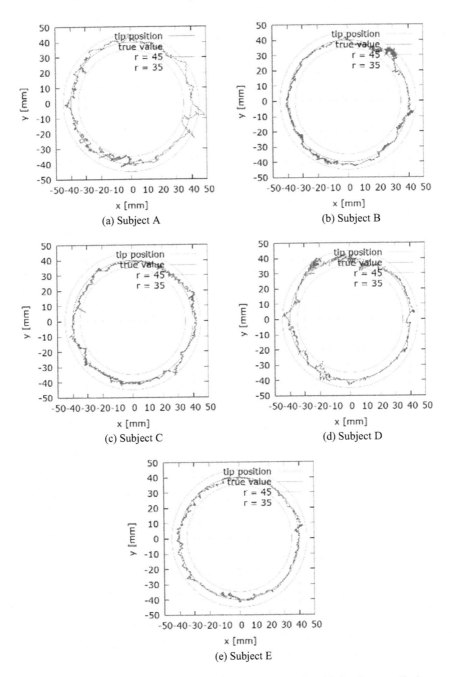

(a) Subject A

(b) Subject B

(c) Subject C

(d) Subject D

(e) Subject E

Fig. 14. Experimental results of trajectory of each subject (Color figure online)

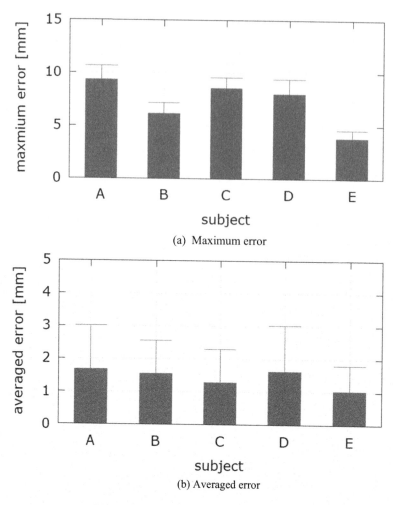

(a) Maximum error

(b) Averaged error

Fig. 15. Navigation error of each subject

7 Navigation Experiment

We conducted experiments to validate operator navigation using the new attachment. The task is to trace an invisible target circle with the knife tip based on the LED information. The target circle is set on a flat horizontal table in front of the subject. The diameter of the circle is 80 mm. The attachment cube was fixed to a hard steel rod with 130 mm in length, 6 mm in diameter.

With $(x_{\text{tip}}, y_{\text{tip}})$ as the knife tip position, (x_c, y_c) as the center of the circle, and r as the radius of the circle, a distance L between the knife tip and the circle is calculated from the following equation.

$$L = \left| r - \sqrt{(x_c - x_{tip})^2 + (y_c - y_{tip})^2} \right|$$

The LED array contains 10 LEDs. However, the microcomputer of new attachment has only 9 digital I/O. For this reason, the LEDs are gradually illuminated between $1 \leq L \leq 9$ mm and can navigate over a range in ± 9 mm of the circle.

The five subjects (A to E) are undergraduate students from the Osaka Electro-Communication University, not surgeons. The experimental results of the trajectory of the tip position are shown in Fig. 14. The green circle is the target circle and the purple dots show the trajectory. The LEDs turn on within the range between the blue and yellow circles. The maximum and averaged navigation errors for each subject are shown in Fig. 15. The results show that it was possible to navigate with the maximum error of 9.3 mm only with the output of the LED array. This is nearly within the navigable range by the LED array, and the usefulness of the new device was shown.

8 Conclusion

We developed a compact, lightweight, inexpensive wireless surgical knife attachment which can display proximity by gradually illuminating LEDs using ArUco markers and a microcomputer with Wi-Fi module. To investigate the characteristics of the positioning of the ArUco marker, we measured the repetitive accuracy of the position of the marker by changing statically in the position and posture of the marker, and clarified the marker has a suitable angle for stable and robust use. We also conducted a navigation experiment to five subjects. The subject held the knife with the attachment in hand and traced the knife tip to the invisible circle by watching the illuminated LEDs on the attachment. The LEDs are gradually illuminated according to the distance between the knife tip and the circle. As a result, it was shown that navigation is possible within the presentable range and the new attachment has comparable navigation accuracy to the previous one.

In the future, we will consider the use of high resolution USB camera, examination of marker size, use of multiple cameras for more precision, robustness and stabilization.

Acknowledgement. This research was supported by Grants-in-Aid for Scientific Research (No. 26289069) from the Ministry of Education, Culture, Sports, Science and Technology (MEXT), Japan.

References

1. Knee Navigation Application - Brainlab. https://www.brainlab.com/en/surgery-products/orthopedic-surgery-products/knee-navigation/
2. ClaroNav - Dental and ENT Navigation Solutions. http://www.claronav.com/
3. Surgical Theater - Surgical Navigation Advanced Platform (SNAP). http://www.surgicaltheater.net/site/products-services/surgical-navigation-advanced-platform-snap
4. Yano, D., Koeda, M., Onishi, K., Noborio, H.: Development of a surgical knife attachment with proximity indicators. In: Marcus, A., Wang, W. (eds.) DUXU 2017. LNCS, vol. 10289, pp. 608–618. Springer, Cham (2017). https://doi.org/10.1007/978-3-319-58637-3_48
5. Noborio, H., Onishi, K., Koeda, M., Mizushino, K., Kunii, T., Kaibori, M., Kon, M., Chen, Y.: A fast surgical algorithm operating polyhedrons using Z-Buffer in GPU. In: Proceedings of the 9th Asian Conference on Computer Aided Surgery (ACCAS 2013), pp. 110–111 (2013)
6. Noborio, H., Watanabe, K., Yagi, M., Ida, Y., Nankaku, S., Onishi, K., Koeda, M., Kon, M., Matsui, K., Kaibori, M.: Experimental results of 2D depth-depth matching algorithm based on depth camera kinect v1. In: Proceedings of the International Conference on Intelligent Informatics and Biomedical Sciences (ICIIBMS 2015), Track 3: Bioinformatics, Medical Imaging and Neuroscience, pp. 284–289 (2015)
7. Onishi, K., Noborio, H., Koeda, M., Watanabe, K., Mizushino, K., Kunii, T., Kaibori, M., Matsui, K., Kon, M.: Virtual liver surgical simulator by using Z-buffer for object deformation. In: Antona, M., Stephanidis, C. (eds.) UAHCI 2015. LNCS, vol. 9177, pp. 345–351. Springer, Cham (2015). https://doi.org/10.1007/978-3-319-20684-4_34
8. Watanabe, K., Yoshida, S., Yano, D., Koeda, M., Noborio, H.: A new organ-following algorithm based on depth-depth matching and simulated annealing, and its experimental evaluation. In: Marcus, A., Wang, W. (eds.) DUXU 2017. LNCS, vol. 10289, pp. 594–607. Springer, Cham (2017). https://doi.org/10.1007/978-3-319-58637-3_47
9. MicronTracker - ClaroNav. http://www.claronav.com/microntracker/
10. Noborio, H., Kunii, T., Mizushino, K.: GPU-based shortest distance algorithm for liver surgery navigation. In: Proceedings of the 10th Anniversary Asian Conference on Computer Aided Surgery, pp. 42–43 (2014)
11. OSX10201-GYR1 - AKIZUKI DENSHI TSUSHO CO., LTD. http://akizukidenshi.com/download/ds/optosupply/OSX10201-XXXX.PDF
12. Garrido-Jurado, S., Muñoz-Salinas, R., Madrid-Cuevas, F.J., Marín-Jiménez, M.J.: Automatic generation and detection of highly reliable fiducial markers under occlusion. Pattern Recogn. **47**(6), 2280–2292 (2014)

Accurate Evaluation of Rotational Angle and Translation Movement of Our Organ-Following Algorithm Based on Depth-Depth Matching

Hiroshi Noborio[✉], Saiki Kiri, Masatoshi Kayaki, Masanao Koeda,
and Katsuhiko Onishi

Department of Computer Science, Osaka Electro-Communication University,
Kiyotaki 1130-70, Shijo-Nawate, Osaka 575-0063, Japan
nobori@osakac.ac.jp

Abstract. We present an algorithm, based on simulated annealing, that causes a virtual liver to mimic an actual liver. We evaluate its precision using the concordance rate of range images of both virtual and actual livers. This concordance rate is evaluated by superimposing a range image, in which a liver polyhedron standard triangulated language form is put through graphical z-buffering using the computer graphics of a PC and a depth image of the actual liver taken with Kinect v2. However, when the actual liver moves in a translational and rotational manner, we are unable to evaluate how accurately the concordance rate corresponds to the actual movement. In this study, we first manufacture a mechanical system that moves a replica of an actual liver in a translational and rotational manner for measurement. This system has two translational degrees of freedom (i.e., X, Y) and three rotational degrees of freedom (i.e., yaw, roll, pitch). This enables the system to move the replica of an actual liver in an extremely accurate manner. Next, we precisely move the actual liver and investigate how much the simulated annealing-based algorithm moves the virtual liver, and we evaluate its accuracy. Whereas previous experiments were conducted under fluorescent lamps and sunlight, our experiment is conducted in an operating room lit by two shadow-less lamps. The Kinect v2 captures depth images utilizing a shade filter to prevent interference from the infrared light of the shadow-less lamps. The past concordance rate and precision of the amount of translational and rotational movement are also evaluated.

Keywords: Digital imaging and communications in medicine
Virtual liver polyhedron standard triangulated language form
Replica of an actual liver · Simulated annealing · Liver surgery navigator

1 Introduction

There are many surgical navigation systems [1, 2]. In almost all cases, we used 3D mechanical or 2D non-mechanical probes with ultrasonic sensors. Unfortunately, since the image resolution of an ultrasonic sensor is not accurate, we cannot detect the position,

© Springer International Publishing AG, part of Springer Nature 2018
M. Kurosu (Ed.): HCI 2018, LNCS 10902, pp. 27–42, 2018.
https://doi.org/10.1007/978-3-319-91244-8_3

orientation, and shape of a real liver precisely for manipulating it in surgical navigation systems. In addition, the calculation of the position, orientation, and shape of the liver is immensely time consuming by many approaches based on combination calculation between enormous cloud points [3, 4].

To address this, we manufactured a liver surgery navigator having the goal of decreasing surgical procedural risk for the liver. We then evaluated its precision using a mechanical system that moves the liver replica translationally and rotationally with a high degree of precision. We previously demonstrated that depth image-matching is quantitatively more useful than matching based on comparing point groups (i.e., the point cloud library) for enabling a virtual liver (i.e., liver polyhedron standard triangu- lated language (STL) form) to follow an actual liver (i.e., liver replica) at high speed [5]. We also investigated two statements about this virtual world: that depth image-matching is useful [6]; and that sufficient following precision can be obtained by evaluating a liver- following algorithm based on the method of steepest descent under natural light or fluorescent lamps in a laboratory [7]. Next, we compared following algorithms based on the method of steepest descent [8] and simulated annealing [9] under shadow-less lamps in an actual operating room, evaluating the latter to be more precise. This revealed that even better following precision is obtained when shadow-less lamps are covered with shade filters [10].

For this study, we manufacture a mechanical system that moves the replica of an actual liver translationally and rotationally with a high degree of precision. We run a simulated annealing algorithm that uses, as a search evaluation indicator, the difference between an actual depth image obtained from the Kinect depth sensor and a virtual depth image based on the z-buffer obtained from OpenGL. When an actual liver is accurately moved translationally and rotationally using a mechanical system that move the replica likewise, we evaluate the precision using the actual amount of translational and rota- tional movement, rather than previous concordance rates.

Section 2 of this paper describes experimental elements, such as the virtual liver, the actual liver, and the shade filter. Section 3 describes the liver surgery navigator. Then, Sect. 4 describes the results of experiments evaluating the liver navigator. We conclude with a summary of our study in Sect. 5.

2   Experimental Elements

This chapter describes the experimental elements used in this study (i.e., the virtual liver, the actual liver, and the shade filter).

2.1   Liver Polyhedron STL Form (i.e., Virtual Liver)

STL is a system that manifests three-dimensional (3D) shapes, including models from small triangular aggregates, having become the standard format in the rapid prototyping industry. In this study, STL created from a hospital patient's magnetic resonance imagery tomography images are used as a liver polyhedron STL form. Figure 1(a) shows the STL human liver model.

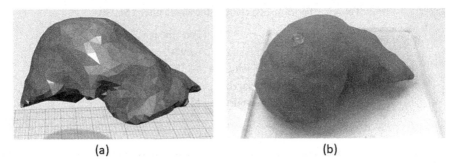

(a)   (b)

Fig. 1. (a) Liver polyhedron STL Form, (b) Skin gel liver model.

2.2   Skin Gel Liver Replica (i.e., Actual Liver)

The STL skin liver model shown in Fig. 1(b) was created using a 3D printer, and skin gel was poured into the concave form of the generated model to produce the skin-gel liver model. The liver model produced using skin gel is comparable to an actual liver during surgery and is used as the liver replica.

2.3   Shade Filter SL999

SL999 is a heat shielding and insulating film sold by Nextfil. This film can shield and insulate infrared light, UV light, and heat, without blocking visible light rays. By affixing it to the target object, we can block 99.9% of infrared light over 1,000 nm and 98% of UV light. Table 1 shows the performance of SL999, whereas Fig. 2(a) shows a graph of its spectrum transmittance.

Table 1. Performance chart of the shade filter SL999.

Items	Performance
Visible light transmittance	76%
Solar radiation transmittance	35.3%
Solar radiation reflectivity	6.3%
Solar radiation absorption	58.4%
UV blocking	98%

2.4   Shade Filter TS6080

TS6080 is a heat shielding and insulating film sold by Cyber Reps. This film can shield and insulate infrared light, UV light, and heat without blocking visible light rays. By affixing it to the target object, we can block 98% of UV light. Table 2 shows the performance of TS6080, whereas Fig. 2(b) shows a graph of its spectrum transmittance.

Table 2. Performance chart of the shade filter TS6080.

Items	Performance
Visible light transmittance	62.9%
Solar radiation transmittance	44.3%
Solar radiation reflectivity	41.8%
Solar radiation absorption	13.9%
UV blocking	97%
Shading coefficient	0.55
Heat transmission coefficient	5.5 W/m^2 K

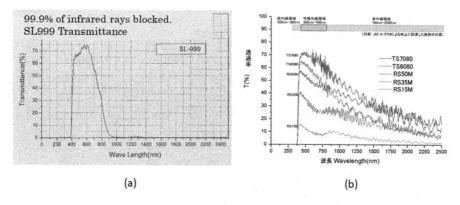

(a)   (b)

Fig. 2. (a) Spectrum transmittance of SL999, (b) Spectrum transmittance of TS6080.

3 Liver Surgery Navigator

This chapter first describes each type of graphical window of the liver surgery navigator. Then, it explains how to find the concordance rate among them.

3.1 Windows of the Liver Surgery Navigator

This section describes our liver navigator, which semi-automatically performs initial alignment of the liver replica and the liver polyhedron STL form. While looking at an image of the livers, the operator first superimposes the liver replica on the liver polyhedron STL form over as wide an area as possible. Next, the liver navigator automatically moves the liver polyhedron STL form and minimizes the difference between it and the depth image. Finally, when the concordance rate is large enough (i.e., 90% or more), the liver replica is moved and interlocking precision evaluation begins.

Figure 3 illustrates the various windows that control our liver navigator. The top-right window displays the liver replica and a depth image of the liver polyhedron STL form. It also shows the concordance rate of the liver replica and the liver polyhedron STL form. In the window located to the right-of-center, on the bottom, concordance rate evaluation and the range of initial alignment can be set. The colored image window on the bottom-right is a real-time image taken by Kinect v2; it allows researchers to monitor the movements of the liver replica. Finally in the window located to the left-of-bottom, we can see positions and angles of 5 degrees-of-freedom concerning to translational and rotational movements.

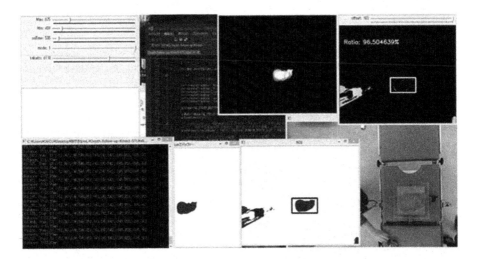

Fig. 3. Windows of the liver surgery navigator that uses simulated annealing.

3.2   Precision Evaluation in Past Following Algorithms (i.e., Concordance Rate)

This study uses the difference in movement distance between the liver replica and the liver polyhedron STL form to evaluate liver navigator precision. Evaluation is conducted by measuring the degree of distance from the axis position of the liver polyhedron STL form in the liver navigator and the liver replica in the translational/rotational movement generator. We then calculate the difference between the movement distance estimated from the initial position of the liver replica and the movement distance of the liver polyhedron STL form. The initial position of the concordance rate is set to 90% or greater. The concordance rate is a value derived from the difference between the depth value and the z-buffer. Figure 4 shows an example of how to find it. First, the depth value obtained using the Kinect to photograph the liver replica and the z-buffer value of the virtual liver STL polyhedron are compared pixel-by-pixel. When $a1 = 80$ mm, $a2 = 92$ mm, $a3 = 85$ mm, $a4 = 79$ mm, $a5 = 75$ mm, $b1 = 73$, $b2 = 93$, $b3 = 82$, $b4 = 68$, and $b5 = 62$, the difference between configuration a and configuration b is 7, 1, 3, 11, and 13. If the difference derived is less than 10 mm of the threshold set in the liver navigator, it is concordant and is expressed as a percentage. Here, the concordance rate is 60% (i.e., 3/5).

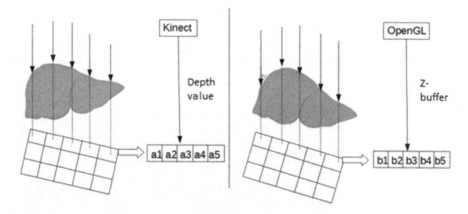

Fig. 4. Concordance rate of actual liver and virtual liver

(a)   (b)

Fig. 5. (a) Translational experiments, (b) Rotational axis of the liver model.

4   Experiments to Evaluate the Liver Surgery Navigator

In this study, experiments are performed in a laboratory and an operating room. In the laboratory, experiments are conducted using an operating bed and shadow-less lamps. To move the liver translationally and rotationally, a translational/rotational movement generator is set atop the operating bed. A 25-cm square acrylic plate 2 cm thick is placed on top; the liver replica is placed on top of that. A robotic arm capable of up and down movement is mounted on the Kinect and set so that the distance between the Kinect and the liver replica can be changed as needed. The Kinect v2 is set up horizontally, in relation to the operating bed, at a position 90 cm above the liver replica atop the translational/rotational movement generator. The Kinect v2 is fixed to the operating bed by placing a metal rod in a clamp installed on the operating bed and fixing it to the rod.

Our experimental methodology follows. First, the axes of the translational/rotational movement-measuring device are adjusted to the initial movement position, the acrylic plate is set up, and the liver replica is placed atop the plate. Next, the initial positions of the liver replica and the liver polyhedron STL form are aligned with the liver navigator that uses simulated annealing, and the concordance rate is set to 90% or greater. Then, measurement of the various axes (i.e., X, Y, yaw) begins. As for movement, both X and Y axes are moved 1 cm at-a-time until they reach 7 cm. Although 360° of movement is possible for the yaw axis, owing to the range of movement of an actual liver, we rotate the yaw axis 5° at a time until it reaches 45° (Fig. 5). Figure 6(a) shows what the experiment looks like in the laboratory, whereas Fig. 6(b) shows what the experiment looks like in the operating room.

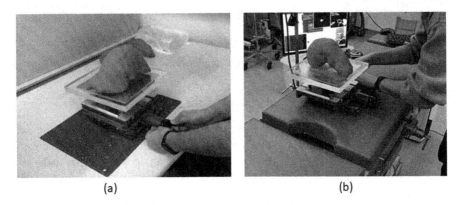

(a)   (b)

Fig. 6. (a) Experiment in the laboratory, (b) Experiment in the operating room.

4.1   Experiment with Exposure to Two Shadow-Less Lamps

This experiment was conducted in a space lit with two shadow-less lamps and operation room lighting. Kinect v2 took images, starting from the initial alignment of the liver replica, using it and the translational/rotational movement generator, until the conclusion of translational and rotational movement. The experiment was conducted using this imaging data. Figure 7(a) shows the lighting from the two shadow-less lamps.

4.2   Experiment with Two Shadow-Less Lamps Covered with TS6080 and SL999

This experiment was conducted in a space lit by two shadow-less lamps and operation room lighting using TS6080 and SL999. As with the experiment sans-lighting from shadow-less lamps, to compare the movement distance of the liver replica to the movement distance of the liver polyhedron STL form, images of the experiment were taken with the Kinect v2 and the captured data was used for evaluation. We attached the TS6080 and SL999 with tape so that they covered the shadow-less lamps; the separator side faced the shadow-less lamps. The TS6080 was affixed to both shadow-less lamps. Figure 7(b) shows what a shadow-less lamp looks like when covered with TS6080.

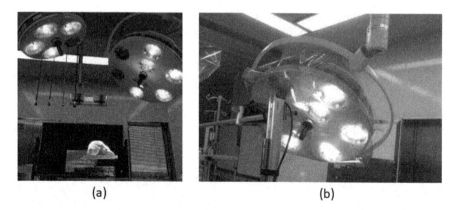

(a)   (b)

Fig. 7. (a) Lighting from two shadow-less lamps, (b) Shadow-less lamp covered with TS6080.

4.3   Translational Movement Experiment on the X-Axis

Here, we evaluated how accurately the liver polyhedron STL form followed the liver replica when it was moved translationally along the X axis in several environments: in a laboratory under natural light or fluorescent lamps, in an operating room under two shadow-less lamps, and in an operating room under two shadow-less lamps covered with two types of shade filters.

Experimental Results in the Laboratory
We moved the liver replica translationally and confirmed that the liver polyhedron STL form was linked to that movement. As shown in Fig. 8(a), the concordance rate during movement consistently exceeded 90%. As for changes in the amount of movement from the liver polyhedron STL form, the error value increased as movement distance increased, as shown in Fig. 8(b). The largest error observed, in comparison to the amount of liver replica movement, was 2.9 mm. This result is slightly better than the experimental results from the operating room, as described in the next section.

Experimental Results Using SL999
We moved the liver replica translationally and confirmed that the liver polyhedron STL form was linked to that movement. The concordance rate during movement was about the same as the rate without shadow-less lamps and, as shown in Fig. 9(a), it consistently exceeded 90%. As seen in Fig. 9(b), results regarding changes in the amount of movement from the liver polyhedron STL form differed from the results for the TS6080 shade filter. Thus, with the SL999 shade filter, there was less fluctuation in errors for each movement distance, and there were fewer errors overall. The largest error, compared to the amount of liver replica movement, was −3.6 mm, similar to those obtained in the TS6080 shade filter experiment. Additionally, the concordance rate was also slightly lower, meaning that it also functioned as an evaluation indicator of movement error.

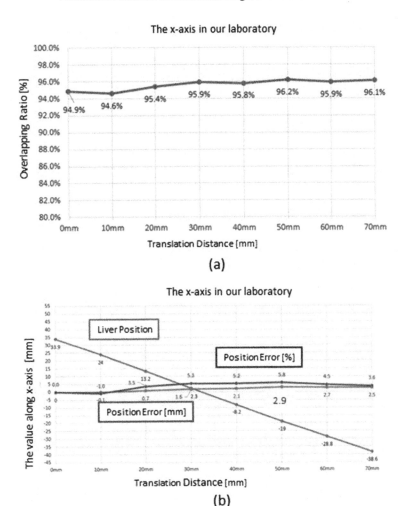

Fig. 8. We describe translational experimental results along the x-axis in the laboratory. (a) Changes in the concordance rate manifested by the liver polyhedron STL when the liver replica is moved (Vertical axis: concordance rate (%); horizontal axis: movement distance (mm)), (b) Movement distance errors (mm) and error rate (mm).

4.4 Translational Movement Experiment on the Y-Axis

Here, we evaluated how accurately the liver polyhedron STL form followed the liver replica when it was moved translationally along the Y axis in several environments: in a laboratory under natural light or fluorescent lamps, in an operating room under two shadow-less lamps, and in an operating room under two shadow-less lamps covered with two types of shade filters.

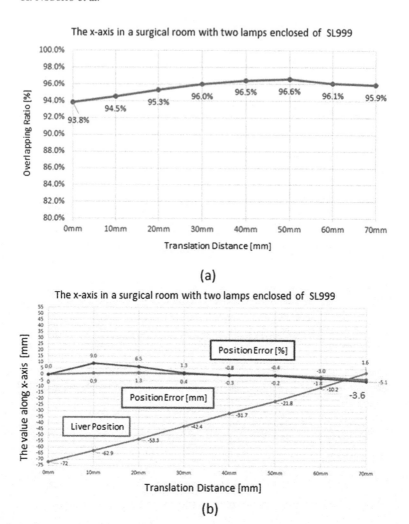

Fig. 9. We represent translational experimental results along the x-axis in a surgical room with two lamps enclosed of SL999. (a) Changes in the concordance rate manifested by the liver poly-hedron STL when the liver replica is moved (Vertical axis: concordance rate (%); horizontal axis: movement distance (mm)), (b) Movement distance errors (mm) and error rate (mm).

Experimental Results in the Laboratory

We moved the liver replica translationally and confirmed that the liver polyhedron STL form was linked to that movement. As shown in Fig. 10(a), the concordance rate during movement consistently exceeded 90%, as measured on the X axis. As can be seen in Fig. 10(b), overall errors were observed in results regarding changes in the amount of movement from the liver polyhedron STL form. Furthermore, large errors were observed from 4 cm-on, with a maximum error of −10.3 mm.

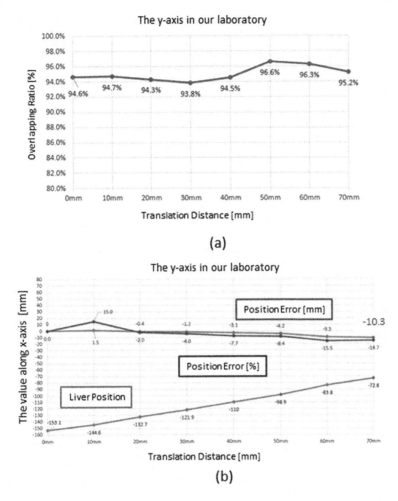

Fig. 10. We describe translational experimental results along the y-axis in the laboratory. (a) Changes in the concordance rate manifested by the liver polyhedron STL when the liver replica is moved (Vertical axis: concordance rate (%); horizontal axis: movement distance (mm)), (b) Movement distance errors (mm) and error rate (mm).

Experimental Results Using SL999

We moved the liver replica translationally and confirmed that the liver polyhedron STL form was linked to that movement. As shown in Fig. 11(a), the concordance rate during movement consistently exceeded 90%, just like the rate without shadow-less lamps. When compared to the TS6080 shade filter, the SL999 results were superior, with errors sustained below half, as shown in Fig. 11(b). There were almost no large errors. The largest error, compared to the amount of liver replica movement, was only −5.3 mm. This was better than any other experimental result to date. However, the concordance rate was not good, demonstrating that it is not necessarily appropriate as an error evaluation indicator for translational movement.

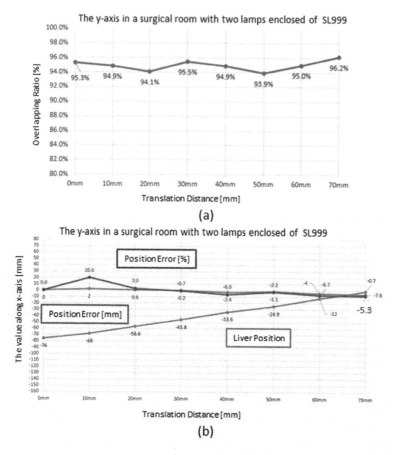

Fig. 11. We represent translational experimental results along the y-axis in a surgical room with two lamps enclosed of SL999. (a) Changes in the concordance rate manifested by the liver polyhedron STL when the liver replica is moved (Vertical axis: concordance rate (%); horizontal axis: movement distance (mm)), (b) Movement distance errors (mm) and error rate (mm).

4.5   Experiments on Rotational Movement Around the Yaw Axis

Here, we evaluated how accurately the liver polyhedron STL form followed the liver replica when the liver replica was moved rotationally around the yaw axis in several environments: a laboratory under natural light or fluorescent lamps, an operating room under two shadow-less lamps, in an operating room under two shadow-less lamps are covered with two types of shade filters.

Experimental Results in the Laboratory
We moved the liver replica rotationally and confirmed that the liver polyhedron STL form was linked to that movement. As shown in Fig. 12(a), the concordance rate during movement consistently exceeded 90%, just as measured on the X axis. As can be seen in

Fig. 12(b), changes in the amount of rotational movement from the liver polyhedron STL form generally followed predictions calculated from initial position. There were few errors that excluded initial movement, and we confirmed that it was more consistent that translational movement. The largest error, compared to the amount of liver replica movement, was 2.3°.

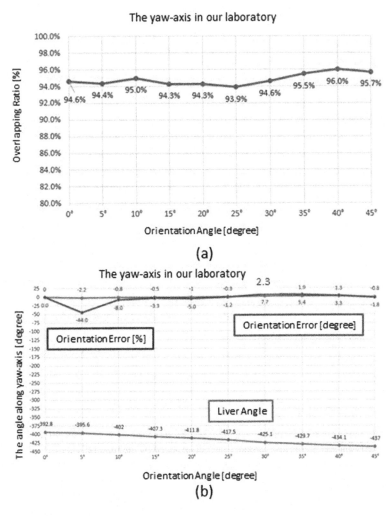

Fig. 12. We describe rotational experimental results along the yaw-axis in the laboratory. (a) Changes in the concordance rate manifested by the liver polyhedron STL when the liver replica is moved (Vertical axis: concordance rate (%), horizontal axis: (°)), (b) Movement distance errors (°) and error rate (°).

Experimental Results Using Two Shadow-Less Lamps
We moved the liver replica rotationally and confirmed that the liver polyhedron STL form was linked to that movement. As demonstrated by Fig. 13(a), the concordance rate during movement was better than in previous results and nearly always exceeded 96%.

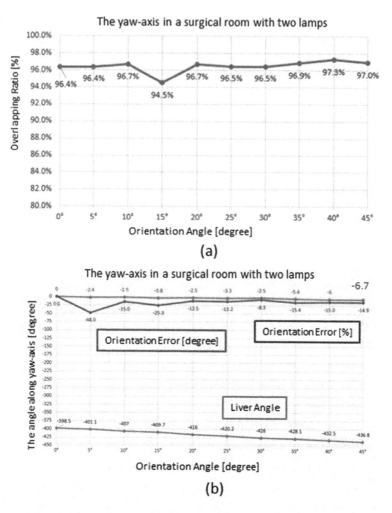

Fig. 13. We represent rotational experimental results along the yaw-axis in a surgical room with two lamps. (a) Changes in the concordance rate manifested by the liver polyhedron STL when the liver replica is moved (Vertical axis: concordance rate (%), horizontal axis: (°)), (b) Movement distance errors (°) and error rate (°).

Meanwhile, as shown in Fig. 13(b), errors were gradually added to the initial value as the amount of rotational movement from the liver polyhedron STL form changed. Although there were few errors for each movement, errors accumulated as the angle of movement increased, and large errors ultimately remained. No noticeable differences were observed when using just one shadow-less lamp. The largest error, compared to the amount of liver replica movement, was $-6.7°$.

To summarize these results, whereas the concordance rate was better than in experimental results from the laboratory and there were no large errors for rotational movement, the errors grew larger. Therefore, we learned that concordance rate is not an indicator for error evaluation in rotational movement.

5   Conclusion

Using a mechanical system that precisely generates translational/rotational movement, this study evaluated the precision of a liver-following algorithm based on simulated annealing. The results empirically demonstrated the following three things.

(1)   The experimental results in the operating room under shadow-less lamps were often superior to the experimental results in the laboratory under natural light. Additionally, using filters to block the infrared spectrum from the shadow-less lamps produced better results. We are currently selecting a shade filter that can reliably remove, from the shadow-less lamps, spectra interfering with the infrared pattern projected by the Kinect v2.

(2)   Concordance rate, which has been used to evaluate liver following algorithms in the past, often could not be used (i.e. was not correlated) for evaluating error in translational movement or rotational movement, globally (i.e., overall comparison of each experiment) or locally (i.e., comparison of multiple times in each experiment).

(3)   When the algorithm was evaluated in the past using concordance rate, rotational movement was evaluated as more precise than translational movement in nearly all cases. However, the results of this study showed the opposite. The movement precision of rotation, especially the degree of roll and pitch, was poor. This revealed that, when depth images are compared, small angle differences between the liver replica and liver polyhedron STL form are not being successfully evaluated.

Moving forward, we will first investigate shade filters that are better fitted to cameras that measure depth images. Next, unlike the lever for translational movement, the lever for rotational movement is in an extremely small area. This causes the operator to move the liver replica by accident. Additionally, because the graduation of rotational movement is done in far smaller increments than that of translational movement, the proper amount of rotational movement is not obtained, particularly for the angles of roll and pitch. This urgently needs improvement.

Acknowledgment. This research has been partially supported by the Collaborative Research Fund for Graduate Schools (A) of the Osaka Electro-Communication University, and a Grant-in-Aid for Scientific Research of the Ministry of Education, Culture, Sports, Science and Technology (Research Project Number: JP26289069).

References

1. Satou, S., Aoki, T., Kaneko, J., Sakamoto, Y., Hasegawa, K., Sugawara, Y., Arai, O., Mitake, T., Miura, K., Kokudo, N.: Initial experience of intraoperative three-dimensional navigation for liver resection using real-time virtual sonography. Surgery **155**(2), 255–262 (2014)
2. Morita, Y., Takanishi, K., Matsumoto, J.: A new simple navigation for anatomic liver resection under intraoperative real-time ultrasound guidance. Hepatogastroenterology **61**(34), 1734–1738 (2014)
3. Rusu, R.B., Cousins, S.: 3D is here: point cloud library (PCL). In: IEEE International Conference on Robotics and Automation, pp. 1–4 (2011)
4. Wu, Y.F., Wang, W., Lu, K.Q., Wei, Y.D., Chen, Z.C.: A new method for registration of 3D point sets with low overlapping ratios. In: 13th CIRP conference on Computer Aided Tolerancing, pp. 202–206 (2015)
5. Noborio, H., et. al.: Motion transcription algorithm by matching corresponding depth image and Z-buffer. In: Proceedings of the 10th Anniversary Asian Conference on Computer Aided Surgery, pp. 60–61 (2014)
6. Watanabe, K., et al.: Parameter identification of depth-depth-matching algorithm for liver following. Jurnal Teknologi Med. Eng. **77**(6), 35–39 (2015). Penerbit UTM Press
7. Noborio, H., et al.: Experimental results of 2D depth-depth matching algorithm based on depth camera kinect v1. J. Bioinform. Neurosci. **1**(1), 38–44 (2015)
8. Noborio, H., Watanabe, K., Yagi, M., Ohira, S., Tachibana, K.: Algorithm experimental evaluation for an occluded liver with/without shadow-less lamps and invisible light filter in a surgical room. In: Marcus, A., Wang, W. (eds.) DUXU 2017. LNCS, vol. 10289, pp. 524–539. Springer, Cham (2017). https://doi.org/10.1007/978-3-319-58637-3_41
9. Watanabe, K., Yoshida, S., Yano, D., Koeda, M., Noborio, H.: A new organ-following algorithm based on depth-depth matching and simulated annealing, and its experimental evaluation. In: Marcus, A., Wang, W. (eds.) DUXU 2017. LNCS, vol. 10289, pp. 594–607. Springer, Cham (2017). https://doi.org/10.1007/978-3-319-58637-3_47
10. Noborio, H., Yoshida, S., Watanabe, K., Yano, D., Koeda, M.: Comparative study of depth-image matching with steepest descendent and simulated annealing algorithms. In: Proceedings of the 11th International Joint Conference on Biomedical Engineering Systems and Technologies (BIOSTEC 2018) - BIODEVICES, pp. 77–87 (2018)

A Useful Robotic-Mechanical System for Measuring a Surgical Area Without Obstructing Surgical Operations by Some Surgeon

Masahiro Nonaka[1], Yuya Chikayama[2], Masatoshi Kayaki[2], Masanao Koeda[2], Katsunori Tachibana[2], and Hiroshi Noborio[2(✉)]

[1] Kansai Medical University, Hirakata, Osaka 573-1010, Japan
[2] Osaka Electro-Communication University, Shijo-Nawate, Osaka 575-0063, Japan
nobori@osakac.ac.jp

Abstract. In this study, we constructed and tested the usability of a surgical area-measuring robot-mechanical system, which does not obstruct the movements of doctors, assistants, or nurses during surgery, under two operating lights in an operating room. This study revealed that using the robotic slider to move the camera up and down did not result in excessive vibration or inconsistent depth measurements before, during, and after the movement. For example, if a doctor moves the camera out of the way to move a microscope to the upper part of the surgical area for microsurgery and then brings it back, the system could accurately retain the depth image alignment.

Keywords: Surgical area sensing · Robotic-mechanical system · Microsurgery
Surgical operation navigation

1 Introduction

In recent years, many groups have conducted extensive research on surgical operation navigation systems. Often, they develop navigation systems in the field of orthopedic surgery because bones have few variations. Navigation systems have also been suggested for neurosurgery and otolaryngology [1, 2], which deal with fairly immobile organs that are surrounded by bones. Surgical navigation systems focusing on the kidney and liver are also being explored; these include endoscopic and/or laparoscopic surgery systems [3, 4] and robot surgery systems [5].

We have supported doctors by designing a sensor-based surgical operation navigator for the liver and brain [6–13]. For this, it was essential to accurately measure the surgical area with a depth camera to obtain a depth image. To accomplish this, last year we built a new surgical area-measuring robot-mechanical system and assessed the correlation between the distance the robot traveled and the change in distance of the depth image [14–16].

For example, this robot-mechanical system allows a surgeon to raise multiple cameras simultaneously to insert a microscope into the surgical area. Then, when the

© Springer International Publishing AG, part of Springer Nature 2018
M. Kurosu (Ed.): HCI 2018, LNCS 10902, pp. 43–52, 2018.
https://doi.org/10.1007/978-3-319-91244-8_4

microsurgery is finished, the surgeon can lower the cameras back into the surgical area. The robot knows the distance that the group of cameras was raised or lowered, so it can achieve consistency in the precision of the depth image before, during, and after the cameras are moved. The system captures images from multiple angles in the surgical area because during long surgeries, the surgeon's head and arms block parts of the surgical area. Using one camera proved insufficient for acquiring an accurate depth image, so we increased the number of cameras and controlled their infrared pattern emissions to acquire stable and accurate depth images.

The robotic-mechanical system is constructed in such a way that there is a pole next to the surgical area and the system is mounted directly onto the operation bed, which obstructs various tasks performed during surgery. Therefore, in this study, we mounted the pole on the operation bed by the patient's feet, and using it as a base, we designed and built a new robotic-mechanical system to support the group of cameras in the surgical area. Here we will evaluate the measurement precision.

In Sect. 2 of this study, we will compare the old and new surgical area-measuring robotic-mechanical systems. In Sect. 3, we will evaluate the surgical area-imaging robotics-mechanical system in an operating room that has two operating lights. Finally, in Sect. 4, we will summarize the assessment test and discuss future projects.

2 Comparison of the Old and New Robotic-Mechanical Systems

First, we will introduce the specifications of the Intel Real Sense SR300, and then we will introduce the old and new surgical area measuring robotic-mechanical systems.

2.1 Intel Real Sense SR300

In this study, we used three Intel Real Sense SR300 cameras to acquire serial depth images of the surgical area (Fig. 1, Table 1).

Table 1. Real Sense SR300 specifications.

Items	Specifications
Depth image resolution	640 × 480 (60 fps, 30 fps, 10 fps)
Depth measurement method	Time of flight
Depth measurement range	200–1200 mm
Color field	68° horizontal, 41.5° vertical
Depth field	71.5° horizontal, 55° vertical

2.2 Previous Surgical Area-Imaging Robotic-Mechanical System

We constructed a robotic-mechanical system that gives doctors an unobstructed view of the surgical area while being able to freely raise and lower a group of cameras (Fig. 2(a), (b), (c)) [14–16]. In this system, the three cameras alternate emission of an infrared pattern, and upon receiving the signal, the system was able to acquire a stable depth image [16].

Fig. 1. Real Sense SR300.

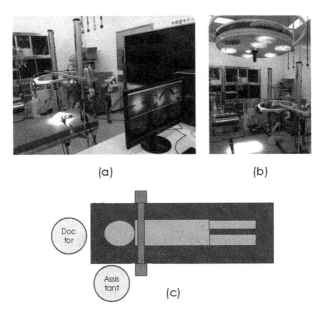

(a)   (b)

(c)

Fig. 2. (a), (b) Previous robotic-mechanical system (includes the display in the front of the depth image from the three cameras), (c) aerial view of the basic layout.

However, when the system was tested, we discovered a flaw. The poles that attach the robotic-mechanical system to the operating bed would often obstruct access to the patient. Therefore, to solve this problem, we built a robotic-mechanical system with the supporting pole located by the patient's feet.

2.3   The New Model of the Surgical Area-Imaging Robotic-Mechanical System

We constructed a robotic-mechanical system supported by a pole that does not obstruct the doctor, assistant, or nurse from accessing the patient (Fig. 3(a), (b), (c)). Then we evaluated the robotic-mechanical system's vibrations when the cameras are raised or lowered using the change in the depth image. We will describe the test results in the next section.

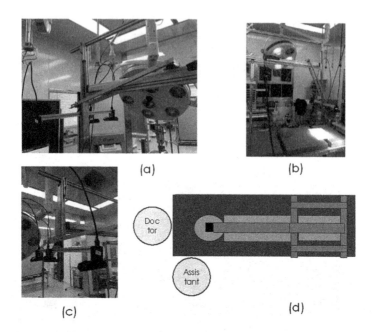

Fig. 3. (a), (b), (c) The new robotic-mechanical system (including the placement of the three cameras and robotic slider), (d) aerial view of the basic layout.

3 Assessment of the Surgical Area-Imaging Robotic-Mechanical System in the Operating Room

We attached the new surgical area-imaging robotic-mechanical system to an operating bed in an operating room with two shadow-less operating lights. We verified that the center Intel Real Sense SR300 depth camera could acquire a stable depth image when the operating lights were off. Then, using the robotic slider, we raised and lowered the camera approximately 50 cm, 100 cm, and 200 cm to verify that the depth image also changed by 50 cm, 100 cm, and 200 cm, accordingly. Here, we averaged a depth of 30 pixels in the depth image for the depth at each time point. The sampling time was set to 30 frames per second. Then, we evaluated the extent of the robotic-mechanical system's vibrations by the change in depth over time. Next, we performed the same experiment, but with the operating lights on using the same evaluation described above.

3.1 Change in Depth Over Time (Without Operating Lights)

First, we raised the camera 50 mm, 100 mm, and 200 mm from the starting point (310 mm), and then we lowered it 200 mm, 100 mm, and 50 mm. The resulting graphs shown in Fig. 4 reveal that the depth of the top camera of the surgical area-imaging robotic-mechanical system increases and decreases are approximately equal.

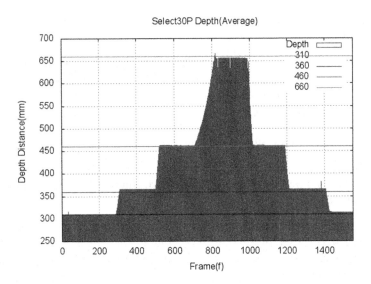

Fig. 4. Graph of the change in depth recorded by the top depth camera of the surgical area-imaging robotic-mechanical system while the operating lights were off (The frame rate is 30 fps).

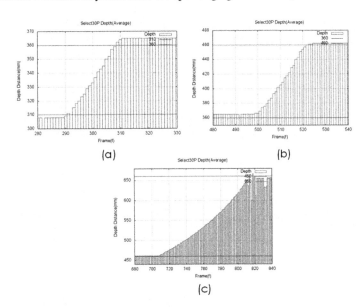

Fig. 5. Graph of vibrations, evaluated as the change in depth recorded when the robotic-mechanical system's camera was raised (a) 50 mm, (b) 100 mm, and (c) 200 mm with the operating lights off (The vibration time is less than 30 frames < 1 s).

3.2 Vibrations While Raising the Robotic-Mechanical System (Without Operating Lights)

The results for when we raised the camera 50 mm, 100 mm, and 200 mm are shown in Fig. 5(a), (b), (c). There was almost no vibration when it was raised 50 mm and 100 mm. When it was raised 200 mm, however, it vibrated at most 1 s. This shows that the differences in the depth images before and after raising the camera is significant. However, typical surgical operations last 3–4 h and laparotomies take about 20 min, so this vibration has very little effect on the surgical operation navigation.

3.3 Vibrations While Lowering the Robotic-Mechanical System (Without Operating Lights)

The results from when we lowered the camera 50 mm, 100 mm, and 200 mm are shown in Fig. 6(a), (b), (c). There was almost no vibration when it was lowered 50 mm and 100 mm, however, when it was lowered 200 mm, it vibrated when it started moving. Fortunately, the vibration time is less than 30 frames < 1 s, which is quite smaller than real periods of several surgeries.

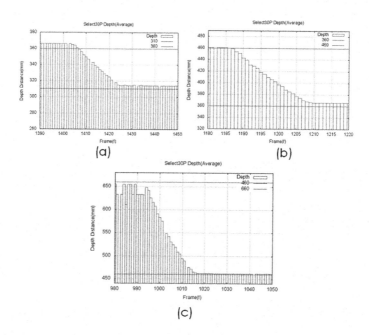

Fig. 6. Graph of vibrations, evaluated as the change in depth recorded when the robotic-mechanical system's camera lowered (a) 50 mm, (b) 100 mm, and (c) 200 mm with the operating lights off (The vibration time is less than 30 frames < 1 s).

3.4   Change in Depth Over Time (with Two Operating Lights)

First, we raised the camera 50 mm, 100 mm, and 200 mm from the starting point (310 mm), and then we lowered it 200 mm, 100 mm, and 50 mm. The resulting graph, which is shown in Fig. 7, reveals that the depth of the top camera of the surgical area-imaging robotic-mechanical system increases and decreases are approximately equally. The depth is more accurate when the camera is on a flat plain and the operating lights are on, which means the operating lights have a positive effect on sensing.

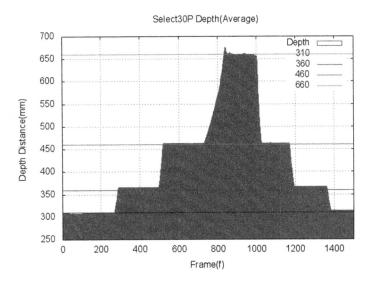

Fig. 7. Graph of the change in depth recorded by the top depth camera of the surgical area-imaging robotic-mechanical system while the operating lights were on.

3.5   Vibrations While Raising the Robotic-Mechanical System (with Operating Lights)

The graph of when we raised the camera 50 mm, 100 mm, and 200 mm is shown in Fig. 8(a), (b), (c). There was almost no vibration when it was raised 50 mm and 100 mm, however, when raised 200 mm, there were vibrations, which lasted for a shorter time compared to when the operating lights were off, and the depth was more constant after the vibrations stopped. This means the operating lights have a positive effect on sensing. From these results, we can see that the depth image comparison before and after raising the camera is significant. Typical surgical operations last 3–4 h and laparotomies take about 20 min, so this vibration has very little effect on the surgical operation navigation.

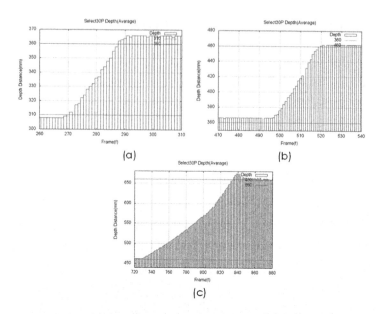

Fig. 8. Graph of vibrations, evaluated as the change in depth recorded when the robotic-mechanical system's camera was raised (a) 50 mm, (b) 100 mm, and (c) 200 mm while the operating lights were on.

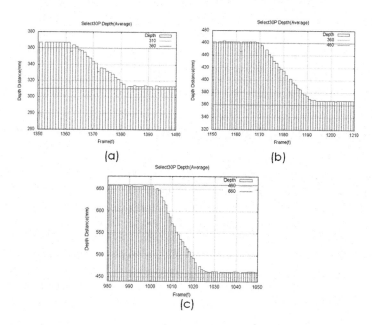

Fig. 9. Graph of vibrations, evaluated as the change in depth recorded when the robotic-mechanical system's camera was lowered (a) 50 mm, (b) 100 mm, and (c) 200 mm while the operating lights were on.

3.6 Vibrations While Lowering the Robotic-Mechanical System (with Operating Lights)

The results when we lowered the camera 50 mm, 100 mm, and 200 mm are shown in Fig. 9(a), (b), (c). There was almost no vibration when it was lowered 50 mm, 100 mm, or 200 mm, and depth is more accurate when the camera is on a flat plain and the operating lights are on, which means the illumination from the operating lights has a positive effect on sensing.

4 Concluding Remarks

In this study, we built a new surgical area-measuring robotic-mechanical system with a pole attached to the operating bed that does not obstruct access to the patient. Then, we evaluated the usability of the system by graphing the change in depth measured by the top camera. Our results showed that under two lit operating room lights, even if the robotic slider raised or lowered the camera, there were no abnormal vibrations and the system was able to stably acquire a depth image of the target object.

In future studies, we will examine calculating depth by averaging depths at randomly selected 30 pixels (instead of averaging depths at a fixed set of 30 pixels), which we believe will cancel out errors and provide better results. After that, we plan to change the number of frames to obtain a more stable average depth value (and individual depth values).

We will strengthen the theoretical formulas for moving the robotic slider and camera up and down based on the geometric properties of the robotic-mechanical system and its targets (various organs) as well as the geometric properties of the position of the three cameras and their targets (various organs). In addition, we will calibrate the relationship between the movement of the robot and the movement of the average depth value. We believe this will allow us to more precisely measure the target object.

Acknowledgment. This research has been partially supported by the Collaborative Research Fund for Graduate Schools (A) of the Osaka Electro-Communication University, and a Grant-in-Aid for Scientific Research of the Ministry of Education, Culture, Sports, Science and Technology (Research Project Number: JP26289069).

References

1. Matsumoto, N., et al.: A minimally invasive registration method using surface template-assisted marker positioning (STAMP) for image-guided otologic surgery. Otolaryngol. Head Neck Surg. **140**(1), 96–102 (2009)
2. Hong, J., Hashizume, M.: An effective point-based registration tool for surgical navigation. Surg. Endosc. **24**(4), 944–948 (2010)
3. Ieiri, S., et al.: Augmented reality navigation system for laparoscopic splenectomy in children based on preoperative CT image using optical tracking device. Pediatr. Surg. Int. **28**(4), 341–346 (2012)

4. Mahmud, N., Cohen, J., Tsourides, K., Berzin, T.M.: Computer vision and augmented reality in gastrointestinal endoscopy. Gastroenterol. Rep. (Oxf.) **3**(3), 179–184 (2015). https://doi.org/10.1093/gastro/gov027. Accessed 1 Jul 2015

5. Pessaux, P., Diana, M., Soler, L., Piardi, T., Mutter, D., Marescaux, J.: Towards cybernetic surgery: robotic and augmented reality-assisted liver segmentectomy. Langenbecks Arch. Surg. **400**(3), 381–385 (2015)

6. Watanabe, K., et. al.: Brain shift simulation controlled by directly captured surface points. In: Proceedings of 38th Annual International Conference of the IEEE Engineering in Medicine and Biology Society, Sessions: Ignite_Theme 2_Fr2, Poster Session III, Orlando Florida USA (2016)

7. Yano, D., Koeda, M., Onishi, K., Noborio, H.: Development of a surgical knife attachment with proximity indicators. In: Marcus, A., Wang, W. (eds.) DUXU 2017. LNCS, vol. 10289, pp. 608–618. Springer, Cham (2017). https://doi.org/10.1007/978-3-319-58637-3_48

8. Watanabe, K., Yoshida, S., Yano, D., Koeda, M., Noborio, H.: A new organ-following algorithm based on depth-depth matching and simulated annealing, and its experimental evaluation. In: Marcus, A., Wang, W. (eds.) DUXU 2017. LNCS, vol. 10289, pp. 594–607. Springer, Cham (2017). https://doi.org/10.1007/978-3-319-58637-3_47

9. Sengiku, A., et al.: Augmented reality navigation system for robot-assisted laparoscopic partial nephrectomy. In: Marcus, A., Wang, W. (eds.) DUXU 2017. LNCS, vol. 10289, pp. 575–584. Springer, Cham (2017). https://doi.org/10.1007/978-3-319-58637-3_45

10. Onishi, K., Miki, Y., Okuda, K., Koeda, M., Noborio, H.: A study of guidance method for AR laparoscopic surgery navigation system. In: Marcus, A., Wang, W. (eds.) DUXU 2017. LNCS, vol. 10289, pp. 556–564. Springer, Cham (2017). https://doi.org/10.1007/978-3-319-58637-3_43

11. Noborio, H., et. al.: Fast surgical algorithm for cutting with liver standard triangulation language format using Z-buffers in graphics processing unit. In: Fujie, M. (ed.) Computer Aided Surgery, pp. 127–140. Springer, Tokyo (2016). https://doi.org/10.1007/978-4-431-55810-1_11

12. Noborio, H., Aoki, K., Kunii, T., Mizushino, K.: A potential function-based scalpel navigation method that avoids blood vessel groups during excision of cancerous tissue. In: Proceedings of the 38th Annual International Conference of the IEEE Engineering in Medicine and Biology Society (EMBC 2016), pp. 6106–6112 (2016)

13. Noborio, H., Kunii, T., Mizushino, K.: Comparison of GPU-based and CPU-based algorithms for determining the minimum distance between a CUSA scalper and blood vessels. In: BIOSTEC 2016, pp. 128–136. The SCITEPRESS Digital Library (2016)

14. Watanabe, K., et. al.: A mechanical system directly attaching beside a surgical bed for measuring surgical area precisely by depth camera. In: Proceedings of the 10th MedViz Conference and the 6th Eurographics Workshop on Visual Computing for Biology and Medicine (EG VCBM), pp. 105–108 (2016)

15. Watanabe, K., et. al.: Capturing a brain shift directly by the depth camera kinect v2. In: Proceedings of 38th Annual International Conference of the IEEE Engineering in Medicine and Biology Society, Sessions: Ignite_Theme 4_Fr1, Poster Session II, Orlando Florida USA (2016)

16. Nonaka, M., Watanabe, K., Noborio, H., Kayaki, M., Mizushino, K.: Capturing a surgical area using multiple depth cameras mounted on a robotic mechanical system. In: Marcus, A., Wang, W. (eds.) DUXU 2017. LNCS, vol. 10289, pp. 540–555. Springer, Cham (2017). https://doi.org/10.1007/978-3-319-58637-3_42

A Novel Liver Surgical Navigation System Using Polyhedrons with STL-Format

Satoshi Numata[✉], Daiki Yano, Masanao Koeda, Katsuhiko Onishi,
Kaoru Watanabe, Hiroshi Noborio, and Hirotaka Uoi

Osaka Electro-Communication University, Shijonawate, Osaka 5750063, Japan
numata@osakac.ac.jp

Abstract. We have developed the liver surgical navigation system composed of three subsystems: the liver position and orientation estimator, the surgical knife position estimator and the liver surgical navigator. These subsystems work separately for estimating the liver position and the knife position, and the liver surgical navigation system will use those positions to navigate surgeons accurately. The liver position is estimated by comparing two depth images; an image come from a depth camera targeting the liver and an image rendered by OpenGL using the Polyhedrons with STL-format data previously scanned from a patient. The knife position is estimated by tracking markers put at the top of the knife. The surgical navigation system holds precise data such as positions of vessels or the surgical steps, and show appropriate navigation data to the surgeons. In this paper, we describe the overview of this system and how we integrated these subsystems into the liver surgery supporting system.

Keywords: Liver surgery support · Navigation · Inter-process communication

1 Introduction

Liver surgery requires extremely delicate treatment for several types of blood vessels such as arteries or veins while they are living inside the soft organ. Surgeons often use X-ray imaging, computed tomography (CT) scanning or magnetic resonance imaging (MRI) previously to the surgery for determining precise positions of those vessels in the liver. However, those vessels are naturally located sterically in our three dimensional world and surgeons face to difficulties in matching those imaging and scanning data to the real liver of the patient. In most of the cases, surgeons have to use projected data around the liver on two dimensional monitors during the surgery. To solve the problem, some approaches are suggested such as making 3D vessel models using 3D printer [1] or matching postures of a virtual liver on a computer and a real liver of the patient in real time for the computer navigation as we have developed [2].

The goal of our system is to navigate surgeons according to the paths previously prepared using the liver models scanned from patients, and to alert surgeons visually and audibly to be careful around the high risk areas.

© Springer International Publishing AG, part of Springer Nature 2018
M. Kurosu (Ed.): HCI 2018, LNCS 10902, pp. 53–63, 2018.
https://doi.org/10.1007/978-3-319-91244-8_5

2   Liver Surgical Navigation System

2.1   System Overview

Our liver surgical navigation system is composed of two cameras located above the liver and the surgical knife and a computer that communicates with those cameras as shown in Fig. 1. These cameras have different features and each camera will be used by different program.

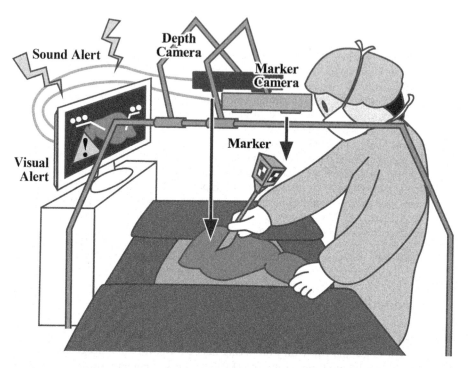

Fig. 1. System overview of our liver surgery support system

One camera (illustrated as a yellow camera in Fig. 1) is a marker tracking camera, which can track multiple two dimensional markers in real time. This marker tracking camera is used by the knife position estimator. As shown in the figure, multiple markers are put on the bottom of the surgical knife, and those markers will be captured and tracked by the camera. The knife position estimator uses position data of those markers put on the bottom to estimate the position of the knife tip.

Another camera (illustrated as a black camera in Fig. 1) is a depth camera, which can capture depth images in its measuring range. The liver position estimator repeatedly gets the depth image of the liver and perform an image processing for estimating current position and rotation of the liver.

We are currently using MicronTracker 3 as the marker tracking camera and Kinect v2 sensor as the depth camera, however, those cameras can be replaced with other cameras or sensors if precision allows.

2.2 Knife Position Estimator

The knife position estimator periodically gets marker data from the marker camera, and utilize the recognized marker information including positions and rotations for estimating the position of the knife tip. This estimator firstly calculate the average position of the markers put on the bottom of the knife, and then calculate the tip position by sliding the average position from the bottom to the top according to the preset length of the knife. Figure 2 shows how 2D markers are put on the bottom of the knife. The tip position is then converted to the depth camera coordinate, as it is well discussed in the next chapter.

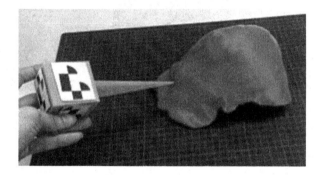

Fig. 2. A knife model with markers and a 3D printed liver model

2.3 Liver Position Estimator

The liver position estimator periodically gets a depth image using the depth camera, and then comparing the shape with Polyhedrons loaded on the memory for finding the exact location of the liver and its orientation. Figure 3 shows how the real liver model (A) is captured as a depth image (B) and how it will be compared with the depth images (C) rendered on the graphics memory using OpenGL.

Fig. 3. Real liver model (A), a depth image (B) and a rendered liver image (C)

2.4   Liver Surgical Navigator

The liver surgical navigator reads and integrates the knife position data and the liver position data from the named shared memories. It also loads the polyhedrons data with STL-format independently, for separately showing sub parts of the liver such as the hepatic artery, the portal vein, lobes and so on for the surgical navigation. In Fig. 4, the experimental implementation of the navigator is shown.

Fig. 4. The liver surgical navigator using knife and liver data from estimators

2.5   Testing Setup

Unfortunately, it is very difficult to attempt to verify our system repeatedly on human bodies. Instead, we have prepared DICOM based liver images captured by MRI, and integrated those images into polyhedrons with STL (Standard Triangulated Language) formatted data. Thereafter, we can make a 3D liver model from the STL data using a 3D printer, and the STL data also can be loaded in a computer memory to be rendered from any direction (Fig. 5).

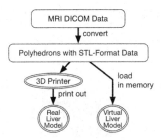

Fig. 5. A real liver model and a virtual liver model

The polyhedrons with the STL formatted data will be printed out as a real 3D model and also rendered on a graphics memory as depth images using OpenGL. The 3D liver model will be used for moving its position and rotating its orientation, and then it is captured by a depth camera connected to the liver position estimator. The result of the liver position estimation can verify the precision of our system.

Of course, it is important not mind the influence of surgeons' shadows and the characteristics of surgical lighting (for heat reduction and shadow dilution) after the verification is well performed. But it is totally efficient way to construct the base of the liver position estimator of our system.

Figure 6 shows 3D printed surgical knife models used with the 3D printed liver model to verify the precision of the knife position estimator. The first model was introduced in [3], and it was totally made from course plastic and it had an average 2.5 mm error. An improved version was introduced in [4], and it was made from fine plastic. It had an average 2.0 mm error. The well improved version introduced in [5] is currently used and it has an average 0.8 mm error.

Fig. 6. Three types of 3D printed surgical knife models with bottom markers

3   Inter-process Communication

3.1   Data Flow

As we described above, three subsystems called the knife position estimator, the liver position estimator and the liver surgical navigator will work simultaneously and communicate each other. As each subsystem can be verified and improved each other, those subsystems are separately developed and are working as different programs in different processes.

Figure 5 shows how and what kind of data is flowed between the subsystems. The knife tip position is repeatedly written by the knife position estimator at a regular intervals. The position and the rotation of a liver is also repeatedly written by the liver position estimator at a regular intervals. Those data are written into separate named shared memories as illustrated in Fig. 5.

Shared memory is the memory that can be accessed by different processes simultaneously. Comparing to the other inter-process communication methods such as socket communication or named pipe, it is expected to be much faster as it is just writing and reading to/from the memories (Fig. 7).

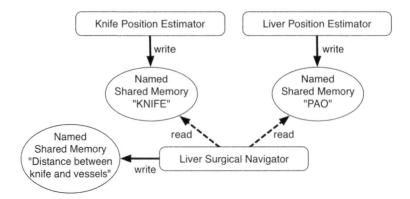

Fig. 7. Data flow in our system using named shared memories

The knife position estimator writes the knife tip position data in the shared memory named "KNIFE." The knife position is expressed as three double values (x, y, z). The unit used in the position value is discussed in the next section about the coordinate conversion.

The liver position estimator writes the liver position and the rotation in the shared memory named "PAO." (The name "PAO" for the liver position and rotation comes from "Position And Orientation," while the knife tip data has just the position.) The liver position is expressed as three float values (x, y, z) and rotation is expressed as three float values (roll, pitch, yaw). Those six float values are continuously written in position-orientation order. The unit used in the position values is discussed in the next section about the coordinate conversion. The unit used in the rotation values is degree.

The data flow design is very simple and they would not do other work. That is very important design to make subsystems so robust that they can continuously work and will not stop during the surgery.

3.2 Coordinate Conversion

In this section, the coordinate conversion between multiple data is precisely discussed. Because there are two cameras and the virtual rendered liver is located in the OpenGL space, those data should be converted in a common coordinate system.

In Knife Position Estimator. Multiple marker positions are captured by the marker tracking camera, and by calculating an average position of those positions, the knife position estimator calculates the tip position of the knife. Those calculations are performed in the coordinate system of the marker tracking camera. Because the body of the marker tracking camera and the body of the depth camera should be located in different position, and because they have different characteristics, those camera uses different coordinates. Therefore, the eight-point algorithm is used to calculate a conversion matrix after setting up those cameras. That conversion matrix is used to convert the knife tip position to the coordinate system of the depth camera, and the matrix is held as long as the same set up is used.

In Liver Position Estimator. A depth image is captured by the depth camera. As shown in Fig. 8, the STL-formatted liver model is loaded at the launch time and rendered from some different directions using an OpenGL renderer for one depth image. The number of the rendered image depends on the machine power, as the rendering process will be terminated after a certain duration has passed (currently the duration is set as ten processor time units in our implementation). Thereafter, the simulated annealing method is used to match the depth image with those rendered images to estimate the closest position and orientation of the liver. To simplify the comparison, the OpenGL rendering uses the same value of the actual depth camera characteristics for making a projection matrix: currently the field of view is set to 90 degrees and the aspect ratio is approximately 1.21. Here we can assume that the rendered images and the depth image are in the same coordinate system of the depth camera.

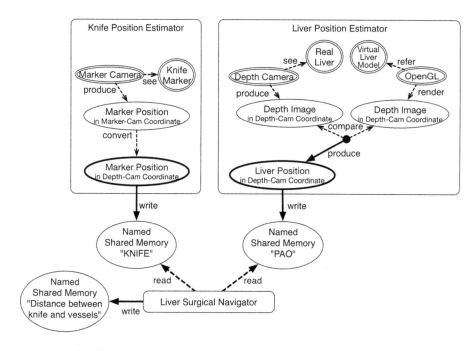

Fig. 8. Coordinate conversion between multiple camera coordinates

In Liver Surgical Navigator. As the knife position estimator and the liver position estimator now use the same coordinate system of the depth camera, the liver surgical navigator can read those data from each shared memory and combine those data for simulating the liver surgery. The liver surgery navigator independently loads STL formatted data and calculates distances between the knife tip and some vessels. Those distance data is also written in a named shared memory for the future application such as visual or sound alerts.

4   System Performance

In this chapter, performance of the whole liver navigation system is discussed, especially focusing on the knife and the liver position estimators while the navigation system is currently implemented as an experimental version. In our laboratory, a Windows PC is being used for the liver navigation system, with which the knife position estimator and the liver position estimator are simultaneously working. The PC has 6 cores of Intel Core i7-7800X CPU (@ 3.50 GHz) and 12 logical processors with 32.0 GB RAM and a graphics card of NVIDIA GeForce GTX 1080, on which Windows 10 Home edition is working. The QueryPerformanceCounter() function was used for the measurement, which can record a high resolution (under 1 ms according to the Microsoft API document) time stamp. Therefore, we assume that the measuring method gives us enough precision when counting in milliseconds.

4.1   Inter-process Communication Cost

At first, we measured the cost of writing and reading to/from the named shared memories both in the knife position estimator and the liver position estimator. However, writing or reading to/from each named shared memory took just one or two CPU clocks, that is less than 0.001 ms. As we described above, it is absolutely faster than any other inter-process communication methods like the BSD sockets.

4.2   Performance of the Knife Position Estimator

The knife position estimator is currently working on the OpenGL rendering flow with GLUT (OpenGL Utility Toolkit). The display callback function specified by glutDisplayFunc() function is repeatedly called in constant intervals, and within the callback function, marker positions captured by the marker camera are checked and the tip position is calculated by getting an average position of the markers.

An experiment was performed for measuring the performance of the knife position estimator. We firstly checked the callback intervals, secondly checked the, by changing the number of the marker captured by the marker camera from zero to two.

The callback intervals were almost constant with any number of captured markers, and the average duration of the interval was 16.668 ms that is precisely equivalent to 1/60 s, which is the basic vertical synchronizing signal interval of today's displays.

The calculation of finding the average position including coordinate conversion took 0.016 ms in average, for any number of markers captured. As Fig. 10 plots the calculation times for each frame within 500 frames (8.33 s), we can see that there is no explicit difference between the different number of captured markers for calculating the average position. Because the average 0.016 ms is definitely small comparing to 16.668 ms (= 1 frame), the calculation around the knife position estimation does not affect the callback ratio of the display function (Fig. 9).

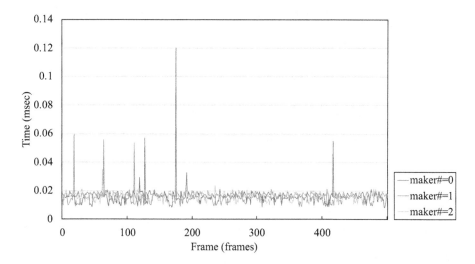

Fig. 9. Time for calculating knife tip positions

As the summary, we can say that the knife position estimator is running and writing the estimated data on the shared memory at 60 frame per second ratio, and the number of makers will not affect the rate.

4.3   Performance of the Liver Position Estimator

For the liver position estimator, we measured how many neighboring liver positions and orientations can be rendered using OpenGL and compare them to the depth image captured from the real liver. In our system, a parameter called "saTime" (prepared as a global variable) can be changed to specify the cutoff time for each simulated annealing process. The unit of the "saTime" variable is clocks per second same as the clock() function declared in time.h as a standard C language function.

Figure 10 shows how many times the liver position estimator can try neighboring liver positions and orientations at the specific saTime (shown as "saΔ" in the figure). Figure 11 shows how many simulated annealing processes (one process including multiple neighboring calculations) can be performed in a second at the specific saTime (shown as "saΔ" in the figure).

We can see that count of the neighboring calculation can be increased by increasing saTime as shown in Fig. 10. Even Fig. 11 also shows us that the simulated annealing performing count will not drastically changed with the different saTime setting, however, the performing count will not be decreased so much around the saTime between 150 to 300 clocks. It is strongly considered that the setting of this parameter should be well discussed in the future.

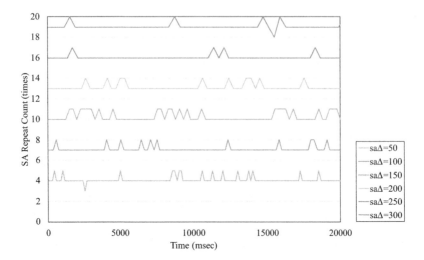

Fig. 10. Simulated annealing repeat count in one calculation

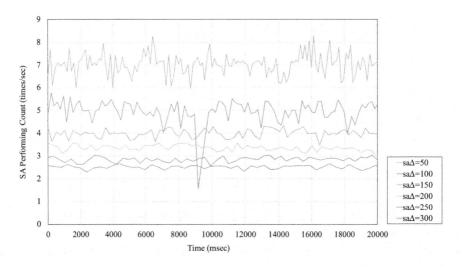

Fig. 11. Simulated annealing performing count in one second

5   Conclusion

In this paper, we described the overview of our liver surgical navigation system composed of subsystems and its data flow between different coordinate systems. The performance of our estimators are discussed and the data showed how the inter-process communication using the named shared memories is effectively transmitting the knife position and the liver position data needed in the liver surgical navigator.

For the future enhancements of our system, few things should be mentioned. First, the performance of the liver position estimator varies quickly by changing the parameter named "saTime." That parameter setting should be well discussed with the other parameters described in [6]. Second, the way of mutual exclusions over the usage of the named shared memories should be deeply concerned because it affects the performance of the entire system. The names of the shared memories currently do not have the unity among the system (the names of "KNIFE" and "PAO" do have asymmetry just now), so it should also be improved in the future. The "KNIFE" and the "PAO" shared memories have different data types by the historical circumstances, but it should be properly measured and united in the future.

Acknowledgement. This research was supported by Grants-in-Aid for Scientific Research (No. 26289069) from the Ministry of Education, Culture, Sports, Science and Technology (MEXT), Japan.

References

1. Kuroda, S., Kobayashi, T., Ohdan, H.: 3D printing model of the intrahepatic vessels for navigation during anatomical resection of hepatocellular carcinoma. Int. J. Surg. Case Reports **41**, 219–222 (2017). ISSN 2210-2612
2. Koeda, M., et al.: Depth camera calibration and knife tip position estimation for liver surgery support system. In: Stephanidis, C. (ed.) HCI 2015. CCIS, vol. 528, pp. 496–502. Springer, Cham (2015). https://doi.org/10.1007/978-3-319-21380-4_84
3. Doi, M., Koeda, M., Tsukushi, A. et al.: Kinfe tip position estimation for liver surgery support. In: Proceedings of the Robotics and Mechatronics Conference 2015 in Kyoto (ROBOMECH 2015), 1A1-E01, May 2015
4. Doi, M., Yano, D., Koeda, M. et al.: Knife tip position estimation using multiple markers for liver surgery support. In: Proceedings of the 2015 JSME/RMD International Conference on Advanced Mechatronics (ICAM 2015), 1A2-08, pp. 74-75, Tokyo, Japan, December 2015
5. Doi, M., Yano, D., Koeda, M. et al.: Knife tip position estimation for liver surgery support system. In: Proceedings of Japanese Society for Medical Virtual Reality (JSMVR 2016), pp. 36–37, September 2016
6. Watanabe, K., Yoshida, S., Yano, D., Koeda, M., Noborio, H.: A new organ-following algorithm based on depth-depth matching and simulated annealing, and its experimental evaluation. In: Marcus, A., Wang, W. (eds.) DUXU 2017. LNCS, vol. 10289, pp. 594–607. Springer, Cham (2017). https://doi.org/10.1007/978-3-319-58637-3_47

Calibration Experiences of Multiple RGB/Depth Visions for Capturing a Surgical Area

Katsuhiko Onishi[1]([✉]), Yuichiro Tanaka[1], Kiminori Mizushino[2], Katsunori Tachibana[1], Kaoru Watanabe[1], and Hiroshi Noborio[1]

[1] Osaka Electro-Communication University, Shijonawate, Japan
onishi@oecu.jp
[2] Embedded Wings Cooperation, Minoh, Japan

Abstract. In the last year, we developed some multiple camera system to measure a surgical area and get several capturing results in our laboratory. In this paper, in order to evaluate the multiple camera system, we first check how to calibrate three RGB/Depth cameras based on many landmarks. Then, when a doctor uses a microscope for the microsurgery, he/she raises or lowers the camera. In this case, we evaluate depth changes at each pixel or the average of all pixels within depth image of each camera in distance. In the evaluation method, it is measure the depth values at five different distance. Through this evaluation, we study about the performance of our capturing system.

Keywords: Robotic system · Depth cameras · Capturing a surgical area

1 Introduction

In neurosurgical surgery, it is common to take an image of the head with CT/MRI in order to grasp the condition of the diseased part in advance before surgery. The image is showed on the display like LCD display etc. to confirm the surgical planning during surgery. However, it is often difficult to mapping the image and real condition of the diseased part. Therefore, it is needed to support surgery by mapping the image and real surgical area, which is like navigation system.

There are many methods for capturing a surgical area that includes multiple kinds of organs and/or several medical tools in an abdominal or laparoscopic surgery using different types of surgical operative procedures [1–3]. In past years, we designed and constructed several prototypes to capture the surgical area for supporting the neurosurgical surgery [4–7]. One of that used one robot and one camera to capture a wider visible surgical area. The unique characteristic of this prototype is that the camera and robotic slider are connected to a surgical bed. By this connection, even though a surgeon controls the surgical bed rotationally or translationally, the relative position and orientation between the camera and surgical area are completely fixed, and therefore our proposed position, orientation, and shape transcription algorithms [4–6] can be directly used in real surgeries. Another prototype used multiple cameras and two robots to capture more widely visible surgical area than that of before [7]. The characteristic of this prototype

© Springer International Publishing AG, part of Springer Nature 2018
M. Kurosu (Ed.): HCI 2018, LNCS 10902, pp. 64–71, 2018.
https://doi.org/10.1007/978-3-319-91244-8_6

is that it can eliminate many types of occlusion in a surgical area by a surgeon's hand, head, and/or microscope. However, it has not evaluated detailed performance yet.

In this paper, we introduce about the performance evaluation to the multiple camera systems. In order to evaluate the system, we first check how to calibrate three RGB/Depth cameras based on many landmarks. Then, when a doctor uses a microscope for the micro-surgery, he/she raises or lowers the camera. In this case, we evaluate depth changes at each pixel or the average of all pixels within depth image of each camera in distance. In the evaluation method, it is measure the depth values at five different distance. Through this evaluation, we study about the performance of our capturing system.

2   Prototype Capturing System with Multiple Cameras

In this section, we introduce our prototype system to capture a visible surgical area by using multiple camera and two robotic sliders. Figure 1 shows the system overview.

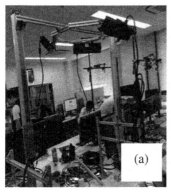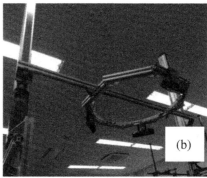

Fig. 1. (a) Three cameras are steadily controlled by two robotic sliders in an up and down manner, (b) Three smaller cameras are located on a ring between two robotic sliders.

Our prototype system set the cameras around over the surgical operation area by using a circle ring mount. Moreover, they can be able to set their vertical position by using two robotic sliders. Using this type of multiple camera system, if a diseased part cannot be caught by initial camera images, it can be captured by other cameras. As a result, our proposed position/orientation/shape transcription algorithms become active with the support of the captured data.

The cameras used in our system are Intel RealSence SR300 [8] (Fig. 2). It is able to capture RGB and Depth images. The principle to capture depth image of this camera is measuring a reflected structured pattern projected an object from each infrared light projector. The position of the reflected light pattern depends on the distance to the reflecting surface, determined through simple geometry. Hence, with bit of trigonom-etry, it is possible to reconstruct a three-dimensional (3D) scene. As shown in the explanation, a structured pattern of infrared light is projected to a target object (in our study, this is a human organ). If two or more cameras project structured patterns of infrared light simultaneously, corresponding confusion can occur, and thus, no depth images can be obtained by any of the cameras. To overcome this obstacle, we use multiple cameras whose depth images are controlled by time shearing to avoid any interference [7]. Figure 3 shows the time sharing schedule model of our system. It uses the number of capturing frames (Nc) and the number of skipping frames (Ns).

Fig. 2. Intel RealSence SR300.

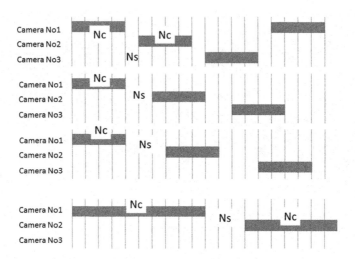

Fig. 3. Time sharing schedule model.

Our prototype system to capture an object is showed in Fig. 4. It moves up or down the ring on which three cameras are attached by using two robotic sliders. Then, it captures depth parameters at 30 points around an object. These points are enable to be arbitrarily defined.

To measure the depth value from the ring adequately, our system has a calibration method to match the positions of the three cameras in advance. Figure 4 shows the calibration markers. At first, marker board A/B (Fig. 5(a) and (b)) is used to measure position of each camera in global coordinate system. Then, point markers (Fig. 5(c)) is used to align each camera in global coordinate system. In this paper, we use two types of marker board, marker board A/B, to evaluate the measurement precision.

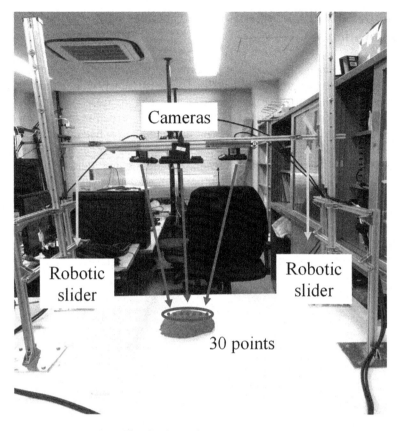

Fig. 4. Capturing environment.

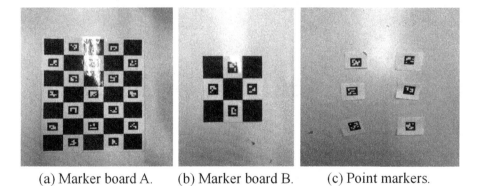

(a) Marker board A.   (b) Marker board B.   (c) Point markers.

Fig. 5. Calibration markers.

3   Comparative Experiments on Differences with/without Calibration

We conduct experiments to clarify the performance of calibration implementation. In this experiment, we compare the depth values from each camera with/without execution of calibration. It is measured distance values between brain model, which is set on our system, and the cameras. The point to measure in this experiment is average of 30 measurement points acquired by the system. It is measured at five different position of the ring. The distance of each position is placed at regular intervals of 100 mm.

Figure 6 shows the result of non-executing calibration procedure before measuring points. Figure 7 shows the result of executing calibration procedure before measuring it. In this calibration procedure, we use marker board A (Fig. 5(a)). Figures 6 and 7 are showed three cameras results. It is confirmed that the results of executing calibration procedure in Fig. 7 is enable to capture more points and to capture more stable than that of in Fig. 6. Especially at camera 1 (Figs. 6(b) and 7(b)), it is clear that the value of the most far position between models and camera is acquired stably.

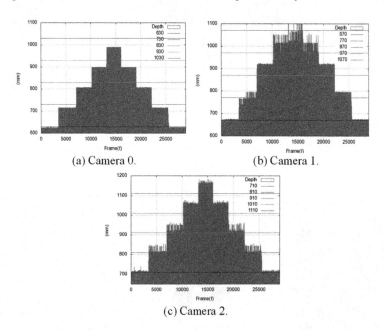

(a) Camera 0.   (b) Camera 1.

(c) Camera 2.

Fig. 6.   Experience results without calibration.

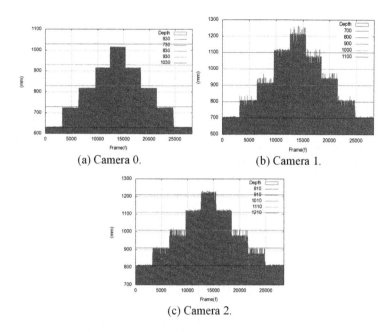

(a) Camera 0.   (b) Camera 1.

(c) Camera 2.

Fig. 7. Experience results with calibration.

4   Experiments by Using Small Calibration Board

For use in actual surgery, it is necessary to consider the size of the marker to be attached to the surgical. Therefore, another experiments were conducted as to whether difference in precision was obtained using the small marker, marker board B in Fig. 5(b). The experiment procedure is the same as before one. It is measured distance values between brain model, which is set on our system, and the cameras. The point to measure in this experiment is average of 30 measurement points acquired by the system. It is measured at five different position of the ring. The distance of each position is placed at regular intervals of 100 mm.

The results are showed in Fig. 8. As a result, it is understood that a substantially constant distance has been acquired. However, concerning the measurement value of the camera 1, fluctuation and a difference from the actual measurement value were observed.

Figure 9 is another result of this experiments. In this result, the time-sharing schedule, which is controls capture frames and skipping frames of the cameras, is changed different value from result in Fig. 8. As a result, it is understood that a substantially constant distance has been acquired. However, concerning the measurement value of the camera 1, fluctuation and a difference from the actual measurement value were observed.

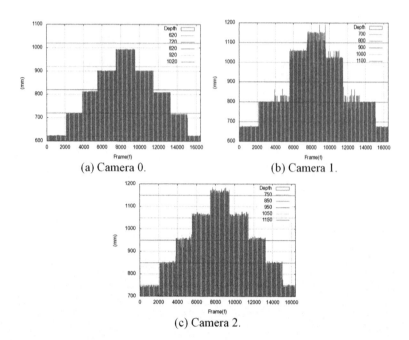

(a) Camera 0.   (b) Camera 1.

(c) Camera 2.

Fig. 8. Experiments results by using small calibration board, marker board B.

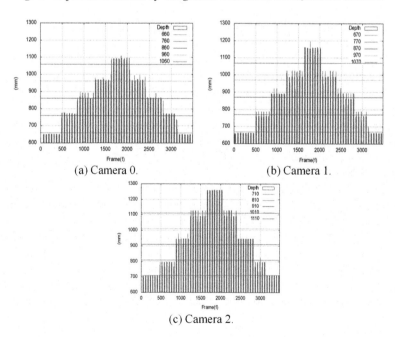

(a) Camera 0.   (b) Camera 1.

(c) Camera 2.

Fig. 9. Another result by using small calibration board, marker board B.

5   Conclusions

In this paper, we evaluate our capturing system that is developed for neurosurgical naviga-tion system presented in last year. A marker based calibration method is implemented on our system. In addition, it is studied about the performance evaluation. As a result, it is clear that the performance is good for capturing the object. Therefore, it is confirmed that our method is enable to use at real surgical room.

As future work, we will conducted experiments at real surgical room with shadow-less lamp.

Acknowledgement. This work was supported by JSPS KAKENHI Grant Number JP17K00420.

References

1. Logan, W.C., Prashanth, D., William, C.C., Benoit, M.D., Robert, L.G., Michael, I.M.: Organ surface deformation measurement and analysis in open hepatic surgery: method and preliminary results from 12 clinical cases. IEEE Trans. Biomed. Eng. **58**(8), 2280–2289 (2011). https://doi.org/10.1109/TBME.2011.2146782
2. Xu, A., Zhu, J.F., Zhang, D.: Development of a measurement system for laparoendo-scopic single-site surgery: reliability and repeatability of digital image correlation for measurement of surface deformations in SILS port. JSLS **18**(3) (2014). https://doi.org/10.4293/JSLS.2014.00267, PMCID: PMC4154418
3. Kang, N., Lee, M.W., Rhee, T.: Simulating liver deformation during respiration using sparse local features. IEEE Comput. Graphics Appl. **32**(5), 29–38 (2012). https://doi.org/10.1109/MCG.2012.65
4. Watanabe, K., Kayaki, M., Mizushino, K., Nonaka, M., Noborio, H.: A mechanical system directly attaching beside a surgical bed for measuring surgical area precisely by depth camera. In: Proceedings of the 10th MedViz Conference and the 6th Eurographics Workshop on Visual Computing for Biology and Medicine (EG VCBM), Bergen, Norway, pp. 105–108, 7–9 September 2016 (2016). ISBN 978-82-998920-7-0 (Printed), ISBN 978-82-998920-8-7 (Electronic)
5. Watanabe, K., Kayaki, M., Mizushino, K., Nonaka, M., Noborio, H.: Brain shift simulation controlled by directly captured surface points. In: Proceedings of the 38th Annual International Conference of the IEEE Engineering in Medicine and Biology Society (EMBC 2016), Category: Late Breaking Research Posters, Theme: BioMedical Imaging and Image Processing, Sessions: Ignite_Theme 2_Fr2, Poster Session III, Orlando Florida USA, 16–20 August 2016 (2016)
6. Watanabe, K., Kayaki, M., Mizushino, K., Nonaka, M., Noborio, H.: Capturing a brain shift directly by the depth camera kinect v2. In: Proceedings of the 38th Annual International Conference of the IEEE Engineering in Medicine and Biology Society (EMBC 2016), Category: Late Breaking Research Posters, Theme: Computational Systems & Synthetic Biology; Multiscale Modeling, Sessions: Ignite_Theme 4_Fr1, Poster Session II, Orlando Florida USA, 16–20 August 2016 (2016)
7. Nonaka, M., Watanabe, K., Noborio, H., Kayaki, M., Mizushino, K.: Capturing a surgical area using multiple depth cameras mounted on a robotic mechanical system. In: Marcus, A., Wang, W. (eds.) DUXU 2017. LNCS, vol. 10289, pp. 540–555. Springer, Cham (2017). https://doi.org/10.1007/978-3-319-58637-3_42
8. Intel RealSence SR300. https://software.intel.com/en-us/realsense/sr300

Research of a m-Health App Design
for Information Management of MDTMs

Qiong Peng[1,2,3(✉)]

[1] Department of Culture and Art, Chengdu University of Information Technology,
Chengdu, China
pengqiongsjtu@gmail.com
[2] Faculty of Industrial Design Engineering, Delft University of Technology,
Delft, The Netherlands
[3] Department of Industrial Design, Eindhoven University of Technology,
Eindhoven, The Netherlands

Abstract. The m-Health apps have been adopted broadly in both medical and family environment. They hold potential to support the work of medical staff and provide help in individual health care. However, the emphasis on the benefits of mobility and the functionality is not enough. Relatively little empirical research guides for the app development. The m-Health apps should be developed for specific purposes with the consideration of the specific users and using contexts. This paper introduces a research for a m-Health app design in support of information management for multidisciplinary medical team meetings (MDTMs) in order to enhancing meeting efficiency. The contextual design methods were used as the guideline for the design. The app design based on tablet was developed and tested by medical teams in this study. The results indicated that the most medical staffs held positive and supportive attitudes to the m-Health app as an intervention in their medical meetings. The recommended app helped medical staffs including oncologists and nurses etc. to improve their meeting efficiency through information management such as setting up meeting schedule, making records for meetings, updating the patients' information, etc. The results also revealed that the choices of different mobile platforms should be taken into account when developing m-Health apps since it would greatly influence user experience in utility and usability in the specific contexts. Design recommendations were summarized for future design.

Keywords: m-Health app · MDTM · Contextual design
Information-management

1 Introduction

M-Health apps have been popular nowadays in our work and daily life. They are the applications for mobile health which as defined covers "medical and public health practice supported by mobile devices, such as mobile phones, patient monitoring devices, personal digital assistant and other wireless devices" [1]. The apps for lifestyle and wellbeing used for personal health guidance, information reminders [2] etc. are also

© Springer International Publishing AG, part of Springer Nature 2018
M. Kurosu (Ed.): HCI 2018, LNCS 10902, pp. 72–82, 2018.
https://doi.org/10.1007/978-3-319-91244-8_7

included in. As an emerging and rapidly developing field in HCI, the benefits of m-Health apps in medical practice as well as healthcare management have been recognized. It is worth mentioning that in medical practice which is complex depending on different users, contexts and purposes, the adoption of m-Health apps is usually taken seriously by taking many factors into account. The medical staffs like doctors and nurses usually work busily with various medical activities. Especially for these working with cancers, for instance, the paediatric oncologists in a children's hospital, the multidisciplinary medical team meetings (MDTMs) which are supposed to discuss of patients' status, to exchange medical treatment ideas, to get helps from internal or external support and to make critical decisions, etc. are often scheduled. To ensure the efficiency of MDTMs, paediatric oncologists should make enough information preparation before the meetings, concentrate on the information during the meeting process, and make use of the information from the meeting afterwards for medical practices. It seems a big burden for paediatric oncologists as they need to do much extra work except their ordinary jobs. However, literatures and designs focusing on either improve meeting efficiency by technology [3], information sharing at MDTMs [4] or the collaboration of multidisciplinary team members [5], little touch the problem of meeting information management by taking the holistic process: pre-meeting——during meeting — post-meeting into account. Tools or devices for instance, appropriate m-Health apps are potentially helpful to support their management of the information for MDTMs. With these questions as a starting point: Whether medical staffs need such a tool as a support to deal with the MDTMs, what the tool would be, how it would work to support, this research was based on the contextual design methodology including observation of the daily work of paediatric oncologists and interviews to get insights into user needs and design directions. Next, a mobile app design was proposed by prototyping and then tested by the paediatric oncologists. Finally, results were collected and discussed for further the development.

2   Related Work

Multidisciplinary medical team meeting (MDTM) is common in medical field. As team work is a tradition in healthcare [3], it means that people with different disciplines backgrounds in healthcare meet together in a meeting at a given time to discuss patients and treatment decisions [6]. MDTMs are also possible to be held with people distributed thanks to the modern technology of teleconference. They serve as a mean to improve communication and decision-making by involving in medical and surgical personnel, nurses and allied health professionals [7]. MDTMs have been becoming a standard practice worldwide for teamwork in the field of healthcare, to formulate an expert-derived management plan, to ensure quality and safety in the delivery of health care services.

Cancer care is such a complex process involving activities such as diagnosis, treatment, rehabilitation and the related supportive care and therefore a wide range and numbers of healthcare professionals involve in it. Treatment for Paediatric oncology is a huge challenge for medical professionals because the patients are young and even more fragile. In many countries nowadays, regular MDTMs have been considered as an integral part of medical care and they have been used widely in paediatric cancer treatment due to children's physiological and psychological conditions. Efficient MDTMs can improve coordination and communication between multidisciplinary medical team members, and enhance discussion and decision-making for treatment with more positive outcomes as well.

In the Netherlands, about 500 children between 0–18 years diagnosed with cancer every year [8]. The collaborative nature of the cancer diagnosis and treatment calls for more meetings for discussion and collaboration. Weekly MDTMs seem to take place in all the hospitals with a paediatric cancer centre. The Dutch Journal of Medicine published an article with the title "Better multidisciplinary consultation fits better care" [9], giving an overview of criteria which can be used to test the efficiency and quality of the MDTMs, including preparation, roles, responsibilities, discussion of case history, meeting, recommendation. Nearly all of the criteria are related with medical information. That means medical information management such as information input and output, information storage, information sharing etc. is a vital factor influencing MDTMs. Efficient and effective information management can greatly improve MDTMs' efficiency. Hence, it is necessary and important to develop appropriate tools to assist information management for multidisciplinary medical team meetings.

Multidisciplinary medical team meeting is a dynamic interaction in nature. It is often conducted through talk, and sometimes by sharing documents, images and videos. Meanwhile, as healthcare system is highly mobile because of multiple clinical locations such emergency departments, operating rooms, intensive care units, etc. [10], information for MDTMs might refers to many other related aspects besides the information during the meetings. Hence, the information management referring to MDTMs is a system involving three main stages: pre-meeting management, during meeting management and post-meeting management as well. It is more complex especially when teleconference is involved in. It requires high flexibility and personal control of the information inherently. However, mobile apps provide possibilities to tackle these challenges.

Mobile devices such as smart phones, tablets are increasing viewed as handheld computer due to their powerful on board computing capability, capacious memories, large touch screen and open operating system [11]. Mobile health application (m-Health app) is a rapid growing trend in healthcare which can support information collection and management [12]. With the convenience and flexibility to download m-Health apps, medical resources become available. Both in theory and practice, it has been very obvious that m-Health apps can help medical professionals to better utilise their valuable working time, simplify communication, enhance working efficiency and effectiveness. In MDTMs, m-Health apps might facilitate in many aspects such as reducing medical errors, providing more flexibility, improving discussion and decision making for treatment etc. As the information technology develops, there have been many kinds of m-Health apps for different purposes. Functionalities such as communication, remote diagnosis, education, even visualisation of medical images are the main focus. The user interface and interaction design of these apps become quite favourite as well. However, there are some limitations during their development, for example apps are often designed with little health professional involvement [12] and patients' information security is usually a potential problem of medical risk. There have been many apps for medical information system, most of which are focused on self-care information and open medical information accessing, but little are specially for information management for MDTMs.

The motivation of this research is to find a way in which design can contribute to MDTMs. We visited several main hospitals with paediatric cancer department in the Netherlands. There is a weekly MDTs including paediatric oncologists, radiotherapists, children radiologist, nuclear medicine physician, paediatric surgeon, nurse specialist etc., to discuss and evaluate patients' conditions and treatment. And then decisions are formally made for further steps. Most of the multidisciplinary medical team members are always busy with work. Thus, it usually happens with inadequate clinical information or lack of necessary information before and during the MDTMs. It may have some negative effects on the discussion and decision-making in MDTMs. At the same time, we noticed that nearly all the medical professionals have a smart phone or iPad and use these mobile devices from time to time for working or personal purposes even they are always busy with work. The visits indicated that m-Health apps are the possible solutions which can assist information management for MDTMs with useful functionality and user-friendly interface and interaction, so that the efficiency of MDTMs can greatly enhanced and more children patients can be cured.

3 Methodology

Four phases were included in this research, and contextual design methodology, a structural and well-defined UCD process providing methods to collect information or data about users, and interpret data in a structural way [13] was used as the guideline. The first phase referred to user study and we carried out research by visiting the paediatric oncology department in several main hospitals in the Netherlands to collect user needs and identify concerns of medical professionals about MDTMs. During the visiting, observation was conducted and recorded by video both in the daily work of the paediatric oncologists as well as other MDT members like nurses and in the MDTMs. Semi-structured interviews focused on perspectives on MDTMs were made to get more feedback. In the second phase, after all the documents were analysed, we identified the design directions and developed it with prototyping. Then in the final stage, a test was proposed aided by a questionnaire and interview to gather comments on functionalities and usability. the questionnaire was based on USE questionnaire [14] which is popular in getting feedback of acceptance. Finally, we made discussion and reflection to identify how it might be further developed as a better support.

4 Results

4.1 Results of the User Study

According to contextual design process, three different work models set by us to represent the work of the medical professionals of MDTMs. The flow model showed the situation of roles and responsibilities of it is concluded that usually an oncologist is in charge of each case, there is no clear structure in the meeting. The communication between multidisciplinary team members is not so effective and interactive in this relaxed and informal atmosphere due to the lack of a hierarchy of the meeting and information need to be organized. It is imperative (Fig. 1).

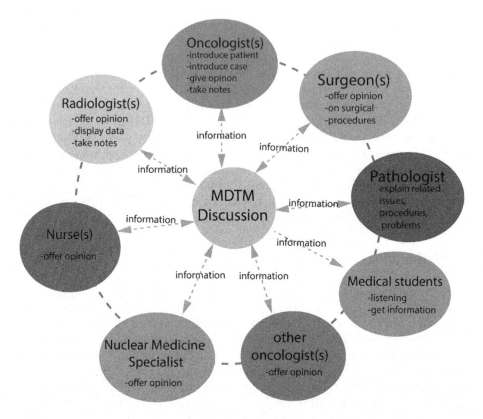

Fig. 1. The flow model

The sequence model (see Fig. 2) indicated the general structure of a MDTM. It is usually followed a linear structure, however, there was no specific steps into sequence to summarize the draw final conclusions. There was also some discussion not included in the list making the meeting chaotic and hard to be followed by people who were late or joined in half-way. During the meeting, oncologists might make presentation, review patient cases, pose a problem for discussion. Others took part in the discussion, contributed their points of view or relevant information. Then decisions were made for future further care and treatment. Sometimes a teleconference was needed to involve external specialists in. MDTMs Provide opportunities for multidiscipline team members to discuss recommendations and get help.

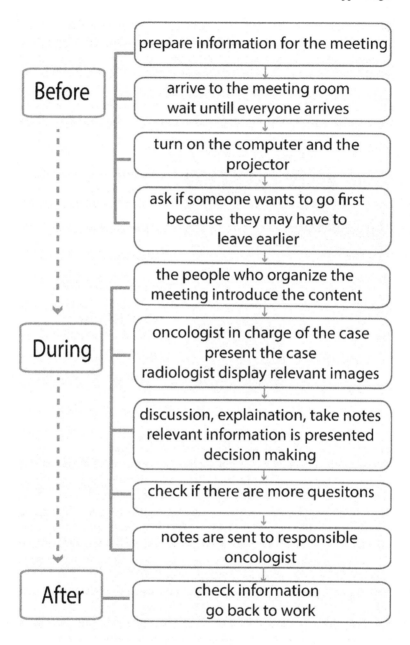

Fig. 2. The sequence model

The artefact model (shown in Fig. 3) offered insights into what documents and what information were needed for MDTMs. Except the meeting room environment, useful devices for the meeting, the agenda is the most important one. Usually, an agenda is printed out with patient's names on it. The responsible oncologists can add any patient to the agenda. However, it was not completely followed during the meeting due to the dynamic changing order. There was a note-taker particularly, and every oncologist took note if needed. Then the notes were shared around. It may be not timely and not everyone can figure out as the notes are made by hand-writing. From this artefact model, it is concluded that if there is a design can help oncologists to organize, recorded and share the meeting documents, quickly, the efficiency of meetings can be improved greatly.

Artefact for MDTMs

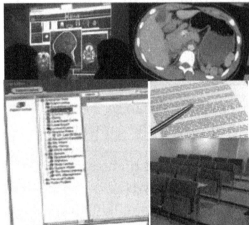

Medical images
(X-ray images, MRI images...)

Patient documents (Treat Record...)

Previous Notes

Agenda of this meeting

Related Software
(Philips Intellispace--PACS,
 teleconfernce software...)

Computer, Projector, Big Screen

Fig. 3. The artefact model

These three work models indicated that all the activities like communication, discussion and decision-making happened before, during and after MDTMs is based on information. For most of the medical professional who work for long hours per day, free time is such a luxury. The MDTMs usually last for one hour and much cases or documents are needed to reviewed. Hence, in such a long time, how to make the meeting more effective, and how to better support the related MDT members especially like the oncologists for their work are the issues needed to solved. Information (including the physical medical documents, images, notes etc. and the talks, discussion) management seems to play an important role to improve the efficiency MDTMs.

Besides the work models, the records of observation and interviews were transcribed and analysed. Quotes about information of MDTMs were selected and categorized by researchers. The concerns about both the information and the meetings were identified and categorized into the three phases: pre-meeting, in meeting and post-meeting (shown in Fig. 4). In pre-meeting phase, the activities and concerns indicated that information management should focus on preparation for the meeting, which includes meeting arrangement, preparation of patients' information to discuss and collection of related information, etc. During the meeting, the dynamic information should be managed effectively and efficiently with the consideration of the meeting context and the possible issues which would happen during the meeting process. After the meeting, oncologists would go back to work based on the information at hand. Thus, checking and updating information is very important.

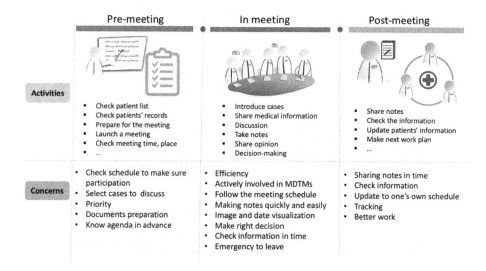

Fig. 4. Analysis of the three phases with activities and concerns

4.2 Prototyping Development

A m-Health app for information management was proposed as the possible solution (shown in Fig. 5). It was developed based on the three phases and pay attention to the dynamic characteristics of the information. Taking the using context into account, it was based on iPad because compared with smart phones, iPad has bigger touch screen, powerful on board computing capability, capacious memories [11] and can be connected to a smart keyboard which potentially better supports the activities of information management like taking notes and making records digitally and making editions if necessary. Meanwhile, we used some bright colours for the interface design with the consideration that medical staffs are easy to get tired due to their busy work for a long time everyday, and the bright colours are potentially positive in adjusting working emotions.

There were four main functionalities: (1) Meeting agenda supports pre-arrangement of MDTMs, with which oncologists can updating the newest information, check related information and making a list for discussion. They can also add important information to the meeting agenda to share with other in advance so that others might have enough time for preparation. (2) My patients, is actually the management of daily work. Compared with the traditional notes-taking, oncologists can make record of each patient at any time any place digitally, and it is easy to edit and update information. It is very important for the meeting since oncologists can not only use it to prepare for the meeting, but also to check related information if needed during the meeting. (3) Taking note is a particular support for the meeting. The app based on iPad offered opportunity to use finger input on interface or a keyboard. Digital notes are easy to store and share with others. (4) Account was a consideration of personal information security. One oncologists usually are in charge of several patients and each patient has his/her own treatment. In account, oncologists can log in and work in their own accounts. They can also customize in the account to set up their preferred styles for information management such as changing colours or list patterns, setting up priorities or reminders, storing information on cloud, etc.

Fig. 5. The prototyping design

4.3   Results of the Prototyping Test

However, only five oncologists participated in the prototyping test because they were too busy to make an appointment with. After they tried to use the prototype, questionnaires about the acceptance of the app were answered and an exit interview was used to get feedback. The collected record was analysed and the results were summarized as follows: All the five oncologists showed positive attitudes to use a mobile device and m-Health apps to support their daily work. As an intervention in their work, they believed that this app was useful to support their management in the information related to MDTMs with the provided functionalities. They also agreed that the app was easy to use with a clear architecture. However, the improvement was still needed since it was only a prototype with some interaction problems when using it.

5   Discussion

This paper introduced the research of the design of a m-health app for information management. It was based on contextual design methodology which emphasizing the importance of deeply understanding users. It indicated that it is promising to combine mobile technology and devices in healthcare and medical practice to support medical staff's work. Our exploration was in accordance with the trend, for instance, healthcare professional use m-Health apps as management [12] or electronic libraries [15] which support storing and sharing information.

However, there were some limitations in this research:

Firstly, this study was proposed based on the investigation in paediatric oncology department of children hospital and we focused on paediatric oncologist. However, there are many other medical staffs involved in multidisciplinary medical team meetings. The needs for information management exist broadly. It is necessary to take the related issues of other stakeholders into concern.

Secondly, there were limited participants involved in the test because of busy schedule of the paediatric oncologists. However, the collected feedback was beneficial for improvement. Prototyping is a highly valuable UX technique to help providing a clear vison of the interface and the user interaction [16].

Thirdly, the app was developed on iPad. Though iPad owns many benefits in interface and input, it is a little heavy to take around in oncologists' busy working routine. It indicated that the choice of platform is an issue needed to be taken into account because m-Health apps should be designed based on many factors including the using context and users' habits.

6   Conclusion

In this paper, we presented a research of a m-Health app design which was supposed to support information management for MDTMs. MDTM is a system that needs to maintain the integrity and effectiveness of the information in order to guarantee the medical activities like treatment. Based on contextual design methodology, a m-Health app was developed and tested with the conclusion that it can facilitate paediatric oncologists in information management before, during and after meetings. Both the positive feedback and suggestions for improvement built the confidence for further development. The goal of this research was not only to develop an app as support, but also to explore more possible solutions to better support medical activities by making full use of mobile and digital technologies. Our future work will be intended to address these challenges through further investigation.

Acknowledgements. The research reported in this paper was supported by the 2017 project (WLWH17-23), 2016 project (2016Z036) and 2014 project (GY-14YB-13) of Sichuan Province Education Department of China. Thanks to all who were involved in this research.

References

1. Kay, M., Santos, J., Takane, M.: mHealth: new horizons for health through mobile technologies. World Health Organ. **64**(7), 66–71 (2011)
2. Green Paper on mobile health ('mHealth'). Digital Single Market. https://ec.europa.eu/digital-single-market/en/news/green-paper-mobile-health-mhealth
3. Kane, B., Luz, S.: Multidisciplinary medical team meetings: an analysis of collaborative working with special attention to timing and teleconferencing. Comput. Support. Coop. Work CSCW **15**(5–6), 501–535 (2006)
4. Kane, B., Luz, S.: Information sharing at multidisciplinary medical team meetings. Group Decis. Negot. **20**(4), 437–464 (2011)
5. Li, J., Robertson, T., Hansen, S., Mansfield, T., Kjeldskov, J.: Multidisciplinary medical team meetings: a field study of collaboration in health care. In: Proceedings of the 20th Australasian Conference on Computer-Human Interaction: Designing for Habitus and Habitat, pp. 73–80 (2008)
6. Fleissig, A., Jenkins, V., Catt, S., Fallowfield, L.: Multidisciplinary teams in cancer care: are they effective in the UK? Lancet Oncol. **7**(11), 935–943 (2006)
7. Jalil, R., Ahmed, M., Green, J.S., Sevdalis, N.: Factors that can make an impact on decision-making and decision implementation in cancer multidisciplinary teams: an interview study of the provider perspective. Int. J. Surg. **11**(5), 389–394 (2013)
8. Treatment of children with cancer in the children's oncology centre of the VUmc - Google Search. https://www.google.nl/search?q=Treatment+of+children+with+cancer+in+the+children%27s+oncology+centre+of+the+VUmc&oq=Treatment+of+children+with+cancer+in+the+children%27s+oncology+centre+of+the+VUmc&aqs=chrome..69i57j69i60.796j0j8&sourceid=chrome&ie=UTF-8
9. Beter multidisciplinair overleg past bij betere zorg - Google Search. https://www.google.nl/search?ei=CwB2WsC6JM2ZkwX7xa3AAg&q=Beter+multidisciplinair+overleg+past+bij+betere +zorg&oq=Beter+multidisciplinair+overleg+past+bij+betere +zorg&gs_l=psy-ab.3..0i19k1.45430.45430.0.46631.1.1.0.0.0.0.467.467.4-1.1.0....0...1c.2.64.psy-ab..0.1.467....0.AHIn1uaPqrc
10. Mosa, A.S.M., Yoo, I., Sheets, L.: A systematic review of healthcare applications for smartphones. BMC Med. Inform. Decis. Mak. **12**(1), 67 (2012)
11. Boulos, M.N.K., Wheeler, S., Tavares, C., Jones, R.: How smartphones are changing the face of mobile and participatory healthcare: an overview, with example from eCAALYX. Biomed. Eng. Online **10**(1), 24 (2011)
12. Craven, M.P., Lang, A.R., Martin, Jennifer L.: Developing mHealth apps with researchers: multi-stakeholder design considerations. In: Marcus, A. (ed.) DUXU 2014. LNCS, vol. 8519, pp. 15–24. Springer, Cham (2014). https://doi.org/10.1007/978-3-319-07635-5_2
13. Beyer, H., Holtzblatt, K.: Contextual Design: Defining Customer-Centered Systems. Elsevier, Amsterdam (1997)
14. USE Questionnaire: Usefulness, Satisfaction, and Ease of use. http://garyperlman.com/quest/quest.cgi?form=USE
15. Payne, K.F.B., Wharrad, H., Watts, K.: Smartphone and medical related App use among medical students and junior doctors in the United Kingdom (UK): a regional survey. BMC Med. Inform. Decis. Mak. **12**(1), 121 (2012)
16. van Boeijen, A., Daalhuizen, J., Zijlstra, J., van der Schoor, R.: Delft Design Guide: Design Methods. BIS Publishers, Amsterdam (2014)

Laparoscopic Forceps with Force Feedback

Atsuro Sawada[1]([✉]), Jin Kono[1], Atsushi Sengiku[1], Naoto Kume[2],
Junichi Fukuda[3], Toshinari Yamasaki[1], and Osamu Ogawa[1]

[1] Department of Urology, Graduate School of Medicine, Kyoto University, Kyoto, Japan
atsuro7@kuhp.kyoto-u.ac.jp
[2] EHR Research Unit, Graduate School of Informatics, Kyoto University, Kyoto, Japan
[3] Suzuki Precision Co., Ltd., Tochigi, Japan

Abstract. There are two main aspects of safety and effectiveness in laparoscopic surgery. The first is ensuring an appropriate operation field and maintaining this throughout the procedure. The second is finding the correct tissue plane and applying appropriate traction and counter-traction. To accomplish these requirements, surgeons must know the appropriate pressure to apply to the target organ or tissue. For example, weak operation of the forceps in the left hand during laparoscopic surgery leads to poor visibility owing to a small operational field. Furthermore, poor traction at the point of incision on the dissected plane decreases the dissection efficiency. In contrast, when excessive force is applied, there is an increased risk of organ injury or bleeding from capillary vessels during traction; this is clearly detrimental to the overall safety of the procedure. It is difficult for surgeons to master a feeling for the appropriate pressure to apply. Imitating the techniques of skilled surgeons is essential; however, surgical techniques cannot be imitated on first sight. With the aim of assisting this learning process, we developed Forceps Guiding Correct Operation (FOGCOP), new laparoscopic forceps with sensors. Although they are the same shape as Maryland dissecting forceps, FOGCOP can measure the pressure applied on the shaft of the forceps in three axis directions (X, Y, and Z) and on the jaw. The measured pressures are displayed in real time. Surgeons can insert this device into a 5-mm trocar in the same manner as normal forceps. We conducted experiments to verify the effectiveness of the device. 30 students with no experience of laparoscopic surgery participated in this study. Using a training box, students performed a task to press and pull a rubber plate. We compared the performance of a group of students using FOGCOP (group 1, n = 10) with that of a group using conventional forceps (group 2, n = 10). The results suggest that the feedback provided by FOGCOP may be useful for understanding the force delivered by forceps. To verify the usefulness of the device, FOGCOP was also used in laparoscopic nephrectomy of a pig, a procedure that is part of the training course for laparoscopic surgery. It was possible to dissect a tissue plane in the same manner as with conventional forceps. However, the wire from the sensor sometimes interfered with operation. In future, we intend to upgrade FOGCOP by including a wireless sensor, to improve operability to be closer to that of normal forceps, and to allow this device to be used as an educational tool.

Keywords: Laparoscopic surgery · Force feedback · Education

© Springer International Publishing AG, part of Springer Nature 2018
M. Kurosu (Ed.): HCI 2018, LNCS 10902, pp. 83–95, 2018.
https://doi.org/10.1007/978-3-319-91244-8_8

1 Introduction

There was a time when most laparotomies required surgeons to come into direct contact with internal organs and perform operations such as the peeling, ligating, and cutting of tissue. Young surgeons who had little surgical experience participated in surgeries as assistants, thus having many opportunities to come into direct contact with internal organs. Through the resulting accumulation of experience, these young surgeons developed a sensual understanding of the elasticity, firmness, and fragility of each organ, depending on which surgeons learned how to safely and efficiently apply force in surgery.

However, the spread of laparoscopic surgeries since the 2000s has implied a corresponding decrease in opportunities for surgeons to directly come into contact with internal organs and an increased need to understand the elasticity, firmness, and fragility of internal organs using the tactile sense, as conveyed by forceps, and understanding changes in the shape of organs, as seen on monitors during laparoscopic surgeries. Moreover, the use of robots in many types of surgeries has proliferated in recent years, and because robotic surgeries do not involve the use of the tactile sense, it has become extremely difficult to understand the elasticity, firmness, and fragility of internal organs or to learn how to appropriately use force. In addition, surgeons in robotic surgeries manipulate a camera and three arms, performing most of the surgeries alone, which largely does away with opportunities to touch internal organs even where a younger surgeon does participate in a surgery as an assistant.

Although surgical methods have changed, understanding the elasticity, firmness, and fragility of organs, as well as learning the appropriate amount of force to be applied to these organs, is necessary for maintaining the balance between safety and efficiency in surgeries. The knowledge of how to properly apply force ensures a good surgical theater and allows the peeling of tissue with an awareness of plane and proper traction. Accordingly, young surgeons who lack surgical experience must learn to efficiently apply force in laparoscopic surgery.

Learning this, however, is not easy. Even after watching an expert performing a surgery, it can be difficult for an inexperienced surgeon to understand and imitate the application of exactly the same amount of force that the expert applied and that too in the direction the expert did so.

For this reason, we have studied surgical education to aid in understanding organ elasticity and firmness and in learning how to properly use force in laparoscopic surgeries. To assist the study of the elasticity and firmness of organs, we developed an instrument called Pressure Measuring Grasper (PMEG) and reported on its ability to collect data [1].

We have now developed a new device to aid the efficient study of how to apply force in laparoscopic surgeries and call it the forceps guiding correct operation (FOGCOP). In this paper, we introduce the FOGCOP in detail and examine its utility.

2   Materials and Methods

2.1   Device Design

The most basic surgical tool used in laparoscopic surgeries is the Maryland forceps. The open/close function of the forceps is used to grasp and separate tissue. Efficiency is improved as a working space is created through the drawing up and pushing down on tissue and organs, with the addition of traction. Maryland forceps were used as the model of the basic design of FOGCOP, which can measure all of the various forces placed on it on any of the shaft's axes—X, Y, or Z—as well as the force used to open or close the forceps. Our aim was to display these forces in real time. Through the provision of real-time visibility of the forces on the forceps, young surgeons can analyze their use of force in comparison with that of experts, thereby more quickly acquiring expert skills.

We had three requirements for the creation of these forceps.

Requirement 1: Have the Same Level of Operability as Normal Maryland Forceps to the Extent Possible

Maryland forceps have a variety of tip shapes, and shaft thickness can be 3 mm, 5 mm, or 10 mm. The variety of tip shapes and the different shaft thicknesses can change the way force is applied to the forceps. We designed the shape of the FOGCOP's tips to be that of the most common type of Maryland forceps, as seen in Fig. 1, and we made the shaft thickness 5 mm. The handle was also designed and fabricated to be similar to that of a standard Maryland forceps. Thus, we were able to ensure the same level of operability for the FOGCOP as that for the standard Maryland forceps and acquired the ability to measure the force used in normal surgical techniques.

Requirement 2: To Allow all Forces Applied by the Surgeon to Be Measured

In laparoscopic surgery, surgeons grasp, open, push, and pull and apply other forces in various combinations on the forceps. These forceps must allow the measurement of all the forces that a surgeon may apply on them. Particularly, this means all forces on the X, Y, and Z axes of the shaft, as well as opening and closing forces on the forceps. In addition, in laparoscopic surgeries, the relationship between the force applied to the tips of the forceps and the force of the hand of the surgeon differs according to the depth of the unit. Thus, according to the principle of leverage, the force applied by the surgeon increases at the tips if the forceps are inserted shallowly and decreases as the depth increases (Fig. 2). Expert surgeons can control the force they apply by adjusting the depth of the forceps, thereby operating it safely and efficiently. Inexperienced surgeons must learn this technique of adjusting depth. Because of this, our forceps needed to be able to measure the amount of force applied by the surgeon not only on the tips of the forceps but also on the handle of the forceps.

Requirement 3: The Forceps Must Be Usable in Animal Laboratories

Current laparoscopic surgery training is done primarily in two ways: through the use of a dry box and by practicing on pigs in animal laboratories. Training in animal laboratories is of course more effective because it is much closer than a dry box to the actual surgical environment. However, opportunities to train in an animal laboratory are extremely rare and limited because of costs and the enforcement of animal rights. We wanted the FOGCOP to be used in animal laboratories to improve the quality of training during these valuable opportunities and for it to be useful in the study of how requisite force can be applied in a short period of time. For these reasons, we felt it necessary to enable the FOGCOP to withstand usage in wet environments, such as those found inside animals.

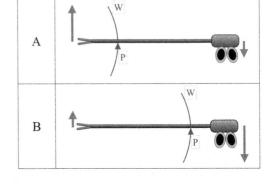

Fig. 1. Tips of standard Maryland forceps

Fig. 2. In laparoscopic surgery, the force applied and force used changes depending on the depth of the part being operated and in accordance with the principle of leverage. A; Operation in shallow section B; Operation in deep section W; Body wall P; Point where shaft meets body wall

After a trial-and-error process of meeting the above three requirements, we designed the FOGCOP as shown in Fig. 3.

The sensors for measuring the amount of force are all in the handle area and are able to measure the force applied on the forceps by the surgeon. By concentrating the sensors in this area, we were able to make the tips and the shaft of the same shape as normal Maryland forceps, enabling the shaft to be inserted into a 5-mm trocar. No sensors are affixed near the tips of the forceps, and because sensors near the handle are covered, the forceps can be used in a wet environment, such as inside the body of an animal.

Codes from the sensor are output to a computer by connecting the forceps to a data logger, thus enabling real-time display of the force used (Fig. 4).

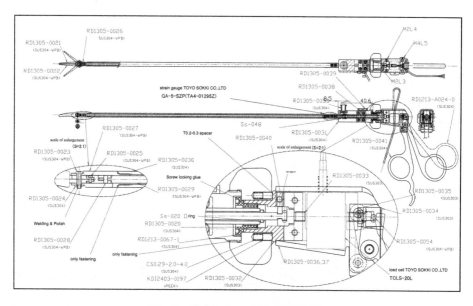

Fig. 3. The design of the FOGCOP

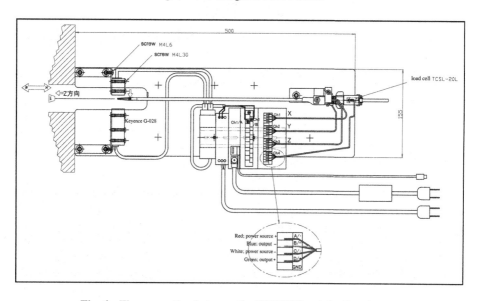

Fig. 4. The connection between the FOGCOP and the Data logger

However, the measurement of force is done with a load cell and a very slightly deflected metal, meaning that the amount of deflection is not absolute. The relationship between the amount of force and the amount of deflection of the metal is expected to differ on the basis of various environmental factors, such as temperature and humidity. We made a test bench to calibrate the device by the use of weights each time prior to use. In so doing, we were able to observe the relationship between the amount of deflection and the absolute amount of force.

2.2 Validation Experiments

Validation Experiment 1. We needed to confirm whether the sensor-equipped FOGCOP that we had made was actually useful for learning "how to apply force to forceps." There existed the possibility that a validation experiment using people who had experienced or seen laparoscopic surgeries would be biased; hence, we conducted the experiment in cooperation with university students who were not studying medicine. Details of the experiment are as follows:

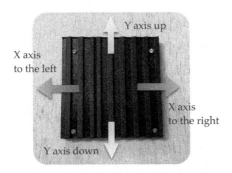

Fig. 5. Using the FOGCOP, a rubber sheet was pushed left and right on the X axis and upward and downward on the Y axis. In the same way, it was pushed and pulled on the Z axis, and was held and spread.

(a) Subjects: 30 university students, none of whom were medical students and none of whom had experience of laparoscopic surgeries. These 30 students were randomly paired into two groups, A and B, numbering 15 each.

(b) Method: A rubber sheet with a slit was affixed within a dry box. Force was applied to the FOGCOP to push the rubber sheet to the right (on the X axis to the right) (Fig. 5). A target level of force was set for this operation. Group A students were shown the amount of force output by the FOGCOP in real time, and they viewed this output as they controlled the amount of force that they were applying so that they could remember the target force level. Conversely, Group B students were not shown the output of the FOGCOP and were asked to adjust the amount of force that they applied on the basis of a target level that was conveyed to them orally; in other words, these students were prompted to "apply more force" if the force that they were using was lower than the target value and to "apply less force" if it was greater. By repeating these instructions, we prompted Group B students to remember the level of target force. Both groups were given one minute to remember the target value using the above methods. A 30-s interval was then provided, after which a test was administered wherein students were asked to apply the target level of force. This same test was also conducted by moving the sheet on the X axis to the left, on the Y axis-upward, and on the Y axis-downward; pushing the sheet on the Z axis; pulling the sheet on the Z axis; and opening and closing the forceps within a 30-s interval, after which the students were again tested for their ability to create the target level of force.

Validation Experiment 2. We needed to ascertain whether the sensor-equipped FOGCOP was able to measure force in an actual wet environment, such as an animal laboratory, without failure.

We brought the FOGCOP into a training conducted in an actual animal laboratory and had four surgeons use it for a total of one hour. After use, we ascertained, using a test bench, whether the sensors had malfunctioned.

3 Results

3.1 A Subsection Sample

Figure 6(A) shows an overview of the FOGCOP. The forceps tips, shaft, and handle are all similar to those found on normal Maryland forceps although, by locating sensors near the handle, the FOGCOP is able to measure, by using a load cell, the amount of force applied on the shaft on the opening and closing of the forceps. Connecting a data logger for the code output from the sensors allows the graphing and display of forces applied to the X, Y, and Z axes, as well as the opening and closing of the forceps. Graphs are color-coded, and each of the measurements can be displayed simultaneously as well as individually (Fig. 7). As the structure of the handle, as well as the tips, is similar to that found in normal Maryland forceps, the device has a familiar feel when used, which met requirements 1 and 2.

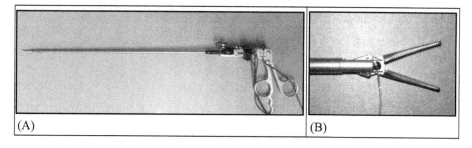

(A)   (B)

Fig. 6. This is an overview of the FOGCOP. Sensors are located near the handle, along with output codes. (B): These are the FOGCOP tips. They are shaped similarly to those on standard Maryland forceps; there is a hole in them through which a thread can be placed though, making provision for weights to be hung on the thread for use in calibration.

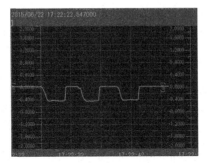

Fig. 7. Connecting a data logger for the code output from the sensors allows the graphing and display of forces applied to the X, Y, and Z axes, as well as the opening and closing of the forceps. Each forces of the measurements can be displayed simultaneously as well as individually.

Figure 8 shows the calibration of the FOGCOP on a test bench. As can be seen in Fig. 6(B), there is a small hole near the tips of the forceps, through which a thread with a weight attached can be threaded for calibration. The handle is fixed to the test bench, and by hanging various weights from the tips using the thread, we can determine the relationship between force and shaft deflection in that environment.

(A)

(B)

Fig. 8. The calibration of the FOGCOP on a test bench. (A) The FOGCOP is affixed to a test bench, and (B) by hanging various amounts of weights from the tips, we can determine the relationship between force and deflection in that environment.

3.2   Results of Validation Experiments

Validation Experiment 1.   The results of the tests for Groups A and B are shown herein. Figure 9 is a plot of all data, with forces plotted as relative values, and with 1 being the target value. Figure 10 presents a comparison of the groups and shows the differences between the forces applied and the target value. Group A had significantly smaller variances between the forces on the Y axis-upward and downward, Z axis-push and the closing of forceps. This suggests that the group using the FOGCOP was able to learn how to apply force more accurately in a shorter amount of time.

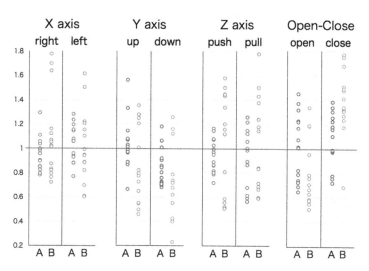

Fig. 9.   This is a plot of all data, with forces plotted as relative values, and with 1 being the target value. Group A students were shown the amount of force output by the FOGCOP in real time. Group B students were not shown the output of the FOGCOP.

Validation Experiment 2.   On the day of the experiment, the animal laboratory had a temperature of 26 °C, with a humidity of 67%. Prior to using the FOGCOP, the device was calibrated using a test bench. Over the course of an hour, the FOGCOP was used to peel and open tissues in the body of a pig (Fig. 11). During this time, the tips and shaft of the forceps were continually exposed to blood and fat from the pig; however, a post-use recalibration on the test bench showed no deviations in the measured values from the sensors after use as can be seen in Fig. 11(B). This shows that the FOGCOP met requirement 3.

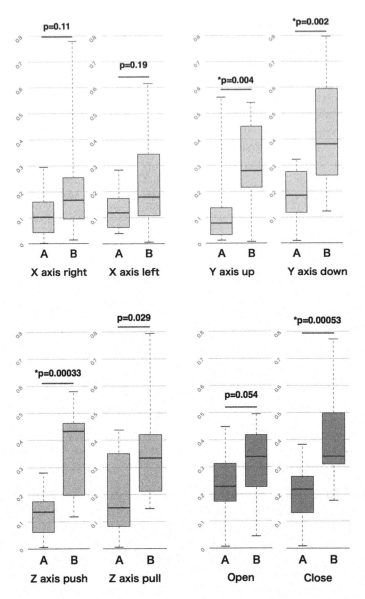

Fig. 10. (A) The differences between the forces applied and the target value. This shows the results of X axis and Y axis. (Mann–Whitney U test) (B) The differences between the forces applied and the target value. This shows the results of Z axis and Open-Close. (Mann–Whitney U test)

4   Discussion

During surgical operations, the amount of force and the direction in which the force is applied are very important. For example, when applying traction to internal organs using laparoscopic forceps, a force that is excessively strong runs the risk of causing a puncture or rupture to an organ. However, conversely, if the force applied is too weak, with insufficient traction on the organ, the working space may become too small and the efficiency of peeling would be reduced. In addition, depending on the direction of the force, the same level of force may introduce an increased risk of forceps puncture and thus lowered safety. Safe and efficient surgeries require that surgeons learn the proper levels and direction of force (Fig. 12).

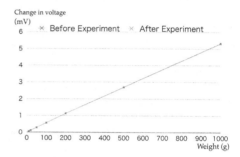

Fig. 11. The usage of the FOGCOP in the animal laboratory

Fig. 12. Assessment of use on test bench after wet laboratory experiment

Various reports in the past have noted differences between experienced surgeons and beginners in the application of force in laparoscopic surgeries. Yoshida et al. attached 2-centimeter square pressure sensors to the middle of the shaft of Hera forceps and reported differences in the use of force with the forceps, which depended on the skills of surgeons [2]. In addition, Yamanaka et al. discussed sensor-equipped Maryland forceps, and Araki et al. reported on the differences between the gripping forces of experienced and novice surgeons using these same forceps [3, 4].

However, past studies have not reported specifically on how surgeries have improved with a more sensitive application of force or how the application of force can be learned more efficiently, nor have they investigated this issue from the perspective of surgeon training and development [5–7]. When an expert surgeon uses a FOGCOP, the complex application of force is made visible and can be analyzed. When a novice surgeon uses the FOGCOP, they can see how they are applying force; hence, the FOGCOP could be very useful as these young surgeons learn how to apply force effectively by studying and imitating expert surgeons in a relatively short period of time.

In validation experiment 1, Group A students were able to more accurately reproduce the level of force required than Group B students. However, we noticed something else from Fig. 9. There is no plot for Group B near the target value 1 for the movement down on the Y axis, push and pull on the Z axis, and so on. This means that almost no one in that group could reproduce the target level of force with oral instructions alone. In an experimental setting, surgical teaching is delivered primarily through oral instruction. We can expect the FOGCOP to be a useful device in the education of surgeons in the future as they learn how to apply force more efficiently.

We must stress once again that it is the surgeon's application of force that is important here. If hand movements are fine-tuned, everything else is determined by the force on the tips of the forceps in accordance with the principle of leverage. It is important for inexperienced surgeons to understand the hand movements of experts and to learn how to imitate the application of force. For this reason, the next issue to be studied should include the collection and analysis of data from expert surgeons applying force using the FOGCOP.

However, one problem is that the FOGCOP will be used in various environments. The code output from the sensors can interfere with surgical operations, depending on the movements of the surgeon when rotating the forceps. Accordingly, an improved model should be equipped to collect force data wirelessly.

5   Conclusion

We developed new sensor-equipped forceps that can be used like a normal Maryland forceps and that can measure and display all the forces applied on the X, Y, and Z axes and the opening and closing of the forceps. We call this device the forceps guiding correct operation, the acronym for which is FOGCOP. The operation of the forceps is very similar to that of a normal Maryland forceps, and it can be used with a 5-mm trocar. They have a vinyl cover on them that allows them to be used in wet environments, such as animal laboratories. Our study suggests that this device is useful in learning how to apply force more efficiently during surgical procedures. We propose that this device be used in surgical education to enable not only researchers and inexperienced doctors to learn the proper application of force but also medical students, who can also use it in practice and experience the joy and difficulty of laparoscopic surgery.

References

1. Sawada, A., Kume, N., et al.: Development of a novel tool for assessing deformation and hardness of real organs: Pressure Measuring Grasper (PMEG). Adv. Biomed. Eng. **5**, 68–75 (2016)
2. Yoshida, K., Kinoshita, H., et al.: Analysis of laparoscopic dissection skill by instrument tip force measurement. Surg. Endosc. **27**(6), 2193–2200 (2013)
3. Yamanaka, H., Makiyama, K., et al.: Measurement of the physical properties during laparoscopic surgery performed on pigs by using forceps with pressure sensors. Adv. Urol. **2015**, Article ID 495308, 10 pages (2015)
4. Araki, A., Makiyama, K., et al.: Comparison of the performance of experienced and novice surgeons: measurement of gripping force during laparoscopic surgery performed on pigs using forceps with pressure sensors. Surg. Endosc. **31**(4), 1999–2005 (2017)

5. Puangmali, P., Althoefer, K., et al.: State-of-the-art in force and tactile sensing for minimally invasive surgery. IEEE Sens. J. **8**(4), 371–381 (2008)
6. Trejos, A.L., Patel, R.V., et al.: A sensorized instrument for skills assessment and training in minimally invasive surgery. J. Med. Devices **3**(4), 041002 (2009)
7. Ly, H.H., et al.: Grasper having tactile sensing function using acoustic reflection for laparoscopic surgery. Int. J. CARS **12**(8), 1333–1343 (2017)

HCI for Health and Wellbeing

Bringing Nature into Our Lives

Using Biophilic Design and Calm Computing Principles to Improve Well-Being and Performance

Carla Barreiros[1]([✉]), Eduardo Veas[2]([✉]), and Viktoria Pammer[2]([✉])

[1] Graz University of Technology, Graz, Austria
cbarreiros@know-center.at
[2] Know-Center GmbH, Graz, Austria
{eveas,vpammer}@know-center.at

Abstract. In the context of the Internet of Things (IoT), every device have sensing and computing capabilities to enhance many aspects of human life. There are more and more IoT devices in our homes and at our workplaces, and they still depend on human expertise and intervention for tasks as maintenance and (re)configuration.

Using biophilic design and calm computing principles, we developed a nature-inspired representation, BioIoT, to communicate sensor information. This visual language contributes to the users' well-being and performance while being as easy to understand as traditional data representations. Our work is based on the assumption that if machines are perceived to be more like living beings, users will take better care of them, which ideally would translate into a better device maintenance. In addition, the users' overall well-being can be improved by bringing nature to their lives.

In this work, we present two use case scenarios under which the BioIoT concept can be applied and demonstrate its potential benefits in households and at workplaces.

Keywords: Biophilia · Calm computing · Positive computing
Persuasive technology · IoT

1 Introduction

In the concept of the Internet of Things (IoT), industrial environments contain a vast number of electronics and IT systems [1]. It is estimated that by year 2020 fifty billion devices will coexist in our environments, connected and interacting with each other. Industrial equipment has embedded sensors and can communicate real-time sensory data. As the machinery grows increasingly complex, such tasks as configuration and maintenance demand higher human expertise, and operators have to specialize in handling complex systems. Moreover, the IoT concept of connected machines extends beyond industrial environments to daily life. Domestic machines are equipped with chips and sensors as well, and servicing them may be rather demanding.

© Springer International Publishing AG, part of Springer Nature 2018
M. Kurosu (Ed.): HCI 2018, LNCS 10902, pp. 99–109, 2018.
https://doi.org/10.1007/978-3-319-91244-8_9

A calm technology implies that humans are informed but not overloaded with information and that technology should only require the user's attention when necessary. To that end, based on the biophilic design and calm computing principles, we developed a nature-inspired visual language, BioIoT, to communicate sensor information.

In this work, we explored how to convey information about complex, real-time processes via nature-inspired visualizations. Our objectives were multi-levelled. First, we aimed to achieve a representation that is both easy to understand and aesthetically engaging and that increases the overall well-being. Second, we tested our hypothesis that if machines were perceived to be more like living beings, operators would take better care of them, which ideally would translate into a better (preventive) machine maintenance.

In this paper, we introduce the BioIoT concept and we present two use case scenarios under which it can be applied and we demonstrate its potential benefits in households and at workplaces.

2 (Re)designing Human-Machine Interaction via the Biophilic Hypothesis and Calm Computing

We propose to use nature-inspired representations to communicate IoT information in an appealing and engaging manner. In the BioIoT concept, an IoT device can connect to a living proxy that reflects the general state of device.

The user interacts with both the IoT device and the nature representation, as depicted in Fig. 1.

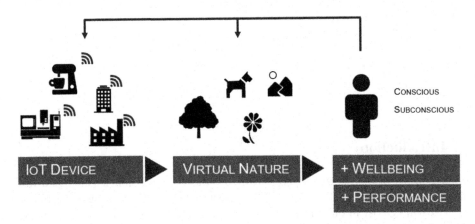

Fig. 1. BioIoT concept - IoT device generates sensory information, which is communicated through virtual nature-inspired representations.

The BioIoT concept is based on four theoretical premises:

- Biophilic Design: by incorporating contact with virtual nature elements into everyday tasks, we expect to contribute to the user's overall well-being;

- Calm Computing: by presenting substantial amounts of IoT data via a single peripherally noticeable representation, we expect to decrease the information overload and only request the user attention when necessary;
- Persuasive Technology: by exploring and stimulating the human tendency to perceive devices as social actors, we expect users to interact with the devices as though they were alive. As a result, behavior or attitude promoting greater care about the device can be enforced, ultimately improving its performance;
- Positive Computing: by designing and developing technology that enhances well-being factors, e.g., positive emotions, empathy and compassion, we expect to positively affect the users' psychological welfare.

2.1 Biophilic Design and Technobiophilia

The biophilia hypothesis states that humans are attracted to nature and all living processes [6]. Research confirms the human preference for natural environments and shows that our well-being, productivity and creativity greatly improve merely by being in direct contact with nature, e.g., gardens, parks and nature window view [7]. The contact with nature analogues, e.g., nature-resembling colors, patterns, materials and art, as well as natural-like light and sounds, also proved to be beneficial [4, 12].

Living in urban environments does not satisfy this human inclination. Efforts have been made to re-design cities, buildings, workplaces and homes to include natural elements. Biophilic design [4] is a method of constructing work and living spaces in a way that fulfils the humans' fundamental need to connect with nature.

The positive effects of biophilic design extend beyond the workers' well-being and job satisfaction and can be translated into economic advantages for employers since human productivity increases upon contact with nature. Both direct (e.g., the number of pieces produced and time required for task completion) and indirect metrics (e.g., illness, absenteeism, staff retention, learning rates, stress levels and fatigue) productivity metrics clearly indicate a remarkable growth, upon which organizations can capitalize [12, 13].

The notion of technobiophilia within the biophilia hypothesis refers to the 'innate tendency to focus on life and lifelike processes as they appear in technology' [22]. Technology can provide access to nature when nature is not available and can help to fulfil the human' attraction to nature [22].

Nature representations, e.g., artificial gardens and pets, as well as easily accessible feedback to data, can lead to reflection and posterior behavioral change [1, 2, 11]. For example, Data Fountain uses water jets to show the currency rates of Euro, Yen, Dollar to achieve a general 'feeling' of interconnection between the currencies [15]. Similarly, plant displays have successfully been employed to represent data and provide affective feedback [3].

2.2 Calm Computing, Persuasive Technology and Positive Computing

Weiser's vision of calm technology [16, 17] is now within reach due to the Internet of Things. Calm technology emphasizes calm, suggesting that humans need to be informed but not overloaded with information. As such, technology should be transparent and only require attention when needed. For example, in industrial environments, the perceived system complexity from the operators' perspective should be reduced [18].

With that regard, establishing the balance between esthetic and informational quality is crucial. Some messages (e.g., fire alarms) are too urgent to be subtle and must be delivered unambiguously. Yet even in the case of potential disaster, the level of urgency can gradually be built up over time. This increasing urgency should be presented 'calmly' in the environment in order to create optimal conditions for vigorous human action to control the damage or even prevent the accident from happening [15].

Research has been carried out to study how people interact with machines, e.g., robots [8]. Human perception of the machines' intelligence and consciousness, combined with anthropomorphic factors, i.e., appearance, gestures and emotions, is known to change the dynamics of human-machine interactions. A possible explanation is that machines tend to be perceived as social actors. In that context, some studies [9] indicate that social rules and dynamics should be applied to design systems that have the potential to change the user's behavior. For example, the reciprocity rule "If you help me, I feel that I should help you" is also valid for human-machine interaction [10]. Humans are hardwired to be social and to experience emotions towards others humans and living beings, e.g., empathy and compassion.

Bartneck et al. designed a study in which two groups of users were asked to play a game collaboratively with a talking cat robot [19]. In one group the robot was very helpful, while in the other one not so much. Eventually, the groups were instructed to turn the robot off. The users' perception of the robot's intelligence and agreeability had a strong effect on the ease of switching it off. The group with the most helpful robot hesitated almost three times as long to switch it off since 'killing' the machine was difficult because of an emotional connection with the machine [20].

Persuasive technology refers to technology designed to change the users' attitudes or behavior through persuasion and social influence [21]. B.J. Fogg proposes the functional triad framework for thinking about the roles technology plays. The functional triad shows that technologies can function as tools (increasing capability), media (providing experience) or social actors (creating a relationship). These functions capture how people use or respond to any technology and most technologies are a mix thereof.

A tool can be persuasive, for example, by making a target behavior easier to establish. A medium can be persuasive by allowing people to rehearse a behavior and a social actor can be persuasive by rewarding people via a positive feedback or modeling a target behavior or attitude.

Technology should be designed not only to impact productivity but also to enhance the humans' well-being. Positive computing is a research area and practice that uses well-established methods in such fields as psychology, neuroscience and economics to design and develop new technologies that foster psychological well-being and human potential [14].

Positive computing relies on psychological principles of motivation, engagement, relatedness, autonomy, competence and compassion to design technology that enhances human lives. The objectives of our work were to communicate sensory information of machines in a meaningful way based on the concepts of biophilia and positive computing and to add value by increasing human well-being via representations of nature.

3   Concretizing the BioIoT Concept

The BioIoT concept contains four main elements, as depicted in Fig. 2:

- an IoT device that generates sensory data and communicates it using a lightweight messaging protocol, e.g., MQTT - Message Queue Telemetry Transport;
- a backend application that handles communication and encodes the IoT data using a nature-inspired language;
- an output-specific user interface, e.g., display with 2D visualization, a head-mounted display with 3D augmented reality visualization;
- a nature-inspired language for encoding the IoT data, e.g., visual elements, sounds, smells.

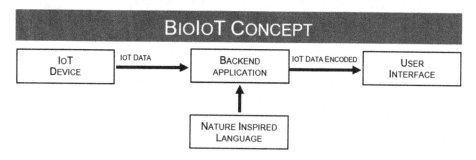

Fig. 2. BioIoT concept: an IoT device generates sensory data communicated through virtual nature-inspired representations.

3.1   Nature-Inspired Visual Language: A Virtual Tree

To implement our concept we designed a virtual tree model for the following reasons:

- Trees are appreciated and recognized as a fundamental part of a natural environment.
- Changes in a tree's condition are easily recognized by everyone, regardless of culture. We intended to minimize the effort required to learn a new language by exploring this prior knowledge.
- Trees have a limited number of parts that can change: flowers, branches, leaves, trunk, and roots. This is of advantage while designing the virtual tree model since it reduces the design complexity. However, this can also be considered a disadvantage since number of variations is limited.

The appearance of the designed virtual tree depends on the foliage density, the foliage color, the presence and size of flowers, and the size of the trunk. The roots of the tree were not considered since we aimed to create a realistic environment, in which they are not visible. In addition, to enhance the virtual tree model we integrated the wind and sun light effects.

We created the virtual tree using the SpeedTree modeler and made it available in 2D and 3D versions.

The proposed virtual tree model has several levels of encoding complexity.

Foliage Color

Tree foliage colors typically vary between green and red. Figure 3 shows two virtual trees with green and red foliage. To achieve a realistic foliage, the leave colors were not completely uniform.

Fig. 3. Two examples of virtual trees with different foliage colors. Left: a tree with green leaves; Middle: a tree with red leaves; Right top: detail of the green leaves; Right bottom: detail of the red leaves. (Color figure online)

Foliage Density

Tree foliage densities vary greatly. Figure 4 provides four examples of virtual trees with different degrees of foliage density.

Fig. 4. Four examples of virtual trees with different degrees of foliage density. Left top: foliage not present; Left middle: low foliage density; Left bottom: medium foliage density; Right: high foliage density.

Flowers

In the tree model, the flowers can be present or absent. When present, the flowers can have three sizes (small, medium and large) (Fig. 5).

Fig. 5. Four examples of virtual trees with/without flowers. Left top: flowers absent; Left middle: small flowers; Left bottom: medium-size flowers; Right: large flowers present.

Sun Light and Wind Animation

The sunlight and the wind animation add movement to the virtual tree model, creating a more realistic effect. The wind had various degrees of intensity (low, medium and intense), and the sunlight effects could be present or absent (Fig. 6).

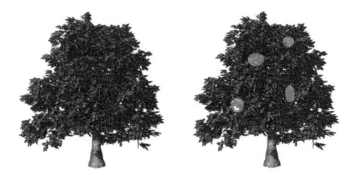

Fig. 6. Two virtual trees without (left) and with (right) of the sunlight effect.

4 Use Case Scenarios – Bringing Nature to Our Lives

The following use case scenarios describe two applications of the BioIoT concept.

Peter and Anna live and work in an urban area and, like many of us, have little or no chance of contact with nature in their daily lives. However, technology and data seem to be present at all times.

4.1 Use Case A: Peter Has a Green Thumb

Peter works in an office and every morning enjoys a cup of coffee while checking his calendar and messages. The coffee machine in Peter's office is a new IoT model, but the machine is a nuisance for him: 'It's a nightmare! No one services the machine or performs maintenance unless it stops brewing coffee! The other day all warning lights were on… Everyone wants to drink coffee, but no one cares for the machine until it stops working'.

The following day, next to the coffee machine there was a screen with a beautiful virtual tree. Everyone was informed that the tree reflects the coffee machine's condition.

A few days later, Peter notices that his colleagues (and he himself) began to interact with the coffee machine in a more positive way, making sure that it was serviced and maintained in time.

After reflecting on his own actions, Peter explains "I just want to make sure that the tree looks its best. And it seems that no one wants to be responsible for killing it!"

Due to this change of behavior and attitude, Peter is now able to fully appreciate his morning coffee.

Study: A Green IoT Coffee Machine

We conducted a study to validate the participants' ability to understand the proposed nature-inspired visual language (virtual tree) and evaluate the appeal of the BioIoT concept [5, 23].

To that end, we created an IoT coffee machine prototype enhanced with sensors and able to communicate the IoT data to a MQTT server. In addition, we developed a desktop application in Unity to encode the IoT data from the coffee machine, creating a multi-surface projection of the tree (four cameras) onto a holographic display.

We encoded the IoT coffee machine's sensors data as follows:

- The foliage density represents the three fill levels of the water tank.
- The foliage color represents the temperature.
- The presence or absence of flowers represents the maintenance status.
- The size of the flowers represents the time until maintenance is required.
- The dead tree (no leaves) represents critical error.
- The presence/absence of the sun light animation represents the presence/absence of a coffee capsule.

Twelve individuals (8M, 4F) participated in the study, which confirmed that the nature-inspired encodings are readable. The participants recognized the status of the machine based on the virtual tree features. However, the comprehension declined when a large amount of sensor information was displayed in a single visualization. All participants considered the interaction with the BioIoT pleasant and agreed that the machine states representations were overall aesthetically satisfying. They also felt more inclined to perform machine maintenance (take "care" of the machine) than they would if classic state representations were to be applied.

4.2   Use Case B: Anna Enjoys Walking Between the Trees

Anna works in a warehouse and is responsible for equipment maintenance, e.g., conveyors, picking stations, storage towers. Anna performs several tasks daily to ensure that the operations run smoothly. Some examples of Anna activities are: installing and (re)configuring equipment, performing preventive maintenance and diagnosing and solving problems (e.g., repairs, spare parts). In addition, Anna has to constantly monitor the warehouse to identify problems with the equipment. She typically wears a head-mounted display and uses the augmented reality performance support system. According to Anna, the system has three very useful features: step-by-step instructions while servicing a machine, direct communication with experts for solving specific problems and access to in-context information dashboards about the warehouse.

A new version of this system offers a nature view feature, with information encoded using virtual trees. Anna personalizes the encoding and defines which equipment or clusters of equipment are connected with each tree. Now, when Anna is monitoring the warehouse, the nature view is activated and she can enjoy walking through a virtual forest.

Anna is very satisfied: 'It is much nicer to be informed via the trees than via red lights! And it is gratifying to see the beautiful trees after solving the issue.'

Study: Scaling the BioIoT Concept

We conducted a study to validate the participants' ability to perceive visual changes and fast-changing states on a larger number of IoT devices encoded using the nature- inspired visual language [20, 23].

Following on Healey et al. work on pre-attentive processing of visual features [24], we investigated accomplishing target detection tasks by relying on variations in hue and in form. The former was represented by the foliage color green or red, and for the latter we applied our virtual maple tree model and a palm tree. We developed a factory model composed of 49 IoT machines and a Unity mobile application that randomly-generated states of the machines and overlaid an augmented reality tree next to the machine.

Sixteen individuals (12M, 4F) participated in the study, which showed that the BioIoT concept can be applied to a larger number of IoT devices and that changes in the hue and form features are pre-attentively perceived (200 ms or less).

5   Discussion

As we increasingly engage with IoT technologies it becomes necessary to find new ways to interact with such large amounts of data. The BioIoT concept proposes to communicate sensory information through nature inspired representations.

As referred, the BioIoT concept is grounded in four theoretical premises: biophilic design; calm computing; persuasive technology; and positive computing.

The biophilic design and calm computing are the base of our concept, which aims to impact positively the wellbeing of the users. In addition, our concept persuades the user to change their behavior.

Accordingly with Fogg's taxonomy persuasive technologies can function as tools, media, or social actors [12]. The BioIoT concept comprehends these three functions.

Firstly, it functions as a tool by providing all the necessary information to infer the general state of an IoT device in a single visualization, which allows an earlier detection of issues. For example, if the user notices that the tree foliage density is decreasing, it is likely that there is lack of water in the machine. Therefore the user can act before the lack of water becomes a critical problem.

Secondly, it functions as a media by allowing users the opportunity to explore cause-and-effect relationships, e.g. if the user does not take care of the machine, the tree will degrade or even die. Up to now we used nature inspired visual representations, e.g. virtual trees in augmented reality. However, we consider to extend it to enrich the user's experience, e.g. addition of audio or scents.

Lastly, it has a strong social actor functional role. It persuades the user in multiple manners, such as: reinforcement of the emotional connection with the IoT devices, e.g. empathy and kindness towards the virtual tree; the act of caring for the IoT device rewards the user through an aesthetical and pleasant visualization, e.g. a beautiful tree is shown if the device is timely serviced and maintained, which motivates the user to establish or strengthen the desired behavior.

So far we performed two studies to validate the BioIoT concept design. Both studies had a strong focus on perceptual aspects of decoding information encoded using our nature inspired representations. Our representations were understood by users, even while performing an activity, e.g. coffee machine maintenance. The BioIoT concept can be scaled to a larger number of devices (forty nine devices), and still users are able to detect changes in the status of these devices.

In the future, we intend to conduct long-term studies to investigate the impact of the BioIoT concept in the users' behaviors and attitudes towards the IoT devices.

Acknowledgements. This work was funded by the LiTech K-project and by KnowCenter GmbH. Both are, funded by the Austrian Competence Centers for Excellent Technologies (COMET) program, under the auspices of the Austrian Federal Ministry of Transport, Innovation, and Technology; the Austrian Federal Ministry of Economy, Family, and Youth; and the Austrian state of Styria. COMET is managed by the Austrian Research Promotion Agency FFG.

References

1. Consolvo, S., et al.: Activity sensing in the wild: a field trial of UbiFit garden. In: Proceedings of the SIGCHI (CHI 2008), pp. 1797–1806 (2008)
2. Froehlich, J.E., et al.: UbiGreen: investigating a mobile tool for tracking and supporting green transportation habits. In: Proceedings of the SIGCHI (CHI 2009), pp. 1043–1052 (2009)

3. Chien, J.T., et al.: Biogotchi! An exploration of plant based information displays. In: Proceedings of the SIGCHI (CHI EA 2015), pp. 1139–1144 (2015)
4. The global impact of biophilic design in the workplace global report. Technical report, Human Spaces (2015)
5. Barreiros, C., Veas, E., Pammer, V.: BioIoT - communicating sensory information of a coffee machine using a nature metaphor. In: ACM CHI Conference on Human Factors in Computing Systems - CHI 2017 (2017)
6. Wilson, E.: Biophilia, 12th edn. Harvard University Press, Cambridge (1984)
7. Largo-Wight, E., Chen, W.W., Dodd, V., Weiler, R.: Heathy workplaces: the effects of nature contact at work on employee stress and health. Public Health Rep. **126**(Suppl 1), 124–130 (2011)
8. Duff, B.R.: Anthropomorphism and the social robot. Robot. Auton. Syst. **42**(3–4), 177–190 (2003)
9. Fogg, B.J., Nass, C.: How users reciprocate to computers: an experiment that demonstrates behavior change. In: Proceedings of CHI EA – Conference on Human Factors in Computing Systems Extended Abstracts, pp. 331–332 (1997)
10. Nass, C., Yen, C.: The man who lied to his laptop - what machines teach us about human relationships (2010)
11. Donath, J.: Artificial pets: simple behaviors elicit complex attachments. In: Bekoff, M. (ed.) The Encyclopedia of Animal Behavior. Greenwood Press, Santa Barbara (2004)
12. The Economics of Biophilia. Technical Report, Terrapin Bright Green (2012)
13. Miller, N., Pogue, D., Gough, Q.D., Davis, S.M.: Green buildings and productivity. J. Sustain. Real Estate **1**(1), 65–89 (2009)
14. Calvo, R.A., Peters, D.: Positive Computing – Technology for Well-being and Human Potential. MIT Press, Cambridge (2014)
15. Eggen, B., Van Mensvoort, K.: Making sense of what is going on 'around': designing environmental awareness information displays. In: Markopoulos, P., De Ruyter, B., Mackay, W. (eds.) Awareness Systems. Human-Computer Interaction Series. Springer, London (2009). https://doi.org/10.1007/978-1-84882-477-5_4
16. Weiser, M., Brown, J.S.: The coming age of calm technology. Xerox PARC, Palo Alto (1996)
17. Weiser, M.: The computer for the 21st century. Sci. Am. **265**(3), 94–104 (1991)
18. Ziefle, M., Röcker, C. (eds.): Human-Centered Design of E-health Technologies: Concepts, Methods Applications. IGI Publishing, Niagara Falls (2011)
19. Bartneck, C., van der Hoek, M., Mubin, O., Mahmud, A.A.: "Daisy, daisy, give me your answer do!" Switching off a robot. In: Proceedings of the HRI Conference on Human-Robots Interaction (HRI 2007), pp. 217–222 (2007)
20. Barreiros, C., Veas, E., Pammer, V.: Pre-attentive features in natural augmented reality visualizations. In: IEEE International Symposium on Mixed and Augmented Reality (ISMAR 2016) (2016)
21. Fogg, B.J.: Persuasive Technology – Using Computers to Change What We Think and Do. Morgan Kaufmann Publishers, San Francisco (2003)
22. Thomas, S.: Technobiophilia – Nature and Cyberspace. Bloomsbury, London (2013)
23. Barreiros, C., Veas, E., Pammer, V.: Can a green thumb make a difference?: using a nature metaphor to communicate the sensor information of a coffee machine. IEEE Consum. Electron. Magaz. **7**(3), 90–98 (2018)
24. Healey, C.G., Booth, K.S., Enns, J.T.: Visualizing real-time multi-variate data using preattentive processing. ACM Trans. Model. Comput. Simul. **5**(3), 190–221 (1995)

Social Robotics and Human Computer Interaction for Promoting Wellbeing in the Contemporary City

Nimish Biloria[✉] and Dimitra Dritsa

University of Technology Sydney, Ultimo, NSW 2007, Australia
{Nimish.Biloria,Dimitra.Dritsa}@uts.edu.au

Abstract. Within today's environment of relentless urban growth, socio-technical approaches towards enhancing wellbeing within the urban have started gathering momentum. Situated in this context, the research paper presents an approach to actively instigate physiological and psychological behavioral change within people for promoting wellbeing via context aware augmentation of physical environments. This involves harnessing a trans-disciplinary approach wherein, the domains of data sciences, HCI, embedded robotics, computational simulation and user-centric interaction design merge in order to promote real-time responsive augmentation (physical, ambient, social and structural) of the built environment. The paper elaborates upon two projects: RoboZoo and FLUID, both built and tested in The Netherlands, representing two different scales; Small scale: object/product scale, which operate within urban open public space and Large scale: indoor public installation.

Keywords: Social robotics · Interaction design · Health and wellbeing

1 Introduction

1.1 Underpinning

The unprecedented pace, with which urbanization is advancing, is principally driving the emergence of Smart Cities on a global scale [1]. A predictive urban growth of 1.84% per year between 2015 and 2020 alone, mapped by Global Health Observatory data [2], already outlines the challenges facing the built environment community. Within this fast-paced demand of urban growth, mostly led by developer led commercial lobbies, issues pertaining to urban health and wellbeing at the urban planning phase appear secondary on the agenda. It is thus critical to explore strategies for re-furbishing and re-purposing the urban environment so that it may proactively reduce health risks and promote wellbeing. Fostering user awareness pertaining to healthy practices, promoting physical mobility and increasing user engagement in community drives for promoting wellbeing via socio-technical mediations within the urban context are all deemed as vital proactive measures.

Within this context, the research paper presents an approach where context aware augmentation of physical environments by harnessing the domains of social robotics and human computer interaction to actively instigate physiological activity and social

© Springer International Publishing AG, part of Springer Nature 2018
M. Kurosu (Ed.): HCI 2018, LNCS 10902, pp. 110–124, 2018.
https://doi.org/10.1007/978-3-319-91244-8_10

wellbeing is deployed. The approach involves incorporating a fusion of an interdisciplinary approach (spatial sciences, social science, human physiology and human behavior) and an intra-disciplinary approach (data sciences, robotics, computational design and human-machine interaction) to promote real-time multi-scalar adaptation (physical, ambient, social and structural) in the built environment. Binding People, Technology and Space into a comprehensive inter-activating looped system to enhance health and wellbeing within the contemporary city is thus a vital characteristic of the elaborated project.

The paper, in order to elaborate upon this approach, is organized in the following sections: Sect. 1.2, will lay the foundation of health and wellbeing within the urban context via a concise literature review, Sect. 1.3, shall dive into the domain of social robotics, its connection with human computer interaction, Sect. 2 and its sub-sections shall elaborate upon the two real-time interactive physical installations: RoboZoo and FLUID, and Sect. 3 shall conclude by engaging in a discussion on the findings of the experiments and the future research work which needs to be conducted within the domains of social robotics and HCI.

1.2 Wellbeing Within an Urban Context

As earlier efforts towards the examination of the philosophical roots of wellbeing and its interpretations among different disciplines have shown, the formulation of a single definition of the term that captures the full spectrum of wellbeing has proved to be an incredibly difficult task. This difficulty stems from the broad and undefined nature of the term, a fact that becomes particularly apparent throughout the varying linguistic interpretations of the term comes forth in non-English-speaking countries, complicating the conduction of comparative research and the formulation of context-aware health policies [3]. Due to this confusion, wellbeing is conceptualized as a term considered to be interchangeable with other terms of equally broad and undefined nature, such as 'quality of life', and it has been widely used as such [3–5].

Three major dimensions have been most commonly associated with wellbeing, the physiological, psychological and social dimension, and in the majority of the studies within fields such as sociology, anthropology and economics, wellbeing is examined in connection to the attribute mostly associated with the field [4]. In the field of biomedicine, wellbeing is commonly discussed in relation to physiological functioning, while psychologists associate wellbeing with a sense of self and interpersonal connectedness [5]. As for its assessment, while morbidity and mortality become the objective components measured in indicators commonly used by health policy makers, in recent literature there is also reference to the difficulty to integrate self-assessed elements and dimensions of subjective wellbeing in the assessment process [3]. Earlier efforts towards the creation of the assessment tools such as that of Kaplan [3] attempted to encompass both the physical and social dimension in a single tool, while other tools such as the Psychological General Well-Being Index [7] have focused on the measurement of a single dimension. A significant step towards that was the development of the WHO-5 Well-Being Index as a generic tool for the subjective measurement of wellbeing, applicable to different age groups and able to capture improvement of wellbeing over time without overlapping with significant disease-related symptoms [8].

Since wellbeing is a term with such a multifaceted nature, it is critical for studies that undertake the task of enhancing wellbeing, to define which of its dimensions are explored within the scope of the study. The focus of this paper will be on discussing technology mediated social and physiological wellbeing, by exemplifying upon two projects. The two projects RoboZoo and FLUID, also operate on two different scales within the urban domain: an object/product scale and an architectural installation scale and thus have different socio-technical approaches towards approaching the topic of wellbeing.

Furthermore, a fact that has emerged in recent literature is the shift from the approach that viewed the absence of psychological or physiological dysfunction as the primary indicator of wellbeing, towards an approach that views wellbeing as a positive multi-faceted attribute [3, 4]. Following this shift, the focus of the study is on positive functioning, and how public interactive spaces and social interactive robots can act towards its advancement in the physiological and social domain.

1.3 Social Robotics and HCI in the Urban Sphere

Public interactive installations, such as the Tactical Sound Garden by Mark Sheppard and Dotty Tate by Jason Bruges Studio [9] commonly incorporate smart technologies which can enhance the sensorial experience of places and stimulate physical activity; despite this fact, there is little to no literature examining public interactive spaces through the lens of wellbeing. Single dimensions of wellbeing, such as social functioning, are addressed more intensively is Social Robotics; the impacts of interacting with social robots have been studied in environments ranging from elderly nursing homes to educational facilities, work environments and public spaces [10]. Within the larger field of Social Robotics, Assistive Robotics (AR), Social Interactive Robotics (SIR) and Social Assistive Robotics (SAR) have emerged as subclasses, defined by a robot's main purpose to give aid, engage in some form of interaction or interact with the aim to provide assistance [11].

The subclass Social Assistive Robotics (SAR) has been particularly productive in terms of enhancing physiological wellbeing, with its most notable contributions belonging in the field of physical therapy, therapeutic play or post-stroke rehabilitation exercises, where the robotic assistant plays a motivational or instructive role [12]. Certain aspects of physiological wellbeing, such as physical activity, have been also addressed indirectly in studies with a focus in the assessment of social interaction between robots and humans; such a case is the study on the sociopsychological effects of living with therapeutic robots in an elderly care facility [13] that, among other metrics, measured the time spent in public spaces as a performance indicator.

As for the contribution of Social Robotics towards the enhancement of social wellbeing, research conducted towards the promotion of social interaction in the elderly and individuals with cognitive disorders is particularly noteworthy; significant research has been carried out towards the development of companion robots for the reduction of stress and depression in the elderly, as well as for therapeutic purposes for children with autism

[10]. The emergence of robotic pets as companions has been mostly connected with this field, as a way to harvest the benefits of animal assisted therapy, but without the constant care that an animal would require [10, 13, 14]. While such studies explore social interaction scenarios as therapeutic interventions towards the treatment of physiological and psychological dysfunctions, a number of studies also explore the enhancement of positive functioning via social interaction. Such a case is that of Cooney et al. [15] that explored the enhancement of social wellbeing through affectionate play, via interaction with a small companion robot.

For social robots deployed in public space, as happens with the two projects that will be further discussed, advanced adaptability as well as response to unexpected scenarios is required [10], while the range of the users expands considerably and the robot has to be capable of interacting with more than one human. Additionally, in the wider field of HCI, other social aspects that technology mediated interaction in public spaces can bring forth have also surfaced lately within the discourse on urban HCI; since one or multiple users can be involved in interaction scenarios within the public space, the public realm becomes a space for people to share creative experiences [16, 17]. With the introduction of user-controlled interactive elements, public spaces become realms where technology enhances the social agency of the users by enabling them to manipulate the barriers between public and private space and negotiate their desired degree of social interaction [18].

2 Urban Social Robotics Experiments

The aforementioned discussion on social robotics and HCI serves as a rich context for embedding the research experiments. The two projects that will be further discussed in this paper examine how social robotics and HCI driven urban interactive interventions can act as potential enhancers of physiological health and mental wellbeing. The projects represent two different scales; Small scale Object/Product oriented, which operate within Urban open public space and Large scale indoor public Installations. Both projects bind critical performative demands imposed by the clients, the solution sets for which involve impacting human behavior through tangible interaction. The projects have been prototyped, experimented and tested in The Netherlands and Spain, and serve as proof of concepts of a trans-disciplinary mode of operation.

a. RoboZoo, Real-time interactive bots in urban public spaces (Fig. 1(a))
b. FLUID, Real-time interactive public installation at Science Museum, Amsterdam (Fig. 2(b))

2.1 RoboZoo: Real-Time Interactive Bots in Urban Public Spaces

RoboZoo is an experiment in social robotics consisting of an ecology of small scale robotic-bots which, operate on the premise that motion/movement and non-verbal communication can be understood as interfaces of emotional interaction and cognition. The installation harnesses swarm computing and ubiquitous computing tools and techniques to develop real-time data communication abilities per robotic bot and amongst a community of these bots and their human counterparts. An important aspect of RoboZoo is the subtle transition from a reactive to a pro-active mode of engagement with its users.

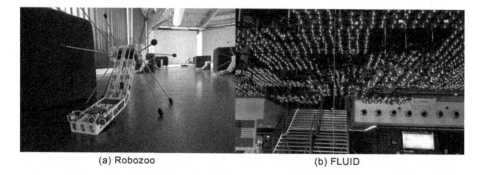

(a) Robozoo   (b) FLUID

Fig. 1. (a): RoboZoo, an ecology of small-scale mobile bots. (b): FLUID, a large scale indoor public installation designed for the NEMO Science Museum in Amsterdam.

With a focus on challenging conventional modes of perception, movement and associated behavioral attributes, the installation operates on the boundaries of science, art and architecture. The client, in this case was the European Union. The RoboZoo installation was developed as a part of a European Union Culture grant, titled METABODY. The research agenda in this case was set towards enhancing physiological response as well as psychological comfort, for instance via offering a mode of companionship. Based on the planned public exhibition locations and urban open environments for exposing RoboZoo, our target audience, apart from the regular visitors of the exhibition, comprised of pre-teenage children (below 10 years) and the elderly who tend to suffer from loneliness. A variety of techno-centric experiments (such as the ones dealing with Ambient Intelligence) have a tendency to be situated in discrete structured environments. A disadvantage of this tendency is that the functional scope of such solutions does not extend beyond their deployment domain. RoboZoo on the other hand is developed as an installation which operates both, within urban open spaces and within controlled home environments. The socio-technical aspect of the installation implied at critically examining the manner in which the divide between humans and machines can be blurred to an extent where aspects of empathy and shared emotional agency become emergent consequences of interactions between the two. Instigating a healthier community engagement, as a critical aspect of wellbeing in urban public spaces via actively merging human and machinic agencies, wherein ambiguity and diffused affordances take center stage, thus provoking pro-active engagements for creating new social structures became a primary objective of RoboZoo.

RoboZoo, as an interactive swarm of robots is conceived as an ecology of small-scale mobile bots, which, operate on the basis of a multi-agent swarm computing model. The design evolution of the bots in itself went through a series of iterations. This primarily focused on the morphology of the bots rather than the communication protocols between them at the primary stage. The form factor, including the material usage, the scale and size of the bots as well as the nature of their movement, was intensively tested within a research lab setting, where both children and elderly were invited regularly for commenting and criticizing the developmental phase. The bots, due to their mobile nature, were always compared with an animal form, however, their morphological makeup and their mobility aspects were directly perceived from an emotive angle. For instance, the first few iterations were conceived as being nervous, too frantic, scary as well as too insect like. The material make up in this case too was perceived as too sharp, very angular, very stiff or too flexible (Fig. 2). Such feedback from the users within a controlled setting was further coupled with technical issues being encountered by the design team while deploying the early phase prototypes in an urban open space. For instance, the friction between rough ground and the ability to propel itself as well as change direction effortlessly, became issues which were coupled together with the aforementioned emotional response.

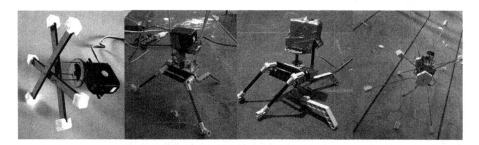

Fig. 2. From left to right: progression of the iterations of RoboZoo according to user feedback.

Fig. 3. Final iterations of RoboZoo, deployed at an indoor and outdoor environment. (Color figure online)

The final iteration (Fig. 3), acquired the form of a slender grasshopper like body structure with two wheels fabricated from bent metal spokes with rubber endings. The body in itself is made out of simple to fabricate, 3d printed profiles, which also host a range of electronics. Each bot operates as an individual agent, with embedded proximity sensors (located prominently as eyes), a micro-controller (located at the heart's position), LED strips (embedded within the 3d printed chassis) and two servo motors (connected with the two wheels), powered by a battery pack. The scale factor was also maintained in a manner that the bot does not become imposing and could be easily lifted up and spatially re-positioned even by small children. Hopping motion vs a smoother wheel based locomotion further helped both technically as well as from an emotional response perspective since the users now expressed a sense of familiarity accompanied with lesser skepticism about the directional movement and intensity of movement of the bots. The LED lighting and its subtle communication such as Red for appearing confused, Green as having registered the presence of a person and Blue for representing a calm state were also equally understood and welcomed as an additional feature by both age groups. Each agent is further programmed with control rules (akin to a swarm) which enables it to sense its context (people and obstacles), sense the speed of movement/approach of people as well as other agents towards it and thus propel itself towards people (based on how they approach: gentle movement equates to a friendly approach vs sudden and rapid movement equates to an unfriendly, imposing approach), while maintaining contact with other agents in its vicinity.

RoboZoo, was ultimately deployed at two large scale public events within two prominent indoor exhibition areas: The Media Lab Prado, Madrid, Spain as well as at AULA, Congress centrum at the TU Delft, Netherlands. Apart from this, the ecology of bots was also deployed at various outdoor locations within the TU Delft: during a major open to public science event frequented by children and elderly alike as well as in an outdoor setting at one of the most frequented pubs at the Faculty of Architecture, TU Delft (Fig. 4). An observational analysis approach, accompanied with informal interview sessions with the users at the aforementioned events resulted in the following conclusions: The bots and humans inter-activate each other in order to create novel social patterns and in the process constantly redefine space via establishing unspoken ecological dependencies. Movement (speed, directionality and pause) based expression of each independent agent evokes instantaneous response in the environment and invites people (who are otherwise organized in clusters/ghettoes) to create dynamic relations on the fly. A special focus was given towards the elderly and children who were interacting with the bots during the public events.

Fig. 4. Deployment of RoboZoo in Madrid (upper left and bottom left image) and Delft (upper right and bottom right image)

A rather comforting observation, which was reinforced with the informal interview sessions with the elderly suggested that they did not perceive the bots as machines, but looked at them as pets and some were even willing to name them and take them home. The fact that some of elderly even went out of their way to pick up and re-position the bots which were stuck or were being mishandled by the younger visitors of the public exhibitions was in itself a testament of them developing an emotional and caring attitude towards RoboZoo. It was also observed by the RoboZoo team that though the electronics were exposed through the framework of the bots, the elderly did not show any signs of fear, however, some suggestions of covering these and adding a top cover module with a softer feel to it were also made. Physical activity such as bending, increased walking and stretching as well as multi-generational engagement were observed as common characteristics shared by both elderly and children. Children, specially were observed to be highly engaged with RoboZoo. However, frantic and rapid movement by children were at times not registered as inviting gestures by the bots. Children around the age of 5 to 7 were particularly involved with the bots. They were not only involved in physically playing with the bot but were surprisingly interested in how the bots were made and how they communicated with them as well as the other bots. A definite increase in physiological activity in addition to mental engagement was observed.

An active alteration of behaviors via shared agency thus starts becoming the norm. This mutual communication between people and bots actuate spatial (manner in which space is used) and social reconfiguration, thus promoting wellbeing via physical and psychological activeness.

2.2 FLUID: Real-Time Interactive Public Installation

FLUID, takes a different take on social robotics and HCI at an architectural scale. The installation thus instead of acquiring an object/product scale like RoboZoo, which operates at an emergent real-time interaction mode, operates at a one to one interaction level with the users. FLUID, also differs in another manner, it only operates within an indoor setting/in a controlled environment and is a social interaction experiment which addresses a specific client demand.

FLUID is a commercial project commissioned by the NEMO Science Museum in Amsterdam, The Netherlands. Some critical issues raised by NEMO specifically pointed towards solving two operative issues with one solution: reduce the amount of effort and resources spent on hiring staff to help reduce the noise in the entrance lobby created by a huge number of school going children who visit the museum, while at the same time keeping them physically active and allow for parents to be focused and organized while purchasing tickets and collecting information from the NEMO staff. This translated into the following research tasks for the FLUID design team: altering user behavior to reduce noise made by kids visiting the museum either via active or passive modes of interaction, inculcating behavioral change in the users to make them self-organized and engaged while waiting in the entrance hall and the active enhancement of pro-active physical activity via physically engaging users (both kids and adults).

As a response, FLUID is conceived as an installation which is suspended from the ceiling of the entrance hall of NEMO. FLUID takes its inspiration from a natural phenomenon: wind flow and the manner in which directionality of wind flow affects objects such as trees etc. to create dynamic fields of flow. Directional swaying of trees, movement of leaves due to the wind force etc. are some examples of such dynamic flows. FLUID aims to reimagine such dynamic flow patterns via replicating natural forces like the wind with the tracked movement pattern of visitors. Interfacing these tracked patterns of visitor movements with integrating embedded robotics and ambient media in a comprehensive manner, FLUID converts an otherwise static assemblage of objects into a dynamic fluid landscape via the physical augmentation of its system components. FLUID thus involves an active interaction approach where the unison of user behavior and mechanic operations are united into one seamlessly.

FLUID went through multiple iterations during the design development phase, which articulated the artistic vision in multiple ways from data communication as well as the physical components constituting it. One of the most prominent ideas, which was further refined into the final version, incorporated linear aluminum sheet based strips, which would run the entire length of the entrance hall and were directly connected to a series of electronic pistons suspended from the ceiling. A camera based tracking system, which would track and interpolate the position of users under this so called false ceiling would then act as a trigger for pushing the flexible aluminum strips on top of the aggregated cluster of users, thus transforming the otherwise static form of the ceiling. However, after discussing the idea with multiple stakeholders, including NEMO personnel, groups of children as well as their parents, the design team arrived at a conclusion that this mode of physical augmentation still did not capture the directional wind-flow based distortion of a physical collection of objects but instead rather projected a heavy, and rather linear cross sectioning of air-space, which lacked a higher resolution of interaction and promoted feelings of fear, anxiety and lack of self-control.

The design team thus came up with a much more refined alternative to address this user feedback and developed a much more fragmented (subdivided clusters of interactive modules instead of the linear strip idea), fragile (in appearance) and location sensitive (with inbuilt sensing systems per interactive module) proposal.

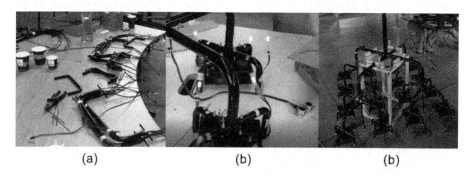

(a)   (b)   (b)

Fig. 5. (a): Setting up the construction of each cluster by passing the wiring through the hollow pipes. (b): Individual sensor testing after the construction of each cluster. (c): Four clusters are connected in order to formulate a supercluster. (Color figure online)

This new articulation of FLUID consists of 40 self-similar ornamental clusters made up of hollow aluminum pipes (Fig. 5(a)), which serve as a host for all the electrical wiring, microcontrollers and external physical elements. Each cluster is populated with the following system components: 4 microcontrollers (Arduino boards), 4 ultrasonic sensors, 4 custom made PCB's, which control 256 RGB LED's, 16 computer fans (which directly impart variable air pressure to tilt 256 pivoted CD's, which are painted an orange color on one side only) and 1 electronic piston (which vertically displaces the cluster) (Fig. 5(b) and (c)). The installation runs on an inter-integrated circuit protocol (I2C) and addresses user behavior by an intricate tracking of the visitor's directionality of movement and the amount of time they spend below each cluster via its embedded sensors (Fig. 7). The 40 clusters are divided into 4 groups and each group's microcontrollers in turn have a master controller (Arduino) attached to another custom made PCB. These master controllers are directly responsible for controlling the movement of electronic pistons connected to each interactive cluster within the group which they are in charge of (Fig. 6(b)).

Fig. 6. (a): The computer fans and the LED's are actuated by tracking the movement below each supercluster. (b): On-site configuration of the movement of the electronic pistons. (c): Testing the movement of the hinged disks before the official launch of the installation (Color figure online)

Fig. 7. Left: Exploded view of the clusters and cluster-to-supercluster assembly. Right: FLUID interacting with the audience within NEMO Science Museum

The directional movement of the children and other visitors is communicated via triggering the fans (Fig. 6(b)) on directly above the tracked location of the visitor (accompanied with a change in the LED color as an added indicator of recognition and physical movement of the interactive cluster). This switching on of the fans makes the hinged disks (Fig. 6(c)), with their orange color exposed to the users, tilt instantly (revealing a different color: the silver colored data reading and writing side) and then regain their horizontal position gradually once the fan slows down to eventually switch off. The visitors are instantly drawn towards this self-impacted dynamic color pattern configurations and are able to easily register that these are produced due to their own movement below the installation. Children, specifically are triggered into a gameplay scenario where they are focused towards producing colored patterns and propagating these patterns by physically moving below the installation. A rapid increase in step count and social interaction amongst the children was witnessed.

Furthermore, each cluster is able to detect the time spent by the visitor under it (a timer which would register the presence of the same person below the cluster for a minimum of seven seconds) and accordingly triggers the attached actuator to vertically push the cluster down towards the visitor, also accompanied by a corresponding change of the LED color and fan speeds. This physical displacement (vertical) of the cluster towards the user is specifically captivating to the user standing below since it gave an expression as if the installation wants to approach and embrace the user. An immediate observed reaction of the visitors, especially children is to reach out for the clusters accompanied by a jumping action with outstretched arms as well as occasional squatting and jumping actions. Apart from this, an independent self-organized structural behavior akin to playing a choreographed game thus started emerging amongst the children visiting the Museum, resulting in pro-active physical engagement and the reduction of noise owing to their self-organized behavior. A result of this engagement of the children in active gameplay is a lower supervision by the staff deployed on ground to cater to unruly and often noisy user behavior of the children. Once the children were engaged in gameplay within the safe confines of the entrance hall and below the virtual boundary of the installation, their parents tendency to be more relaxed and stress free allowed them to be more focused on tasks such as buying tickets for the entry into the museum as well be more focused while gathering information from the NEMO staff. It was also observed that when the parents were not engaged in such tasks, they were involved with the children in activities such as trying to decipher how the installation works or else trying to organize them below the installation in order to trigger one of the two behaviors of FLUID. Apart from these two behaviors of the installations, if the system detects multiple sensors being triggered (more than 70%) or if it detects inactivity in the entrance hall, an automated three dimensional pattern formation from the interactive clusters is set in motion. This involves triggering the vertical displacement of the clusters in multiple pre-programmed patterns, accompanied by the fans switching on and the LED's changing their colors.

Overall, the ornamental character of FLUID coupled with its simple yet effective behavioral communication modes as well as its scale, which allowed for an immersive experience addressed the issues raised by the Museum and more importantly engaged the audience both physiologically and psychologically via promoting pro-active behavior in real-time.

3   Conclusions and Future Research

The paper outlines the role of social robotics within the urban environment via two real-world experiments. Apart from elaborating upon the socio-technical nature of these experiments, the paper also reports upon the findings of both observational analysis and informal interview outcomes. The two projects, operating at different scales, adhere to the brief presented to the design team by the clients (European Union and NEMO) while at the same time strategically derive solutions that adhere to enhancing physiological activity and mental wellbeing in both children and the adults alike. Different modes of activating children to engage in physical activity were initiated (scale dependent). These range from inculcating a pet like behavior via RoboZoo and thus enhancing activities such as running, bending, squatting and following as opposed to an embracing/reaching out gesture promoted by FLUID, which instinctively activate reactions such as reaching out with arms outstretched, jumping, and focused physical movement in order to trigger color changes. Besides this, both installations enhanced mental engagement within children and the elderly alike. This was apparent during group formation and social engagement and interaction activities that materialized while being engaged with both social robotics experiments. RoboZoo however, was especially enticing for the elderly since they developed empathy towards the bots owing to the anthropomorphic embodiment and the tangible interaction they promoted. The higher rates of social connectedness that were identified in this user group might be associated with higher rates of loneliness that are usually demonstrated in the elderly, which as it has been reported, increase the chances of human-like properties to be attributed to non-human agents [19]. Another vital characteristic difference, dealt with the emergent behavior, which, RoboZoo inherits owing to the swarm robotics principles applied within the project. This implies that the bots not only established interactions with the users but at the same time were constantly interacting with each other in terms of the distance that they maintain between themselves and the manner in which they would propel towards each other upon spotting each other. The role of agency of the social robot in this case thus moved beyond displaying an Individualistic to a more Group oriented interaction.

Looking back at the literature review, it is noteworthy that, in the past, discussions on social robotics positioned social robots as agents that can be seen as a part of a larger heterogeneous group, while having a distinguished "individual social" agency and behavioral attributes, in contrast to the "group social" behavior that a member of a multi-agent robotic formation would have [20]. Currently, combined research in swarm intelligence and collective robotics tends to be more focused on task-specific applications, such as robot-assisted search-and-rescue response scenarios [21], or object manipulation [22]. Our study however suggests that there is potential in working with swarm robotics for the case of social interaction and thus be able to impact aspects of physical health and mental wellbeing.

A vital question for future research by the authors can be formulated as follows: Could a multi-robot scenario (in contrast to a scenario with a single robotic agent) increase the perceived social agency of the robot? This research question also stems from the observations of Alac et al., which suggest, that the social agency of the robot is not a mere product of its programming but is also largely dependent on the multimodal interactions between the humans that are engaging with the robot. In their study towards the identification of features that determine the social agency of a robot, it was found that the moment that a human addressed a robot as a being with assumed social intelligence and engaged in conversation with it, the chances of other humans interacting with it increased significantly [23].

While models of multimodal interaction have been explored within Social Robotics applications, such models commonly include one robot and multiple humans. It would be of interest to investigate how the social agency of the robot would be influenced in the case that another robot enters the multimodal interaction scenario; further experimentations with RoboZoo could implement an investigation towards this direction, in order to determine if the perceived social agency of the robotic agents in a multi-robot scenario is influenced by the fact that, apart from interacting with other humans, the robots are also seen interacting with each other.

Besides this, the quantification of observed interactions in terms of interaction time, degree of engagement and attention span etc. would certainly be among the next steps for both research projects. Longitudinal studies of social robots interacting with humans show that the novelty effect often wears off quickly and humans lose their initial interest in the robot [10]. It would thus be of interest to investigate if multimodal interaction including multiple robots interacting with each other would assist in retaining their initial interest owing to the emergent behavior that they embody. Both spatial (FLUID), Interactive and Assistive modes of engagements and the impact of scalar variations should thus be examined and enriched further. Finally, further studies in enhancing perceptual capabilities to increase the robot's awareness of social cues coupled with research in terms of morphological and behavioral attributes of the experiments would highly benefit the manner in which we envision the research to progress.

Acknowledgements. We would specially like to thank the research and design team members involved in the RoboZoo and FLUID projects: Javid Jooshesh, Veronika, Laszlo, Ricardo Galli, Chrysostomos Tsaprailis, Leslie Che, Jiarui Sun, Yağız Söylev, Tanya Somova, Nick van Dorp, Hua Fan, Y. Lyu, Danny Cheng, R. Chheda. Additionally we would like to thank the European Union Culture Grant as well as NEMO for providing us with the opportunity and for funding the two social robotics and HCI based projects.

References

1. Solanas, A., Patsakis, C., Conti, M., Vlachos, I., Ramos, V., Falcone, F., Postolache, O., Pérez-Martínez, P., Di Pietro, R., Perrea, D., Martínez-Ballesté, A.: Smart health: a context-aware health paradigm within smart cities. IEEE Commun. Mag. **52**(8), 74–81 (2014). https://doi.org/10.1109/MCOM.2014.6871673
2. WHO Homepage. http://www.who.int/gho/urban_health/situation_trends/urban_population_growth_text/en/. Accessed 6 Feb 2018
3. Fleuret, S., Atkinson, S.: Wellbeing, health and geography: a critical review and research agenda. NZ Geogr. **63**(2), 106–118 (2007). https://doi.org/10.1111/j.1745-7939.2007.00093.x
4. Dodge, R., Daly, A., Huyton, J., Sanders, L.: The challenge of defining wellbeing. Int. J. Wellbeing **2**(3), 222–235 (2012). https://doi.org/10.5502/ijw.v2i3.4

5. Cronin de Chavez, A., Backett-Milburn, K., Parry, O., Platt, S.: Understanding and researching wellbeing: its usage in different disciplines and potential for health research and health promotion. Health Educ. J. **64**(1), 70–87 (2005). https://doi.org/10.1177/001789690506400108

6. Kaplan, R.M., Bush, J.W., Berry, C.: Health status: types of validity and the index of well-being. Health Serv. Res. **11**(4), 478–507 (1976)

7. Grossi, E., Groth, N., Mosconi, P., Cerutti, R., Pace, F., Compare, A., Apolone, G.: Development and validation of the short version of the psychological general well-being index (PGWB-S). Health Qual. Life Outcomes **4**(1), 88 (2006). https://doi.org/10.4172/2167-7182.1000412

8. Winther Topp, C., Østergaard, S.D., Søndergaard, S.: The WHO-5 well-being index: a systematic review of the literature. Psychother. Psychosom. **84**(3), 167–176 (2015). https://doi.org/10.1159/000376585

9. Haque, U.: Distinguishing concepts: lexicons of interactive art and architecture. Archit. Des. **75**(1), 24–31 (2005)

10. Leite, I., Martinho, C., Paiva, A.: Social robots for long-term interaction: a survey. Int. J. Soc. Robot. **5**(2), 291–308 (2013). https://doi.org/10.1007/s12369-013-0178-y

11. Feil-Seifer, D., Mataric, M.J.: Defining socially assistive robotics. In: 9th International Conference on Rehabilitation Robotics (ICORR 2005), pp. 465–468 (2005). https://doi.org/10.1109/icorr.2005.1501143

12. García-Vergara, S., Brown, L., Park, H.W., Howard, A.M.: Engaging children in play therapy: the coupling of virtual reality games with social robotics. In: Brooks, A.L., Brahnam, S., Jain, L.C. (eds.) Technologies of Inclusive Well-Being. SCI, vol. 536, pp. 139–163. Springer, Heidelberg (2014). https://doi.org/10.1007/978-3-642-45432-5_8

13. Wada, K., Shibata, T.: Living with seal robots-its sociopsychological and physiological influences on the elderly at a care house. IEEE Trans. Rob. **23**(5), 972–980 (2007). https://doi.org/10.1109/TRO.2007.906261

14. Kidd, C.D., Taggart W., Turkle, S.: A sociable robot to encourage social interaction among the elderly. In: Proceedings of the 2006 IEEE International Conference on Robotics and Automation, pp. 3972–3976. IEEE, Orlando (2006)

15. Cooney, M.D., Nishio, S., Ishiguro, H.: Designing robots for well-being: theoretical background and visual scenes of affectionate play with a small humanoid robot. Lovotics **1**, 1–9 (2014). https://doi.org/10.4172/2090-9888.1000101

16. Fischer, P.T., Hornecker, E.: Urban HCI-interaction patterns in the built environment. In: Proceedings of the 25th BCS Conference on Human-Computer Interaction, pp. 531–534. Newcastle-upon-Tyne (2011)

17. Kuikkaniemi, K., Jacucci, G., Turpeinen, M., Hoggan, E., Müller, J.: From space to stage: how interactive screens will change urban life. Computer **44**(6), 40–47 (2011). https://doi.org/10.1109/MC.2011.135

18. Kostakos, V., O'Neill, E., Penn, A.: Designing urban pervasive systems. Computer **39**(9), 52–59 (2006)

19. Epley, N., Waytz, A., Cacioppo, J.T.: On seeing human: a three-factor theory of anthropomorphism. Psychol. Rev. **114**(4), 864–886 (2007). https://doi.org/10.1037/0033-295x.114.4.864

20. Fong, T., Nourbakhsh, I., Dautenhahn, K.: A survey of socially interactive robots. Robot. Auton. Syst. **42**(3–4), 143–166 (2003). https://doi.org/10.1016/S0921-8890(02)00372-X

21. Liu, Y., Nejat, G.: Multirobot cooperative learning for semiautonomous control in urban search and rescue applications. J. Field Robot. **33**(4), 512–536 (2016). https://doi.org/10.1002/rob.21597

22. Song, P., Kumar, V.: A potential field based approach to multi-robot manipulation. In: Proceedings of the 2002 IEEE International Conference on Robotics and Automation, pp. 1217–1222. IEEE, Washington, DC (2002). https://doi.org/10.1109/robot.2002.1014709
23. Alac, M., Movellan, J., Tanaka, F.: When a robot is social: spatial arrangements and multimodal semiotic engagement in the practice of social robotics. Soc. Stud. Sci. **41**(6), 893–926 (2011). https://doi.org/10.1177/0306312711420565

Interactive Stress-Free Toy Design
for Students Studying Overseas

Robert Chen[✉] and Tse-Ming Chuang

School of Design, De Montfort University, Leicester, UK
rchen1@dmu.ac.uk, fiyingwater518@gmail.com

Abstract. The aim of this project is to create a relaxing product to release East-Asian international students' stress in order to be in a better health. The direction of this project focuses on handling the students' negative emotions produced by stress to avoid negative consequences happening such as depression. This project begins in secondary research about stress followed by case studies of the existing products along with an interview with the target users. The case studies use the KJ method to find the design elements of existing relaxing products. Moreover, there is deeply understanding of the students' stress and the effective method of releasing the students' stress through the interview of East-Asian international students. After the research, the author transfers the information from research into design rationales and decides the design direction of this project with the design rationales. The design direction of this project is to design an interactive robot to increase the interaction between the students and their family to achieve the goal of relaxation. There is an initial focus group to gain the user's feedback from after the initial design, and a redesign with the feedback. Finally, there is a final focus group to evaluate the final design and the final design uses the user's feedback as the reference to amend and develop in the future.

Keywords: Stress-free · Interactive design

1 Introduction

1.1 Background and Motivation

With the development of economy and growing technology, human lifestyles are changing rapidly and people receive more information every day. However, these events also bring stress to people because people need to adapt to the changes rapidly and to deal with the massive information. Although certain kinds of stress would make people grow stronger, overloaded stress lowers people's work efficiency and even causes negative impacts on people's physical and mental health. Besides, these overload stresses cause negative emotions to people and then people would have the negative reactions such as depression and nervousness. However, different stresses are from different events for different people, so how to handle stress becomes a vital issue of modern life. Moreover, the negative reactions from the stress might be the root causes of some social problems, of which suicide is an example. According to World Health Organization [16]

© Springer International Publishing AG, part of Springer Nature 2018
M. Kurosu (Ed.): HCI 2018, LNCS 10902, pp. 125–144, 2018.
https://doi.org/10.1007/978-3-319-91244-8_11

report, "Major depression is linked to suicide. Most people who commit suicide are also clinically depressed." Also, this report also shows that depression is predicted to become the second-leading cause of global disability burden by 2020. Therefore, releasing stress has been an important issue to the modern society.

Nowadays, Students also have more stresses because need to learn and understand more from school and absorb more knowledge from the generation of information explosion. Especially, international students would meet more difficulties in school life because of different language, strange surroundings, and culture wall. Thus, stress for international students might be stronger than local students and the overload stress might have the negative impact on the international students' health to both physical level and mental level. The author of this project is also a case because the author, Taiwanese, has heavy stress while studying in the UK due to the language barrier and low academic performance. The author used to release the stress through eating more and consequently gains 10 KG within three months. The stress has influenced the author's physical and mental health seriously. This situation is also a reason why the author tries to find a way to release the international students' stress to be better health in physical level and mental level.

1.2   Aims and Objectives

The aim of this project is to analyse the stress that has the negative impact on the mental and physical health of international students who study in the UK and the author try to design a relaxing product for the international students to vent the negative emotions and to be in a better health. In order to achieve these aims, there are eight objectives in this project as follows:

(1) To review related and relevant literature, including understanding the system of stress, interaction design, and robotics.
(2) To do an analysis of existing products, including relaxing methods and the important elements of relaxing products
(3) To interview international students to find out their stress and what methods make them relax
(4) To integrate information from research into design rationales
(5) To develop concept with design rationales
(6) To conduct the prototype
(7) To evaluate final design (focus group)

1.3   Related Research Works

With the technology growing, there are more communication media and interaction methods invented and these technological products minimize distance between people. The international students can contact their family and friends with smartphones, communication software, social media, and Apps. However, the interactions of these solid products and software are limited in 2D world; for example, texting in Facebook, Face time in the IPhones' screen, emoticons and stickers in social Apps. Thus, this project tries to create a 3D solid product to bring a new interaction experience for people like face-to-face and make the international students have a better interaction with their family and friends. Moreover, the product vents the students' negative emotions to reach the effect of relaxing with increasing interaction between the international students, family and friends.

1.4 Limitation

The target group of this project focuses on East-Asian international students who study in the UK. The fist reason is that stress is a complex system because people have different cognition as people meet the same event. The impact factors of people's cognitions include different backgrounds, cultures, environments, and personality traits. Hence, the target users are minimized into East-Asian international students to decrease the complexity of the impact factors because of the similar background and culture. The second reason is that the author of this project is studying in the UK, so finding international students who study in the UK to be interviewed is easier than other countries and the information would be more accurate for this project. After all, the academic year is just one year, so the author needs to find an effective research manner for this project.

2 Secondary Studies

The purpose of this project is to create a relaxing product for releasing East-Asian international students' stress, so the first step is to understand what stress is and the system of stress. The literature review of stress helps the researcher understand the process of stress produced and which stage of the stress system may be a suitable opportunity to deal with. Since the final direction of this project is to create a relaxing interaction robot, the range of the literature review is extended to interaction design and robotics. Interaction design might be helpful to create a better interaction experience between the robot and the users. Besides, the robotics is an important knowledge for designing and setting this toy interactively.

2.1 Stress Definition

There were many specialists trying to define stress with different approaches and one of the famous specialists in this field of stress research was Richard Lazarus who was a psychologist. Lazarus has done stress research for nearly 50 years and indicated that the meaning of stress is a whole factors relating with interaction between the stressor and reaction, including stimulus, cognitive appraisal of threat, and response. The stressor meant a stimulus with a potential for activating the stress response and had a threat of personal security [6, 7]. Moreover, Lazarus declared that the psychological operation system was not stimulus-response models (S-R) and was stimulus-organism-response models (S-O-R) since people have individual motivations and cognitions [4]. Thus, different people with the same stressor might produce different results and even there is no stress reaction. However, Greenberg [6, 7] supposed that the range of Richard

Lazarus's definition in stress is too broad for the management of stress, and Greenberg [6, 7] assumed that the term "stress" contains a stressor and stress reaction. Furthermore, if the two factors do not exist together, there is no stress as the stressor just has a potential for activating the stress reaction. For instance, if two people are redundant from their jobs, and the event that the first person is a stressor, then he starts to worry how to be employed again to support his family after the event. So, people experience stress because of the stress reactivity. On contrast with the first people's reaction, the second one wants to change the job before being redundant and s/he gets a vacation to rest, thus, s/he does not feel stressful on this event because there is no stress reaction.

The above two definition of stress explained that stress produced need to reach two conditions, including stressor and stress reactivity. Moreover, there are a lot of factors influencing the generation of stress between stressor and stress reactivity, because these factors have influence on people's cognition. These factors include personal experience, individual motivation, and so on.

2.2 Interaction Design and User Experience

Interaction design is like a bridge connecting people and products. The purpose of inter-action design is to create a better interaction between people and products. By interaction design, Rogers et al. [14] expressed "designing interactive products to support the way people communicate and interact in their everyday and working lives." Saffer [15] viewed that interaction design as "the art of facilitating interactions between humans through products and services". Therefore, the result of interaction design might be not only an interactive product but also a service. Moreover, designing an interaction between human and products needs other fields to support, so the range of interaction design is wide.

Rogers et al. [14] pointed out that "Designers need to know many different things about the users, technologies, and interactions among them in order to create effective user experiences." The central of interactive design is user experience (UX) because a good interaction design depends on the feeling of use. User experience means how a product works and is used by people in the real world. Another definition of user experience from Nielsen and Norman [12] is "all aspects of end-user's interaction with the company, its services, and its products." When someone uses every product, there is a user experience produced [5]. Therefore, user experience happened in people's life every day and contained all interactions among users, products, and services.

2.3 Interaction Design Process

Rogers et al. [14] indicated that there were four basic activities in the process of inter-action design and that were shown in follow:

(1) Establishing requirements
(2) Designing alternatives
(3) Prototyping
(4) Evaluating

The four activities is a repeating cycle and inform one another. The evaluating step is a heart of interaction design because designers can know what has been built and ensure the interactive product is appropriate. There are many different approaches to achieve the evaluation, including interviews, and observing users and focus group. These approaches make products more user-centred and close people's requirements.

In the process of developing an interactive product, the objectives can be divided into two types in terms of usability and user experience goals to be clearer, though the two types affect each other. Since the usability has influence on the quality of user experience and, in contrast, user experience is associated with how usable the product is [14]. The usability goals more focus on products and more objectives such as efficiency to use. On the other hand, user experience goals are subjective qualities and concerned how users experience the interactive product from user's viewpoint; for instance, satisfying and enjoyable. Thus, a good interactive product not only achieves the usability goals but also the user experience goals.

2.4   Emotional Interaction

People have personal emotions, as there is an interaction with products. Emotional interaction is about what makes people produce emotions such as happiness, angry, nervousness, and so on, and using the knowledge to inform the design of user experience [14]. However, there are a lot of reasons that might affect people's mood and feelings, which might be the weather or winning a game. Designers, therefore, need to research how the users express the emotion and how the users read other people's expressions to understand how user's emotions and behaviours affect each other. [13] suggests that the positive emotion of mind can make people more creative and less focus. In contrast, the negative emotion of mind makes people to be less tolerant.

2.5   Robotics and Balance System of Robots

Balance plays an essential role in movement and performance of a robot. Generally, the balance system of robot consists of sensors and actuators to lead a complex system [8]. Today, the three common sensors are gyroscopes, accelerometers, and tilt switches. Although tilt sensor is the cheapest, the sensor does not have higher accuracy and a lower frequency response.

Accelerometer Sensor. In 2013, Goodrich [9] explained that "an accelerometer is an electromechanical device used to measure acceleration forces. Such forces may be static, like the continuous force of gravity or, as is the case with many mobile devices, dynamic to sense movement or vibrations". Today, accelerometer is popularly used in compass Apps and other mobile devices to identify orientation. In addition, the accelerometer measures the amount of static acceleration due to gravity, and then the users can find out the angle the device is tilted at with respect to the earth. Thus, through the accelerometer sensing the amount of acceleration, the users can understand and analyse how the device is moving. Therefore, this type sensor can measure a robot's movement and assist the robot to keep in a balance. However, the accelerometer can measure the orientation of a stationary object with relation to Earth's surface but senses the rotation. As accelerating in a specific direction, an accelerometer is unable to classify between the acceleration and the acceleration from Earth's gravitational pull.

Gyroscope. A gyroscope is a device that is used to determine orientation by Earth's gravity. The structure of a gyroscope consists of a freely-rotating disk on a spinning axis in the centre of a larger and more stable wheel. As the axis turns, the freely-rotating disk stays stationary to show the central gravitational pull [9]. Hence, the gyroscope is able to measure the rate of rotation around a particular axis and the technology also use in balancing robots.

2.6   Connection Function

Teleoperation. Teleoperation is a kind of remote interaction system between human and robots and indicates the operation of a machine at a distance [1]. Moreover, the technique is commonly associated with robotics and mobile robots. The structure of teleoperation is shown in Fig. 1 and people can use electronic devices to control a robot from a distance through the Internet and get the feedback from the robot.

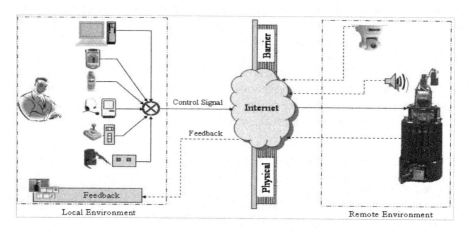

Fig. 1.   Remote interaction system (Salichs 2014)

Bluetooth. Bluetooth technology is the global wireless standard enabling the Internet of Things and created in 1994. This technology was seen as a wireless alternative to data cables by exchanging data using radio transmissions [2]. In the past, Bluetooth had a limitation that the rate of data transfer is about 3 megabits per second this is lower than Wi-Fi. But, now the rate of data transfer has reached 24 megabits per second combining with Wi-Fi [11]. Although the rate of data transfer is still lower than Wi-Fi, it is enough to play music and receive single for robots. However, there is still a limitation of Bluetooth technology in terms of distance limitations because the best effective distance between Bluetooth devices is less than 10 m.

2.7   Design Rationales for Releasing Stress

Design Rationales

S1: experience emotion before the physical arousal and the negative consequence might an effective approach.

S2: good interactive product focuses on not only usability but also user experience.

S3: emotion and behaviour affect each other.

S4: anthropomorphism might be an effective method to increase interaction between people and interactive products.

S5: combination of Gyroscope and Accelerometer sensors has a more accurate measurement and a better balance in robots.

S6: use teleoperation technology to solve the problem that controlling robots in a long distance.

3   Case Studies

3.1   Introduction

The purpose of this case study is to analyse the existing products' features to find out design elements and to rank these elements to discover the important elements, moreover, these relaxing methods and design elements are used into the questions for interview survey. In order to achieve the aims, there are a series of objectives as follows: (1) To make a research plan, (2) To collect twenty kinds of existing relaxing products from shops and websites, (3) To find the features and relaxing methods of these products with KJ method, (4) To integrate the features of these products into simple elements, (5) To compare these elements with Intra-action analysis (Matrix-A), (6) To conclude important elements for design rationales and transfer these information into the options of the interview questions.

3.2   Methods Used in This Case Studies

KJ (Kawakita Jiro) Method.   KJ method was a research method, which was used in organizing massive information into a few groups in a certain field to find key points and the trends quickly, and Kawakita Jiro, Japanese anthropologist, introduced his KJ method in 1960s [10]. There are 5 main steps in KJ methods, i.e. (1) decide the topic, (2) collect information or products, (3) write down every piece of information that you need to organize onto a separate sticky note, (4) sort all sticky notes into groups as the notes are similar, and (5) find main trends and relationships between these groups.

Intra-action Analysis (Matrix-A) Analysis.   The Matrix-A is to compare each element with itself and every other inside element to find the importance of each pair of those relationships, moreover, the purpose of the matrix-A chart method for design research is designed to permit a systematic search for connections between the elements (of an aimed product) involved within a design research problem [3]. Therefore, there is an

Intra-action analysis in this project to find the importance of design elements of the existing relaxing products.

Existing Products Analysis. There are twenties relaxing products chosen to explore the features, both physical level and mental level, and these features were transferred into design rationales through KJ method and Matrix-A analysis. The researcher followed the KJ method to find the relaxing manners and common design points of current products. First of all, the researcher wrote down the relaxing method and the features of these existing products on the sticky notes, one product for one sticky note as showed in Fig. 2. This method is helpful to find out the each relaxing method because some products include more than one type of relaxing methods; for instance, the stuffed animals with two relaxing elements: accompanying and soft touch. Furthermore, the research can discover the common design elements from these sticky notes.

Fig. 2. Sticky notes

After analysing these sticky notes, the researcher made a list of the various relaxing approaches (see Table 1) that were found on these sticky notes and grouped these relaxing method in two groups i.e. physical level and mental level.

Then, the researcher grouped these relaxing methods into mental level and physical level showing in Fig. 3. There was a finding that most of these relaxing methods had the relaxing effect of the mental level so people might require relaxation mentally and physically.

Besides, there are some common elements from these relaxing products as the follows: (1) Easy to use, (2) Easy to carry, (3) Attractive appearance (e.g. Adorable, Delicate, and beautiful). After the analysis of existing relaxing products in KJ method, the researcher separated 10 design elements from these relaxing products, and compared the 10 design elements to rank a priority of these products using the Intra-action analysis (Matrix-A) shown in Fig. 4.

Table 1. List of relaxing methods.

Massage (e.g. Shaking, Rolling, and scratching)	Massage is a kind of physical methods in releasing stress and makes people feel comfortable quickly. Moreover, more and more additional functions are combined into the massage function such as playing music
Soft touch (e.g. Stuffed dolls)	Soft touch is also a kind of physical ways making people relax through the sense of touch. The most common relaxing products with soft touch are stuffed dolls. When people are hugging the stuffed doll, people feel comfortable even expressing sentiments
Interaction (e.g. actions feedback, voice feedback, and move function)	The interaction means the behaviour between the users and the products. For instance, people press the button of the TED 2 and then the TED 2 has a response to people, and the process is an interaction. There are a lot of types of interactions in relaxing products and this element is often combined with other relaxing methods such as changing people's attention
Music	Music is a common relaxing method today because people have a change of the mood in listening to music. According to a journal of Psychology of Music shows that one of many functions for music, as it is an emotional expression, so music is an approach to for people to vent their negative emotions
Smell (e.g. Essential oil)	This way is to make people relax physically through the sense of smell such as perfume
Accompanying	People usually have the sense of insecurity facing strange surroundings and changes in the life, and the negative sense affects people physically and psychologically, including the negative thinking and nervousness. However, accompanying is a kind of mental senses that makes people feel safe and have a stable emotion, so accompanying is helpful to solve problems of insecurity
Visual communication	Vision is also a way to change people's emotion and then makes people relax. The factors that affect people's emotions directly through vision including colour, shape, moving, and still
A simple behaviour (e.g. Shouting and rubbing)	Some simple behaviour has impacts on human's emotional and sometimes the impact occurred in cognitive system or from people's instinct. For example, some people feel relaxed in shouting because the behaviour makes people relax the body with a good mood
To satisfy personal desire (e.g. famous products and collecting)	Most people have personal desires and satisfying personal desire usually makes people have a delightful feeling. However, a control of personal desire is necessary because wants are unlimited

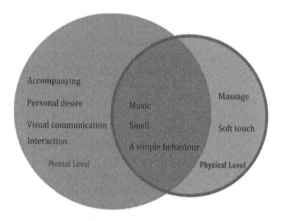

Fig. 3. A relationship of the relaxing methods

Elements	The effect of relaxing	Colour	Grip	Texture	Interaction	Easy to use	Exterior	Funny	Easy to carry	Massage			Total
The effect of relaxing	█	1		2	2	2	1	2	1	2	10	3	13
Colour	1	█		1	1		2				2	3	5
Grip			█	2	1	2	1	2	1		6	3	9
Texture	2	1	2	█	2				2	2	10	1	11
Interaction	2			2	█	2	1	2	1	1	8	3	11
Easy to use	2		2	2		█	1	1		2	8	2	10
Exterior	1	2	1		1	1	█	2	1	1	4	6	10
Funny	2			2	2		2	█			8	0	8
Easy to carry	1			2	1	1	1		█	2	4	4	8
Massage	2		1	2	1	2	1		2	█	8	3	11

█ 2	Direct connection
░ 1	Indirect connection

Fig. 4. Intra-action analysis of relaxing products

The 10 design elements included the effect of relaxing, colour, grip, texture, interaction, easy to use, exterior, funny, easy to carry, and massage. Then, these elements were compared with other elements to gain a score in the relationship of the connection. If the two elements having a direct connection, the score was 2, showing in the blank. If the two elements have an indirect connection, the score is 1, showing in the blank. However, if there is no connection between the two elements, the blank is empty. The final step sums up all scores and there is a total score for each element. After that, the researcher gained a rank of the connectional relationship from the total score for each element. The highest priority is the effect of relaxing, so this element is still the most important element for designing a relaxing product. Besides, the elements, including interaction, texture, massage, easy to use, and exterior also gain the high priority.

3.3 Summary and Design Rationales

The authors found out the relaxing approaches and some common points in these relaxing products. Another finding is that most effects of these relaxing approaches are to release stress in mental level. Hence, people might feel stressed in mental level more than physical level or release the stress in mental level might avoid the stress from occurring in physical level. Besides, the researcher evaluated design elements of the relaxing products in the connectional relationship and had a priority of the importance for these design elements. Finally, the researcher integrated these findings from the case studies into design rationales as follows, C1: Interaction, C2: Easy to use, C3: Music, C4: A simple behaviour, C5: Massage, C6: Funny, C7: Attractive appearance, C8: Easy to carry, C9: Accompanying, C10: Soft touch, C11: To change attention.

4 Interview Studies

This chapter was to obtain the in-deep information from East-Asian international students through an interview, and the information included the causes of the students' stress, how the students deal with these stresses, and which relaxing method the students feel a good effect in releasing the stress. Besides, the design rationales that are from case studies are also used in the questions of the interviews, and there is a rank of the effect of releasing the stress depending on the interviewees' choices. Therefore, the researcher can get accurate and realistic problems the students meet today and a direction of the possible solution with analysing the information that contained the interviewees' thinking, opinions, and feeling. The purpose of this interview is to understand the potential root causes of the students' stresses from the interviewees' responses and gain the possible solutions based on the analysis of the interviewees' feedback.

4.1 Subjects' Selection

There were 8 interviewees in this interview and all of these students were East-Asian international students who are studying in the UK. Moreover, these students' native language is not English. The 8 interviewees contained 5 female students and 3 male students, which all interviewees' experience of studying abroad under two years except the fourth interviewee, and the ages of all interviewees are during 20–30 years old.

4.2 The Questions

The researcher created the questions from the target users' thinking since the researcher is also in the target group of this project and has studied in the UK over one year. Thus, the author of this project created the possible issues the target users might meet when the questions through personal experience and used a calculation to find the main causes that made the students feel stress and there was a negative impact on the student's health.

Before the author started to ask questions to the interviewees, the interviewee needed to sign a consent form. The purpose of the consent form is to confirm that the interviewee understood the purpose of this interview and the researcher's basic information. The most important of this consent form is that the interviewer needs to get the agreement from the interviewee if the researcher would like to use the interviewee's feedback in this project. Besides, the interview is conducted face-to-face with an audio record, so that it also needs the interviewee's consent. The questions of this interview sheet was designed in step by step, the first part of the questions is personal information, after that the interviewee was asked the questions about what aspects the interviewee cannot adapt to during studying abroad. The reasons of this question are that the stress occurred was made in life situations, including changes, troubles, and threats in people's life [6, 7]. When people met a change in life, people began to adapt the new situation. However, people felt stressed during the process of adapting the new situation and even more stress, as people cannot adapt the change. Thus the first step was to understand the issues of the students' adaption and the issues might be the root cause of the students' stress. Then, the second step is to ask the interviewee whether the situation the student cannot adapt to cause the negative reactions of the student's health in mental level and physical level. Afterward, the interviewee was asked how improve and deal with the situation that make the interview feel stress. The next question listed relaxing methods for the interviewee to evaluate the effect of relaxing each method and these relaxing methods were collected from the case studies. Finally, the researcher can get possible problems the students met with these questions and have a direction of the initial idea through this interview.

4.3   Summary and Design Rationales

According to the interviewees' feedback of this interview, the root causes of the students' stress were focused on a worry for academic performance, family expectation, self-expectation and communication problems due to the language barrier and culture difference. These issues had the negative impacts on the students' mental reactions, including the negative emotions and thinking. Then these mental reactions caused the students to have the negative physical reactions such as depression, a difficulty in concentrating, and insomnia. For instance, the student met the life situation: studying abroad, and then the adaption issues happened. If the student perceives the adaption issues as stress, there were the negative emotions happening. Moreover, the physical reactions happened resulting from the negative emotion is not released, and even the worst consequence is the disease such as the depression. However, the two key points needed to be considered. The first point was the cognition stage of stress because the different cognitions are produced different people met the same life situation. For example, the two interviewees did not perceive that academic performance caused the stress due to the fact that the two interviewees' English was better than other interviewees. The second point was that the stress has not only negative influences but also positive influences and people just need to handle the excessive stress. The non-excessive stress made the growth of people. For instance, the stress of language issue also made the students have an effort of learning English to reach a better English level. It is not necessary to remove these stressors because the stressors stimulate the East-Asian international students to be more mature.

Therefore, to handle the stress of East Asian international students in the stage of emotional arousal, which is between the stage of physical arousal and perceiving as stress, might be a possible solution. The root causes of the stress are complex as different cognitions so that the stress produced is not easy to control. Moreover, to deal with the negative emotions before the excessive negative emotions become physiological arousal is simpler than the control of the stress produced. To sum up the evaluation of relaxing methods from the eight interviewees and gain a final rank are shown in Table 1. All relaxing methods from the case studies got score, so the situation expressed that these methods all had value to be design rationales. An interaction with people was scored the highest rank and these students all felt that chatting and an interaction with friends and family were helpful to relax and vent the emotion. Therefore, increasing interaction between the East Asian international students to vent the students' negative emotions became the design direction of this project. Most of these summaries were transferred into the design rationales (i.e. I1: for handling the students' stress in the emotion stage of the stress model; and I2: for increasing interaction with friends and family.

5   Design Development

The initial design was to develop the idea from the author's conceptual development and design rationales that are from secondary research and primary research. After that, there was a testing step, including a 3D modelling of the initial design and an initial focus group using this 3D model. Then, the designer redesigned the initial design according to the user's feedback of the initial focus group, and did detail design to complete the final design. Finally, there was a final focus group to evaluate the final design.

Today, there were many contact ways between people such as texting, calling, and video. Moreover, the contact media was also multifarious, including smart phones, webcams, and projectors; however, these contact approaches were limited in a 2D world or just an image. The author, therefore, tried to combine contact ways and medias with robots as shown Fig. 5 and created an interactive robot with contact function to increase the students' interaction with friends and family.

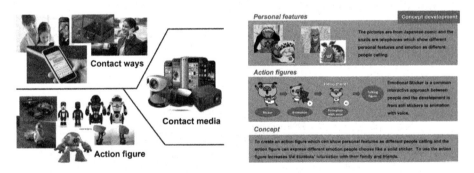

Fig. 5. Mood board   **Fig. 6.** Concepts/ideas

Figure 6 showed the concept development of this project, including the two design elements. The first one was a personal feature and this idea was from a Japanese comic. The snails were telephones that showed different personal features as different people called and expressed the emotion with the calling people's moods. The second factor was to create an action figure that can express the emotion like a 3D emotional sticker. This idea was from the emotional sticker because the process of the sticker development was from still stickers to animation stickers with voice. Hence, the author thought that a vivid solid sticker might attract people to have interactions with it. Finally, the concept is to create an action figure that can show personal features as different people are calling and the action figure can express different emotions people choose like a solid sticker, and further to use the action figure to increase students' interactions with family and friends.

Figure 7 showed the concept sketch and the prototype of this robot that is from one of the author's colleagues, Miss Sue, so the author named this robot with Robot (Sue v1.0).

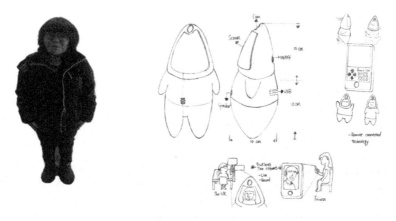

Fig. 7.   Concept sketch

5.1   Initial 3D Printed CAD Model for Testing

The Figs. 8 and 9 showed the first step was to create a 3D model of Robot Sue v1.0 using Rhino and the semi-finished model.

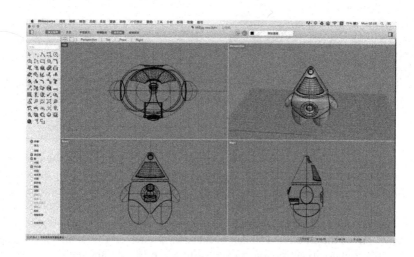

Fig. 8.   3D modelling (Robot Sue v1.0 in Rhino)

Fig. 9. Semi-finished 3D modelling

5.2 Focus Group Testing

In order to understand the users' feelings, the researcher did the initial focus group with the target users and these students were same as the interviewees. The following information is the feedback from the focus group:

Advantage. (a) The appearance makes the users feel friendly and funny, (b) It is effective way to increase interactions with family and friends, (c) The feeling of using this robot is stronger than 2D stickers, (d) The half size is easy to carry.

Improvements. (a) The size of the screen is too small, (b) To add move function makes family and friends see the students' surroundings more, (c) Additional functions: clock…etc.

The designer confirmed that the initial design achieved the main design rationales that to increase the student's interaction with family and friends through this focus group. However, there were some issues to improve, including the size of the screen is too small, a requirement of moving function, and more additional functions.

6 Final Design

6.1 Balance System

Robot Sue v2.0 uses a combination of gyroscope and accelerometer to keep the body in balance.

6.2 Connect Function

Robot Sue v2.0 uses the two connection functions, including teleoperation technology and Bluetooth. If the distance between users and the robot is over 10 m, the user needs to connect the robot via the network. For instance, the parents want to connect the student's robot and the parents need to connect via the network. In contrast, if the distance less than 10 m, the user can use Bluetooth.

6.3   Charging

Figure 10 showed that Robot Sue v2.0 uses wireless charging technology and choose Wireless Power Consortium (Qi) standard because this standard is the most common today. Moreover, if the user's smartphone supports this standard, the smartphone also can be charged using this wireless charger.

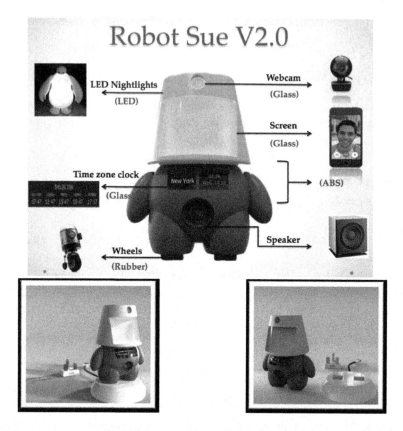

Fig. 10.   Introduction to Robot Sue v2.0

6.4   Emotion Performance

Robot Sue expresses emotions through expressions, actions, and voice. The designer adds colour factor into expressions to enhance feelings of emotions and the idea is from a popular movie "Inside out". Figure 11 showed the different expressions with different emotion colours; for instance, angry expression comes with red colour.

Fig. 11. Emotional colour and performance (Color figure online)

6.5   User Interface in App

Figure 12 showed the user interface in App of Robot Sue. The functions of the App include Bluetooth, Network, play music, nightlights, time zone clock, remote mode, camera, video, and emoticon. As the user enters the App, the user needs to choose Bluetooth or Network to connect the robot. After connecting the robot, the user can click remote mode, and then the screen will show the control surface. The user can move the robot through the virtual joystick and take photos, record videos, and send emoticons. When the user clicks the emoticons, the robot will have emotion performance, where the most important step is to choose connect approaches depend on the distance between the smartphone and the robot.

Fig. 12. User interface (App)

7   Discussions

With technology development, people received much more information unconsciously everyday than past and this situation also caused overload on people's body. Moreover, there were more new things people needed to adapt to rapidly and challenge and these changes caused people to feel stressed both mentally and physically. This situation was also the possible reason why more mental diseases and society problems have been occurring. International students also met the difficulties, including adaption of new surroundings and different language. The author of this project was also a Taiwanese international student and has been studying in the U.K., so the author can understand the stress on studying abroad. The stress caused the author gained 10 kg within three months, so the author decided to choose this topic and understand deeply the causes of the stress.

Through the secondary research, the author found that stress system is complex because of personal cognition. There were a lot of factors influencing people's cognition, including culture background, family background, and personality traits. Different people had different responses while meeting the same life situation, so this increasing situation made it more difficult to find the root causes of the student's stress. Therefore, the author minimized the range of target group into East-Asian international students to decrease the complexity and did an interview to understand the stress of the student and tried to find the possible solution. However, the result of the interview showed that there were different causes of the student's stress and different stress reactions even if the students met the same situation. Although the most of the root causes were collected in academic performance, culture shock, family expectation, and self-expectation, the stressful level was different in the students.

Besides, the author found that these root causes of the students' stress also made the students grow up, so the direction might be amended to just handle the excessive stress and not remove all stress. Thus, the author thought that if it is impossible to control the students' cognition; however, to vent the emotion after the stress happened and before the negative physical arousal and the ensued consequences might be a possible direction.

After that, the researcher found a method in which all the interviewees had a relaxation, and this method is interacting with friends and family. Moreover, the researcher understood that behaviours and emotions affected each other from the research of interaction design, so positive behaviours can give people positive mood such as happiness. Moreover, Anthropomorphism is an effective way to attract people to have an interaction with the product. Thus, the researcher decided to design an interactive robot and this robot can increase interaction between the students and family to vent the emotions further in order to achieve the aim of relaxation. However, the researcher met some difficulties in designing the interactive robot. Firstly, the author is strange to robotics and the limitation of the academic period, so the author just can design a conceptual model and combine it with the generally existed technology. Secondary, there is no design background for the author, so the author dealt with a lot of design in the first time, including user interface design of Robot Sue's App and the use of materials.

Although the interactive robot is in a concept stage, the result of the final evaluation showed that Robot Sue is effective to increase the students' interaction with family and friends, and has the effect of venting the students' emotion. Thus, continuing to develop this project with this concept, Robot Sue might be manufactured in real products and a solution for releasing the East- Asian international students' stress.

8   Conclusions and Recommendations

8.1   Conclusions

With the development of civilization and information delivering rapidly, people's life became more convenience and to replace old things also became fast. However, this situation also caused the people to have heavy stress and increased mental illness. Thus, to release the stress has become an important issue today. International students also had heavy stress resulting from adaption problems of oversea life. The author of this project was also an international student who studied in the UK, so the author had the stress experience. Moreover, the stress made the author to gain 10 kg in three months and had the negative impact on the author's health. Thus, the author decided to research this topic and tried to find the solution to improve this situation.

8.2   Recommendations

Due to the limited academic period, the final design is just a concept model and shows a general structure with functions. In the future, the robot can be developed more to be customized using 3D printing technology and divided into assembly parts. Besides, the author just set five basic emotion performances in the final design, so it is not enough. It is possible to attract the users as the more emotion performances developed, including more types of actions, expressions, and a wider range of voice. For environmental friendly, a service design of replaceable assembly parts and a recycle of ABS plastic can reduce the waste.

References

1. Aboudaya, E.: Mobile teleoperation of a mobile robot (2010). http://www.doria.fi/bitstream/handle/10024/64282/. Accessed 18 July 2016
2. Bluetooth SIG: What is Bluetooth technology? (2016). https://www.bluetooth.com/what-is-bluetooth-technology/bluetooth. Accessed 17 July 2016
3. Chen, R.: Intra-action Analysis, from Designer's Systematic Tools and Techniques. De Montfort University, Heritage House, Leicester (2016)
4. Cooper, C.L., Dewe, P.: Stress: A Brief History. Blackwell, Oxford (2004)
5. Garrett, J.J.: The Elements of User Experience: User-Centered Design for the Web and Beyond, 2nd edn. New Riders Press, Berkeley (2010)
6. Greenberg, J.S.: Comprehensive Stress Management. McGraw-Hill, New York (2008)
7. Hargreaves, D.J., North, A.C.: The functions of music in everyday life: redefining the social in music psychology. Psychol. Music 27(1), 71–83 (1999)
8. George, D.: How a robot can keep its balance and stand up even if gets kicked-case study (2014). http://www.smashingrobotics.com/how-a-robot-can-keep-its-balance-and-stand-upeven-if-it-get-kicked-case-study/. Accessed 16 July 2016
9. Goodrich, R.: Accelerometers: what they are & how they work, live science (2013). http://www.livescience.com/40102-accelerometers.html. Accessed 17 July 2016

10. Martin, B., Hanington, B.M.: Affinity Diagramming, Universal Methods of Design: 100 Ways to Research Complex Problems, Develop Innovative Ideas, and Design Effective Solutions. Rockport Publishers, Beverly (2012)
11. McClain, S.: What are the limitations of bluetooth? eHow (2016). http://www.ehow.com/list_6495445_limitations-bluetooth_.html. Accessed 15 July 2016
12. Nielsen, J., Norman, D.: The definition of user experience (2014). www.nngroup.com/articles/definition-user-experience/. Accessed 15 July 2016
13. Norman, D.: Emotional Design: Why We Love (or Hate) Everyday Things. Basic Books, New York (2005)
14. Rogers, Y., Preece, J., Sharp, H.: What is Interaction Design? Interaction Design: Beyond Human-Computer Interaction, pp. 8–9. Wiley, Chichester (2015)
15. Saffer, D.: Designing for Interaction: Creating Smart Applications and Clever Devices, 2nd edn, p. p4. New Riders Press, Indianapolis (2010)
16. World Health Organization: MENTAL HEALTH: A Call for Action by World Health Ministers, Geneva, pp. 6–7 (2001). http://www.who.int/mental_health/media/en/249.pdf. Accessed 1 Dec 2015

Assessing Patient Needs for the Enhancement of Stroke Rehabilitation Services: A Customer Value Perspective

Yu-Hsiu Hung[1(✉)], Yu-Ching Lin[2], Wan-Zi Lin[1], and Pin-Ju Chen[1]

[1] Department of Industrial Design, National Cheng Kung University, Tainan, Taiwan
{idhfhung,P36051066,P36054080}@mail.ncku.edu.tw
[2] Department of Physical Medicine and Rehabilitation, National Cheng Kung University, Tainan, Taiwan
richelin@mail.ncku.edu.tw

Abstract. Continuous participation in stroke rehabilitation programs enables function recovery and quality of life. However, research showed that stroke rehabilitation services do not necessarily meet the needs and the expectations of stroke patients. To address this issue, in this study, patient needs was assessed from the perspective of customer value. Customer value was defined using the service dimensions in SERVQUAL. Contextual Inquiry (CI) was conducted with three stroke patients and their therapists. Critical incidents (i.e., service gaps) were identified and categorized by the service dimensions. A follow-up survey was conducted with 11 stroke patients and 11 therapists to obtain subjective ratings on the critical incidents to provide quantitative insight that corroborated the findings from the CI in improving current stroke rehabilitation services. Results of the CI revealed that most occurred critical incident was related with reliability when therapists provided instructions on the rehabilitation activities. Results of the survey showed that (1) for stroke patients, all service dimensions were equally important; responsiveness was the least satisfied dimension; (2) Therapists believed that all service dimensions were addressed by their services; assurance was the most important dimension. The perceptual differences of the two groups on customer value led to recommendations on the current rehabilitation services. The outcomes of the study provided insight on critical stroke patient needs and contributed to the design of stroke rehabilitation therapy services.

Keywords: Stroke rehabilitation · Customer value · Service quality

1 Introduction

Nowadays the advancements in medical technologies have reduced the stroke death rate. However, the number of stroke patients did not drop accordingly [1]. It was found that the age of first-ever stroke decreased gradually [2]. The stroke recovery rate depends on the severity of stroke and individual patient's unique situation. Most patients recovering from a mild stroke can recover most function within 3–6 months of rehabilitation. The recovery rate starts to decline after 6 months [3]. Stroke recovery is not limited by time. Research

© Springer International Publishing AG, part of Springer Nature 2018
M. Kurosu (Ed.): HCI 2018, LNCS 10902, pp. 145–157, 2018.
https://doi.org/10.1007/978-3-319-91244-8_12

shows that continuous participation in rehabilitation programs enables function recovery and quality of life [4], even for severe stroke patients [5, 6]. Thus, for stroke patients, to improve health and adjust to life at home, actively joining rehabilitation programs becomes necessary. This suggests that effectively engaging patients in their recovery process through adequate rehabilitation services is critical.

Studies showed that stroke rehabilitation services do not actually meet the needs and the expectations of stroke patients. For example, Klein [7] and Newborn [8] indicated that most rehabilitation services did not incorporate patients' life interests and goals in their rehabilitation activities. Brandriet et al. [9] revealed that the efficacy of rehabilitation services was not assessed with regards to preparing patients returning to their lives. Moreover, Shapero [4] noted that stroke rehabilitation services were not holistically designed to meet patients' needs after inpatient rehabilitation, particularly how follow-up rehabilitation should be provided to make great strides in recovery.

For identifying patients' needs and preferences on the stroke rehabilitation, Laver [10] found that patients cared about functional recovery, preferred one-on-one rehabilitation services, and showed less preference on intensive rehabilitation as well as computer-assisted therapies. In addition, Jones et al. [11] identified four patient needs for developing stroke rehabilitation services: (1) offering the information on stroke prevention, (2) providing unobstructed counseling channels, (3) long-term supports, and (4) integrating therapies into patients' daily life activities.

In fact, patients' opinions become increasingly important in assessing rehabilitation service and are considered to be the indicators of the quality of rehabilitation services [11]. According to Crawford et al. [12], patients' participation in the planning and development of healthcare service is important. In a similar vein, Ashworth et al. [13] and Guadagnoli and Ward [14] showed that integrating with the views and needs of both professional therapists and patients could not only shorten the gap between the services and patient actual needs but also help to improve the quality of rehabilitation services.

In practice, there is few attempt developing/improving stroke rehabilitation services on the basis of customer value [15] – i.e., patients' needs and expectations in exchange for what they pay in the service. In most cases, patients' needs, wants, and expectations were not seriously considered or understood, eventually leading to low service quality and patients' complaints [16]. Despite that researchers proposed innovative rehabilitation services, however, most of which lacked inputs from both field experts (i.e., professional therapists) and stroke patients, thus making the service outcomes deviate from actual patients' expectations [17].

The above studies suggested that (1) most stroke rehabilitation services were not adequately designed to reflect patient needs and customer value in the field [18]; (2) in addition to adopting opinions of professional therapists, taking into account the customer value is imperative for improving/developing stroke rehabilitation services. In reflecting these findings, the purpose of this study, therefore, was to assess patient needs (from the perspective of customer value) for the enhancement of stroke rehabilitation services. First, CI (observations with follow-up interviews) was conducted with both stroke patients and their therapists to ethnographically uncover patients' latent needs and their gaps - defined as critical incidents - with the customer values (i.e., the dimensions of service quality identified in SERVQUAL). Second, survey was conducted to reveal which critical incidents deviated the most from the customer values and which should be first improved. The survey data were used to provide quantitative insight that supported the findings in CI in improving current stroke rehabilitation services.

2 Literature Review

2.1 The Need to Understand Work Practices to Develop Medical Innovations

Conventional interview and needs assessment techniques are limited to demographic data and end-user opinions. However, detailed information about actual work processes and practices can provide critical information for developing relevant and useable systems [19]. The most-used technique for understanding work practice information is Contextual Inquiry (CI) [20]. It is an ethnographic based method that integrates observation and semi-structured interview to investigate field challenges that influence users' interactions with technologies/services/systems. CI provides tacit, explicit, and implicit qualitative details of work practices. It is a user-centered design method that helps designers in the design process to do in-depth understanding and exploration of user needs.

In the medical domain, CI has been massively used to identify innovative spaces and systems. For example, Cawood et al. [21] attempted to create an optimal cross-department office space for hospital staff. In their study, Cawood et al. [21] conducted contextual inquiries with 21 staff (such as examining the work behaviors and their related attitudes, needs, and processes, etc.). Cawood et al. [21] also conducted static observations over 12 locations (such as watching movement and interactions that occurred around and through and in every place, etc.). In addition, co-design workshops were conducted to explore the functional and emotional needs of the staff, as well as innovative office space solutions. This study used a human centered design process (involving 'hear', 'create', deliver' phases) that can not only produce an effective design, but also improve employee engagement and the level of satisfaction with the final workspace.

Gurses et al. [22] attempted to identify hazards in the cardiovascular operating room (CVOR) to guide improvement efforts to improve patient safety. Gurses et al. [22] conducted direct observations (including 20 on-pump cardiac surgeries) and contextual inquiries with 84 healthcare providers to identify and classify safety hazards in the CVORs in five hospitals. Results of the study revealed 55 types of hazards related to the five components of the CVOR work system. They are related with provider, task, tools and technologies, physical environment, as well as organization. Results of the study identified common hazards across operating rooms: non-compliance with evidence based guidelines, usability problems of tools and technologies, practice variations among care providers within the same institution, poor teamwork, and hierarchical nature of the organizational culture. Gurses et al. [22] suggested that, to improve patient safety in the CVOR, efforts should focus on: (1) creating a culture of safety, (2) increasing compliance with evidence based infection control practices, (3) improving communication and teamwork, and (4) designing better tools and technologies through partnership among all stakeholders.

The above studies demonstrated the potentials of CI in identifying contextual challenges and eliciting explicit and latent needs of patients in the medical environment.

2.2 Customer Value in Stroke Rehabilitation Services

Delivering value to customers is important to healthcare and service providers. According to Woodruff [15], customer value can be generally defined as: "a customer perceived preference for and evaluation of those products attributes, attribute performances, and consequences arising from use that facilitate (or block) achieving the customer's goals and purposes in use situations." Simply put, value is what a customer gets in exchange for the price he/she pays. In the context of stroke rehabilitation, to be willing to pay, patients would derive value from the service they get. Patients' needs are the values that patients want and desire from paying their medical/insurance bills.

In the literature, studies were conducted to explore the rehabilitation needs of stroke patients. For instance, Jones et al. [11] conducted semi-structured interview and focus group to unveil service priorities in stroke rehabilitation. Results showed that, from the viewpoints of stroke patients and caregivers, service priorities included: (1) offering information on stroke prevention, (2) providing unobstructed counseling channels and long-term supports, (3) integrating therapies into patients' daily life activities. In addition, to find out the problems in stroke rehabilitation and needs of stroke patient, Kamalakannan et al. [23] administered questionnaire and in-depth interview with stroke patients, caregivers, and nursing professionals. Kamalakannan et al. [23] found that establishing easily accessible treatment services, offering patient-centered rehabilitation services, and taking into account cultural backgrounds were critical to customer satisfaction. Moreover, to uncover stroke patients' preferences for rehabilitation, Laver et al. [10] performed face-to-face interview with stroke patients. Results showed that most stroke patients were concerned about functional recovery, strongly preferred one-on-one treatment, and less preferred intensive rehabilitation and computer-assisted therapies. Furthermore, with respect to the gaps between patients' expected services and their received ones in stroke rehabilitation, Parasuraman [24] administered SERVQUAL (a multidimensional questionnaire to measure patients' perceptions of service quality). Results showed that reliability, responsiveness, assurance, empathy, and understanding/knowing the customer, were five key measures to predict patients' satisfactions on stroke rehabilitation.

To sum up, patients' needs reflect the value that patients want/desire in the rehabilitation. The benefits that patients get have to outweigh what they pay. In general, patients desire to understand the details of the rehabilitation programs, to receive customized rehabilitation, to recover from functional deficits, to become functional independent in daily and social life, and to obtain unobstructed counseling channels and long-term supports. In addition, to understand the performance of a service in regards to customer satisfaction, reliability, responsiveness, assurance, empathy, and understanding/knowing the customer are important dimensions to look at in stroke rehabilitation.

3   Method

The purpose of this study was to assess patient needs (from the perspective of customer value) to enhance stroke rehabilitation services. CI (observations with follow-up interviews) was conducted in the first place with both stroke patients and their therapists to ethnographically understand patients' latent needs and the gaps between the needs and the provided rehabilitation services. The service quality dimensions suggested in SERVQUAL [24] were used to guide CI to identify the service gaps. The service gaps were treated as critical incidents and were then shown to patients and therapists via survey. Both participant groups were asked to rate on the critical incidents with regards to satisfaction and importance. The data were used to provide quantitative insight that supported service design decisions in improving current stroke rehabilitation services.

3.1   Contextual Inquiry: Identification of Needs

Participants
A convenience sample of three stroke survivors and their onsite occupational/physical therapists participated in this study. Inclusion criteria required that stroke participants be at least 6 month post-stroke, experience upper-extremity hemiparesis, and receive rehabilitation services more than one time. Exclusion criteria included inability to give informed consent, a diagnosis of any cognitive deficits. The therapists were required to have at least 6 month work experience related with stroke rehabilitation. Both participant groups were recruited in the occupational therapy rehabilitation center in a teaching hospital in the Tainan city in Taiwan.

Procedure
Two trained observers followed the participants throughout the whole rehabilitation process (from checking in to leaving the rehabilitation center). Patient participants were observed during their scheduled time slots for rehabilitation. Prior to CI, the observers ensured that participants understood the goals of the study and were comfortable with the process. This protocol helped the observer attain a certain level of trust and openness. The CI would not start until obtaining participants' consents. In addition, during the observation, the observers were taught to identify 'critical incidents' using the critical incident technique [25]. A critical incident in this study was defined as any observable rehab service elements (either tangible or intangible) or incidents that were against the customer value – including the following five dimensions of service quality in SERVQUAL [24].

- **Assurance** means knowledge of competence, courtesy of staff, and respects of customers.
- **Empathy** means treating the customers as individual and understanding their needs and wants, customer easily access to the staff of the organization and to their service and information.
- **Reliability** means providing the promised service regularly, consistently, timely and accurately to the consumers.

- **Responsiveness** means the prompt attention to requests and questions, and willingness to sort customers' problems and help.
- **Tangible** means visual appealing, physical facilities, equipment, employees and communication materials.

In this study, the observers noted participants' emotional reactions to the critical incidents. They also asked the patients and the therapists follow-up/clarification interview questions about the observed critical incidents (e.g., whys or/and attitudes and motivations behind needs and behavior). These interview questions were used to get a deeper understanding of the patients' latent needs. Therapists' responses helped identify the gaps and disconnections between patients' needs and the rehabilitation services. During the CI, one observer was responsible for asking questions and the other took notes on any critical information relevant to this study.

3.2 Subjective Quantification of Critical Incidents (Service Gaps)

Participants

A convenience sample of 11 stroke survivors and 11 occupational/physical therapists participated in this study. The inclusion and exclusion criteria for the stroke participants were the same with those indicated in the CI. The screening criterion for the participated therapists was the same with that in the CI as well.

Procedure

After the CI and before investigating the service gaps, researchers explained the purpose of the study to the participants. Descriptions of the critical incidents (i.e., service gaps between patient expectations and the rehabilitation services provided at different stages) were provided to every participants. Participants were then instructed to rate their levels of satisfaction (1–5, from the least satisfied to the most satisfied) and their perceived importance (1–5, from the least important to the most important) on each critical incident related with the service quality dimensions in SERVQUAL.

4 Results and Discussion

The purpose of this study was twofold: (1) to elicit patients' rehabilitation needs from the viewpoint of customer value and conducting CI and (2) to make recommendations on stroke rehabilitation services. This study looked at inpatient/outpatient rehabilitation services where therapists mainly helped patients maintain and refine motor skills physical functions. The participants being observed were aged 25–71 acute/chronic patients and senior therapists with averagely 13 years of work experience. The CI identified the following 5 stages for the current stroke rehabilitation therapy services:

- **Check-in:** Nurses confirmed patients' identity, accessed records of patients' rehabilitation progresses, and informed therapists of patients' arrival.

- **Warm-up:** Therapists gave massages to patients to reduce their muscle tension and help patients relax. Some patients were directed to do basic level exercises (e.g., slow walking) and warm-up stretching.
- **Preparation/Instructions:** Therapists explained training the session, and the exercises, and prepared patients to get ready to perform rehabilitation activities.
- **Rehabilitation/Treatment:** Therapists engaged patients, depending on their disabilities, in passive/active exercises, and/or progressively helped patients perform complex and demanding tasks.
- **Assessment:** After the treatment, therapists identified decline or changes in patients' physical function and cognition that may or may not respond well to treatment and then entered the information into the computer system. Therapists might also review patients' stroke discharge check-list and go through follow-up assessment on patients' recovery and address points where patients may need help.

Table 1 shows the identified critical incidents. There were a total of 14 critical incidents identified from the observation and interview with three stroke patients and their therapists. Among these incidents, eight fell under reliability that occurred while therapists prepared patients for their rehabilitation exercises. Most of them were about therapists failing to regularly/consistently explain how the selected modalities, equipment, and movement related with patients' paralysis, spastic and involuntary muscle movement. Such problem not only made patients less engaged in the rehabilitation activities, but also lowered patients' motivations to continue receiving the rehabilitation therapy services.

The problem of reliability could be found from the utterances of three patients in the interview:

- *"I had no idea where the admission form and the doctor's order were. They might be probably handed to my family members."*
- *"When I started a new treatment, my therapist would explain what hand functions were to be improved. However, along the way in the rehabilitation process, he did not explain every adjustment he made. I would anyway ask him about it as I wanted to do the same thing at home."*

The most common incident (happening 3 times) was that therapists failed to do good care and understand patient wants on an individual level (falling under empathy). This issue was respectively found in the stages of warm-up, therapists' preparation for rehabilitation, and patients' rehabilitation exercises.

In addition, our CI also identified incidents related with responsiveness (e.g., nurses and therapists did not promptly respond to patients' requests), tangible (e.g., equipment was not set up properly before patients began exercises), and assurance (e.g., therapists did not necessarily provide instant feedback and clear discharge instructions needed for patients to transit into their next stage, such as referrals to community resources, dietary instructions, medication instructions, and home therapy schedules and programs, etc.).

To further understand which gaps deviated the most from customer values and which should be first improved, our study conducted a survey with 11 patients and therapists on each of the critical incident relevant to patients' customer value. Table 2 shows the demographic information of the participants. From Table 2, most participants were elder people (around the age of 60) with chronic disorders (for above 1 year). Half of them were males

Table 1. Critical incidents (service gaps) in the stroke rehabilitation service

Service stage	Deviation from customer value	Critical Incident (CrI) (s)
Check-in	Reliability	CrI 1 - Patients did not always bring with them their patient admission forms and their doctor's signed orders. Therapists could not have critical therapeutic information needed for rehabilitation in the first place
	Responsiveness	CrI 2 - Nurses were busy and did not respond to all patients' requests promptly. Depending on the situation, nurses might let patients wait in the waiting area until they finished their job at hand
Warm up	Empathy	CrI 3 - Therapists did not actively show patients their cares with respect to their recovery progress
Preparation/ Instructions	Empathy	CrI 3 - Therapists did not actively show patients their cares with respect to their recovery progress
	Reliability	CrI 4 - Therapists did not always thoroughly explained to the patients how to properly use the rehabilitation equipment, making patients possibly exercise with the wrong posture. Patients also had no idea when the exercise would finish and when to move to the next rehabilitation exercise
		CrI 5 - Therapists did not always explain whether the treatments patients received would help them reach the preset goal. Therapists sometimes explained about it after being asked
		CrI 6 - Therapists did not always or in the first place explain how each physical movement was linked to their functional recovery. Patients' willingness to participate in the rehabilitation program might be decreased accordingly
		CrI 7 - Therapists did not particularly explain to patients the modalities they used in the treatment. Therapists normally would not explain until being asked
	Tangible	CrI 8 - In the beginning, therapists did not set up all tools/equipment in the right place
Rehabilitation/ Treatment	Empathy	CrI 3 - Therapists did not actively show patients their cares with respect to their recovery progress
	Reliability	CrI 9 - Exercises and activities were not planned according to patients' physical strength and the session timeframe, making patients easily feel exhausted after the treatment
		CrI 10 - Therapists did not always provide patients with or suggested adequate treatments according to their post-stroke conditions
	Responsiveness	CrI 11 - Therapists were not able to perform one-on-one rehabilitation because of the shortage of man power, making them hard to instantly keep track on patients' activity progress. Dealing with multiple patients at one time also made patients feel ignored
Assessment	Assurance	CrI 12 - Therapists did not provide summative feedback on patients' recovery progress right after the therapy session unless being asked
		CrI 13 - Therapists did not provide patients' with practical advices/ tips on caring themselves at home unless being asked
	Reliability	CrI 14 - Patients did not regularly receive assessments in stroke recovery every time after their rehabilitation

and half were females. One half of the participants had left-side paralysis while the other half had right-side paralysis. Most participants were in Brunnstrom stage 3 of stroke recovery. On the other hand, most therapists were young (in the age of 30 s) and had sufficient work experiences (generally around 8 years).

Table 2. Characteristics of the participants responding to the identified critical incidents

	Stroke patients (n = 11)	Therapists (n = 11)
Female/Male	5/6	2/9
Age (mean ± SD)	60 ± 12.3	32.6 ± 10.8
Onset duration (mean ± SD) (months)	40.9 ± 24.4	
Paretic Limb (left/right)	6/5	
Brunnstrom-upper	3.6 ± 1.1	
Work Experience (mean ± SD) (years)		8.6 ± 9.4

Table 3 shows participants' ratings to all the incidents under the five customer values. Overall, participants' ratings were greater than 3, suggesting that participants thought that the identified customer value, i.e., service quality, were important and that participants generally felt satisfied with the rehabilitation therapy services. Both patients and therapists tended to rate assurance the most important value (Mean = 4.41, SD = 0.66; Mean = 4.82, SD = 0.40). In terms of satisfaction, empathy was rated highest by both group of participants. It appeared that empathy was addressed by the current services. In addition, the least important customer value for the patients appeared to be different than that for the therapists. Empathy was rated the lowest by the patients while tangible was rated the lowest by the therapists. Both groups gave responsiveness the lowest satisfaction ratings.

To verify which customer value was considered the most important/the least satisfied and to be particularly addressed by the current rehabilitation services, inferential statistics were conducted (in Minitab 15) on the rating scores of the participants. The one-way ANOVA tests indicated that, for the stroke patients, their ratings on importance were not significantly different across the 5 customer values, $F(4, 50) = 0.16, p = 0.957$. However, their ratings on satisfaction were significantly different across the values, $F(4, 50) = 3.12, p = 0.023$. Despite that the ratings for the 5 customer values were generally high, the Tukey pairwise comparisons showed that the ratings for responsiveness was significantly lower than those for empathy. This suggests that, from the perspective of stroke patients, despite that the importance of the 5 values were not considered different, responsiveness could be improved in the current rehabilitation services. In fact, there were participants complained about therapists' lack of responsiveness in the interview.

- For instance, as one patient articulated, *"My therapist usually treated 2-3 patients. I sometimes needed to wait. It might be due to the lack of manpower…"*
- In addition, empathy appeared 3 times in the CI. Some patients stressed its importance in the interview, *"My therapist always chatted with me during my training session. It made me feel relax and happy."*

Table 3. Participants' subjective ratings on the identified critical incidents and the service quality dimension

Customer value – service quality dimension	Critical incident	Stroke patients				Therapists			
		Importance		Satisfaction *		Importance *		Satisfaction	
		Mean (SD)		Mean (SD)		Mean (SD)		Mean (SD)	
Assurance	CrI 12	4.55 (0.93)	4.41 (0.66)	4.55 (0.93)	$4.27^{a,b}$ (0.61)	4.82 (0.40)	4.82^{a} (0.40)	4.27 (0.47)	4.18 (0.34)
	CrI 13	4.27 (1.27)		4.00 (118)		4.82 (0.40)		4.09 (0.30)	
Empathy	CrI 3	4.09 (1.38)	4.09 (1.38)	4.82 (0.40)	4.82^{a} (0.40)	4.18 (0.60)	$4.18^{a,b,c}$ (0.60)	4.36 (0.50)	4.36 (0.50)
Reliability	CrI 1	3.36 (0.92)	4.34 (0.35)	3.64 (0.67)	$4.40^{a,b}$ (0.46)	4.09 (114)	$4.55^{a,b}$ (0.36)	4.00 (0.63)	4.17 (0.26)
	CrI 4	4.73 (0.65)		4.36 (0.92)		4.91 (0.30)		4.27 (0.47)	
	CrI 5	4.45 (0.82)		4.09 (114)		4.82 (0.40)		4.09 (0.54)	
	CrI 6	4.36 (1.03)		4.45 (0.93)		4.91 (0.30)		4.18 (0.40)	
	CrI 7	4.55 (0.82)		4.55 (0.69)		4.36 (0.67)		4.09 (0.30)	
	CrI 9	4.82 (0.40)		4.73 (0.90)		4.00 (0.63)		4.00 (0.63)	
	CrI 10	4.82 (0.40)		4.55 (0.69)		4.55 (0.52)		4.18 (0.40)	
	CrI 14	3.64 (1.36)		4.82 (0.40)		4.73 (0.65)		4.55 (0.52)	
Responsiveness	CrI 2	4.09 (1.38)	4.27 (1.01)	4.55 (0.93)	4.09^{b} (0.83)	3.73 (0.90)	$3.86^{b,c}$ (0.67)	4.27 (0.65)	3.86 (0.67)
	CrI 11	4.45 (1.21)		3.64 (1.75)		4.00 (0.89)		3.45 (0.93)	
Tangible	CrI 8	4.18 (1.40)	4.18 (1.40)	4.73 (0.47)	$4.73^{a,b}$ (0.47)	3.73 (0.90)	3.73^{c} (0.90)	4.27 (0.65)	4.27 (0.65)

Note: * denotes significant difference of participants' ratings among the 5 customer values (i.e., service quality dimensions), $p < 0.05$; Means that do not share a letter are significantly different.

The one-way ANOVA tests also indicated that, for the therapists, their ratings on satisfaction were not significantly different across the 5 customer values, $F_{(4, 50)} = 1.49, p = 0.218$. However, their ratings on importance were significantly different across the 5 values, $F_{(4, 50)} = 6.28, p = 0.000$. The Tukey pairwise comparisons showed that tangible received the lowest ratings and was the least important customer value. The most important customer value was assurance. Regarding assurance, both groups of participants confirmed its importance in the interview.

- As articulated by one therapist, *"Patients are more willing to complete the training session after they were shown the purpose of the activities."*
- Two patients made similar comments, *"I would like to know what daily exercises I can do with my affected hand at home as my rehabilitation recovery supplement."*

"I preferred doing activities rather than doing the assessments. Now I don't have to do the assessment often, and I think it's good. Besides, my therapist always let me know if I made good progress on my hand function. I felt being cared."

The above analyses yielded interesting findings and service recommendations:

- First, the analyses showed that therapists believed that their therapy services universally addressed and satisfied the 5 customer values. However, from the viewpoint of the stroke patients, despite that they felt satisfied with the overall service quality, the 5 customer values were not consistently addressed in the services. Particularly, *responsiveness* is the 1 among the 5 values that could be looked at and make improvements. In other words, therapists and/or nurses should react to patients' requests, wants, and needs more promptly and proactively during patients' rehabilitation process.

- Second, the analyses revealed that, for the therapists, (1) the 5 customer values were not equally important; (2) among the 5 values, a*ssurance* is the one that comparatively was the most critical in the services (with the mean rating of 4.82, almost close to 5). The findings contradicted with what we observed in the CI, meaning that although *assurance* was considered important, there were still 2 critical incidents related with it. In other words, what the therapists believed as important did not reflect what they actually delivered in the field. From our interview with the therapists, the lack of manpower and the heavy workload could have been the causes making them have difficulties addressing assurance in their services. Thus, to resolve the problem, the management of the rehabilitation center should revisit the work and task design to balance patients' demand and therapists' capabilities so that therapists are more able to provide instant feedback to help patients progress their training and recovery.

- Third, the CI found that 8 out of 14 critical incidents were related with *reliability*, especially while therapists prepared patients for their rehabilitation activities. It appeared that therapists did not necessarily provide individualized instructions on the treatment, the equipment, as well as the rehabilitation plan/goal/timeline/process, etc., thus easily making patients lose patience, motivation, and trust in the services. To deal with this problem, therapists should provide the needed instructions to patients in a consistent manner to maintain good service quality.

5   Conclusions

Taking care of patients is what healthcare is all about. It may be hard for some people to think of patients as customers, but they definitely are. The goal of this study was to assess patient needs (from the perspective of customer value) for the enhancement of stroke rehabilitation services. CI (involving observation and interview) was conducted with 3 stroke patients and their therapists to identify the critical incidents (i.e., service gaps) in the rehabilitation services related with the customer values (i.e., the service quality dimensions identified in SERVQUAL). A survey was conducted with 11 stroke patients and 11 therapists to obtain subjective ratings on the critical incidents to provide quantitative insight that supported the findings in CI in improving current stroke rehabilitation services. Results of the study revealed 14 critical incidents, most of which were related with reliability, occurring when therapists prepare patients for rehabilitation activities. Empathy was another customer value deserving the attention as it occurred multiple times throughout the rehabilitation services. Results of the survey showed that, overall, participants' ratings were greater than 3. Patients generally thought that the 5 customer values were equally important. Patients were less satisfied with the responsiveness of the therapists (compared with other customer values). In addition, therapists thought that, among the customer values, assurance tended to be the most important; tangible tended to be the least important. However, all customer values were equally addressed by their services and were satisfied by stroke patients. The recommendations to the current rehabilitation services were as follows:

- Therapists and/or nurses should react to patients' requests, wants, and needs more promptly and proactively during patients' rehabilitation process.
- The management of the rehabilitation center should revisit the work and task design to balance patients' demand and therapists' capabilities so that therapists are more able to provide instant feedback to help patients progress their training and recovery.
- Therapists should provide the needed instructions to patients in a consistent manner to maintain good service quality.

Most healthcare services were mainly developed from the perspective of the healthcare providers, causing the gaps between the patient needs and the provided services. Few services were developed from the angle of customer value. The outcomes of the study provided insight on critical stroke patient needs and contributed to the design of stroke rehabilitation therapy services.

References

1. Clark, M.S.: Patient and spouse perceptions of stroke and its rehabilitation. Int. J. Rehabil. Res. **23**(1), 19–29 (2000). Internationale Zeitschrift fur Rehabilitationsforschung. Revue internationale de recherches de readaptation
2. Basteris, A., et al.: Training modalities in robot-mediated upper limb rehabilitation in stroke: a framework for classification based on a systematic review. J. Neuroeng. Rehabil. **11**(1), 111 (2014)
3. Wade, D.T., et al.: The hemiplegic arm after stroke: measurement and recovery. J. Neurol. Neurosurg. Psychiatry **46**(6), 521–524 (1983)
4. Sabari, J.S., Meisler, J., Silver, E.: Reflections upon rehabilitation by members of a community based stroke club. Disabil. Rehabil. **22**(7), 330–336 (2000)
5. Carey, L.M., Matyas, T.A., Oke, L.E.: Sensory loss in stroke patients: effective training of tactile and proprioceptive discrimination. Arch. Phys. Med. Rehabil. **74**(6), 602–611 (1993)
6. Yekutiel, M., Guttman, E.: A controlled trial of the retraining of the sensory function of the hand in stroke patients. J. Neurol. Neurosurg. Psychiatry **56**(3), 241–244 (1993)
7. Klein, B.S.: An ally as well as a partner in practice. Can. J. Occup. Ther. **62**(5), 283–285 (1995)
8. Newborn, B.: Surviving stroke: a perspective on the role of OT. OT Pract. **3**, 28–32 (1998)

9. Brandriet, L.M., Lyons, M., Bentley, J.: Perceived needs of poststroke elders following termination of home health services. Nurs. Health Care off. Publ. Natl League Nurs. **15**(10), 514 (1994)
10. Laver, K., et al.: Early rehabilitation management after stroke: what do stroke patients prefer? J. Rehabil. Med. **43**(4), 354–358 (2011)
11. Jones, S.P., et al.: Engaging service users in the development of stroke services: an action research study. J. Clin. Nurs. **17**(10), 1270–1279 (2008)
12. Crawford, M.J., et al.: Systematic review of involving patients in the planning and development of health care. Br. Med. J. **325**(7375), 1263 (2002)
13. Ashworth, P.D., Longmate, M.A., Morrison, P.: Patient participation: its meaning and significance in the context of caring. J. Adv. Nurs. **17**(12), 1430–1439 (1992)
14. Guadagnoli, E., Ward, P.: Patient participation in decision-making. Soc. Sci. Med. **47**(3), 329–339 (1998)
15. Woodruff, R.B.: Customer value: the next source for competitive advantage. J. Acad. Market. Sci. **25**(2), 139 (1997)
16. Dobkin, C., Shabani, R.: The health effects of military service: evidence from the Vietnam draft. Econ. Inq. **47**(1), 69–80 (2009)
17. Walker, M.F.: Stroke rehabilitation: evidence-based or evidence-tinged? J. Rehabil. Med. **39**(3), 193–197 (2007)
18. Tistad, M., et al.: Unfulfilled rehabilitation needs and dissatisfaction with care 12 months after a stroke: an explorative observational study. BMC Neurol. **12**(1), 40 (2012)
19. Blechner, M., et al.: Using contextual design to identify potential innovations for problem based learning. In: AMIA Annual Symposium Proceedings, vol. 2003. American Medical Informatics Association (2003)
20. Beyer, H., Holtzblatt, K.: Contextual Design: Defining Customer-Centered Systems. Elsevier, Burlington (1997)
21. Cawood, T., et al.: Creating the optimal workspace for hospital staff using human centred design. Intern. Med. J. **46**(7), 840–845 (2016)
22. Gurses, A.P., et al.: Using human factors engineering to improve patient safety in the cardiovascular operating room. Work **41**(Supplement 1), 1801–1804 (2012)
23. Kamalakannan, S., et al.: Rehabilitation needs of stroke survivors after discharge from hospital in India. Arch. Phys. Med. Rehabil. **97**(9), 1526–1532 (2016)
24. Parasuraman, A., Zeithaml, V., Berry, L.: SERVQUAL: a multiple-item scale for measuring consumer perceptions of service quality. Retail. Crit. Concepts **64**(1), 140 (2002)
25. Flanagan, J.C.: The critical incident technique. Psychol. Bull. **51**(4), 327 (1954)

Towards Encouraging a Healthier Lifestyle and Increased Physical Activity – An App Incorporating Persuasive Design Principles

Sunny Ladwa[1], Tor-Morten Grønli[2], and Gheorghita Ghinea[1,2(✉)]

[1] Brunel University, Uxbridge UB8 3PH, UK
sunnyladwa90@gmail.com, george.ghinea@brunel.ac.uk
[2] Westerdals Oslo School of Arts, Communication and Technology,
Oslo, Norway
tmg@westerdals.no

Abstract. The number of young adults becoming overweight leading to obesity is on an unceasing rise. Attempts have been made to tackle this epidemic throughout the UK through varied technology platforms including video games and more recently through ubiquitous mobile applications. With a significant increase of smartphone usage, mobile applications have become the ideal platform to reach out to young adults. This paper addresses the obesity epidemic and the fundamental value of healthy living through the development of an app which encourages eating a balanced diet and particularly increasing the time spent exercising by incorporating it into an individual's daily routine. It focuses on tackling the common barriers currently preventing individuals from increasing their level of physical activity and aims to provide a solution to the problem domain by implementing persuasive design principles, models and frameworks in an android mobile application to successfully change or modify behaviors and attitudes within young adults to increase the time spent on exercise and a healthy lifestyle.

Keywords: m-Health · Obesity · Persuasive design

1 Introduction

One of the most common health concerns in the UK is related to obesity and being overweight, which results in poor quality of life, illnesses and even resulting in mortality. Obesity is a condition where a person accumulates a vast amount of body fat that negatively affects an individual's health and in which weight has been gained to the point of seriously endangering one's health. There has been a significant increase in the proportion of the UK population who are now categorized as overweight or obese, with 27% of adults classed as obese and a further 36% who are overweight, making a total of 63% who are either overweight or obese [36]. The impact of obesity is so severe that a recent study claims that being overweight can cut life expectancy between 1–10 years [20]. Consequently, failing to address the obesity epidemic will place an even greater burden on the UK's National Health Service resources with an existing cost of approximately £6.1billion in 2014–2015 alone. The annual spend is currently on an

M. Kurosu (Ed.): HCI 2018, LNCS 10902, pp. 158–172, 2018.
https://doi.org/10.1007/978-3-319-91244-8_13

upward trend and according to Public Health London, the UK-wide NHS costs attributable to overweight and obesity are projected to reach a staggering £9.7 billion by 2050, with wider costs to society estimated to reach £49.9 billion per year which will continue to rise to treat overweight and obesity related health problems [36]. Obesity is a serious health implication that in fact can easily be prevented with a balanced diet and regular exercise.

Smartphones are ubiquitous and with an increase in usage amongst young adults has led to mobile phones being considered as a necessity. A study conducted by Statista in 2017 reports that the main smartphone owners are aged 16–24 with a confounding 96% of market share [43]. This in turn has led the younger generation to use their smartphones for all their daily activities from shopping online, communicating with friends and family to playing games. The sheer popularity and ease of access to smartphones has resulted in numerous developments of mobile applications within the Mobile-Health (m-Health) division with it being the fastest-developing sector, with over 100,000 health applications (apps) currently available [13, 15, 31, 41, 42]. Furthermore, the concept of changing an individual's behavior using mobile applications has become the optimal choice to increase obesity prevention awareness, additionally, with modern features integrated into mobile phones such as GPS and pedometers; it provides the ideal platform to embolden exercise amongst young adults [12].

In order to introduce behavior change via technology, persuasive design principles are becoming increasingly common in mobile applications. B.J Fogg was the first to articulate the concept of 'Captology', a term used to describe the overlap between persuasion and computers. Fogg [11] defines persuasive technology as 'any interactive computing system designed to change people's attitudes or behaviors' and has created the Fogg Behaviour Model (FBM). This poses a question on how persuasive technology can be utilized to improve the lives of young adults through exercise and adopt a healthier lifestyle

In addressing this issue, the aim of the study reported in this paper is to gain an understanding of how persuasive design principles can be integrated in the form a modern mobile application that encourages young adults to lead healthier lifestyle and increase their motivation to exercise frequently. Accordingly, the structure of this paper is as follows: Sect. 2 details work done in respect of obesity prevention, with a particular emphasis on approaches involving Information and Communication Technologies. Section 3 then presents the main principles behind the persuasive systems design mode, whilst Sect. 4 details our contribution, namely PowerFIT, an app for obesity prevention incorporating persuasive design principles. Lastly, conclusions are drawn and opportunities for future work identified in Sect. 5.

2 Obesity and Its Prevention

Obesity amongst young adults is a key health concern due to its correlation with chronic diseases such as type-2 diabetes, cardiovascular diseases, hypertension and cancer. These in turn are primary drivers of healthcare costs, disabilities and cause a decrease in life expectancy [45]. According to a study by the Public Health England, recent estimates suggest over 62.9% of adults were overweight or obese of which

67.8% were men and 58.1% women [36]. With a large proportion of the population being classed as overweight, it is imperative to highlight the dangers of weight gain and endorse increased levels of physical activity to prevent health and lifestyle complications. Additional studies also suggest that moderate weight gain from early to middle adulthood is associated with significantly increased risk of major chronic diseases, mortality and decreased odds of healthy aging [49].

With the growing number of young adults in scope for obesity, it is vital that changes to their lifestyles are made to increase both the quality and longevity. Considerable evidence has increased over the last few decades with an emphasis on physical activity that can reduce the risk of heart disease. Longer periods of inactivity have proven to lead to not only obesity but also expose individuals to major heart diseases. Further evidence has also accumulated linking physical inactivity to an increased risk for other chronic conditions, including stroke [17], cancer [46] and non-insulin dependent diabetes [5]. It is evident that obesity has detrimental health and social implications however these findings may help counsel patients regarding the risks of weight gain along with understanding whether or not they are in fact overweight.

2.1 Preventing Obesity

It is common knowledge that a balanced diet combined with moderate exercise can prevent obesity yet this practice is often followed by few due to the lack of knowledge amongst individuals. According to a recent study on the related factors causing obesity, education levels of the subjects appeared to be the most important factor in controlling body weight [39] therefore, every effort should be made to increase the level of education on healthy nutrition and the significance of regular physical activity.

An increase in regular physical activity and healthy eating amongst adolescents must become a lifestyle choice, as opposed to dieting and unhealthy weight control behaviors, which may be counterproductive. Though dietary weight loss interventions often result in weight loss, weight maintenance on a long-term basis is the key problem in obesity treatment [1]. There are concerns that "obesity prevention efforts may also lead to the development of eating disorders" [14], as a result, it is vital to ensure that obesity prevention and treatment is conducted appropriately with a focus on a healthy lifestyle and "positive eating and physical behaviors that can be maintained on a regular basis" are encouraged [30].

In order to prevent obesity, a basic understanding on the factors causing weight gain as wellbeing perceptive as to why there has been no significant decline in the epidemic will provide a prospect to design the mobile application to ensure the existing hindrances are accounted for.

Physical activity has far-reaching benefits to individuals. There has been extensive research supporting the notion on the positive effects of exercising, including physical and psychological well-being. Anderson and his team conducted an in-depth study on how moods are affected by the level of physical activity, suggesting, "acute exercise can have beneficial effects on the mood" [3]. Studies have linked physically activity with increased happiness where recent findings revealed that individuals who are more physically active are actually happier. These individuals tend to be happier in the moments when they are more physically active [22].

However, the duration of physical activity became an important variable to consider. For instance, experiments have been conducted on individuals based on duration and intensities, the results of which showed consistently positive effects of acute exercise at low intensities, with a duration of up to 35 min for low to moderate exercise doses [38]. To complement this, research reported in [35] compared studies that measured physical activity and daily mood and concluded that light and moderate physical activities were also associated with positive daily affect, but vigorous activity was not.

Mobile applications are providing an exciting platform to develop physical activity interventions with researchers beginning to base the design of applications on established health and persuasive theories. With applications such as Pokémon Go being the most downloaded iOS app of 2016 [25] which uses local geo-location information to encourage participants to exercise, it is obvious that the broad reach of mobile applications is phenomenal and highlights how the world of ubiquitous computing can target large audiences, resulting in potential exceptional behavior changes. The application provides challenges in the form of "hatching eggs" where the user must walk a specific distance to "hatch" the egg; the challenge aspect was a considerable motivation for players.

These findings indicate how exercise plays an important role in improving ones' lifestyle and can potentially prevent obesity; therefore, exercise should be viewed as an obligation and be considered the norm in order to lead a healthy prolonged life.

2.2 Healthy Eating

Eating a healthy balanced diet along with frequent exercise is known to be beneficial for one's health and can potentially reduce the risks of obesity. Though this is common knowledge, few lead this lifestyle. To reap the benefits of a healthier lifestyle it is imperative to stay motivated however the number of barriers preventing healthy eating is increasing. Paradoxically, the prevalence of both eating disorders and obesity has been increasing in developed countries during the past few decades and ironically, dieting has been viewed as contributing factor to both problems [28]. Clearly the consumption of unhealthy meals as well as lack of meals can contribute to the obesity epidemic.

Eating behavior can be affected through both, physical and psychological barriers, which could have either a positive or a negative impact. Physical barriers include time, cost and unavailability whilst willpower and eating habits are considered psychological [29]. In addition, according to a study on determinants of eating behavior amongst students, the individuals eating habits were influenced by "individual factors (e.g. taste preferences, self-discipline, time and convenience), their social networks (e.g. (lack of) parental control, friends and peers), physical environment (e.g. availability and accessibility, appeal and prices of food products), and macro environment (e.g. media and advertising)" [9].

Motives to eating healthy can be categorized in terms of being intrinsic or extrinsic. An intrinsic motive includes 'self-image' and 'personal health' which leads to rewards that are internal to the individual as opposed to extrinsic motives which leads to external rewards or punishments such as approval or disapproval of others [29]. According to Deci [8], intrinsic motivation is also associated with a reward but focuses on the physiological pleasure or satisfaction such as leading a healthy lifestyle to 'look good' and have self-confidence for their own reasons. Alternatively, extrinsic motivations are defined as "engaging in an activity to obtain and outcome that is separable from the activity itself" [7, 24] where the reason for an activity would solely revolve around the rewards or punishment aspect. For example, extrinsic motives can include pressures to conform to society's perspective of being 'good looking' or having the medias perception of an ideal figure. Moreover, societal pressures have been indicated as one of the principal factors which lead to individuals initiating losing weight [44]. Indeed, it is argued that some degree of dissatisfaction may be helpful and necessary to motivate individuals to engage in health behaviors such as exercise [17].

Moreover, several studies have concluded that food has a momentous impact on the behavior and moods of individuals as well. Unhealthy and unbalanced diets that consist of high sugar content and starch filled carbohydrates lead to internal problems such as hypoglycaemia [27], which causes the brain to secret glutamate at levels that cause agitation, depression and anxiety. Moreover, healthier diets support cognition, problem solving and memory, which are noted benefits leading to brain development [27].

2.3 Persuasive Technology and Captology

Persuasive technology is defined as any interactive computing system designed to change or alter individual's attitudes or behaviors by applying psychological principles of persuasion including principles of credibility, trust, reciprocity and authority [11]. It has been used in many disciplines including advertising, marketing, games and healthcare. Particularly, it has been used in encouraging good eating habits [19] and Internet advertising [23]. The use of persuasive technology to motivate healthy behavior change is a growing area of research within human computer interaction (HCI) and ubiquitous computing, with the evolving field increasingly being targeted to influence behavior in the area of health and wellness [34]. With mobile phones dominating individual's lives in today's generation, it is imperative to utilize this platform to promote healthier lifestyles through mobile applications. Mobile phone applications, benefiting from their ubiquity, have been progressively used to address obesity. In order to increase the applications' acceptance and success, a design and development process that focuses on users, such as user-centred design, is necessary [16].

Fogg describes the development of applying persuasive techniques in computing technology as 'captology', whereby the design, research and analysis of interactive computing products are created to alter the attitudes and behaviors [11]. As a result, captology can be viewed as the overlap between computers and persuasion, which correlates around influencing behavior, and attitude change alongside computing technology. The combination of persuasion and technology lead to a well-structured background on persuasive technology.

Captology is defined as "the study of user's interactions with computers, focusing on the psychological drivers involved for pursuing an intended goal defined as change in people's behaviors or attitudes without coercion or deception" [11]. Although defined as a study of computers, it is in fact not limited to computer systems only but is open to other platforms such as websites, games, or for the context of this research, mobile applications. Development of applications using persuasion within healthcare to motivate people towards healthy behavior have been identified as resulting in a possible delay, or even preventing medical problems [33].

Humans are arguably the strongest persuaders [18]. They tend to offer a presence and a valuable impact in persuading others to commit to long-term goals however, Fogg [11] suggests that technology can now have a number of distinct advantages over human persuaders. Some of which can allow anonymity, access and control to an unlimited store of data, of which these advantages are to be more persistent [18]. However, looking at distinct types of sync-able technology such as wearables and Android applications to match, it is clear that technology is now a necessity during physical activity.

3   The Persuasive Systems Design Model

To create efficacious persuasive technology, it is evident that unique design principles need to be taken into consideration with the design process for a higher possibility to modify user behaviors and attitudes. The Persuasive Systems Design Model, also known as the PSD model was introduced by Oinas-Kukkonen and Harjumaa [33] and is, to the best of our knowledge, currently the only comprehensive methodology for developing and evaluating persuasive systems. The PSD configures the design processes and provides a comprehensive list of system features and requirements that can be used during the development process. The PSD model has been used in the development of Behavioural Change Support Systems (BCSS) in order to define the overall process [2], to analyze the persuasion context [37, 48] and to design system qualities [10, 22]. Further related research associated with the use of the PSD model has been applied in the evaluation phases of existing systems by providing heuristics for expert evaluations [6] and systematic ways to analyze user experience data [4, 40].

The three phases are based on the principle that before any system is developed or implemented, it is central to understand the fundamental issues behind persuasive systems, which is the first stage of the model. Only once a reasonable level of understanding has been obtained, can the system be analyzed and designed. During the second stage of persuasion context analysis, the intent, event and strategies for using the persuasive application is a prerequisite to progress onto the final stage. The concluding stage consists of designing the system qualities for the proposed application or evaluating the features of an existing application [33].

Upon conducting conceptual analysis and empirical work, Oinas-Kukkonen and Harjumaa [33] have defined seven postulates which should be addressed when designing or evaluating persuasive systems. These entail how we see the users in general, persuasion strategies and addressing actual system features:

1. Information technology is never neutral.
2. People like their views about the world to be organized and consistent.
3. Direct and indirect routers are key persuasion strategies.
4. Persuasion is often Incremental.
5. Persuasion through persuasive systems should always be open.
6. Persuasive systems should aim at unobtrusiveness.
7. Persuasive systems should aim at being both useful and easy to use.

The second stage within the PSD requires an in-depth analysis and concrete understanding on the persuasion context. This constructs as an integral aspect which is vital in promoting the slightest behavior or attitude change. Analyzing the persuasion context requires a thorough understanding of what happens in the information-processing event, namely understanding the roles of persuader, persuadee, message, channel, and the larger context [32].

The final stage within the PSD model is System Qualities; here the designers must ensure the system incorporates a set of non-functional requirements [47]. There are 28 dissimilar principles organized into four categories that reflect the design of the system qualities including primary task support, dialogue support, system credibility and social support [33].

- **Primary Task Support**
  The design principles associated with primary task support essentially aid the user in carrying out the user's primary task. These include reduction, tunnelling, tailoring, personalisation, self-monitoring, simulation and rehearsal.
- **Dialogue Support**
  The dialogue support category relates directly to the actual interactive system that provides a degree of feedback to its users. An example of this may be a dialogue box providing ongoing moral support to the user as they reach closer to their goal. The design principles include praise, rewards, reminders, suggestions, similarity, liking and social role.
- **System Credibility**
  System credibility describes how to accurately design a system ensuring it is credible and persuasive. The design principles can include trustworthiness, expertise, surface credibility, real-world feel, authority, third-party endorsements, and verifiability. For example, if a user is searching for medical advice, they are likely to trust an established government organisation such as the NHS as opposed to a blog by a third year medical student.
- **Social Support**
  Social support defines how to design the system ensuring it motivates users by leveraging social influence. The design principles within this category include social facilitation, social comparison, normative influence, social learning, cooperation, competition, and recognition.

4   The PowerFIT App

Prior to beginning development work, a set of low-fidelity diagrams were generated to provide a foundation for developing the application. Developing a working application for evaluation is considered to be impractical [26], therefore a low-fidelity prototype was created on the basis of the gathered user requirements and persuasive design principles. User requirements were gathered through two iterations with a focus group comprising 10 participants and were complemented by best practice identified from the state-of-the-art literature on usability and persuasive systems design.

4.1 Splash and Welcome Screens

To begin with, the user will view a splash screen as shown in Fig. 1. The screen allows the user to begin using the application using the 'Start' button; alternatively, the application will automatically continue onto the main screen after a few seconds. Though the splash screen does not explicitly highlight that the application is free, this is evident whilst downloading the application from the play store. A free application should enable the user to reciprocate and repay the favor (the reciprocation principle). The color scheme and button format have been deliberately designed with curved edges for a soft look and feel to application with a light color scheme. Figures 1 and 2 show the Android application being run on a Google Nexus 7. Figure 2 shows the welcome screen with the options to Register, Login or view Help. The welcome screen also provides the user with the option to go 'Back' and exit the application.

Fig. 1. PowerFIT   splash screen

Fig. 2. PowerFIT welcome screen

4.2 Login and Home Screens

Once users have completed registration, they are directed to the 'Login' page to input their email and password as highlighted in Fig. 3. The password is encrypted as the users for security purposes. Upon logging in, the user is directed to the main page as shown in Fig. 4. From here, the user can opt to use any of the following features: Route Tracker, Track My Steps, Reminders or Food & Calorie Log.

4.3 Route Tracker

The 'Route Tracker' functionality allows the users to define a route for their journey using google maps within the application. The user can specify a 'From' and 'To'

Fig. 3. PowerFIT   login screen

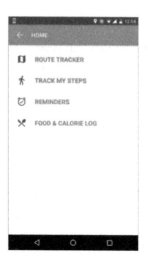

Fig. 4. PowerFIT   home screen

Fig. 5. PowerFIT   route tracker

Fig. 6. Destination   auto selection

destination and select 'Draw Route' which will highlight the route on the map and has the ability to search any location from the text box (Fig. 5).

The functionality includes the Google Maps API which is required to work alongside the 'Pedometer' feature. Given most mobile applications already have a map feature, the use of google maps will be a familiar function for the user and prevents them from having to learn the feature again. The map provides a visual view of the route for the user making the feature self-explanatory and user friendly and thus allows the user to track their physical activity session for jogging or walking.

To ensure the application is easy to use and convenient, the starting and ending destinations can be selected from an auto-populated suggestion. Figure 6 illustrates the destination suggestions depending on the initial characters typed.

The use of a social actor in the form of a small character has been incorporated to guide users through various processes and provide motivation. The social actor will display a series of randomly generated motivational quotes, and praises to help the user attain the best performance. The intention is to utilize this character to tempt the individuals to pick a longer route and to encourage a healthy challenge to accomplish as well as provide motivation when the users may lack the urge to increase physical activity.

The Route Tracker and the Pedometer correlate to one another as the user can draw their desired route in the Route Tracker screen and select 'Track' which will direct the users onto the 'Pedometer screen'.

4.4 Calorie Log

Possessing the ability to count your calories throughout the day is an important task that should be completed when setting out physical exercise goals. Physical activity yields a significant amount of benefits alone, however to maximize the results an in-depth log of the individual's calories must be counted and logged. This will provide the individual an insight to whether they need to promote a calorie surplus or a calorie deficit. This feature will enable the individual to successfully search for the food they have consumed and be able to add this to their log that can then be totaled towards the end of the day of week. The calorie log successfully searches for food and adds the total onto the table on screen (Fig. 7).

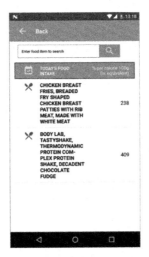

Fig. 7. PowerFIT calorie log

4.5   Evaluation

An individual think aloud session was held with the original participant group to evaluate and analyze the final solution. The purpose of expending the think aloud approach is to facilitate systematic data collection in a controlled environment and support the identification of usability problems that are experienced in the use of the application [21]. Participants were asked to explore the app without restrictions throughout the session and provide their honest thoughts on the design, features available and usability. The intention was to understand the user's attitude towards the application and to assess whether they are likely to use the application long term. The session will follow the very same process as the data gathering sessions but will be categorized against the requirements.

The data collated from the think aloud sessions have been grouped into common themes in relation to this project. Generally, the participants favored the application and provided positive feedback as well as constructive negative feedback. All users stated that they were inclined to use and explore the application and seemed enthusiastic to view their progress over a period of time. The feedback has been categorized into common themes as outlined below in Table 1 below:

Table 1. Think aloud evaluation summary.

Theme 1: Aesthetics

The application was well received amongst the participants, particularly the bright base and the logo. Due to the negative perception on the Fitness Pal logo which was perceived as targeted for males only, the logo for PowerFIT was exceptionally well received with users reacting positively to the color scheme and gender neutral design. All participants found the application formatting to be visually appealing and preferred the minimalistic design approach

Theme 2: Ease of Use

Applications should be effortless and make things easier for the user (Whalen 2011). Participants mentioned that the application was self-explanatory with the navigation and usability of the application being 'straightforward' and 'easy to understand'. They favored that all functions were visible and not hidden. A minority of participants stated that they would prefer and 'Help' page on each screen as opposed to going back to the Home screen

Theme 3: Color Scheme

Following on from the initial data gathering sessions it was evident that all participants preferred a neutral color scheme. This was then taken in to consideration and implemented into the application which was well received and considered to be one of the key favorite aspects as the application was 'fresh' and 'inviting'. The consistency has remained throughout the application in the form of color scheme and fonts however, some negative responses included that the use of pink and blue felt to be too diverse when selecting fields to type in, they preferred it stayed the same color. Additionally as the logo had shades of yellow present, users expected yellow in the application

(continued)

Table 1. (*continued*)

Theme 4: Features
All participants likened the motivational prompts as well as the ability to view their progress on the pedometer and the calories lost. Users stated that the ability to create the timing of the reminders was convenient as their routines changed; making it easier to suit the app to the users' needs though, they did find this to be a manual task. This represents 'status quo' as the concept is adaptable to fit the users' life (Whalen, 2011). To add, the option to configure the journey pace as 'Walk' or 'Run' was pleasing for all participants as they felt they had control over the pace of the exercise. The consistency of having an existing functionality such as Google maps on a phone that has been incorporated into the application received positive feedback, as all users knew how to use the feature. It is significant that the application is consistent as it provides the user with familiarities, which increases its likeability

5   Conclusions

The aim of the work reported in this paper was to investigate whether persuasive design principles can be integrated in the form a modern mobile application that encourages young adults to lead a healthier lifestyle and increase their motivation to exercise frequently.

A fundamental achievement highlighted following an evaluation of the developed mobile application is that persuasive design principles do have a positive impact on users and it has the potential to determine the success or failure of a mobile application. Although it is difficult to assess whether the application can change behavior long-term and whether or not it assists in tackling obesity, it is evident that users are encouraged to use the application and attempt the new behavior, which is likely to change their behavior for the time being.

References

1. Ahlgren, C., Hammarström, A., Sandberg, S., Lindahl, B., Olsson, T., Larsson, C., Fjellman-Wiklund, A.: Engagement in new dietary habits—obese women's experiences from participating in a 2-year diet intervention. Int. J. Behav. Med. **23**(1), 84–93 (2016)
2. Alahäivälä, T., Oinas-Kukkonen, H., Jokelainen, T.: Software architecture design for health BCSS: case onnikka. In: Berkovsky, S., Freyne, J. (eds.) PERSUASIVE 2013. LNCS, vol. 7822, pp. 3–14. Springer, Heidelberg (2013). https://doi.org/10.1007/978-3-642-37157-8_3
3. Anderson, R.J., Brice, S.: The mood-enhancing benefits of exercise: memory biases augment the effect. Psychol. Sport Exerc. **12**(2), 79–82 (2011)
4. Basic, J., Yadamsuren, B., Saparova, D., Ma, Y.: Persuasive features in a web-based system for weight-loss team competition. In: Stephanidis, C. (ed.) HCI 2013. CCIS, vol. 374, pp. 125–129. Springer, Heidelberg (2013). https://doi.org/10.1007/978-3-642-39476-8_26
5. Brancati, F.L., Kao, W.L., Folsom, A.R., Watson, R.L., Szklo, M.: Incident type 2 diabetes mellitus in African American and white adults: the Atherosclerosis Risk in Communities Study. JAMA **283**(17), 2253–2259 (2000)

6. Chang, T.-R., Kaasinen, E., Kaipainen, K.: Persuasive design in mobile applications for mental well-being: multidisciplinary expert review. In: Godara, B., Nikita, K.S. (eds.) MobiHealth 2012. LNICST, vol. 61, pp. 154–162. Springer, Heidelberg (2013). https://doi.org/10.1007/978-3-642-37893-5_18

7. DeCharms, R.: Personal Causation: The Internal Affective Determinants of Behavior. Academic Press, New York (1968)

8. Deci, E.L.: Effects of externally mediated rewards on intrinsic motivation. J. Pers. Soc. Psychol. **18**, 105–115 (1971)

9. Deliens, T., Clarys, P., De Bourdeaudhuij, I., Deforche, B.: Determinants of eating behaviour in university students: a qualitative study using focus group discussions. BMC Public Health **14**(1), 53 (2014)

10. Derrick, D.C., Jenkins, J.L., Nunamaker Jr., J.F.: Design principles for special purpose, embodied, conversational intelligence with environmental sensors (SPECIES) agents'. AIS Trans. Hum. Comput. Interact. **3**(2), 62–81 (2011)

11. Fogg, B.J.: Persuasive Technology. Morgan Kaufmann Publishers, Amsterdam (2003)

12. Gao, C., Kong, F., Tan, J.: Healthaware: tackling obesity with health aware smart phone systems. In: Proceedings IEEE International Conference on Robotics and Biomimetics (ROBIO), pp. 1549–1554. IEEE (2009)

13. Ghinea, G., Spyridonis, F., Serif, T., Frank, A.O.: 3-D pain drawings–mobile data collection using a PDA. IEEE Trans. Inf Technol. Biomed. **12**(1), 27–33 (2008)

14. Golden, N.H., Schneider, M., Wood, C.: Preventing obesity and eating disorders in adolescents. Pediatrics **138**(3), e20161649 (2016)

15. Hansen, J., Gronli, T.M., Ghinea, G.: Cloud to device push messaging on android: a case study. In: Proceedings 6th International Conference on Advanced Information Networking and Applications Workshops (WAINA), pp. 1298–1303. IEEE (2012)

16. Hermawati, S., Lawson, G.: Managing obesity through mobile phone applications: a state-of-the-art review from a user-centred design perspective. Pers. Ubiquit. Comput. **18**(8), 2003–2023 (2014)

17. Hu, F.B., Stampfer, M.J., Colditz, G.A., Ascherio, A., Rexrode, K.M., Willett, W.C., Manson, J.E.: Physical activity and risk of stroke in women. JAMA **283**(22), 2961–2967 (2000)

18. IJsselsteijn, W., de Kort, Y., Midden, C., Eggen, B., van den Hoven, E.: Persuasive technology for human well-being: setting the scene. In: IJsselsteijn, W.A., de Kort, Y.A.W., Midden, C., Eggen, B., van den Hoven, E. (eds.) PERSUASIVE 2006. LNCS, vol. 3962, pp. 1–5. Springer, Heidelberg (2006). https://doi.org/10.1007/11755494_1

19. Intille, S.S., Kukla, C., Farzanfar, R., Bakr, W.: Just-in-time technology to encourage incremental, dietary behavior change. In: Proceedings AMIA Annual Symposium Proceedings, p. 874 (2003)

20. Kivimäki, M., Kuosma, E., Ferrie, J.E., Luukkonen, R., Nyberg, S.T., Alfredsson, L., Knutsson, A.: Overweight, obesity, and risk of cardiometabolic multimorbidity: pooled analysis of individual-level data for 120 813 adults from 16 cohort studies from the USA and Europe. Lancet Public Health **2**(6), e277–e285 (2017)

21. Kjeldskov, J., Stage, J.: New techniques for usability evaluation of mobile systems. Int. J. Hum Comput Stud. **60**(5–6), 599–620 (2004)

22. Langrial, S., Oinas-Kukkonen, H., Wang, S.: Design of a web-based information system for sleep deprivation – a trial study. In: Eriksson-Backa, K., Luoma, A., Krook, E. (eds.) WIS 2012. CCIS, vol. 313, pp. 41–51. Springer, Heidelberg (2012). https://doi.org/10.1007/978-3-642-32850-3_4

23. Lee, J.K., Lee, J.W.: Internet advertising strategy by comparison challenge approach. In: Proceedings of the 5th International Conference on Electronic Commerce, pp. 450–457 (2003)
24. Lepper, M.R., Greene, D.: The Hidden Costs of Reward. Lawrence Erlbaum Associates, Inc., Hillsdale (1978)
25. Leswing, K.: Pokémon Go was most downloaded iOS app worldwide in 2016, Apple says. Business Insider (2017)
26. Lim, Y.K., Pangam, A., Periyasami, S., Aneja, S.: Comparative analysis of high-and low-fidelity prototypes for more valid usability evaluations of mobile devices. In: Proceedings of the 4th Nordic Conference on Human-Computer Interaction: Changing Roles, pp. 291–300. ACM (2006)
27. Linus Pauling Institute Cognitive Function in Depth. http://lpi.oregonstate.edu/mic/health-disease/cognitive-function. Last Accessed 20 June 2017
28. Lowe, M., Levine, A.: Eating motives and the controversy over dieting: eating less than needed versus less than wanted. Obes Res. **13**(5), 797–806 (2005). North American Association for the Study of Obesity
29. Michaelidou, N., Christodoulides, G., Torova, K.: Determinants of healthy eating: a cross-national study on motives and barriers. Int. J. Cons. Stud. **36**(1), 17–22 (2012)
30. Neumark-Sztainer, D.: Preventing obesity and eating disorders in adolescents: what can health care providers do? J. Adolesc. Health **44**(3), 206–213 (2009)
31. Nikolaou, C.K., Lean, M.E.J.: Mobile applications for obesity and weight management: current market characteristics. Int. J. Obes. **41**(1), 200 (2017)
32. Oinas-Kukkonen, H., Harjumaa, M.: A systematic framework for designing and evaluating persuasive systems. In: Oinas-Kukkonen, H., Hasle, P., Harjumaa, M., Segerståhl, K., Øhrstrøm, P. (eds.) PERSUASIVE 2008. LNCS, vol. 5033, pp. 164–176. Springer, Heidelberg (2008). https://doi.org/10.1007/978-3-540-68504-3_15
33. Oinas-Kukkonen, H., Harjumaa, M.: Persuasive systems design: key issues, process model, and system features. Commun. Assoc. Inf. Syst. **24**(1), 28 (2009)
34. Orji, R., Moffatt, K.: Persuasive technology for health and wellness: state-of-the-art and emerging trends. Health Inf. J. **24**, 66–91 (2016)
35. Poole, L., Steptoe, A., Wawrzyniak, A.J., Bostock, S., Mitchell, E.S., Hamer, M.: Associations of objectively measured physical activity with daily mood ratings and psychophysiological stress responses in women. Psychophysiology **48**(8), 1165–1172 (2011)
36. Public Health England. https://www.gov.uk/government/publications/health-matters-obesity-and-the-food-environment/health-matters-obesity-and-the-food-environment–2. Last Accessed 07 Feb 2018
37. Purpura, S., Schwanda, V., Williams, K., Stibler, W. Sengers, P.: Fit4life: the design of a persuasive technology promoting healthy behavior and ideal weight. In: Proceedings of the SIGCHI Conference on Human Factors in Computing Systems, pp. 423–432. ACM, New York (2011)
38. Reed, J., Ones, D.S.: The effect of acute aerobic exercise on positive activated affect: a meta-analysis. Psychol. Sport Exerc. **7**(5), 477–514 (2006)
39. Salici, A.G., Sisman, P., Gul, O.O., Karayel, T., Cander, S., Ersoy, C.: The prevalence of obesity and related factors: an urban survey study. Endocr. Abstr. **49**(EP679) (2017). https://doi.org/10.1530/endoabs.49.ep679
40. Segerståhl, K., Kotro, T., Väänänen-Vainio-Mattila, K.: Pitfalls in persuasion: how do users experience persuasive techniques in a web service? In: Ploug, T., Hasle, P., Oinas-Kukkonen, H. (eds.) PERSUASIVE 2010. LNCS, vol. 6137, pp. 211–222. Springer, Heidelberg (2010). https://doi.org/10.1007/978-3-642-13226-1_22

41. Serif, T., Ghinea, G.: Recording of time-varying back-pain data: a wireless solution. IEEE Trans. Inf Technol. Biomed. **9**(3), 447–458 (2005)
42. Spyridonis, F., Hansen, J., Grønli, T.M., Ghinea, G.: PainDroid: an android-based virtual reality application for pain assessment. Multimed. Tools Appl. **72**(1), 191–206 (2014)
43. Statista. Annual number of mobile app downloads worldwide 2021|Statistic. https://www.statista.com/statistics/271644/worldwide-free-and-paid-mobile-app-store-downloads/. Last Accessed 03 June 2017
44. Stevenson, C., Doherty, G., Barnett, J., Muldoon, O., Trew, K.: Adolescents' views of food and eating: identifying barriers to healthy eating. J. Adolesc. **30**(3), 417–434 (2007)
45. Sturm, R.: The effects of obesity, smoking, and drinking on medical problems and costs. Health Aff. **21**(2), 245–253 (2002)
46. Verloop, J., Rookus, R.A., van der Kooy, K., van Leeuwen, F.E.: Physical activity and breast cancer risk in women aged 20-54 years. J. Nat. Cancer Inst. **92**(2), 128–135 (2000)
47. Wiafe, I., Alhammad, M.M., Nakata, K., Gulliver, S.R.: Analyzing the persuasion context of the persuasive systems design model with the 3D-RAB model. In: Bang, M., Ragnemalm, E.L. (eds.) PERSUASIVE 2012. LNCS, vol. 7284, pp. 193–202. Springer, Heidelberg (2012). https://doi.org/10.1007/978-3-642-31037-9_17
48. Young, M.M.: Twitter me: using micro-blogging to motivate teenagers to exercise. In: Winter, R., Zhao, J.L., Aier, S. (eds.) DESRIST 2010. LNCS, vol. 6105, pp. 439–448. Springer, Heidelberg (2010). https://doi.org/10.1007/978-3-642-13335-0_30
49. Zheng, Y., Manson, J.E., Yuan, C., Liang, M.H., Grodstein, F., Stampfer, M.J., Willett, W.C., Hu, F.B.: Associations of weight gain from early to middle adulthood with major health outcomes later in life. JAMA **318**(3), 255–269 (2017)

User Acceptance Factors for mHealth

Adam Pan[1](✉) and Fan Zhao[2]

[1] Physicians Regional Hospital, Naples, FL, USA
adamsp824@gmail.com
[2] College of Business, Florida Gulf Coast University, Fort Myers, USA
fzhao@fgcu.edu

Abstract. There used to exist a vision of telemedicine in which healthcare became universally connected. mHealth is a manifestation of that vision. However, studies that demonstrate theoretical user acceptance factors of mHealth are limited. We are still just neophytes in this area of research with the full potential of mHealth being an unknown. Through the use of literature review and qualitative we examined the effectiveness of mHealth use in a clinical setting, the factors inhibiting the proliferation of mHealth technologies, and the future expectations of mHealth. In this qualitative study twenty random patients between the ages of 25–94 were surveyed on their usage and expectations of mHealth related apps. Of the twenty patients that were sampled, only five had reported of past experience with mHealth related applications. Of those five with past experience in use of mHealth apps, only two reported to have continued with mHealth use on a daily basis. Reasons cited for discontinuation of use included difficult to understand interface, failure to provide precise diagnosis, and time required for data entry. Concerns that patients had for mHealth included security risks, ease of use, and accuracy of disease prediction. Key features that patients expect for the future of mHealth included medical record consolidation, easier appointment scheduling and prescription refills, integration with wearable health monitoring devices, and facilitation of direct patient-to-patient and physician-to-patient communications. Future studies of mHealth will require a greater sample size to verify the validity of these concerns and find solutions to meet the future expectations of mHealth.

Keywords: mHealth · Acceptance · Application

1 Introduction

The term eHealth has been used interchangeably by individuals of various academic intuitions, health facilities, professional bodies, and funding organizations [1]. Even as the term became recognized internationally, a unanimous agreed upon definition has yet to be determined [1]. In a systematic review of eHealth bibliographic databases, it was determined that the term carried 2 universal themes of health and technology. In particular, it has become widely accepted that eHealth is the utilization of "ICTs (information and communication technologies), including Internet technologies to manage health, arrange, deliver and account for care, and manage the health care system" [2]. In another

© Springer International Publishing AG, part of Springer Nature 2018
M. Kurosu (Ed.): HCI 2018, LNCS 10902, pp. 173–184, 2018.
https://doi.org/10.1007/978-3-319-91244-8_14

systematic review of eHealth impact on the quality and safe of health care, it was noted that there is a large gap between the hypothesized benefits of eHealth and the empirically demonstrated benefits [3]. Despite its promotion by many policymakers and tech enthusiasts, eHealth required further studying to fully comprehend its implementation risks as well as cost-effectiveness.

mHealth system is a category of eHealth that typically involves the implementation of a mobile device [4]. This specific category of eHealth has been maturing and evolving at a rapid rate for the past decade with the advances in mobile cellular technology and artificial intelligence. The full potential of mHealth has yet to be understood, but some practical applications of mHealth today include its implantation in the field of fitness and lifestyle application and its use as a tool to promote health monitoring in less developed regions of the globe, predominantly in Africa and South America [4]. Its adoption by health care professionals is becoming widespread on multiple levels of clinical practice such as information and time management, health record maintenance access, communications and consulting, and patient management and monitoring [5]. In a previous Research/Physician Channel Adoption Study, it was found that doctors' ownership and use of mobile devices is pervasive, with 87% using a smartphone or tablet device in their workplace, compared to the 99% using a computer [6]. The use of mobile applications in healthcare also extends to patients. It was estimated that 500 million patients will have utilized mobile applications in management of their health [7]. According to a survey done in 2012, the global penetration of cellular services and data use had reached 87% with no sign of decrease [8]. In the momentum of this mHealth burgeoning, it becomes ever more important to address our deficiencies in the lack of understanding of this area of research.

In 2015, number of mHealth related apps was estimated to be over 100,000 in the iOS App Store alone with 98.19% of those available to people living within the United States [9]. However, in a national cross-sectional survey conducted in 2015, it was found that only 58.23% of those sampled downloaded a health-related mobile app [10]. Even worse, 45.7% of those individuals eventually stopped using the application after one year. Interestingly, most of those surveyed felt that the apps had improved their health [10]. Previous research found several reasons why users discontinued their mhealth applications [11]. However, studies that demonstrate theoretical user acceptance factors of mHealh applications are limited. This is the first study with experimental design to evaluate the users' perspectives on mHealth applications.

2   Literature Review

Despite its recognition as a significant issue, the obesity epidemic continues to plague the United States. It was estimated that approximately 34% of the adult US population are obese [12]. Poor diet management was cited as one of the leading causes of obesity. Consequences of obesity include hypertension, hyperlipidemia, and type 2 diabetes [13]. The lack of available continuous health monitoring programs with physicians can be a contributing factor to this issue. A 2013 study focused on the use of mobile applications in diet and fluid intake self-monitoring of adults receiving hemodialysis [14]. In a six-week intervention program, 24 participants monitored their own diet and fluid intake through the use of the Dietary Intake Monitoring Application (DIMA). Results of the study suggested that intervention via the integration mHealth application is feasible. Similarly, mobile applications were studied as tools for personal lifestyle check-up and improvement suggestions [15]. A 23-question survey was presented based on items in the Korean National Health and Nutrition Examination Survey (KNHANES). Data from 25,124 participants were analyzed and it was concluded that the difference between participants' usual lifestyles and lifestyles after using the program was statistically significant. People also reported of greater motivation to continually make improvements to their own lifestyle after using the program. During office visits with physicians, a very limited amount of time is spent on weight-loss counseling and lifestyle choices [16]. Commercially available mobile applications were analyzed and were found to have the potential to improve factors such as motivation and stress management. Despite evidence for the practical application of mHealth, the issues of integration and acceptance remain.

VTT Technical Research Centre of Finland studied the user acceptance of mobile services based on a series of case studies [17]. A Technology Acceptance Model for Mobile Services was formed based on the case studies. According to the model, user acceptance is built on three factors: perceived value of the service, perceived ease of use, and trust. Midwives in rural Ghana were studied in the integration of mHealth in their daily care [11]. mHealth was found as a significant mechanism for improving the efficiency and effectiveness of their care, but participants felt that the interface would be too time intensive and cumbersome to use progressively. Currently, many mHealth intervention programs are designed on the basis of pre-existing healthcare system constructs that do not necessarily consider the consumers. These programs may not be as effective as those that involve the end users in the design process [18].

The accessibility of mHealth apps, in terms of their ease of use, was cited by multiple studies as being a key contributor, if not the top contributor, of an individual's determination in the consistent use of these applications [10]. People's perception of ease of use is defined to be the degree to which a certain system can be utilized free from additional effort [19]. Key system requirements can be identified when users are involved in the design process [18]. User-centered design (UCD) mHealth app was studied in a group of adolescents with type 1 diabetes [20]. The participants and their family caregivers were interviewed regarding their past experiences and UCD was then utilized to develop the mobile app bant. By the end of the study, it was concluded that the use of UCD and incentives increased frequency of blood glucose monitoring in adolescents and participants were more likely to take actions to improve their glycemic control. UCD can also be utilized as a tool for personal lifestyle check-up and improvement [15].

Perceived risk can be described consumers' sensitivity to possible losses while using the technology [20]. For mHealth users, the perceived risk is generally associated with the security of their private health information [21]. The Health Insurance Portability and Accountability Act (HIPAA) of 1996 is the standard security protocol to which all electronic health information is being regulated [22]. Typically, mHealth systems must conform to the standards of confidentiality, integrity, audit control, user authentication, and access control [22].

Security risks are becoming areas of concern for some individuals using mHealth applications. According to one survey, approximately 73% of physicians text other physicians regarding work related issues [23]. A concern amongst patients is that of the HIPAA privacy protection [24]. Potential threats to the breach of security include theft or loss of the mobile device, improper disposal of the device, and interception of transmission by unauthorized personnel [23]. This privacy concern extends to the use of mHealth applications. In 2013, University of Michigan studied the potential use of mobile applications in the care and management of diabetic patients [25]. Although mobile health apps have great potential for improving chronic disease care, they lacked integration and acceptance due to concerns regarding the threats to safety and privacy [25]. There are over 35,000 mHealth applications on the iOS and Android operating systems [26]. Of the 600 most commonly used apps, only 183 (30.5%) had privacy policies. Two thirds (66.1%) of privacy policies did not specifically address the app itself. The privacy policies that are available do not make information privacy practices transparent to users, require college-level literacy, and are often not focused on the app itself. A study of 256 participants across twenty-four groups measured consumers' attitudes and perceptions towards mHealth [27]. Findings had indicated that consumers were primarily concerned regarding the tradeoffs between the privacy/security of using and the potential benefits. In order to address the security concerns, it was recommended that health care providers and technology developers consider tailoring mHealth accordingly to various types of information in the health care setting, as well as according to the comfort, skills, and concerns individuals may have with mHealth technology [27].

mHealth can be also be viewed as a more secure platform of communication through data encryption [28]. mHealth had been successfully implemented as an intervention in children dealing with anxiety [28]. Patients engaged in cognitive behavioral therapy (CBT) directly with their therapists via mHealth apps. Goal setting with rewards increased patients' active participation with their therapists, leading to more successful outcomes.

In the study above, the SmartCAT app was able to successfully bypass traditional text message or email exchanges, which poses potential threats to security and confidentiality of sensitive health data [28]. Figure 1 demonstrates this protocol.

Given the prior evidence of positive effects, it is imperative that these mHealth apps be understood more closely in regard to an improved adoption rate. Ultimately, adoption will be based on the users' perceived value of mHealth. Research in the area of perceived value has been beset by "inadequate conceptualization and the lack of a validated scale" [29]. Six point-of-care applications were examined for their usability in a clinical setting on four different devices [30]. The applications studied included DynaMed, DynaMedPlus, Epocrates, Essential Evidence Plus, Medscape, and UpToDate. Overall, there was no significant difference between the various point-of-care tools with regard to information coverage. Selection of point-of-care tools was found to be highly dependent on the individual preference based on ease of use, perceived benefits, and perceived risks. Interviews with post hospital care patients are beneficial for insight into qualities of a mHealth application that are deemed "valuable" [31]. These values include, but not

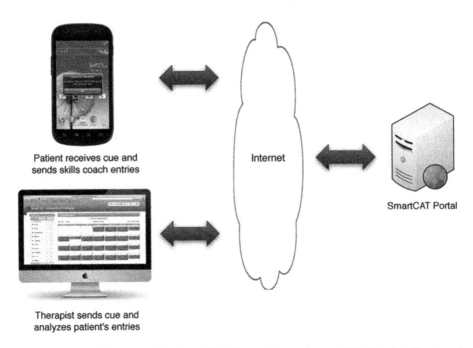

Fig. 1. Functional diagram of the SmartCAT (Smartphone-enhanced Child Anxiety Treatment) platform [28].

limited to, meeting basic accessibility, usability and security needs; encouraging patient-centeredness; facilitating better, more secure communications; and supporting personalized management by providers. Principal factors for mHealth acceptance in accordance with the literature are displayed in Table 1.

Table 1. Factors for mHealth acceptance in accordance with the literature review

Principal factors considered when using mHealth applications	References
Perceived ease of use	Kaasinen [17], McCurdie et al. [18], Cafazzo et al. [20], Curioso and Mechael [40], Estrin and Sim [41], Lewis and Wyatt [45], Jonas et al. [43], Curioso and Mechael [40]
Trust	Kaasinen [17], Pramana et al. [28], Zubaydi et al. [22], Bajwa [38], Arora et al. [21]
Perceived value of service	Kaasinen [17], Aranda-Jan et al. [37], Wildenbos et al. [49], Johnson et al. [30], Akter et al. [29]

3   Research Method

A qualitative study, face-to-face interview, was undertaken to collect users' information of mHealth application usage. Items of inquiry included the subject's hours of use on a mobile device, purpose of usage, uses of mobile device, previous experience with mHealth related applications, and expectations of mHealth apps in the future. The study was conducted with the consent of random patients who presented to the Physicians Regional Walk-in Clinic in Naples, FL. Physicians Regional Clinic was ultimately chosen because of the convenience of access as to the researchers. Twenty random patients, in total of 8 males and 12 females, were interviewed.

Ages of the participants ranged from 25–94 with 45% of these individuals over the age of 65. Of those sampled, individuals within the ages of 25–30 used their mobile devices for everything including communication, entertainment, and media consumption. On average, the patients in this group used their phone between 4–6 h. Individuals between the ages of 51–64 are generally those are still in the labor force and they typically see primary use of their mobile devices in communication and work-related activities with an average of 3–4 h of phone use daily. Those who were 67 years and older generally admitted that they were "casual phone users". Consistently, the participants in this group stated that they used their devices for communication and news update, but no more than 2 h of use daily.

4   Discussions

Responses from the twenty participants in this research were analyzed and the factors are shown in Table 2 in order of importance as noted by the interviewees.

Table 2. Factors for mHealth acceptance in accordance with patient interviews

Principal factors considered when using mHealth applications	References
Interface/Ease of use	Kaasinen [17], McCurdie et al. [18], Cafazzo et al. [20], Curioso and Mechael [40], Estrin and Sim [41], Lewis and Wyatt [45], Jonas et al. [43], Curioso and Mechael [40]
Scheduling for appointments/ Prescription refills	
Patient-to-physician communication/ Physician-to-physician communication	Pramana et al. [28]
Accuracy of diagnosis/Disease prediction	Alepis and Lambrinidis [33]
Integration with wearable health monitoring devices	Dobkin and Dorsch [34], Poon et al. [36], Mercer et al. [46]

It was found that sixteen had cited ease of use or ease of learning a new interface as an expectation for them to accept mHealth applications into their daily routine. Perceived of use was discussed as a major contributing factor in the literature review. It is important to note that some of the participants of the study that had past experience with mHealth as a diagnostic tool found that the diction of these apps can be confusing or difficult to understand. In particular, one patient noted, "Sometimes it's frustrating having to look up a certain term and be taken out of the app to do so." Information presentation is equally as important as the quality of information in enticing users to continually dedicate time for mHealth apps. Engaging users in the design process can significantly improve patient adherence to use of these mobile applications [18].

Integrating appointment scheduling and prescription refills into mHealth apps are functionalities that have not been fully explored in past studies. Patients noted the difficulty of scheduling for appointments especially during the months when Florida sees an increase in its population due to the influx of patients from the north. One patient surveyed states that she tried calling the scheduling center but was given an appointment in 3 months for an acute bronchitis that needed to be resolved as soon as possible. Patients who are not able to be scheduled with their usual primary care physician were given the option of seeing another physician or going to a walk-in-clinic. Neither option was optimal as these physicians lacked the information and understanding of the patient's past medical history. For instance, the patient above with bronchitis may have had a history of asthma or used an ACE inhibitor, which would have indicated cough as a potential side effect. Electronic health records have improved methods of recording patient records, but with a majority of patients reporting of less than 20 min spent with their physicians [32], there may not be adequate time for another physician to review the patient's complete medical records and address the pertinent issues. With mHealth applications, patients hope that future scheduling can be done on the urgency of medical issue. Patients expect that the mHealth system will be able to determine whether the issue is acute or chronic and whether the issue needed to be addressed immediately. Appointments can then be offered based on the nature of their issues. For simple issues such as prescription refills, patients hope that the system would be able to fill them if they have been taken on a long-term basis. For prescriptions that are tightly regulated, patients hope to establish a direct line of communication to their providers through mHealth, who will then determine if the patients should be seen immediately. This leads to the following factor taken into consideration: mHealth as a means of facilitating patient-to-physician communication.

As indicated in the study of CBT for children with anxiety disorders, mHealth was able to be successfully implanted as a communication device between the provider and the patient [28]. This achievement is extraordinary in that it was able to successfully merge the functions of an advanced online patient health portal with that of a mHealth app. In the interviews with patients, a majority (65%) had indicated integration with existing health portals as an expectation of future mHealth apps. Online health portals are essentially conduits to contacting their health providers. In the typical health portal, one can gain access to their lab results, vaccination records, and records of past visits. It can also sometimes be used as a means of contacting physicians through a secure messaging system. Four of the twenty patients interviewed had indicated that they were seasonal patients, which meant spending Winter months in Florida and the rest in their home state. They state that even though they would request medical records to be sent from their home state to providers in Florida, records would still sometimes be absent from their charts in Florida. Patients hope to extract medical records securely from their health portal to their mHealth app, then uploading that information to the other health portal that needs to be supplemented. In this manner, mHealth will have become a web of information, connecting patients' care teams nationally. One particular patient from Massachusetts noted the difficulty of having her different physicians in different states to agree on certain medical treatments. She hopes mHealth to also be utilized as a means of facilitating direct physician-to-physician communication. More research for this feature is required to ensure that the it can be compliant with HIPAA regulations.

Although seven of the twenty patients had expected mHealth as an accurate diagnostic tool in the future, there were five in the study that remained skeptical. One patient who had used mHealth to diagnose her husband noted that the app was unable to ask questions strictly pertaining to the experienced symptoms. The provided possible diagnoses were in various fields of medicine, which caused her to have more questions than answers. Some of the patients interviewed remained skeptical of the mHealth's future capability in this regard as it would lack the patients' medical records and would be unable to perform a physical exam. However, a past study has applied the concept of Analytical Hierarchical Process algorithm to infer the presence of an illness in the subjects, or lack thereof [33]. The system was able to extrapolate data from the corresponding subjects' electronic health records and incorporate this data into the system's decision making and diagnosis. A more advanced system is currently being studied to also incorporate patient's image related health tests, which include X-Rays, ultrasounds, and MRI's, Future integration of wearable health technologies may also potentiate the credibility of mHealth as a diagnostic tool.

"The great promise of mHealth is to enable evidence-based practices to wirelessly reach into the homes and communities of people who cannot readily or affordably access health care [34]." Three patients surveyed in this study noted active use of smartwatches in the tracking of their fitness routine. However, they state that they have not used the devices beyond simple tracking of steps taken and heart rate. Previous trials had indicated effectiveness of ankle triaxle accelerometers, gyroscopes, and pressure-sensitive textiles combined with wireless communication to provide monitoring of patients with impaired ambulation [34]. The live data received by patients' health providers allowed the clinicians to provide feedback for better self-management of home-based rehabilitation programs. High cost was cited as one of the chief reasons for the lack of widespread use of these devices. However, these sensor technologies are becoming increasingly integrated into our daily lives. As mentioned above, smartphones now are becoming natively equipped with sensor technology to measure the body's oxygen saturation and pulse. Even smartwatches are becoming integrated in the monitoring of home-based dementia patients [35]. Developments such as wearable cuff-based blood pressure monitor device can allow the clinical staff to continually observe variability in patients' vital signs remotely [36]. It's important to recognize that the future of mHealth may not be limited to certain mobile based applications, but the inclusion of multiple sensors and monitoring devices working in tandem with the app.

5 Conclusions

Applications involving mHealth have been maturing since 1995. However, it remains that there is no unanimous definition of mHealth. It can be understood that mHealth is an enabler of participatory health that includes not only mobile devices, but also possible add-on health monitoring applications. But with the rapid advancements of wireless communication technologies in the last decade, our understanding of mHealth has not yet reached the level to fully comprehend the full potential of mHealth and factors for greater user acceptance.

Through the extensive literature review, three dominant factors were found to have significant influence in users' decision to integrate mHealth applications. These include perceived ease of use, trust, and perceived value of service. Patients who were interviewed in this study listed five principal reasons that they believe were integral for the acceptance of mHealth. These factors included ease of interface, appointment scheduling, physician communication, accuracy of disease prediction, and integration with existing wearable health monitoring device. New findings from the patient interviews can expand upon the value of service as noted in the literature review. These additional features include the app's native ability to communicate with healthcare providers, refill prescriptions and schedule appointments, and accurately predicate acute diseases. Strangely, security was not a primary concern amongst the patients that were interviewed. A greater sample size will be required to validate these findings.

This study addressed some new patient concerns regarding mHealth generally not found in past studies. As there are still gaps within our understanding of mHealth and its full potential, fellow researchers can utilize the information from these interviews to further expand upon the existing foundation of mHealth. Besides conducting additional surveys, researchers can examine the plausibility of these future mHealth expectations and find ways to fulfill these expectations. mHealth is still in the nascent stage of development and proliferation. However, it has the potential to improve the care of healthcare providers. It may be possible for providers to continuously monitor vitals of critical care patients or communicate directly with other physicians to work out a plan of care straight from the mHealth application.

Limitations of this study include the small sample size, limit of a single clinic as area of research, and the majority of the city population being greater than 65 years of age and are generally less integrated with the advances of modern smartphone technologies. Future studies should streamline the survey to random participants from around the country. Focus should be placed on perfecting the interface module of the mHealth application. Prior research has shown the effectiveness of mHealth apps in improving the health of individuals who continued consistent use of the app [15]. Unfortunately, many individuals cease use of these applications within the first year [10]. Patients sampled in this study point to laborious interface as the main reason for discontinuation of use. This was also cited as one of the main reasons for discontinuation of use by a previous study [11]. The development and implementation of a successful mHealth application interface will be critical to the future of our healthcare.

References

1. Oh, H., Rizo, C., Enkin, M., Jadad, A.: What is eHealth (3): a systematic review of published definitions. J. Med. Internet Res. **7**, e1 (2005)
2. Pagliari, C., Sloan, D., Gregor, P., Sullivan, F., Detmer, D., Kahan, J.P., MacGillivray, S.: What is eHealth (4): a scoping exercise to map the field. J. Med. Internet Res. **7**, e9 (2005)
3. Black, A.D., Car, J., Pagliari, C., Anandan, C., Cresswell, K., Bokun, T., Sheikh, A.: The impact of eHealth on the quality and safety of health care: a systematic overview. PLoS Med. **18**, e1000387 (2011)
4. Waegemann, C.P.: mHealth: history, analysis, and implementation. In: Moumtzoglou, A. (ed.) M-Health Innovations for Patient-Centered Care, pp. 1–19. Medical Information Science Reference, Hershey (2016)
5. Tomlinson, M., Rotheram-Borus, M.J., Swartz, L., Tsai, C.A.: Scaling up mHealth: where is the evidence? PLOS Med. **10**, e1001382 (2013)
6. Ventola, C.L.: Mobile devices and apps for health care professionals: uses and benefits. Pharm. Ther. **39**, 356 (2014)
7. Ghose, S., Littman-Quinn, R., Kyer, A., Mazhani, L., Seymour, A., Kovarik, C.L., Anolik, R.B.: Use of mobile learning by resident physicians in Botswana. Telemed. e-Health **18**, 11–13 (2012)
8. van Heerden, A., Tomlinson, M., Swartz, L.: Point of care in your pocket: a research agenda for the field of m-health. Bull. World Health Organ. **90**, 393–394 (2012)
9. Xu, W., Liu, Y.: mHealthApps: a repository and database of mobile health apps. JMIR Mhealth Uhealth **3**, e28 (2015)
10. Krebs, P., Duncan, D.T.: Health app use among US mobile phone owners: a national survey. JMIR Mhealth Uhealth **3**, e101 (2015)
11. Velez, O., Okyere, P.B., Kanter, A.S., Bakken, S.A.: Usability study of a mobile health application for rural Ghanaian midwives. J. Midwifery Womens Health **59**, 184–191 (2014)
12. Mitchell, N., Catenacci, V., Wyatt, H.R., Hill, J.O.: Obesity: overview of an epidemic. Psychiatr. Clin. North Am. **34**, 717–732 (2012)
13. Ogden, C.L., Carroll, M.D., Kit, B.K., Flegal, K.M.: Prevalence of obesity in the United States, 2009-2010. Centers for Disease Control and Prevention (2012)
14. Welch, J.L., Astroth, K.S., Perkins, S.M., Johnson, C.S., Connelly, K., Siek, K., Scott, L.L.: Using a mobile application to self-monitor diet and fluid intake among adults receiving hemodialysis. Res. Nurs. Health **36**, 284–298 (2013)
15. Youm, S., Park, S.H.: Development and evaluation of a mobile application for personal lifestyle check-up and improvement. Telemed. e-Health **20**(11), 1057–1063 (2014)
16. Pagoto, S., Schneider, K., Jojic, M., DeBiasse, M., Mann, D.: Evidence-based strategies in weight-loss mobile apps. Am. J. Prev. Med. **45**(5), 576–582 (2013)
17. Kaasinen, E.: User acceptance of mobile services - value, ease of use, trust and ease of adoption, Espoo (2005)
18. McCurdie, T., Taneva, S., Casselman, M., Yeung, M., McDaniel, C., Ho, W., Cafazzo, J.: mHealth consumer apps the case for user-centered design. Biomed. Instr. Technol. **46**, 49–56 (2012)
19. Schnall, R., Higgins, T., Brown, W., Carballo-Dieguez, A., Bakken, S.: Trust, perceived risk, perceived ease of use and perceived usefulness as factors related to mHealth technology use. Student Health Technol. Inf. **216**, 467 (2015)
20. Cafazzo, J.A., Casselman, M., Hamming, N., Katzman, D.K., Palmert, M.R.: Design of an mHealth app for the self-management of adolescent Type 1 diabetes: a pilot study. J. Med. Internet Res. **14**(3), e70 (2012)

21. Arora, S., Yttri, J., Nilsen, W.: Privacy and security in mobile health (mHealth) research. ARCR **36**, 143–151 (2014)
22. Zubaydi, F., Saleh, A., Aloul, F., Sagahyroon, A.: Security of mobile health (mHealth) systems. In: IEEE Xplore Digital Library (2016)
23. Greene, A.H.: HIPAA compliance for clinician texting. J. AHIMA **83**(4), 34–36 (2012)
24. Centers for Disease Control and Prevention: HIPAA privacy rule and public health. Guidance from CDC and the US. Department of Health and Human Services. MMWR Morb. Mortal. Wkly. Rep. (2003)
25. Lee, J.M., Eng, D.S.: The promise and peril of mobile health applications for diabetes and endocrinology. Pediatr. Diabetes **14**, 231–238 (2013)
26. Sunyaev, A., Dehling, T., Taylor, P., Mandl, K.: Availability and quality of mobile health app privacy policies. J. Am. Med. Inf. Assoc. **22**, e28–e33 (2014)
27. Atienza, A., Zarcadoolas, C., Vaughon, W., Hughes, P., Patel, V., Chou, S., Pritts, J.: Consumer attitudes and perceptions on mHealth privacy and security: findings from a mixed-methods study. J. Health Commun. **20**(6), 673–679 (2015)
28. Pramana, G., Parmanto, B., Kendall, P.C., Silk, J.S.: The SmartCAT: an m-Health platform for ecological momentary intervention in child anxiety treatment. Telemed. J. e-Health **20**, 419–427 (2014)
29. Akter, S., D'Ambra, J., Ray, P.: Development and validation of an instrument to measure user perceived service quality of mHealth. Inf. Manage. **50**, 181–195 (2013)
30. Johnson, E., Ren, J., Emani, V.: Breadth of coverage, ease of use, and quality of mobile point-of-care tool information summaries: an evaluation. JMIR mHealth uHealth **4**, e117 (2016)
31. Sanger, P., Hartzler, A., Lober, W., Evans, H., Pratt, W.: Design considerations for post-acute care mHealth: patient perspectives. In: AMIA Annual Symposium Proceedings, pp. 1920–1929, 14 November 2014
32. Lin, C.-T., Albertson, G.A., Schilling, L.M., Cyran, E.M., Anderson, S.N., Ware, L., Anderson, R.J.: Is patients' perception of time spent with the physician a determinant of ambulatory patient satisfaction? Arch. Internal Med. **161**, 1437–1442 (2001)
33. Alepis, E., Lambrinidis, C.: M-health: supporting automated diagnosis and electonic health records. SpringerPlus **2**, 103 (2013)
34. Dobkin, B.H., Dorsch, A.: The promise of mHealth: daily activity monitoring and outcome assessments by wearable sensors. Neurorehabil. Neural Repair **25**, 788–798 (2011)
35. Boletsis, C., McCallum, S., Landmark, B.F.: The use of smartwatches for health monitoring in home-based dementia care. In: Zhou, J., Salvendy, G. (eds.) DUXU 2015. LNCS, vol. 9194, pp. 15–26. Springer, Cham (2015). https://doi.org/10.1007/978-3-319-20913-5_2
36. Poon, C.C., Wong, Y.M., Zhang, Y.: M-Health: the development of cuff-less and wearable blood pressure meters for use in body sensor networks. In: IEEE Xplore Digital Library (2006)
37. Aranda-Jan, C.B., Mohutsiwa-Dibe, N., Loukanova, S.: Systematic review on what works, what does not work and why of implementation of mobile health (mHealth) projects in Africa. BMC Public Health **14**, 188 (2014)
38. Bajwa, M.: mHealth security. Pak. J. Med. Sci. **30**, 904–907 (2014)
39. Conway, N., Campbell, I., Paula, F., Cunningham, S., Wake, D.: mHealth applications for diabetes: user preference and implications for app development. Health Inf. J. **22**, 1111–1120 (2015)
40. Curioso, W.H., Mechael, P.N.: Enhancing 'M-Health' with south-to-south collaborations. Health Aff. **29**, 264–267 (2009)
41. Estrin, D., Sim, I.: Open mHealth architecture: an engine for health care innovation. Science **330**, 759–760 (2010)

42. Hamida, S.T.-B., Hamida, E.B., Ahmed, B.: A new mHealth communication framework for use in wearable WBANs and mobile technologies. Sensors **15**, 3379–3408 (2015)

43. Jonas, S.M., Deserno, T.M., Buhimschi, C.S., Makin, J., Choma, M.A., Buhimschi, I.A.: Smartphone-based diagnostic for preeclampsia: an mHealth solution for administering the Congo Red Dot (CRD) test in settings with limited resources. J. Am. Med. Inf. Assoc. **23**, 166–173 (2016)

44. Khalid, H., Shihab, E., Nagappan, M., Hassan, A.E.: What do mobile app users complain about? IEEE Softw. **32**, 70–77 (2014)

45. Lewis, T.L., Wyatt, J.C.: mHealth and mobile medical apps: a framework to assess risk and promote safer use. J. Med. Internet Res. **16**, 210 (2014)

46. Mercer, K., Giangregorio, L., Schneider, E., Chilana, P., Li, M., Grindrod, K.: Acceptance of commercially available wearable activity trackers among adults aged over 50 and with chronic illness: a mixed-methods evaluation. JMIR mHealth uHealth **4**, e7 (2016)

47. Naples city, Florida Demographics. Retrieved from United States Census Bureau (2016). https://www.census.gov/quickfacts/fact/table/naplescityflorida/PST045216

48. Sherry, J.M., Ratzan, S.C.: Measurement and evaluation outcomes for mHealth communication: don't we have an app for that? J. Health Commun. **17**, 1–3 (2012)

49. Wildenbos, G.A., Peute, L.W., Jaspers, M.W.: A framework for evaluating mHealth tools for older patients on usability. Stud. Health Technol. Inf. **210**, 783–787 (2015)

Healthy Hankerings: Motivating Adolescents to Combat Obesity with a Mobile Application

Farzana Rahman[1(✉)], Paul Henninger[2], David Kegley[2], Keegan Sullivan[2], and James Yoo[2]

[1] Florida International University, Miami, FL 33172, USA
farahman@fiu.edu
[2] James Madison University, Harrisonburg, VA 22807, USA

Abstract. Obesity has become a major public health issue in most countries around the world. In addition, adolescent obesity is increasing in an alarming rate all over the world. Many attempts have been made to address this issue that ranges from doing exercise to following a diet plan to playing games. While the existence of the above works indicates the past and ongoing efforts to combat adolescent obesity, they are clearly not enough since it is still rising. Researchers have found that adolescent obesity controlling has a lot to do with combating unhealthy cravings that needs strong will power and motivation at such an age. Often, young people and their caregiver struggle to find healthy and nutritious recipes that would fulfill the craving of young people. In order to motivate unfit adolescents towards healthy eating, our research tries to provide them with alternative tasty yet healthier food options using a mobile application. In this paper, we present the design and development details of a mobile application, *Healthy Hankerings*, which has the potential to help deal with adolescent obesity by motivating its users to choose a healthier food option when they have craving for unhealthy or junk food. To find a healthy recipe, the application uses a recognition algorithm, a decision tree based learning algorithm that considers user's meal intake history and current cravings. To evaluate our application, we also present the usability study of the prototype in this paper.

Keywords: Mobile application · Obesity · Healthcare · Decision tree
Yummly database

1 Introduction

In recent years, obesity has become a major health problem in the world that affects people of all ages [6]. Adolescent obesity has increased to epidemic levels in recent decades [6]. It can lead to problems including increased risk of cardiovascular disease, diabetes, and cancer in addition to psychosocial problems, functional limitations, and disabilities. Many attempts have been made to address the adolescent obesity issue that involves taking medication, doing exercise, dieting or playing games.

The main challenge in any healthcare related application lies in both sparking a subject's interest and then sustaining it to produce sustained improvements. The advantage of using motivation and social connection to motivate versus techniques such as gaming is

© Springer International Publishing AG, part of Springer Nature 2018
M. Kurosu (Ed.): HCI 2018, LNCS 10902, pp. 185–194, 2018.
https://doi.org/10.1007/978-3-319-91244-8_15

that friends and social acquaintances theoretically can sustain interest over long periods through social interaction. Game motivators will often lose user interest over time unless continuous novel changes are introduced. Researchers and practitioners have also advocated for a combination of approaches, such as following a diet plan and exercise [6, 7]. While the existence of the above works indicates the past and ongoing efforts to combat adolescent obesity, they are clearly not enough since it is still rising. Researchers have found that adolescent obesity control has a lot to do with combating unhealthy cravings that needs strong will power and motivation at such an age [9].

The emergence of personal mobile devices and the potential for Smartphone applications to improve adolescents' eating behaviors is promising, given existing evidence that mobile phone-based interventions can influence health-related behaviors. Along this avenue, we have developed an application that targets adolescents towards combating obesity. In order to motivate unfit adolescents towards healthy eating, our research tries to provide them with alternative tasty yet healthier food options using a mobile application.

Our Contribution: In this paper, we present the design and development details of a mobile application, ***Healthy Hankerings***, which has the potential to help deal with adolescent obesity by motivating its users to choose a healthier food option when they have craving for unhealthy or junk food. The idea is based on the fact that cravings are often unhealthy, and providing healthy options could potentially help adolescent satisfy their cravings without eating unhealthy foods. To find a healthy recipe, the application uses a recognition algorithm, a decision tree based learning algorithm that considers user's meal intake history and current cravings.

Features in Our Application: Healthy Hankerings takes in users' personal food hankering at any given time and provides healthy recipes that fit users' immediate preference. It lets people discover healthy recipes based on their current cravings. In addition to this main feature, we included a grocery store locater and a custom recipe maker, taking a picture of their prepared meal and a social connection with peer feature. In our application, rather than entering in a specific food item, the user goes through a quick and fun process of selecting various flavors. We then run a query in our database, selecting recipes that are healthy and that match with the user's preferences. Another innovative feature of our app is that it completes the entire cycle of creating a food dish. We provide the recipe, the directions to the grocery store, option to share in social platform to motivate connected friends in healthy eating.

The rest of the paper is organized as follows: Sect. 2 describes relevant related work. Section 3 briefly presents the development details of our application. Section 4 presents the prototype implementation of the application. Section 5 presents usability study results of the prototype's user interface. Finally, Sect. 6 concludes the paper.

2   Background and Related Work

The use of smart-phones as a tool for achieving improved healthier lifestyle is on the rise, which makes mobile health technology a very promising field. There are several noteworthy apps which had significant research invested behind the development i.e. Kalico [1]. This app helps users to instantly make a healthy choice in restaurants while keeping within the budget. A study on effectivity of mobile technology to support healthy eating habit among ethnic minority students [5] proved that such interventions facilitate healthier practices using data gathered from this project. MyBehavior [4] is one such recommendation system that operationalized theories from behavior change literature i.e. low-effort [3] and self-efficacy [2] into machine-learning optimization functions to generate suggestions based on automatically logged data from the phone sensors. A 14-week study on 16 participants showed significant improvement in physical activity and dietary measures while using this app. There are a number of apps that are also focused on recipes. For instance, there is ChefTap, an app that imports recipes from websites. ChefTap is different from our app because the user selects specific recipes. It is more about organizing recipes than finding new ones. Another competitor app is Fooducate Healthy Weight Loss. Fooducate allows user to scan barcodes to see what is in your food. It has the capability to provide healthy alternatives that is what we aim to do as well. While Fooducate focuses strictly on weight loss, which has been found to be demotivating after some time to adolescent user base, Healthy Hankerings is a more casual way to help user find a healthier recipe.

3   Design and Development of Healthy Hankerings

The design diagram of Healthy Hankerings application is shown in Fig. 1. The User Interface (UI) module resides in the user's device and it works like a client application. The UI takes input from the user and communicates with a Decision Maker (DM) module in cloud. The DM is the most important module of the application since this is in charge of using a decision tree based learning algorithm [10], which generates the keywords (i.e. ingredients, cuisine and etc.) to search the database for a healthy meal recipe that satisfies user's current cravings. The DM module communicates with the Database module retrieves recipe result, which is then replayed back to the user.

The home screen of the application is implemented with a button in the center and a menu in the top right corner allowing the user to access the grocery store finder and the custom recipe creator. Within menu, there is two other activities-one corresponding to meal history and another corresponding to sharing in social network. In the main activity, there is a button "what am I hankering?" which in turn takes user to enter their cravings in another activity. The taste, spice, and cuisine activities are implemented with radio buttons. After the user submits all the craving options, they are saved using shared preferences. The recipe results activity is started, which gets the user input from shared preferences. The user input is passed on to the Decision Maker (DM) module in the cloud. The DM module then uses user cravings input along with users' previous meal intake history to create a decision tree. This decision tree then generates some key ingredients, which is then used to run a query on the database using an HTTP get request. An HTTP response, along with a healthy recipe, generated based on the learned DM modules output, is sent back to the activity, which is parsed to display the title, a picture,

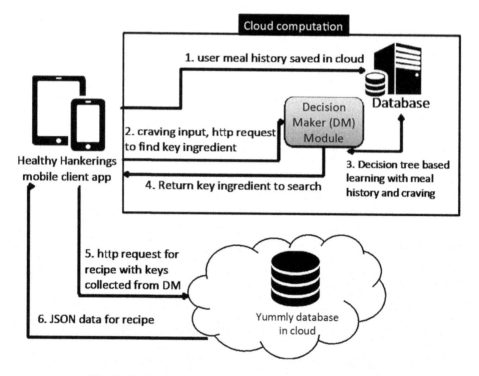

Fig. 1. System design and architecture of Healthy Hankerings

and a link to the recipe. The development details of the app are briefly described in the following subsections.

3.1 Decision Tree Based Learning to Select Healthy Recipes

We use Decision Tree to train our DM module, which allows us to generate healthy keywords to be used to search the database. Decision tree are either classification trees or regression trees. If the sample for the training is given then the decision tree algorithm make trees, which has leaves containing the classification results. With a proper training dataset, the decision tree going to use a correct path from the root of the tree to the correct leave by taking step by step decisions in every branches beforehand.

The DM module is naïve at the beginning without any prior history input. The users are encouraged to enter their consumed meals couple of times a day which is stored in the cloud for training the DM. With time, as the DM module learns more information (i.e. consumed meals) about user, it can train itself to provide better key ingredients which in turn can search better recipes from the database. Since the DM does not have any meal history the first time, it uses some random key ingredients along with user craving input to generate a decision tree. Every time, user searches a healthy recipe using this app is also stored in DM module for future training. For example, if the user has consumed French fries in the past and the current craving of the user is (savory, medium spicy, American cuisine), then the decision tree in our case uses vegetable, fry, spicy as a the key ingredients to search in the database. When a query is made with these key ingredients, the database in turn determines Spicy Zucchini Fry as the output and redirects this recipe to the user.

3.2 Finding Recipe Using Yummly Database

The Yummly database is an integral part of our application. Users can select their desired tastes, spice levels, and cuisine and then receive recipes. The DM module of Healthy Hankerings connects to the Yummly database by performing an HTTP Get request, passing in the information provided by the DM module. Connecting to the database involves opening an HTTPClient through android and sending a request to the Yummly API The response is a JSON object which we then parse and create POJOs (Plain Old Java Objects). Once we have the list of recipes, we are then able to display a list of recipes on the results page. Results are shown along with a picture of the returned recipe and a link to the yummly site where the user can view the recipe in its entirety.

3.3 Custom Food Imaging with Camera Sensor

In our application, we have used camera sensor for our custom recipe feature. We allowed users to be able to take a picture of their own recipe and add its information to a local database so that it could be found after a new search. We implemented a camera feature that took a picture and displayed that image of the custom recipe page by launching camera intent and saving the image to the device and take that source's name to the image view.

3.4 Social Connection Capabilities

As we described in the application design, in order to allow for social interaction the menu activity of the application displays all stories posted by friends of the active user. The users are allowed to share the healthy recipes they have searched. They are also allowed to share the picture of the healthy meal prepared using the recipe so the connected friends can get motivated and interested to try this instead of the unhealthy meal. For example, in case of our spicy zucchini fries, the shared post will contain the recipe link of spicy zucchini fry. The post will also contain "Try zucchini fry instead of French fry". If a user taps on a friend's name within the news feed, that user's profile is displayed with latest updates from last two days. If there is no update from a friend in last two days, the activity provides an option to the user to post a "poke" message with any new healthy recipe tried within last 7 days. The healthy recipe list tried in last 7 days are displayed as a list to the user which can be selected and posted on this friend's profile with the hope that the friend might be interested in trying this meal.

Our social connection feature also maintains a scoreboard, which lists the top 5 users who have searched for most number of healthy recipes in a week. This feature helps the user to be in a healthy competition where they want to try different healthy recipes. In future, we would like to make the scoreboard more efficient by considering who have posted picture of a prepared healthy meal, and who have helped their peers by posting a poke message.

4   Prototype Implementation

As a first step towards validating our proposal, we created a prototype application that allows users to navigate through the various activities. In our app, the home screen includes a large button in the center with our logo. Pressing this button starts the recipe discovering process. After starting, there are three screens of food options (corresponding to taste, spice and cuisine) that require selecting one option per screen. Once complete, the user presses the "What am I hankering?" button to get the recipe.

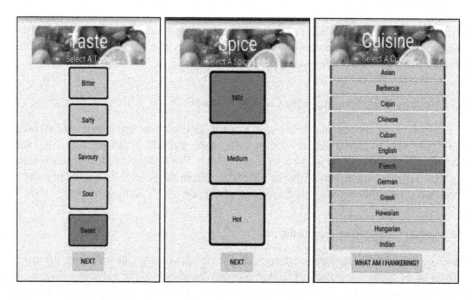

Fig. 2. Select taste, spice, and cuisine to find recipes for craving

Since, the decision maker module has no user data points the first time, it presents a recipe based only on the user choice of taste, spice and cuisine. With time the DM module learns user meal intake history and uses those to train the decision tree to provide better keywords to search the database for better recipe matching user's interest. The recipe screen shows the name of the recipe, a picture, and a link to the ingredients and instructions. To train the decision maker module, the user can go to the meals tab and enter various meals taken at different times of the day. Once some of the meal items are entered, the data is used to train the model and from then on the decision tree is used to determine a healthy recipe considering user's previous food choices and current craving (taste, spice, cuisine). At any point the user can press the menu button in the top right corner of the screen to access the grocery store finder page, custom recipe page and social connection page. Figure 2 through Fig. 4 shows the various screens of our prototype (Fig. 3).

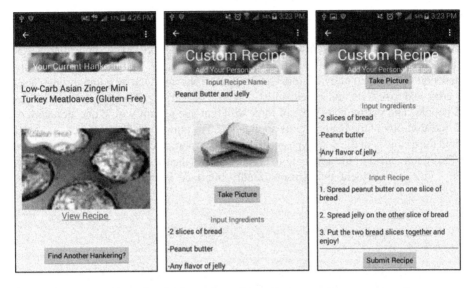

Fig. 3. [left to right] display recipe, taking picture, creating a custom recipe

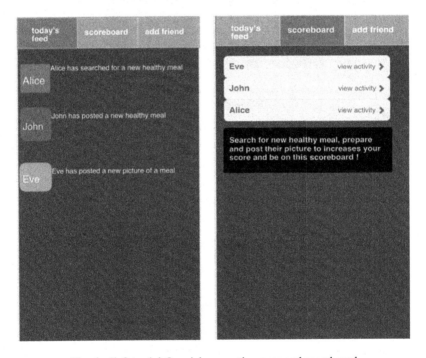

Fig. 4. [left to right] social connection page and scoreboard

5   User Study of the Prototype

In order to evaluate the ***usability*** of the Healthy Hankerings prototype application's user interface, we have used the cognitive walkthrough strategy. This strategy [8] encompasses one or a group of evaluators who inspect a user interface by going through a set of tasks and assess its understandability and ease of learning. The survey included the 25 people. The participants were of three different age groups with a questionnaire of 17 questions about the feature of the application. The questionnaire contained questions about the usability of the prototype and the overall importance of certain concepts related to the effectiveness of the application. Figure 5 shows the survey results. From the graph (Fig. 5(a)) it is evident that a user-friendly interface is the most important feature

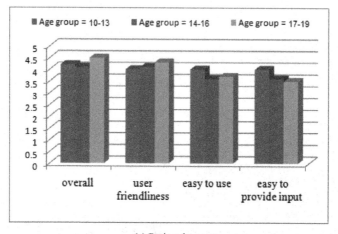

(a) Ratings by users

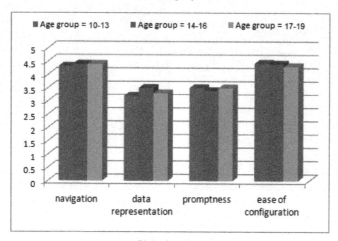

(b) Ratings by users

Fig. 5. Usability study results of Healthy Hankerings app

according to the users. The category shown in Fig. 5(b) reveals that the prototype requires enhancement in data representation and promptness from which we can infer that we need to minimize our computation in the cloud decision maker module and query searching in the Yummly database. Both of these issues are part of future research directions.

6 Discussion on Evaluation Methodology

In order to evaluate the effectiveness of Healthy Hankerings application in combating obesity, we intend to conduct human subject studies. We are currently applying for IRB approval to conduct such studies. There are numbers of NIH initiatives to support obesity prevention in the past have specified that the primary outcomes must include a measure of weight and/or Body Mass Index (BMI) as one of the primary outcomes. For our study, we intend to study middle/high/college school students. We plan to recruit sample with various age, BMI index, height, race, educational backgrounds. Furthermore, we plan to recruit two groups of students: those with normal weights and those with weight/ obesity issues. For both, we would let them keep a track of their food/meal intakes weeks before trying our applications so that we can investigate if our application provides motivations for them to change their meal preferences.

7 Conclusion

In this paper, we present the design and development of an application, healthy hankering, which is targeted to help control obesity by promoting and motivating healthy eating among young adolescent. A future research direction is to include a feature of physical activity to help control obesity. We plan to have a participating user invite friends to view his/her physical activity achievements and meal intakes so they can form teams to compete with one another to achieve a certain weight goal milestone. Additionally, we intend to conduct a large-scale evaluation of our application with a control group consisting of population with normal weight and over weight so we can determine if our system can have an impact on the target population.

For citations of references, we prefer the use of square brackets and consecutive numbers. Citations using labels or the author/year convention are also acceptable. The following bibliography provides a sample reference list with entries for journal articles [1], an LNCS chapter [2], a book [3], proceedings without editors [4], as well as a URL [5].

References

1. Anwar, M., Hill, E., Skujins, J., Huynh, K., Doss, C.: A smartphone application for health-smart menu selection within a budget. In: Proceedings of ICSH, pp. 113–121 (2013)
2. Bandura, A., McClelland, D.C.: Social Learning Theory. Springer, Berlin (2013). https://doi.org/10.1007/978-3-642-28753-4

3. Fogg, B.J.: A behavior model for persuasive design. In: Proceedings of Persuasive 2009, pp. 40:1–40:7, New York (2009)

4. Rabbi, M., Aung, M.H., Zhang, M., Choudhury, T.: Mybehavior: automatic personalized health feedback from user behaviors and preferences using smartphones. In: Proceedings of UbiComp 2015, pp. 707–718 (2015)

5. Rodgers, R.F., Pernal, W., Matsumoto, A., Shiyko, M., Intille, S., Franko, D.L.: Capitalizing on mobile technology to support healthy eating in ethnic minority college students. J. Am. Coll. Health **64**(2), 125–132 (2016). PMID: 26630479

6. National Heart Lung and Blood Institute (NHLBI) Obesity Education Initiative, The Practical Guide to the Identification, Evaluation and Treatment of Overweight and Obesity in Adults. NIH Publication Number 00-4084 (2000)

7. Puska, P., Nishida, C., Porter, D.: Obesity and overweight, world health organization (who) - global strategy on diet, physical activity and health fact sheets. Fact Sheet 2 (2003)

8. http://www.pages.drexel.edu/~zwz22/CognWalk.htm

9. Adler, N.E., Stewart, J.: Reducing obesity: motivating action while not blaming the victim. Milbank Q. **87**(1), 49–70 (2009)

10. Safavian, S.R., Landgrebe, D.: A survey of decision tree classifier methodology. IEEE Trans. Syst. Man Cybern. **21**(3), 660–674 (1991)

Research on Office Chair Based on Modern Office Posture

Xinxin Sun[(✉)], Xiaoyan Lan, Di Zhou, and Bin Jiang

School of Design Arts & Media, Nanjing University of Science and Technology,
Xuanwu Area, Nanjing 210094, China
`sunxinxinde@126.com`

Abstract. The office sitting position of the staff is closely related to the design of the office chair. We use the dynamic capture system of Microsoft Kinect sensor to study office sitting posture, in order to capture sitting posture and form three-dimensional coordinate data and RGB images, and then with the help of GBR and FCM methods to cluster Kinect data in MTATLAB data analysis software, getting the average sitting posture and sitting position type and transformation rules. The results show that there are four types of office posture. The data shows that these four types of postures can be divided into skill posture, adaptive posture and initiative attitude, and then analyzed corresponding task scene, office tasks and office equipment. Category 1 posture scenario is using computer, which belongs to the skill posture. Category 2 posture scene is mobile working, which is initiative attitude; Category 3 posture scene is to talking on the phone, belonging to the adaptive posture; Category 4 pose is a rest scene, belonging to the adaptive posture. The time of Category 1 of changing sitting position is 11.6 min; The time of Category 2 of changing sitting position is 13.7 min; the time of Category 3 of changing sitting position is 2.8 min; the time of Category 4 of changing sitting position is 17.2 min.

Keywords: Behavior clustering · Sitting posture · Kinect sensor
Office chair

1 Introduction

Office chair is one of the most intimate office furniture that contact with the body. The body in the seat will vary in sitting posture according to the task, and the comfort of the body. Design of improve the comfort for the human sitting posture has always been a major task in furniture design because ergonomic sitting can cause uncomfortable or low levels of comfort and easily lead to diseases such as lumbar muscle strain [1]. The prevention of such diseases requires regular exercise and correct sitting posture [2]. At the same time, office tasks have a significant impact on the posture, and understanding the impact of the tasks on the posture will enable designers to better design chairs to improve office comfort and productivity [3]. In addition, due to the greater differences in work posture among individuals [4], the richness of posture is even greater. Therefore, it is necessary to obtain the average posture from the abundant and different sitting postures, and to study the interdependence and interaction between the user's

© Springer International Publishing AG, part of Springer Nature 2018
M. Kurosu (Ed.): HCI 2018, LNCS 10902, pp. 195–205, 2018.
https://doi.org/10.1007/978-3-319-91244-8_16

sitting posture, the task and the design attributes of the chair, so as to develop the functional design of the chair according to the current user's sitting habits.

In the global research project of the Steelcase in the United States, the observation method was used to cluster the posture photographs of the global workers using office equipment, and nine kinds of sitting behavior were obtained, so as to design a chair that emulates the user's body activity. Bull focuses on the postures and gestures that people use to communicate with each other in their seats, by using photographs, sketches and videos, recording the tilt and position of the body's torso, hands on hips and body open degree, and through the method of role-playing, interpreting the user's posture and gesture in a design way [5]. Graf studies data of user's sitting behavior in two hours, generates matrices based on the position of the shoulders, spine, upper body and legs, and divides data into 5 types [6]. In the above studies, the observer only relies on photos and videos to cluster the behavior posture by his own senses, which requires strong classification ability of the observer. At the same time, many researchers place sensors on the backrest and the seat of chair to study the relationship between the pressure distribution and the sitting posture [7]. However, this method is vulnerable to external instability factors such as ambient noise, deviation and crosstalk, and the pressure distribution is not only related to sitting posture, but also subject to body shape, weight and the location of sitting, causing the resulting data is difficult to understand [8]. Grafsgaard believes that kinect is a non-intrusive device for experimental environments and does not affect user behavior. And the accuracy of human posture recognition is high enough to capture small movements that are usually overlooked or very difficult to classify during manual observation [9]. Therefore, it has become a new turn of research to analyze human sitting posture objectively by Kinect sensing technology.

However, the current domestic research is still inadequate: First, there is insufficient research on the clustering of office sitting posture; Second, the application of Kinect sensors are more used in the field of computer [10] and interactive design [11], but less in the study of furniture design. Therefore, in this study, Kinect dynamic capture system is introduced into the study of sitting posture, and the 3D coordinate data and RGB image are formed by using the task-setting Kinect device to capture the office posture. The GBR and FCM methods are used to cluster the data in the MTATLAB data analysis software, and the average posture of each class is obtained, and then the task types and the transformation rules of the office sitting posture are analyzed.

2   Sitting Posture Experiment

2.1   Experimental Equipment

This experiment uses the Microsoft's Kinect V1.0 sensor device to capture office sitting posture. The device has an infrared laser transmitter and an infrared camera with its own depth sensor, which provides the third dimension of range data [12]. When users make different actions on the seat, Kinect can track the coordinates of the user's joints and retrieve the angle information of the skeleton, so as to realize the recognition of the human posture. The steps include: (1) acquiring the 3D coordinate data of the points of human joint relative to the Kinect skeletal coordinate system; (2) transforming the captured 3D skeletal coordinate system into the 2D coordinate system of the screen; (3) constructing the human skeleton according to the human skeletal topology, and presented it as an image [13].

Kinect uses 3D space coordinates, the origin of which ($x = 0$, $y = 0$, $z = 0$) is defined at the center of the infrared camera of the Kinect in the experiment; the x-axis direction is the left direction of the vertical Kinect irradiation; The y-axis direction is the upward direction along the Kinect irradiation direction; the z-axis direction is the irradiation direction along the Kinect.

2.2 Experimental Subjects

The experiment selected fifteen subjects who were healthy, no humpback phenomenon and cervical, lumbar discomfort, including eight males and seven females. Their mean age was 30.5 years, of whom 8 were 20–29 years old and 7 were 30–40 years old. The subjects were all knowledge workers in Nanjing whose jobs were quite different. Their daily office hours were about 8–9 h and office equipment are mainly laptops or desktop computers.

2.3 Experimental Environment

In order to improve the accuracy of posture capture, reduce the interference to users and make the users present the office sitting posture in the real scene, and beneficial to the experimenters to observe and record the testing process, the experiment was conducted in a user research laboratory with unidirectional glass, empty interior and flat ground. There is no obstruction between the Kinect device and the user's seat, and the distance between them was 1 m. Laboratory provided the subjects with desks, office chairs, desktop computers, laptops, tablets, mobile phones, etc. to simulate the real office scene. Among them, the experiment using breathable mesh high-back office chair, brand mymaioffice, with rotating, lifting features.

2.4 Custom Mark Human Body Joints

In experiments, Kinect was programmed by the Processing software [14], which set the device to automatically capture the human sitting posture and three-dimensional coordinate data every second. Images were saved in Jpg format and each point of human joint data was saved as an Excel file.

Custom label every key points of the tester's movement, and customize the device to label the data of head, left hand, right hand, left elbow, right elbow, left foot, right foot, left hip bone, right hip bone, left Knee, right knee, left shoulder, right shoulder, neck and torso.

2.5 Experimental Process

In this study, the subjects were arranged to the experimental room, and adjust the office chair to a comfortable height at first. Then the subjects made the action of outstretching arms while they kept standing and the test for catching joint points was carried on by Kinect. After the joint points catching displayed normally on the computer, the subjects were arranged to sit on the appointed office chairs to do their daily office tasks with each subject tested for an hour, as shown in Fig. 1. The experimental process was recorded into video throughout. The experimenter observed the Kinect test displayed on the computer interface on the other side of the unidirectional glass. Then get the three-dimensional coordinate data.

Fig. 1. The experimental process

3 Data Analysis

As described in Sect. 2.4, a total of 15 body joint sites were collected for three-dimensional position information in this experiment. For Kinect only collects the (X, Y) two-dimensional information on the trunk area, the depth information Z is lacking. Therefore, we only selected the three-dimensional position information of the remaining 14 body joints except the trunk area for further analysis. The body joint data set in this experiment is $R^{7178 \times 42}$, where 7178 is the number of all acquired gestures and 42 (14 × 3) is the data dimension of each posture.

Because of the lack of data class label information for the body-joint data sets used, in order to classify all the acquired postures accurately, the experiment was performed according to the following steps: Firstly, GBR (Graph-based relaxed clustering) method is used to determine the number of clusters in the body joint data set R; then according to the determined number of clusters, the FCM clustering method is used to segment the body joint data set accurately, and the corresponding class label is marked on each data sample.

All experiments were performed in Matlab, 2.4 GHz Intel Core i5, 4 GB 1600 MHz DDR3.

3.1 Determination of Cluster Number of Body Joint Data Set

In the experiment, we first use the graph-based relaxed clustering method GBR to determine the cluster number of the body joint data set $R = [v_1, v_2, \ldots, v_{7178}]$. Specific steps are as follows:

Step 1:   According to formula (1)–(3), calculate the Laplace matrix L of data matrix R

$$D(i, i) = \sum_{j}^{N} W(i,j), \quad i = 1, 2, \ldots, N; \quad j = 1, 2, \ldots, N. \tag{1}$$

$$W(i,j) = \exp\left(\frac{-\delta(v_i, v_j)^2}{2\sigma^2}\right), \sigma > 0 \tag{2}$$

$$L = D - W \tag{3}$$

Wherein: $\delta(.)$ denotes similarity function, σ denotes Gaussian kernel bandwidth, and v_i & v_j respectively denotes two different sample vectors in the body joint data set R.

Step 2:   Convert clustering problem of data set R into quadratic programming problem as shown in formula (4):

$$\begin{aligned} &\min y^T L y \\ &\text{s.t. } Ay = \varphi, \ \varphi \neq 0. \end{aligned} \tag{4}$$

Wherein, y denotes the constraint solution, that is, the number of clusters in the body joint data set R; A denotes e^T, $(e^T = (1, 1, \ldots 1))$; φ denotes the truth value of the sum of the elements of the constrained solution y. Through the analysis and derivation, the optimal solution y^* of formula (4) is:

$$y^* = (AL^{-1})^T (AL^{-1}A^T)\varphi \tag{5}$$

In this experiment, y^* represents the optimal cluster number of body joint data set R.

3.2 Body Joint Data Set Clustering

After formula (5) determines the clustering number y^* of body joint data sets R, the fuzzy C-means clustering FCM algorithm can be used to cluster data sets R accurately and classify each sample with a label. The principle of the FCM algorithm is to minimize the objective function shown in formula (6):

$$J_m = \sum_{i=1}^{7178} \sum_{j=1}^{C} \mu_{ij}^m \|v_i - c_j\|^2, \quad 1 \leq m < \infty \tag{6}$$

$$\sum_{i=1}^{C} \mu_{ij} = 1, \quad \forall j = 1, 2, \ldots, N \tag{7}$$

Wherein m is the fuzzy index and v_i is the i th data sample measured, μ_{ij} indicates v_i belonging to membership of category j, c_j is the cluster center of class j, C is the number of clusters of data set, and $||.||$ means the similarity between any measured data and cluster center.

Divided the body joint data set $R = [v_1, v_2, \ldots, v_{7178}]$ into y^* categories, the specific steps are as follows:

Step 1: Initialize the membership matrix U, so that it satisfies the constraints in formula (7).

Step 2: Calculate the center vector:

$$c_j = \frac{\sum_{i=1}^{N} u_{ij}^m \cdot v_i}{\sum_{i=1}^{N} u_{ij}^m} \tag{8}$$

Step 3: Update membership matrix:

$$u_{ij} = \frac{1}{\sum_{k=1}^{c} \left(\frac{||v_i - c_j||}{||v_i - c_k||} \right)^{\frac{2}{m-1}}} \tag{9}$$

Step 4: If $||U^{(k+1)} - U^{(k)}|| < \varepsilon$, stop the iteration, where ε is the threshold. Otherwise, go back to step two

According to the above steps, the body joint data set R is clustered, and after the FCM converges, the corresponding class label of each sample can be automatically obtained.

4   Results and Analysis

4.1   Clustering of Sitting Posture

By using the GBR method in Sect. 2.1, the optimal cluster number for the body joint data set $R = [v_1, v_2, \ldots, v_{7178}]$ is determined to be $y^* = 4$. For the convenience of displaying, after dividing 7,178 gestures into 4 classes using the FCM method in Sect. 2.2, this experiment also averaged the postures of each class and shown the resulting average posture for each class. Specific results are as follows:

(1) Class 1, see Fig. 2(a), the average sitting posture obtained is that the arm is stretched forward and has no point of contact with the seat, legs is drooping, the torso is leaning forward, and the head is advanced.

(2) Class 2, see Fig. 2(b), the average sitting posture obtained is that the body leans back against the backrest, with both hands facing inwardly, arms resting on the armrests, and the legs dropping.

(3) Class 3, see Fig. 2(c), the average sitting posture obtained is that the user tilted back, legs stretched, one hand close to the head, the head tilted to one side, the other hand placed on the armrest.

4) Class 4, see Fig. 2(d), the average sitting posture obtained is that the body lean back on the backrest with both hands resting on the armrests, the head resting on the headrest and the legs extending forward.

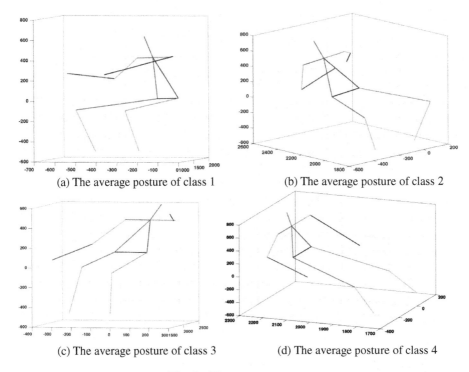

(a) The average posture of class 1   (b) The average posture of class 2

(c) The average posture of class 3   (d) The average posture of class 4

Fig. 2. The average posture

4.2   The Task Types of Office Sitting Posture

Office tasks is the main reason for affecting office sitting posture. The tasks posture of knowledge workers are subdivided into task proficiency (e.g. ensuring that core tasks are properly completed), task adaptability (e.g. adapting to new equipment and processes in core tasks) and task initiative (e.g. developing new approaches to core tasks) [15]. Chair as a tool to support the completion of the office tasks, the office posture of users on which can be divided into three types according to their tasks: skill posture, adaptive posture and initiative posture. In this way, the four main types of office posture obtained above are explained in task.

As shown in Table 1, skill posture refers to the trained or repeated skilled behaviors performed by the user in order to complete the work tasks, as shown in the type 1, which the users present in using the desktop or laptop computers; initiative posture refers to the self-creation behavior of users using mobile devices such as smart phones and tablets in the process of completing their work tasks, as shown in Type 2, which the user present for more convenient operation of the smart phone; Adaptive posture refers to behavior that the user dependent on the existing furniture products, to complete the work, rest and other tasks, such as type 3 posture is in the scene of the user in the office process to answer the phone, and type 4 refers to the user with office chairs, handrails, headrests and other components, present the sitting posture on rest state in the office process.

It can be seen from the current office sitting posture, posture scenes of office equipment and tasks will affect the type of office sitting posture. The skills required to operate the computer are high, requiring the user to pay the most attention, and rest requires minimal attention. The attention required for mobile office and dialing is between the two.

Human body as a set of integrated system change in the office process, taking an interlinked approach [16]. Therefore, the design of the chair needs to be integrated with the sitting posture in different scenes to better assist the user to achieve sitting posture transformation and optimize the office experience.

Table 1. Mission analysis of posture type

	Posture type 1	Posture type 2	Posture type 3	Posture type 4
Posture scene	Operate the computer	Mobile office	Answer the call	Rest
Task type	Skill posture	Initiative posture	Adaptive posture	Adaptive posture
Attention level	Highest	Medium +	Medium +	Lowest
Office equipment	Desktop computer, laptop	Tablet, smart phone	Phone, smart phone	———

4.3   Sitting Posture Transformation and Time

Although the body size varies greatly from person to person, the overall variation pattern of human sitting posture is consistent [17, 18]. The experiment edit the recorded office video of 15 subjects, extract four types of postures as separate video files, analyze four office posture duration and sitting conversions and draw the following.

(1) Type 1, this type of posture is derived from the use of computer that people need to tap the keyboard and look at the screen so that the torso is tilted forward. The desktop and keyboard can not provide support for the user's elbows and forearms, which is mainly caused by the force on the bottom of the hips and thighs. This kind of posture needs worker to pay more attention to in order to pursue higher work efficiency. The subjects usually adopt this posture at the beginning stage. The average time of changing sitting position is 11.6 min; and then torso alternately tilted forward and backward to relieve fatigue.

(2) Type 2, the body is more relaxed at this moment, which perform leaning backward, one hand and seat armrest contact, lumbar curve arc is more relaxed than the type 1 due to the relatively soothing sitting position at this time and mainly the buttocks and back by force. With the immersion of a tablet and phone, the average time of posture shift was 13.7 min, holding longer than type 1. The left and right arms will alternate as a support point to relieve the arm fatigue.

(3) Type 3, the user answered the phone in the office process, interrupted the previous task and the trunk lean forward, legs stretched out, one hand closed to the head, the other arm elbow placed in the Seat armrests. The average time of changing sitting position is 2.8 min, and the torso alternately tilts forward and backward to relieve fatigue.

(4) Type 4, with the trunk leaning back, the subject puts both hands on the armrests instead of touching the table and rests his head on the headrest, legs slightly stretch forward. Users have the most contact points with office seats at this time. All parts of the body can be supported by the office seat and lumbar curve is the most relaxed arc. The average time of changing sitting posture is longest and reach for 17.2 min, and then conversion of both feet support position.

Therefore, the change of workers' posture is the result of both the purposefulness and the subconscious adjustment. In the design process, the structure of the office chair should be in accordance with the sitting activity as much as possible for the user in office will lean on the backrest and place arms on the armrest of the seat to use the mobile phone and the tablet for a long time. The emergence of these new postures puts forward new needs and design opportunities for chair design. For example, the design needs to consider to provide appropriate armrest height, increase the width of the adjustment range and armrest angle adjustment function, in order to provide the corresponding support.

5 Conclusion

The research of this paper aims to improve the design insight of the changing rules of sitting posture under the multitask type of knowledge workers. Therefore, the Kinect dynamic capture system is introduced into the study of office sitting posture. The conclusions of the experiments are as follows:

(1) People's sitting posture is not a fixed way. There are four types of office sitting posture, each type contains abundant subtypes. The positions of posture transformation are mainly concentrated in the trunk, arms and legs, see Fig. 2.

(2) The posture and transformation behavior of knowledge workers are affected by their work tasks. In accordance with the tasks, the four types of sitting posture is divided into skill posture, adaptive posture and initiative posture. Type 1 posture is the scene of operate the computer, belonging to the skill posture; type 2 posture is the scene of mobile office, belonging to the initiative posture; type 3 posture is the scene of answer the phone, belongs to the adaptive posture; type 4 posture is the scene of rest, belongs to the adaptive posture. Knowledge work includes a variety of tasks and chair design needs to support corresponding postures and actions of various tasks.

(3) Based on the experimental video, we analyzed the duration and sitting transformation of four kinds of sitting posture, and concluded that sitting duration of type 1 was 11.6 min, and then the trunk alternately lean forwards and backwards. The average time of changing sitting posture of type 2 was 13.7 min, and then the left and right arms alternately transformed; the average time of changing sitting posture of type 3 was 2.8 min, and then the trunk alternately lean forwards and backwards; the average time of sitting duration of type 4 was the longest, reaching 17.2 min, and then feet transformed to support position.

(4) Office chairs needs to be compatible with sitting posture in the structure and function for the user's regular sitting habits and subconscious adjustments, to provide adequate compatibility and ensure adjustable and comfortable of a variety of posture.

Acknowledgement. The authors are grateful for the financial support provided by "The general project of Humanities and social sciences of Ministry of Education" (17YJA760022).

References

1. Vink, P., Hallbeck, S.: Comfort and discomfort studies demonstrate the need for a new model. Ergonomics **44**(8), 781–794 (2012)
2. Van Dieën, J.H., De Looze, M.P., Hermans, V.: Effects of dynamic office chairs on trunk kinematics, trunk extensor EMG and spinal shrinkage. Ergonomics **44**(7), 739–750 (2001)
3. Groenesteijn, L., Ellegast, R.P., Keller, K., et al.: Office task effects on comfort and body dynamics in five dynamic office chairs. Appl. Ergonomics **43**(2), 320–328 (2012)
4. Ebe, K., Griffin, M.J.: Factors affecting static seat cushion comfort. Ergonomics **44**(10), 901–921 (2001)
5. Bull, P.E.: Posture & Gesture, pp. 20–25. Elsevier (2016)
6. Graf, M., Guggenbühl, U., Krueger, H.: An assessment of seated activity and postures at five workplaces. Int. J. Ind. Ergon. **15**(2), 81–90 (1995)
7. Zhu, M., Martinez, A.M., Tan, H.Z.: Template-based recognition of static sitting postures. In: 2003 Conference on Computer Vision and Pattern Recognition Workshop, CVPRW 2003, vol. 5, pp. 50. IEEE (2003)
8. Xu, W., Huang, M.C., Amini, N., et al.: eCushion: a textile pressure sensor array design and calibration for sitting posture analysis. IEEE Sens. J. **13**(10), 3926–3934 (2013)
9. Grafsgaard, J.F., Boyer, K.E., Wiebe, E.N., et al.: Analyzing posture and affect in task-oriented tutoring. In: FLAIRS Conference (2012)
10. Meng, M., Yang, F.B., She, Q.S., et al.: Human motion detection based on the depth image of Kinect. Chin. J. Sci. Instrum. **36**(2), 386–393 (2015)
11. Wang, Y., Zhang, Z.Q.: Gesture recognition based on kinect depth information. J. Beijing Inf. Sci. Technol. Univ. **28**(1), 22–26 (2013). (Natural science edition)
12. Cao, G.G., Cao, L.: Human motion recognition based on skeletal information of Kinect sensor. Comput. Simul. **31**(12), 329–333 (2014)
13. Li, H.B., Ding, L.J., Ran, G.Y.: Analysis of human identification based on Kinect depth image. Digital Telecommun. **39**(4), 21–26 (2012)
14. Han, J., Shao, L., Xu, D., et al.: Enhanced computer vision with microsoft kinect sensor: a review. IEEE Trans. Cybern. **43**(5), 1318–1334 (2013)

15. Xie, J., Wang, L.: Empowering leadership, trust in supervisor and knowledge workers task behavior: evidence from a survey. South China J. Econ. **32**(1), 77–88 (2014)
16. Xu, J.F., Zhang, H.N., Cui, T.J.: Office chair design and creation based on sitting behavior. Packag. Eng. **8**, 52–56 (2013)
17. Huang, L., Yang, Y., Peng, B.: Three-dimensional parametric modeling of human body for analysis of seat comfort. J. Eng. Graph. **32**(1), 10–15 (2011)
18. Yang, H.B., Jiang, H.M., Wang, X.: Research of health office chair design based on ergonomics. Design. **2**, 24–25 (2012)

Eudaimonic Gamification to Engage Cancer Patients in Positive Coping Strategies

João Ventura[1], Sandy Ingram[1(✉)], Maurizio Caon[1], Maya Zumstein-Shaha[2], Omar Abou Khaled[1], and Elena Mugellini[1]

[1] University of Applied Sciences and Arts Western Switzerland, Fribourg, Switzerland
{joao.ventura,sandy.ingram,maurizio.caon,omarabou.khaled,
elena.mugellini}@hes-so.ch
[2] Department of Applied Research and Development in Nursing,
Bern University of Applied Sciences, Bern, Switzerland
maya.zumsteinshaha@bfh.ch

Abstract. This paper presents a mobile gamified application encouraging positive coping strategies for patients of serious and possibly fatal illnesses. The application concept is based on the analogy between one's lifetime memories and future bucket lists and a journey in the sea of remembrance, traveling back and forth between past and present positive moments and future wish-lists, whilst being aware that life as water, goes on. This concept was co-designed by a team of UX researchers, engineers, and domain experts applying the principles of Eudaimonic design. The iterative development process brought to the final prototype: a multimedia diary with a gameful interface, which is thoroughly described, along with the relative heuristic and empirical evaluations, in this paper.

Keywords: Gamification · Co-design · Ehealth · Eudaimonic design
Palliative care

1 Introduction

Technology is nowadays pervasive and ubiquitous, profoundly shaping human life. It should be designed to assist individuals in improving the quality of their lives. In particular, following the "positive technology" concept, the quality of experience should become the guiding principle in the design and development of new technologies [1]. However, often the development of technology aiming at providing a quality experience and support the flourishing of users is not thought in the context of the end of life. In particular, despite the popularity of video-games and gamification, it is rare to find digital solutions that are designed for people nearing death adopting a "gameful" approach. In the scientific literature, it is possible to find some works concerning the development of serious games designed for people affected by a life-threatening disease. For example, "Time After Time" is a serious game designed to educate men diagnosed with localized prostate cancer about their condition and support them in taking decisions about their treatment [2]. Similarly, "mHealth TLC" is an interactive health game that coaches lung cancer patients toward assertive communication strategies during first-person virtual clinics visits [3]. Another

© Springer International Publishing AG, part of Springer Nature 2018
M. Kurosu (Ed.): HCI 2018, LNCS 10902, pp. 206–218, 2018.
https://doi.org/10.1007/978-3-319-91244-8_17

popular example is "Re-Mission", which is a game designed to engage young cancer patients through entertaining game play while impacting specific psychological and behavioural outcomes associated with successful cancer treatment [4]. These examples are indeed designed for people affected by cancer with their life at risk, but they aim at supporting the coping with the treatment or the disease itself, rather than with death. An outstanding example of game designed to guide the player through the analysis of death is "That Dragon, Cancer" [5]. This is an immersive, narrative videogame that retells Joel Green's 4-year fight against cancer through about two hours of poetic, imaginative gameplay that explores themes of death, hope and love.

This paper presents the result of an interdisciplinary work focused on eudaimonic design, between the department of applied research in nursing of the Bern University of applied sciences, and the "HumanTech" institute of the Fribourg university of applied sciences. A mobile storytelling application targeting patients with life threatening diseases, is developed to promote positive coping strategies using a gamification approach.

The remainder of this paper is structured as follows: the next Section reports the different types of coping strategies that can be developed by people affected by fatal illness. Afterwards, Sect. 3 is dedicated to the description of the concept of Eudaimonic design. The following section, presents the concept and how the application design has been thought to empower the users in order to adopt the positive strategies to cope with the finitude of life. Section 5 reports the entire iterative design process performed by the interdisciplinary team and the relative heuristic and empirical evaluations. The final section contains the conclusion and the next steps of this project, which aims at evaluating this mobile application with actual cancer patients.

2   Coping Strategies

Cancer remains associated with a potential fatal outcome, despite tremendous advances in diagnostics and treatment. Patients with cancer experience shock and disruption in the short and long term. Once diagnosed with this disease, patients can experience thoughts about death, anxiety and fear as well as a modification in their outlook on life in general.

When confronted with life threatening diseases such as Cancer, people develop different coping strategies, some of which are reported in the literature, as positive, and some others as negative. Among the positive coping strategies are realising one's achievements and maintaining and enlarging one's social support network. Denying the disease or its impact on life is considered to be one of the negative coping strategies. For patients to better manage the confrontation with life's finitude, mobilising positive coping strategies can be helpful.

Six main coping strategies were found in the literature, three are considered positive (Group A) and three negative (Group B). Referring to [6–8].

Group A is composed of the following strategies:

- Palliative: reducing stress doing something enjoyable.
- Optimism: positive thinking.
- Facing the situation: constructive resolution of problems.

Group B is composed of the following strategies:

- Fatalism: Pessimism, loss of hope, feeling a lack of control of the situation.
- Avoidance: Avoid or delay the confrontation to the problem.
- Emotion centered coping: Releasing emotions, impulsiveness, auto-accusation.

To date, existential concerns in cancer patients are not systematically assessed. No specific interventions promoting the mobilisation of positive coping strategies are regularly proposed to support cancer patients. Current trends in digitalisation and gamified design are interesting and propose alternatives to traditional interventions. Hence, it is warranted to develop and test a digital gamified application aiming to promote the mobilisation of positive coping strategies for cancer patients.

3   Gamification and Eudaimonic Design

Gamification was originally defined as "the use of game design elements in non-game contexts" [9]. The application's specific context requires a design with a meaning. Eudaimonic design inspired the whole design process. Aristotle's concept of Eudaimonia refers to "human flourishing" and is defined as "the autotelic, self-determined exercise and perfection of one's innate capacities for its own sake and proper pleasure" [10]. Eudaimonic design is defined as the process of creating potential tools for "positive design" actively supporting human flourishing. Applying this principle, gamification is not anymore a mere integration of game mechanics in the system, but focuses on the experience and what is called "social software" and empowerment, passing from the deterministic stimulus-effect pattern to the theories of game enjoyment, "from designing games as interventions deployed within certain contexts, to designing contexts as interventions, informed by game design" [10].

4   Application Concept

The general concept is based on the analogy between one's lifetime memories and future bucket lists and a journey in the sea of remembrance, traveling back and forth between past and present positive moments and future wish-lists, whilst being aware that life as water, goes on. The application has been thought as a personal diary or multimedia album where the user can shed light on the most meaningful moments of her past and present life, reflect on and share future plan. The principles of Eudaimonic design guided the development of this concept, which aims at providing the user with an empowering tool enabling self-reflection and transforming remembrance in a coping strategy while providing a pleasant experience. The tempo and the "room" or space that each shared moment or thought takes, is decided by the user. The interface presents a customisable boat in a sea with four icons on the bottom part of the screen (Fig. 1). The user can touch the screen to navigate forward or backward. The sea is divided in sections. Each section represents a specific period of the user's life and they are also represented on the bar in the right-hand top corner of the screen; the sections are customisable (Fig. 1). The user can drag and drop each of the four icons on the bottom part of the screen, to create a new multimedia "memo". This memory can be a text, a picture, an audio file or a video (Fig. 2).

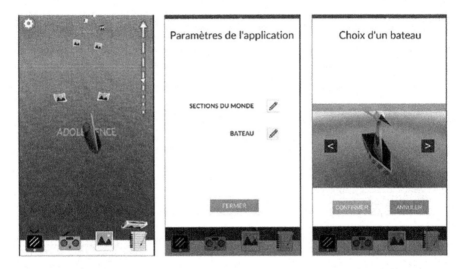

Fig. 1. User interface of the developed application with the option to personalize the boat travelling across life moments.

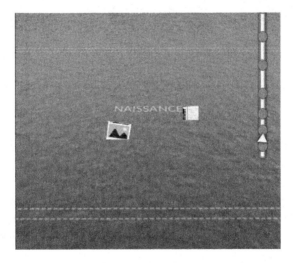

Fig. 2. This image shows two memos of different types, floating in the sea, within a specific region ("birth"), along with customizable navigation bars.

This application supports the aforementioned positive coping strategies: it allows facing the current situation allowing the user to express her feelings through the personalisation of multimedia content and life episodes. The default section concerned with actual patient's illness is particularly useful in encouraging the patient to face and discuss his illness. The application design supports optimism as it allows users to reflect on their accomplishments, to remember the people they loved and think of the good moments; finally, the application was designed to be also palliative providing a default life section dedicated to the user's future to be used as bucket list or to plan future important activities (e.g., travels or family reunions). The particular interface based on the boat metaphor with multimedia contents also aims at providing an enjoyable experience designed to have a less formal and tedious interaction than standard electronic diaries, leveraging again the palliative coping strategy (Fig. 3).

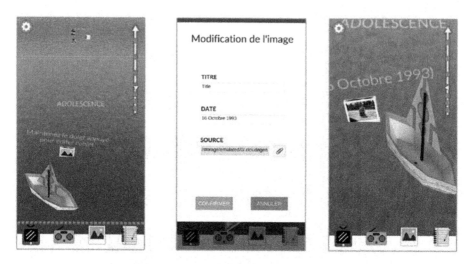

Fig. 3. Creating a memo: modifying a labeled image.

5   Design Process

An iterative design process is adopted. The process focuses on positive coping strategies, and positive reinforcement as opposed to negative punishment. The overall flow of the design process is as described in the following sub-sections and depicted in Fig. 4.

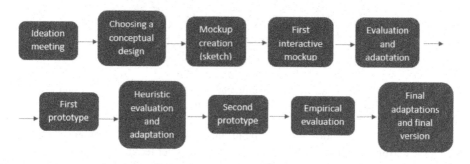

Fig. 4. Design process flow.

5.1 Conceptual Design

An ideation session was organized to find and discuss design alternatives, which were later grouped in an affinity diagram. After consulting with the health partner, the idea of an interactive diary that can be shared with others, was chosen. A mobile application immersing the user in a game-like environment was conceived. The health research partner indeed reported patients' need to maintain a diary during their treatment, reinforcing the concept's adequacy and strength. The user (the patient) controls a boat in a 3D world, navigating in a 2D plane of water. The vertical axis of the world represents an open-ended timeline of the user's life, starting at the user's birth continuing to his/her future. The user's birth is a suggestion by default, knowing that timeline events can be redefined so that they stop earlier or after the user's birth. As the user navigates in his/her boat, along the past, present, and future sections on the timeline, he/she can drag and drop artefacts or memos in the water. Four types of artifacts are supported: video, recording, image and text (Fig. 5). The concept design covers the four positive strategies presented in Sect. 2. The palliative strategy is covered by the upper part of the world as the future section can be thought of as a bucket list and a way of planning a trip or other activities. The confrontation strategy is covered by inciting users to express their feelings, thoughts and talk about their daily challenges; an explicit section dedicated to the patient's illness is defined by default. The palliative and optimistic strategy is covered, by also emphasizing the future section, and encouraging user to define a bucket list, mention future trips and plans in general.

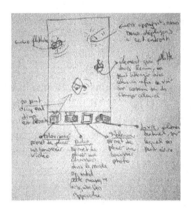

Fig. 5. First sketch of the conceptual design.

The first prototype consisted of an interactive mid-fidelity mockup developed using Unity. This mockup lets the user navigate with a primitive boat by tapping on the screen (Fig. 6). The user could also choose a type of memo out of four possible options, define it, and drop it into the water. The application "world" was not yet divided into separate timeline regions.

A small survey was conducted to examine whether the perceived usefulness of lower bar with the four memo types and to assess the chosen icons' usability and affordance.

Fig. 6. First interactive mockup.

The conclusions were that the two of the chosen icons were hardly understandable, more specifically the icons representing the text and image media types, and so alternatives were found in the second prototype.

5.2 Second Application Prototype

The second prototype was a high-fidelity one developed in Unity 3D, built for Android, and covering all functionalities (Fig. 7). All interactions were more precisely defined using use case diagrams and storyboards. The two problematic icons were changed, and the notion of sections was introduced. The world was separated in 7 sections as a reference to the "seven seas". These sections are: before birth, birth, childhood, adolescence, adulthood, illness and future.

5.3 Heuristic Evaluation

A heuristic evaluation conducted on the second prototype, helped identifying key usability issues. Each feature of the application was examined by two usability experts and the health partner as a domain expert, and the following problems were discovered:

- The newly added bar at the top lacked usefulness. It presented N (north) and S (south) marks at each end which were deemed inappropriate for the temporal representation of the world.

Fig. 7. Second prototype with location awareness, the two rightmost icons have been changed. A polaroid represents the image media and a notebook represents the text media.

- The representation of world artefacts was independent of the user's proximity to them; one would expect to get more information about each artefact as we approach it.
- There was a lack of user guidance towards the action that can be undertaken.

The following interactions with the four objects were implemented: place in the world (via drag and drop), consult, edit content (add metadata such title, date and artefact URL), delete. An additional bar was added at the top right corner, making the user aware of the timeline region, their boat is currently in.

5.4   Third Application Prototype

The third prototype tackled the problems reported in the heuristic evaluation as well as introduce few new features.

The following adaptations were done:

- The bar at the top don't present the N and S marks anymore and a "fast travel" function was added when the user presses on one of the points in the bar for a certain number of seconds.

- When pressing one of the elements of the bottom bar, immediate feedback is provided: the chosen element slightly moves up showing the user that it is currently being selected.
- The artefact or memo edition interfaces was changed to be full screen rather than occupy a small portion of the screen to facilitate edition and improve readability (Fig. 8).

Fig. 8. Changes made to the size of elements

- As the user boat approaches dropped "memos", a tooltip appears displaying the memo title and date. For the graphical media (image, video) a small preview of the content is displayed directly at the memo location.

  The following new features were added:

- The possibility to change the position of already dragged & dropped world artefacts.
- A Zoom feature activated by pinching.
- An introductory popup displayed once during the first usage of the application (Fig. 9 left).
- A setting that let the user rename and resize each default section of the world timeline (Fig. 9 right).

5.5   Empirical Usability Evaluation

A usability test was organized to evaluate the usability of the third prototype. 9 subjects, were involved. Subjects were given a set of actions to accomplish, covering all the application features. They were then invited to rate the difficulty of accomplishing each

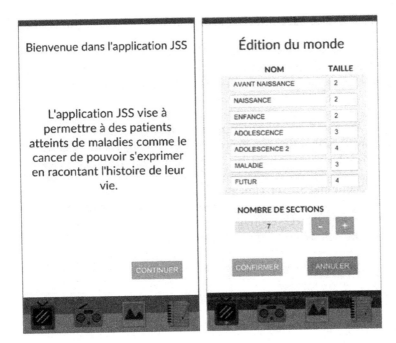

Fig. 9. Introductory message (left) and section modification menu (right).

required action in a scale from 1 to 10, 1 being "succeeded from the first try" and 10 being "didn't succeed". Users could also comment on each action performed.

This empirical evaluation shed lights on the features that required usability improvements. Each action performed is listed below followed by its evaluation results:

Move Around in the World: the average difficulty of performing this task was 2.11/10 with values ranging from 1 to 4. 3 out of 9 subjects succeeded from the first trial. Two subjects commented that they would prefer that the boat continued to move forward for as long as the finger was pressed on the screen, rather than having to tap and release the finger for each new direction. One of the subjects thought at first that you had to move the boat with your finger by drag & drop (as is the case for dropped artefacts). A change was made to the prototype in which the boat follows the finger of the user if it is touching the screen.

Drop an Artefact in the World: the average difficulty of performing this task was 1.78/10 with values ranging from 1 to 4, 6 out of 9 subjects were able to deposit an artefact or "memo" in the sea world from the first attempt. Two subjects started by tapping, but since the "memo" is automatically moved upwards they could understand that it was necessary to drag & drop it.

Assign Content to an Artefact: the average difficulty of this task was 3.56/10 with values ranging from 1 to 5. 3/9 subjects reported the fact that it took too long to open the content edition menu (the waiting time being set during this prototype at 2 s as a default value), as such the time to open the menu was reduced by half prior to the evaluation.

View the Content of an Artefact: the average difficulty of performing this task was 1.78/10, with values ranging from 1 to 5, 6/9 subjects were successful from the first try. One subject was not able to view the videos.

Remove an Artefact from the Environment: the average difficulty of performing this task was 1.56/10, with values ranging from 1 to 3, 5/9 subjects were successful from the first trial. One subject first pressed the "X" button (a button that simply closes the menu).

Modify the Name and Size of Timeline Sections: the average difficulty of performing this task was 1.67/10 with values ranging from 1 to 5, 78% of the subjects were successful on the first try. One subject reported that while it is not currently possible, it would be nice to allow users to move sections relative to one other.

Fast Travel to Another Section: the average difficulty of performing this task was 3.33/10, with values ranging from 1 to 10, one of the subjects failed to complete the task, 2 out of 9 succeeded from the first trial. One subject found that the activation surface of the "fast travel" was not big enough and that the boat started to slow down too early. Another subject found that the action lacks indications and that they had to guess that the "fast travel" action requested was related to the timeline bar at the top right. Another subject noticed that sometimes only the targeted section name was displayed and the "fast travel" did not start. The only change made to the fast travel function prior to the evaluation was to mention the function existed during the introductory message that is displayed the first time the user enters the application. Other changes to the UI that would the interaction more intuitive would be welcome, but the set amount of time for the realization of the project didn't allow for the exploration of ideas in that direction.

Move an Artefact Around the Environment: the average difficulty of performing this task was 1.89/10, with values ranging from 1 to 4, 6 out of 9 subjects were successful from the first attempt. One person commented that they did not know that this action was possible before the survey asked them to do it.

Evaluation of the "Look and Feel" or Visual Aspect: in addition to testing the application features, users were asked to rate the visual aspect in a scale of 1 (very bad) to 10 (very good). The average of the answers was 7.22/10, the minimum value being 5, and the maximum value being 10. Two subjects reported that the application felt too bland, too sad and that in the context of such an application it would be necessary to use more vivid colors (Fig. 10).

The domain expert also supported this claim and the need for a more colorful application. As such, changes were made to the overall appearance of the interface. Users were also allowed to customize, personalize their boats.

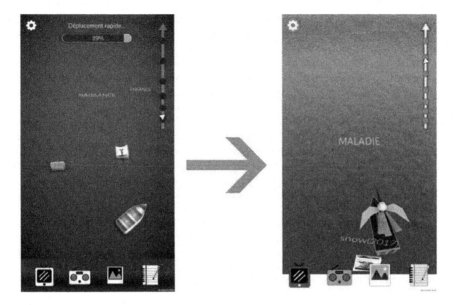

Fig. 10. Colorfulness change.

6   Conclusion and Future Work

This paper presented the iterative design process and prototypes of a mobile storytelling application, encouraging patients with life threatening diseases to adopt positive coping strategies. Patients are immersed in a game-like environment, adopting the metaphor of a boat travelling throughout time to share good memories, current thoughts and concerns, and future wish-lists and plans. In this case, gamification is not intended as a mere application of game mechanics to a non-game context but as the design of an experience able to empower the user towards the self-realization and enjoyment informed by the principles of game design. Heuristic and empirical evaluations were conducted to improve the application usability. Future steps include longitudinal studies led by the health partner with actual cancer patients in order to evaluate the actual usage and perceived usefulness and impact of the proposed application.

References

1. Riva, G., Banos, R.M., Botella, C., Wiederhold, B.K., Gaggioli, A.: Positive technology: using interactive technologies to promote positive functioning. Cyberpsychol. Behav. Soc. Netw. **15**(2), 69–77 (2012)
2. Reichlin, L., Mani, N., McArthur, K., Harris, A.M., Rajan, N., Dacso, C.C.: Assessing the acceptability and usability of an interactive serious game in aiding treatment decisions for patients with localized prostate cancer. J. Med. Internet Res. **13**(1), 188–201 (2011)
3. Brown-Johnson, C.G., Berrean, B., Cataldo, J.K.: Development and usability evaluation of the mHealth Tool for Lung Cancer (mHealth TLC): a virtual world health game for lung cancer patients. Patient Educ. Couns. **98**(4), 506–511 (2015)

4. Beale, I.L., Kato, P.M., Marin-Bowling, V.M., Guthrie, N., Cole, S.W.: Improvement in cancer-related knowledge following use of a psychoeducational video game for adolescents and young adults with cancer. J. Adolesc. Health **41**(3), 263–270 (2007)
5. That Dragon, Cancer: http://www.thatdragoncancer.com/#home. Accessed 02 Mar 2018
6. Asiedu, G.B., Eustace, R.W., Eton, D.T., Radecki Breitkopf, C.: Coping with colorectal cancer: a qualitative exploration with patients and their family members. Fam. Pract. **31**(5), 598–606 (2014). https://doi.org/10.1093/fampra/cmu040
7. Manne, S.L., Myers-Virtue, S., Kashy, D., Ozga, M., Kissane, D., Heckman, C., Rosenblum, N.: Resilience, positive coping, and quality of life among women newly diagnosed with gynecological cancers. Cancer Nurs. **38**(5), 375–382 (2015). https://doi.org/10.1097/NCC.0000000000000215
8. Palese, A., Cecconi, M., Moreale, R., Skrap, M.: Pre-operative stress, anxiety, depression and coping strategies adopted by patients experiencing their first or recurrent brain neoplasm: an explorative study. Stress Health **28**(5), 416–425 (2012). https://doi.org/10.1002/smi.2472
9. Deterding, S., Dixon, D., Khaled, R., Nacke, L.: From game design elements to gamefulness: defining gamification. In: Proceedings of the 15th International Academic MindTrek Conference: Envisioning Future Media Environments, pp. 9–15. ACM, September 2011
10. Deterding, S.: Eudaimonic design, or: six invitations to rethink gamification. In: Fuchs, M., Fizek, S., Ruffino, P., Schrape, N. (eds.) Rethinking Gamification, pp. 305–331. Meson Press, Lüneburg (2014)

Sports IT and Digital Wellness:

Three Waves of Digital Transformation in Sports and Training

Charlotte Wiberg[✉]

Department of Informatics, Umeå University, 901 87 Umeå, Sweden
charlotte.wiberg@umu.se

Abstract. In the recent twenty years, people have developed a close relationship with digital technology in conducting sports and training. Initially, approximately 1995–2005, the first wave of Sport IT included technology as GPS watches and pulse measurement equipment connected to rudimentary digital services, designed by the brand delivering the watch and only available for the single user's needs. In the second wave, between years 2006–2010, APIs and platforms started to emerge, facilitating the data to flow between artefacts, services, brands and facilities. Aesthetics in information visualization and other User experience (UX) aspects become popular and the audience becomes broader. The third wave, in the interval of 2011 and forward, could be described as the maturing wave. People now become fanatic about showing results to others – in sport platforms and on general social media. Further, what symbolizes this wave is that the focus in use becomes more on hi-fi information rather than low-fi data. In the third wave, the usage is widely spread and covers a wide range of requirements from a wide range of users.

The paper gives a more thorough description of the three waves of Sports IT when it comes to applications and user cases. A thorough description of related work for each wave is given with the main goal to pinpoint where research has given fruitful insights and contribution. In order to give a deeper understanding of the waves, one detailed example of a typical digital service of each wave is presented. Finally, the phenomenon of Sports IT and digital wellness is discussed based on findings shown earlier in the paper.

Keywords: Sports IT · Digital wellness · Quantified self · GPS
Digital service design

1 Introduction

Through the recent history, say the last fifty years, Information Technology (IT) has been one of the most significant changes in people's lives. Of course, IT can be blamed for people staying inside in front of a computer or game console, sometimes with health problems as one of the results (c.f. Vandewater et al. 2004, Hesketh et al. 2007, Forster et al. 2010). However, besides being a cause for unhealthy ways, it has also provided people with support, motivation and inspiration for a healthier way of living where, so

© Springer International Publishing AG, part of Springer Nature 2018
M. Kurosu (Ed.): HCI 2018, LNCS 10902, pp. 219–227, 2018.
https://doi.org/10.1007/978-3-319-91244-8_18

called, pervasive computing, wearables, etc. including technology as cameras, pedometers, accelerometers and other sensors (c.f. Chi et al., 2005; Baca et al., 2009; Dourish, 2001). This usage of IT started to develop and spread around 1995. In this context, we call it Sports IT.

Initially, Sports IT included technology as Global Positioning System (GPS) watches and pulse measurement equipment connected to rudimentary digital services, mainly as stand-alone application on your PC. These included statistics of collected data, for single-user need only. You were only collecting and visualizing the data for yourself and your own needs. This type of Sport IT and use we here define to be the first wave of Sport IT – 1995 to approximately 2005. The main user group was high end sports people like elite athletes, marathon runners or triathlon athletes. The main goal here could be described as efficiency, i.e. the results were measured to control efficiency in training for maximum results. Also, worth noting in relation to this wave is that the data was only processed and available in this, brand dependent, closed digital environment.

In the second wave, between years 2006–2010, the technology became more mature and also more open. Collected data became generally more accessible for different types of platforms and applications through, so called, Application Programming Interfaces (API)s that were business standards and globally adapted by sports industry. This, including the fact that large technology platforms started to emerge from large sports actors such as Nike and others, truly facilitated the data to flow between artefacts, services, brands and facilities. The focus was the quantified self (c.f. Lupton 2016), i.e. the person could measure all sports activity conducted and this data could be stored anywhere and abstracted by any stand-alone digital Sports IT service or platform. During this time, the target group using the technology are a wide audience, from novices in training and sports to more hard core users. Many of the artefacts use much more low-fi data, i.e. the accuracy is not in focus, however the user experience and information visualization was important, since motivation and inspiration for a healthier life through use of Sports IT technology was the main theme during this period. Finally, in this phase, the game industry reacted to the trend of sports and fitness and fitness games and consoles appeared – where both software, i.e. games and hardware, i.e. consoles were developed with this theme.

The third wave, in the interval of 2011 and forward, could be described as the maturing wave. An important parallel trend in this third wave is the emerging trend of using social media. This also became important in Sport IT use, since it became very popular in relation to visualize sports-, training-, and dieting results to others. The driving force here was that it became an inspiration to people by showing results to your friends. Further, what also has become important is to carefully choose genre of artefact based on underlying theories and models, e.g. it is not only important to monitor your weight curve or count calories, but to choose *type of* diet and to also record and monitor BMI-value and fat percentage – both in your upper and lower body. As it turned out in the very technology deterministically driven phase 2, i.e. what could be measured were measured and stored without initial idea of what theoretical baseline to use. In this third phase, the services were designed with a specific basis for measurements in combination with proper information visualization in relation to this basis are the winners when it comes to downloads and use. Examples of personas using the Sport IT in this phase are

(1) people already doing sports, training, exercise or dieting, (2) people inspired to start to train or diet where Sports IT can facilitate and inspire the person by supporting not only by monitoring the quantified self but also facilitating, often personalized, learning about the activity and/or diet. Further, communication channels with coaches and trainers are often included if needed, i.e. *your personal trainer online*. Overall, the third phase are characterized by personalized digital service based on specific persona – i.e. elite athlete, team members, member at sports facility, marathon runners, student at sports academy, dieting people that have chosen program to join etc. This third wave could be seen as the time where the Sports IT became a *mature technology*, individualized for each person's needs in order to make each person achieve the goals set by him- or herself – not seldom shown to others in social media.

2   The First Wave – "Because I Have Technical Support to"

In 1995, sports watches were big and clumsy and gave only general data. It was expensive because of no critical mass in selling, and the main target audience was people very interested in their progress in training – elite athletes down to amateur long distance runners with high goals in their training. The main goal here could be described as *efficiency*, i.e. the results were measured to control efficiency in training for maximum results. Also, worth noting in relation to this wave is that the data was only processed and available in this, brand dependent, closed digital environment. The expression *"because I have technical support to"* refers to a technological deterministic view of IT use (for discussions about technological determinism c.f. Smith and Marx 1994, Binber 1994). Hard core athletes had driven technology development in this area and at this time it was *possible* to measure heartbeats, steps and geographical data – so they *did*. The technological deterministic view is "There is technology – I will use it". Often, this view is present early in a technology development cycle generally, where social aspects and consequences are not in focus. The user just try out technology without reflection. The connection between technology and user are therefore quite loose, since the technology often is designed/developed without any thoughts on user requirements.

2.1   First Wave Case – GPS Hard Core Technology for Marathon Runners

Marathon runners on different levels train an enormous number of hours in order to be able to complete a race. Usage of Sport IT is very frequent in this group, and the reason is to keep track of training data – hours, length of runs, pace etc. The main focus here is efficiency, i.e. to use training hours in the most efficient way to reach the best race result. A secondary goal is to keep motivated. By using self-monitoring technology like Sports IT devices, the motivation could be kept on high levels as it may be motivating to see how many hours, miles etc. you have completed. However, the last aspect is not vital to this group to stay motivated to do their sport (Fig. 1).

Fig. 1. When running a marathon, wearable Sport IT is used in first wave of Sport IT (Photo by Filip Mroz on Unsplash)

The two most common measures are finished number of miles by using GPS and measurement of someone's pulse. Most of the technology measure both of the types of data. However, depending on what the platform came from – from the GPS world or measuring pulse world – interfaces and forefront data was different. Important to note is that interface design and aesthetics were not in focus here – only displayed data counted. The more data, the merrier were the paradigm here (Fig. 2).

Fig. 2. Many marathon runners using Sports IT equipment for measurement of personal data during the race. (Photo by Mārtiņš Zemlickis on Unsplash)

3   The Second Wave – "Because I Feel Motivated by Using It"

In the second wave, between years 2006–2010, APIs and platforms started to emerge, facilitating the data to flow between artefacts, services, brands and facilities. The focus was the quantified self, i.e. the person could measure all sports activity conducted and this data could be stored anywhere and abstracted by any stand-alone digital Sports IT service or platform. During this time, the target group using the technology are a wide audience, from novices in training and sports to more hard core users. Many of the artefacts use much more low-fi data, i.e. the accuracy is not in focus, however the user experience and information visualization was important, since motivation and inspiration for a healthier life through use of Sports IT technology was the main theme during this period. If the paradigm in the first wave was efficiency, here User Experience (UX) is in center (For a thorough discussion about UX c.f. Wiberg 2003, Swallow et al. 2005, Forlizzi and Battarby 2004, Hassenzahl 2008, Karapanos et al. 2009).

3.1   Second Wave Case – Nike+ - Aesthetics and Fun

The showcase in this wave is the global collaboration between Nike and Apple, which became a groundbreaking success due to some core aspects. First, two huge platforms, and existing customer groups joint together. This was groundbreaking at the time. Second, the timing was right for a larger and less hardcore runner audience to adopt Sport IT technology. Finally, the concept was playing with simplicity and aesthetics which was new in Sport IT world. Earlier, platforms, artefacts and interfaces were more functional and at its most usable. To also include more pleasure values was new and very attractive to the audience. Below, an example of one shoe using the built-in pedometer that sent information through a plug-in to an iPod, which gave audio feedback to the runner regarding time, pace etc. The interfaces as well as the accuracy in measurements were leaning towards a general audience. It was good looking but with rudimentary measurements (Fig. 3).

Fig. 3. In the second wave, a broader group of people were targeted for the Sports IT concepts, where facility and aesthetics were up front. The image shows Nike+ sensor and connected iPod.

4   The Third Wave – "Because Others See Me Doing It"

The third wave, in the interval of 2011 and forward, could be described as the maturing wave. People are not only measuring calories, pace and weight – they also get inspiration by receiving (positive) feedback by positing results and images from their Sport IT activities on social media. Social media suddenly became full with number of kilometers, curves of average speed of bike rides etc. As social media get more and more graphical, images of scales, plates with food etc. appear frequently. Finally, when the selfie hit the ground as a trend, the gym image taken through a mirror becomes mainstream.

Another important aspect in this third wave was not only to do a random diet, but to choose app or platform based on *what type of* diet, or theoretical framework to base training, sport or diet on. The number of apps on Appstore for diets exploded and they were filled with recipes etc. As it turned out in the very technology deterministically driven phase 1 and 2, i.e. what could be measured were measured and stored without initial idea of what theoretical baseline to use. In this third phase, the services clear of their basis for measurements in combination with proper information visualization in relation to this basis are the winners when it comes to downloads and use. The target audience in this phase are (1) people already doing sports, training, exercise or dieting, (2) people inspired to start to train or diet where Sports IT can facilitate and inspire the person by supporting not only by monitoring the quantified self but also facilitating, often personalized, learning about the activity and/or diet. Overall, as the technology use matured in Sports IT, the user group got wider and the applications grew in number. As we can see a strong development curve in the sensor technology, the number of interesting artefacts grow. Besides posting information online into social media, the direct communication between people in relation to Sports IT grow. Trainer to client, client to client etc. grow. The third wave – the mature wave – of Sports IT gives both developers and clients great business and motivation to continue to develop technology as well as use.

4.1   Third Wave Case – Lifesum and Runkeeper

In order to show upon real cases, two platforms are described below. First, Lifesum is described and discussed – a platform for monitoring weight, exercise with a large number of add-ons like receipts and more. Secondly, Runkeeper is described. This is a platform from the exercise part of wellness. So, here focus is more on that part. Together, they give an overview of the third wave Sports IT spectrum.

Lifesum includes goal bar of what weight to reach in your weight loss. Further, it has a database of calorie counted food and beverages which helps in the food diary. Another feature is that it gives notifications as drinking sounds during the day in order to remind you to drink water. You take notes in the app how many you had (Fig. 4).

Runkeeper includes features as GPS – map support, music control, interval sounds, i.e. when you have reach a specific number of kilometers or miles for instance, you hear a sound. All to get you motivated to keep going (Fig. 5).

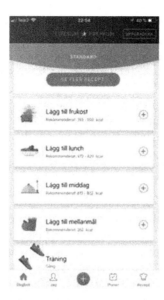

Fig. 4. Screenshot of Lifesum – an app mainly for diet control. However, it also includes exercise and water drinking.

Fig. 5. Screenshot of Runkeeper – an app originating from the exercise/running world.

5 Discussion

Sports IT as a technology phenomenon is definitely here to stay – it is not a short term trend. Hopefully, the diversity will be motivating in itself for people, so that they get more interested because of the flexibility in Sport IT technology when it comes to personalization in the platforms and apps. Another significant thing is the technology development speed – everything is getting more and more accurate, wearable and more UX friendly, which help in IT adaptation. However, looking at Sports IT throughout those three waves in history, gives some insights. Below, these are further developed.

5.1 Industry Standards vs. Market Value

It is important that platform owners and producers globally come together and even further discuss and collaborate when it comes to APIs, and other industry standards, in order to further facilitate for users to bring the data seamless between platforms, in order to avoid lock-in effects. These are negative for all involved – customer, developer and platform owners. To bring or spread the data is vital in this technology segment.

On the other side, some actors believe that a protectionist way is the right way. If I lock in the clients they will stay – forever – seems to be the model. All with the purpose to keep a high rate of market share to get a high market value. The sports and wellness industry has to look beyond this short-term advantage in order to build a sound market in total.

5.2 Function, Usability and Experience – User's Needs

Throughout the three waves of Sport IT use, different levels of user's need has been in focus. (c.f. Jordan 2000). Initially, especially in early part of first wave, functionality was the main or only aspect at stake. The user wanted the data, and user was very persistent so even if he or she didn't actually understand the interface initially, she had motivation to complete task even if usability was poor. Later on, however, with a wider user group, usability became as important as functionality. In the second and third wave, the third aspect in Jordan's stairs of user needs, i.e. pleasure/(or UX) is highly important as well. So, Sports IT is a typical example where Jordan's theory apply – it is deterministic that over time user needs will evolve from not only need for functionality but also usability and finally UX.

5.3 There is an App for that vs. Individualization

In Sport IT of today, the flood of apps handling registering of food and training is enormous. There is a danger that platforms will not gain enough attention to survive. The balance here is to make it general enough but with a thought of personalization as well. The negative side of personalization part of the scale is that it gets more complicated to interact with the app or artefact whenever individualization/personalization is around if not done in a smart way. This aspect might be the most vital in order to succeed in Sports IT in the future.

References

Foster, D., Linehan, C., Kirman, B., Lawson, S., James, G.: Motivating physical activity at work: using persuasive social media for competitive step counting. In: Proceedings of the 14th International Academic MindTrek Conference: Envisioning Future Media Environments (MindTrek 2010), pp. 111–116. ACM, New York (2010)

Forlizzi, J., Battarbee, K.: Understanding experience in interactive systems. In: Proceedings of the 5th Conference on Designing Interactive Systems: Processes, Practices, Methods, and Techniques (DIS 2004), pp. 261–268. ACM, New York (2004)

Hassenzahl, M.: User experience (UX): towards an experiential perspective on product quality. In: Proceedings of the 20th Conference on l'Interaction Homme-Machine (IHM 2008), pp. 11–15. ACM, New York (2008)

Hesketh, K., Wake, M., Graham, M., Waters, E.: Stability of television viewing and electronic game/computer use in a pro- spective cohort study of Australian children: relationship with body mass index. Int. J. Behav. Nutr. Phys. Act. **4**, 60 (2007)

Jordan, P.: Designing Pleasurable Products: An Introduction to the New Human Factors. Taylor & Francis, London (2000)

Karapanos, E., Zimmerman, J., Forlizzi, J., Martens, J.-B.: User experience over time: an initial framework. In: Proceedings of the SIGCHI Conference on Human Factors in Computing Systems (CHI 2009), pp. 729–738. ACM, New York (2009)

Lupton, D.: The Quantified Self. Wiley, Cambridge (2016). ISBN: 1509500618

Smith, M.R., Marx, L.: Does Technology Drive History?: The Dilemma of Technological Determinism. MIT Press, Cambridge (1994). ISBN: 0262691671

Swallow, D., Blythe, M., Wright, P.: Grounding experience: relating theory and method to evaluate the user experience of smartphones. In: Proceedings of the 2005 Annual Conference on European Association of Cognitive Ergonomics (EACE 2005). University of Athens, pp. 91–98 (2005)

Vandewater, E.A., Shim, M., Caplovitz, A.G.: Linking obesity and activity level with children's television and video game use. J Adolesc **27**(1), 71–85 (2004)

Wiberg, C.: A measure of fun. Extending the scope of web usability. Department of informatics. Umeå University (2003)

An Innovative Mattress Design to Improve Sleep Quality and Thermal Comfort

Fong-Gong Wu[✉], Tsu-Yu Shen, and Su-Huey Tan

National Cheng Kung University, Tainan, Taiwan
fonggong@ncku.edu.tw, jjessiem6@gmail.com, sh030265@gmail.com

Abstract. Different body segments have different thermal characteristics and sleeping postures change unconsciously during the night. Thus, the movements of the extremities should be taken into consideration in a bedding system design. The design guidelines propose in this study is enhance pressure balance, the physiological balance of microclimate, and improvement of distal skin blood circulation. An innovative mattress design has been developed in this study. The proposed mattress has a five-layer sandwiched structure. Twelve healthy participants had general level in BMI were recruited in 3-day sleep monitoring including one habit adjustment night in simulated laboratory condition to evaluate the original and design mattresses. The consequence indicated mattress design considered thermal comfort efficiently on the basis of position change improved sleep efficient, loss sleep disturbance by loss mean activity and arousal time.

Keywords: Sleep position · Thermal comfort · Sleep quality · Mattress design

1 Introduction

The thermoregulation system composed of core body temperature (CBT) and skin temperature [1] acts as a signal of both sleepiness and wakefulness regulation. Increasing the phase of lower CBT is correlated with sleep initiation and maintenance [2]. Simply stated, the decline and the rise rhythm of CBT inversed to skin temperature rhythm [3] respectively herald initiation and termination of sleep.

Body temperature influences blood circulation and then the sleep quality. Research showed that cardiovascular capacity reduced during REM sleep [4]. In normal sleep cycle, shorten of rapid eye movement (REM) stage results in bad sleep quality. Compare to low skin temperature which causes sleep onset latency, over-high skin temperature alerting CBT causes arousal. Both skin temperature and sensitivity to thermal stimulus differs from area to area on the body surface [5]. Skin temperature contains distal skin temperature (e.g., hand, calf, ankle, foot and, toe) and proximal skin temperature (e.g., thigh, rectal, forehead and abdomen). Increasing in skin temperature to improve sleep quality. To refrain alerting CBT, a mere increase (0.4 °C) in skin temperature assists people have trouble initiating sleep or early morning awakening to accelerate sleep onset, decrease arousals, and increase SWS (slow wave sleep) [6]. The effect on physiology reduced as confining the heated area from full to the lower extremities [7]. The effects on position change are considered

© Springer International Publishing AG, part of Springer Nature 2018
M. Kurosu (Ed.): HCI 2018, LNCS 10902, pp. 228–237, 2018.
https://doi.org/10.1007/978-3-319-91244-8_19

to enhance blood circulation, avoid or decrease the pressure on certain areas of the body, and regulate body temperature [8].

2   Methods

One new design mattress was implemented and evaluated experimentally to examine whether the goals to improve sleep quality and enhance sleep thermal comfort were achieved, and the flow chart of mattress design process is shown in Fig. 1.

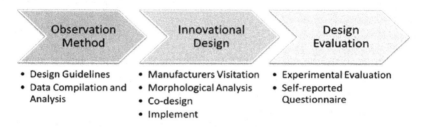

Fig. 1. Flow chart of mattress design process

Through investigating the skin temperature change and discussing particular sleep posture during sleep. The correlation of crucial sleep posture and skin temperature change were analyzed to quarry the specify requirement of body segments and develop design guidelines. All the participants is standard body ($18.5 < BMI < 24$), and with no medicine taking and caffeine or alcohol consuming during the experiment. The use of actigraphy records the sleep patterns, including sleep onset latency, sleep onset time, total sleep time, total awake time, and sleep efficiency whole night to evaluate the quality of sleep.

2.1   Procedure

The aim of observation method was to collect all night sleep posture, sleep quality and skin temperature. Through this procedure, the prior grasp of physiological requirements under certain situation during sleep. Before the day into the laboratory, all participants conducted one week adaptation night to adjust their sleep time for experiment need. For the laboratory night, participants came to the laboratory one hour before their habitual bedtime and they will dress the specific pajamas, and sleep on an installed mattress with a bed sheet in a constant room temperature at 25 °C and in a relative humidity at 50%. The thermistors stuck on proximal (forehead, abdomen, thigh) and distal skin (forearm, calf, hand and foot) by using surgical tape to monitor temperature every 30 s; the Digital Video was set up overhead for all night sleep posture recording; and the actigraphy was worn on non-dominant wrist to investigate sleep pattern, shown in Fig. 2. Time cues are given for the participants' arousal, and after the laboratory sleep night, participants were asked to do the subjective sleep quality questionnaire with self-reported sleep disturbance. An eight hours sleep from at 11:30 pm to the alarm clock went off at 8 am.

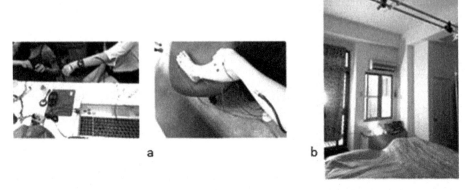

Fig. 2. Experiment environment and device. (a) Thermistors making and sticking condition (b) Laboratory environment and digital video handling overhead

2.2 Data Compilation and Analysis

To obtain the relation between body segment location and the distribution on sleep surface, sleep position recorded by digital video were categorized visually by the author. Sleep positions defined as the position that was maintained more than one minute were analyzed for the whole night [9]. Sleep positions were printed from the video, and the heights of the participants in each image were adjusted to a standard scale before the images were overlaid. The image captured was analyzed according to the body parts of the participants. The joints of the body segments (shoulder, elbow, wrist, fingers, knee, ankle, heel and toes) were illustrated as circle with different proportions and colors. To obtain the distributions of sleep positions on a sleeping surface, the images captured of the participants were overlaid based on the marker which was drawn on the pillow.

By means of sleep monitoring data analysis, main sleep position percentage and specific sleep positions of body segments corresponding to mattress were obtained. The outcome presented as Fig. 3 which data collection of temperature and sleep position recording was at the testing night. Despite of time as x-axis, sleep posture and proximal and distal skin temperature change to understand (1) specific position on sleep onset and before arousal (2) specific position change when temperature change. The proportion of every sleep position in total sleep time related to sleep quality was another key point of analysis.

2.3 Innovation Mattress Ideation and Implementation

Understanding of existing products is a non-ignored preparation before ideating. For satisfying various requirements of body parts, the study developed design ideas by morphological analysis and co-design. The exterior and inner structure of existing mattress. After the existing mattress comprehension, morphological analysis was conducted for classification of vertical-layer functions and horizontal surface parallel to sleep surface division.

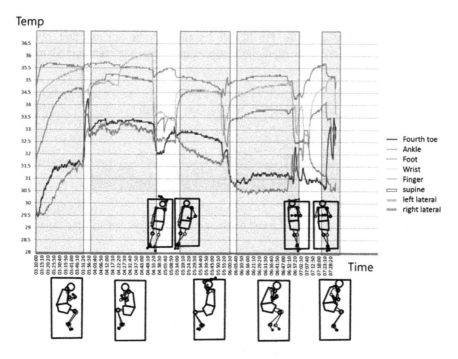

Fig. 3. Skin temperature change and body position change at testing night

Through outcomes of observational experiments, sleep surface is divided into multi zones which fit the movements of body segments and the crucial sleep posture and skin temperature change of each sleep stage are found. Body segment on mattress represented the distribution area. First step was to develop functions by co-design for vertical layer through observation information and design guidelines of improvement of thermal comfort from literature.

A group of six designers gathered to create numerous ideas following the design guidelines to improve thermal comfort induced sleep quality for one and a half hour. In the beginning, the author presented the observation results for the six designers for realizing the actuality condition, then, they started to ideate ideas. For specific position in certain sleep stage, the sleep characteristics of the observation were adopted to provide a reference to conduct the mattress design to satisfy the design guidelines and needs of different body parts. Therefore, the ppt showed the specific positions when they developed ideas. The three design guidelines were the main purpose should achieve through design criteria aligned in the column based on the design guideline. Through co-design, the preliminary attributes of the mattress and the possible solutions for requirements of each body parts of different positions were generated.

Morphological analysis was adopted to generate different kinds of mattress matrices. For co-design, the possible designed area of a mattress in vertical layers and horizontal spaces (corners, edges, and middle) were aligned in the bottom of the design criteria column. Horizontal division design considered different sleep position, and the location of body segments on mattress (Fig. 4). Designers selected the proper design area of horizontal surface due to the position of real condition. And also, they chose the proper design layer for vertical structure. Finally, all design would be category and found out the best solution not only satisfied the design guidelines but recommend to local improvement.

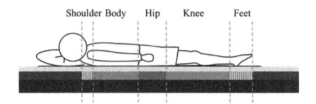

Fig. 4. Vertical layers of mattress and body segments corresponding to sleep surface

2.4   Experimental Assessment

The study was designed to achieve two critical efficacies: Improve sleep quality and enhance sleep thermal comfort by physiological and perception evaluation. One innovative mattress design implements and the original one were conducted for experimental assessment and self-reported questionnaires for subjective and objective evaluations to practical inspect all night usage of new design mattress. The original mattress called Mattress O in this research was a seven area latex mattress showed as Fig. 3. Ambient room temperature was kept at approximately 25 °C.

To investigate the skin temperature and sleep position, besides other sleep disorders, eight standard body (18.5 < BMI < 24) participants were involved in this study. All participants were informed to conduct sleep adaptation to reduce effect on sleep quality owing to unfamiliar sleep environment. Throughout a week sleep habit adjustment, eight good sleep-wake cycle participants filter for taking the laboratory night monitoring. During the experiment, all the participants complied with the provisions of no medicine taking and caffeine or alcohol consuming.

Participants were required to be at laboratory one hour before sleep time at 00:00 were then prepared for actigraphy and fitted with thermistors for proximal and distal skin temperature manipulation. At midnight, lights were turned off and participants were allowed to sleep until am 08:00 h. After first night sleeping in the laboratory, participants returned for a second night, and then the third night. The experiment environment shows as Fig. 5. The original mattress and mattress implement were examined alternately and randomly among three days. The original one was the multi-zone latex mattress.

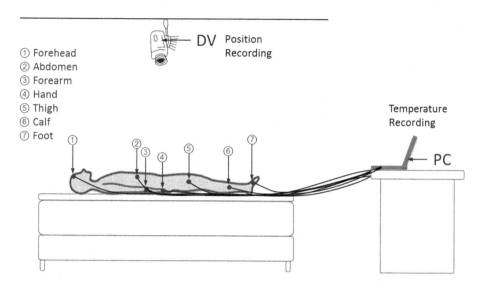

Fig. 5. Laboratory experiment environment

3   Results

A number of interesting findings emerged from this design process, and this report concludes three main results of an innovative mattress design process concerning local and dynamic physiological requirements during sleep, design ideate and product implement, and experimental assessment of mattress design.

There were three design guidelines that a mattress design should cover: (1) enhance pressure balance, (2) the physiological balance of microclimate, (3) improvement of distal skin blood circulation.

Design guidelines were applied to the major sleeping posture (supine and lateral) in order to meet the requirements of different body parts. The detailed information is presented in Fig. 6.

Through sleep monitoring of whole night, the study found out the basic physiology phenomenon change during sleep. By analyzing temperature correlate to specific sleep position of different sleep quality, to gain key sleep position as design inspiration. As the major movements of each participant were repeated, therefore the changes of sleep position were categorized as supine, lateral and semi-lateral according to the direction and angle of their torsos to the mattress, and the direct definition due to the turns of their torsos.

Sleep position distribution represented the location of body segments with overlay of major sleep position and semi-lateral was integrated to lateral. The results showed that the covered sleeping surface of supine was larger than the latera. In lateral position, the positions of their shoulders inclined to one side and opposite to the side of their hips. When change into supine, sleepers bent their bodies to match the size of the mattress, especially their foot. It was the reason why some covered surface was higher than knee.

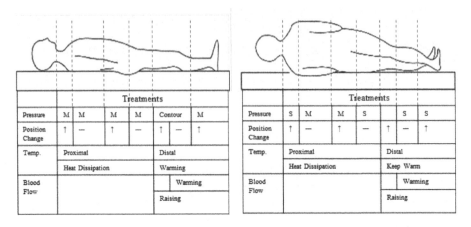

Fig. 6. Specific requirements of different body parts

The distributed area of legs in lateral was larger and placed separately during their sleeps. By understanding of the body distribution on the mattress combined with the design guideline connected with body part will later both use in mattress design. The union of body parts distribution on mattress would later as design parallel to mattress surface consideration of mattress to fit location of body part.

Compare of traditional and a better mattress, the quality was not about as many layers as the mattress involved, but about function and nature of material which was benefit to mattress structure. There presented a certain effect of each layer in mattress, and the common existing mattress structure analyzed by morphological analysis. Vertical layers arrangement was due to function and the horizontal distribution was due to the space division.

All of the ideas were classified into five items and named each one of it. No matter the design was for whole or partial of mattress. After design classification, the design of each layer was chosen. The priority was that the design can achieve more than one design criteria.

The final decision was planned. The size of the single mattress is 100 * 190 cm and 150 cm height. The proposed mattress has a five-layer sandwiched structure. The first layer had a V-shaped division line between the hip and leg and fulfilled different needs of trunk, hip and feet. For leg parts, increasing the friction between the skin and the mattress for warming, and a different material had been used to increase the heat dissipation of the torso and hip; the second layer had a rectangle on the bottom of egg shape material for keep warm and a little leg raising; the third layer is designed for ventilation and moisture transmission; the bottom layer is designed for pressure redistribution and the corrugated shape on the top was for position change. The first and third layers were designed according to physiological balance of microclimate). The second layer was for improvement of distal skin blood circulation. The top and bottom layer were for enhancing pressure balance.

All participants were standard-bodied young women aged 20–25. Sleep quality data were analyzed by PC based MotionWare Software. In composed of seven data each mattress, the results indicated the relationships among sleep quality and mattress design were what was expected, that is, mattress D enhanced sleep quality. Exclude one outliners, participant 7's data showed great difference evenly in most situation, and almost every index was opposite to others. The results of four representative index, sleep efficiency, sleep latency, actual wake and mean activity, were showed as following. Mattress D had 3.38% higher sleep efficiency, five minutes shorter sleep latency, 2.57% less actual wake, and 1.85 epochs less mean activity. Expect for outliner a, every index illustrated the sleep quality of mattress D was better.

A t-test analysis indicated a significant difference of actual wake time; $t(5) = 3.34$, $p = 0.021$, and sleep efficient; $t(5) = -5.48$, $p = 0.003$, between the means of two groups, but there was not significant in the sleep onset latency; $t(5) = 1.55$, $p = 0.183$ and mean activity, $t(5) = 1.24$, $p = 0.270$.

4 Discussion

Comparison between traditional and a better mattress, the quality was not about as many layers as the mattress involved, but about functions and nature of material which were benefit to mattress structure. There were several physiological factors associated with comfort and interface skin temperature also included in those factors [10]. The innovative mattress of this study combined three aspects of mattress design factors that influenced efficiency of thermal comfort improvement to propose the design guidelines. Design guidelines included enhance of pressure balance, physiological balance of microclimate, and improvement of distal skin blood circulation. To increase nature character of innovative mattresses, both of the design excluded heating system which reduced the effect on fast-deducing thermoregulation. Another reason that heating-considering design was not chosen was that in previous studies, passive heating products were usually suggested to operate under the condition of low ambient temperature. It may reduce cold stress, thereby supporting sleep stability and thermoregulation during sleep [7]. Compared to the innovative design implant in the mattress structure of this study, numerous interrelated products which are used to improve sleep thermal comfort increase in recent years. Most of those products were not integrated to the bedding system, such as electronic temperature control devices (electric blanket and ChiliPad) or focus on the textiles substitution, such as foam and fabrics [5].

This study enhances the previous studies' finding by integrating effect factors of whole body and local needs of mattress design. The result of this study developed an innovative mattress fulfilled local need according to physiological condition information. Owing to sleep pattern and habitual sleep posture are personal, Tsai and Liu (2008) referred the good bed is the familiar one to achieve the local need of body sites [10, 11]. The information of position change provides mattress design a virtual condition for designers to ideate design. For guideline of this study, a mattress design is required to conform to the body contours to avoid local point pressures on the human body tissue especially at the location of bony prominence and it should support human to change their sleep position when they felt uncomfortable and tried to reduce sleep discomfort by redistributing the interface pressures of the body. The first layer had a V-shaped division line between the hip and leg and fulfilled different needs of trunk, hip and feet. For leg parts, increasing the friction between the skin and the mattress for warming, and a different material had been used to increase the heat dissipation of the torso and hip; the second layer had a rectangle on the bottom of egg shape material for keep warm and a little leg raising; the third layer is designed for ventilation and moisture transmission; the bottom layer is designed for pressure redistribution and the corrugated shape on the top was for position change.

5   Conclusion

Exile investigation of continuous sleep position change information provided a benefit resource to valid sleep surface comfort with more physiological message other than body temperature. The images of sleep monitoring attempts to account for most of particular temperature change and sleep quality affected by body movement. To conclude the thermal comfort achievement of this study, the design of Mattress D was benefit for heat dissipation to distal skin, and had comfort feeling in extremities and whole body thermal comfort promotion.

The mattress design due to sleep position change was contributed to reduce minor position period to enhance sleep quality during sleep. The relationship between sleep position, skin temperature and sleep quality needs further exploration. A t-test analysis indicated a significant difference of actual wake time and sleep efficient. Furthermore, despite of one of seven participants had poor sleep quality when slept on Mattress D, and others had a better sleep at the night on new Mattress. Two participants reported that they took more than half an hour to fall asleep and four participants had chance to wake up in the middle of the night when slept on original Mattress.

References

1. Romanovsky, A.A.: Skin temperature: its role in thermoregulation. Acta Physiol. **210**(3), 498–507 (2014)
2. Raymann, R.J.E.M., Swaab, D.F., Van Someren, E.J.W.: Skin temperature and sleep-onset latency: changes with age and insomnia. Physiol. Behav. **90**(2–3), 257–266 (2007)
3. Fronczek, R., Raymann, R.J., Romeijn, N., Overeem, S., Fischer, M., van Dijk, J.G., Lammers, G.J., Van Someren, E.J.: Manipulation of core body and skin temperature improves vigilance and maintenance of wakefulness in narcolepsy. Sleep, **31**(2), 233–240 (2008)
4. Viola, A.U., Tobaldini, E., Chellappa, S.L., Casali, K.R., Porta, A., Montano, N.: Short-term complexity of cardiac autonomic control during sleep: REM as a potential risk factor for cardiovascular system in aging. PLoS ONE **6**(4), e19002 (2011)
5. Amrit, U.R.: Bedding textiles and their influence on thermal comfort and sleep. AUTEX Res. J. **8**(4), 252–254 (2007)
6. Anders, D., Gompper, B., Kräuchi, K.: A two-night comparison in the sleep laboratory as a tool to challenge the relationship between sleep initiation, cardiophysiological and thermoregulatory changes in women with difficulties initiating sleep and thermal discomfort. Physiol. Behav. **114–115**, 77–82 (2013)

7. Okamoto-Mizuno, K., Tsuzuki, K., Ohshiro, Y., Mizuno, K.: Effects of an electric blanket on sleep stages and body temperature in young men. Ergon. **48**(7), 749–757 (2005)
8. Caldwell, J.A., Prazinko, B., Caldwell, J.L.: Body posture affects electroencephalographic activity and psychomotor vigilance task performance in sleep-deprived subjects. Clin. Neurophysiol. **114**(1), 23–31 (2003)
9. De Koninck, P.G., Lallier, S.: Sleep positions in the young adult and their relationship with the subjective quality of sleep. Sleep **6**(1), 52–59 (1983)
10. Tsai, L.L., Liu, H.M.: Effects of bedding systems selected by manual muscle testing on sleep and sleep-related respiratory disturbances. Appl. Ergon. **39**(2), 261–270 (2008)
11. Lin, L.Y., Wang, F., Kuklane, K., Gao, C., Holmér, I., Zhao, M.: A laboratory validation study of comfort and limit temperatures of four sleeping bags defined according to EN 13537. Appl. Ergon. **44**(2), 321–326 (2013)

HCI in Cultural Heritage

Interaction and Interactivity: In the Context of Digital Interactive Art Installation

Salah Uddin Ahmed[✉]

Høgskolen i Sørøst Norge, Ringerike, Norway
Salah.ahmed@usn.no

Abstract. Different people define 'interaction' in the context of digital interactive art in different ways. The confusion comes from the fact that the meaning of interaction is different in different fields. Medical science, social science, information technology all define interaction in a way that is different from the meaning in the other field.

In this article, we would like to point out how interaction and interactivity is defined in different fields that has some sort of relevance and applicability in the area of digital interactive art and how these varied definitions are related and what they mean when applied in the context of digital interactive art. In particular, we would like to identify the various types of interactions and communication that take place and have some meaning and significance in the context of a digital interactive art installation.

Keywords: Interactivity · Interaction · Digital interactive art · Digital art
Interactive art · Digital interactive art installation

1 Introduction

In the recent years, number of technology dependent artworks have increased because of the increased availability, accessibility and development of computer technology. The intersection of the two fields, art and technology, has interested many artists, researchers and theorists in the recent years. This is reflected in the recent art festivals like Transmediale (www.transmediale.de), Read_Me (http://readme.runme.org), ARS Electronica (www.aec.at), Make Art (http://makeart.goto10.org), FILE (www.file.org.br), Trondheim MatchMaking (http://matchmaking.teks.no), in the literature and in online artist community sites and blogs where plenty of examples of artists using technology in their artworks are visible. As a result of this trend of using more technology in artwork, more and more artists-technologists collaboration is taking place. In SArt project, we collaborated with several artists, and participated and observed the development of several digital interactive artworks (Ahmed 2011). From our experience, we have seen that definitions of different terms in the intersection of art and technology are not very well defined. While doing research in the context of digital interactive art, we have seen that interaction and interactivity in the context of artwork is defined differently by different artists and technologists. This is due to the reason that the definitions of different genres of artwork in the intersection of art and technology are overlapping and not mutually distinct. Besides intersection

© Springer International Publishing AG, part of Springer Nature 2018
M. Kurosu (Ed.): HCI 2018, LNCS 10902, pp. 241–257, 2018.
https://doi.org/10.1007/978-3-319-91244-8_20

of art and technology involves people from various background where the definition of a term such as interaction can get different meaning (Ahmed et al. 2009).

In this paper, we would like to see how interaction and interactivity is defined in different fields that has some sort of relevance and applicability in the area of digital interactive art, how these varied definitions are related, and what meaning they offer when applied in the context of a digital interactive art. Since digital interactive art is a multidisciplinary field that brings in people from different fields together, it will be interesting to see the different viewpoints of interactivity viewed from different discipline. In particular, we would like to identify the various types of interaction and communication, and their meaning and significance in the setting of a digital interactive art installation. Finding the different meanings and uses of interaction will remove the confusion about interaction among artists, technologists and others involved in the digital interactive art, and help them to better identify, define and design the desired interactions that they are interested in a certain context.

The rest of the article is organized in the following way. Section 2 provides some background information; a brief introduction of intersection of art and technology and digital interactive art. It also presents the inconsistencies among researchers and artists about the definition of interaction and interactivity in digital interactive art. Section 3 provides a description of how interaction and communication is defined in different disciplines. Section 4 presents interactivity in the context of digital interactive artwork.

Section 5 presents our results. We present the different kinds of interactions that are possible in the context of a digital interactive art installation. With reference to the definitions in the literature, we identify the interactions and their types and the meaningfulness and significance of them in the given context. Section 6 is the conclusion.

2   Background

2.1   Intersection of Art and Technology

As increasing number of artists are using technology and the advent of different tools and technologies enabling different kinds of collaborations between art and technology, we see various new types and genres of art in the intersection of art and technology. As an example, digital art, computer art, internet art, software dependent art, digital interactive art, generative art, interactive art installations etc. are only a few to mention in this regard. Often the distinction between different genres are not very clear; one genre collides with others. Some genres are not well defined and some overlap with others since there are no mutual exclusive criteria that distinguish them. Often, one genre is derived from another, and one can have several sub genres or sub categories; thus making the categorization and classification blurry and overlapping.

As an example, internet art is a sub-category of digital art and both of them belongs to the new media art. Many digital arts are interactive in nature; hence, they are interactive art as well. However, not all digital arts are interactive art. Again not all interactive arts are digital art. How to draw distinctions between computer art, digital art, and Internet art when they overlap and combines so much? Again, all these genres can be placed under the larger umbrella term new media art. New media art is usually defined as a genre that encompasses artworks created with new media technologies. But defining new media is difficult; as Pereira (2015) puts it in the following way.

"What is digital art? What is new media art? What are the boundaries of new media art? I am afraid there are no clear answers to these questions,…" He continues the puzzle as,

"…when we see definitions of new media art or digital art, we are left a bit confused, and with a lot of questions to be posed. New media art is usually defined as a genre that encompasses artworks created with new media technologies, including digital art, computer graphics, computer animation, virtual art, Internet art, interactive art, video games, computer robotics, 3D printing, and art as biotechnology. But, then we could pose questions such as: What is new media? What is digital art? What is the difference between interactive art and new media art?" (Pereira 2015).

In this puzzle of these linked and overlapped terms, clarifying the concept of digital interactive art deserves some special attention as it touches many other categories of art. Defining a concept of something in the context of a concept that is not very clear and overlaps with several other concepts can be fuzzy and misleading. So is the case with defining interaction in the context of digital interactive art. In the next section, we describe digital interactive art tracing it from the genres: digital art and interactive art.

2.2   Digital Interactive Art

"Digital interactive artwork" or "Interactive digital artwork" as some others name it refers to a genre of artwork which are interactive and where digital technology is an essential component for the creation of the artwork. Whatever name it is called, either *digital interactive art* or *interactive digital art,* it refers to a combination of two terms: *(i) digital art* and *(ii) interactive art.*

Wikipedia defines *digital art* as "an artistic work or practice that uses digital technology as an essential part of the creative or presentation process". British art organization Tate (http://www.tate.org.uk) defines the term digital art to describe "art that is made or presented using digital technology".

Interactive art on the other hand is defined by the Wikipedia as "a form of art that involves the spectator in a way that allows the art to achieve its purpose. Some interactive art installations achieve this by letting the observer or visitor "walk" in, on, and around them; some others ask the artist or the spectators to become part of the artwork". As Edmonds (2011) describes, "interactive art is distinguished by its dynamic behaviour in response to external stimuli, such as people moving and speaking". Art becomes interactive when audience participation is an integral part of the artwork. Audience behavior can cause the artwork itself to change. In making interactive art, the artist not only considers how the artwork will look or sound to an observer, but the way it interacts with the audience is also a crucial part of its essence (Edmonds 2011).

In the recent years extensive use of digital technology in artwork and audience interaction gives us an impression that all digital art is interactive, or on the other way, all interactive art is digital. As an example, we can cite the artworks of Gregory Lasserre & Anais met den Ancxt. They are two artists who work as a duo under the name Scenocosme and develop the concept of interactivity in their artworks by using multiple kind of expression: art, technology, sound and architecture. In their website, they have a list of interactive installations. It is not surprising that all of the interactive installations in their list are actually digital art considering the fact that one of the artists is a Computer Science graduate (Lasserre and Ancxt 2018). However, similar is the case with many other artists in the area of art and technology where artists are either collaborating with technologists or hiring some expertise to develop the technical part of their artwork if they do not know the technology by themselves (Ahmed et al. 2009) (Ahmed 2011). Thus in the recent lists of interactive artworks, in most of the cases, the digital and the interactive part smoothly joins as two sides of a coin.

However, the concept of interactive art is older than the concept of digital art and digital interactive art. Interactive art engages the audience with the artwork. While Interactive art became a large phenomenon due to the advent of computer based interactivity during the 1990s, but the theoretical concept of audience participation and interaction with the artwork been developed by the British artist and theorist Roy Ascott as early as 1966 (Schraffenberger and van der Heide 2012). Thus, interactive art does not necessarily have to be digital art; non-digital art can be interactive as well. At the same time, digital arts can be non-interactive too.

Besides, not all digital-interactive art is interactive in the sense of *interactive art*. As Lopes (2001) mentions, "Interactivity is a buzzword used rather indiscriminately to describe everything from computer games to Internet shopping, and it is not the case that all computer-based art is interactive in any interesting sense. Indeed". The main idea of interactive artwork is audience's interaction with the artwork, audience's participation and engagement in the artwork in such a way that the activity of engagement becomes part of the artwork.

2.3 Different Approaches of Interactivity in Digital Interactive Art

Several artists and researchers define digital interactive art in different ways. In fact, the variety and richness of existing approaches are so wide that the relevance of interaction in interactive art is suggested to be a broad and interdisciplinary field of research (Schraffenberger and van der Heide 2012). Here we mention only three different approaches.

Trifonova and Jaccheri (2007) presents art installation Flyndre as an example of interactive art installation. Flyndre has an interactive sound system that has the goal to reflect the nature around the sculpture. Flyndre takes as input parameters from the environment such as the local time, light level, temperature, water level and depending on these parameters creates music by exploiting algorithmic composition techniques (Ahmed 2008). While the artwork is interactive in the sense that it interacts with the outer world by taking some sensor data, but considering interaction with the audience, it is not interactive.

While defining interactive digital art Nardelli (2012) mentions, "Digital films/videos are usually not examples of IDA (Interactive Digital Art), nor is digital music, since they both lack the contribution of the user to the content production. But when the outcome of video animations or music pieces is modified according to user interaction they are examples of *interactive digital art*". This definition focuses on the content generation part rather than the audience experience of interaction.

Satomi and Sommerer (2007) calls "game_of_life" an interactive art installation that lets spectators walk through the virtual city by using their own eye gaze movement. Even though they call it only *"interactive art installation"*, it is a digital interactive art as it depends heavily on the digital technology. On the other hand, this is a true interactive art, as here the audience becomes a part of the artwork expression.

Immediately from these three examples, we can find three different interactions, (i) artwork interaction with non-user parameters (environment), (ii) audience interaction with artwork for content accessibility or content generation and (iii) audience interaction with the artwork for user experience and being a part of the artwork expression.

In this paper, we want to see why and how these various types of interaction finds a relevance in the digital interactive art context by investigating some relevant disciplines. Since digital interactive art brings together different genres of art and brings together people and knowledge from different disciplines, we would like to see if the variations of meaning and approaches of interaction are due to that multi-disciplinary involvements and origin. In the next section, we present how the concept *interaction* is defined in some disciplines and how it is mixed with a different concept *communication* in some cases.

3   Interaction and Communication

Encyclopedia Britannica defines *communication* as the exchange of meanings between individuals through a common system of symbols. Merriam-Webster defines communication as a process by which information is exchanged between individuals through a common system of symbols, signs, or behavior. It also defines *communications,* the plural form, as a system (as of telephones, or computers) for transmitting or exchanging information.

The Merriam Webster dictionary defines *interaction* as mutual or reciprocal action or influence. The meaning of the concept 'interaction' depends on the context in which it is used. As Jensen (1998) mentions, different disciplines have quite different meaning of interaction. For example, in medical science it refers to the interplay between two medications applied at the same time, whereas, in engineering it refers to the relationship between two different materials under stress. Statistics and linguistics have all different meaning of interaction. However, none of these fields are related to the context of digital interactive artwork. The fields that are more related to concept of interaction in the context of digital interactive art are the concepts of interaction in (i) social science, (ii) communication and media studies, and, (iii) information technology. In the following sections, we present how interaction is defined in these relevant fields. Besides, we also show how *interaction* is related with or different from *communication* according to the various discipline-specific definitions.

3.1   In Social Science

In social science, interaction refers to the reciprocal relationship between two or more people (Duncan 1989) who, in a given situation, mutually adapt their behavior and actions to each other. Partners involved in interaction are located in close physical proximity and some form of symbolic interaction exists which leads to a mutual exchange and negotiation regarding meaning in that social context (Jensen 1998).

Social interaction is the process by which we act and react to those around us. Thus, a quick conversation with a friend is a kind of social interaction. Influential sociologist of twentieth century Erving Goffman argues that even though conversation with a friend may appear as a trivial and insignificant form of social interaction, but they are of major importance in sociology (Moffitt 2018). In sociology, social interactions include such large number of behaviors that interaction is usually divided into five categories: exchange, competition, cooperation, conflict and coercion (Moffitt 2018).

The difference between interaction and communication in social science is that of response, reply and reciprocity. In communication, the receiver may or may not respond, whereas in interaction, there is requirement of a response for it to be an 'inter'-action. It is noted that when two people interacts according to the definition of social science, mutual exchange and negotiation regarding meaning takes place between partners as a result of the interaction. Therefore, interaction in social science includes communication.

3.2   In Communication and Media Studies

In communication and media studies, the concept of interaction is not clearly defined as in social science. Interaction in communication and media studies is used as a broad concept that covers the processes that takes place between media message and its receiver. For example, reading a text, a literary work is an interaction between its structure and its recipient (Iser 1989). In that way listening to radio, watching TV etc. and other forms of communication which take place through technologies of various kinds such as telephone, internet, presentations are also sort of interaction (Horton and Richard Wohl 1956). Thus, we can see that, in communication and media studies, the reciprocity nature in the social science sense is not required, and interaction can be one sided and non-dialectical.

When media technologies opened up for input from the user later on, media researcher still did not use the concept of interaction as reciprocity in the sense of social science for quite a while (Jensen 1998). Interaction was predominantly considered as one way by the media researchers and it referred to the actions of an audience or recipients in relation to media content. After the arrival of new media, the interactive nature of media started to gain attention of the researchers.

3.3   In Informatics

The concept of interaction in information technology refers to the relationship between people and machines, which is known as human computer interaction or man-machine interaction. The term 'interactive' historically originates from batch processing. Batch processing refers to a process where a series of tasks are executed by a computer without any human interruption. Contrary to the batch processing, interactive processing is the situation where a user can observe partial results, interrupt the program and continually influence the flow and performance of the program by giving input to the program. Thus, 'interaction' in the context of information technology or computer science refers to the process that takes place when a human user interacts with the machine with a goal to influence its processing. Though the reciprocity nature of interaction is taken from the social science sense, but in informatics it does not refer to the interaction between two persons, rather it refers to the interaction between a machine and a user.

There is a difference between interaction and communication in informatics. When two people communicate with each other through a machine, that is communication mediated by computer, it is not termed as interaction; rather it is called computer-mediated communication. Whereas in terms of communication and media studies that could still be called as an interaction.

In summary, we can say that, 'interaction' in the sociological sense refers to reciprocal relationship between two people, but in informatics sense, it refers to the relationship between people and machine. Communication mediated by computer is not interaction in the informatics sense, whereas, according to communication and media studies it can be interaction. In social science, since interaction is between two human beings, it is not possible to have interaction without communication, but communication without interaction is possible for example reading a text, paper, watching TV etc. In media and communication study, interaction is possible even with static information or one-way flow of contents; interaction and communication is somewhat similar here. Finally, in informatics, interaction happens only when a user interacts with a machine, and is not between two human beings, so it is possible to have interaction (with machine) without human-human communication.

4   Interactivity

The concept of interactivity extends from the concept of 'interaction'. Interactivity refers to the extent to which something is interactive. The Merriam Webster dictionary defines interactive as (i) "mutually or reciprocally active", or (ii) involving the actions or input of a user; especially: of, relating to, or being a two-way electronic communication system that involves a user's orders or responses. Oxford English dictionary defines it as, "(of two people or things) influencing each other". It also includes a definition from the viewpoint of computing as below:

"Allowing a two-way flow of information between a computer and a computer user; responding to a user's input". In the following sections, we present the concept of interactivity of media artefacts and digital interactive artworks.

4.1   Interactivity of Media Artefacts

Social science does not usually use the term interactivity, but in informatics and media studies, the concept of interaction and interactivity is used synonymously (Jensen 1998). In this section, we put some notable definitions of interactivity that researchers used to define whether a media artefact is interactive or not. The definitions in this section were mainly used in the context of media artefact or communication systems.

Interaction is a style of control, interactive systems exhibit that style and interactivity defines the level/extent to which the system is interactive. Rogers (1986) defines interactivity as the ability of the communication system to talk back, and he considers it as a variable: some systems are low interactive and some are highly interactive.

Jensen (1998) argues that a large number of new media artefacts can be addressed if we consider interactivity as a continuum rather than a criteria and the interactivity can be presented in varying degrees. As an example, Klaus Schrape's five levels scale of interactivity which considers a TV/radio with only the user functions of turn on and off and changing channels as level 0 interactive and video phone which offers two way communication is given level 4, the highest level on the scale (Schrape 1995). Thus, the level of interactivity in media refers to how much control the user has over it.

Laurel (1990) has argued that "interactivity exists on a continuum that could be characterized by three variables" specifically: (1) "frequency" in other words, "how often you could interact", (2) "range", or "how many choices were available" and (3) "significance", or "how much the choices really affected matters".

Sheizaf Rafaeli's concept focuses on the responsiveness of the media in dialogue with the user and distinguishes between level of responsiveness: reactive and fully interactive. Rafaeli (1988) mention three progressive levels: (i) Two way communication- message flows in both ways but do not depend on previous message, (ii) reactive - a later message reacts to a previous message but does not consider history (iii) full interactivity- later message responds to a sequence of previous messages, i.e., history of interaction.

Based on Bordewijk and Van Kaam (1986) matrix of information traffic pattern, Jensen (2008) defines four types of interactivity of a media considering who controls content creation and distribution or, in other way, user's influence on creation and distribution of content:

(1) *Transmissional interactivity,* where information is both produced and distributed by center. It is a one-way flow of information where user has no influence except choosing for example a channel in multichannel TV.
(2) *Conversational Interactivity,* where information is both produced and distributed by consumer. For example, chat, news groups, emails etc.
(3) *Consultational interactivity*, where information is produced by center, distributed by consumer. User can choose from an existing selection of pre-produced information in a two-way media system with a return channel. For example, true video on demand, online information services, WWW etc.
(4) *Registrational interactivity* is where media allows the user to register information but does not allow distribution control to the user. For example, home-shopping, surveillance systems, intelligent agents etc.

From the above discussion, it is clear that, there are not only various concepts of interaction but also various concepts of interactivity. The levels of interactivity of media artefacts address several aspects, such as media's ability to talk back, degree of reciprocity, user's level of control on the media, user's level of control on content of the media etc. In this scenario, it will be interesting to see which definitions and aspects of interactivity suits the context of digital interactive art.

4.2 Interactivity of Digital Interactive Artworks

In the previous section, we have listed some concepts of interactivity in the context of media. Here we will present some definitions that is more relevant for interactive artworks and multimedia installations.

Digital interactive art is part of new media art. As Steinkamp (2001) puts it, "They obviously can be considered part of the new media art genre because of their origins in, and reliance upon, computer-based technology". Therefore, it is interesting to see how interactivity is defined in the sense of new media. Particularly we will see how the digital interactive art positions its definition of interactivity compared to the media studies and new media. We will note the differences of aspects in the definitions along the way as we go from a general multimedia application to the more specific digital interactive artwork.

Interactivity is one of the main characteristic of the new media. As mentioned in (Jensen 1998), interactivity of new media is defined as the ratio of response or initiative on the part of the user to the offer of the source or sender.

In the context of multimedia applications, Hannington and Reed (2002) discusses three distinguished types of interaction: passive, interactive and adaptive. *Passive* interaction is where the content has a linear presentation and users interact by only starting and stopping the presentation; *interactive* is when users are allowed to choose a personal path through the content; *adaptive* is the interaction in which users are able to enter their own content and control how it is used.

In the context of interactive artwork and edutainment, Mignonneau and Sommerer (2005) identifies two types of interaction that they have observed in existing interactive artworks: *pre-designed* or *pre-programmed, and evolutionary. Pre-designed* or *pre-programmed* paths of interaction refers to interaction as in interactive CDs where the viewer can choose his/her path, but the possibilities are limited. E*volutionary* refers to situation in which the artwork's processes are linked to interaction and is evolving continuously.

Based on the relationship between the artwork, artist, viewer and environment, Edmonds et al. (2004) discuss four categories of artwork: *static, dynamic-passive, dynamic-interactive* and *dynamic interactive (varying)*.

In static, the art object is mainly static and does not change itself in respect to its context. There is no interaction between the viewer and the object. Even though the viewer may experience personal psychological or emotional reactions, but that is internal and personal to the viewer. Example of this type of art are traditional art such as painting or sculpture. Art consumers can view a painting or a sculpture, listen to an audio tape and talk to one another about an art on the wall.

Dynamic-Passive type artwork changes with time but remains passive in response to user interaction. The change mechanism of the artwork is pre-designed and the change is controlled by an internal mechanism (algorithm or mechanical/physical process etc.). Environmental factors such as temperature, sound, light etc. can play a role in the changes. Sculptures such as George Rickey's (1979) kinetic pieces that move according to internal mechanisms and also in response to atmospheric changes in the environment fall into this category.

In **Dynamic-Interactive**, the user has an active role in the change of the artwork. Usually artwork has some sensors that take values such as touch, movement, gestures, proximity etc. from the user, which serve as an input for the artwork changes based on a predefined algorithm.

Dynamic-Interactive (Varying) artworks are similar to dynamic interactive with the addition that artwork evolves over time and changes from its original specification. In this case, all the changes of the artwork due to the interactions are accumulated and the state of the artwork at a particular time depends on the history of the interactions. The future status of the artwork is therefore unpredictable.

From the above discussion, we see that from the static digital art to dynamic multi-media applications and to the highly interactive art installations, artworks at the lower end of the interactivity spectrum uses interaction in the sense of media and communication studies, mainly to refer to the degree to which user can have control on the media or its contents. In the higher end, in the interactive art installations, interactivity is used in the sense of informatics, to refer to the degree to which a user can control the output of the system and the reciprocity nature of the artefact.

5   Identifying the Interactions in Digital Interactive Art Installation

Now that we have some idea about the interaction and communication, and interactivity of artwork, we would like to identify the different kinds of interactions that can take place in the context of a digital interactive art installation. However, before describing the possible meaningful interactions with a digital interactive artwork, we give an example of a digital interactive art installation from where it will be easy to understand the components of the artwork and the relationships and interactions between them.

5.1   A Digital Interactive Art Installation

Sonic Onyx is an exemplary project of digital interactive art installation in public space in which we participated as researcher and collaborated with the artists and technologists. This artwork brings into many sought after interactions and aspects that artists are interested in public space installation.

Sonic Onyx is an interactive sound sculpture that is placed in front of a secondary school (Ahmed 2012). The sculpture has seven loudspeakers located in seven arms and a subwoofer located in ground at the center making it possible to provide 3D sound effects within the space created by the sculpture (Fig. 1). People can communicate with the sculpture by sending text, image, and sound files from their Bluetooth enabled hand-held devices. These media files are processed and converted into unrecognizable sound by mixing with randomly selected algorithms. The converted audio is then played by the sculpture. Audience interact with the sculpture by sending files and try to reflect how their files are modified and converted into different sound files. A website archives previously sent and modified files that were played by the sculpture. Students from music class can create an account and upload the music composed by them to be played by the sculpture in its idle time, i.e., when no one interacts with it by sending files via Bluetooth.

The sphere on the top contains a light bulb that dynamically changes its color based the outside weather condition such as light, dark, gloomy etc. We find the example of Sonic Onyx very interesting as it covers many aspects of interaction with the artwork. Audience can directly interact with the artwork, it allows inter-audience communication within the space, and audience can communicate indirectly via the website. Artist can even get ideas and insights about the audience interactions through the website.

Fig. 1. Users interacting with Sonic Onyx

5.2 Components of a Digital Interactive Art Installation

As we can see from the previous example, there are essentially four components in an art system they are: (i) Artwork, (ii) Audience, (iii) Environment, and (iv) Artist (Fig. 2).

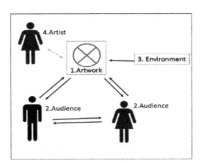

Fig. 2. Components of an artwork system

There could be several relationships between different components which might be meaningful and interesting in respect to interactive artwork such as:

1. audience – artwork,
2. audience–audience,
3. artwork–environment.

In the traditional sense, artist might not be a part of the artwork system, but as researchers consider that the artist and the audience play integral participant roles in today's interactive art (Edmonds et al. 2004), therefore we have put the artist as part of the system. We have shown artist in the artwork system as loosely connected and the interaction between artist and artwork system is shown with dashed line. In one hand, artist is not an integral part of the system as like an audience (unless the artist him/herself takes part as an audience), but on the other hand, in the context of today's digital interactive artworks, artist might be interested in getting feedback about audience interaction with the artwork. Considering artist as part of the system, two other relationships:

4. artist–artwork, and
5. artist–audience,

appears in the scenario. Artist and audience relationship can take place either as a direct artist-audience interaction or through the artwork as artist-artwork-audience interaction (in the sense of communication). With the ability of the artwork to register its audience input, the artist can get direct contact with its audience and uses the feedbacks from audience as like a co-creative process. As it is mentioned in (Beyl and Bauwens 2010).

"Thinking about art as a process of social communication, i.e. an exchange of symbolic content between the meaning creator and the meaning receiver, we explore how the relationship between the artist and his audience is shaped and potentially altered in an interactive Internet environment. On the one hand, this media technological advancement could allow the artist to engage in a more direct contact with his audience. On the other hand, it permits the beholder to inspire the artist from a co-creative point of view."

Considering the artwork as a system that evolves and changes with time depending on audience feedback and participation, there could be one last relationship,

6. artist-artwork system,

that includes artist's all other relationships with the audience, artwork and the environment as a whole system.

5.3 Identifying the Interactions

In this section, we identify the possible interactions that can happen between two or more components of the artwork. We identify all possible interactions and categorize them according to the definitions. If there are more than one type of interactions, we mark which ones are prominent in the context of an interactive art installation. Among the six possible relations in the artwork system, there could be several meaningful or interesting interactions as noted below:

(i) *Audience - Artwork:* The interaction between artwork and audience is in the sense of informatics, in the form of human machine interaction. This is the dominant type of interaction in a digital interactive artwork. In the Fig. 3, this is shown in capital "D".

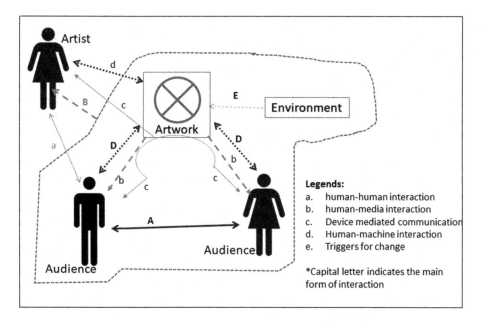

Fig. 3. Interactions in a digital art installation

Interaction in the sense of media studies is also possible, for example, analogous to the mental and psychological effect of reading a book or article, a user can have similar the mental and psychological effect by observing and interacting with the artwork. However, this interaction is less prominent at least when interactivity of the artwork is talked about. In the Fig. 3, it is shown as small letter "b".

(ii) *Audience - Audience:* This sort of interaction is the interaction in the sense of social science which is otherwise called social interaction. Social interaction between audiences can take place even in the case of a traditional non-interactive art such as painting or photography while visiting a museum or a gallery. However, in case of an interactive art, artists often carefully design and observe the social interaction so as to make the interaction an integral part of the artwork system. In Fig. 3, this is marked as capital "A".

When the artwork is considered as a media device, there could be also device mediated communication between two audience, like computer mediated communication. In the Fig. 3, it is shown as small letter "c". However, this is not interactivity in the sense of reciprocity between the audience and the artwork, or in the sense of social interaction between audience and audience, rather it is a non-prominent communication that can take place between audience – audience or artist - audience.

(iii) *Artwork - Environment:* Some artworks interact with some environmental factors or events. For example, artwork may change based on light, temperature, wind or other changes of the environment.

The interaction between the environment and artwork is not an interaction. It is not interaction in the sense of neither social interaction, nor media studies or informatics - since there is not at least one human being (as the user) involved in the interaction. But some artists and researchers still call it as interactive artwork as the nature and the technical design of the artwork is quite similar to an interactive artwork that would otherwise interact with similar inputs from an audience instead of from the environment (for example, by reading similar values from sensors). It can be grouped as dynamic-passive artwork according to Edmonds et al. (2004). However, if the user can, in no way, change or control the output of the artwork, for a user this would rather appear as a dynamic passive artwork where the rules for changes are triggered by some environment factors. In Fig. 3, this is marked as capital "E", as this is the only and prominent interaction between artwork and environment. Since this is not any true interaction in the sense of any relevant disciplines that we have discussed in this article, we have named this relationship as "triggers for change" instead of calling it interaction or communication.

(iv) *Artist - Artwork:* This is very similar to *audience-artwork* interaction only except the fact that artist is the creator of the artwork. Artist's personal interaction with the artwork may give him insight about the audience interaction and feedback for future changes or modification of the artwork. However, this is not a sought after interaction in a digital interactive art installation, since the artwork is supposed to have main interaction with its audience rather than the artists him/herself. In Fig. 3, it is shown with small letter "d".

(v) *Artist - Audience:* Most of the cases, artist is not directly interacting with the audience unless the artist is actively participating in the artwork for the sake of the artwork expression. However, in some cases, if the artist wants, or if that is planned in the artwork expression, this can happen in the sense of social interaction.

Apart from direct interaction, the artist- audience interaction can also take place in the sense of media studies interaction (rather, we can say it, communication) via the artwork. This is device mediated communication that is already mentioned in *audience - audience* interaction in point (ii). In the Fig. 3, this is marked with small letter "c" between artist and audience.

(vi) *Artist - Artwork system:* In an interactive artwork artist not only considers audience as an integral part of the artwork, but also considers the artwork as an evolving agent which changes and updates over time. Artists carefully design the interaction between artwork and audience, and between audience-audience, and over time, considers the feedback and responses of the audience to make future changes and improvements of the artwork system. Artists are more interested in this approach and this is the prominent communication pattern they look after from the whole system. This is an interaction in the sense of media and communication studies, and it is shown in Fig. 3 as capital "B". The artwork system is shown as dotted outline that includes all the components of the figure except the artist.

6   Conclusions

In this article, we have presented the concept of interaction in different fields and shown what it means when we refer to interactivity of digital interactive art. We have presented different kind of interactions that are possible in the context of an artwork or art installation and compared different concepts of interactivity. We narrowed down the definitions from the context of a general media artefact to new media artefacts and then drew towards more specific digital interactive artworks. We have presented the interactions in the context of a digital interactive art installation in an open space, since this kind of artwork gives the opportunity to have the most possible interactions considering spatial and environmental factors.

As we have seen that different artists, technologists, researchers define interaction and interactivity of artwork differently, finding the different meanings and uses of interaction will thus remove the confusion and make clear the blurry concepts about interaction among them. As we have noticed in the article, the concept of interactivity in digital interactive art gets the influence of interactivity concepts from several fields like: media artefacts, new media, digital art and interactive art. We have noticed that the approach and depth of interactivity changes from field to field. In the context of media artefacts, interaction refers to some sort of user control over the media artefact, whereas in highly interactive new media artefacts interactivity refers to user's ability to the creation and distribution of contents. In digital art, it refers to user's control over the processing or the output of the system, whereas in pure interactive art it refers to user's participation and being a part of the artwork. These variations are linked to the various meanings of interaction that we have found in different disciplines for example, control over a process, reciprocity, communication via a media, and interpretation of some communication. In this article, we have defined and identified all these various meanings in context of digital interactive art to make it clear and unambiguous. We believe that our work will help the artists and technologists to better classify their artwork, define the concepts of interactivity of an artwork from a particular viewpoint, and help them to identify, define and understand the desired interactions that they are interested in a certain artwork from a certain context. It will also help the multidisciplinary stakeholders of an artwork to understand each other better. Besides that, since interaction and user experience is the main idea in a digital interactive art, it will help the different stakeholders in designing, developing and evaluating their artworks.

References

Ahmed, S.U.: Achieving pervasive awareness through artwork. Paper presented at the Proceedings of the 3rd International Conference on Digital Interactive Media in Entertainment and Arts, Athens, Greece (2008)

Ahmed, S.U.: Extending Software Engineering Collaboration towards the Intersection of Software and Art. NTNU, Trondheim (2011)

Ahmed, S.U.: Developing software-dependent artwork: artist and software developers' collaboration. Leonardo **45**(1), 92–93 (2012)

Ahmed, S.U., Jaccheri, L., Sindre, G., Trifonova, A.: Conceptual Framework for the Intersection of Software and Art. In: Handbook of Research on Computational Arts and Creative Informatics, pp. 26–44. IGI Global (2009)

Beyl, J., Bauwens, J.: Understanding the social meaning of art on the internet. Univ. Melb. Refereed E-J. **1**(5) (2010)

Bordewijk, J.L., Van Kaam, B.: Towards a new classification of tele-information services. Intermedia **14**(1), 19–21 (1986)

Duncan, S.J.: Interaction, Face-to-Face International Encyclopedia of Communications. Oxford University Press, New York (1989)

Edmonds, E.: Interactive Art. In: Candy, L., Edmonds, E. (eds.) Interacting: Art, Research and the Creative Practitioner, pp. 18–32. Libri Publishing Ltd, Faringdon (2011)

Edmonds, E., Turner, G., Candy, L.: Approaches to interactive art systems. Paper presented at the Proceedings of the 2nd International Conference on Computer Graphics and Interactive Techniques in Australasia and South East Asia, Singapore (2004)

Hannington, A., Reed, K.: Towards a taxonomy for guiding multimedia application development. Paper presented at the Ninth Asia-Pacific Software Engineering Conference (APSEC 2002), Gold Coast, Queensland, Australia, 4–6 December 2002 (2002)

Horton, D., Richard Wohl, R.: Mass communication and para-social interaction: observations on intimacy at a distance. Psychiatry **19**(3), 215–229 (1956)

Iser, W.: Interaction between text and reader. In: Hawthor, J.C.J. (ed.) Communication Studies. An Introductory Reader. Edward Arnold, London (1989)

Jensen, J.F.: Interactivity: tracing a new concept in media and communication studies. Nordicom Rev. **19**, 185–204 (1998)

Jensen, J.F.: The concept of interactivity – revisited: four new typologies for a new media landscape. In: Proceedings of the 1st International Conference on Designing Interactive User Experiences for TV and Video, pp. 129–132 (2008). https://doi.org/10.1145/1453805.1453831

Lasserre, G., Ancxt, A.: met den (2018). Scenocosme. http://www.scenocosme.com/index_e.htm. Accessed 3 Feb 2018

Laurel, B.: Interface agents: metaphors with character. In: Laurel, B. (ed.) The Art of Human-Computer Interface Design. Addison-Wesley, Reading (1990)

Lopes, D.M.M.: The ontology of interactive art. J. Aesthetic Educ. **35**(4), 65–81 (2001)

Mignonneau, L., Sommerer, C.: Designing emotional, metaphoric, natural and intuitive interfaces for interactive art, edutainment and mobile communications. Comput. Graph. (Pergamon) **29**, 837–851 (2005). https://doi.org/10.1016/j.cag.2005.09.001

Moffitt, K.: Social Interactions: Definition and Types (2018). https://study.com/academy/lesson/social-interactions-definition-types-quiz.html. Accessed 3 Feb 2018

Nardelli, E.: A classification framework for interactive digital artworks. In: Alvarez, F., Costa, C. (eds.) User Centric Media. UCMEDIA 2010. Lecture Notes of the Institute for Computer Sciences, Social Informatics and Telecommunications Engineering, vol. 60, pp. 91–100. Springer, Heidelberg (2012). https://doi.org/10.1007/978-3-642-35145-7_12

Pereira, L.: Why is it So Difficult to Define New Media Art? (2015). https://www.widewalls.ch/new-media-art-definition/. Accessed 3 Feb 2018

Rafaeli, S. (ed.): Interactivity: From New Media to Communication, Newbury Park (1988)

Rickey, G.: A Retrospective. Guggenheim Museum, New York (1979)

Rogers, E.M.: Communication Technology. Free Press, New York (1986)

Satomi, M., Sommerer, C.: "game_of_life": interactive art installation using eye-tracking interface. Paper presented at the Proceedings of the International Conference on Advances in Computer Entertainment Technology, Salzburg, Austria (2007)

Schraffenberger, H., van der Heide, E.: Interaction models for audience-artwork interaction: current state and future directions. In: Brooks, A.L. (ed.) ArtsIT 2011. LNICSSITE, vol. 101, pp. 127–135. Springer, Heidelberg (2012). https://doi.org/10.1007/978-3-642-33329-3_15

Schrape, K.: Digitales Fernsehen Marktchancen und ordnungspolitischer Regelungsdedarf, München (1995)

Steinkamp, J.: My only sunshine: installation art experiments with light, space, sound and motion. Leonardo **34**(2), 109–112 (2001)

Trifonova, A., Jaccheri, L.: Towards good software engineering practices in interactive installation art. Paper presented at the International Conference on Software Engineering (ICSE) 2008, Leipzig, Germany (2007)

Towards Cross-Generational System Design

Maurizio Caon[✉]

University of Applied Sciences and Arts Western Switzerland, Fribourg, Switzerland
maurizio.caon@hes-so.ch

Abstract. This paper introduces the concept of cross-generational system, which indicates an information technology system designed to allow different generations interacting through centuries or, even, millennia. In the era of digital immortality and advances in artificial intelligence, there will be not only the problem of preserving and accessing data, but the emergence of digital clones will bring new challenges for technology development, interaction design and ethics. This paper provides an overview of societal transformation towards digital immortality, then describes the vision of cross-generational system design, investigates the relative future challenges and proposes the eventual socio-ethical questions.

Keywords: Digital immortality · Cyber world · Digital curation
Artificial intelligence · Blockchain

1 Introduction

Using the term "cross-generational" in any field and, in particular, in communication refers to the interaction between older and younger people [1]. However, humanity is currently living a transition towards a more and more technological society and, most importantly, growingly composed of digital natives. This means that digital systems have now been present for decades, outliving a growing number of human beings. In this intergenerational change, there is also an exchange of goods and items, which are progressively becoming more and more digitalised. This implies that new trends in society are rising. For example, researchers found that some users already keep talking to deceased people on social media [2]. This phenomenon has been called thanatechnology, which is defined as the use of technology to allow people to remember the deceased loved ones [3].

At the same time, people can communicate messages and ideas to the next generations, leaving a trace for the future. In a landscape where the number of digital items people possess continues to grow, there is also the question of inheriting digital possessions (e.g., photos, books, movies, online videogame characters and items, Inter-net domains, cryptocurrencies). The ubiquitous computing and Internet of Things will provide new opportunities for remembrance and communication with future generations [3]. Enabling the secure transmission of digital information and virtual objects to future generations represents for humanity the achievement of a first type of digital immortality [4].

In this era of profound digital transformation, where also the fast evolution of artificial intelligence is playing a crucial role, it is important to start thinking about the correct approaches and methodologies for the design of the systems of the future, which will allow cross-generational communication beyond death. This is the right time to start discussing about the importance of developing new systems designed with the purpose of interacting with several human generations through time.

As already mentioned, this paper wants to provide an opportunity for reflection about the challenges in designing systems in the era of digital immortality. It starts providing a description of the ongoing process of digital transformation, which is impacting everyone's life. This description will introduce the concept of digital clones and how these would imply a further evolution of the meaning of digital immortality. Following the analysis of this imminent progress towards digital immortality, the challenges in designing systems in this context are preliminarily explored and exposed. Before concluding this vision paper, a modest Section is also dedicated to the possible ethical questions that this technological evolution will, or at least should, raise in a not-so-distant future.

2   From Digital Dark Ages to the Digital Immortality Era

Because of Industry 4.0, social media, Internet of Things and multimedia, humanity is currently generating data at a record rate (often referred to as "big data") [5]. In 2016, global users produced as much data as in the entire history of humankind through 2015 [6]. Hundreds of thousands of Google searches and Facebook posts are generated every minute. The amount of information generated by users is growing exponentially not only because of the increased time spent on the Internet but also because of the ubiquity of connected devices. Indeed, the number of internet-connected devices is growing and are already exceeding the number of people on Earth. It has been predicted that by 2020, there will be on average approximately seven internet-connected devices per person for a total of 50 billion devices [7]. Ubiquitous computing is indeed enabling a digital transformation towards the so-called cyber world [8]. This term was first defined by T. L. Kunii in 2004 as "worlds on cyberspace as computational spaces, either intentionally or spontaneously, with or without design" [9]. Later, J. Ma provided a further definition, in which the cyber world is "a digitized world created on cyberspace inside computers interconnected by networks including the Internet" [10]. Always J. Ma stated that these cyber worlds represent the next phase of human evolution and will bring a number of unknown phenomena, and novel challenges such as digital explosion in data, connectivity, services and intelligence [11].

2.1   Preserving Digital Human History

It is interesting to note that it is clear that society is building this cyber world as a reflection of the physical one, which represent together two dimensions of future human life. This implies that the cyber world should be built in order to last in time as, at least, the physical one does. However, although it is obvious that the digitisation of information is already happing fast and at a large scale, the management and preservation of digital information are still not mature, and this raises a number of issues. The euphoria brought by the technological revolution is making everyone focus more on the generation of data forgetting the important and consequent act of preserving digital information. On this matter, T. Kuny wrote "as we move into the electronic era of digital objects, it is important to know that there are new barbarians at the gate and that we are moving into an era where much of what we know today, much of what is coded and written electronically, will be lost forever. We are, to my mind, living in the midst of digital Dark Ages; consequently, much as monks of times past, it falls to librarians and archivists to hold to the tradition which reveres history and the published heritage of our times" [12]. The ongoing process of digitalisation of the society is not taking into account the severe threat of total loss of a broad swathe of the scientific record and cultural heritage in digital form. Indeed, since the democratisation of the personal computer, enormous amounts of digital information are already lost forever. Once lost, digital history cannot be recreated by individuals or organizations. The raising awareness of risking to further extend the duration of these digital dark ages brought the foundation of digital curation domain. The digital curation has been defined as "the act of maintaining and adding value to a trusted body of digital information for both current and future generations of users: in other words, it is the active management and appraisal of digital information over its entire life cycle" [13]. Often, the causes of such losses were as trivial as the lack of archive management or because information was stored in out-dated formats. For these reasons, it is important to start designing systems that can integrate effective fail-safe mechanisms to support the rescue of endangered digital information and the constant update of their storage formats.

2.2 Achieving Digital Immortality

Preserving and transmitting information to next generations has been defined as one-way immortality: allowing communication with the future [4]. This type of digital immortality would already enable sharing ideas and memories through time, making it possible to democratise knowledge and enhance the conservation of cultural heritage.

Passing digital information to next generations could also bring other novel applications and unprecedented opportunities. For example, preserving scientific data in an adequate and intelligible manner may give to those data more than one life: as scientific ideas advance, new concepts may emerge from study of observations that led earlier to different kinds of insights [14]. This would accelerate scientific progress and, at the same time, reduce the cost of research and innovation. In this way, the research could virtually be conducted from researchers lived in different eras giving to collaboration a new dimension independent from time and augment the potential of human intellect.

The relentless evolution of technology is not just touching its pervasiveness but also its potential. The progress made in machine learning in the last decade made the vast majority of the researchers quite optimistic about the future of artificial intelligence (AI) [15]. Several researchers in AI are working toward the ultimate goal: the creation of a machine able to mimic the human mind [16]. Several researchers actually think that the AI is positioned to become smarter than humans [17].

This context stimulated the generation of a further vision, which depicts a future where the evolution of AI will make possible to develop virtual agents based on the personality of deceased users, transferring their minds into the machine becoming digitally immortal [18]. These agents will not only be repository of the dead people's knowledge but will act generating new information in the cyber world according to the personality. This is called *two-way immortality*: "allowing you, or at least part of you, to communicate with the future in the sense that artefact continues to learn and evolve" [4]. This will introduce a new level of interaction between different generations: users will be able to co-create original information with deceased people. A kid can ask his grand-grand-grandfather opinion about the new political scene. Designing such interaction will face many unprecedented challenges, such as the difference of language and the update of the deceased people awareness of new technologies and socio-political events.

Finally, digital immortality can be defined more in general as "a continuum from enduring fame at one end to endless experience and learning at the other, stopping just short of endless life" [4].

3 Emergence of Digital Clones

The process of digital transformation is causing the emergence of the cyber world, which means creating a digital copy of every entity present in the physical world, and this phenomenon includes the human beings. Many research works introduced the concept of digital avatar to model the characteristics of each individual. For example, the European Commission initiated the Virtual Physiological Human (VPH) initiative, which aims at developing an integrated model of human physiology at multiple scales from the whole body through the organ, tissue, cell and molecular levels to the genomic level [19]. The ultimate goal of the VPH is to support the development of patient-specific computer models and their application in personalised and predictive healthcare [20]. This initiative allowed collecting and integrating heterogeneous and data predictive models to obtain unprecedented results in the interpretation and prediction of the progress of diseases and of the effectiveness of relative treatments. Many projects stemmed from this initiative to tackle specific problems or diseases [21], or also to provide personalised motivational interventions [22]. However, the ultimate goal is to have a comprehensive model of each individual to provide personalised treatments. A new European project, with this vision, has just been created: the Health EU. This project aims at developing human avatars that will allow healthy individuals and patients to prevent, intercept and cure any disease [23]. The Health EU project is positioned to revolutionise the human model development by leveraging data from omics analyses, medical and imaging data, environmental and life style big data that are continuously updated by a multitude of biosensors at an unprecedented scale. In particular, this health avatars will be able to update their information directly uploading data from the most advanced organ-on-chip and implantable smart nanosensors.

Although the aforementioned projects already represent the avant-garde of digital avatars, it has been predicted that future digital representations of individuals will be able to simulate also thoughts, ideas and emotions. Indeed, J. Ma stated that the effort of research to digitise also the human beings will lead to the creation of the Cyber-Individual (or Cyber-I), which is a digital clone of a human individual able to simulate the original human being from the behaviours to the mind/thinking through the continuous collection of personal data [11]. The digital clone is an identical copy of its original individual with the difference that it exists in the cyber world, although it may be embedded within a physical entity or object present in the physical world, e.g., a humanoid robot. Since it has been predicted that it will be possible to copy any entity in the cyber world, J. Ma provided also a more general definition of digital clone, which is "a digital copy of a creature, a plant or something related to an individual with certain life characteristics" [11].

The research conducted by J. Ma on the creation of the Cyber-I aims at creating a digital clone through the continuous collection of personal data not only for precision medicine treatments for life prolongation, but also to make individual-aware applications for the provision of desired services to everyone living in both the physical and cyber world [11]. The Cyber-I would enable new computing modes for personalized services (e.g., individual-aware search engines) and other novel applications (e.g., suitable service discovery and community simulation) [11]. It is possible to imagine that there could be multiple uses of the Cyber-I in favour of the original individual. For example, the digital clone could work on behalf of the original individual, or the Cyber-I could run a myriad of simulations to suggest the best action to the original human being in every context and at every moment. However, it is clear that at this moment in time, there are still many open technical challenges for the realisation of such digital clones, starting from the continuous aggregation of personal data, to running a model of the human mind.

4   System Design in the Era of Digital Immortality

The previous sections introduced the cyber world and the concept of digital clones. In this era of digital immortality, it will be possible to interact with copy of oneself or digital simulations of other people, who could have already died even centuries before. The development of systems allowing to interact with multiple digital clones, to receive and send information through centuries, and generating personalised services will surely introduce new challenges at both user interface and data management levels.

4.1   Interaction

First, it is important to state the obvious: in the era of digital immortality, users will be able to interact with information coming from the past and send data to the future in a deterministic way. These cross-generational systems should be designed following two principles:

1. Link to the past: integrating the possibility of accessing information and inheriting digital items left from the deceased ones.

2. Link to the future: integrating an interface allowing to produce information that will be transmitted to the next generations after the user's death.

These systems will be used by several different generations through time, maybe centuries or even millennia. This means that huge amounts of information will be accumulated through time. This would also imply that the cross-generational systems will have to provide the possibility to users to access data in an effective and agile manner. This issue becomes more evident when considering the fact that the adoption of lifelogging technologies is a current growing trend. Lifelogging offers the ability to capture an individual's life experiences through digital means, and to eventually retell and share them with other people, possibly with future generations. Taming such voluminous multimodal collections is very hard: a lifelogging device collects every moment of one's life [24]. It is easy to understand that this implies that filtering and elaborating the best moments would take more than a lifetime. For this reason, it will be indispensable to automatise the filtering but allowing access to the correct information. A user would like to access a particular moment without knowing specific information concerning the picture and its metadata. For example, the user could search a picture describing the memory of an emotion or the song played when it was taken or an event that occurred the same day. Performing such advanced searches requires the use of artificial intelligence. This implies that users wanting to simply access information should probably interact with an intelligent digital entity. Interaction modalities will move towards more natural language, such as writing and talking like while interacting with another human being. Indeed, this trend can be seen in the current explosion of chatbot services and virtual assistants (e.g., Apple Siri, Google Assistant, Microsoft Cortana). This kind of interface is currently also populating homes for domotics, such as with the use of Amazon Echo and Google Home. In order to provide effective personalised services, the AI should be able to understand the user's preferences and needs.

Preparing the information to be purposely shared with the future generations will require applying advanced techniques of digital storytelling [25]. This will encourage the formation of timeless communities and adding the possibility to reuse and adapt these stories will also represent the opportunity for the generation of collective intelligence and collaborative artistic creation.

The amount of digital information will be so vast that current interfaces will not be adequate to interact with it, not only, as already mentioned, for the difficulty of managing it, but also because devices will be able to record new kind data that will lose their value when just represented in audio-visual formats. In particular, virtual reality, augmented reality and mixed reality will enable new forms of interaction with data and the cyber world. Current interfaces are falling short with reference to the level of immersion, indeed they just rely on two senses, i.e., vision and hearing, missing the opportunity to convey information through the others, which can augment the bandwidth of the communication between digital and physical individual. Future interfaces will probably stimulate all the human senses, probably also through the use of implanted connected technology [26]. So far, implanted systems are perceived as sensors, a useful source of data about the subtlest human signals. Hopefully, the future implantable systems will be able to provide feedback and connect the humans directly to the cyber world through all the senses.

4.2   Technology

The underlying technology will need to evolve in order to allow information preservation through millennia. As already state in Sect. 2.1, cross-generational systems will have to integrate effective fail-safe mechanisms to support the rescue of endangered digital information and the constant update of their storage formats. Currently, the standard procedures for digital curation rely mainly on human labour [13]. Future systems will be required to integrate automatic services for the preservation of digital materials during its whole life-cycle. Automatic and periodic conversion of files and databases will be effectuated. When this would require more complex tasks like translation or selection or restoration, a specialised AI will take on the job.

Another issue related to information that is supposed to be shared by multiple generations in different eras is linked to how granting access and privileges for editing the contents to the different users. When sharing this information, the original user cannot know who her/his descendants will be. Therefore, it will be necessary to develop novel security systems based on heritage rules and biometric data recognition (probably, based on DNA).

As already mentioned, the preservation of digital information through centuries will require conversion and migration of the stored data. Moreover, multiple users will access this information through time, with also the possibility to apply changes. Information will need to be stored in place that could be accessible although in continuous update. A solution could be based on centralised databases controlled by a single society that is able to guarantee security. However, breaches in third parties' data centres could may induce the adoption of new decentralized systems [27]. Moreover, having a third party to control all the data is risky because there is no guarantee that it will last centuries or millennia. For all these reasons, a decentralised system for the preservation of digital information while providing privacy could be based on the blockchain technology. Memories could be stored on blockchain, tracking who accessed them and if they have been modified. Pushing this concept further, it might be possible to work with digital mindfiles (uploads of full human mind files) in the future, which could be also stored using blockchain [28]. This could enable lifelogging as personal thinking blockchains, meaning that it will be possible to "capture and safely encode all of an individual's mental performance, emotions, and subjective experiences onto the blockchain, at minimum for backup and to pass on to one's heirs as a historical record". Hence, the blockchain could be an elegant solution for the storage of Ma's Cyber-I [11].

Although the blockchain can be seen as an excellent technological solution for the storage of the Cyber-I, running the simulation of an individual mind raises new technical challenges. To this day, it does not exist a computer that can simulate the functioning of the human brain. However, the European Commission supported the creation of the Human Brain Project [29]. This project aims at developing a Brain Simulation Platform, which is an internet-accessible collaborative platform designed for reconstruction and simulation of brain models. Hopefully, in a not-so-distant future, it will be possible to run comprehensive simulations of an individual's mind.

5   Ethics

Naturally, the vision presented in this paper about the future of systems in the era of digital immortality brings a number of ethical questions. In particular, a main question concerns the actual identity of these digitally immortal entities that will populate the cyber world [8]. Would this technology be democratic or just an advantage for the rich? Will these digital clones have rights or just treated as property? Will digital clones be treated as physical clones or will their intangibility change their value? Would it be ethical to delete or shut down a digital clone? Who could have the right to do it and why? Would a Cyber-I have a conscience? Would a digital mind be considered alive?

Going beyond the confinement of the definition of digital clones as just a copy of an individual, can they clones have access to unlimited amount of data? Would omniscient digital clones be allowed to evolve? This could imply that they would advance far beyond human capabilities; would they represent the transcendence of humanity towards divinity? Would digital clones with access to unlimited resources become digital gods?

6   Conclusion

This paper wanted to provide an overview of the current transformation of a society apparently destined to achieve digital immortality. This transition towards the digital domain will imply creating a parallel cyber world that will be populated with intelligent digital copies of physical entities. These so-called digital clones will bring a number of unprecedented advantages. However, this transformation is already raising several challenges. In this paper, some of these challenges concerning interaction with digital information, possible technological solutions for its preservation and related socio-ethical questions. This paper is only a preliminary discussion about this complex matter and future work is needed in multiple domains for the development of adequate cross-generational systems.

References

1. Lindley, S.E.: Shades of lightweight: supporting cross-generational communication through home messaging. Univ. Access Inf. Soc. **11**(1), 31–43 (2012)
2. Goldschmidt, K.: Thanatechnology: eternal digital life after death. J. Pediatr. Nurs. **28**(3), 302–304 (2013)
3. Gilbert, K.R., Massimi, M.: From digital divide to digital immortality: thanatechnology at the turn of the 21st century. In: Dying, Death, and Grief in an Online Universe. For Counselors and Educators, pp. 16–27 (2012)
4. Bell, G., Gray, J.: Digital immortality (2000). https://www.microsoft.com/en-us/research/publication/digital-immortality/. Accessed 09 Mar 2018
5. Hashem, I.A.T., Yaqoob, I., Anuar, N.B., Mokhtar, S., Gani, A., Khan, S.U.: The rise of "big data" on cloud computing: review and open research issues. Inf. Syst. **47**, 98–115 (2015)
6. Helbing, D., Frey, B.S., Gigerenzer, G., Hafen, E., Hagner, M., Hofstetter, Y., van den Hoven, J., Zicari, R.V., Zwitter, A.: Will democracy survive big data and artificial intelligence. In: Scientific American (2017)

7. Liu, H., et al.: A review of the smart world. Future Gener. Comput. Syst. (2017). http://dx.doi.org/10.1016/j.future.2017.09.010

8. Ma, J.: Cybermatics for cyberization towards cyber-enabled hyper worlds. In: 2016 4th IEEE International Conference on Mobile Cloud Computing, Services, and Engineering (MobileCloud), pp. 85–86. IEEE, March 2016

9. Kunii, T.L.: The potentials of cyberworlds - an axiomatic approach. In: 2004 International Conference on Cyberworlds, pp. 2–7. IEEE, November 2004

10. Ma, J., Yang, L.T., Apduhan, B.O., Huang, R., Barolli, L., Takizawa, M.: Towards a smart world and ubiquitous intelligence: a walkthrough from smart things to smart hyperspaces and UbicKids. Int. J. Pervasive Comput. Commun. 1(1), 53–68 (2005)

11. Ma, J., Huang, R.: Digital explosions and digital clones. In: 2015 IEEE 12th International Conference on Ubiquitous Intelligence and Computing and 2015 IEEE 12th International Conference on Autonomic and Trusted Computing and 2015 IEEE 15th International Conference on Scalable Computing and Communications and Its Associated Workshops (UIC-ATC-ScalCom), pp. 1133–1138. IEEE, August 2015

12. Kuny, T.: The digital dark ages? Challenges in the preservation of electronic information. Int. Preserv. News 17, 8–13 (1998)

13. Pennock, M.: Digital curation: a life-cycle approach to managing and preserving usable digital information. Libr. Arch. J. 1, January 2007. http://www.ukoln.ac.uk/ukoln/staff/m.pennock/publications/docs/libarch_curation.pdf

14. National Research Council: Preserving Scientific Data on Our Physical Universe: A New Strategy for Archiving the Nation's Scientific Information Resources. National Academies Press (1995)

15. Arel, I., Rose, D.C., Karnowski, T.P.: Deep machine learning-a new frontier in artificial intelligence research [research frontier]. IEEE Comput. Intell. Mag. 5(4), 13–18 (2010)

16. Minsky, M.: The Emotion Machine: Common Sense Thinking, Artificial Intelligence, and the Future of the Human Mind. Simon and Schuster (2007)

17. Grace, K., Salvatier, J., Dafoe, A., Zhang, B., Evans, O.: When Will AI Exceed Human Performance? Evidence from AI Experts. arXiv preprint arXiv:1705.08807 (2017)

18. Swan, L.S., Howard, J.: Digital immortality: Self or 0010110? Int. J. Mach. Conscious. 4(01), 245–256 (2012)

19. Viceconti, M., Clapworthy, G., Jan, S.V.S.: The virtual physiological human—a European initiative for in silico human modelling. J. Physiol. Sci. 58(7), 441–446 (2008)

20. Kohl, P., Noble, D.: Systems biology and the virtual physiological human. Mol. Syst. Biol. 5(1), 292 (2009)

21. Spanakis, E.G., Kafetzopoulos, D., Yang, P., Marias, K., Deng, Z., Tsiknakis, M., Sakkalis, V., Dong, F.: MyHealthAvatar: personalized and empowerment health services through internet of things technologies. In: 2014 EAI 4th International Conference on Wireless Mobile Communication and Healthcare (Mobihealth), pp. 331–334. IEEE, November 2014

22. Caon, M., Carrino, S., Lafortuna, C.L., Serrano, J.C., Coulson, N.S., Sacco, M., Khaled, O.A., Mugellini, E.: Tailoring motivational mechanisms to engage teenagers in healthy life-style: a concept. In: AHFE Conference on Advances in Human Aspects of Healthcare, July 2014

23. Health EU Project: https://www.health-eu.eu/. Accessed 09 Mar 2018

24. Byrne, D., Jones, G.J.: Towards computational autobiographical narratives through human digital memories. In: Proceedings of the 2nd ACM International Workshop on Story Representation, Mechanism and Context, pp. 9–12. ACM, October 2008

25. Lambert, J.: Digital storytelling: Capturing Lives, Creating Community. Routledge, New York (2013)

26. Holz, C., Grossman, T., Fitzmaurice, G., Agur, A.: Implanted user interfaces. In: Proceedings of the SIGCHI Conference on Human Factors in Computing Systems, pp. 503–512. ACM, May 2012
27. Zyskind, G., Nathan, O.: Decentralizing privacy: using blockchain to protect personal data. In: 2015 IEEE Security and Privacy Workshops (SPW), pp. 180–184. IEEE, May 2015
28. Swan, M.: Blockchain thinking: the brain as a decentralized autonomous corporation [commentary]. IEEE Technol. Soc. Mag. **34**(4), 41–52 (2015)
29. Markram, H.: The human brain project. Sci. Am. **306**(6), 50–55 (2012)

Exploring Technology Use in Dance Performances

Klaudia Çarçani[1(✉)], Veronica Wachek Hansen[2(✉)], and Harald Maartmann-Moe[2(✉)]

[1] Østfold University College, Halden, Norway
klaudiac@uio.no
[2] University of Oslo, Oslo, Norway
veroniwh@ifi.uio.no, harald.maartmann-moe@mn.uio.no

Abstract. The objective of the paper is to critically reflect on how research through design (RtD) can be used to gain knowledge of a new design context within HCI. We use the design research triangle presented by Fallman [1] as the framework for analyzing and to reflect upon the RtD process. The design context to which this new knowledge was applied to is within the area of dance and technology. Our design inquiry, therefore, using the term we coined – addhance, seeks to either add a sort of novel experience, or enhance a dance performance. We, thus, taking an RtD approach, explored how the dancers could compose music by moving their bodies. We designed a Kinect based system that captures dancer's movements and translates them into music. Intending to addhance the choreography, enlighten dancers' movements and bring a new disrupted workflow of both creating and enjoying a dancing performance.

Keywords: RtD · Dance · Technology · HCI

1 Introduction

Design contexts for Human-Computer Interaction (HCI) are becoming increasingly complex. While HCI designers understand the traditional tools of the HCI trade (research and design methods, e.g. [2]), contexts in which they work, and their complexities, may be less familiar. Research through Design (RtD) [3–9] is gaining traction in HCI as a way to explicitly engage in combining design studies, design experimentation and design practice. The approach offers, through the design of an artefact and its use, an opportunity to gain a deeper understanding of the context, as well as the fit between the context, the designed artefact and its use.

The objective of this paper is to critically reflect on how research through design inquiry can be used to gain new knowledge within a novel design context, i.e. context that is not familiar to HCI designers. We make use of the interaction design triangle presented by Fallman [1] to structure and describe our process of repeated drifts between design studies, design practice and design exploration.

The backdrop for the practical part of our project was a large European research and innovation project, The People's Smart Sculpture. It focuses on effects of technology and digitalization on urban living. In particular, the evolution of the urban cultural sphere was of interest. As a consequence, in the context of real-life, project based RtD course, we were challenged to explore the use of technology in dance. The timeframe for the project was only five weeks. Dance and technology span a challenging design space, with some beautiful examples of work [10–14] yet not too many HCI researchers and designers are working in this space. One of the reasons for this situation is that dancers often needed to wear sensors that would limit their movements or were required to pay attention and relate to different technologies while dancing [10, 13], something that may be disrupting the flow of the movements.

A dance performance, as an artistic and cultural form, engages both visual and auditory senses. The music, in a usual workflow of a dance performance set up, is chosen prior to work on choreography. Thus, music leads the choreography, dance and the performance and contributes to building a coherent visual and auditory experience [15].

With the inquiry as broad as the one we started with, we initially questioned how the technology can be used to enhance, or bring something new to a dance performance, coining the term addhance to describe our aim. However, by engaging in design studies and HCI literature around possibilities to addhance the performance, we have discovered an opportunity to disrupt the common workflow by making dancers movements the primary driver of the experience, thus producing music as a result of performing movements.

In what follows we describe how the explorations were carried out, and what insights were gained. We challenged ourselves to think big, to think how digital design and designed artefacts could truly revolutionize the dancing experience. The outcome of our design practice, i.e. the artefact we made, shows a much more constrained set of opportunities than what our vision is. However, the designed artefact, Musical Moves, is a research product [16] that enables further exploration of the design space and possible relations between the dance and the technology. Musical Moves is based on a movement capture using the Microsoft Kinect. Watching numerous exemplars of dance performances and carefully analyzing how the body parts move, we have developed an initial language that translates specific movements into sounds. Thus, the movements captured by Kinect are translated into a series of harmonious sounds and provide a new opportunity for finding joy in dance movements, also for others than dancers, e.g., children.

2   Methodology

We adopted a research through design (RtD) approach to carry out a series of exploratory activities to deepen our understanding of the relation between dance and technology. The term "research through design" comes from Frayling [17] when he presents a descriptive framework for research in arts. However, the term was later expanded, and here, we use it as defined in ([6], p. 3):

> [...] a type of research practice focused on improving the world by making new things that disrupt, complicate or transform the current state of the world. [...]

This definition of RtD helps us argue that the chosen methodology is suitable for our work. In his paper on research through design [5] emphasizes the importance of conceptual articulation in leading design practice. In [6], by using Koskinen et al.'s [18] framework, is described how critical design approach can play an important role in RtD project cases. Led by a critical approach, researchers make provocative artefacts that drive people to think and reconsider some aspects of the world.

In our case, we focus not just on design explorations and practice, but we engage in reflections and critical thinking toward a conceptual formulation and maturation [5, 6]. We took a concept driven critical design approach, where theory and concept, lead our design decisions. The intention of our project was to change the current workflow of making a choreography. Through this, we want to provoke a new way of thinking and a different perspective on the dance performance and consequently stimulate discussion and make new knowledge contributions [19, 20].

RtD represents a combination of research and making. Differently from the design practice where the intention is to design commercially successful products, in RtD arte-facts are designed to be carefully crafted questions, questioning "what it might be" rather than "what it is" [5, 19]. Also, by making things and placing them into the world, RtD can change the current state, creating new situations and new practices for anthropologist and researchers to investigate [6]. Additionally, Gaver's approach on RtD [5] is more ludic, where the designed artefact is more explorative and open. Rather than trying to solve a problem, or do the right thing [17], the design researcher tries to explore towards some goal, such as what supports pleasurable experience with the artifact. This approach is pertinent to our case as we aim to addhance the dancing experience.

2.1   Fallman's Triangle

Fallman's model, a triangle, aims to integrate the theoretical reflections with design practice and explorations as well as to shape the interaction design research discipline and give researchers a useful tool to control and keep up with their project efforts, see Fig. 1.

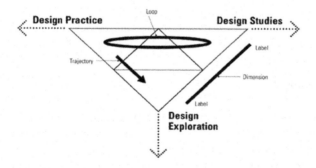

Fig. 1. Interaction design research triangle [1]

Design practice – this relates to the kind of activities that the interaction design re-searcher would undertake if he was practicing interaction design outside of the academia, such as producing commercially successful products. He joins the design team and engages in design practice as a designer but does so with a design question or inquiry in mind, which may or may not be related to the overall scope of the project.

Design explorations – has similarities with design practice in its synthetic and provocative approach to designing a new solution. However, it has a different perspective: Questioning "what if" takes precedence and the main intention of the de-sign is to provoke, criticize and to be proactive and societal in its expression.

Design studies – Other activities related to RtD involve the intellectual tradition within the discipline and the contribution that the researcher will bring in the ongoing discussions. Design studies are more focused on seeking general knowledge and to describe and understand the design process.

Fallman argues that interaction design research happens when design studies, explorations and practice are integrated into a project. To enable discussion on tensions and movements in the model describes the following terms: Trajectories - sought moves between two or more activity areas in the model, Loops - the ability to freely move between theory and practice, and Dimensions –subsets of the model and refer to discussions and tensions about the relevance of the activities presented in the extremities of the Fallman's triangle.

3   Applying RtD to Dance

At the outset of our project, we were encouraged to explore the field of dance and technology freely. Below we will describe how we applied RtD in the context of a dance and technology project. Moreover, we will make use of Fallman's framework to reflect on our project effort at a time.

3.1   Defining a Design Concept

Fallman states that projects can start in different extremities of the triangle. This is influenced by the perspective of the project and the tradition in which your research is rooted. Led by the choice of our methodology and the fact that we designed within a field of which we didn't have deep knowledge, we started the project with design explorations, searching exemplars on how technology had been integrated in dance performances or described in the HCI literature.

The first search was broad and helped us get an overview of existing work within this specific context. Also, it helped us to identify new opportunities for design. Figure 2 shows some of the initial exemplars that caught our interest.

We were fortunate enough to have Bill Gaver as a guest lecturer at our university and share his view on RtD. Annotated portfolios were presented as a way of communicating design research and generating new knowledge within HCI. [21] defines annotations as "textual accounts of artefacts, including any theoretical pronouncements about them…annotated portfolios may serve an even more valuable role as an alternative to more formalized theory in conceptual development and practical guidance for design". Referring to Gaver's annotated portfolio, we can argue that through searching for exemplars, we created a portfolio of artefacts designed within dance and technology. Annotating these exemplars helped us gain insights into the field, and these, in turn, guided our design process. Although this way of working was not really in tune with Gaver´s

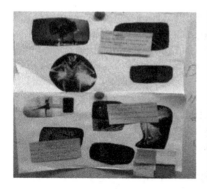

Fig. 2. Annotated exemplars

use of annotated portfolios, it was helpful, perhaps because the design space was an unfamiliar one and it provided some structure for discussing ideas and concepts.

We used Bowers' [8] features of annotation as a frame to annotate our portfolio of exemplars. He highlights that portfolios can be annotated in different ways based on the purpose and interest. In the beginning, we started with a limited number of exemplars and the purpose of annotating was to explore which role the technology was playing in the dance performance.

After that, we went back to collect even more exemplars. In total, we gathered more than 60 exemplars (see Fig. 2) of technologies used for adding or enhancing a dance performance. In the second round, the purpose of annotations changed. At this point, they reflected how the technology was used in each case and its role in the dance performance.

We experienced this annotation process as creative, and helpful in defining, and later refining, our conceptual inquiry. For example, amongst our annotations, one of the categories, that we called "added senses", stood out to us. Deciding to further explore this category, we discussed which senses could be involved in a dance performance, and whether they could add to, or enhance, the performance. The discussion about whether we could add or enhance lead us to create a new term, addhance, that harmoniously combines the two.

In parallel with collecting and annotating exemplars, we worked towards theoretical and conceptual explorations of the design space. Thus, once addhance comes into focus, this exploration entailed asking, why, how and whose (dancers, audience) senses could be affected during a performance. Of relevance was the "Eclipse" project [22] which presents an interactive dance costume that creates its own visual and sonic environment based on the wearer´s movements. This project inspired questions as: What if dancers could wear sound? Or, what if they generated sound? Would this addhance the performance? After several brainstorming sessions, we found the concept of making dancers identity audible to be of great interest, and it defined the direction for further inquiry.

To challenge the concept, we moved in Fallman's triangle from design explorations toward design practice and prototyping. Three low fidelity prototypes were made. Experimenting with material and technological aspects of these prototypes, discussing them with others, we concluded that the concept of identity was too ambiguous and could create confusion. As we were not able to achieve conceptual maturation, we drifted back into design exploration.

We started looking into ways to addhance a performance using sound in a different, possibly disruptive way. We had numerous brainstorming sessions and reading hours to related concepts and theories we could find in the literature with the annotated exemplars and insights gained. The inquiry was always accompanied by the "what if" question. The intention was to bring something that would create a change or would boost a discussion within the dance and technology context and maybe lead a change in the society at large.

While investigating in the relationship between music and choreography, we found an interesting case which inspired and guided our conceptual thinking. It exhibits distinctive movement vocabularies: Errand into the Maze, a ballet with the music scare by Menotti. The first choreography was by M. Graham. The movement, framework and visual imagery of her choreography were created before Menotti's music was added [15]. His score was then 'shaped to fit the demands of Graham's movement scenario' [23]. The second choreographer, G. Bodenwieser, had a more traditional approach to choreography. She "laid the movement phrases on top of the sound, shaping them in time and style to the music" [23]. While Bodenwieser's represent the common workflow of making a choreography we were fascinated by Graham's experience. She was giving expression to movements by making the individual movements audible in a harmonious way. This led to our idea of turning the tables in regard to the way music is played during a dance performance. The article "Gesture $\approx$ Sound Experiment: Process and mapping" [10] was also important for our work. The paper describes the development of a system which supports kinaesthetic-auditory synchresis, where human body motion is mapped with sound in such a way that sound production becomes an inherent and unavoidable consequence of moving the body" [10]. We built on the concept of kinaesthetic-auditory synchresis presented in that paper. We wanted to give expressive sonic capabilities to the whole body in motion, with the aim of producing music.

Thus, we finalized our design concept: Producing music through body movements – Musicify movements to include music as a dimension of choreography, rather than the means for leading it. We define 'producing music' as bringing into existence, making or providing vocal or instrumental sounds combined in a harmonious way. Also, we define 'movement' as the act, process or result of moving or not moving/the absence of movement.

3.2 Musical Moves

Once we had a well-defined concept, we moved again into technological explorations and further design practice and prototyping. The first discussion was related to the kind of technology we could utilize to implement our concept. The questions raised were: what technological tools can be used for motion detection and what technological tools can be used to produce sound. In motion detection, the technologies discussed were wearables and optical motion sensors. While wearables may be more accurate in detecting motion, they can as well restrict the dancer movements [13]. Similarly, to [10] work, we seek to create performances which engage the whole body, and hence avoid dependence on hand-based sensor input or 'interface artefacts' which draw attention (of both performer and audience) away from the body towards the artefact. Hence, they chose the Kinect motion sensors to implement the kinaesthetic-auditory synchresis concept. Another case where the motion sensors have been implemented is in the SoundEffects project [24]. The author explores how dynamically adapting musical beat and rhythm can be used to stimulate and motivate physical activity in older adults. The prototype developed used an optical motion sensor (Microsoft Kinect), to detect motion and Max MSP, as a sound synthesizer [25]. We decided to apply the same technology, thus using Kinect as a motion sensor for detecting body movement and Max for producing music, as the two main pillars of our solution. However, we are aware that the Kinect system has weaknesses, and we have taken these into consideration when implementing our solution.

Exploring Mappings Between Sounds and Movements

We once more started prototyping to further explore and challenge our concept. Technological explorations went hand in hand with our attempt of creating a map between dance moves and sounds, which when performed by a dancer would produce harmonious music. Continuous explorations of possible mappings encouraged the iterative implementation of our prototype.

The journey of implementing our solution started with exploring possible mappings. The design practice and the prototyping were always influenced by the "what if" questions that we raised during our design explorations. Every improvement in the solution came after long hour hours of brainstorming in conceptual terms and then translating those discussions into the prototype.

To compile a first mapping, we relied on the dancing expertise of one of our team members, supplemented with numerous dance performance observations, body movement analyzations and music element relations. These explorations provided useful information for the technical solution. This helped in deciding on what data was relevant to read through Kinect for recognizing specific movements. Inspired by previous research projects that have used Kinect as part of their installations [10, 24] and as well testing it ourselves and with colleagues, we could build a better understanding of what data the Kinect could reliably read and modified our code to better recognize movements based on these data streams.

We mapped the set of movements previously mentioned to selected instruments and sound files diverse enough to produce multiple styles of music. After long hours of reviewing the literature, brainstorming and going through dance examples we concluded on a first mapping.

The initial tests and adjustments produced inharmonious sounds. The dancer had control of a digital orchestra, but the moves were not orchestrating harmonious and pleasant music. To address this, we iteratively looped between design practice and design explorations. We experimented with adjusting pitch, volume, type of instrument, sound file seed, or the ease of triggering sound, and tested the system ourselves. We paid attention to what degree the music was, in fact, harmonious, as well as the coherence of music and movements. Unfortunately, the results were unsatisfactory. Hence, we brought in two experts on music and technology. We presented our concept and the ongoing process, demonstrated the system, and gave them the opportunity to test themselves. The suggestions were to map the dance moves with notes produced by only one instrument. The piano became our instrument of choice. We were also advised to employ chords as they are, by definition, a harmonic set of pitches made up by multiple notes. Moreover, we were advised to utilized compatible chords to produce a harmonious music. Thus, considering these guidelines, we went back to refine our mapping.

We took a top-down approach in planning out the mapping. We now rooted our choices in music-, and body movement theory. The exploration phase helped us map a set of common dance movements, which we further integrated into a short choreography. The choreography was made up of a set of four different movements. We planned each of the movements in the choreography as a set of three body parts moving simultaneously. This, to be compatible with the music theory and the experts' recommendations about utilizing chords as a way for achieving a harmonious music. Chords are typically made out of three or four notes. We focused on three notes chord.

Mapping technique: Each dance move was mapped to a chord. Thus, each body part movement of the dance move was mapped with a piano note. The aim was to achieve a system where one body movement would produce a single note, hence, a dance move would produce a chord, while multiple dance moves would produce music. We decided to utilize a "pop-music-heuristic" in striving for harmonious music production: "4 chord songs" [26]. As demonstrated by the band, Axis of Awesome, these 4 chords are all made up of the C-major scale (see Fig. 3, left) and can be combined rather freely to produce harmonious music. In our system, this would translate to freedom in combining dance moves, maintaining a harmonious musical outcome. The mapping process was accompanied with brainstorming and rooted in principles of mapping [27].

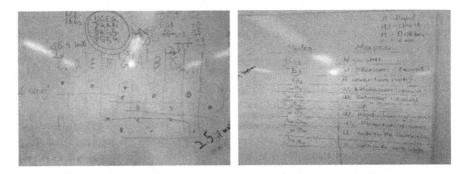

Fig. 3. Illustrates the thought process and the final mapping

The theoretical and technological explorations led to the final vocabulary (see Fig. 3, right), where each dance move was mapped with a piano note, as presented in the picture. After implementing the mapping, we began testing the prototype ourselves. The results immediately seemed more harmonious to us. We then fine-tuned the parameters as well as the ease of triggering for each note, before moving on to testing different styles of dance with the system. We perceived a greater degree of movement-music style coherence with this implementation.

3.3 Testing

After several rounds of testing the prototype ourselves and making use of the dance experience of one of our team members, we had the opportunity to test it with professional dancers. No prior instructions were given to them and both girls were encouraged to freely explore the system and improvise choreographies. We produced a video scenario to show their experience with our system[1]. In Fig. 4 on the left is shown one of the dancers testing the system, with a mirroring of the computer screen in the corner and on the right is the MAX code running in the background, to produce harmonious music.

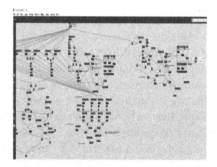

Fig. 4. Dancer testing the system (left) and what is happening in MAX (right)

Their feedback was positive, pointing at the freedom that the system gave to the dancer and the enjoyment of learning how to compose harmonious music by exploring different combinations of moves. Testing with professional dancers gave us confidence in the concept of our design. Moreover, it was a lesson learned for further refining the technological solution.

4   Drifting in the Fallman's Triangle

The process described above was conducted with the intention of learning how to apply Research through Design. We will, as mentioned, use Fallman's triangle [1] as a framework to discuss our case. In this section, we will elaborate on how we moved and drifted within the different parts of the model as a mean on reflecting on our process.

Looping between design practice and design explorations - While in design explorations we worked toward conceptual maturation by formulating an inquiry and suggesting new design alternatives that would provoke discussion, in our design practice we focused on making our idea feasible and bring change through the design of an ultimate particular [1]. An example of this loop was the concept of: making identity audible. While design explorations led us to the concept of making identity audible, the design practice made us aware that there were weaknesses in the concept, consequently

---

[1] https://youtu.be/E7vJKoWOARI.

not leading in a conceptual maturity. This was the first loop that we went through during our four weeks of learning and applying RtD. The second loop happened once we had defined the idea of wanting to make music through body movement (Sect. 3.1) and move on into technological explorations (Sect. 3.2), leading to conceptual maturation. Technological explorations and further prototyping are other examples of these loops.

The activities in each extremity and the looping between design exploration and practice was orchestrated by design studies. Using the concept of trajectories, we argue that the theories and previous work in the design field and as well in dance and technology, influenced our choices during the project. [21] annotated portfolio led our exemplars exploration. Concept driven design influenced our work and helped us maintain focus in the formulation of a final concept, which would later be further implemented as a design artefact. Moreover, RtD principle on designing artefacts which enhance a critical thinking and boost discussion, is noticeable in our final solution.

We did not use the concept of dimension as described in [1], as the intention of this paper is to use the triangle as a framework for reflecting on our case and not discussing on the subsets of the model itself.

The reflection above shows our RtD process prompted in the Fallman's model. We have included what kind of activities has happened in each extremity and as well the kind of movements that we took among these extremities. Furthermore, we can argue that critically reflecting on design practices and explorations can bring new knowledge in design studies. This is consistent with RtD. On the one hand the theories feed and trigger the design of new provocative solutions and on the other hand, the artefacts designed will serve as further explorations of desired changes in society. The artefact itself serves as a mean for furthering critical discussions both in design studies and in the new context for which that is designed. Similarly, our system intends to further discussion in the context of dance and technology, by questing the origin of the music in a dance performance. Positioning the artefact in dance schools can, for example, trigger the discussion on how music and dance are integrated in a choreography. Moreover, touching on the subject of annotated portfolio [21], putting our prototype in the same portfolio along with [10, 22, 24] etc. prototypes, could contribute to further knowledge in the context of dance and technology design as well as in novel interactions and forms of participation. We hope that this paper may serve for furthering knowledge on how to apply RtD in simple, time constrained innovative projects. We can argue that Fallman's model is very helpful for the researcher to keep track of its design efforts and as Fallman states the interaction design research in possible only when the three extremities of the triangle model are integrated with each other in the project.

5   Contributions and Further Explorations

Sharing our design process through this paper our aim is to contribute in the field of RtD in two dimensions: knowledge about learning and applying RtD, and knowledge of applying RtD in a novel context. We hope that our approach will motivate others to explore how to apply RtD. We believe that the field might benefit from what [28] calls "the method stories", in which designers share their stories and the challenges that they have faced in design projects. Moreover, our contribution is in applying RtD in a new and interesting context, that is, use of technology and dance as a means for contributing in culture. Music and dance are considered art and consequently an important part of cultural heritage. Musical Moves' interactivity is important to its function, but the concept on which it was designed is more important, producing music through body movement. Although we initially designed the system with dancers as future users thinking that this experience would support them in dance classes, the tool is flexible. Thus, it can be applied in a different context and enhance a whole new pleasurable experience.

We were invited in an exhibit for children where we had the chance to present and test our new design as well as its flexibility to adapt to different contexts and user group. Some technical, system, modifications were thought to be necessary to be able to test the flexibility of the concept with a new user group. We modified the system to estimate the distance between the shoulders of users, and scale the minimum distance required to produce sound proportionally. The exhibit took place at Sentralen (Oslo), on the 13th and 14th of January, as a part of an initiative called CityKids (see Fig. 5).

Fig. 5. Moments from the CityKids experience

We noticed that children had a playful experience while interacting with the system. We used observations and kept notes about all the children visiting our room. They seemed to be attracted by the music and the Kinect skeletons who mirrored them, on the screen. The element of silence seemed essential to the users perceiving their control of the music, which in turn seemingly contributed to them grasping the concept. We observed users stopping or starting movement once noticing that the music followed their lead. Similar cases occurred on multiple occasions, more frequently when the system was solely being used by one person. Another interesting aspect that we noticed was that although initially hesitant to test the system, once the children movements started producing music that increased the motivation to continue dancing. Moreover, it seemed difficult for children to understand the fact that the more rhythm they incorporated in their movements, the more pleasurable and harmonious the music would be.

Our experience with City Kids sparked the interest in exploring the adaptation of our system to design for a more ludic experience, where exploration, playfulness, reflectivity and openness become the leading design concepts [29]. Leaving the dancer to explore for himself and find meaning in this system, designed to musicalise moves, seems very interesting and intriguing. This demonstrates a strength of applying RtD, where the designs are often generative. One makes a generic prototype that can be tweaked to particular use situations. We aim to further expand our vocabulary of moves and music hope our research would inspire further research in the use of technology in dance.

Acknowledgements. This project was, in part, financed by the EU Creative Europe project "The People's Smart Sculpture", under the grant number EC-EACEA 2014-2330. We are grateful to Katie Coughlin, the leader of Oslo Children's Museum and the organizer of the City Kids exhibit. Further, we want to thank Alma Culén for discussions and comments on the paper. Finally, thanks are due to dancers who helped us fine tune Musical Moves and CityKids visitors who tried it.

References

1. Fallman, D.: The interaction design research triangle of design practice, design studies, and design exploration. Des. Issues **24**(3), 4–18 (2008)
2. Lazar, J., Feng, J.H., Hochheiser, H.: Research Methods in Human-Computer Interaction. Morgan Kaufmann, San Francisco (2017)
3. Fallman, D.: Design-oriented human-computer interaction. In: Proceedings of the SIGCHI Conference on Human Factors in Computing Systems. ACM (2003)
4. Culén, A.L., Mainsah, H., Finken, S.: Design practice in human computer interaction design education (2014)
5. Gaver, W.: What should we expect from research through design? In: Proceedings of the SIGCHI Conference on Human Factors in Computing Systems. ACM (2012)
6. Zimmerman, J., Forlizzi, J.: Research through design in HCI. In: Olson, J.S., Kellogg, W.A. (eds.) Ways of Knowing in HCI, pp. 167–189. Springer, New York (2014). https://doi.org/10.1007/978-1-4939-0378-8_8
7. Bardzell, J., Bardzell, S., Hansen, L.K.: Immodest proposals: research through design and knowledge. In: Proceedings of the 33rd Annual ACM Conference on Human Factors in Computing Systems. ACM (2015)
8. Bowers, J.: The logic of annotated portfolios: communicating the value of'research through design'. In: Proceedings of the Designing Interactive Systems Conference. ACM (2012)
9. Dalsgaard, P.: Research in and through design: an interaction design research approach. In: Proceedings of the 22nd Conference of the Computer-Human Interaction Special Interest Group of Australia on Computer-Human Interaction. ACM (2010)
10. Bencina, R., Wilde, D., Langley, S.: Gesture ≈ Sound experiments: process and mappings. In: NIME. Citeseer (2008)
11. Halpern, M.K., et al.: MoBoogie: creative expression through whole body musical interaction. In: Proceedings of the SIGCHI Conference on Human Factors in Computing Systems. ACM (2011)
12. Castellano, G., et al.: Expressive control of music and visual media by full-body movement. In: Proceedings of the 7th International Conference on New Interfaces for Musical Expression. ACM (2007)
13. Birringer, J., Danjoux, M.: The sound of movement wearables: performing UKIYO. Leonardo **46**(3), 232–240 (2013)
14. Culén, A.L., Rosseland, R.: Ecologies of spaces for enjoyable interactions. Int. J. Adv. Netw. Serv. **6**(3), 361–373 (2014)
15. Mason, P.H.: Music, dance and the total art work: choreomusicology in theory and practice. Res. Dance Educ. **13**(1), 5–24 (2012)

16. Odom, W., et al.: From research prototype to research product. In: Proceedings of the 2016 CHI Conference on Human Factors in Computing Systems. ACM (2016)

17. Frayling, C.: Research in Art and Design. Royal College of Art, London (1993)

18. Koskinen, I., et al.: Design Research Through Practice: From the Lab, Field, and Showroom. Elsevier, Oxford (2011)

19. Forlizzi, J., Zimmerman, J., Evenson, S.: Crafting a place for interaction design research in HCI. Des. Issues **24**(3), 19–29 (2008)

20. Zimmerman, J., Forlizzi, J., Evenson, S.: Research through design as a method for interaction design research in HCI. In: Proceedings of the SIGCHI Conference on Human Factors in Computing Systems. ACM (2007)

21. Gaver, B., Bowers, J.: Annotated portfolios. Interactions **19**(4), 40–49 (2012)

22. Ucar, E.: Eclipse. http://www.ezgiucar.com/. Accessed 19 Feb 2018

23. Vincent, J.B.: An Errand into two minds: The music of Gian Carlo Menotti in the choreography of Martha Graham and Gertrud Bodenwieser. Brolga Aust. J. Dance (27), 7 (2007)

24. Rosseland, R.B.: Design and evaluation of an interactive music system for exercise and physical activity with Alzheimer's patients. SoundEffects-An Interdisc. J. Sound Sound Experience **6**(1), 4–22 (2016)

25. MAX. https://cycling74.com/products/max/. Accessed 19 Feb 2018

26. Awesome, T.A.o. 4 Chords Song. https://www.azchords.com/t/theaxisofawesome-tabs-43687/4chordslive-tabs-355925.html

27. Norman, D.: The Design of Everyday Things. Verlag Franz Vahlen GmbH (2016)

28. Lee, J.-J.: The true benefits of designing design methods. Artifact **3**(2), 5.1–5.12 (2014)

29. Gaver, W.W., et al.: The drift table: designing for ludic engagement. In: CHI 2004 Extended Abstracts on Human Factors in Computing Systems. ACM (2004)

From Interpretation to Deduction: A Study on the Experience Design Method of Digitized Communication of Cultural Heritage

Zhigang Chen[1]([✉]) and Jing Ma[2]

[1] Shanghai Academy of Fine Arts, Shanghai University,
Shanghai 200444, People's Republic of China
410432675@qq.com
[2] Department of Landscape Design, Shanghai Xian Dai Architectural Design Group,
Shanghai, People's Republic of China

Abstract. Based on the present situation of digital communication of cultural heritage at home and abroad, this article compares, analyzes and summarizes the current typical methods of digitized communication. At the same time, from the perspective of "interpretation and deduction", combining with the scientific nature illustrated and artistry induced in the process of strategic analysis communication of experience design, typical theories and methods on digitalized communication of cultural heritage are analyzed and induced.

This article will explore the design method system of digitized communication of cultural heritage from the perspective of science and technology. The obtained data and information are of scientific and technological value. It will also provide scientific and methodological guidance for the status quo of the present cultural heritage. And from the point of view of creation, the artistic and cultural values behind the heritage will be reasonably and artistically induced and communicated.

Keywords: Cultural heritage · Digitization · Communication
Experience design

1 Introduction

There have been dozens of conventions, recommendations, charters, declarations and principles born out by the international community since the 20th century in the field of cultural heritage protection. Through these international documents, many international organizations are constantly creating new consensus and using advanced protection concepts in this field, combining with the latest achievements of heritage protection practices, and making cultural heritage protection a concept of social consensus. As economic, social and technological developments continue to evolve and update, the protection of a single element of material and cultural heritage has developed towards the direction of the comprehensive protection of intangible elements such as society, environment and nature in which the heritage is located.

M. Kurosu (Ed.): HCI 2018, LNCS 10902, pp. 281–289, 2018.
https://doi.org/10.1007/978-3-319-91244-8_23

The production, dissemination, use and preservation of information resources are increasingly being digitized. After the process of digitized acquisition, digital preservation, digital representation, and digitized reconstruction, and cultural heritage goes through digital media interpretation; the deduction of cultural heritage with the digital media after scientific interpretation is now the main form of cultural heritage. In the process of digitized communication of cultural heritage, new characteristics are presented, which objectively put forward new requirements on the design methods in the process of communication experience.

2 Influences of Intervention of Digital Technology on Communication of Cultural Heritage

First of all, the deep intervention of digital technology in modern society makes the heritage subject to the impact of transformation of "media", the unique attributes of digital media have an impact on the whole process of recording, describing, rebuilding, interpreting, deducing and transmitting of cultural heritage. The digitalization of the heritage itself has changed its experience and mode in cultural heritage and communication.

Second, the use of technologies such as computers, the Internet and new media in the field of heritage digitization has changed the original simple subject-object relationship of the heritage, and formed a complex subject-object relationship that involves heritage owner – heritage manager – government – expert – audience and other stakeholders. The digitalized inheritance of cultural heritage will inevitably balance the relationship among all parties (inter-subjectivity).

Finally, the digital technology divides the audience of the heritage and different ways of viewing, accepting and participating in the interaction are formed. The understanding of the cultural essence and connotation of the heritage is also different. Different audiences also have different knowledge and interpretations of the digitalized heritage, which also influence each other (i.e., the inter-textuality of the heritage), and the inter-textuality brings more possibilities of interpretation and deduction of heritage.

Therefore, the field of cultural heritage, it refers to the intervention in the stages of "record – presentation – description – reconstruction – interpretation – deduction" by means of digital technology and the use of digital media to effectively convey the connotation of the value of cultural heritage. Digital cultural heritage, as a "bit-shaped" heritage, is a form of digital simulation of cultural heritage itself in the process of media conversion. It can present the system and value of the heritage itself from different attributes, levels and dimensions.

3 Essential Connotation of Digitalized Communication of Cultural Heritage

The history of communication tells us: "People seek a more expressive means of media, so as to understand the material world in a more accurate, faster, more realistic way."

From a media point of view, the development of communication is the media's optimal choice. As McLuhan argues, "media technology is determined and irresistible in changing people's perception patterns." As a natural existence and historical existence, the digitalized process of cultural heritage is a traditional cultural regeneration model of cultural modernity, which connects the past and shows the process aesthetics of differentiated acquisition and modernity in terms of dimension (Fig. 1).

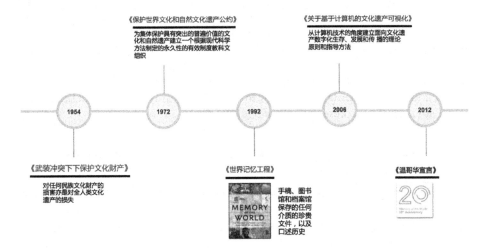

Fig. 1. International convention from 20th century

From the Memory of the World (MOW) of UNESCO in 1992, UNESCO Charter on the Preservation of the Digital Heritage which went into effect in 2003 and to Vancouver Declaration on the occasion of the 20th anniversary of MOW, the international community has brought enormous efforts to the digitalized preservation, protection and communication of cultural heritage. This span of 20 years has given people more understanding and consensus on the protection, development and utilization of digitalized cultural heritage. However, in the tide of digitalization, many difficulties such as the following have to be solved from the perspective of methodology in the process of digitized collection, protection, presentation and communication of cultural heritage:

3.1   Digitalized Protection of Cultural Heritage Is Greater Than the Protection of Embedded Value of Heritage

The original intention of digital protection was to transform the cultural heritage of material and nonphysical forms into digital forms widely used and easily communicated on computers and the Internet by technological means to achieve the permanent preservation and widespread communication of the heritage. At this stage, the digital process focuses on the recording, collection and preservation of data, the so-called "digital heritage protection" is merely storage of computer collected data in the hard disk, like "specimens" in the museum. It is still in the data "preservation" stage, and study on the connotation and extension values and other relevant elements with data and information has not yet been carried out in-depth.

3.2 The Digitized Media Presentation of Cultural Heritage Is Greater Than the Exploration of Its Content

Digitalized heritage is relatively untouchable, insensible, in-sniffable, invisible and inaudible as its natural form, and its nature and functions are demonstrated by means of other carriers. McLuhan, a Canadian scholar, has pointed out that "media is information" in his works. The characteristics of the media lead directly to people's cognition of the cultural heritage they express. Therefore, the right medium shall be selected to comprehensively restore the natural environment, social environment and cultural environment in which the cultural heritage is located to change the status quo in the digitalization field that values media presentation and neglects heritage value.

3.3 Continuous Media and Content Updates Bring About "Heritagization" of Digitalized Heritage

The major difference between "bit" and "atom" is that bit cannot be touched, smelled, seen or heard, it can only demonstrate its feature and function with the aid of other carriers, so digitized cultural heritage also face such problem, the characteristics of media can directly affect people's cognition on the characteristics of cultural heritage. Therefore, the ultimate goal of cultural heritage digitization is to choose the right media and restore the original cultural heritage truthfully, including the natural environment, social environment and humanistic environment.

3.4 The Ways of Expression of Cultural Heritage in the Process of Digitized Communication Is Homogenized

The process of globalization promoted by the rapid development of information and communication technologies has created unprecedented conditions for the intensification of cultural interactions, which have also affected the coexistence of cultural diversity. Cultural diversity is not only reflected in the style of development in a specific historical, geographical, cultural and economic environment, but also in the unique and pluralistic forms adopted by cultural groups in expressing and demonstrating their own cultural identity. The protection of cultural heritage is based on the global consensus on the protection of "cultural diversity." The diversity and differentiation of cultural heritage are also the values of cultural heritage. Their tradition, artistry and scientific nature also show the basis on which common ground with all countries and nationalities are sought for. The ways in storage, exhibition, and communication expressed and showcased in digitalized cultural heritage protection are homogenized, which is in conflict with the original intention of diversity in expressions of heritage protection and that is also a problem in the field of digitalized heritage exhibition and communication.

4   Experience Design Method in Digitalized Communication Process

John Dewey argued that "communication, while being characteristic, has an instrumental and ultimate character, when it frees us from the weight of events and makes sense to our lives, it is instrumental.[1]" Whether it is digitalized heritage or tangible heritage, its transmission with communication as a tool and symbols as a consensus, restructures and communicates the value of cultural heritage in the perspective of elaboration. The study of communication of heritage is to examine various social processes how a significant symbolic shape is created, understood, and applied. The meaning of cultural heritage is not inherent, but is generated from specific interpretation activities (Fig. 2)."

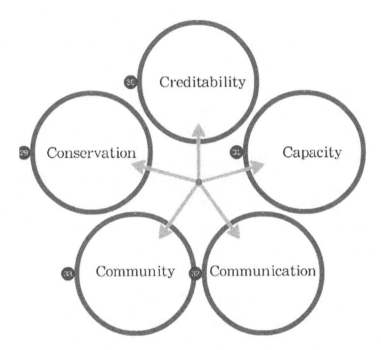

Fig. 2.   5"C" strategy of culture heritage preservation

Communication and experience are inextricably linked, and all communication is to create a process experience of information transmission. It can also be considered that the content of communication is experience: the experience of information, the experience of value, the experience of ritual and the experience of meaning. Information, values, ritual and meaning are lacking in the form of definite materialization in real life. This is especially true of the cultural heritage, and in some ways, digitalized heritage is a replica, which is consistent with Benjamin's judgment of art in the era of mechanical reproduction. The "glow" effect of the value of patronage in the digital age, compared with the era of mechanical duplication, is much more weakened, and its display value is also gradually diversified with the richness of the display media, that is to say, it has more opportunities for "display" in the public digital existence and the value of display is more diluted. Therefore, the "experience value" of heritage needed to be explored in depth (Fig. 3).

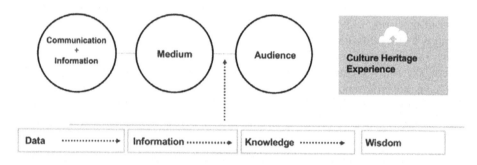

Fig. 3. Model of culture heritage experience

As a form of heritage in the information age, the digitalization of digitalized heritage is a process of constant selection. Reconstruction and interpretation are the starting points of digital communication activities. The heritage experience design is a new method of digital protection and inheritance of heritage. Digital technology as the "language" of the computer in "information age" considers "cultural heritage" as the target "statement" to be expressed, it expresses the "semantic meaning" of digitized existence of the public in the stage, so the realization of the cultural value experience behind the heritage is more natural, the author is convinced that the digital communication experience of shaping of the cultural heritage can proceed from the following points:

4.1 Context Fusion - Diachronic and Synchronic Combination

Heritage is the art of time. Therefore, in the process of experience design of digitalized heritage, the historic context and the realistic context of heritage are unavoidable in this process. The diachronic context of the heritage answers the environment in which it forms, develops and declines. Through the restoration of history, the essence of the cultural heritage can be manifested and the metaphorical meaning of the "heritage" under the prevailing environmental conditions can be reflected rather than simply demonstrating the artistic height of the heritage itself from a visual art perspective. The synchronic context can find the content, media and narrative way of cultural heritage in the realistic environment in line with the cognition, values and aesthetic orientation of modern people. Under the objective premise of not violating the original intention of cultural heritage, the two should be interpreted under the diachronic and synchronic contexts so as to shape the value experience that heritage can feel in terms of time dimension.

4.2   Combination of Virtual and Reality - Cross-Complementing Form and Content

The in-depth development of the digital living model has not changed people's "physical character" and still needs a carrier that is sensible, accessible, smelling, audible and visible to provide a basic sense of existence and to balance the proportion of "virtual and reality" of content and media. Both the tangible and intangible cultural heritages have tangible and intangible characteristics, and are not isolated. In the process of digitization, especially in the process of deduction, communication and display, the proper balance of the tangible elements and intangible elements of the heritage shall be maintained so that the tangible material and cultural heritage may accompany "invisible" social and cultural practices and rituals and the intangible cultural heritage can be sensible, touchable, sniffable, audible, visible and carried by "visible" entities.

4.3   The Balance of "Interpretation" and "Deduction" - Science Interprets Process and Art Deduces Values

Heritage protection began with the protection of its artistic value, and the process of digitization was the process of describing, restoring and displaying the artistic and scientific values of the cultural heritage. There is a difference between the digital form of the heritage and the heritage itself, and the heritage itself has a strong "readiness" without the need for other media-assisted self-exhibitions. The digital heritage changes the "format" of existence, and the state of heritage in the space and time is modeled. Therefore, under this "context", it is necessary to fully express the artistic value characteristics of cultural heritage and make reasonable art interpretation, set appropriate art guidance and expansion, bring the audience into the atmosphere artistic interpretation creates; the scientific, rational, natural ways of presentation shall be demonstrated and communicated in a balanced way.

4.4   Online Demonstration and Offline Verification

The virtual environment built by computers and the Internet is the main stage of heritage experience, and digitalized interactive technology can also trigger the viewer's curiosity about real collections. Indian scholar Amrit Sudar holds the same view: "The easier it is to see the imagery of the collection, the more likely you are to have a strong desire to face it." Amrit Sudar has not had a chance to go to one of these museums in person for many years, and this regret became his motivation to set up Google's art project. The digitalized form of cultural heritage reorganizes the heritage itself, dissolves the geographical restrictions of the heritage, and gives the audience more freedom and choice to extend the depth and breadth of the heritage itself. Therefore, the online cultural heritage shaped by digital technology can play a demonstrative role, and the communication coverage of heritage experience is more extensive, and this can promote more people to come to reality to experience in person (Fig. 4).

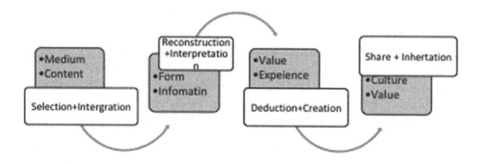

Fig. 4. Process of culture heritage experience communication

5   Conclusion

The process of digitized dissemination of cultural heritage can be regarded as a process of interpreting its information and value and deducing its meaning. Interpretation of cultural heritage, including its historical, artistic, technological and cultural values, is an important foundation in the process of communication. The scientific nature of the interpretation determines the authenticity and validity of the communication. The process of digitizing cultural heritage is the process of describing, restoring, displaying the artistic and scientific values of the cultural heritage. The heritage of digital form has changed the "format" of its own existence. Under the "simulated" state of space and time, it is necessary to fully represent the artistic value and characteristics of cultural heritage, carry out reasonable artistic deduction, and display and communicate the scientific nature, rationality and nature in a balanced way.

As another form of existence of heritage, it is a product of technological evolution and socio-economic development and a process of digitized existence of heritage. The introduction of the concept of experiential communication evades the "digital dilemma" currently facing the domain of heritage and combines the information presentation, interactive technology and environment construction involved in the digitalized design field of heritage. The "interpretation" and "deduction" carried out in the two dimensions of technology and science provide different audiences with a context suitable for the communication of heritage experience, create a new way for exchanges, interactions and communication among different cultures, and present some available theories, methods and tools for protection and display of cultural heritage, museum management, cultural and creative industries and other fields.

References

1. Schofield, J., Szymanski, R.: Local Heritage. Global Context. Ashgat, Farnham (2011)
2. Lytras, M., de Pablos, P.O., Damiani, E., Diaz, L.: Digital Culture and E-Tourism: Technologies, Applications and Management Approaches, 1st edn. IGI Global, Hershey (2010)

3. Runnel, P., Pruulmann-Vengerfeldt, P., Viires, P., Laak, M.: The Digital Turn: User's Practices and Cultural Transformations. Peter Lang International Academic Publishers, Frankfurt (2013)
4. Bautista, S.S.: Museums in the Digital Age: Changing Meanings of Place, Community, and Culture. AltaMira Press, Lanham (2013)
5. Tzanelli, R.: Heritage in the Digital Era: Cinematic Tourism and the Activist Cause. Routledge, Abingdon (2013)
6. Din, H., Wu, S.: Digital Heritage and Culture: Strategy and Implementation. World Scientific Publishing Company, Singapore (2014)
7. Waterton, E., Watson, S.: Culture, Heritage and Representation. Ashgate, Farnham (2010)
8. Pricken, M.: Creative Strategies: Idea Management for Marketing, Advertising, Media and Design. Thames & Hudson, London, New York (2010)
9. Toler-Franklin, C.: Matching, archiving and visualizing cultural heritage artifacts using multi-channel images. Princeton University (2011)
10. Ajlouni, A., Ahmad, R.: Development and evaluation of a digital tool for virtual reconstruction of historic Islamic geometric patterns. Texas A&M University (2005)
11. Liu, S.B.: Grassroots heritage: a multi-method investigation of how social media sustain the living heritage of historic crises. University of Colorado at Boulder, Computer Science (2011)
12. Cherry, T.K.B.: Online cultural heritage materials and the teaching of history in the schools: a concept analysis of state archives and collaborative digitization program web resources. The University of North Carolina at Chapel Hill, Information & Library Science: Library Science (2010)
13. Webmoor, T.A.: Reconfiguring the archaeological sensibility: mediating heritage at Teotihuacan, Mexico. Stanford University (2008)
14. Zavalina, O.L.: Collection-level subject access in aggregations of digital collections: metadata application and use. University of Illinois at Urbana-Champaign (2010)
15. Yeung, A., Yin, T.C.: The Gap between personal vs institutional digital archives of researchers. University of Calgary, Canada (2011)
16. Grace, J.A.: Adapting preservation policy in archives to the digital age. Queen's University at Kingston, Canada (2000)
17. Moulaison, H.L.: A framework for cultural heritage digital libraries in the developing world: access to non-textual information for non-literate people in Morocco. Rutgers the State University of New Jersey - New Brunswick, Graduate School - New Brunswick (2010)
18. Dougherty, M.: Archiving the Web: Collection, documentation, display, and shifting knowledge production paradigms. University of Washington (2007)

Bias in Perception of Art Produced by Artificial Intelligence

Joo-Wha Hong[✉]

University of Southern California, Los Angeles, CA 90089, USA
joowhaho@usc.edu

Abstract. Some perceive AI as encroaching on human capacities, perchance affecting their perceptions of AI. Applying Schema theory, this study examines whether and to what extent human judges are biased in ascribing "creativity" to the artwork of artificial intelligence. To begin to examine whether an artist's perceived identity (i.e., as an artificially intelligent agent (AI) or human) might produce different reactions in judging the same artwork, participants blocked by subject characteristics (e.g., graduate, undergraduate) were randomly assigned to one of two types of focus groups. The groups differed only in that they were led to believe the same artwork was the product of a human or the product of an AI artist, triggering very different identity schemas about the artist. Participants were asked to (a) define art; whether AI can (b) make art and (c) if given art (which was the same in all groups) is "art." Both focus groups types similarly associated art with expression, creativity, providing a message, and broadly conceived the boundaries of what was art. They differed in that the "Human Artist group" had an interactive view of art (perceiving, providing feedback) but the "AI Artist group" said any sense (visual, auditory, etc.) stimulus was art. The "Human Artist group" thought AI could make art while the "AI Artist group" disagreed. Both types of focus groups believed that the given art piece is art. Implications of findings for applications and theory are discussed.

Keywords: Schema theory · Artificial intelligence · Art evaluation
Mixed methodology

1 Introduction

Technological advances have threatened the jobs of many Americans. According to an article from Forbes, almost 47% of current jobs are vulnerable due to automation (Quora 2017). These jobs have mostly involved jobs involving physical labor. Now, another big technological threat pertaining to a technology-based non-human competitor is coming, Artificial Intelligence. For example, in an event involving human and AI competitors, an AI Go player, AlphaGo, beat all the highly ranked human Go players: The competitive cognitive abilities of AI compared to humans demonstrated the limitation of human intellectual prowess. Moreover, even one of Silicon Valley superstars, Elon Musk, warned that in the near future many people would lose their jobs due to technological innovations such as these and be forced to depend on government

© Springer International Publishing AG, part of Springer Nature 2018
M. Kurosu (Ed.): HCI 2018, LNCS 10902, pp. 290–303, 2018.
https://doi.org/10.1007/978-3-319-91244-8_24

handouts. Even though Musk's views are extreme, a dynamic change in the job market due to AI would be consistent with the history of the emergence and disappearance of jobs due to technological development.

However, an optimistic view toward this AI threat is the perspective that some domains remain the exclusive purview of humans. Creativity is one such domain that is sometimes considered the final wall that AI cannot breach. One World Economic Forum article suggests creativity will become one of the most important ability domains for job seekers in 2020 (Gray 2016). However, AI developers are trying to build a system that can also conquer the area of creativity, using tools such as Google's DeepDream making works of art (Stecher 2017). So, academics have begun to ask whether creativity is a sacred terrain that is a domain restricted to human beings or whether this is a domain where artificial intelligence can also excel. The approach of this study is to see if human judges are likely to ascribe creativity to the artistic creations of artificial intelligence compared to humans when those human judges are judging objectively the same art: That is, do stereotypes and biases affect human perceptions of art when the character- istics of the artists are differentially described (i.e., as AI or human).

Communication involving messages is often construed as involving a sender and a receiver: This is also the case for human-computer interaction. Google and other AI companies, who are developing their AI capacity to make artwork have already demon- strated that perceivers cannot differentiate whether the artwork is produced by humans or produced by AI, essentially passing the Turing Test (Emerging Technology from the arXiv 2017). This suggests that these companies in their role as "sender" have already made great strides. What we don't know, however, is how participants would react differentially as "receivers" to art that they are told was produced by AI (versus a human). Indeed, not only is there very little research examining this issue, the topic has not even been acknowledged as a frontier for future investigation (Russell et al. 2015), perhaps due to the fact that relatively few researchers operating in this domain are communica- tion scholars. Thus, one goal of this study is to broaden the perspective that ability or capacity of artificial intelligence should not be measured solely in terms of its potential societal effects (economically, legally, ethically, etc.), but also in terms of human's perceptions of the meaning of what AI does.

Some (Erden 2010) have argued that artificial intelligence can only seem to be crea- tive, but it is not actually creative. Similarly, others have argued that what makes art – art—involves the intentions of artists, which of course, AI lack (Searle 2007). However, I argue here that typically most people in evaluating art do not, in fact, are less influenced by intentions of the artist (Omasta 2011). What they do know is what they perceive: That is that they perceive the work to be art or not. My research question is whether people are willing to deem the product that is made by artificial intelligence as "art." Therefore, this study concerns investigating the perception of audiences. I argue that if artificial intelligence can be seen to be creative and people cannot prove it is not tech- nically creative, then it is creative, based on the idea that the world is the world we see. In this study, the purpose was to find out the difference in evaluation of the same artwork based on two different schemas triggered by noticing identity of the artist differently, using experimental focus group discussion setting.

2   Theoretical Background

Schema Theory provides a useful theoretical framework for understanding audience perceptions of art based on the identity of the artist. Schema theory has philosophical roots but also more modern psychological underpinnings that are applied here in the current research (Dahlin 2001). Schema is "an active processing data structure that organizes memory and guides perception, performance, and thought" (Norman and Rumelhart 1981). Schemata, for example about art, would include knowledge about art concepts, our perceptions of what makes art more or less artistic, art we have viewed and enjoyed or not, situations in which we have viewed art, and so forth. Humans also have schemata that include stereotypes about artificial intelligence and the creativity of AI. According to Dixon (2006), "These stereotypes are part of an associative network of related opinion nodes or schemas that are linked in memory, and activating one node in network spreads to other linked nodes" (p.163). Schemas, based on prior experience, can be activated when we are interpreting new given information. Thus, it is possible to say that schema and bias (or stereotype) function similarly in the cognitive process (Dixon 2006). Schema theory is an adequate theory to illustrate how a stereotype may affect cognitive processing: For example, when we view someone of another race, we may activate a schema that affects how we process information about that person. Not surprisingly, Schema theory is widely used in media influence studies where researchers are interested in how bias affects individuals' media portrayals of certain ethnicity and influence media users' perceptions. I argue that an art piece is a medium with messages, so schema theory is applicable to research focused on artwork. Hence, the theory was applicable to understand how stereotypes toward artificial intelligence and its creativity may alter perceiver's views toward artificial intelligence's artwork.

3   Research Question

This study examines the interplay of schema about the creativity of artificial intelligence and the evaluation of AI creating art and its artworks. The creativity is what often deemed as the property of human beings and artificial intelligence (Finn 2017). Thus, this research tried to seek how an understanding of an artist in such way, artificial intelligence that is believed to have less creativity in this case, influences the understanding general idea of AI creating art and its artwork.

- RQ 1: How different assumptions about the identity of the painter (AI or human) of the same art piece will influence the evaluation of the art piece?
- RQ 2: How different assumptions about the identity of the painter (AI or human) of the same art piece will influence the idea of artificial intelligence creating art?

4   Method

4.1   Overview and Design

Two types of focus groups (one knowing an artist of a painting as a human and the other knowing it as AI) were formed through group blocking in order to keep the same ratio of educational level and gender in each group and within that ensure random sampling. Across all groups, as participants arrived, a picture was presented on a monitor screen. When all participants were present, they were told that the picture was either produced by a human or by AI. Then, based on the impression from the picture, participants engaged in a discussion based on the following: (a) participants were asked to define art (b) participants were asked whether AI can make art and (c) participants were asked if given work (which was the same in all groups) is "art." A group with information that a painter of a shown image was artificial intelligence was put as an experimental group and a group with information that a painter is a human artist was put as a control group. The responses from two groups are compared.

4.2   Participants

Twenty-eight participants were recruited from University of Southern California, both undergraduate and graduate students from various fields. The aim here was to capture diverse points of view toward the concept of art and more generalizable mutual understandings of artificial intelligence. Still, participants were recruited from a single school (USC) to make research participants feel more relaxed, and thereby more likely to participate openly in the focus group (Corfman 1995). Also, the identity of participants was not revealed until the study was finished. This was accomplished by having participants use a fake name and not sharing any further personal information, such as their major and whether undergraduate or graduate students. This led to the presumption that other participants are also recruited students. Such limited information sharing functioned not only to protect personal information but also to have a comfortable setting through assuming homogeneity of the population. Even though the research involved randomly sampling within a single university, there was a gender bias with 24 participants who were female, and 4 participants who were male. The average age of participants was 22.4 years (SD = 4.3). Table 1 contains a summary of participants' other key demographic data.

This study involved multiple focus-groups (4 in all; two of each type) and the similar ratio of educational level and gender was maintained. This was done, since if one group consists of all graduate students and the other groups consist of undergraduate students, differences between two groups may due to educational level (rather than a response to the knowledge about the identity of the artist). Thus, two graduate students and five undergraduate students were deployed in each of four groups, while keeping a similar gender ratio. Before the experiment began, a researcher briefed students on the purpose of the study and how the study will proceed with the focus group moderator. After providing necessary information and procedure of the study, the moderator collected informed consent before starting the focus group discussion. Because there was no reward for participating the research, the survey was completed by students who are interested in the study.

Table 1. Focus group participants' demographic characteristics (n = 28)

Characteristic	AI Artist group (n = 14)	Human Artist group (n = 14)
Ethnic background		
Caucasian	7	5
African American/African/Black	2	0
Hispanic/Latino/Latina	0	2
Asian/Asian American	3	5
Persian	1	1
Not Reported	1	1
Gender		
Male	2	2
Female	12	12
Level of education		
Undergraduate	10	10
Graduate	4	4

4.3   Procedures

The research method was mainly a focus-group discussion given that the understanding of art requires diverse and unexpected perspectives, considering the ever-changing nature of art (Fokt 2017). Even though focus group method was applied, there was a difference with a regular focus group due to its setting. In general focus-group discussion, participants are recruited with a single characteristic (e.g., cultural background, social position, etc.) that meets the purpose of research (Poindexter and McCombs 2000). However, this was a more experimental approach since the independent variable here was whether participants eventually were told that the artwork was made by AI or human. Unlike the general focus group discussion, a goal of the study was to compare participants' reactions in the two types of focus groups.

For both groups, a picture of "Standing in the sky" by Tanya Schultz (2014), a piece of hand-crafted artwork with pastel tone patterns was presented that appears digitally/graphically constructed (see Fig. 1). The reason for this selection was to avoid identification of the artist as the image is vague to determine whether it is handcrafted or digitally produced. While showing the same picture of artwork to every group, two groups were notified that the art is produced by a human artist (hereinafter "Human Artist Group") (n = 14) and the other groups were notified that the art was produced by artificial intelligence (hereinafter "AI Artist Group") (n = 14). Before the focus-group discussion, an open-ended survey with the same questions from the focus-group discussion was given to prevent the Bandwagon effect, participants following arguments of opinion leader despite their actual belief. The questionnaire asked about three general sets of questions, which all involved the impression about the given artwork, their own definition of art, and the artificial intelligence's eligibility to produce artwork. After the focus group discussion, participants received a debriefing sheet that tells the actual goal of this research and the actual identity of the artist.

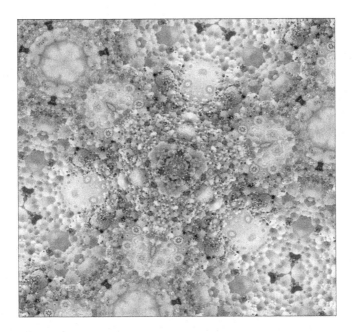

Fig. 1. Standing in the sky.

4.4 Coding and Analysis

After the responses from series of focus discussions were gathered by audio recording, the recordings were transcribed and the transcriptions were organized using NVivo, a quantitative research tool. Using the programs, commonly used terms and words from the conversation were colored and put into categories. Also, terms with similar meanings that can be drawn from their contexts were colored, even though the words that participants used were not identical. The analysis of these data was done by comparing groups of colored terms and themes between two research groups based on three categories from the research question of this research.

5   Results

The issues discussed in four focus group discussions were broadly classified into the following categories: (1) deeming the shown work as art, (2) definition of art, and (3) capability of AI making art.

5.1 Deeming the Shown Piece as an Art

We assumed art pieces we face are generally made by a human artist. Thus, for participants in the "Human Artist Group," a question asking whether the given artwork seems to be "art" was identical with a question of asking the artistic value of a piece of modern art. Thus, the evaluation they made was focused solely on the artistic value of the image without any bias about its artist. On the other hand, participants in the "AI Artist Group" had in mind that the image was produced by artificial intelligence when evaluating it. Thus, while assessing the pure artistic value of the work, there was another layer of cognitive process that involved the consideration that the artist is not human.

26 out of 28 participants in both the "Human Artist Group (n = 14)" and the "AI Artist Group (n = 12)" answered that they thought that the given image was "art." It was an interesting outcome as there were those in the "AI Artist Group" with the knowledge that the shown image is made by an artificial intelligence program, who also said that artificial intelligence could not make art. One distinctive argument for deeming the work as "art" was that it was based on their impression, not logical approaches. For example, one participant in the "AI Artist Group" said, "I like the colors and it makes me happy" and another participant in the "Human Artist Group" stated that "This piece of work evokes my emotion and therefore I consider it art." However, deeming it as art did not always lead to high satisfaction of the work. There was an opinion from a person thinking it as art saying, "It is very trippy. It is also not very traditional, though." There was a participant who rated the artwork two out of five with a mention "I have no inherent attraction to it" while saying she thinks the piece was still art. It is also found that both of the two participants who did not deem the work as art were from "AI Artist Group." A person who said the piece is not art made rather a logical approach to determining the type of the image, not focusing on how he felt, saying, "it really is like computer graphics."

5.2 Definition of Art

An individual's personal definition of art is one of schemas people have since its meaning is constructed through cumulated knowledge and experience (Harris and Sanborn 2014). The "AI Artist Group" versus the "Human Artist Group" differed in that the former group was shown an image of a supposed AI artist's artwork while the latter group presented with the same image was told that this art was produced by a human artist. So only the former group ("AI Artist group") could have had a schema of artwork modified by this manipulation (i.e., now potentially inclusive of AI artwork in the general schema of artwork).

When comparing the terms participants used to define art between two groups, it was found that there were terms shared in both groups, which were that art was "an expression", "creativity", "a comprehensive approach", and "a message." "Expression" was the 1st ranked and "message" was the 5th ranked term within each group for conceptualizing "art." Even though the same terms were used, there was a difference shown in the frequency of the term usage between these two groups from 2nd to 4th ranked terms (see Table 2). The participants in the "Human Artist Group" stressed creativity (2nd ranked term) as a crucial factor in understanding the art concept while the "AI Artist Group" participants' 2nd ranked term was "comprehensive approach" by which they meant a broad definition of art (e.g., "anything can be art", "whatever a person calls out", "Anything", and "there are so many ways to be artistic"). However, for the "Human Artist Group" a "comprehensive approach" was the 3rd ranked concept of art, and by the "comprehensive approach" they meant something quite different. That is the art itself had to be "created" - a view that strongly implicated the causal role of the human in creating art (e.g. "anything that is created", "something created by human", and "anything created in some way." Thus, the art-making-artificial intelligence-schema was not activated for the "Human Artist Group," meaning that those participants apparently had no idea that art could be produced by an entity other than a human. Thus, the word "created" frequently within the "Human Artist Group" indicates that which is only "created by a human artist," clearly excluding the "AI artists" from this conceptualization.

Table 2. The terms used in the definition of art discussion and its ranking

Rank	Human Artist group	AI Artist group
1st	Expression	Expression
2nd	Creativity	Comprehensive art concept
3rd	Comprehensive art concept	Creativity
4th	Interactivity	Sense stimulus
5th	Message	Message

Another difference between two groups is a unique term that was only used within each group. The term that was used only by the "Human Artist Group" was "interactivity." One participant in the group said, "(art is) a form of expression for interacting with the audience, transmitting intentions, and expressing idea and feelings." Another participant in the group said, "art is a tool for communication" and communication here is, again, between artists and audiences. How the "AI Artist Group" participants approached the concept of art distinctively was in seeing art objects as stimuli that can arouse sense perceptions. What was said related to this context was "(art should) aesthetically engage viewers" and "(art should be) something that stirs emotion or some sort of reaction." The difference between these two groups' unique approach was that one ("Human Artist group") required mutual and two-way message sending and receiving while the other ("AI Artist group") sees art as one-way communication.

5.3 Capability of AI Making Art

A direct question "Can AI make art?" led to further insights into help focus group participants conceptualized AI art. This was the first question for the "Human Art group" to be asked about their view about artificial intelligence. Hence, unlike the concept of artificial intelligence could be only seen to the "AI Artist group" in the previous two questions, this question enables us to put both groups in the same stance. Moreover, as the priming effect had brought up the most recently activated stimuli, the "AI Artist Group" in which AI creativity related schema was apt to have been actively activated due to the discussion based on previous questions (Jeong and King 2010). On the other hand, the "Human Artist Group" was at the stage where AI creativity related schema was far from being activated. Therefore, it is still possible to compare cognitive outcomes due to the influence of the schema.

For both groups who agree with the given statement, it could be found that there were two reasoning themes for the argument that were identical in both groups. One same theme between the two groups was "art with a different value." The participants argued artificial intelligence can make art, but the art it makes should be distinguished with art that human artists make. The arguments related to this opinion were, "yes, but not original art", "It is art but less valuable due to less uniqueness", and "instinctively perceive it as an art but not like traditional artworks." First two statements were based on the idea that originality and uniqueness are values of art that artificial intelligence cannot perform or not as good as a human is capable of. Also, a word "instinctively" can be linked to the impression-based decision of deeming the given art piece as "art." The other theme was "personal preference," such as "Because I liked it, I would still feel it as an art, no matter who made it." Similarly, another participant in the "AI Artist Group" said, "No matter how it is produced, it is art if I like it." Even though both groups shared similar reasonings, there were also two different reasonings to reach the same idea that AI can make art.

The "Human Artist Group" participants who agreed that artificial intelligence could make art employed two distinctive themes to support their argument. The most often argued theme among overall themes of reasoning was "the artificial brain." This indicates their presumption that artificial intelligence would function as same as human brain functions, even though it is artificially made. The relevant statements were, "There is a possibility that AI might have a feeling later on if it functions identically with a human brain, and this gives the possibility of AI making art" and "Because it is built to be similar to a human as much as possible, its creation should be deemed as a human creation." Also, there was a view that having "intention" to create art is an important factor to consider the capability of AI making art. When there was a conversation related to this topic, there was a question that "what is more artistic between artworks painted by an elephant and produced by artificial intelligence?" One participant said, "Unlike an elephant can't be an artist, AI is more of an artist as it possesses the intention of producing art coming from its programmer since its development."

There were also two themes that were shown distinctively among the "AI Artist Group." One was "defined by purpose." One participant said AI could make art "if it is programmed to do so." His view oriented from the idea that purpose is what defines an action, no matter how others perceive it. If a programmer built an AI to make art, he thought everything created by the AI should be deemed as "art." This is dissimilar to the theme "intention" as "defined by purpose" saw AI as a purely passive tool. Another approach that supported the capability of artificial intelligence creating art was "comprehensive approach." It is the same theme that was shown in the previous discussion of deeming the given image as "art." The approach made here was to broaden the concept of art from the art that we see in an art museum. One participant said, "AI itself could be deemed as art so its creation should also be deemed as art...I am art, too" (see Table 3).

Table 3. Themes in the capability of AI making art discussion (agreed) and its ranking

Rank	Human Artist group	AI Artist group
1st	Artificial brain	Art with different value
2nd	Art with different value	Defined by purpose
3rd	Personal preference	Comprehensive approach
4th	Intention	Personal preference

Unlike participants who agreed, participants who disagreed that artificial intelligence can make art had no distinctive difference between the groups. Both groups chose "lack of human value", "authority", and "incapacity of AI" as main reasons artificial intelligence cannot produce artwork. The most frequently supported theme was artificial intelligence's lack of human values. Many of the "lack of human value" arguments from the "AI Artist Group" were focused on "feeling," such as "No computer's going to tell him, 'Oh this is how I felt, so I drew this.' No, I don't think that's ever going to happen.", "It's already creative, but you can't have feelings", "it has a brain (thinking process), but it does not have the heart (feeling)", and "You need expression, thought, and feelings to make art." However, this theme was not limited to feeling only, and there was "an instinctive denial." One participant said, "Even though admitting the possibility of AI being creative, I don't want to admit anything produced by AI as art once knowing that it is made by AI. I think making art only belongs to a human." She said she could not eloquently explain the reason that she felt that way, but she could not accept the fact that what artificial intelligence makes can be viewed as art. "Human Artist Group," on the other hand, said the same argument that AI cannot make art due to the "lack of human value" with different approaches. Participants in the group said "Even though it mimics or possesses emotion, what it produces cannot be art as it does not have a human spirit and the AI emotion is not human emotion" and "The effort that is put to make art by a human is different compared to the effort of AI." Even though both of these two arguments appealed the lack of human values, they made dissimilar approaches as one is based on a measurable value (effort), while the other is based on what cannot be measured (spirit). One interesting fact in this discourse was that the "AI Artist Group" was particularly more active when arguing artificial intelligence cannot make art due to the "lack of human values."

"Authority" is an argument based on the human role, especially programmers, in the creativity of artificial intelligence. It is revealed well in their statements, "The AI art is an extension of whoever created the AI" and "It is still the programmer who makes art, not AI." As seen here, the idea of the authority of creativity is linked to the doubt that artificial intelligence is fully independent of its creator. "Incapacity of AI" was another theme both groups used to support their argument that AI cannot make art. They focused on the inherited structure of artificial intelligence that limits its capacity to make art. For instance, a participant in the "AI Art Group" said, "AI might have feeling, but its feeling would not be as delicate as human's emotion." This is different with the "lack of human value" theme since it still admits artificial intelligence can have emotion. Similarly, a person in the "Human Artist Group" said, "biologically living things have emotion but

AI cannot since it is not naturally born." This argument did not focus on the fact that AI is not human, but rather focused on the fact that AI is not "biologically" created. The person talked about feeling, like pain, which she thinks can be felt only by biologically constituted entities. Even though artificial intelligence can have emotion, such feelings were deemed to be impossible for it. There was a theme that was only shown in the "AI Artist Group," which was "perfect and logical." One participant said "Creativity comes out from unexpected circumstances or even through mistakes. However, AI perfectly calculates to avoid such mistakes." Another participant in the same group used terms "preprogrammed" and "predictable" which he believed those are contradictory to the concept of art (see Table 4).

Table 4. Themes in the capability of AI making art discussion (disagreed) and its ranking

Rank	Human Artist group	AI Artist group
1st	Lack of human value	Lack of human value
2nd	Authority	Incapacity of AI
3rd	Incapacity of AI	Perfect and logical
4th		Authority

6 Discussion

This study aimed to identify the influence of bias and schema toward artificial intelligence creating art in order to develop the idea that the ontology of creativity of artificial intelligence is based on the audience's perception. In this section, major findings of this study, the limitations and implications for future research will be discussed.

6.1 Major Findings

This study showed that admitting the capability of AI to create art can be done based on what contexts are used when it is asked. When participants in the "AI Artist group" were asked, "Can AI make art?" quite a few participants (n = 10) answered "no" based on a logical approach involving letter-triggering schema. The participants added that artificial intelligence could not create art because it cannot have a feeling, intention, and the possibility of creating mistakes. However, when the same participants were shown an image with the information that it was produced by artificial intelligence and asked, "Do you think this image is 'art'?" most of the participants (n = 12) said "yes" based on an impression-based approach involving image-triggering schema. The participants answered based on how they felt after seeing the picture and argued that their feeling was crucial when deciding what is "art." There was a participant who believed that anything produced by artificial intelligence should not be viewed as "art." While informed that a shown image is produced by artificial intelligence, she deemed it as "art" because she thought it was "cool." Thus, application of the creativity of artificial intelligence in the real world would be done apart from how it is viewed in related discourses. In other words, even though there are pessimistic views toward artificial intelligence being creative, the markets of products created by artificial intelligence may function independently from such views based on how it is marketed. Therefore, the context of the message should be analyzed beforehand to persuade consumers the creativity of artificial intelligence.

Another outcome of a question asking the capacity of AI creating art was that the "Artist as AI" schema aroused stronger disapproval toward artificial intelligence creating art among the "AI Artist group," compared to the "Human Artist group." The information that a painter of a shown image is artificial intelligence was only given to the "AI Artist group." In other words, the "AI Artist group" had a recent experience with an AI-made painting, while the "Human Artist group" did not. In this setting, the "AI Artist group" was triggered by the schema about artificial intelligence, but the "Human Artist Group" possesses a similar opinion with the public as they do not have any triggered schema. Thus, the "AI Artist group" was set as an experimental group and the "Human Artist group" was set as a control group. In comparing the two major types of focus groups, what was distinctive was the outcome that the "Artist as AI" schema led to a stronger tendency toward the belief that AI cannot produce art. Among those who argued that artificial intelligence cannot make art in both groups, the "AI Artist group" was more active during the discussion and used more various terms and attempted diverse approaches to strengthen the argument, compared to the "Human Artist group." Contrarily, the "Human Artist group" was more active compared to the "AI Artist group" among those who argued that artificial intelligence can make art.

One unexpected finding from the discussion was about the origins of AI creativity. The conversation related to the authority of the creativity was often mentioned during the discussion, which was one approach to argue the limitation of artificial intelligence to create art, based on its structure. There were arguments that artificial intelligence cannot be creative because it is a mere representation of its programmer's creativity. Jennings (2010) argued that creativity of artificial intelligence can be fulfilled only when automation of the system from its programmer is guaranteed, such as artificial intelligence altering its own evaluation standard without any input from its programmer. The participants' reactions related to the authority may be due to the insufficient trust toward the autonomy of artificial intelligence, even though the brief explanation of artificial intelligence, including its autonomy, was given before the discussion. Thus, the reaction is less likely due to the misunderstanding of the concept but rather due to assumptions that creative artificial intelligence creating data by itself is hypothetical, as one participant remarked: "Would it still need input to make any output?" Hence, one way to diminish a negative stereotype toward artificial intelligence being creative is to successfully persuade the public its autonomy. This is similar to Colton's (2008) argument that providing information on how a software functions is crucial to prove the creativity of a computational system.

6.2 Limitations

Even though the study was carefully planned and conducted, there were limitations that should be considered for future studies. First, there was an imbalance of gender distribution of participants. For this study, there was no distinctive gender-based difference shown in perspectives of both contents or participation. Still, since this study used an experimental approach, having balanced gender distribution would have increased both internal and external validity, since the issue of artificial intelligence or art is not a single gender-related topic. Also, there was an issue of using both quantitative and qualitative research methods, since this study employed the QUAN-qual design, starting a question from the quantitative theoretical idea and using the qualitative method as supplement component (Morse et al. 2006). There were few disadvantages in using the research design. For participant recruitment, the focus group discussion requires homogeneity of participants while experiments receive higher validity through random-sampling. Also, it was incapable to conduct focus group discussion with the number of people that fulfills the analytical validity requirement.

6.3   Implications for Future Research

Wilson (1983) conducted a study about art-producing artificial intelligence before AI was familiar to the public, emphasizing the role of audiences, as this present study did. However, his study did not extend the inquiry to audience bias and understanding of creativity of artificial intelligence, which this research attempted. This study started with the idea that the stereotype toward artificial intelligence being creative would cause different perceptions and cognitive understanding of the artwork produced by AI. A positive relation between accepting AI producing art and deeming art created by AI as "art" was predicted, but results showed a contrary outcome. Through comparing two groups, two major findings were found: (1) there was a tendency that schema influenced the logical decision, and (2) this tendency strengthened the idea that artificial intelligence cannot create art. However, the schema did not alter the impressionistic process, how they felt about a painting produced by artificial intelligence, which leads to admitting it as "art." Because this was not an anticipated result, an inquiry designed to investigate the discrepancy is needed. Further studies focusing on how different contexts of similar messages influence the schema processing will bring insight.

Also, in employing a qualitative research method, it was possible to more deeply investigate how bias toward artificial intelligence influences the perception of what it is and what it is capable of, through investigating what values audiences had and used to make decisions. These values can be utilized to develop the scale for measurement of perception and evaluation of artworks created by artificial intelligence. These findings can support future quantitative research on the perception and cognitive process involved when receiving unfamiliar information about new technology. The speed with which technological developments occur often leave the public with very little technical knowledge of them and require expert explanation. This lack of understanding of new scientific information can lead to the public assumption that the development is a threat to them (Haynes 2013). Further research about how the public understands artificial intelligence and new technologies can help to explain technological development more persuasively and make them more accessible.

References

Colton, S.: Creativity versus the perception of creativity in computational systems. In: AAAI Spring Symposium: Creative Intelligent Systems, vol. 8, March 2008

Corfman, K.: The importance of member homogeneity to focus group quality. Adv. Consum. Res. **22**, 354 (1995)

Dahlin, B.: Critique of the schema concept. Scand. J. Educ. Res. **45**(3), 287–300 (2001)

Dixon, T.: Psychological reactions to crime news portrayals of black criminals: understanding the moderating roles of prior news viewing and stereotype endorsement. Commun. Monogr. **73**(2), 162–187 (2006)

Emerging technology from the arXiv. Can this computer-generated art pass the turing test? 30 June 2017. https://www.technologyreview.com/s/608195/machine-creativity-beats-some-modern-art/. Accessed 29 Nov 2017

Erden, Y.: Could a created being ever be creative? some philosophical remarks on creativity and AI development. Mind. Mach. **20**(3), 349–362 (2010)

Finn, E.: How algorithms are transforming artistic creativity. Aeon Essays, 06 October 2017. https://aeon.co/essays/how-algorithms-are-transforming-artistic-creativity?utm_source=Aeon%2BNewsletter&utm_campaign=b9f0697292-EMAIL_CA%E2%80%A6

Fokt, S.: The cultural definition of art. Metaphilosophy **48**(4), 404–429 (2017)

Gray, A.: The 10 skills you need to thrive in the fourth industrial revolution. World Economic Forum, 19 January 2016. https://www.weforum.org/agenda/2016/01/the-10-skills-you-need-to-thrive-in-the-fourth-industrial-revolution/

Harris, R.J., Sanborn, F.W.: A Cognitive Psychology of Mass Communication, 6th edn. Routledge, New York (2014)

Haynes, R.: From alchemy to artificial intelligence: stereotypes of the scientist in western literature. Publ. Underst. Sci. **12**(3), 243–253 (2003)

Jennings, K.E.: Developing creativity: artificial barriers in artificial intelligence. (Report). Mind. Mach. J. Artif. Intell. Philos. Cogn. Sci. **20**(4), 489–501 (2010)

Jeong, Y., King, C.: Impacts of website context relevance on banner advertisement effectiveness. J. Promot. Manag. **16**(3), 247–264 (2010)

Morse, J., Niehaus, L., Wolfe, R., Wilkins, S.: The role of the theoretical drive in maintaining validity in mixed-method research. Qual. Res. Psychol. **3**(4), 279–291 (2006)

Norman, D.A., Rumelhart, D.E.: The LNR approach to human information processing. Cognition **10**(1), 235–240 (1981)

Omasta, M.: Artist intention and audience reception in theatre for young audiences. Youth Theatre J. **25**(1), 32–50 (2011)

Poindexter, P.M., McCombs, M.E.: The Research Phase and The Research Expert. Research in Mass Communication: A Practical Guide. Bedford/St. Martin's, Boston (2000)

Quora: How We Can Embrace the Replacement of Jobs by Artificial Intelligence. Forbes. https://www.forbes.com/sites/quora/2017/03/20/how-we-can-embrace-the-replacement-of-jobs-by-artificial-intelligence/#29b62fb02bae. Accessed 20 Mar 2017

Russell, S., Dewey, D., Tegmark, M.: Research priorities for robust and beneficial artificial intelligence. AI Mag. **36**(4), 105–114 (2015)

Searle, J.: Dualism revisited. J. Physiol. Paris **101**(4–6), 169–178 (2007)

Stecher, B.: This robot is probably more creative than you. World Economic Forum. https://www.weforum.org/agenda/2017/04/this-artist-is-creating-amazing-artwork-oh-and-its-not-human. Accessed 7 Apr 2017

Research on Personalized Learning Pattern in Traditional Handicraft Using Augmented Reality: A Case Study of Cantonese Porcelain

Yi Ji[1(✉)], Peng Tan[1(✉)], and Henry Been-Lirn Duh[2(✉)]

[1] School of Design Arts and Design, Guangdong University of Technology,
Yue Xiu District of Dong Feng East Road No. 729, Guangzhou 510000, China
jiyi001@hotmail.com, 297470555@qq.com
[2] Department of Computer Science and Information Technology, La Trobe University,
Bundoora, Melbourne, VIC 3086, Australia
B.Duh@latrobe.edu.cn

Abstract. Recently, technology-enhanced learning research has increasingly focused on emergent technologies such as augmented reality. Educational researchers of traditional handicraft have used emergent technologies to inject affective and cognitive learning in teaching. However, numerous studies have highlighted content display of traditional handicraft in teaching based on emergent technologies. As far as we know very little work emphasized personalized learning and experience based on augmented reality in traditional handicraft. In order to address these problems, the researchers present an AR-based experiential learning method for traditional handicraft, with the purpose of shifting the pattern of learning from content-centered to experience-centered. Our approach is Augmented Reality-based Personalized Learning Pattern (ARPLP) for traditional handicraft, and it can be divided into four phases. In addition, a case of Cantonese Porcelain is presented to support this pattern in experience interface of application. The results of research produced an experience interface framework of traditional handicraft based on ARPLP, it contributes to the value of augmented reality as well as experiential learning of students for Cantonese Porcelain.

Keywords: Cantonese Porcelain · Teaching · Augmented reality
Personalized learning pattern · Experiential learning

1 Introduction

In recent years, there has been an increasing interest in applying Augmented Reality(AR) to create meaningful teaching and learning in intangible cultural heritage [1]. Cantonese Porcelain is one of the important categories in the intangible cultural heritage. The current practice in public education applied to Cantonese Porcelain is based on face-to-face teaching and student apprenticeship [2]. With the advent of the era of experience, people have a new motivation and anticipation of experience from Cantonese Porcelain the learning of Cantonese Porcelain [3, 4]. Learning is no longer transmission process of

© Springer International Publishing AG, part of Springer Nature 2018
M. Kurosu (Ed.): HCI 2018, LNCS 10902, pp. 304–316, 2018.
https://doi.org/10.1007/978-3-319-91244-8_25

teachers and students, but rather it is a personalized learning process focusing on the individual needs of students with intent and conscious. Therefore, we need to explore a student-centered learning pattern to adapt to the learning of Cantonese Porcelain in a new context.

However, the main channel of learning Cantonese Porcelain is based on offline workshop teaching (see Fig. 1). This channel is mainly based on the text of the textbook to help users without a knowledge background to learn and not meet the user's personalized learning needs. On the one hand, the Cantonese Porcelain production requires a clear understanding of the production process. The text-based textbooks cannot dynamically display the production process of Cantonese Porcelain, and it is difficult to realize the natural interaction between textbooks and users. On the other hand, the traditional forms of workshop teaching are still mainly face-to-face. Text-based textbooks always emphasize the learning of contents but lack of the attention to user experience in the learning process.

Fig. 1. Traditional craftsman is making face-to-face tutorials in offline workshops.

In order to solve this problem, this paper proposes a personalized learning pattern based on AR technology for Cantonese Porcelain learning. This pattern integrates interaction technology (AR) with its visualization, user cognition and behavior, learning content (Cantonese Porcelain), and interaction context. The pattern will help users to enhance the Cantonese Porcelain learning experience in special interactive context. In this article,

(1) we will be defining the current problems faced by traditional handicraft teaching and analyzing how AR can affect traditional handicraft teaching.
(2) we will be exploring how users can personalize learning through AR interface in different stages of experience with a case study of traditional handicraft.

The following is the paper framework. In Sect. 2, we conduct a literature study including the application of AR technology in Cantonese Porcelain teaching, as well as the theory of experiential learning and personalization. In Sect. 3, we proposes a

Cantonese Porcelain personalized learning pattern based on AR technology from the Kolb's experiential learning theory. In Sect. 4, we analyses users' AR application strategies in different stages of experiential learning based on personalized learning pattern with a case study of Cantonese Porcelain.

2　Related Work

2.1　Augmented Reality in Traditional Handicraft Teaching

The application of augmented reality technology in traditional handicraft teaching is mainly focused on the digitization of contents to enhance the user's interaction and experience. Traditional handicraft teaching has been developed traditionally in learning scenarios where educators offer to scholars predetermined curricula using traditional teaching strategies. Kang (2012) developed AR Teleport, a mobile AR application that reorganizes destroyed historical and cultural sites in Korea based on movement-based interaction [11]. Puyuelo et al. (2013) presented the use of AR transcends its own specific functions to favorably create a renewed image of the monument, promoting the active perception of this historic site as well as the receptiveness of user groups who not frequently use these types of technologies [12]. Mendoza et al. (2015) presented the use of emerging technologies such as augmented reality in heritage education is promising in both formal and informal contexts, observing that heritage and natural environments are suitable for contextualized learning development processes [13]. Kim et al. (2016) presented contextualized content retrieval according to user preference will be possible for AR applications in the cultural heritage domain [14]. Dieck et al. (2017) presented AR is considered to be a way to preserve history, enhance visitor satisfaction, generate positive word-of-mouth, attract new target markets and contribute to a positive learning experience [15]. In the past 5 years, the rapid development of smart mobile devices has raised the potential for AR to move from the experimental development stage to deployment as a ubiquitous learning tool in traditional handicraft teaching.

Many studies corroborate the benefits of AR for improving the learning performance and motivating students [16–18]. The advantages of AR in educational settings includes learning gains, collaboration, increase the experience and just-in-time information [19]. However, these advantages need to be further explored in order to understand the real benefits of AR-based learning experiences. In this paper, we will discuss how augmented reality can improve the efficiency of user experiences in traditional handicraft teaching.

2.2　Experiential Learning Theory

"Experience" is an activity, and it is also a result of activity. ISO 9241-210 [20], defines user experience as "a person's perceptions and responses that result from the use or anticipated use of a product, system or service". User experience highlights non-utilitarian aspects of such interactions, shifting the focus to user affect, sensation, and the meaning as well as value of such interactions in everyday life [21]. Users gain knowledge and emotion through experiences of everyday life. Experiential learning is the process of learning through experience, and is more specifically defined as "learning through reflection on doing" [22]. Experiential learning differs from teacher-centered didactic instruction in that it emphasizes independent judgment, free thinking, and personal experience [23]. Through interactive learning processes, students gain personal experience from Cantonese Porcelain they derive an understanding of the core elements of learning tasks and explore the relation between activity concepts and implications. Learners convert the experience gained through the learning activity into an integral part of their lives, thus transforming their attitudes and prompting further reflection on extrinsic behaviors.

Beginning in the 1970s, David A. Kolb helped to develop the modern theory of experiential learning (1984), arguing that learning is a process of experience conversion [24]. The experiential learning cycle includes four cyclical learning stages (see Fig. 2): (1) concrete experience, (2) observation and reflection, (3) forming abstract concepts and generalizations, and (4) testing in new situations. Learners must go through this cycle to complete the learning experience. The four stages are continuous and experience occurs at any time. Each experience will affect the formation of future experiences.

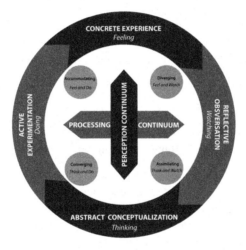

Fig. 2. Reflection Models and Learning Styles by David A. Kolb (1984). (image from University of Toronto Mississauga website).

Experiential learning theory emphasizes the correlation between concrete experience and learning, Cantonese Porcelain matches the ostensive purpose of improving Cantonese Porcelain teaching. However, learning of Cantonese Porcelain is still based on text-based teaching, Cantonese Porcelain leads to low efficiency of learning and experience. Accordingly, this study seeks to integrate experiential learning into Cantonese Porcelain of the experience process and system design, thereby strengthening the effectiveness of experiential learning.

2.3 Personalization Motivation and Experiential Learning

Personalization for promoting an inclusive learning using AR is also a growing area of interest. Personalization is considered for meeting the needs and interests of the individual learners. A thematic analysis of the definitions of personalization include (a) a purpose or goal of personalization, (b) what is personalized (interface, content, etc.), and (c) the target of personalization (user, consumer, etc.) [25]. To enhance personalization, learning preferences as context in Cantonese Porcelain learning occurs were explored [26]. In addition, context-aware and engagement are also seen as one of the most important ways to personalize [27, 28]. In the educational arena, motivation can be defined as the student's desire to engage in a learning environment [29]. Experiential learning enables users to acquire knowledge, enhance participation and achieve personalized user demands through their behavior [30, 31]. A key distinguisher of experiential learning from other learning approaches is the requirement for students to continually self-evaluate their progression in the learning process through constant reflection [32]. The process of Personalization motivation is the process of experiential learning, it will drive user to experience their activity.

Based on previous findings, the present study of experiential learning need to pay attention to how to realize personalization. Furthermore, we should focus on the factors of influences personalization, including content, functionality, user interface and channel/information access [33, 34].

3   Methodology

3.1 Personalized Learning Pattern Based on Augmented Reality

In the current workshop of Cantonese Porcelain teaching, text-based textbooks have greatly influenced the user experience, efficiency and usability. Therefore, to allow users to become immersed in environmental exploration and interaction with AR-enhanced learning information in workshops of Cantonese Porcelain, this study developed an innovative learning pattern, AR-based personalized learning pattern (ARPLP) for Cantonese Porcelain (Fig. 3). ARPLP integrates AR technology with the four stages of Kolb's experiential learning cycle (Kolb, 1984) (concrete experience, reflective observation, abstract conceptualization, and active experimentation) [24] and interaction of online and offline experience. Furthermore, AR technology and mobile devices are coupled to build an experiential learning AR-based user interface framework. The framework plays three roles in experiential learning: (1) it helps users navigate the learning of Cantonese Porcelain and reduces user's mistakes; and (2) realize real-time interaction of online and offline experience; and (3) convert physical content to virtual content of traditional handicraft to strengthen the impact of exploratory learning.

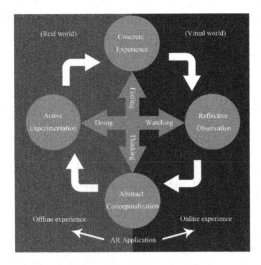

Fig. 3. Augmented Reality-based Personalized Learning Pattern (ARPLP)

3.2   Four Stage of Learning Cantonese Porcelain

Concrete Experience (Feeling and Watching)
The user's perception of the Cantonese Porcelain includes the user's understanding of the basic schema of the learning content (short-term memory), mainly through the perception of learning content. AR intervention can be digitized by learning Cantonese Porcelain content, including the schematization (decomposition and combination) of Cantonese Porcelain content and the natural human-computer interface design (dynamic display, gesture interaction). The purpose is to enable users to import schema of Cantonese Porcelain.

Reflective Observation (Watching and Thinking)
Users learn Cantonese Porcelain modeling, colors, patterns and other contents through the observation. Combined with the existing knowledge to deepen the cognition of Cantonese Porcelain. AR intervention to gain knowledge primarily through online video and interaction with offline of the authentic Cantonese Porcelains.

Abstract Conceptualization (Doing and Thinking)
Users acquire cognition primarily through interactive experience with Cantonese Porcelain. In this process, user obtain more knowledges through the practice of production for further memory (long-term memory). AR intervention to guide users through natural and efficient learning processes, including narrative teaching, real-time integration with offline experience, and natural human-computer interaction experience with the goal of enabling users to build custom behavioral memory.

Active Experimentation (Doing and Feeling)
Users gains cognition through self-reflection and re-creation of the creative learning process, Cantonese Porcelain is a further development. AR intervention can be based

on the user's learning data in real-time personalized recommendations similar to the custom content and interactive experience with offline content.

4   Cantonese Porcelain as a Case Study

4.1   Problem of Learning Cantonese Porcelain

Cantonese Porcelain is a traditional ceramic art in Guangzhou, China (Fig. 4). It is an important representative of China's intangible cultural heritage. With the development of society, the teaching of Cantonese Porcelain workshop is facing many problems. Table 1, according to the channels learned from Cantonese Porcelain, current channels for learning Cantonese Porcelain mainly fall into two forms: online learning and offline learning.

Fig. 4.   Flower butterfly plate Cantonese Porcelain in Qing Dynasty

Table 1.   Learning problems of Cantonese Porcelain

Learning channels	Learning problems
Online learning	Single way of human-computer interaction
	Lack of interactive with offline experience
	Can not effectively enhance the cognitive
Offline learning	Choice of content is relatively small
	Handmade is difficult
	Limitations of time and context
	Less opportunities to try error of the experience

Online Learning

Cantonese Porcelain online learning channels are mainly mobile applications and websites as the main learning context. The user learning through the online based on the process of simple work, which mainly exist online interactive mode of a single, lack of interactive experience with the offline and learning process cannot effectively promote the user cognition of Cantonese Porcelain.

Offline Learning

Cantonese Porcelain offline learning channel is mainly based on museums and other workshops and schools as the main learning context. Under the certain circumstances is face to face between the teacher and the user based on the contents of the teacher's work to learn. In addition, there are relatively few optional contents for learning. Cantonese Porcelain is difficult to practice and has limited learning time and context.

4.2 Modeling

3D intangible culture modeling is the key to realize the system. Generally, fabrication of an intangible culture model requires the following steps: (1) Select exhibits (material object is the best or detailed picture information shall be required as support); (2) Collect information (take pictures of material object from different angles, summarize corresponding literature and images as background introduction); (3) 3D intangible culture model fabrication (use ads Max and CLO professional intangible culture modeling software to fabricate the model and save the model in fbx format); (4) Make maps (make maps on the basis of pictures taken in Step (2) with help of Photoshop and save them in jpg format); (5) Model format conversion (use unity 3D game engine to compose the documents in Step (3) and Step (4) into u3d format). (6) Upload model to background database of 3D somatosensory image matching system. After display system is started up, it would detect data updating and intangible culture model in the database can be downloaded via wireless network [35].

Based on the characteristics of Cantonese Porcelain be divided into color, Instrumental type and pattern (Fig. 5). There are five kinds of colors, eight Instrumental types, seven patterns. The above classification criteria reference Cantonese Porcelain authoritative books and master's suggestion.

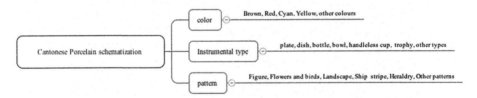

Fig. 5. Modeling of Cantonese Porcelain

4.3 The Process of AR-Based Learning

The production of the AR-based instructional channel was also an analytic activity as it addressed the learning process from three perspectives:

Online Experiential Learning: (Fig. 6)
E-learning is mainly based on the virtual content being learned by the user prior to the beginning of a practical activity through the mobile device. It contains historical background and process characteristics and production process learning of Cantonese Porcelain. This stage is mainly experiential learning early from concrete experience (feeling and watching) to reflective observation (watching and thinking).

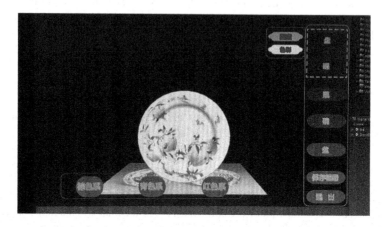

Fig. 6. Learning content display based on AR

Offline Experiential Learning: (Fig. 7)
It is a real-time interaction between the user and Cantonese Porcelain in the real environment based on the AR recognition function in the mobile device. Users acquire information through scanning real objects. In addition, users can also scan images 2D and then the system will automatically convert to 3D. This stage is mainly experiential learning mid-term from reflective observation (watching and thinking) to abstract conceptualization (doing and thinking).

Fig. 7. Model from 2D to 3D based on AR

Mixed Online and Offline Experiential Learning: (Fig. 8)

This stage is mainly experiential learning mid-term from abstract conceptualization (doing and thinking) to active experimentation (doing and feeling). Users can experience the creation of Cantonese Porcelain online through mobile device. After having a certain knowledge base, users can go to offline workshops for creative practice. They can personalize their own work based on personal interests.

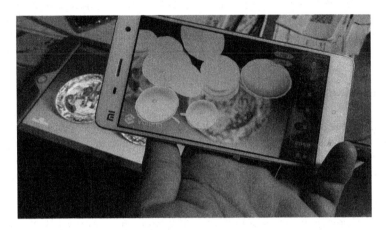

Fig. 8. Virtual and realistic interaction based on AR

4.4 User Interface Design

Chinese characteristics are kept in the user interface design of display system and symmetric layout is used in the main interface and secondary interface (Fig. 9) to highlight traditional intangible culture. Four columns in the main interface are clearly

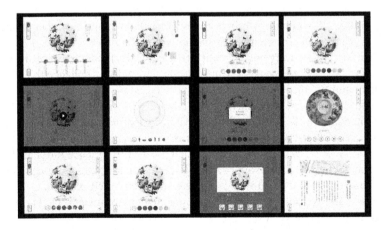

Fig. 9. User interface AR-based of Cantonese Porcelain

arranged from top to bottom and different columns are connected by the hick lines and blurry clouds. It shows different themes are associated somehow. Illustration is used in the secondary interface. Form features of different intangible cultures are outlined by simple lines and simple and light colors match their themes accordingly.

The first level application page includes three levels of understanding, production and testing. The module of understanding is mainly linear history dynasties show Cantonese Porcelain works. The module of production be divided into color, Instrumental type and pattern of Cantonese Porcelain through the dismantling and combination of schema. The module of testing is order to learning of Cantonese Porcelain through the graphical jigsaw puzzle and unit questionnaire to test the user level.

5 Discussions

After testing, it is found that augmented reality technology has some limitations in the traditional handicraft teaching. For example, showed limitation in the studies reviewed are "difficulties maintaining superimposed information". Students may feel frustrated if AR application does not work properly or the device in order to see the augmented information. Another limitation, the use of AR applications allows users to rely on virtual information and reduce the interaction with the real world. These effects will limit the user's natural interaction with the real world. In addition, a case study of Cantonese Porcelain: limitations are "designed for a specific knowledge field" and "users cannot create new learning work", and so on. In summary, the suggestion of this research is that the development of augmented reality mobile application should be centered on the user's behavior and cognition. Integrating the cultural connotation of traditional handicraft and the cognitive psychology of users, we can effectively realize the mixed interaction and experience both online and offline.

6 Conclusions and Future Work

Traditional handicraft are treasures of China and important component in traditional Chinese culture. AR technology brings a new presentation form for intangible culture and endows traditional culture more exuberant vigor. To make up for text-based textbook limitations, we used augmented reality to dynamically render traditional handicraft content: static display changes to dynamic display. In order to enhance the user experience and cognition, the study proposes a theory based on experiential learning: from content-centric to experience-centric, and design a personalized learning pattern for traditional handicraft. To explain the personalized learning pattern, we designed a learning scheme that stimulated students' creative design learning motivation, and a case study of Cantonese Porcelain. We also designed the user experience interface by referring to the characteristics of AR application. Users can learn content through AR applications interacting with the real world to create an effective AR scenario.

In future work, we will examine the personal and environmental factors that affect personalization and creative design. At the same time, we will improve the AR prototype system of this study, which will be applied to the local traditional arts and crafts teaching classroom. In addition, we will focus on the natural interaction and experience of AR mobile applications online and offline in the traditional handicraft teaching environment, and enhance the interactive experience value of mobile applications. Thus, our aim is to ensure that AR technology plays an increasing role in the future of general technology personalized (creative) learning courses.

Acknowledgments. This research was supported by the 2018 Guangdong College Students cultivate special funds for technological innovation projects, Guangdong University of Technology Youth Hundred Talents Fund under grant No. 220413137. The completion of this study benefited from the tireless efforts of every teacher and classmate in the project team. Special thanks for the technical support given from the research team of Professor Henry Been- Lirn Duh from La Trobe University.

References

1. Bibri, S.E., Krogstie, J.: ICT of the new wave of computing for sustainable urban forms: their big data and context-aware augmented typologies and design concepts. Sustain. Cities Soc. **32**, 449–474 (2017)
2. Wei, X., Weng, D., Liu, Y., Wang, Y.: Teaching based on augmented reality for a technical creative design course. Comput. Educ. **81**(C), 221–234 (2015)
3. Russon, J.: Sites of Exposure: Art, Politics, and the Nature of Experience (2017)
4. Pine, B.J., Gilmore, J.H.: The Experience Economy (1999)
5. Mou, Q.C., et al.: Making children's education products of "TuTuLe" based on AR technology. Comput. Inf. Technol. (2017)
6. Wei, S., Wang, B.: Application of AR technology in intangible cultural heritage and cultural tourism industry. J. Jianghan Univ. **44**(4), 364–368 (2016)
7. Ilic, U., Yildirim, O.G.: Augmented reality and its reflections on education in Turkey. In: International Dynamic, Explorative and Active Learning (2015)
8. Hirve, S.A., Kunjir, A., Shaikh, B., Shah, K.: An approach towards data visualization based on AR principles. In: International Conference on Big Data Analytics and Computational Intelligence, pp. 128–133. IEEE (2017)
9. Heun, V., Kasahara, S., Maes, P.: Smarter objects: using AR technology to program physical objects and their interactions. In: Extended Abstracts on Human Factors in Computing Systems CHI 2013, pp. 2817–2818. ACM (2013)
10. Zhang, Y.X., Zhu, Z.Q.: Interactive spatial AR for classroom teaching. In: International Conference on Augmented Reality, Virtual Reality and Computer Graphics, pp. 463–470. Springer, Cham (2016). https://doi.org/10.1007/978-3-319-40621-3
11. Augmented reality. In: IEEE International Conference on Trust, Security and Privacy in Computing and Communications, pp. 1666–1675. IEEE, fchencq
12. Puyuelo, M., Higón, J.L., Merino, L., Contero, M.: Experiencing augmented reality as an accessibility resource in the unesco heritage site called "la lonja", valencia. Procedia Comput. Sci. **25**, 171–178 (2013)
13. Mendoza, R., Baldiris, S., Fabregat, R.: Framework to heritage education using emerging technologies. Procedia Comput. Sci. **75**, 239–249 (2015)
14. Kim, E., Kim, J., Woo, W.: Metadata schema for context-aware augmented reality applications in cultural heritage domain. In: Digital Heritage, vol. 2, pp. 283–290. IEEE (2016)
15. Dieck, M.C.T., Jung, T.H.: Value of augmented reality at cultural heritage sites: a stakeholder approach. J. Destin. Mark. Manag. **6**(2), 110–117 (2017)

16. Chang, K.-E., Chang, C.-T., Hou, H.-T., Sung, Y.-T., Chao, H.-L., Lee, C.-M.: Development and behavioral pattern analysis of a mobile guide system with augmented reality for painting appreciation instruction in an art museum. Comput. Educ. **71**, 185–197 (2014)

17. Di Serio, Á., Ibáñez, M.B., Kloos, C.D.: Impact of an augmented reality system on students' motivation for a visual art course. Comput. Educ. **68**, 586–596 (2013)

18. Jara, C.A., Candelas, F.A., Puente, S.T., Torres, F.: Hands-on experiences of undergraduate students in automatics and robotics using a virtual and remote laboratory. Comput. Educ. **57**(4), 2451–2461 (2011)

19. Bacca, J., Baldiris, S., Fabregat, R., Graf, S., Kinshuk: Augmented reality trends in education: a systematic review of research and applications. J. Educ. Technol. Soc. **17**(4), 133–149 (2014)

20. International Organization for Standardization. Ergonomics of human system interaction - Part 210 (2009)

21. Human-centered design for interactive systems (formerly known as 13407). ISO F ± DIS 9241-210:2009

22. Law, E., Roto, V., Hassenzahl, M., Vermeeren, A., Kort, J.: Understanding, scoping and defining user experience: a survey approach (PDF). In: Proceedings of Human Factors in Computing Systems conference CHI 2009, Boston, MA, USA, 4–9 April 2009

23. Huang, T.C., Chen, C.C., Chou, Y.W.: Animating eco-education: to see, feel, and discover in an augmented reality-based experiential learning environment. Comput. Educ. **96**, 72–82 (2016)

24. Dunlap, J., Dobrovolny, J., Young, D.: Preparing eLearning designers using Kolb's model of experiential learning. J. Online Educ. **4**(4), 1–6 (2008)

25. Fan, H., Scottpoole, M.: What is personalization? perspectives on the design and implementation of personalization in information systems. J. Organ. Comput. **16**(3–4), 179–202 (2006)

26. Mayeku, B.: Enhancing personalization and learner engagement in context-aware learning environment - a pedagogical and technological perspective (2015)

27. Li, M., Ogata, H., Hou, B., Uosaki, N., Yano, Y.: Personalization in context-aware ubiquitous learning-log system. In: IEEE Seventh International Conference on Wireless, Mobile and Ubiquitous Technology in Education, vol. 16, pp. 41–48. IEEE (2012)

28. Kucirkova, N., Messer, D., Whitelock, D.: Parents reading with their toddlers: the role of personalization in book engagement. J. Early Childhood Literacy **13**(4), 445–470 (2012)

29. Keller, J.M., Litchfield, B.C.: Motivation and performance. Trends Issues Instr. Des. Technol. **2**, 89–92 (2002)

30. Lidón, I., Rebollar, R., Møller, C.: A collaborative learning environment for management education based on experiential learning. Innov. Educ. Teach. Int. **48**(3), 301–312 (2011)

31. Roosta, F., Taghiyareh, F., Mosharraf, M.: Personalization of gamification-elements in an e-learning environment based on learners' motivation. In: International Symposium on Telecommunications, pp. 637–642. IEEE (2017)

32. Townsend, R.: A Handbook for Teaching and Learning in Higher Education: Enhancing Academic Practice, 3rd edn. Kogan Page, New York (2009)

33. Kwon, K., Kim, C.: How to design personalization in a context of customer retention: who personalizes what and to what extent? Electron. Commer. Res. Appl. **11**(2), 101–116 (2012)

34. Felicia, P.: Handbook of Research on Improving Learning and Motivation, p. 1003 (2011)

35. Hisatomi, K., Tomiyama, K., Katayama, M., Iwadate, Y.: Method of 3D reconstruction using graph cuts, and its application to preserving intangible cultural heritage. In: IEEE International Conference on Computer Vision Workshops, pp. 923–930. IEEE (2010)

An Essay About the Impact of the Digital Revolution on Higher Education in Art and Design

Hendrik Wahl[(✉)]

American University in Dubai, Dubai, UAE
hendrik@optio-n.com

Abstract. This paper focuses the shift in human culture and society, delivered by the digital revolution. Due to an expected dematerialization of the most future products and services the contradiction between the classical value of a commodity, negotiated in the traditional exchange systems and the digital economy will further increase. This again will contribute to dramatic changes in production, rendering gigantic industrial complexes obsolete, which puts the personal creativity as an eternal, never expiring source of inspiration, art, design and high elaborated products into the focus.

Starting from this point we want to explore how future-oriented education can meaningfully interlink the widely chaotic processes of art and design production, the absolute necessary fuzziness of an artist's mind with the cool and sometimes unforgiving logic of the digital machines. We are deeply convinced that this is not a matter of interface-design anymore. That's why we want to go beyond any conventions and rethink higher education in the domain of art and design related creativity, virtuosity and intellectuality under the impact of the digital revolution from the beginning. By conducting an analytic review of the mindsets and methods applied here, we are expecting to face the major challenge in defining the criteria, which are allowing us to establish and to sustain a dynamic balance between the needs of the carbon beings and the possibilities of their siliconized representations - far apart from buzzword centered platitudes.

Keywords: Art · Design · Higher education · Digital revolution · Human labor
Dematerialization · Fuzziness of the artist's mind · Tectonic shift
Parallels in history · Industrial robotics · Uniformity of mass-production
Philosophy · Creativity · Virtuosity · Intellectuality · Global society
Self-regulating markets · Deviation · Evolution · Success · Ethics
Needs vs. Possibilities · Lifelong learning

1 Introduction

The world we are living in is subjected to a dramatic change. Something deep below in human society has lost coherence. Our certainties, our thinking, our beliefs in enlightenment and progress of the human being, are deeply rocked. At first, subconsciously we get aware of a tectonic shift, delivered to not insignificant extents by the repercussions

© Springer International Publishing AG, part of Springer Nature 2018
M. Kurosu (Ed.): HCI 2018, LNCS 10902, pp. 317–333, 2018.
https://doi.org/10.1007/978-3-319-91244-8_26

of the digital revolution. Interpenetrating any aspect of an increasing number of individual lives, the promises made by the concepts of pure reason and formal logic, to
deliver a reliable order of knowledge and a predictable vision of the future are becoming
astonishingly challenged from an unexpected direction. Suddenly, memories of seemingly long forgotten phenomena deeply believed to be overcome, now arising from
nothingness. Newer variations of protectionism, separatism, discrimination, alternative
facts, speech regulations and backward oriented sentiments are gaining perceivable
relevance within an increasing segment of the population. This development indicates
a climate of precariousness, anxiety and the impression of being individually subjected
to an overwhelming complexity, controlled by an incomprehensible "establishment"
situated somewhere high above.

Since the worldwide networks, the industrial robotics, the magic of digital illusion
and other varieties of the technology driven realm, for a longer period have been
perceived as a playground of nerds and highly qualified people, now have come of age,
unfolding its highly dynamic, chaotic potential on a global scale, a strong urge for
simplicity of life, driven by sentiments of easy to understand, compartmentalized structures, for simple criteria of personal identification and distinction has emerged. What
has been for years the credo of the user interface design, making highly complex logical
systems playful and intuitive accessible for everyone, now shows its flip side - appears
to be a mask, disguising, distracting and disconnecting the common user from the actual
processes underneath. Sensing this, getting aware of the function of this thin layer, makes
an increasing number of people reacting with anger and mistrust in the actually or
seemingly in-transparent mechanisms of the contemporary societies and leads not
seldom to irrational and crude, "alternative" ideologies.

Looking for parallels to this situation in history, we can recognize a similar increment
of social, economic and cultural complexity affecting larger populations - symbolized
in the metaphor of the steam engine, heralding in the first industrial revolution. Considering the thinking, of this period (Smith, A., Marx, K.), which has fundamentally shaped
the understanding of economy, we can recognize that the paradigms established back
then are receiving still highly appreciations in contemporary. Rooted in the conviction
that ethical, on mutual benefit oriented collaboration, trust, and fair exchange are the
fundamental driving forces of human interaction, the ideas of distributed production-
methods and unlimited, self-regulating markets have grown paramount. On the other
side, we can find an analytic criticism of the relation between mechanized and human
labor and the distribution of the in this way aggregated values. Also a consideration of
the metaphor of the assembly line - standing for the industrialized uniformity of mass-
production and contributing significantly to the ideology of an eternal economic growth,
might help to set up a solid proposition, for the attempt to discuss the correlation between
the digital industry and economy on one side and its impact on the commonly as
"cultural" considered processes of art and design creation, distribution and education.

2 Proposition

Relaying the deliberations above to the contemporary situation we want to mention a couple of aspects, which are supporting the thesis of the similarity between the industrial and the digital revolution. Seen from the POV of a common person the picture shows at first thrilling but harmless attractions e.g. the computer-generated creatures in block-buster movies (Tron, Jurassic Park, The Mask,...) comparable with the first mechanical androids e.g. buy Jacques de Vaucanson or Pierre Jaquet-Droz. Next, we want to mention the conflicts about copyrights between the classical music industry and the respective exchange platforms on the Internet in parallel to the emergence of trademarks as D.R.G.M. or MADE IN GERMANY rooted in the British Merchandise Marks Act from 1887. But also this got perceived by the majority to be only a concern of very specific peer groups. Much more severe developments in the domain of industrial robotics, predictive analytics, as well as the activities of security agencies have been for a longer period quite unacknowledged, not to mention the clearly criminal actions in conjunction with digital technology. Also here, we can draw a line to the Luddism in the late 19th century respective to the inventions of Herman Hollerith. In resemblance to the development of various technological supported propaganda methods in the first half of the 20th century, we can see the prosumer contents in the social networks and their influence on democratic and political processes, which has been widely ignored by broader segments of the population - leading now to an increasingly precarious awaken.

Focusing more the domain of industrial robotics and autonomous production it becomes clear, that the distinction between hard- and software describes the frontier where individual human factors as intellectuality, skill-fullness and creativity meets the mechanisms of a global economy and where fundamental changes are taken place. Has the metaphor of the assembly-line established the idea of mass-production as the key to economic efficiency and in extrapolation led to the ideology of a constant growth of welfare, it is nowadays clearly to see that this concept is about to expire. At first, we need to acknowledge that robots are surely able to build robots but never will buy robots. Second, the products of the future will be basically material-less. Since we are able to transfer almost any blueprint and production data in light speed to any place on earth, to any facility, which can generate the specific product without the use of anyone's hand, the era of the gigantic production plants is inevitable over - because the generators of the actual objects e.g. Maker Bots can be dispensed into the residential areas of the cities. This will deliver a major challenge to the concept of diversification of labor and the idea of expanding markets, which are already experiencing the limitation of the globalized economy. Also, the system-constituting concept of the individual effort as the promise for personal success within a community requires an urgent reconsideration. Since the availability of products will become gradually less a matter of shortage in number or overproduction, the paradigm of quantity will be more and more substituted by the qualities a specific solution can offer within a defined timeframe. Thinking about the already existing material-less products, as software, used in mass communication, media and the creative production we can perceive already a process of democratization. In a situation where a movie, can be made with a cellphone, where games and any other software can be developed on a tablet, where all of this can be distributed due to highly effective digital, common accessible channels it become also in the domain of creative, digital production clear, that the people in future can only rely on their own material-less intrinsic values, their intelligence, creativity and maker skills, which brings us now to the core of this deliberation: education and in particular higher education within the domain of art and design, as a mean for the carbon beings to assert them self and to keep control of the digital spirits we have shouted for.

3   The Subject Matter

Art and design are commonly considered to be cultural subject matters, which are only exist in uplifted spheres, governed by logical non-predictable criteria. But facing a situation where art and in particular design has become increasingly a concern of accessibility, of perceptual narratives and dynamic interconnectivity, this appears to be a non-sufficient argument. When a negligent tip on a smartphone can cause economic turbulences, when a tweet can raise international tensions, when the sublime forces of pictures are commonly used to design opinions - it becomes clear that art and design are increasingly gaining relevance far beyond there traditional domains. Therefore newer ideas in art and design education unconditionally need to pay tribute to the highly interwoven structures and processes of the contemporary and expected societies. Not at least, the ethical momentum as the driving force of human interaction needs to be subjected to a deeper reconsideration.

3.1   Education in Art (Fine Art)

The freedom of art is a well conserved and repeatedly used argument to demand a distinguished understanding for a specific quality in human expression. But to find sufficient indications, justifying the specific difference between art and non-art or to define criteria for a genuine proximity to this subject matter, is everything else as trivial. A significant debate in this domain, which may serve us as an access point here, is the discussion between conceptual constituted art and the phenomenological approach, which refers more to perceivable qualities of certain art pieces. In an attempt of clarification between all the arguments and objections brought forward here, we want to distinguish between sublime narrations and manifest notations, between idea and sensation, between concept and percept. Although these criteria do clearly not matter to the processes of the contemporary art marked, on the other side freedom neither does.

In regard to education the separation between conceptual creativity and practical virtuosity, the ability to evoke the impression of speechless relevance in the spectator's mind, can nevertheless serve as a significant cornerstone. In contrast to the well-preserved myth that the origin of a significant art piece is a sudden idea, which the artists get aware by e.g. divine infusion and which she/he subsequently just need to bring in a manifest form, the reality looks usually quite different. In order to make intentions inter-subjective accessible a specific form of expression is necessary, which requires a transformation of an idea, a mood, a speechless certainty into a manifest piece. Since human perception (the artists as well as those of the audience) is extremely sensitive and amenable to deception, widely governed by unconscious influences, the process leading to an expression, which subsequently can be considered to be of a certain quality, to be artistic or just breathtaking is everything else but simple. On the other side fine art, appeals in general to perception, to be sensual recognized and to have a certain effect in the mindsets of an extreme heterogeneous audience. Since everyone (except maybe those who suffer from specific physiological insufficiencies) is able to perceive and since any perception is widely governed by pre- and sub-cognitive judgments [1], it is basically not to comprehend why art in the first place should be a subject of highfalutin deliberations, which only can be conducted by peers of a particular domain, who are claiming not seldom to possess a specific intellectual, mostly not closer described access to the subject matter. The fact, that art is not dependent at all on reason and logical validity, does not support this kind of accords; moreover, it makes clear that art founds its existence fundamentally due to practical efforts. During the process of art production, the same fact of independence constitutes the actual freedom of art. But freedom itself is not a value of its own. It is an opportunity but also the obligation to make decisions. How these artistic decisions are made, how the results of these decisions are evaluated, corrected, emphasized, contrasted or even discarded is the fundamental duty of the artist. This is usually a demanding act and is not subjected to the guidance of a super oriented instance and according to the freedom of art neither dependent on theoretical figures. Moreover, it is the ability of the artist to create based on her/his specific skill-sets a form of expression, which gains relevance due to its sheer existence beyond any convention.

Following from this, we may agree that art due to its fundamental independence from any objective criteria cannot be a subject of systematic teaching. In contrast to this, the development of skill-sets and abilities surely can and must be the goal of a related education. Since creativity and virtuosity can be seen as implicit, tacit knowledge founded largely on sensomotoric constituted certitudes, the method of learning in this domain is less a matter of understanding relations between well-vindicated facts but much more a result of continuous experiments on form, values, contrast, form-ground-relations and so on. The question whether classical methods or digital technology are best suited to support learning in this domain should not be seen as a contradiction. Since the reception and appreciation of art is not a matter of, which methods have been used but how a certain quality has been achieved, classical and digital tools should be applied to supplement each other. In regard to teaching and learning the focus should be laid on the acquisition of the principals, which subsequently supporting the transformation of ideas by a creative act into a manifest form of expression. Since this process is governed to large extents by the application of tacit knowledge, studio classes, which are focused on the development of particular skillsets (classical as well as digital), and which are conjunct each other can be the mean of choice to impart the underlying principals and the advantages of each particular toolset/method.

3.2 Education in Design (Product, Motion, Interaction, Visual)

The distinction between design and fine art is commonalty reasoned by the specific way human creativity is respectively applied. In contrast to the fundamental rejection of any convention rightly demanded by the fine and some performing arts, the domain of design is much more determined by concrete and methodic aspects. Nevertheless also here the common phrase used to appreciate extraordinary design is; to experience something new, a new look or style, a new approach to a formal or gestalt problem, a new manner of user interaction or the application of newer concepts of knowledge as e.g. cloud intelligence, procedural creativity or network distributed automata. Since we are facing a development of dematerialization, functional integration and common accessibility in regards to future products and services in contrast to an astonishing resilience of classical economic exchange methods, design today is less a matter of well established, reductionist approaches as form follows function, phantasy, fun, fiction, emotion and so on. Design today faces much more pivotal questions, referring to the eternal problem about the relation between the un-extended ideas (virtualities) and the actual, extended realms everyone is an inherent part of. The duty of design today (among of course other disciplines), is nothing else but to find practical solutions to define the relation between the increments of complexity we are facing in the interaction with the highly dynamic processes of the contemporary world and the fundamental needs of any individual. These needs are on the first hand not compulsory of an aesthetically nature. Moreover, they are increasingly defined by an individual's relation to it's particular and global environment, they are a matter of mutually beneficial interaction, of a meaningful, balanced life, of the cultivation of needs, of the conscious use of resources and of sovereign interacting within the contemporary society. Design today is a question of the relation between the forms of objects, the forms of dynamics and the forms of intuition.

Conducting an approach towards a contemporary design education - it might be useful for methodical reasons, to pay tribute to reductionism in order to distinguish 3 major elements of equal importance (creativity, virtuosity, intellectuality), which any design process is consisting of. At first and foremost we need to consider creativity. Creativity is characterized as the ability to generate something unprecedented, something, which carries a momentum of surprise, which delivers unconventional solutions and what therefore barely can be a subject of methodical teaching. But looking closer, we can define creativity as the ability to connect given or hypothetical figures in a manner, which can suffice the criteria above. To ignite and to propel this process, various side conditions and methodical measures can be found e.g. in the well establish rules of brainstorming. But using the brain only, which traditional deals with categorization to increase the effectiveness of thinking, might be not enough. When we want to overcome boundaries given by classical formalized notation systems as specific languages or subconsciously established traditions of thinking, it can be very helpful to interconnect the text with nonverbal forms of expression. When we start to scribble, to sketch, to knead a chunk of clay or to run computerized iterations on a simple shape, we can achieve figures, forms and types of connection of which, we would not have a word neither an idea before. Doing this in a team of equitable members in a non-competitive situation will increase the chances to achieve unique solution furthermore. If we complement the realm of rhetoric with the domain of nonverbal expression we are facing the next major element of our canon, practical virtuosity.

A sketch, an accord, a color scheme, a specific type of motion or interaction can trigger our perceptual system in most effective ways and push ideas in unexpected directions, far apart from the boredom of, the extensive use of prefabricated templates, the coward attempts of "luxuryzation", or the hesitantly conducted "brand-cosmetics" so often perceived today. Off course the development of skill-sets, virtuosity and crafts-manship in the domain of visual, procedural or product design is not limited to visual thinking, but moreover a major factor in order to develop ideas further, to gain confi-dence about a particular solution and to communicate process and status of a specific design project. To focus on the development of creative craftsmanship is, therefore, an unconditional necessity for a contemporary whole person education in any field of design. To draw a well tense line, to create constant curvature in freeform (A-class) surfaces, to achieve color consistency or complementary, to reach continuity in time-based media, or to provide smooth blends in interaction is definitely not a question of whether it has attempted but gains relevance when these qualities are just presented to perception. In particular when this takes place on a subconscious way, we can achieve a momentum of surprise, emphasizing the well known quote, which says: outstanding design is invisible. Due to the nature of the implicit, tacit subjects of learning here, we need to understand that the only way to develop mastership, to gain virtuosity is to conduct frequent exercises of the particular skills as e.g. sketching, perspective drawing, rendering, color composition, typography, animation and motion design, virtual and physical prototyping. Since we clearly can not accurately predict the final outcome of a virtuous creative process, since any methodical approach in this regard does not guar-antee a specific effect, we want to suggest to consider the efforts leading to outstanding design solutions as non - reductionist. Facing the significant effect of nonlinear approaches conducted by creative virtuosity, the methodical methods (analog, digital or intellectual) applied here, can be clearly indicated as tools, which only gaining relevance due to their application within the creative process. So the question whether analog or digital techniques are the mean of choice within contemporary design education becomes finally subordinate.

Nevertheless, since we have characterized the actual processes within the realm of design as not linear constituted, we are now on the edge where creativity and virtuosity need to be supplemented and interwoven with intellectual, theoretical deliberations. The role of intellectuality within a state of the art design or applied arts education can in the first instance seen as the development of an open, whitely scoped mind, which is inter-ested in various implications and relations. It is indisputable that an individual, which has developed a well-founded, heterogeneous and wide-ranging knowledge base possesses significant advantages when it is requested to generate highly integrated and unconventional constituted mind maps or to conduct creative explorations. It is also self-evident, that a person who can supplement thinking with visual expressions, emotional narrations and a procedural understanding of form and gestalt will much more likely be able to find sufficient solutions on particular design problems. Therefore theoretical and research-oriented approaches towards design related phenomena are already funda-mental justified. But there is another dimension, which exceeds the traditional theory in the domain of design. Since we are facing a radical increment of the complexity of almost any aspect of everyone's life, we are urged to find solutions at the edge between the overwhelming amount of virtual opportunities, granted by the digital domain, and the basic aspects, which are defining our self-concept as independent individuals. A strategy to find answers to this problem can be oriented in two main directions. On one side we see the obligation of any one to define its own freedom by making well-founded decisions. In the process of contemporary creative design, this must be directed to the acquisition of individual abilities regarding to the creation of unconventional solutions, which are earning appreciations and getting considered to be of a certain, distinguished quality. The efforts to be undertaken in this regard are of an individual, practical nature as the continuous exploration of form, gestalt, interconnectivity, and the lifelong acquisition of knowledge. On the other side and interconnected with the point above, it becomes increasingly important and someone may say difficult, not only to keep up to date with the progressive acceleration within the digital domain. Moreover, it is eminent to define the essential ethical needs of the human being, as social-economical stability, mind- and meaningful interaction, mutual beneficial collaboration and the conscious use of resources as the conditions, which any technological development should be aligned to. The realms of art and design, in this regard are not the worst places to start on. Since predictive analytics are wildly considered to deliver quite reliable forecasts of behaviors within human populations and to model average personalities; the artist, the designer today is nothing else but requested to exceed this average in order to sustain a mindset, which is expressed in the term individual. The means to do so are provided to not insignificant extends by digital technology, but the ways to use them, to act in unpredictable manners are still in the hand of the carbon inter-agent.

In order to close this paragraph, we want to paraphrase the structure-defining elements; a contemporary education in art and design should be committed to. In the first place stands the idea, to focus the actual needs of the human being. Considering beneficial interacting as more important then profit making, brings the problem of how to make things in the focus. This is basically not a matter of numbers or data and conjunct with an emphasis to tacit qualifications, as creativity, virtuosity and the ability of unconventional intellectual reflection. Done frequently and various manners (classical and digital), this aims to a cultivation of sensitivity in perception, creation, interaction and subsequently is a prerequisites to achieve creative, virtuous mastership. By supplementing the practical efforts with theoretical activities in order to foster critical independent minds, which are assessing any promise made by technology, ideology or economy, the answer on the question of design today is a constant approach to the relation between the form of objects, the forms of dynamics and the forms of intuition.

4   Criticism

Coming back to the discussion above, regarding the increment of complexity pervading all aspects of anyone's life due to the progress in the realm of technology, we can identify a series of indications, which are delivering severe repercussions to the economic and social structures of contemporary and expected societies.

At first, we need to recognize, that the idea of an unlimited expansion of the markets is reaching an ultimate boundary, defined by the limitation of the nowadays-actual globalized economy. Facing a situation, in which any physical, as well as any virtual product, can be created everywhere on earth to any extent and subsequently can be distributed due to highly elaborate logistic networks anywhere, the classical merchant doctrine of supply and demand as the ultimate regulating principal is becoming funda-mental questionable. This leads to an emphasis on intensification, in order to sustain the increase of profit. The reaction to this problem, expressed from the standpoint of the classical intuition, is to demand radical deregulation. In particular custom duties, but also variations in technological, social or environmental protection standards as well as specific cultural implications of local markets are seen as significant restraints, detaining the unimpeded flow within the global economy, allegedly guaranteeing an eternal growth of profit and subsequently leading to an increment of common welfare.

On the other hand, we can find strong indications that the idea, which supposes, that common benefits can be only achieved due to the enforcement of individual self-inter-ested behavior does not gain a common appreciation anymore. In conjunction with this, the classical theme of capitalism, insisting that individual success in life is a matter of pure determination, of self-optimization, of acquiring highest grades in education, and delivering maximal performance is losing charmingness. What has been a promise of chance, twists under the conditions of the global economy, automata production and highly distributed labor more and more into in a figure of linear thinking, which delivers sublime threads to the individuals, who are scattered around the globe and requested to offer their abilities to unrestricted marked conditions.

Looking in this regard closer on the economic concept of market prices, which suggests that the final price of a product is constituted, not by the actual expenses on raw material nor by intellectual effort or labor force applied in production, but by the amount a customer is finally willing or convinced to spend, illustrates the situation in which individual creativity, virtuosity, skills, and intellectuality are requested to be offered and applied. The criteria on which the decision to purchase a certain product is made, is in the most cases also less a matter of an actual need, bud widely influenced by implications as limited availability, seasonal trends, the promise of exclusivity or a special discount. This is where the marketing and advertising industry derives its right to exist. Here we can perceive various methods and attempts to gain influence on the equilibrium between supply and demand. In order to achieve or to enforce the desired profit a scope of activities is applied, ranging from reasonable means of customer care over the application of predictive analytics and further to ethical clearly questionable measures. Thinking of production methods fundamentally relying on the exploitation of labor under precarious social conditions around the globe, of marketing mechanisms to enforce overpricing by establishing artificial shortages or alleged exclusivity, of actions which are in regard to existing market regulations are just illegal as price rigging or of even more severe criminal activities, as the conspiracy we have seen e.g. in regard to the "Dieselgate" emissions scandal [2], the unrestricted freedom of economy shows its dark flip side. An indication, that the mindset behind this kind of activities is not a regrettable exception, executed by a small number of ethical mislead individuals, but an inherent characteristics of an ideology, which refers repeatedly and with emphasis to the idea of the freedom of business and markets, can be easily found already by Adam Smith. *"People of the same trade seldom meet together, even for merriment and diver-sion, but the conversation ends in a conspiracy against the publick [sic.], or in some contrivance to raise prices. It is impossible indeed to prevent such meetings, by any law which either could be executed, or would be consistent with liberty and justice. But though the law cannot hinder people of the same trade from sometimes assembling together, it ought to do nothing to facilitate such assemblies; much less to render them necessary"* [3].

Nevertheless, during the age of the uniformity of mass production the relation between supply and demand, of applied labor and more or less fair wages has been, at least within the industrialized nations and due to the constant altercation and strive in a social economical balance. But the character of the actual product has over time become subjected to significant changes. Has the products of the early assembly line helped to content dramatic needs, the capacity of the industrialized mass production soon provided oversupply, putting marketing and the question of the distribution of the generated values into the focus of the intellectual and political discussion. An indication of this development can be seen in the thesis of alienated work, by Karl Marx [4]. The product, which is created in an industrial manner, does not refer to any individual needs anymore. The relation a worker, who assembles just a part of a machine, develops to the product she/he is working on no direct relation but sees the time and energy spend in the factory as a mean to earn a specific salary. Seen from the other side of the table, a specific product also is not of a particular interest, since the quantity of mass production and its average quality deliver the key figures, in which the success of a company is measured. Due to the process of technology and automata in production, the relation between production, distribution, and consumption is drifting even further apart. On one side we can recognize a trend in the creation of value, which more and more finds its expression in virtual processes e.g. within the sector of the finance and reinsurance industry. On the other hand, we are facing a constant dematerialization of contemporary products and services. Conjunct with this development of virtualization we can also perceive an ongoing separation between the design, the development, the actual production process and the manner products and service are distributed and used. Thinking of an production-pipeline of classical machinery to day, it is not difficult to imagine, that a specific finance and business concept is be made in e.g. Great Britain or America, the design of the product and the interaction narratives might be made in Italy or Korea, while software components are developed in Finland or Japan, feeding production facilities in France or Brazil, from where sub-assembled units or the end-product will be finally shipped to the worldwide markets. Thinking further, of the productive collaborations applied in software development, the structure of the creation can be described in a similar way, but without the need of physical logistics already today. Imagining the extreme points of such a development, we may think about a situation where all design data of any product are instantaneous digital accessible everywhere around the globe, just in the way as the 24/7 accessibility to software products is already. Now the actual production of a specific good can be done on demand at the home or e.g. a digital prototyping center in the vicinity of the residential area, where the end-user is situated. This, in consequence renders vast production plants, storage and transportation facilities widely obsolete and brings the point of production to the identical place as the point of sale. The place where the actual design and development of such a product takes place is respectively also not necessarily located at a specific geographical area but can be dispersed to the home offices of the individual developers. Going one step further along this thoughts brings us to a situation, in which the actual physical product might become finally obsolete at all. Since it is not a question whether but moreover when and how we will be able to achieve a level of technical, sensorial and motoric stimulation, which allows evoking any type of impression by seamless blending any kind of virtuality in our cognitive reality, this is not a tail from utopia. Soon, we will be able, by wearing a VT/AR device, or even further having a respective user interface implanted in everyone's brain, to face the opportunity to access any augmented immersion e.g. driving a vintage car on a scenic road, having an exclusive meal at the top of Olympus Mons on mars or to satisfying our deep interwoven desire of competition by fighting virtual creatures in breathtaking game levels, without the presence of any physical product, which is result of an classical design, development or production process. Apart from the idea of augmenting cognitive reality to the maximal extent, in which consequently any interface between technological virtuality and cognitive integrity vanishes away, delivering a singularity, where any discussion leads immediately to an infinite regress and to a denial of individuality, personality, and humanity, we can still find valid access points to think further.

Despite a situation where the concept of the actual product is increasingly less suited to justify a specific value (due to its instant and unlimited availability), we are facing a world full of overwhelming supply of virtual services and digital opportunities, which can be seen as an indication of the shift from expansion to intensification in worldwide economics. Since we just need to talk to Alexa, Siri or the Google Assistant in order to enter full-scale pampered living, questions pointing to the concepts of free will, independent mind, individual creativity and how to prevent that the human being is becoming in consequence, just an expendable appendix of the silicon logic, gaining relevance again. On one side the fully interconnection of any data a individual is "producing" due to the use of digital devices (smartphones, home pods, bracelets) offers great opportunities in regard to obtain living quality for larger populations. On the other side, the way in which the so acquired data are used, delivers serious conflicts in regard to transparency of social-economic processes and private autonomy. This becomes significantly lucid under the aspect of how those data becoming subjects of the traditional capitalistic economy. Under the paradigm, which sees those processes as a law of nature like technological evolution, any attempt to translate all kind of human activity into digital data, into the ultimate raw material for whatever algorithms, capable to predict, to steers and to manipulate social interaction are absolutely justified means to shape future societies. Following this ideology we can recognize a tectonic shift between the concept of quality and quantity, resonating the theme of the industrial mass production further to likes and followers into contemporary. But does this approach, of which the term predictive analytics is standing for and which fundamentally relies on the concept of the average deliver enough system-constituting significance to replace the idea of excellence? Is the logical methodology able to deliver a comprehensive, indisputable narrative, able to operate with any kind of frequently chaotic human behavior, social interaction and political opinion formation? At least the communist ideology, which has claimed similarly by the alleged or proclaimed descendants of Karl Marx, has been obviously proven wrong in this regard.

In a situation, in which the concept of the actual product as the carrier of a specific value is losing significance, where the question of raw material is expected to shift gradually from the exploration of natural resources towards an infinite reproducible and expandable binary matrix, where any product is instantaneous and to any extent accessible, rendering classics merchant doctrine to zero and where computing power is undergoing an dramatic process of democratization, the only source which can be a subject of generating value or profit, in the classical intuition of capitalism is human intellectual and creative ability.

This seems to be formidable news for anyone who sees the field of excellent and lifelong education as the realm where meaningful efforts in the development of the human society can be undertaken. While this is basically not to deny, the contemporary situation delivers severe contradictions. Since we rightly can speak of a creative, intellectual proletariat in order to describe high educated, creative people who are requested to offer there energy and time to an economy which shows a quite stiff resilience to the technological, social and cultural development today - the criticism, which need to be applied does not go to technology, art or design but to the concept of amount and eternal growth of profit, which is apparently incapable to deliver a commonly acceptable vision of the future.

4.1 Looking for Answers

Looking for answers to this unsatisfactory situation can be done along two premises. At first, we need to understand that all of us are subjected to the autopoietic processes of the social systems we are living in [5]. Thinking about the idea of the invisible hand [6] delivers another indication to understand this highly complex processes, as, non-linear and dynamic constituted. In addition, we also perceive a continuously dispute about how the various relations within a human population should be organized best. From the beginning of philosophy [7] up to now, nary methodical approach towards this problem has delivered a commonly accepted metaphor, leading to a coherent narration and further to an ideal constituted government. Despite this, the human society has been undergone significant developments, which usually just post factual has led to respective theories. Therefore we want to consider the processes within a human population as in principal chaotic. This does not mean, that we want to understand those processes as erratic, but neither to be sufficiently characterized in the figure of linear thinking [8]. Moreover, we want to consider the human society with its sub-domains as art, technology, economy, ethics... as a given situation, where a present status, within certain parameter determines the future, but an approximation of the present does not determine a holistic vision of the worlds to come.

Second, we want to consider the capabilities and the limitation of a pure methodical, algorithmic approach towards the non-linear dynamics of human societies. The mindset behind all the activities sub-summarized in the term predictive analytics relies fundamentally on statistics. By quantifying all aspects of human life, by processing this data, by recognizing the pattern in the behavior of a population or an individual, the fundamental conviction expressed here is, to reduce the human being into a quite predictable entity within a social swarm. The contradiction, which emerges from this conception, can be articulated in several ways. We can ask whether it is a good idea to approach social problems with ice-cold technocratic efficiency, whether a government should be organized like a business, whether the human being can and should be comprehensibly measured in numbers and whether the measurable part of the world, represents actually the entire universe. Or is mathematics just a tool, developed by insufficient beings in order to project "Ordo" into their everyday chaotic life. What has been for centuries a practical mean especially of the merchants has grown over time to pure science. Mathematics claims rightly, to be the only discipline, which can make universal valid predictions, has become in the digital age the metabolism of the economy, which in its original meaning refers to counting, comparing, ranking. Since digital economy today is still largely relying on the application of human intelligence and creativity it is easy to understand, where this conviction is rooted and how it aims to the modeling of social-economic processes in mathematical terms. Understanding the processes within the human economy and society, as mentioned above as nonlinear dynamics, the logical approach today goes not to a certain individual (as in the age of enlightenment), or a specific class (as Karl Marx supposed), but "limits" itself to the behavior of any member of the whole population. This approach can be seen, and is not seldom characterized as the ultimate realization of democracy. Only the actual activity of each inhabitant (conscious or unconscious), will be detected, analyzed, evaluated and becomes part of the collective narration, written in binary language. Any need, desire, lust or action will be anticipated and assistance will be provided at any occasion. The only request of the system towards its inhabitants is system conformity, "Brave new world 2.0". As compelling such a scenario may appear to certain people in the first instance, it is highly questionable whether it can reach conformity with the fundamentals of the human nature at all.

First, the basic narrative resulting from such a mindset can be criticized with the argument, that actually any ideology before has promised in similar but could never establish a commonly accepted and sustainable equilibrium within the human society. Second, asking the traditional question "Cui bono?" in this case logically would deliver the answer: everyone. Hard to believe, that in particular digital technology should be inspired by altruistic sentiments. And it is even more unlikely, that a larger group of individuals is willing or actually able to overcome the concept of the individual self (origin and precondition of self-interested, self-centered behavior), which has guaranteed the survival of the human being since the cave age on. Third and most important, if we would accept a social-economic situation, which fundamental relies on system conformity of its inhabitants, or moreover where this is factual enforced (thinking off pre-crime analytics), we would finally drown in boredom, mediocrity, arbitrariness, and conventionality. This would be the end of any ethical, political or intellectual discussion but also creative or artistic activities, because the interaction between humans under the paradigm of total system conformity would require a level of "political correctness" where any meaning, any thinking, any idea vanishes in subordination to the rules of grammar.

Any system in nature on the other side, any species, structure or intellectual concept, which is the result of an evolution, has post-factual proven its right to exist. Due to its ability to adapt to instability or to take advantage of the underlying randomness and noise perceivable at any empirical approach to science, the eternal driving force behind nature is rather to describe as constant alternation then static codification. The mutation in a DNA leads to new sets of abilities, which assessed by the particular environment getting improved or extinguished, a minor deviation in gravity can tip the equilibrium of a cosmic body's trajectory, bringing it on a collision course to earth, a glimmer of hope can motivate people to fight and to overcome any hardship and a modicum of sense renders vast ideologies, committed to the idea of total stability and preservation of the status quo easily obsolete. The momentum of deviation, the unconventionality of creativity, the capacity to make and to understand pictures [9], the ability to overcome self-centered affection and to be inspired by mutual beneficial collaboration, the miracle of falling in love are factors, which are deeply interwoven into the fabric of which human beings are made from. Thinking about, how these aspects can be acquired and reliable transformed into the raw material for pure logical algorithms, can be an inspiring task for people who are looking from the technological side to this problem. There is not a shadow of a doubt that there are countless attempts in this direction (thinking about dating-portals today may illustrate this). To be not misunderstood, each of these attempts is justified in the regard, as it represents a deviation from the status quo. Which and whether an algorithm will gain relevance, is under this mindset largely a question of software Darwinism, isn't it? From the systems point of view, which is not committed to particular interests; this appears to be an example of absolute conformity. Supposed a machine, makes the algorithm, which is an entity of the same kind as the system, everything could be seen, to be quite coherent. If the algorithm is man-made, if it is a product of human labor, effort, of the transformation process of the widely chaotic human creativity into methodical applications, we are starting to sense the tectonic shift underneath. Having an ultra-efficient digital infrastructure on one side, interested in nothing capable to do everything and constituted to be total opaque in regard to the mechanisms inside renders the human being just irrelevant. It neither can compete in speed, endurance, means of perception, the extent of its formalized knowledge base or any other criteria, which matter within the digital networks, nor is it able to acquire a profound understanding of the processes situated behind the masks of the user interfaces. In particular, the last indication can be seen as quite critical. Since the in-transparency of such systems is on one side result of the concept of intellectual property owned and secretly hidden by the system carriers and providers, which theoretically can be overcome - on the other side opacity gradually becomes a contingent feature of such systems, due to self-learning algorithms. These algorithms, which are able to emulate evolutionary principals in order to process data sets of incremental complexity and non-linear dynamics, do apparently deliver logical appropriate solution to given problems. But no one is finally able to understand how these solutions are made (compare: AlphaGo against Lee Sedol, [10]) and which parameter are relevant and which not. This puts the human being under an immense sublime pressure, rendering the system constituting narrative of capitalism, that everyone can reach anything by determination, enhancing of performance and the acquisition of knowledge and skills just meaningless.

4.2   How to Deal with This Situation?

The typical reactions, which are resulting from the evolution of human creativity, in a situation which appears to be dominated by totality (technological, economical, ideological) is not seldom retreat or the establishment of private save-spaces (echo chambers) and the development of idiosyncratic narratives. On the other side, it also can be perceived, that individuals are attempting to reach system conformity at all cost by denying their individuality, by the use of self-enhancement methods (medication on an individual base or e.g. prenatal diagnostic in regard of their descendants) or by employing measures, which are ethical even more questionable, as the implementation of distinct in transparent value systems (thinking about clan structures, lobbyism or nepotism). This can explain the urge for departmentalization and separation to be perceived in contemporarily politics, the boom of cosmetics surgery or respective medi-cation and the rise of cybercrime. Since all these phenomena are indicating an alignment to the concept of intensification, following the leitmotif of the industrial age, of uniformity and mass-production, of an ideology of continues economic growth by piling up commodities and virtual values, it might be helpful to shift the focus in other direc-tions. Being saturated with the idea of problem solving, of being committed to perform efficient accordantly incomprehensible criteria, is something, which narrows attention, limits understanding and extinguishes creativity, which is perceived to be unhealthy and not an expression of the fundamentals of the human nature. Due to the fact, that this unilateral point of view does not considers the unspoken and unspeakable (not mean-ingful formalizable) qualities of human existence, addressed by the implicit, tacit efforts undertaken in the realm of art and design, we want to understand this fraction of the human nature as the actual domain where a related education ion art and design can deliver significant contributions.

5 The Digital Age and Higher Education in Art and Design Today

Turning away from the idea of being surrounded by more or less critical problems, which need to be solved in increasing shorter timespans, in order to be efficient and therefor a valuable member of the society, we can ask: which particular problem have actually been solved by artistic expressions or iconic design pieces as e.g. the painting "Haupt-wege und Nebenwege" (Highway and Byways) by Paul Klee (1929), the "Matteuspas-sion" (Matthew Passion) by Johann Sebastian Bach (1727) or the Lounge Chair by Charles and Ray Eames (1956)? To reduce the answer, to this question to utilitarian aspects, to a matter of prestige by the particular owner or to a question of entertainment will surely fall far to short in this regard. If we have the impression of getting inspired, enriched, touched, by an artwork or an iconic design, by a piece of music or performing arts we are perceiving something, which is not and does not need to be logical, precise or calculable. Despite this, the results from those clearly not problem-solving oriented expressions of the human nature do certainly deliver significant impacts to our percep-tion, mindsets and doing. There is nothing to define in regards to the question, what actually can be the subject or outcome of a creative art and design process. People are interested to create, to express unspeakable certitudes, to transform thoughts by gestures of the visible hand into manifest art or design pieces - from the cave age on. Since then, the products of this deep inherent urge are gaining relevance to other individuals, who are getting inspired, enriched, challenged to do similar or to find new approaches, to change their mind or to provide insights to there individual thinking and doing.

Given a world, which offers any amount of binary raw material, any mean of design and production facility to transform data into physical objects and any kind of distribution channel, it makes no sense at all to compete with technology and the cadence of the machines (today measured in GHz). Also, the idea of mass production, the accumulation and concentration of nonproductive value to insanity, the ideology of an eternal growth of welfare by expanding into untapped markets appears to be increasingly less compelling. In front of this backdrop, the question of "what" to do in order to generate profit turns gradually into the question of "how" to make things, which actually matter to people - and this is basically the access point where education in art and design can connect to. Since the relevance of a product resulting from the creative process is increasingly less restrained from technological limitations, the side conditions under which art and design related efforts can be conducted best, shifts into the focus. Here we can think about concepts, which are aiming to obtain the living, and working conditions of any individual in order to unleash the creative potential, today most applied to suffice the paradigm of the number. This is everything else but trivial, but the three main premises, mention above can serve as a guiding idea.

First, we can think about an education concept referring to the development of interdisciplinary creativity. Since we have characterized creativity as in principal oriented to reach non-conventional results, the act of deviation needs to be emphasized. To propel this act, a high amount of professional and ethical integrity is required in order to establish an atmosphere in which individuals can go beyond their traditional thinking, cultural imprints and practiced behavior. Supplemented by means of visualization, the domain of implicit, tacit knowledge can be seamlessly integrated into the creative process, leading to a much more flow-like interaction with individual thoughts and within the inter-subjective communication. Developing the ability to create compelling visual, haptic or processual designs, which are deliver speechless perfection marks the second domain, in which respective efforts should be oriented. Since implicit, tacit knowledge and skillsets are neither a matter of logical thinking nor do they deliver methodical predictable outcomes, the concept of effectiveness is barely suited to be a guideline of learning a teaching within this domain. Moreover, it is the individual involvement, the relationship between the student and the person (the word teacher would fall to short), who has proven its ability to develop, to communicate and to exemplify the art of speechless expression, which matters most in this regard.

To close the circle, we want again emphasize the momentum delivered by a well-founded sense of quality, by a approach which puts more attention of the necessary instead of the possible, by being mindful and sensible for silence, vague, unspoken expressions and by sensing the manner, how Qualia [11] leaving significant traces in perception and mind, without being a stringent argument. Doing this, with an inner urge to understand the approaches, conducted over centuries, by people who are fundamentally more interested in knowledge than in profit, can constitute a mindset, which is critical against any ideology, interested in the deviation from the common, driven to achieve speechless perfection and resilient to adopt to "Innovations" proclaimed by any type of mainstream. Individuals, who can commit their self to this kind of endeavor, who are willing and able to adapt their perception and mind to the unspoken truth, will be best prepared to apply creativity, virtuosity and ethical principals in order to sustain the independence of the carbon-being, in critical opposition and creative, virtuous conjunction with the silicon logic. Whether this can be achieved in total, is everything else but certain. And totality is not at all the mindset behind this article, but we shall never stop any attempt, to make the human society as congenial and adaptive to further developments, as possible and digital technology is a powerful mean to do so.

References

1. Frey, S.: Im Bann der Bilder. In: Zerdick, A., Picot, A., Schrape, K., Burgelman, J.-C., Silverstone, R., Feldmann, V., Heger, D.K., Wolff, C. (eds.) E-Merging Media. European Communication Council Report, pp. 137–151. Springer, Heidelberg (2017). https://doi.org/10.1007/978-3-642-18600-4_8

2. Dieselgate emissions scandal (The Guardian, 2015). https://www.theguardian.com/business/ng-interactive/2015/sep/23/volkswagen-emissions-scandal-explained-diesel-cars. Accessed 12 Feb 2018

3. Smith, A.: An inquiry into the nature and causes of the wealth of nations (1723–1790). Reprint, Originally published. Clarendon Press, Oxford (1979). (Glasgow Edition of the Works and Correspondence of Adam Smith; 2)

4. Marx, K.: Karl Marx, Friedrich Engels. Werke, Berlin 1968, Band 40, S. 510–523 (1844)

5. Luhmann, N.: The autopoiesis of social systems. In: Geyer, F., Van der Zeuwen, J. (eds.) Sociocybernetic Paradoxes: Observation, Control and Evolution of Self-Steering Systems, pp. 179–192. Sage, London (1986)

6. Smith, A.: The Theory of Moral Sentiments, vol. 1, p. 184 (1976). The Glasgow Edition of the Works and Correspondence of Adam Smith, vol. 7. Oxford University Press

7. PLATO, MENO 71e-72a

8. Laplace, P.S.: A Philosophical Essay on Probabilities (1951). Translated into English from the original French by Truscott, F.W., Emory, F.L. (eds.) 6th edn., p. 4. Dover Publications, New York

9. Jonas, H.: Die Freiheit des Bildens. Homo Pictor und die differentia des Menschen. In: Jonas, H. (Hg.), Zwischen Nichts und Ewigkeit. Drei Aufsätze zur Lehre vom Menschen. Vandenhoeck & Ruprecht, Göttingen (1963)

10. AlphaGo against Lee Sedol (The Guardian, 2016) https://www.theguardian.com/technology/2016/mar/15/googles-alphago-seals-4-1-victory-over-grandmaster-lee-sedol. Accessed 12 Feb 2018

11. Jackson, F.: Philos. Q. 32, 127–136 (1982)

12. Nagel, T.: What is it like to be a bat? Philos. Rev. 83, 435–450 (1974). see p. 436

The Application of Augmented Reality Technology in Digital Display for Intangible Cultural Heritage: The Case of Cantonese Furniture

Xing Xie and Xiaoying Tang(✉)

Guangdong University of Technology, Guangzhou, China
1009415641@qq.com

Abstract. The purpose of research on innovative applications of Augmented Reality technology in digital display for intangible cultural heritage is to promote the way to display and disseminate for collections. We explored the relationship between AR technology and digital display, and then the model of digital display for intangible cultural heritage is designed, and the current status was analyzed. This paper examines how to build a model of a digital display with the example of Cantonese furniture that embodies and reflect history, society, culture, technology, function, and style requirements of different content. Finally, the most important, it is how to practice in actual program combined with AR technology. The conclusion is to provide a reference to disseminate the cultural soft power and to construct digital public service platform through a study on innovative applications of AR technology.

Keywords: Augmented Reality technology · Digital display
Intangible cultural heritage · Cantonese furniture

1 Introduction

New media technology has changed our view of time, space and living conditions. With the background of technology, society, culture, and economy, we have created new thinking on design. When many developed countries such as Britain, the United States, and Japan put forward their cultural and creative ideas as a new growth point and breakthrough point of their country's economy, Chinese leaders are also aware of the importance of design for the transformation of China from a manufacturing power to a creative power and a design power. The Ministry of Science and Technology also explicitly proposed in the "Twelfth Five-Year Plan" for the development of science and technology in modern service industry to strengthen the integrated application of new media technologies such as virtual reality, promote the healthy development of cultural products market, and built the innovative country stage of digital technology for cultural resources.

An Intangible cultural heritage (ICH) means the practice, representation, expression, knowledge, skills—as well as the instruments, objects, artifacts and cultural spaces that are considered by UNESCO to be part of a place's cultural heritage [1]. The social,

© Springer International Publishing AG, part of Springer Nature 2018
M. Kurosu (Ed.): HCI 2018, LNCS 10902, pp. 334–343, 2018.
https://doi.org/10.1007/978-3-319-91244-8_27

cultural and technological developments arguably make ICH careers more challenging than ever before. The protection and inheritance of the ICH have been transformed from the traditional way of oral and graphic records into digitization. However, at present, the display and transmission of the ICH in various parts of China have such problems as the backward forms of cultural transmission, the lack of digital protection and inheritance, and the lack of public education functions [2]. In the context of the development of digital industries, strengthening the study of the digital display is a necessary requirement to ICH in China.

2   Augmented Reality Technology and Digital Display

The early digital display was widely used in the field of cinema art, it was considered broad and easy to spread with the inclusion of projection technique and transmission technology. With the extensive application of many new technologies, such as Internet technology, multimedia technology and virtual reality technology, the concept of the digital display has been given a richer connotation and denotation. The so-called digital display is based on the display content as the mainstay of digital technology as means to achieve through various types of new media technologies to achieve digital display content presentation [3]. Augmented Reality (AR) is a new media technology developed on the basis of Virtual Reality (VR). The essence of AR is to generate generated virtual objects, scenes, audio, video, and animation through computer technology, the system prompt information is superimposed to the real world to obtain a mixture of the real world and the virtual world with enhanced information, and then the display technology is used to present the mixture to the user. Throughout the process, augmented reality technology realizes the perfect combination of the things in the virtual world and the real surroundings, and real-time synchronization between the virtual world and the real world.

In 2012, Wonderbook: Book of Spells, developed by Sony Corporation, was one of the more mature cases at present. Through Sony's Play Station Eye camera device and Play Station Move controller, respectively, a combination of augmented reality and Somatology interaction technology, for the flat display unprecedented immersive unique feeling. And the SCARLET project funded by the British Joint Information Systems Committee - "Using AR Technology to Promote Research and Teaching of Special Collections" helps students study medieval manuscripts, representative versions and document archives collected by the John Lanes Library. Students using the iPad with the AR application installed to capture the original Dante Divine Comedy in the glass case, and the digital image, textual information, relevant online information and related literature resources of the document appear on the screen. Students can zoom in on pictures and observe hard-to-digest details. They can also listen to the audio data in Old English to read the article.

The innovative design of digital display under the AR technology has broken the boundaries of the traditional single media and the traditional thinking, got rid of the shackles of the purely material world, surpassed the limitation of time and space, and the content of the exhibition turned from figurative physical substance to abstract digital immaterial. Through the deep excavation of the cultural connotation of the ICH resources and the formation of a rich digital cultural content product, AR technology integrates the virtual cultural integration of the ICH with the digital cultural contents, and will digitally display the intangible cultural heritage provide a new application of ideas and technical means.

3   Digital Display Model of Intangible Cultural Heritage

3.1   The Information Integration of Core Content

ICH is manifested inter alia in the following domains [4]: (a) oral traditions and expressions, including language as a vehicle of the intangible cultural heritage; (b) performing arts; (c) social practices, rituals and festive events; (d) knowledge and practices concerning nature and the universe; (e) traditional craftsmanship. In this study, according to their attributes and characteristics, they classify and abstract from the core elements including history, society, culture, technology, function, and style requirements.

Digital Display transforms the core content of ICH into digital information that can effectively enhance the perception and understanding of users by applying images and sounds. Stylized text, graphics, colors and sound effects enable viewers to perceive the history, society and cultural habits of their predecessors through visual and auditory stimuli. Technology emphasizes practical experience and skillfulness, and the digitally displayed interactive function can provide more help for users to know the technical process accurately. Function and stylized style requires a stronger audiovisual effect. For example, performing art involves music, movement, sound cavity, environment, etc., and has higher requirements for presence. It can be expanded in combination with information presentation such as animation, video and stereo model Elements that interact with the environment.

3.2   Realistic Environment to Create

The result of the AR technology application is to add virtual objects in a real-world, that is, virtual three-dimensional objects, text, graphics, videos, animations. This addition is a seamless integration of real-world environments and virtual objects, rather than a simple overlay. American scholar Ronald T. Azuma concluded AR technology has three distinct characteristics: virtual reality integration, real-time interaction, three-dimensional registration [5].

The key consideration of the principle of functional interaction in the digital display of ICH is the multi-dynamic display of multidimensional space-time information such as the past state at the time of creation of the ICH, the current state and the future state of the simulated cultural relics [6]. AR technology can be used to create more fun. Its strength is that it creates a scene image that does not exist in reality. The disadvantage is the sense of space is relatively poor. By combining with real objects, these advantages can be complemented well to create more excellent results.

3.3 Multiple Control Methods

In the AR application, people are looking for a natural and harmonious interaction mode. In the real world, they mainly use the following three ways to interact with a virtual object [7]: (1) Menu: AR application for mobile phones and handheld computers, the touch screen can make up the plane Panel information can not interact with the audience shortcomings, designers can integrate more interesting elements in the show, in the flat panels based on the development of new features; (2) special markers: special markers fixed in the interactive Equipment, multimedia technology can be integrated control of lighting, sound, video, etc., with the theme of the show to create a more interesting space; (3) special tools: a simple shape, easy to identify and so on, through the button can trigger a series of events.

3.4 User-Perceived Experience

Based on the audience-centered principle, and focus on the real-time message content and active participation of the audience, the hope is to break through the traditional display model of static exhibits, to achieve the audience from the perspective of passive and active participation changes, the establishment of two-way interactive information dissemination channels [8], so that viewers at Communicate with the exhibition information at the same time, deepen the understanding of the display content and memory.

The principle of digital interaction is based on three main experience processes: space experience, sensory experience, and spiritual experience. By analyzing and evaluating the proportion of experiential design elements used therein, an experiential design module closest to the user's needs can be obtained, and visual design and back-end programming are planned based on this module.

First of all, on the space experience, AR technology superimposes the virtual objects in real time on the related realities such as furniture, picture books, postcards and furniture entities, which can expand the physical space that carries the cultural connotation in the realistic environment and enhance the realistic environment to carry the cultural connotation Ability.

Secondly, on the sensory experience, digital transformation and transformation of intangible cultural heritage resources based on AR technology is the combination of creative ideas, animation, multimedia and digital technologies with the creative, planning, designing and Produced, the static intangible cultural heritage into dynamic digital animation, video, sound and other digital content, so that experience and virtual digital content multi-dimensional, multi-level sensory interaction. From the perspectives of visual, sound, touch, smell and taste, it fully and effectively mobilizes the experience of human perception and information acquisition.

Thirdly, on the spiritual experience, the traditional cultural display can only transmit the cultural knowledge carried by the product within the physical space of the product itself. The cultural display product developed based on the ICH content of the AR technology, not only embedding static cultural contents in physical space, but also other rich cultural contents related to it can be digitally presented to the experimenters, thus enhance the capacity and knowledge in the cultural display products. Create a knowledge atmosphere, which in turn generates more communication, collision and learning.

In order to improve the effectiveness of digital display and information dissemination, fully mobilize the experience of human perception and information acquisition, provide a reference for ICH digital display design. The digital display design model is as shown in Fig. 1, which analyzes and studies AR technology in digital display for ICH, the appropriate content information, and control methods are selected according to the focus of information dissemination, and at the same time, the audiences are given the best experience.

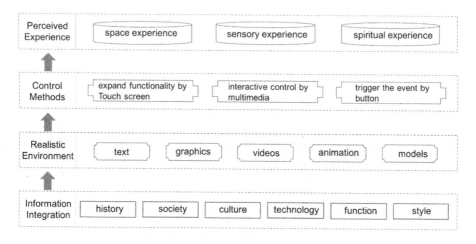

Fig. 1. Digital display design model

4   Digital Display for Cantonese Furniture

4.1   The History of Cantonese Furniture

Located in the Pearl River Delta on the coast of the South China Sea, Guangzhou is the starting point of the maritime Silk Road. It is the earliest city for overseas exchanges with foreign countries. Not only are foreign businessmen gathered in Guangzhou, but also millions of Chinese have emigrated to other parts of the world via Guangzhou. The import and furniture trade has opened up a vast supply and marketing channel. Due to the favorable conditions of both natural conditions and economic conditions, the commercial and handicraft industries in Guangdong during the Qing Dynasty were in a relatively prosperous situation. Cantonese furniture occupies the leading position in geography, geography and people and has led the way in breaking through the original format of traditional furniture for thousands of years in our country. It boldly drew on new forms of furniture such as luxury, boldness, elegance, and luxury in Western Europe and various curves. A traditional furniture-based system to create a new Cantonese furniture. The simple shape of it has been changed, full of dynamic curve modeling replaced. It is characterized by the pursuit of gorgeous, luxurious, delicate, graceful style, but also the use of various decorative materials, blending a variety of artistic expression, forming a modeling atmosphere, exquisite workmanship, luxurious decoration of furniture style, with rich Cantonese Regional characteristics, is an important part of Chinese traditional culture.

Cantonese furniture into a new era, it is also necessary to keep up with the trend of the times, to achieve the inheritance and promotion of the Cantonese furniture culture. The traditional display mode is the physical exhibition in the museum. In a fixed space, according to certain rules, the collection of exhibits and ancillary exhibits are displayed in sequence, accompanied by the captions of the excerpts. The prominent advantage of this exhibition mode lies in the authenticity, but there are some limitations on the information transmission and the experience function of displaying.

4.2 Inner Beauty of Cantonese Furniture

Combined with the above research, in view of the inheritance and newborn design project of Cantonese folk arts and crafts, the digital display application of the inner beauty of Cantonese furniture has been developed. Hidden beneath the minimalist exterior of Cantonese furniture lies a secret: a highly complex mortise-and-tenon joint structure (see Fig. 2), like a three-dimensional jigsaw puzzle in which everything fits intimately together, yet can be easily dismantled. Metal nails are hardly used [9].

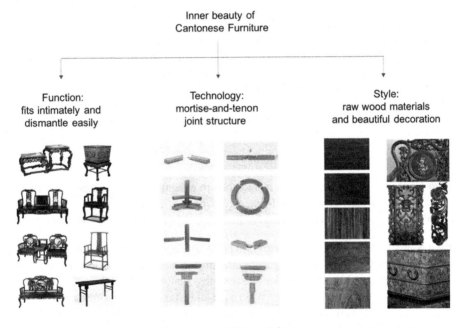

Fig. 2. Mortise-and-Tenon joint structure

Mortise-and-tenon joint structure is a piece of technology with significant practical experience and skill, and therefore emphasizes interactive features in digital display.

The connotation of traditional technology determines that the process of its dissemination has strict procedures. Information nodes will be interactive, allowing users to get the most authentic sense of participation and experience. Take advantage of the ease-of-use features of any type of multi-screen device, giving viewers the convenience to view, and use anytime, anywhere.

According to the characteristics of the mortise-and-tenon technique, the four keywords "prim and proper", "harmony in diversity", "perfect penetration" and "wiping along the edge smooth" can not only represent the cultural connotation and style characteristics of Cantonese furniture, but also embody the four common techniques and morphological structures of mortise-and-tenon joint. And extract the corresponding Chinese keywords "prim", "harmony", "circle", "smooth" to emphasize as the visual presentation of this application (see Fig. 3).

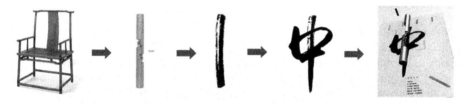

Fig. 3. The relationship between Mortise-and-Tenon joint structure and Chinese keywords

The basic design concept of the digital display application is to demonstrate the three-dimensional model, structural principle, fabrication process and historical background of the tenon-mortise structure through digital interaction based on AR technology. In order to show the above contents, the Chinese traditional calligraphy and writing are used in the design of Augmented Reality Recognition Diagrams. From the perspective of the unique structure features in the four Chinese key words, it shows the position and artistic characteristics of mortise-and-tenon joint in Cantonese furniture.

4.3 Interactive Module Development

Video Capture. When the system is switched to enhance the interaction module, the camera is immediately opened, real-time acquisition of the display environment, and generate a series of real scene images for tracking system registration module to call.

Track Registration. Tracking registration is the core of augmented reality system. The augmented reality system based on artificial marking can accurately locate the virtual model in the real world and maximize the seamless fusion between the actual situation and the actual situation. It has the characteristics of fast, stable and accurate, Therefore, most of the augmented reality tracking registration modules are based on artificial marking method. In this paper, the tracking method is based on the artificial marking method in computer vision technology and use color identification map. Tracking the registration process is divided into the following four steps:

Step1: Collect video images based on video capture device. To meet the real-time, accuracy requirements, AR-VR system by calling the Android mobile camera, capture real-world video images.

Step2: Preprocess the captured image to binarize the captured video image, thus completing the conversion from a color video image to a black-and-white binary image. For any point (x, y) in the image, if The gray value S x, y $\geq$ t can be considered as the background pixel point, otherwise considered the point of interest points, the thresholded image can be defined as:

$$S x, y = \begin{cases} a0, f x, y < t \\ a1, else \end{cases}$$

Usually set a0 = 0, a1 = 1, the result is a binary image. Then, using image segmentation and edge detection techniques to find all the points of interest in the image.

Step3: According to the pattern recognition matching algorithm, the mark image is compared with the template mark image in the mark library to judge whether the mark is a valid mark, and if the matching is successful, it is found that an interesting area is found.

Step4: After the matching of the template succeeds, the specific ID of the current mark is determined and the mark is identified.

Actual and superposition system. After the tracking registration step, the camera position is obtained. In this case, the indoor environment video stream shot by the camera is merged with the generated virtual cultural relics information in real time to form an augmented reality image, and the virtual cultural relic information is finally rendered on the screen, allowing users to experience the realism of a real indoor scene combined with virtual information. This article enhances the development of interactive modules using Vuforia SDK. The Vuforia SDK is a powerful augmented reality development kit that provides API interfaces in Java, C++ and .NET languages and extends it to Unity 3D. Currently more commonly used in the world of augmented reality platforms include AR ToolKit, Aurasma and Vufori.

Experiment and Test Results. The experiment was based on the Unity3D platform and integrated with Vuforia SDK for development. The mobile devices used in the experiment were tested on PC with Intel CoreTM2 Quad CPU, Q8200 @ 3.22 GHz, 4 GB memory and NVIDIA GT9800 graphics card.

After starting the system, the default access to the application, the user can choose according to their own needs to enter the various modules to experience. After switching to the AR system, in order to verify the performance of the system, the tracking angle is defined as the angle between the marker and the camera. The tracking performance is verified by tracking images of 0°, 30°, 45° and 60°, respectively, and the initial tracking moment is 0.2 m. When the initial shooting angle is 0°, the system can not capture the feature information contained in the artificial sign image. When the tracking angle is selected between 30° and 90°, the system collects the feature information in the artificial sign image to achieve real-time Tracking function; when the tracking angle is less than 20°, the loaded three-dimensional model has broken light leakage, which exceeds the normal working range of the system tracking registration function module.

In environmental interference testing practice, the identification chart may exist in the tracking camera in order to test the distance between the mark and the mark on the tracking performance, because the marked distance as shown in the figure changes, the test proved that the identification Pitch larger than the camera and recognition 1/2. It can not track the registration information by identifying the influence of the map.

Therefore, the mark images can be applied to a variety of environments, such as architectural surfaces as the interface, posters, cards, books, etc., while supporting gesture control (see Fig. 4).

Fig. 4. Using environment and gesture control

4.4   Experience Development of Digital Display

In theory, the content of intangible cultural heritage can be transformed digitally by means of digital technology to form corresponding digital content, and AR technology can be used to superimpose the digitized content in real-time scene in real time so as to solve the problem that people are not familiar with the content of intangible cultural heritage Invisible, inaccessible, cannot experience the problem. Taking the mortise-and-tenon joint structure of traditional Cantonese furniture as an example, through the deep excavation of the thematic connotation of the mortise-and-tenon joint structure, the paper digitizes the cultural contents of the mortise-and-tenon by digital image rendering and digital animation, Corresponding digital content.

Firstly, the interactive nature of information nodes enables the most realistic sense of participation and experience. Take advantage of the ease of use in multi-screen devices, allowing viewers to watch and use them anytime, anywhere and quickly. Secondly, although the Cantonese furniture is widely known to the general public, its complicated and professional production processes and procedures behind it are not clear. Digital display can vividly depict the detailed scene and manufacturing details, and can use the interactive method to give users a more direct and easy understanding of the mortise-and-tenon joint structure of Cantonese furniture. Through the classification and display of different shapes, structures, features, in the visual and tactile combination of cultural information to complete the transmission and reception, allowing users to more easily manipulate and understand. Finally, as a mobile application, Cantonese furniture components can be combined and disassembled by 360° rotation to deepen the display of the components and the mortise-and-tenon joint structure, and stimulate the mysteries of classical furniture through a simple and fun interactive experience. As a case of digital display of ICH in mobile intelligent devices, it embodies the new experience of the dissemination, interactivity and interestingness of digital media. And it plays an active role in protecting and inheriting for ICH.

5   Conclusion

AR technology can construct the contents and display forms of intangible cultural heritage, greatly enrich the form of computer information performance, and improve the efficiency of user acceptance of information. At the same time, through interactive design to create the overall user experience, through the media change to rewrite the cultural content, thereby generating the value of social capital, thus contributing to the global users and the continued development of the museum industry, it also provides new opportunities for the education experience of intangible cultural heritage.

Acknowledgments. This study is supported by philosophy and social sciences "Twelve Five" planning project of Guangdong Province (Grant No. GD14XYS17, Technology and Beauty: Inheritance and Rebirth of Cantonese Folk Arts and Crafts in the New Media Age), and Graduate academic forum project of Guangdong Province (Grant No. 2016XSLT_13, The Digital Inheritance of the Intangible Cultural Heritage in Canton).

References

1. Sullivan, A.M.: Cultural heritage & new media: a future for the past. 15 J. Marshall Rev. Intell. Prop. L. **604** (2016)
2. Yuan, L., Gu, J.: Taxonomic research on intangible cultural heritage. Henan Soc. Sci. **6**, 58–62 (2013)
3. Gao, B.: The intangible cultural heritage as a public culture. Lit. Art Stud. **2**, 77–83 (2008)
4. UNESCO Homepage, https://ich.unesco.org/en/convention. Accessed 23 Feb 2018
5. Azuma, R., Baillot, Y., Behringer, R., et al.: Recent advances in augmented reality. IEEE Comput. Graph. Appl. **21**(6) (2001)
6. Qin, J.: Research on the information design methods in digital cultural heritage. Sci. Technol. Rev. **13**, 22–26 (2007)
7. Zhu, M., Yao, Y., Jiang, Y.: a survey on augmented reality. J. Image Graph. **07**, 3–10 (2004)
8. Zhao, L., Qian, W., Cui, J.: Interactive Thinking. China Light Industry Press, Beijing (2007)
9. Fang, H.: Chinesism in modern furniture design. Publication Series of the University of Art and Design Helsinki A 41, pp. 33–34 (2004)

HCI in Complex Environments

Navigation for Visually Impaired Using Haptic Feedback

Siri Fagernes and Tor-Morten Grønli[⊠]

Mobile Technology Lab, Department of Technology,
Westerdals Oslo School of Arts, Communication and Technology,
Oslo, Norway
{siri.fagernes,tmg}@westerdals.no
http://mobiletechlab.no

Abstract. Smartphones have become commodity tools and exist in large multiple in all parts of the population. The typical use of navigation applications focus on aiding users with no impairments. Guidance applications with enhancing features, and facilitating for i.e. people with visual impairments, focus on voice-based feedback. In this paper we focus on the use of haptic feedback as a tool and guidance for navigation, through utilising the vibration mechanism available in mobile phones. Through the development of a prototype application we illustrate how haptic feedback can be used to guide users in cases of visual impairment or hindrance. The preliminary results display a novel contribution to multi-modal navigation and exemplifies active use of receptors for smartphone feedback interpretation.

Keywords: Smartphone · Indoor navigation · Haptic
Multi modal interaction · Universal access · Android

1 Introduction

Mobile phone application development has taken a huge step from its first days of development on monochrome screens. Today, sophisticated features are available and there are a large number of platforms to develop new software on. With smartphones having become a commodity tool and the general household appliances making its way online through the Internet of Things (IoT) movement, we are still moving at a slow pace. Common, and not unseen issues include the lack of complete application implementations, as highlighted by Paganelli et al. [1].

The IoT technologies and applications are still in their infancy [2], and the academic community still have a number of topics to investigate in depth to thoroughly cover the area. Although IoT initially was meant to describe a network of radio frequency enabled devices, it has since been expanded and grown to include in its definition interoperable devices and covers global network infrastructures from traditional cloud computing [3] to small embedded ad hoc networks in fog computing [4]. Interaction is first and foremost based on touch screen input and

© Springer International Publishing AG, part of Springer Nature 2018
M. Kurosu (Ed.): HCI 2018, LNCS 10902, pp. 347–356, 2018.
https://doi.org/10.1007/978-3-319-91244-8_28

the feedback mechanisms rely heavily on audio and visual [5]. The movement of IoT has removed the barrier for interpreting sensor data and innovative solutions may exploit such feeds [6].

According to Perera et al. [7], most of the research done on IoT during the last two decades has been focused around prototypes, systems and solutions with a limited number of data sources. However, as the technology develops, a need to be context - aware and able to utilise a large number of sensors arises, and with this, the need to develop solutions which implement a strong core architecture and is flexible and modular enough to be combined with other IoT solutions. Especially office buildings are currently being enriched with sensor data and mobile ad hoc networks emerge for such sensors and actuators to be added and removed in an ad hoc manner [8]. Context-aware solutions and applications have been around for years and are often the target of research. The ability to successfully enrich applications with contextual dimensions can inherently increase success. To build on previous achievements and utilise context as a source of information is vital for user adaptation, interpretation and interface tailoring [9].

Building on Zhang et al. [8], the motivation in the field of information visualisation is to convey information efficiently to the user, in that the user should be able to do a task as efficiently and with so little cognitive effort as possible [10]. Users are often overwhelmed by large amounts of information to perceive. Designing a user-friendly interface hence involves giving priority to the information that is most crucial and that the user must be able to perceive. Especially in stressed situations, it is important to have clear purpose instructions. Current established solutions fail in one or more of these aspects.

With this as the curtain our research, we focus to investigate a novel exploitation of sensor-based feedback on smartphones and the use of haptic feedback as the primary means of navigation. Building upon general principles [11], now widely accepted through cloud computing and service-oriented architecture, we scale down from large scale distributed systems and focus on in-door mobile and ad hoc distributed systems. Here, smartphones, wearables and IoT-based sensors are widespread and engage actively in communication on themselves and users behalf. The motivation for the project has emerged from the case of developing an evacuation application for fire emergencies, where the situation is that visual and audio-based feedback may be difficult to perceive. However, this can be extended to be a general navigation aid for people that are visually impaired.

The rest of the paper is organised as follows. First, we introduce the scenario with mobile smartphones for navigation. Following this, we introduce the prototype design and architecture, before presenting and discussing the results. Towards the end we around off with our concluding remarks and point out possibilities for future work.

2   Scenario of Using Smartphones for Navigation

Smartphones have become the predominant personal assistant and is by the vast majority of the population brought with them at any given time. Accordingly, they are actively used as a vital source of information, and notifications are the most used feature to invoke the users' attention. This relates both to new information, signs of danger and social interaction. A study by Aranda et al. [12], reports that when a user's context can be decided correctly, and a notification helps them accomplish a task, it is welcomed. Further, the notifications need to be actionable in the moment, and hence this is an important design consideration to take forward in this study.

The use case for this mobile application is a situation where the user is situated in a larger building (e.g. a hotel or office building) where a fire has erupted. The building typically contains several floors, and potentially several possible emergency exits. The building also has a number of sensors for various purposes; like smoke detectors, motion detectors and temperature sensors. Data from the smoke detectors represent the level of danger associated with moving around in the area near that detector, while the temperature sensor data indicate the distance to the actual fire. These data are useful for monitoring how the fire develops but are also important for determining which areas in the building the users should avoid when evacuating the building. Data from the motion detectors can be used to determine the number of people present in the building, and where potential bottlenecks are, due to people gathering in stairways etc.

The idea then is that the application is able to calculate a safe route out of the building, based on the sensor data. The route should be calculated based on the user's current position, and where the shortest safe route of the building is. However, the calculation of route is out of scope for this paper and will be discussed in later work. For this paper, it is assumed that such a route already has been calculated, and that the remaining issue is how to convey this route to the user in an efficient way. Further to this, the application must be able to convey this information to the user, potentially blinded by darkness, smoke from the fire or other similar hazards. Navigation must be facilitated through smartphone navigation without relying solemnly on visual aid.

3   Prototype Design and Architecture

In the aforementioned scenario, the mobile application is the primary guidance aid for the user in the emergency situation. The core functionality of the application focuses on guiding the user out of the building or towards the next given waypoint. To achieve this, design principles, UI guidance and system architecture have designated features to support multimodal interaction and communication with the user.

The prototype application was implemented using the Android Framework [13] using Android SDK version 7.0 Nougat following design principles of Google code style guidelines and material design. The architecture is based on the standard Android model view controller framework implementation [14] and a rigid separation of concerns between view, its related logic and the algorithmic functions. Architecture of the aforementioned classes and components are here visualised together with sensor communication and manipulation packages, Fig. 1.

This component-based approach makes the prototype suitable for being embedded into other applications, if not further expanded on to lay ground for future sensors integration as a framework component.

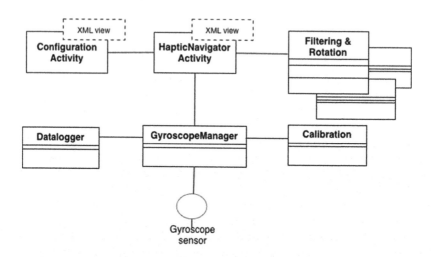

Fig. 1. Prototype class diagram architecture

The current prototype, Fig. 1, has implemented functionality for navigation through haptic feedback. By having set a waypoint, and enabled tracking of direction, the application will help the user to navigate. Based on readings from the gyroscope sensor, received data is interpreted in the *GyroscopeManager*, the bearing of the user is calculated and compared to waypoint. If the user is off track, the haptic feedback will initiate and indicate for the user that s/he is facing in the wrong direction. The *HapticNavigatorActivity* controls haptic feedback and it is intensified the further away from correct direction the user is. When facing the correct direction, the haptic feedback stops indicating success. To be able to calculate this information the gyroscope is exploited as the primary sensor. Due to the extremely rapid sampling rate from the gyroscope sensor (average 0.06 s) a smoothing filter and a mean filter are applied to even out results to map to human hand movement. Further three complimentary filters using respectively orientation, rotation matrices and quaternions are applied for sensor fusion measurements. A Kalman filter based on quaternions and an allowed offset of two degrees are applied to adjust sensitivity and tolerate slight hand movements when the user is walking around. All logic related to these filtering, smoothing and calculation operations are contained in a package collection of *filtering and rotation classes*. A *Datalogger* outputs log data results to file for later analysis purposes and individual adjustments and sensor sensitivity can be adjusted in the *ConfigurationActivity*.

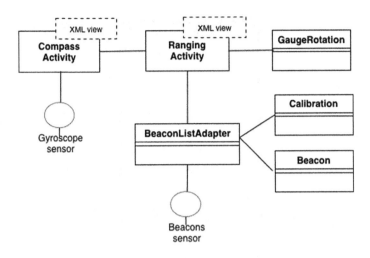

Fig. 2. Beacon application architecture

Further to this we explored the possibilities for indoor navigation using bluetooth beacons as means for way-finding in this mobile ad hoc communication scenario. Figure 2 shows the architecture for this implementation. The core of this test is the *RangingActivity* which calculated the bearing and distance to next informed beacon. All beacon information and associated reading of sensor information is maintained in *BeaconListAdapter, Beacon and Calibration* classes. To further communicate with readings from the gyroscope, the *CompassActivity* class maintains this information. For visual feedback to the user, a *GaugeRotation* implementation class controls this feedback.

4   Result and Discussion

The project is anchored in core Android development architecture and specifications as well as in universal design principles from computer science and mobile development research [14]. Following Perera et al. [7], a loosely coupled, modular and standardised architecture, enhanced the built solution exposing no single point of failure. Building on Android architecture components and patterns, facilitates for a robust design, with testable and maintainable applications. Features from accessibility is incorporated into the application design following API conventions from the model-view-view-model (MVVM) pattern and these Android features support out of the box a backward compatible approach which allows for focus to be put in applications features.

Fig. 3. Navigation application screenshot

4.1   Application Prototype

The evacuation route is presented to the users using several modalities, both visual cues in the form of an arrow showing the direction to take, Fig. 3, possibly also explicit verbal information, in addition to audio-based feedback, giving instructions. In a situation of fire, potentially stressful sounds of fire alarms and difficulty of seeing anything due to smoke, make the ability to perceive such information even more challenging, hence the haptic feedback provided should aid the user to navigate even without the visual and audio-based feedback.

The initial prototype has a simple visual design, showing arrows pointing in the direction the user should move in, in order to follow the correct path out of the building, Fig. 3. The main issue then, is how to use haptic feedback to convey similar information, or how to give the user a sense of direction only using haptic feedback.

To ensure correct information, and assess the given bearing of the application compared with received and interpreted gyroscope information, the application was also tested following a white-box testing approach, Fig. 4. In this round of verification received information was presented on screen and interpreted by the beta-testers. Measurement readings from the sensor were displayed giving bearing and relative position in the X, Y and Z dimension. Following, and further elaborating on, the approach by Aranda et al. [12], this interpreted information was compared with actual sensor positioning. The combination of a simple interface and multi-modal interaction in the final prototype (Fig. 3) underpins the conclusions by Furukawa et al. [10] about keep cognitive load as small as possible.

Fig. 4. Application screenshot

Thirdly it was of high importance to verify placement and manipulation of beacon information in such an ad-hoc scenario. For the approach to be confirmed and to address the correctness of interpreted sensor data, sensor implementations and location-aware API's were investigated including *Altbeacon, EstimoteSDK, Google Nearby API*. Following internet of things properties as laid out by Gubbi et al. [6], the ability to extract associated data from the Beacon/API, offline/online connectivity and user direction mapping were given most weight in the evaluation. Figure 5 shows the manual control interface for the beacons.

When all put together, reviewing the application showcases a navigation approach with beacon information as the primary driver for finding waypoints. Information to the user is conveyed through a simple visual interface, haptic feedback is given when in use and the potential of spoken instructions are facilitated by the component-based architecture. Interesting opportunities, all in line with Furukawa and Yang [10], were explored through testing and showed that haptic feedback can be used not only for confirming correct path, but also be used for signalling when the user diverge from correct path, and even indicating back/forth direction using a push/pull stream of the haptic feedback.

Fig. 5. Adding beacon address

5   Conclusion

This paper investigates exploitation of sensor-based feedback on smartphones and the use of haptic feedback as means of navigation, particularly useful for people who have difficulties perceiving visual information. Building on the work from Aranda et al. [12], Furukawa and Yang [10] and Zhang et al. [8] we built haptic feedback into an Android prototype application. Through beta-testing of our prototype, the technological suitability has been verified. The testing reveals that haptic feedback can be used on commodity smartphones and further adds reason for this to be implemented as a full scale navigation solution building further upon the achieved results.

6   Future Work

The approach shows promising prospects for being extended to general outdoor navigation and existing navigation application such as Google maps and Waze Navigation application. We will continue to extend the prototype and testing also towards these outlooks and think they all are worthy future purse. In future work we will create a full-scale application and pursue to have data representing waypoints supplied to the system through IoT-devices and indoor mobile ad hoc networks. This will help calculate the safest route out of a building or navigating a given path. Using sensor data and information about possible exits, stairways and obstacles reported from users, the system with its smartphone frontend will be able to act as a full-blown navigation solution.

One of the main challenges, is how to convey a sense of direction to the user, solely on the basis on haptic feedback. Given that a correctly calculated path from the user's current position exists, the navigation application should be able to convey the next direction the user should move in. Based on using the current prototype, it remains to be investigated further, what types of vibration patterns are most intuitive to the user. As an example, we are interested in whether the vibrations should be more or less intense, dependent on if the user is close to the correct direction or not. Different options need to be implemented, and a large user study is being planned to evaluate applicability and usability of the system in full scale.

References

1. Paganelli, F., Turchi, S., Giuli, D.: A web of things framework for restful applications and its experimentation in a smart city. IEEE Syst. J. **10**(4), 1412–1423 (2016)
2. Da Li, X., He, W., Li, S.: Internet of things in industries: A survey. IEEE Transactions on industrial informatics **10**(4), 2233–2243 (2014)
3. Mell, P., Grance, T. et al.: The NIST definition of cloud computing (2011)
4. Bonomi, F., Milito, R., Zhu, J., Addepalli, S.: Fog computing and its role in the Internet of Things. In: Proceedings of the First Edition of the MCC Workshop on Mobile Cloud Computing, pp. 13–16. ACM (2012)
5. Minamizawa, K., Fukamachi, S., Kajimoto, H., Kawakami, N., Tachi, S.: Gravity grabber: wearable haptic display to present virtual mass sensation. In: ACM Special Interest Group on Computer GRAPHics and Interactive Techniques (SIGGRAPH) 2007 Emerging Technologies, p. 8. ACM (2007)
6. Gubbi, J., Buyya, R., Marusic, S., Palaniswami, M.: Internet of Things (IoT): a vision, architectural elements, and future directions. Future Gener. Comput. Syst. **29**(7), 1645–1660 (2013)
7. Perera, C., Zaslavsky, A., Christen, P., Georgakopoulos, D.: Context aware computing for the Internet of Things: a survey. IEEE Commun. Surv. Tutorials **16**(1), 414–454 (2014)
8. Zhang, C., Guo, A., Zhang, D., Li, Y., Southern, C., Arriaga, R.I., Abowd, G.D.: Beyond the touchscreen: an exploration of extending interactions on commodity smartphones. ACM Trans. Interact. Intell. Syst. (TiiS) **6**(2), 16 (2016)
9. Strobbe, M., Van Laere, O., Ongenae, F., Dauwe, S., Dhoedt, B., De Turck, F., Demeester, P., Luyten, K.: Integrating location and context information for novel personalised applications. In: Pervasive Computing, p. 1. IEEE (2011)
10. Furukawa, H., Yang, K.: Experimental study on cognitive aspects of indoor evacuation guidance using mobile devices. In: Proceedings of the International Multi-Conference of Engineers and Computer Scientists, vol. 2 (2017)
11. Duquennoy, S., Grimaud, G., Vandewalle, J.J.: The web of things: interconnecting devices with high usability and performance. In: International Conference on Embedded Software and Systems, ICESS 2009, pp. 323–330. IEEE (2009)

12. Aranda, J., Ali-Hasan, N., Baig, S.: I'm just trying to survive: an ethnographic look at mobile notifications and attention management. In: Proceedings of the 18th International Conference on Human-Computer Interaction with Mobile Devices and Services Adjunct, pp. 564–574. ACM (2016)
13. Google Android Inc., Android developer guidelines (2017). https://developer.android.com/index.html. Accessed 12 Jan 2018
14. Google Android Inc., Android developer (2018). https://developer.android.com/topic/libraries/architecture/index.html. Accessed 19 Feb 2018

Supporting Collaboration in Human-Machine Crisis Management Networks

Ida Maria Haugstveit and Marita Skjuve[(✉)]

SINTEF, Oslo, Norway
{imh,Marita.skjuve}@sintef.no

Abstract. Several parts of our modern lives are today taking place in networks where both humans and machines are key actors. With this development follows the increased need and importance of investigating related consequences and understand how we best can design technological systems to support efficient and productive human-machine networks. This paper presents the use of a human-machine network approach to nuance how we think of the interactions and collaboration that takes place in human-machine networks. Specifically, we study the complex network involved in crisis management, and show how such a network's characteristics may have implications for, and affect collaboration. The study is based on the analysis of in-depth interviews with both system provider representatives and end-users of a collaborative tool for crisis management. Three directions in which the design and development of crisis management systems should be guided are proposed.

Keywords: Human-machine networks · Crisis management networks
Collaborative tool

1 Introduction

We live in a highly-connected world where technology has undeniably become an integrated part of our personal and professional lives, supporting us in conducting a range of tasks. Often when we interact with technology, we are a part of a larger human-machine network (HMN), assemblages of humans and machines that interact to produce synergistic effects [1]. This acknowledgement of both humans and machines being vital parts and having active roles in the network, which is often overlooked and a gap in current research, is crucial if we in the future are to tackle the design challenges HMNs constitute [2]. Knowledge and awareness of human and machine actors involved in the network, the interactions between them, and their embedded capabilities and behaviors is a requirement for creating successful networks [1].

The value of HMNs is perhaps especially visible when people have to solve complex tasks that require high degrees of coordination and information sharing. Crisis management represents such a domain, consisting of HMNs where technological systems and a variety of human actors, interact and work together towards achieving the common goal of saving human lives and other values important to society [3]. Technological systems for crisis management have the purpose of facilitating efficient collaboration between humans – a core requirement for successful management – through supporting coordination by providing information, an overview of the situation, and decision support. However, inadequate or the lack of well-designed and well-functioning crisis management systems is often a contributing factor to collaboration failing [4, 5]. There is a strong need for such systems to better support the collaborative work that crisis management entails. As modern crisis management is taking place in networks where both humans and machines are key actors, it becomes increasingly important to investigate related consequences and understand how we best can design technological systems to support efficient management of crisis events.

Through our research, we aim to show how a HMN approach and analysis may influence how we consider and think of HMN and their characteristics. Specifically, we study how the characteristics of a crisis management network may have implications for, and affect collaboration. By this, we aim to provide designers and developers of crisis management systems with an understanding of crisis management as a complex HMN where different dimensions of the network should be considered.

We build our research on the HMN typology proposed by Eide et al. [6], which presents an opportunity to understand and discuss design challenges and issues within HMNs according to the network actors, the relationship among them, its extent, and how the network is organized. Based on this typology, we investigate a crisis management network that draws on information from multiple sources to facilitate dynamic collaboration across the actors of a potential crisis. The study involves in-depth interviews with 6 system provider representatives and 6 end-users of a collaborative tool for crisis management.

2   Challenges of Crisis Management

Crisis management involves several comprehensive phases and activities, including preparedness, prevention, protection, mitigation, response, and recovery [7, 8]. To be able to manage these activities, coordinated collaboration, cooperation, and transparency between people from a variety of agencies and organizations is required [3] - all of whom possess complementary knowledge and skills needed for efficient crisis management. Such collaborative teamwork is often chosen within complex domains where desired outcomes cannot be accomplished by individual efforts alone [5].

Crisis incidents occur in several forms and vary in origin [9], from natural disasters (e.g. floods, snowstorms, droughts), to accidents caused by human or technological errors (e.g. offshore oil spills, traffic accidents, industrial accidents), or man-made as intended acts (e.g. school shootings, terror attacks). As such, the people managing crisis incidents are often working under conditions characterized by uncertainty, stress, time pressure, and lack or overload of information [10].

During recent decades, a variety of technological solution have been developed to support crisis management, especially focusing on the establishment of situation awareness and decision-making [11, 12]. Crisis management systems have been recognized to have the ability to enhance crisis management by, e.g., improving situation assessment and awareness, support decision-making, coordination of actions, and the exchange of information [13]. Designing systems meant to support a variety of people and organizations is obviously a challenge, as each actor might have their own needs that a system should be able to account for. At the same time, the system being generic is exceedingly important for collaboration and shared coordination to be possible.

Improving collaboration in crisis management can have highly positive effects and can contribute to saving human lives. We must therefore strive to gain in-depth knowledge of elements affecting collaboration, and how to best facilitate good collaboration structures where both humans and technology is considered. As crisis management is carried out in collaborative networks where both humans and technological systems are key to efficient management, it becomes increasingly important to study what the current implications on collaboration are, and understand how we best can design such technological systems for the domain.

3   Human-Machine Networks

Human-machine networks are assemblages of humans and machines that interact to produce synergistic effects [1]. As such, crisis management constitute a human-machine network where people and systems interact to solve complex tasks in the environment of crises. By looking at crisis management from a human-machine network perspective, we are able to explore different elements of the network that affect collaboration.

3.1   The HUMANE Typology

The human-machine network typology proposed by Eide et al. [6], named HUMANE, presents an opportunity to understand and discuss design challenges and issues within a network. HUMANE is helpful in understanding which implications the characteristics of the crisis management network has on collaboration, and can provide valuable insight on how to strengthen the design of future crisis management systems to better support collaboration and efficient crisis management.

The proposed typology includes four analytical layers (Actors, Relations, Extent, and Structure), each with two dimensions that should be considered by system designers and developers. Table 1 provides an overview of the analytical layers and dimensions in relation to each other.

Table 1. Overview of analytical layers and dimensions of the HUMANE typology.

Analytical layers	Dimensions
Actors	1. Human actors
	2. Machine actors
Relations	3. Social ties strength
	4. Human-machine relationship strength
Extent	5. Size
	6. Geographical reach
Structure	7. Workflow interdependence
	8. Organization

The analytical layer Actors includes the two first dimensions (1) *human agency* and (2) *machine agency*. This layer and its dimensions consider the capacity and possibilities of the network actors, both humans and machines, in terms of what they are able to do and accomplish. Within this lies the activities the actors can perform, actors' opportunities to freely interact and influence other actors, and behaving unpredictably [2].

The layer Relations consists of the two next dimensions, (3) *social tie strength* and (4) *human-to-machine relationship strength*. This layer addresses the relations that exists both between humans in the network, and between the humans and the machines. One is here interested in looking at the level of which human actors are connected by remote or close affiliation, the duration of the relationship, and if the relationship is of a mutually supportive character. Regarding the relation between humans and machines, the topics of interest are the level of trust and acceptance people experience towards a machine, as well as dependency.

The Extent layer includes the next two dimensions, namely (5) *size* of the network and (6) *geographical reach*. The layer and dimensions concern the number of human nodes in the network, the network's growth rate, transnationality and cultural diversity.

Finally, the analytical layer Structure consists of the final two dimensions, (7) *workflow interdependence* and (8) *organization* of the network. The layer tells the story of how the network is structured, touching the level of interdependencies, coordination, and collaboration between human actors, and to which degree the network is fixed or flexible to change, organized in a centralized or predetermined manner, and regulated by policies.

The scale of each dimension range from low, to intermediate, to high. By using the HUMANE typology to profile crisis management networks, we are able to identify implications of the network characteristics and related design challenges that are helpful in guiding the design and development of future systems for crisis management.

4   Methodology

To explore the elements affecting collaboration in crisis management networks from a human-machine network perspective, we conducted a study that followed the HUMANE approach [6]. This involved defining the network characteristics and creating a network profile, identifying implications connected to collaboration, and providing informed design suggestions.

The study was carried out between September and October 2016 within a Western European country. The scope was public crisis management, and the system or machine in focus was a collaborative tool commonly used by the public crisis management organizations in the respective country, as well as by several private organizations, to maintain shared situational awareness and support decision-making. The tool, which in this paper will be referred to as the Crisis Management Tool (CMT), is a module-based tool with flexible functionalities so that it can be adapted to different organizations' needs. As such, the tool is flexible and fit for supporting the management of a variety of crisis incidents. Due to the CMTs exposure to competition and anonymity promised to the participants of this study, more specific details about the tool and the study context will not be provided.

In the following, details of the study will be described. Figure 1 gives a brief overview of the sample, method, and themes of the study.

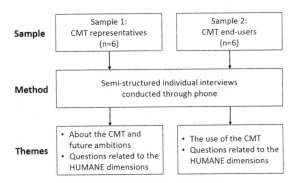

Fig. 1. Study overview

4.1   Participants

Two groups of participants were involved in the study. The first group consisted of six *representatives* of the CMT, which where people working within the company providing the tool. This group of participants were recruited through a contact person within the company, which chose the representative that were seen as appropriate for the study.

The second group consisted of six *end-users* of the CMT, which where people within different public sector organizations working with the management of crises, and that used the CMT in their work. The end-users were recruited by the one of the authors contacting them directly through phone. These end-users were selected based on their extensive experience and involvement with using the CMT.

4.2   Interviews

Semi-structured interviews were chosen as the method for data collection. This method gives the participants opportunity to talk relatively freely about their experiences and perceptions [14], guided by questions related to the interview topic. Two interview guides were developed, one for each group of participants. Participants were interviewed individually through phone by one of the two authors.

In the interviews with CMT representatives, the aim was to get an overview of the CMT and extract information on possible challenges related to the design of the tool. The representatives were first asked to describe the CMT in general, together with the company's future ambitions for the tool. Further, they were asked to describe the current and desired future state of the CMT network, in accordance with the dimensions of HUMANE. The interviews lasted approximately 45-60 min.

In the interviews with the CMT end-users, questions were formulated to specifically extract end-users' thoughts on challenges and implications regarding the current use of the tool and the state of the human-machine network. End-users were first asked to describe how they used the CMT. Following, participants were asked to answer questions related to the HUMANE dimensions, in addition to describing related challenges and implications, and possible solutions. The interviews with the end-user lasted approximately 30-45 min.

4.3 Data Analysis

Interviews were audio recorded and transcribed, which were used as the basis for the analyses. The analyses included visual profiling of the human-machine network in accordance with Eide et al. [6], as well as identification of implications and design suggestions.

To support the profiling activity, the HUMANE Network Profiler was used [15]. The profile of the CMT human-machine network was reached by the two authors first profiling the network individually based on the interviews with CMT representatives and end-users, and then conducting a joint profiling. During the joint profiling session, inconsistencies and disagreements in the profiles were discussed and resolved.

Implications and design suggestions were identified through a thematic analysis [16] of the interview data, conducted by one of the authors. Specifically, themes containing elements affecting collaboration was extracted. The analysis and results were validated in a workshop with the CMT representatives.

5   Findings

The analysis resulted in the development of a profile of the network, as well as the identification of implications and related design suggestions. The elaboration on implications and design suggestions will be concentrated around the dimensions that have clear and reasonable improvement potentials.

5.1   The Network Profile

A visual representation of the CMT network is presented in Fig. 2. The profile is a result of the interviews with both CMT representatives and end-users combined. The numbered circular points connected by the solid line marks the network score as it is today, for each dimension. The smaller circles connected by the dotted line marks the desired future score that can potentially strengthen collaboration in the network.

The closer a point is to the boundary of the octagon diagram in Fig. 2, the higher the score, whereas points closer to the center of the diagram, indicates a lower score. Table 2 lists the current and desired future score of each dimension.

In the reminding of this section, we discuss how to better support and strengthen collaboration within crisis management through the design of such networks. Based on the profile analysis, the following presentation of results and discussion will mainly be concentrated around the dimensions where we have identified deviations in current vs. desired future state. The current scores of the studied CMT network will be described and seen in connection to its implications on collaboration. Suggestions as to how to mediate the current implications and move towards the desired future scores are then proposed.

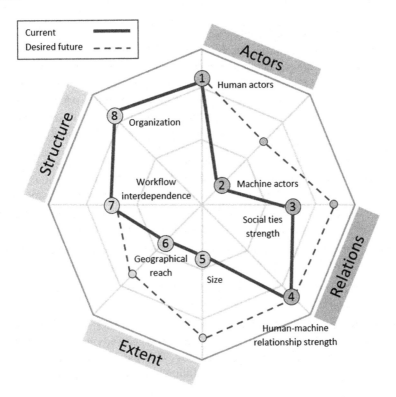

Fig. 2. Visual profile of the CMT network

Table 2. List of dimensions and their current and desired future score for the CMT network

Dimensions	Current	Desired future
1. Human actors	High	–
2. Machine actors	Low	Intermediate
3. Social ties strength	Intermediate	High
4. Human-machine relationship strength	High	–
5. Size	Low	High
6. Geographical reach	Low	Intermediate
7. Workflow interdependence	Intermediate	–
8. Organization	High	–

5.2   Increasing Machine Agency Through Higher Degree of Automation

In the studied CMT network, human agency is today high while machine agency is low. This implies that the humans in the network have a great degree of freedom to adapt the CMT to fit their organizational activities and tasks. Although there is a high level of human agency in the network, the degree of freedom humans are given varies. Within crisis management organizations, users of the CMT may have different roles, which means they are given different authorizations or levels of access in the tool. Some information might for example be protected or limited-access information, only accessible to some individuals. This may have implications on collaboration, e.g. if a person is not given the access to information that he or she needs in order to carry out tasks and actions. At the same time, it is important to make sure information is not distributed to people unnecessarily, as it can lead to information overload.

The CMT performs few tasks on its own. Rather, the tasks performed by the tool are largely predetermined by how human actors in the network has configured the system. In other words, for the CMT to function in an optimal manner where the tool supports the humans in performing their activities, the CMT first needs to be customized and fed with the needed input. A CMT representative explains this as follows.

> "There is not much automation in the CMT. In the vast majority of cases, an event is initiated by a user detecting that something has occurred. From here, the CMT can handle some things automated based on data put in to the tool. Special warnings can be sent out to predefined lists of people, etc., and the CMT can retrieve the correct action and contingency plans according to the input the tool has received." (CMT representative)

Appropriate utilization of the CMT thus requires that its users have the resources to and knowledge of how to configure the tool, which is currently lacking for many users within public crisis management organizations. This has implications for how users experience the tool and its usefulness. The following two quotes exemplify this challenge.

> "We would like to automate the incident potential based on the action plans. And I know that it is possible, but it's just that it needs to be done. The fact that our organization ourselves must do this requires quite a bit. I wish that they could standardized this process a bit more. Unfortunately, we have few resources." (CMT end-user)

> "There are very many clicks, and you have to click here and you have to click there, and you have to somehow create categories. In addition, I don't think it has been easy to find material that describes how this should be done." (CMT end-user)

As the quotes illustrate, some end-users experience the CMT as challenging to use due to the configurations that must be made to the tool. In addition, finding out how to configure the tool is not always intuitive and information on how to do it is not, to a large enough extent, made visible and available. Providing guidance in how to best configure the CMT might help users utilize the tool more effectively.

Systems for crisis management are often intended for use by several crisis response organizations. Therefore, they are usually designed with high levels of human agency and low levels of machine agency, where a systems usefulness relies on the human actors' ability to configure the system to fit their organization's needs. The background for this design rational may be the varying requirements and needs of different user organizations. Thus, such systems are designed to be flexible enough to fit the needs of several different user organizations. When considering automation into the design of crisis management systems, it is important to keep in mind the unpredictable environment in which crisis management takes place, something that is, according to Carver and Turoff [10], often forgotten.

Automation of crisis management systems essentially needs to be under the control of human actors [10], and with the possibility of being overruled. It can, however, be argued that applying higher degrees of automation to certain parts of crisis management systems could potentially streamline such machine networks and make them more efficient [17]. By automating appropriate tasks, such as automatic distribution of warnings or synthesizing of relevant information, the users can be given greater leeway to perform activities that require handling from human actors as they are based on human experience and knowledge. Such activities include collaborative tasks at all phases of crisis management, e.g. making complex decisions, implementing protective measures, and securing coordination across different organizations as a few examples.

5.3   Strengthening Social Ties of Dispersed Human Resources

Humans in the investigated network have medium strong relationship with each other. This is typical within crisis management, as the people working together to solve a crisis event come from different organizations and are often dispersed. The social relations between people in the network vary to some extent, depending on the network scope. Participants point out that internally in the organizations, relations are generally strong, while between organizations they are somewhat weaker. Tie strength also vary depending on the situation in which the network finds itself. During normal state (no on-going crisis), collaboration usually takes place between people with closer relations. However, during handling of a crisis, the network expands and collaboration between magnitudes of people with varying degrees of social ties occurs.

Although social ties are important in crisis management as in all work settings requiring collaboration, participants highlight that knowing the role and authority of others is of equal or more importance within this particular domain. It is assumed that a person within a certain work position will handle his or her responsibilities in a satisfying manner, independent of the strength of the social ties with the persons he or she collaborates with. There is, however, an ambition to strengthen the social ties between human actors in the network, as it is often easier to collaborate with people one knows.

Strong social ties foster successful collaboration, while lack of social ties may have negative implications on collaboration and the use of the CMT. This applies both within and across organizational boundaries. One end-user exemplified how social ties is connected to the commitment to use a common system.

> *"If you and I know each other, it is much harder for you to ignore me when I say that you have to use the CMT. If you do not know me, it is much easier for you not to care and not use the system. So it is like in all other contexts, that relationships fosters commitment, for better and worse."* (CMT end-user)

Establishing strong social relationship is a challenge that exists within the crisis management domain in general, and is not solely connected to the particular network involving the CMT. The challenge is especially apparent during handling of crisis events that require the collaboration between several actors and organizations, where weak social ties can potentially hinder efficient collaboration as the essential knowledge of and trust in each other is missing.

A well-designed crisis management system has the potential to increase social ties and strengthen collaboration between human actors in the network by providing a common platform for collaboration, in addition to information about participating actors and organization, and being a mean for information sharing. Joint and regular training sessions between crisis management organizations was also mentioned by participants as a way of strengthening interpersonal knowledge and social ties. In such training sessions, a natural part of the training should be exercising the use of and collaboration through systems for crisis management. Thus, it is important not to forget that the system is a central part of the network. Forums where users of a system or tool can meet to discuss and learn from each other can also contribute useful arenas for strengthening ones' knowledge of and relationships to colleagues and collaborative partners.

5.4   Extending the Use of a Common Crisis Management System

The size and geographical reach in which the CMT is used is rather limited. Although the global network of people involved in public crisis management is relatively large, the particular network is limited as the use of the CMT within public crisis management organizations varies. The network currently extends over a restricted geographical area, with little variation in culture and jurisdictions. The CMT is mainly used within a few countries and continents. The ambition for the future is to extend the use and the user group of the CMT, and that the tool is being adopted and used worldwide.

The limited size and geographical reach of the network does not directly entail negative implications for the network. However, the varying degree in which end-users in public crisis management organizations utilize the CMT affects collaboration. Ideally, for the CMT to function as common platform, all relevant crisis management actors should be using the tool for information sharing and coordination.

Furthermore, the lack of use among some public crisis management organizations has implications on the network's motivation for using the tool, according to the participants. Users might not see the value of the tool when important collaboration partners are absent. One of the end-users exemplified this point through the following quote.

"There's no point that we send out information, unless it is read at the other end and responded to." (CMT end-user)

There exist a variety of systems for crisis management, and a challenge for collaboration is that different crisis management organizations often use different systems that do not support communication, sharing of information, and coordination across systems. To stay up-to-date on the situation and maintain a holistic operational picture, there is a clear need for collaboration to take place through joint collaborative systems that include information from the several sources participating in the management of an event. As many of the end-user participants stated, such system should hold the possibility for integration with other systems.

The CMT provider's foremost ambitions for extending the network size involves getting more of the public crisis management organizations to use the tool. To function as common platform that can support collaboration through joint coordination, communication, and sharing of information, all relevant crisis management actors and organizations should ideally use the same system. One of the interviewed end-user answered the following when asked how to increase the use of the CMT among public crisis management organizations.

> *"I think it simply has to be a greater degree of commitment or in other words it should be mandatory. And basically, that is not something positive. But yet, I don't think there is anything else that will work, really. Or have the higher authorities use the CMT for information sharing with the public sector organizations so that they [the public sector organizations] actually have to use the CMT to get the information."* (CMT end-user)

Encouraging the higher authorities to use the CMT in communication with public crisis management organizations is, as the above extract states, one possibility of increasing the use of the tool. Another solution is to establish formal requirements for use of the CMT in the public sector.

For technology to serve as intended during the management of crisis events, the users need to be familiar with how to utilize the system in an efficient manner. The technology should therefore also be useful for accomplishing tasks in the before and after stage of a crisis, and preferably be used on a daily basis. One of the CMT representatives expressed how regular use can have beneficial effects when a crisis occurs.

> *"From experience, we know that the more you use a system, the better you use it. So the focus is more and more on using it on a daily basis. We see that those who use the tool daily or at least regularly, they experience increased confidence in using the tool during the management of crisis situations."* (CMT representative)

To emphasis the importance of organizations participating in the use of a common system for crisis management is vital for efficient collaboration. Increased use can be accomplished through arenas where beneficial effects of use are highlighted, preferably exemplified by end-users who themselves have successfully utilized the system. Such arenas can also function as support groups where users can get help and learn from each other, as well as get ideas on how best to make use of the system and its functionalities.

6 Conclusion

In this paper, we have studied crisis management from a human-machine network perspective, and explored how characteristics of a crisis management networks may have implications on and affect collaboration. Arising from this, we have proposed three aspects that should be considered in future design and development of crisis management systems, with the purpose of supporting collaboration throughout the phases and activities that crisis management involve. First, we presented how higher degrees of automation can increase machine agency while at the same time giving human actors greater leeway to perform their tasks. Automation in crisis management systems should essentially be controlled by humans and have the possibility of being overruled. However, if automation is introduced to the correct tasks and elements, it can provide substantial support for the human actors in the network, freeing them to concentrate on more demanding, cognitive tasks. Second, we highlighted the benefits of strengthening social ties or relationships between the dispersed human resources managing crisis events. Knowing the people one works with is recognized to support collaboration. There are several ways in which to strengthen social ties, e.g. through joint training sessions on a regular basis, as well as other arenas for socializing among colleagues. It should also be stressed that a well-design crisis management system functioning as common platform can potentially increase social ties and strengthen collaboration between human actors of a network. Third, we elaborated on how the use of a common crisis management system is crucial for efficient collaboration and effective crisis management. Specifically, it is important to extend the use among central public crisis management organizations by making visible and clearly communicate possible benefits and gains common use might lead to.

The method used, which involved interviews with both CMT representatives and end-users, made it possible to detect differences between the answers of the two groups. However, no noticeable discrepancies were found, and the participants seemed to have the same perception of the network, its implications, and possible solutions. Participants reported that the HUMANE approach provided a structured way to understand crisis management as a human machine network. Some even stated that the approach made them reflect upon elements and topics not frequently reflected on, such as social ties, which clearly have an impact on the collaboration within the network.

As all studies, this as well has its limitations. We acknowledge that the number of participants in the study could have been higher, especially concerning the end-user participants. Even though the interviews conducted provided highly valuable in-depth information, efforts should be made to include a larger sample of participants in similar future studies. Moreover, the sample in this study did not include crisis management personnel that work out in the field during crisis incidents. A suggestion for future studies is therefor to investigate the human-machine network within these groups and identify design challenges and opportunities to better support collaboration. In addition, the development of the profiles is, to some degree, a subjective process. Even though discrepancies were resolved though communication and the profiling were validated by presenting it to the CMT representatives, we recognize that the profiling can, potentially be vulnerable to researcher bias. Validation of the profile is therefore advised.

Designing efficient crisis management systems is certainly challenging due to the complexity involved in crisis management. In addition to meeting the requirements of the different actors involved, a crisis management system should preferably be of a flexible character that gives room for improvisation. It should be useful in all phases of crisis management, and adaptable to support the management of different types of events.

This study has aimed to provide designers and developers of crisis management systems with an understanding of crisis management as a complex human-machine network where different dimensions of the network should be considered. When developing technology, it is of high importance to take into account the purpose and role it is supposed to serve, and the impacts new technology might pose [10]. Technology for crisis management, as well as for many other domains, should be designed to support the human actors, while at the same time be considered as an important actor and team member itself.

Acknowledgements. This work has been conducted as part of the HUMANE project (http:// humane2020.eu), which has received funding from the European Union's Horizon 2020 research and innovation program under grant agreement No 645043. The authors would like to thank the participants of this study for their contributions.

References

1. Tsvetkova, M., et al.: Understanding Human-Machine Networks: A Cross-Disciplinary Survey. ACM Comput. Surv. **50**(1), 35 (2017)
2. Engen, V., Pickering, J.B., Walland, P.: Machine agency in human-machine networks; impacts and trust implications. In: International Conference on Human-Computer Interaction International, Toronto, Canada (2016)
3. Mendonça, D., Jefferson, T., Harrald, J.: Collaborative adhocracies and mix-and-match technologies in emergency management. Commun. ACM **50**(3), 44–49 (2007)
4. Turoff, M., et al.: The design of a dynamic emergency response management information system (DERMIS). JITTA Journal of Information Technology Theory and Application **5**(4), 1 (2004)
5. Human Factors and Ergonomics Society **50**(3), 540–547 (2008)
6. Eide, A.W., et al.: Human-machine networks: towards a typology and profiling framework. In: The 18th International Conference on Human-Computer Interaction International, Toronto, Canada (2016)
7. Hallberg, N., et al.: Rationale for emergency management systems for local communities: a needs assessment. In: Proceedings of ISCRAM 2012 (2012)
8. (FEMA), F.E.M.A. https://www.fema.gov/mission-areas. Cited 22 May 2017
9. Rosenthal, U., Boin, A., Comfort, L.K. (eds.): Managing Crises: Threats, Dilemmas, Opportunities. Charles C Thomas Publisher, London (2001)
10. Carver, L., Turoff, M.: Human-computer interaction: the human and computer as a team in emergency management information systems. Commun. ACM **50**(3), 33–38 (2007)
11. Shim, J.P., et al.: Past, present, and future of decision support technology. Decis. Support Syst. **33**(2), 111–126 (2002)
12. Fogli, D., Guida, G.: Knowledge-centered design of decision support systems for emergency management. Decis. Support Syst. **55**(1), 336–347 (2013)
13. Jefferson, T.L.: Evaluating the role of information technology in crisis and emergency management. Vine **36**(3), 261–264 (2006)
14. Willig, C.: Introducing Qualitative Research in Psychology. McGraw-Hill Education, UK (2013)
15. Profiler, H.N. https://networkprofiler.humane2020.eu/
16. Ezzy, D.: Qualitative Analysis. Routledge (2013)
17. Følstad, A., et al.: Automation in human-machine networks: how increasing machine agency affects human agency. In: International Conference on Man-Machine Interactions (ICMMI 2017), Cracow, Poland (2017)

Evaluating Effects of Hand Pointing by an Image-Based Avatar of a Navigation System

Michiko Inoue[1], Aya Shiraiwa[2], Hiroki Yoshimura[2], Masashi Nishiyama[2,3(✉)], and Yoshio Iwai[2]

[1] Graduate School of Sustainability Science, Tottori University, 101 Minami 4-chome, Koyama-cho, Tottori 680-8550, Japan
s132007@eecs.tottori-u.ac.jp
[2] Graduate School of Engineering, Tottori University, 101 Minami 4-chome, Koyama-cho, Tottori 680-8550, Japan
nishiyama@eecs.tottori-u.ac.jp
[3] Cross-informatics Research Center, Tottori University, 101 Minami 4-chome, Koyama-cho, Tottori 680-8550, Japan

Abstract. We investigate whether the behavior of pointing at a map by an image-based avatar helps a user understand a route in an image-based avatar navigation system. We also evaluate whether this behavior is preferred by the user. Existing avatar-based methods inform the user of a route by this behavior while talking. However, the existing methods do not consider how to incorporate a map. Thus, we consider how to inform the user of a route using an image-based avatar that indicates the route by pointing at a map. In the experiments, after users interacted with the system, we conducted a route depiction test to determine whether a user was able to correctly understand the route on a map and performed a questionnaire-based subjective assessment to determine whether the user liked the image-based avatar system. The results of the experiments show that the pointing behavior significantly increased the likeability of the system but did not help the user understand the route.

Keywords: Navigation system · Hand pointing · Image-based avatar
Route depiction test · Questionnaire

1 Introduction

An interaction system with a life-size display has many potential applications. In particular, there is a demand for a system that uses an image-based avatar [1–5] to smoothly communicate with users. The avatar provides good usability, such when talking about past experiences [1] or acting as a guide at a museum [2]. This paper discusses a route navigation system that uses an image-based avatar for intuitive interaction, that is, as if a real guide were directing the user, as

© Springer International Publishing AG, part of Springer Nature 2018
M. Kurosu (Ed.): HCI 2018, LNCS 10902, pp. 370–380, 2018.
https://doi.org/10.1007/978-3-319-91244-8_30

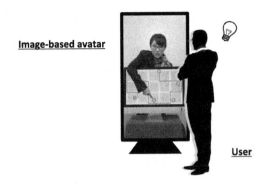

Fig. 1. Route navigation system that uses an image-based avatar that points at a map.

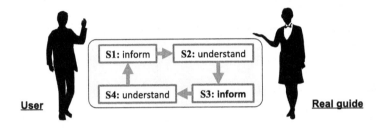

Fig. 2. Cycle of route navigation as performed by people.

illustrated in Fig. 1. We assume the scenario of an information center in a public space, such as a tourist information office.

In the design of a route navigation system [6–9], the aim is for the user to understand the explanation of the route and like using the system. When a user cannot understand the route, he or she will repeatedly ask about the route and then feel uncomfortable using the system. To avoid this problem, we need to consider the interface between the image-based avatar and user.

When designing a user-friendly interface for route navigation, we aim to mimic the behaviors of a real guide. The real guide generally directs the user according the following steps.

S1: The user informs the real guide of the destination.
S2: The real guide understands the destination provided by the user.
S3: The real guide informs the user of the route.
S4: The user understands the route provided by the real guide.

The user's understanding and liking of the system are determined in the cycle of informing and understanding, as illustrated in Fig. 2. In this cycle, S3 is important in terms of smoothly satisfying the demands of the user. We thus focus on developing an interface for S3 using an image-based avatar.

In existing avatar-based methods [10–12] the avatar informs the user of the route by pointing while talking from a first-person viewpoint. The use of the hand for pointing has merit in that it resembles natural communication among people. However, existing methods have not considered incorporating a map with a bird's-eye view. As described in [13], a map is an important part of helping a user to understand a route. A real guide frequently presents a route by indicating it on a map. We thus tackle the challenging issue of how to control an image-based avatar so that it presents the route on a map.

To this end, we investigated the hypothesis that an image-based avatar that indicates a route by pointing at a map helps the user understand it. We also investigated the hypothesis that an image-based avatar that points is preferred by the user. After exposing users to the system, we conducted a route depiction test to determine whether they correctly understood a route on a map, and then performed a questionnaire-based subjective assessment to determine whether they liked the system.

The rest of this paper is organized as follows. Section 2 describes our experimental design, Sect. 3 presents the results of the route depiction test, Sect. 4 describes the results of the questionnaire-based assessment, and our concluding remarks are given in Sect. 5.

2   Experimental Design

2.1   Overview

We assumed that a user accesses the route navigation system in an information center. We explored a scenario in which the user would like to visit some destinations in a particular order in a downtown area. We evaluated the effect when the image-based avatar describes the route on a map using its finger. Twenty-four participants (20 males, four females, average age 21.9 years) participated in the study. The details of our experimental design are described below.

2.2   Route on the Map

We generated a fictional map containing 3×5 square blocks. Figure 3 shows examples of the routes on the map. A route consists of a start point, destination points, and path segments. We randomly set the start point and the destination points during the experiment for each participant. We used six destination points so that the user would not easily remember them. In general, a human can remember 4 ± 1 items in short-term memory time [14]. We believe that using six destination points is a valid way to keep participants from easily getting full marks in the route depiction test. Furthermore, we set the paths that connect the destination points so that they did not cross each other. Note that we fixed the number of the corners in the paths to 12 to keep the experimental conditions the same.

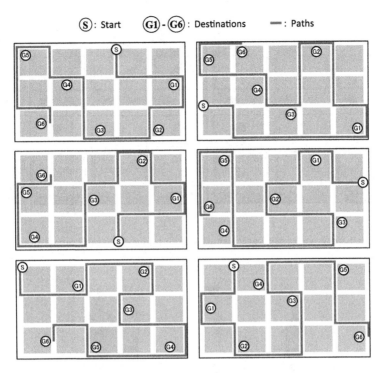

Fig. 3. Examples of the routes, which consist of a start point, destination points, and path segments on the map.

2.3   Interface with the Image-Based Avatar

We tested two interfaces as follows:

I1: An image-based avatar *with* map pointing,
I2: An image-based avatar *without* map pointing.

We generated the video sequences of the interfaces, as illustrated in Fig. 4. Each participant viewed the video sequence of interface I1 or I2 in random order. The length of each video sequence was 90 s. The sentences and speed of the avatar's speech were the same for both I1 and I2.

Figure 5 shows the setup of the interface using the image-based avatar. Each participant stood 1.5 m from the display and viewed the video sequences. We used an 80-inch display with a resolution off 1,920 × 1,080 pixels (Sharp PN-A601) to show the life-sized avatar. We placed the voice speaker (Towa electronic TW-S7B) behind the display.

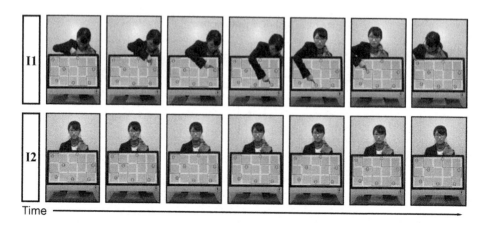

Time

Fig. 4. Video sequence of the interface using the image-based avatar with and without map pointing.

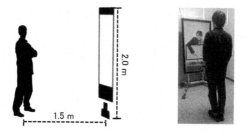

Fig. 5. Setup of the interface using the image-based avatar.

2.4   Procedure

To evaluate the hypothesizes for the interfaces, we executed the following procedure:

P1: We displayed the video sequence of the interface for the participant.
P2: We gave the route depiction test to the participant.
P3: We gave the questionnaire to the participant.

We also gave an easy numerical calculation task to the participant between P2 and P3. We prepared six routes on the map and randomly selected a route when assessing the interface. The order of interface I1 or I2 was randomly chosen.

3   Route Depiction Test

3.1   Overview

We prepared a blank map for the participant, as illustrated in Fig. 6(a), before starting the route depiction test. We slightly shifted the viewpoint of this blank map with respect to the map displayed in the video sequences of Fig. 4. We asked the participants to depict the start point, destination points, and path segments at the same scale as displayed in the video sequence. Figures 6(b) and (c) show the results of the route depiction test with respect to the ground-truth of the route illustrated in Fig. 6(d).

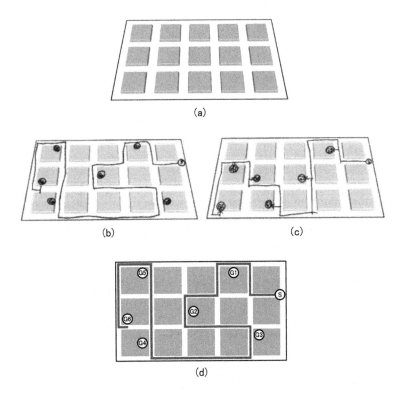

(a)

(b)   (c)

(d)

Fig. 6. Examples of the route depiction test. (a) Blank map. (b) and (c) Results of the route depiction test. (d) Ground-truth.

We evaluated the interfaces using the following three metrics. The first one was the correctness of the start point and destination points. The second one was the correctness of the path segments. The third one was the time taken for the user to complete the depiction. The details of the metrics are described below.

3.2   Metrics in the Route Depiction Test

We first explain the correctness of the start point and destination points. We evaluated whether a point depicted by the participant in the test was at the same location as the point displayed in the video sequence. When checking this correctness, we divided the blocks of the map into $3 \times 3 = 9$ regions. Figure 7(a) shows an example of the regions in a block. The depicted point was considered correct when it was more than half-way within the same region as the displayed point. Figure 7(b) shows an example of a correct case, and Fig. 7(c) shows an example of an incorrect case, where the depicted point is shifted by one region. The maximum number of incorrect points was seven (one starting point and six destination points).

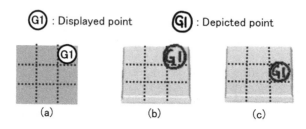

Fig. 7. Example of correct and incorrect destinations in the route depiction test. (a) Regions in the block. (b) Correct case. (c) Incorrect case.

We next explain the correctness of the path segments. We assigned correctness to a path segment when the depicted segment and the displayed segment were the same. Figure 8(a) shows an example of a displayed path segment, Fig. 8(b) shows an example of a correct case, and Fig. 8(c) shows an example of an incorrect case, where the path between the destination points was incorrect even though the locations of the points were correct. The maximum value of path incorrectness was six.

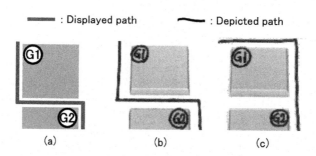

Fig. 8. Example of correct and incorrect path segments in the route depiction test. (a) Displayed path. (b) Example of a correct case. (c) Example of an incorrect case.

We finally explain the time taken by the user to create the depiction. We used a stopwatch to record the times when the participant started the test and when he or she finished.

3.3 Results of the Route Depiction Test

Figure 9(a) shows the number of incorrect start and destination points for each interface. Figure 9(b) shows the number of the participants obtaining an incorrect

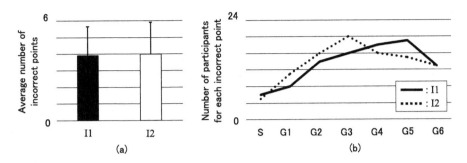

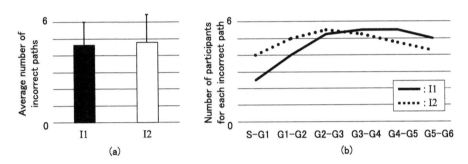

Fig. 9. Results for destination points in the route depiction test.

Fig. 10. Results for path segments in the route depiction test.

answer for each point. We used the Wilcoxon signed-rank test to determine that there is no significant difference ($p < .05$) between interfaces I1 and I2.

Figure 10(a) shows the number of incorrect paths for each interface. Figure 10(b) shows the number of the participants obtaining an incorrect path for each path segment. We used the Wilcoxon signed-rank test and determined that there is no significant difference ($p < .05$) between interfaces I1 and I2.

Figure 11 shows the time taken to depict the route. We used the Wilcoxon signed-rank test and found that there is no significant difference ($p < .05$) between interfaces I1 and I2.

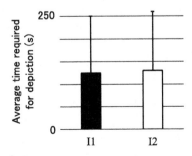

Fig. 11. Results of the average time taken to depict the map.

Hence, we cannot claim that the pointing behavior of the image-based avatar helps the user understand the route.

4   Questionnaire-Based Subjective Assessment

4.1   Items of the Questionnaire

After viewing the video sequences of interface I1 or I2, we asked the participant the following questions:

Q1: Did you like interacting with the avatar?
Q2: Did the avatar provide a navigation service resembling that of a real guide?
Q3: Was it easy to understand where to go on the map?

Each participant provided a rated score using six response levels (1: disagreeable to 6: agreeable) for each question. We also asked the inverse questions of Q1, Q2, and Q3. The purpose of Q1 was to evaluate the hypothesis that the image-based avatar that points to the map was more liked by the user. The purpose of Q2 was to check whether the behavior of the avatar in the interface was close to that of a real guide. The purpose of Q3 was to check whether the user felt that the avatar that pointed at the map had correctly presented the locations on the route.

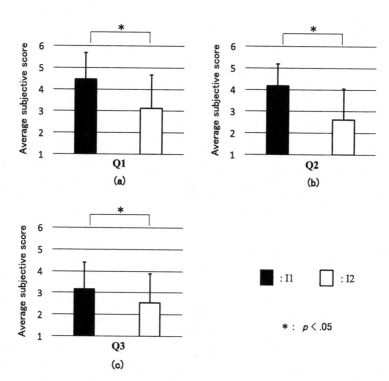

Fig. 12. Subjective scores of the questionnaire-based subjective assessment.

4.2   Results of the Subjective Assessment

Figures 12(a) to (c) show the subjective scores of the questionnaire obtained using the Wilcoxon signed-rank test. In Fig. 12(a), in terms of Q1, there was a significant difference between I1 and I2. We can hence claim that the image-based avatar that points at the map is more liked by the user. In Fig. 12(b) in terms of Q2, there was a significant difference between I1 and I2. We can hence claim that the behavior of the avatar in interface I1 is closer to that of a real guide. In Fig. 12(c), for Q3, there was also a significant difference between I1 and I2. Therefore, we can also claim that the avatar with pointing behavior makes the user feel that the avatar has correctly presented the locations on the route.

5   Conclusions

We investigated two hypotheses regarding an interface with an image-based avatar that points at a map. We evaluated the interface using a route depiction test and a questionnaire-based subjective assessment. We can claim that an avatar that points at a map significantly increases the likeability of the system, but we cannot claim that this avatar better helps the user to understand the route.

In future work, we will expand our assessment of the interactive system and intend to develop a method to add an explanation of landmarks, as used in [15], for the our avatar system.

References

1. Artstein, R., Traum, D., Alexander, O., Leuski, A., Jones, A., Georgila, K., Debevec, P., Swartout, W., Maio, H., Smith, S.: Time-offset interaction with a holocaust survivor. In: Proceedings of the 19th International Conference on Intelligent User Interfaces, pp. 163–168 (2014)
2. Robinson, S., Traum, D., Ittycheriah, I., Henderer, J.: What would you ask a conversational agent? Observations of human-agent dialogues in a museum setting. In: Proceedings of the Sixth International Conference on Language Resources and Evaluation, pp. 28–30 (2008)
3. Nishiyama, M., Miyauchi, T., Yoshimura, H., Iwai, Y.: Synthesizing realistic image-based avatars by body sway analysis. In: Proceedings of the Fourth International Conference on Human Agent Interaction, pp. 155–162 (2016)
4. Jones, A., Unger, J., Nagano, K., Busch, J., Yu, X., Peng, H.I., Alexander, O., Bolas, M., Debevec, P.: An automultiscopic projector array for interactive digital humans. In: ACM SIGGRAPH 2015 Emerging Technologies
5. Miyauchi, T., Ono, A., Yoshimura, H., Nishiyama, M., Iwai, Y.: Embedding the awareness state and response state in an image-based Avatar to start natural user interaction. IEICE Trans. Inf. Syst. E100.D **12**, 3045–3049 (2017)
6. Darken, R.P., Peterson, B.: Spatial orientation wayfinding and representation. Design, Implementation, and Applications. Handbook of Virtual Environments. CRC Press, Boca Raton (2002)

7. Devlin, A.S., Bernstein, J.: Interactive wayfinding: use of cues by men and women. J. Environ. Psychol. **15**(1), 23–38 (1995)
8. Blades, M., Spencer, C.: How do people use maps to navigate through the world? Cartographica: Int. J. Geogr. Inf. Geovis. **24**(3), 64–75 (1987)
9. Makimura, Y., Yoshimura, H., Nishiyama, M., Iwai, Y.: Decreasing physical burden using the following effect and a superimposed navigation system. In: Virtual, Augmented and Mixed Reality, pp. 533–543 (2017)
10. Kopp, S., Tepper, P.A., Ferriman, K., Striegnitz, K., Cassell, J.: Trading spaces: how humans and humanoids use speech and gesture to give directions. In: Conversational Informatics: An Engineering Approach, pp. 1–26 (2007)
11. Bergmann, K., Kopp, S.: Gnetic - using Bayesian decision networks for iconic gesture generation. In: Proceedings of the 9th International Conference on Intelligent Virtual Agents, pp. 76–89 (2009)
12. Bergmann, K., Kopp, S.: Knowledge representation for generating locating gestures in route directions. In: Proceedings of Workshop on Spatial Language and Dialogue, pp. 1–13 (2005)
13. Taylor, H.A., Tversky, B.: The description of routes: a cognitive approach to the production of spatial discourse. Cah. Psychol. Cogn. **35**, 371–391 (1996)
14. Cowan, N.: The magical number 4 in short-term memory: a reconsideration of mental storage capacity. Behav. Brain Sci. **24**(1), 87–114 (2001)
15. Denis, M.: The description of routes: a cognitive approach to the production of spatial discourse. Cahiers Psychologie Cogn. **16**(8), 409–458 (1997)

Using Convolutional Neural Networks for Assembly Activity Recognition in Robot Assisted Manual Production

Henning Petruck$^{(\boxtimes)}$ and Alexander Mertens

Institute of Industrial Engineering and Ergonomics of RWTH Aachen University,
Bergdriesch 27, 52062 Aachen, Germany
{h.petruck,a.mertens}@iaw.rwth-aachen.de
http://www.iaw-aachen.de

Abstract. Due to ever-shortening product life cycles and multi variant products the demand for flexible production systems that include human-robot collaboration (HRC) rises. One key factor in HRC is stress that occurs because of the unfamiliar work with the robot. To reduce stress induced strain for assembly tasks we propose an adjustment of cycle times to the human's performance, so that the stress that is exerted on the working person by a waiting robot is minimized. For an autonomous adaptation of the cycle time, the production system should be aware of the human's actions and assembly progress without the need to inform the system manually. Therefore, we propose an activity recognition in assembly based on a machine learning technique. A convolutional neural network is used to distinguish between different activities during the assembly by analyzing motion data of the hands of the working person. The results show that the network is suitable for distinguishing between nine different assembly activities like screwing with a screwdriver, screwing with a hexagon wrench or general assembly and further activities.

Keywords: Human-robot collaboration · Human-machine systems
Manual assembly · Machine learning · Neural networks
Convolutional neural network · Pattern recognition
Activity recognition · Motion tracking

1 Introduction

In high-wage countries like Germany or the United States of America the amount of automation in production is very large, which creates a large effort for a change of product in these production systems. Consequently these production systems are not suitable to meet the challenges of ever shortening product life cycles and multi variant products without limitation. Human-robot collaboration, which combines the fine motor and cognitive skills of a human with the precision, speed and fatigue-free work of a robot, can contribute to make a production system more flexible. One key factor in effective human-robot collaboration is a user

© Springer International Publishing AG, part of Springer Nature 2018
M. Kurosu (Ed.): HCI 2018, LNCS 10902, pp. 381–397, 2018.
https://doi.org/10.1007/978-3-319-91244-8_31

centered design of the interaction between the robot and the human. To ensure acceptance and reasonable mental and physical load on the working person, the workplace has to be designed ergonomically. Among others, an important aspect regarding these goals is the level of automation of the workplace [1], on which we will focus in the following. How much control over the robot's behavior does the working person need or want to have in order to achieve an effective human-robot collaboration?

In order to deal with this question, we consider a scenario of robot-assisted manual assembly. The process of handover of tools or components is the main interaction between robot and human in this scenario. One characteristic of the handover process is that it always has to be triggered. This trigger can either be an explicit command by the working person or it can be triggered automatically, by analyzing real time data from the working person. For an automated trigger cycle times of assembly can be used for the calculation of the next trigger time. However, by integrating the human in the production process, a great uncertainty emerges, because the human behavior is not as predictable as the motions of a machine or the actions of a computer. The uncertainty is reflected by the occurrence of flaws in production or fluctuating cycle and total process times. It is caused by multiple factors like age, experience, skills, assembly instructions, fatigue, workload, number of repetitions, etc. [2–6]. As a first step the authors developed an adaptive cycle time prediction to deal with these uncertainties [7]. However, as this approach only has the possibility to compare its prediction with the real times at points of interaction between robot and human, it is not sufficient and accurate enough for an autonomous triggering. To support the adaptive cycle time prediction by enabling the possibility to track the assembly progress between interaction points, the recognition of assembly activities is necessary.

Ikeuchi and Suehiro [8] used visual object recognition do identify assembly tasks. Kuniyoshi and Inoue [9] detected objects or hand movements during assembly tasks by using visual object recognition. However the use of image recognition is critical in an operational environment considering data protection regulations. Futhermore, the level of detail in recognition for the depicted method is not sufficient. Therefore, we developed an assembly activity recognition, that distinguishes between different activities by analyzing motion tracking data from the working person. Compared video data, motion tracking data can be handled anonymous. The classification of assembly activities is carried out by a Convolutional Neural Network (CNN), which is pretrained on sample data and implemented in MATLAB.

2   Activity Recognition Based on Sensor Data

Activity recognition based on sensor data is a widely used technique in many different application areas. A familiar example is the Timeline feature of the Google Maps app. In this feature the collected data is used to create a protocol of the daily activities. In the protocol the day is segmented into stays at specific adresses and covered tracks between them. The segmentation even distinguishes between different modes of transport like walking, going for a run, bicycle, car, train or plane.

Both Bao and Intille [10] and Maurer et al. [11] found that decision trees are capable of distinguishing between different physical activities of everyday tasks like walking, sitting, jogging, etc., independent of their place of execution. They used data of multiple accelerometers that were worn by the participants of the study on different parts of the bodies [10] or the combination of a dual axes accelerometer and a light sensor [11]. In both cases the timeseries input of the recorded sensor data was transformed from time-domain to feature domain by calculating, for instance, mean, energy, entropy or correlation. These features were then used as input for the classification algorithms. Kwapisz et al. [12] conducted a similar experiment in which the data of a single tri axial accelerometer was used and found that the most accurate algorithm from the three compared classification methods decision tree, logistic regression and multilayer neural networks varied among the different activities. However, the overall accuracy was best for the neural network.

For the same application domain of daily activity recognition Yang et al. [13] use CNNs, which operate directly on the time series data of the various sensors without transforming the timeseries in another feature domain. Similar approaches to classify multivariate timeseries data by CNNs can be found in [14, 15].

Tapia et al. [16] used state-changing sensors, that registered, for example, the opening of a refrigerator door or a window or the time of turning on the television or iron to recognize activities for two different subjects in their home environment. By definition the data of state-changing is already in feature domain and has been classified with a naive Bayes classifier.

It is important to note that some studies mention the fact, that subject dependent training is necessary for the detection of those activities, that are carried out in a different manner by different people, and therefore lead do different characteristics [10, 11]. This is especially true for the study conducted by Tapia et al. [16], because the individual homes of the different subjects require different setups and numbers of the state-changing sensors, e.g. two different apartments might have different numbers or locations of windows.

The presented methods have proven to be applicable in the domain of activity recognition, however most methods incorporate a transformation from time domain to feature domain before classification, which is connected with a loss of information in most cases. Therefore this paper will focus on using CNNs to classify the motion tracking data during assembly into several different assembly activities.

3   Neural Networks for Classification Tasks

3.1   Neural Networks

A Neural Network, or an Artificial Neural Network, is a structure, that consists of processing elements called neurons and unidirectional channels between them [17]. Such a network consists of layers, which are constructed of neurons and arcs. Biologically motivated by the nerve system, the neurons and arcs represent nerve cells and axons respectively [18]. A simple neural network consists of an input layer, a hidden layer, in which the input is processed to the next layer, and an output layer. Usually, each neuron of a layer is connected to all neurons of the following layer. Such a layer is called fully connected. As a powerful technique in pattern recognition, a common application area of neural networks are classification problems, e.g. face recognition [19]. In a classification problem the input layer receives an input sample of the objects to be classified and returns the estimated output class in the output layer of the network. Therefore, the network has to be trained with reference data of objects from the different output classes [20]. With a larger size of the training set and more diverse characteristics of the output classes, the accuracy of the neural network increases. Such a pretrained network can be used in a steady state to classify objects with unchanging characteristics, but it can also be trained further with new data, e.g. in order to adapt to a specific persons behaviour [21].

3.2   Convolutional Neural Networks

Firstly developed by LeCun et al. [22] for digit recognition, CNNs have been further developed and widely used in image classification and other recognition tasks [23–26]. They represent a subclass of neural networks, that are not constructed from fully connected layers in contrast to ordinary neural networks. The essential difference is that CNNs consider the topographical order of the input neurons, like the pixels of an image, and are able to deal with feature translation invariance [27,28]. In other words, it does not matter, if the face, which we want to detect is on the left or the right side of the picture. Important for the classification are the relative positions of the characterizing features.

The three main ideas of CNNs are local receptive fields, shared weights and subsampling [28]. As already mentioned, not all neurons of consecutive layers are fully connected in CNNs. For the calculation of a neuron, only a local neighbourhood of a neuron in the preceding layer, the local receptive field, is considered for calculation. By using this strategy local features can be extracted from the small receptive field. Features in pictures can be orientated edges, end-points or corners (e.g. [29]). For calculating the value of a neuron a filter kernel (or set of weights) is applied to the local receptive field of the preceding layer. A specific filter kernel stands for a specific feature, that is extracted by using this filter kernel. By applying the same filter kernel on every local receptive field of the input layer, a feature map of input is generated. Although one layer can have several filter kernels, that generate several feature maps, the number of parameters of one layer is bounded by the number of filter kernels and their size.

The most important layer of a CNN is the convolutional layer. The filter kernels of a convolutional layer perform a convolution on the local receptive field of the input, which is basically a dot product of local receptive field and filter kernel with the addition of a bias term. A simple example of a convolution layer is given in Fig. 1.

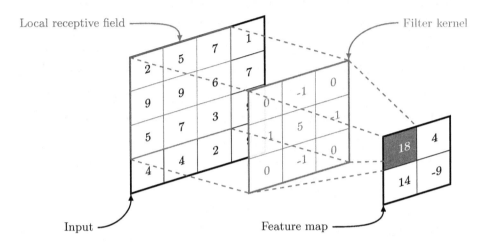

Fig. 1. Simple example of a convolution layer with a 4×4 input matrix, a 3×3 filter kernel and a 2×2 output feature map with zero bias

A pooling layer, which is typically applied after a convolutional layer, calculates the average or maximum of the local neighbourhood of a neuron [27]. The stepsize for applying pooling layers on local receptive fields is usually the same as the size of the local receptive field. Therefore a downsampling is performed. Both pooling layer and convolutional layer contribute to the translation invariant feature detection of CNNs [28]. The sequencing of multiple pairs of convolutional and pooling layers allows the detection of higher level features [28].

The structure of a CNN is built up from an image input layer, followed by an alternating series of convolution and pooling layers, an optional fully connected layer, which combines all features, and an output layer that returns the calculated output class [28,29].

In contrast to ordinary fully connected neural networks, which have a huge number of parameters and therefore are prone to overfitting, the number of parameters in CNNs is comparatively very low, because of weight sharing [29]. The small number of parameters of a CNN makes the network more robust to overfitting and the training effort is much smaller [23,27,29].

4 Assembly Activity Recognition with Neural Networks

4.1 Experimental Data

To conduct the assembly activity recognition on real assembly data, a study was conducted. The participants had to assemble a helical gear unit consisting of 32 components (see Fig. 2), repeatedly for ten times without the assistance of a robot. All participants of this study were right-handed. For more information regarding this study the interested reader is referred to Kuhlenbäumer et al. [30]. The data collected during this study is used to investigate the suitability of CNNs to recognize assembly activities. Therefore, video data, which was taken from the left side of the participants during the assembly process with a frame rate of 25 frames per second, was analyzed and segmented into distinct classes of activities during assembly. Two exemplary video frames from this perspective can be found in Fig. 3. The segmentation of the activity classes was carried out separately for each hand. Otherwise combinations of activity classes for left and right hand would have been considered, which would have resulted in more possible outputs for the neural network and less training data per activity class. The desired effect of keeping the number of possible outcomes to a minimum is a higher accuracy of classification. The activities during assembly were divided into nine distinct classes:

- **Assembly (AS):** This class covers all general movements of the hand in and around the gearbox ((1) in Fig. 4) and holding components except the screwing of the flange with the right hand and screwing of the cover box with both hands.

Fig. 2. All 32 components of the gear unit including housing, groove ball bearings, gearwheels, spacer rings, feather keys, motor shaft, pinion shaft, circlips, caps, flange, gearbox cover and screws

Fig. 3. Screwing of flange with a hexagon wrench (left) and screwing of the gearbox cover with a screwing driver (right) from the camera perspective

- **Assembly Screwing Flange[1] (AS-FL):** The screwing of the flange with the hexagon wrench contains a characteristic movement of the right hand, whereas the left hand mostly is positioned on the gearbox for stabilizing purposes (Fig. 3, left). Therefore this class in only considered for the right hand. The class covers the screwing movements with the screwing flange.
- **Assembly Screwing Gearbox Cover (AS-GBC):** The screwing of the gearbox cover with the screwdriver contains characteristic movements or positions for both hands respectively (Fig. 3, right). The class covers the hand movements and postures during screwing.
- **Mounting Aid (MA):** During the assembly of the complete gear unit two mounting aids are used. The first one is inserted into the gearbox from the drive side before turning the box with the drive side facing bottom, to ensure a leveled contact area. The second aid is a mounting sleeve which is put over the drive shaft before the flange is fitted. Both mounting aids are located on the left side of the working area ((2) in Fig. 4). The class covers the hand movements for getting and putting back the mounting aids in their original place.
- **Components (CO):** The components for the assembly of the gear are originally located in component boxes, which are labeled with the according component ids in the back of the working area ((3) in Fig. 4). The class covers movements which are related to getting components from the boxes or putting them back.
- **Monitor[2] (MO):** In the upper left corner of the workplace a touchscreen monitor with assembly instructions can be found ((4) in Fig. 4). In order to navigate through instructions the participants have to touch the monitor. The activity class covers all movements, that are movements towards the monitor, navigating actions or movements near the monitor. Since only movements towards the monitor by the left hand were observed, this class is only considered for the left hand.

---

[1] Only assigned for right hand.
[2] Only assigned for left hand.

- **On Table (OT):** Sometimes a hand is just resting on the table. This can be the case, when the other hand is used, for instance, to get a component or both hands are placed on the table sometimes, when the participant looks at the assembly instructions.
- **Tool (TO):** A tool holder with the hexagon wrench, screwdriver and two spring tongs can be found at the right side of the working area ((5) in Fig. 4). Whenever the participant reaches out for the toolholder to get a tool or bring it back the tool class is assigned.
- **Miscellaneous (MISC):** The activity class covers all activities, that cannot be assigned to any other defined class, like scratching in the face or rolling up of sleeves.

It is important to note, that the distinction between these classes from video data was and cannot be based on fixed coordinates, which means that a movement towards the monitor e.g. starts with different distances to the monitor and the end of the preceding activity is not defined exactly. Additionally, different activities are merging and it is hard to define the exact point in time between two different activities. This leads to the assumption that especially for the transition area incorrect classifications are to be expected. The workplace used for this study with marked locations of the mentioned areas of the workplace are depicted in Fig. 4.

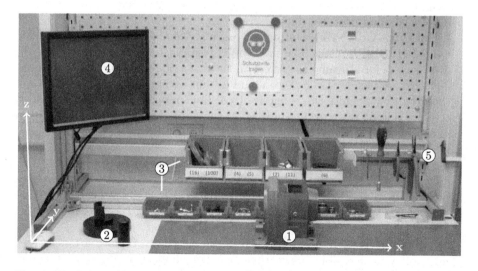

Fig. 4. Workplace of assembly study with marked locations of gearbox (1), mounting aids (2), component boxes (3), touchscreen monitor for assembly instructions (4) and tool holder (5) and reference coordinate system. The coordinate system has been translated with respect to its origin to fit into the picture.

In addition to the time periods of the different activity classes the movements of both hand joints were tracked by a motion tracking system. Therefore markers were attached to the participants hand joints (cf. Fig. 3). The tracking system captures the position of both hands in a three-dimensional cartesic coordinate system, which is aligned with the axes of the workplace (cf. Fig. 4), and the rotation angles of the markers with regard to axes of the reference coordinate system, which gives us a vector of six values per timeframe $\mathbf{t} = \left(p_x, p_y, p_z, r_x, r_y, r_z\right)$ with p denoting the position and r the rotation. The motion data is tracked with a frame rate of 60 frames per second.

4.2   A Neural Network for Assembly Activity Recognition

As acceleration is an important source of information for activity recognition (cf. [10–13]), the derivatives up to the second order of both position and rotation are also considered for the assembly activity recognition. Because for some activities like two-handed assembly the proximity of both hands is a characteristic feature in contrast to a movement to the touchscreen monitor, which is typically performed only with one hand, the relative difference of both hands is also considered including its derivatives up to the second order. The final input vector $\mathbf{i}$ containing 27 values defined as $\mathbf{i} = \left(\mathbf{x}, \mathbf{x}', \mathbf{x}''\right)$ with

$$\mathbf{x} = \left(p_x, p_y, p_z, r_x, r_y, r_z, \Delta p_x, \Delta p_y, \Delta p_z\right) \tag{1}$$

with $\Delta p_x = p_{x,right} - p_{x,left}$ denoting the difference of left and right hand on the x-axis and $\Delta p_y, \Delta p_z$ accordingly. As Yang et al. [13] suggest, the input for the CNN is arranged of sensor data from a sliding window including 30 time steps. Applied to the described input data this is a reasonable sample size, because it describes a movement of roughly half a second and should consequently contain enough information. By arranging 30 consecutive input vectors $\mathbf{i}_k$ as column vectors in a matrix, we get the input Matrix

$$I = \left[\mathbf{i}_k^T \; \mathbf{i}_{k+1}^T \cdots \mathbf{i}_{k+29}^T\right]. \tag{2}$$

The final step is the transformation of this matrix into a picture, so that it can be used as input for a CNN in a MATLAB application. To ensure a high resolution the matrix I is stored as greyscale image with 16 bit color depth which corresponds to a value range of 0 to $2^8 - 1 = 65535$. To achieve the greatest possible resolution for each of the 27 sensor values in the input data, each channel is independently scaled exactly to this range over all activity classes and time steps. Examples of these input pictures are depicted in Fig. 5.

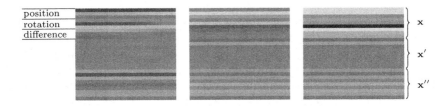

Fig. 5. Example input pictures from assembly study for CNN: getting a component with the left hand (left), screwing the gearbox cover with the right hand (middle) and getting a tool with the right hand (right)

Table 1. Counts of assembly activity classes for both hands

#Left hand	#Right hand	Assembly activity
60,841	54,229	AS
-	5,605	AS-FL
4,964	4,964	AS-GBC
565	165	MA
4,403	3,343	CO
844	-	MO
2,492	2,405	OT
603	2,881	TO
1,110	372	MISC
75,822	73,964	Σ

Table 2. Layers of CNN for assembly activity classification

Nr.	Type	Layer size	Kernel size	#Kernels
1	Image Input Layer	$D = [27 \times 30]$	-	-
2	Convolution Layer	$D = [27 \times 30]$	$K = [3 \times 3]$	16
3	Batch Normalization Layer	$D = [27 \times 30]$	-	-
4	Rectified Unit Layer	$D = [27 \times 30]$	-	-
5	Max Pooling Layer	$D = [27 \times 30]$	$K = [2 \times 2]$	-
6	Convolution Layer	$D = [14 \times 15]$	$K = [3 \times 3]$	32
7	Batch Normalization Layer	$D = [14 \times 15]$	-	-
8	Rectified Unit Layer	$D = [14 \times 15]$	-	-
9	Max Pooling Layer	$D = [14 \times 15]$	$K = [2 \times 2]$	-
10	Convolution Layer	$D = [7 \times 8]$	$K = [3 \times 3]$	64
11	Batch Normalization Layer	$D = [7 \times 8]$	-	-
12	Rectified Unit Layer	$D = [7 \times 8]$	-	-
13	Fully Connected Layer	$D = [8 \times 1]$	-	-
14	Softmax Layer	$D = [8 \times 1]$	-	-
15	Classification Layer	$D = [1 \times 1]$	-	-

Due to time consuming video analysis not all participants of the assembly study were included in the activity recognition study. Video and motion tracking data were segmented for two randomly picked participants of the study. A number of at least two participants is important to validate the transferability of recognition to new subjects. Overall 75,822 images for the left hand and 73,964 images for the right were generated. The detailed distribution over the activity classes can be found in Table 1. The difference in the overall image counts can

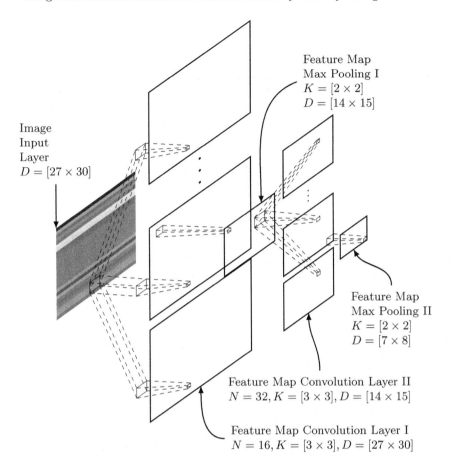

Fig. 6. First five layers of convolutional neural network for assembly activity recognition. D denotes the dimension of the layer/feature map, K the dimension of the filter kernel/local receptive field and N the number of feature maps.

be explained by the fact, that due to occlusions the right hand was not visible in the video at all times. At those times no classification of was conducted for the right hand. The CNN, which we use to classify the assembly activities is constructed of 15 layers. The detailed composition is listed in Table 2. Batch normalization layers are used to normalize the data and facilitate a faster training of the network. A Rectified Unit Layer simply maps a value to the positive range by applying the function $f(x) = max(0, x)$ to every neuron of the feature maps. The softmax layer normalizes the values of the preceding layer, so that their sum adds up to one, so it represents the probabilities of the input image belonging to the different classes. The output layer finally returns the class with the highest probability in the softmax layer. Figure 6 depicts the first nine layers of the network, omitting normalization and rectified unit layers. The network has been implemented and trained using the MATLAB Neural Network Toolbox.

In contrast to Yang et al. [13] an ordinary CNN for image recognition has been chosen, which applies the filter kernels not only to single rows, but on multiple rows, which contain data of multiple sensors. Analysis of different network structures revealed that the results were significantly better for the chosen layers. This can be explained by the fact, that the data contains features, which are distributed over several rows, e.g. x, y and z coordinates in the second layer of the network.

5   Results

5.1   Subject-Independent Validation

The neural network was trained with 70% randomly picked samples of the data of both participants and validated with the remaining 30%. The result of the validation is a confusion matrix, which lists the relative assignments of the validation data to the different activity classes. The rows indicate the true activity class, whereas the columns indicate the predicted class. A confusion matrix with relative frequencies of 100% on the main diagonal and all other elements being zero would be the optimal validation result. The confusion matrices for both hands, which refer to the neural networks trained with data from both participants, are depicted in Fig. 7. The confusion matrix for the left hand shows, that general assembly activities (AS) are correctly assigned with the highest accuracy of 99.18%, followed touching the monitor (MO, 82.21%) and reaching for components (CO, 79.33%). The posture of the left hand while screwing the gearbox (AS-GBC) can be distinguished from all other activities with an accuracy of 68.57%.

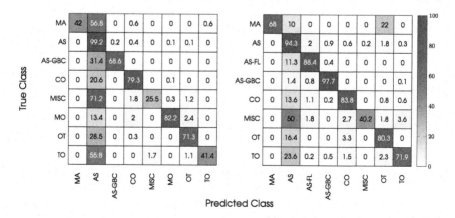

Fig. 7. Confusion matrices for left hand (left) and right hand (right) with data from both participants

For all activities the most incorrect assigned samples were assigned to the general assembly class (AS), the smallest amount of correctly assigned activities and general assembly class adds up to 95.65% for reaching for a tool (TO). On the one hand this can be explained by the fact, that most activities merge with general assembly at the beginning and the end, on the other hand the general assembly data samples were by far the most, so the CNN could be oversensitive to general assembly data.

Poor accuracies lower or equal to 60% are achieved by miscellaneous activities (MISC, 25.53%), reaching for a tool (TO, 41.44%) and reaching to the mounting aid (MA, 42.01%). As miscellaneous activities are very similar to movements during assembly, the poor accuracy is not surprising, as well as for reaching for the mounting aid and tool, as there is no sharp border between these activities and general assembly. Those activities are also, with exception of the touch-screen monitor, the activities with the smallest sample count ($N \leq 1,110$). An increase in accuracy is expected for a larger database. Overall the accuracy of the left hand assembly activity recognition is 63.69%, weighted by their relative frequency the accuracy can even be increased up to 92.96%.

For the right hand the most accurate prediction is achieved for the screwing of the gearbox cover (AS-GBC, 97.65%), followed by general assembly (AS, 94.30%) and screwing of the flange (AS-FL, 88.35%). The drop in general assembly accuracy for the right hand compared to the left hand, might be explained by the fact, that with three assembly activities the network distinguishes between one more direct assembly activity than for the left hand. The high accuracy for the posture of the right hand during screwing the gearbox cover proves, that this is a very characteristic movement.

As for the left side the most activities are assigned either to the correct class or to general assembly, with one exception: 22.00% percent of the mounting aid (MA) samples are incorrectly assigned to hands on table (OT). Considering its sample size ($n = 165$), which is by far the smallest, the odd assignments can be explained. A much larger dataset of this activity is necessary for an accurate recognition. For all other classes the sum of relative assignments to the correct or assembly classes is larger or equal to 90.20% (MISC).

Only by miscellaneous activities poor accuracies lower or equal to 60% are achieved, which could already be observed for the left hand. The amount of data samples for this activity class is the second smallest. The accuracy of reaching for a tool is much larger for the right hand (71.88%), which can be explained by the position of the tool holder. Most of the time the participant reaches to the tool with the right hand, so much more datasamples (cf. Table 1) are available. Overall the accuracy of the right hand assembly activity recognition is 78.05%, weighted by their relative frequency the accuracy can even be increased up to 91.94%.

5.2   Subject-Dependent Validation

To validate the transferability of a neural network to new subjects the neural network has been trained with the complete dataset of the first participant

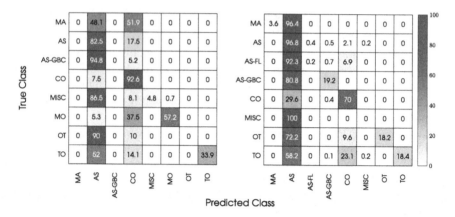

Fig. 8. Confusion matrices for left hand (left) and right hand (right) with training data from the first participant and validation data from the second participant

and afterwards validated with the complete dataset of the second partcipant. Figure 8 shows the corresponding confusion matrices. Both confusion matrices show poor accuracies of the neural networks for validating the data of the second participant. Only for general assembly (AS) and reaching for components (CO) accuracies greater or equal than 70% are achieved. Most of the classes get misclassified for general assembly or reaching to components. Some classes are even never correctly classified (left: MA, AS-GBC, OT; right: MISC). The overall accuracies for the left hand are 33.86% without and 73.28% with weighted calculation, for the right hand without weight an accuracy of 28.31% is achieved compared to 78.81% weighted accuracy. The results indicate that either the amount of training samples is too low, or all activities except general assembly and reaching for components contain subject specific characteristics or features, that the neural network has to be trained on in order to guarantee transferability.

6 Conclusion

The paper shows how machine learning methods like convolutional neural networks can be applied to activity recognition in assembly. They prove to be highly suitable for distinguishing between different activities like screwing, reaching for components, using the touchscreen, etc. For a dataset from two participants satisfactory classifications with a high level of accuracy were conducted. However, a certain amount was still classified falsely, most of it to the general assembly class. Further investigations have to answer the following questions regarding the falsely classified samples: 1. Is each movement mostly classified correctly, except for individual scattered time periods of the whole movement? 2. How are the misclassified time periods distributed over the whole activity time? Do they belong to the transition area between two activities?

Furthermore, the transferability of assembly activity recognition to new subjects has to be further explored. The results raise the question if such a neural network is transferable to new subjects at all or if the amount of training data was just to small. Hopefully, a network, which has been trained on more than one subject will achieve much better results. This finding is crucial as the subject independent training would be hard to implement in a productional company, since it is hardly automatable and would require additional resources for each working person.

For a successful application in an automated triggering of the next actions of the robot, a model is required, which joins the recognized activities and assembly plan and in order to recognize the assembly progress and predict interaction points between human and robot based on that information. When the autonomous triggering is finalized, a higher level research question can be explored: How does the autonomous triggering affect the human working person?

Acknowledgments. The authors would like to thank the German Research Foundation DFG for the kind support within the Cluster of Excellence "Integrative Production Technology for High-Wage Countries".

References

1. Freedy, A., DeVisser, E., Weltman, G., Coeyman, N.: Measurement of trust in human-robot collaboration. In: International Symposium on Collaborative Technologies and Systems, CTS 2007, pp. 106–114. IEEE (2007)
2. Maynard, H.B., Stegemerten, G.J., Schwab, J.L.: Methods-Time Measurement. McGraw-Hill, New York (1948)
3. Chryssolouris, G., Mavrikios, D., Fragos, D., Karabatsou, V.: A virtual reality-based experimentation environment for the verification of human-related factors in assembly processes. Robot. Comput.-Integr. Manuf. **16**(4), 267–276 (2000)
4. Zhang, W., Gen, M.: An efficient multiobjective genetic algorithm for mixed-model assembly line balancing problem considering demand ratio-based cycle time. J. Intell. Manuf. **22**(3), 367–378 (2011)
5. Kuhlenbäumer, F., Przybysz, P., Mütze-Niewöhner, S., Schlick, C.M.: Age-differentiated analysis of the influence of task descriptions on learning sensorimotor tasks. In: Schlick, C., Trzcieliński, S. (eds.) Advances in Ergonomic Design of Systems, Products and Processes, pp. 159–175. Springer, Heidelberg (2017). https://doi.org/10.1007/978-3-319-41697-7_43
6. Krueger, G.P.: Sustained work, fatigue, sleep loss and performance: a review of the issues. Work Stress **3**(2), 129–141 (1989)
7. Petruck, H., Mertens, A.W.: Predicting human cycle times in robot assisted assembly. In: Trzcielinski, S. (eds.) Advances in Intelligent Systems and Computing, AHFE 2017 International Conference on Human Aspects of Advanced Manufacturing, Los Angeles, CA (USA), 17 July 2017–21 July 2017, pp. 25–36. Springer, Cham (2018). https://doi.org/10.1007/978-3-319-60474-9_3
8. Ikeuchi, K., Suehiro, T.: Toward an assembly plan from observation, part i: task recognition with polyhedral objects. IEEE Trans. Robot. Autom. **10**(3), 368–385 (1994)
9. Kuniyoshi, Y., Inoue, H.: Qualitative recognition of ongoing human action sequences. IJCA **I**, 1600–1609 (1993)

10. Bao, L., Intille, S.S.: Activity recognition from user-annotated acceleration data. In: Ferscha, A., Mattern, F. (eds.) Pervasive 2004. LNCS, vol. 3001, pp. 1–17. Springer, Heidelberg (2004). https://doi.org/10.1007/978-3-540-24646-6_1

11. Maurer, U., Smailagic, A., Siewiorek, D.P., Deisher, M.: Activity recognition and monitoring using multiple sensors on different body positions. In: International Workshop on Wearable and Implantable Body Sensor Networks, BSN 2006, 4 pp. IEEE (2006)

12. Kwapisz, J.R., Weiss, G.M., Moore, S.A.: Activity recognition using cell phone accelerometers. ACM SigKDD Explor. Newsl. **12**(2), 74–82 (2011)

13. Yang, J., Nguyen, M.N., San, P.P., Li, X., Krishnaswamy, S.: Deep convolutional neural networks on multichannel time series for human activity recognition. IJCA **I**, 3995–4001 (2015)

14. Zheng, Y., Liu, Q., Chen, E., Ge, Y., Zhao, J.L.: Time series classification using multi-channels deep convolutional neural networks. In: Li, F., Li, G., Hwang, S., Yao, B., Zhang, Z. (eds.) WAIM 2014. LNCS, vol. 8485, pp. 298–310. Springer, Cham (2014). https://doi.org/10.1007/978-3-319-08010-9_33

15. Zheng, Y., Liu, Q., Chen, E., Ge, Y., Zhao, J.L.: Exploiting multi-channels deep convolutional neural networks for multivariate time series classification. Front. Comput. Sci. **10**(1), 96–112 (2016)

16. Tapia, E.M., Intille, S.S., Larson, K.: Activity recognition in the home using simple and ubiquitous sensors. In: Ferscha, A., Mattern, F. (eds.) Pervasive 2004. LNCS, vol. 3001, pp. 158–175. Springer, Heidelberg (2004). https://doi.org/10.1007/978-3-540-24646-6_10

17. Hecht-Nielsen, R., et al.: Theory of the backpropagation neural network. Neural Netw. **1**((Suppl. 1)), 445–448 (1988)

18. Hopfield, J.J.: Artificial neural networks. IEEE Circ. Devices Mag. **4**(5), 3–10 (1988)

19. Lin, S.H., Kung, S.Y., Lin, L.J.: Face recognition/detection by probabilistic decision-based neural network. IEEE Trans. Neural Netw. **8**(1), 114–132 (1997)

20. Hepner, G., Logan, T., Ritter, N., Bryant, N.: Artificial neural network classification using a minimal training set-comparison to conventional supervised classification. Photogram. Eng. Remote Sens. **56**(4), 469–473 (1990)

21. Park, D.C., El-Sharkawi, M.A., Marks, R.J.: An adaptively trained neural network. IEEE Trans. Neural Netw. **2**(3), 334–345 (1991)

22. LeCun, Y., Boser, B., Denker, J.S., Henderson, D., Howard, R.E., Hubbard, W., Jackel, L.D.: Backpropagation applied to handwritten zip code recognition. Neural Comput. **1**(4), 541–551 (1989)

23. Krizhevsky, A., Sutskever, I., Hinton, G.E.: Imagenet classification with deep convolutional neural networks. In: Advances in neural information processing systems, pp. 1097–1105 (2012)

24. Zeiler, M.D., Fergus, R.: Visualizing and understanding convolutional networks. In: Fleet, D., Pajdla, T., Schiele, B., Tuytelaars, T. (eds.) ECCV 2014. LNCS, vol. 8689, pp. 818–833. Springer, Cham (2014). https://doi.org/10.1007/978-3-319-10590-1_53

25. LeCun, Y., Huang, F.J., Bottou, L.: Learning methods for generic object recognition with invariance to pose and lighting. In: Proceedings of the 2004 IEEE Computer Society Conference on Computer Vision and Pattern Recognition, CVPR 2004, vol. 2, p. II-104. IEEE (2004)

26. LeCun, Y., Bottou, L., Bengio, Y., Haffner, P.: Gradient-based learning applied to document recognition. Proc. IEEE **86**(11), 2278–2324 (1998)

27. Hinton, G.E., Srivastava, N., Krizhevsky, A., Sutskever, I., Salakhutdinov, R.R.: Improving neural networks by preventing co-adaptation of feature detectors. arXiv preprint arXiv:1207.0580 (2012)

28. Abdel-Hamid, O., Deng, L., Yu, D.: Exploring convolutional neural network structures and optimization techniques for speech recognition. In: Interspeech, pp. 3366–3370 (2013)

29. LeCun, Y., Bengio, Y., et al.: Convolutional networks for images, speech, and time series. In: The Handbook of Brain Theory and Neural Networks, 3361 pp. (1995). 10

30. Kuhlenbäumer, F., Polis, S., Przybysz, P., Mütze-Niewöhner, S.: Age-differentiated analysis of the influence of the duration of breaks on learning sensorimotor tasks. In: IEEE International Conference on Industrial Engineering and Engineering Management, IEEM2017, 10 December 2017–13 December 2017 (2017)

CoRgI: Cognitive Reasoning Interface

Vinícius Segura$^{(\boxtimes)}$ ⓘ, Juliana Jansen Ferreira, Ana Fucs,
Marcio Ferreira Moreno, Rogério de Paula, and Renato Cerqueira

IBM Research, Rio de Janeiro, RJ, Brazil
{vboas,jjansen,anafucs,mmoreno,ropaula,rcerq}@br.ibm.com

Abstract. Cognitive systems built with artificial intelligence resources
(AI-powered systems) can be defined as software systems that learn at
scale from their interaction with humans and environments. That kind
of system allows people to augment their cognitive potential in order to
harvest insights from huge quantities of data to understand complex situations, make accurate predictions about the future, and anticipate the
unintended consequences of actions. These systems evolve naturally from
such learning, rather than being explicitly programmed. In this approach,
humans and computers work more interconnected to achieve unexpected
insights. In order to be useful, an AI-powered system must be aware of
the users' goals, so it can help him/her by bringing contextual information from multiple sources, guiding through the series of tasks associated
with the goals. The knowledge structuring is a challenge by itself and it
has been the focus of knowledge engineering research. Once the knowledge is structured or organized, the challenge falls on UX researchers to
investigate users and their tasks and goals with that structured knowledge.
Questions like who the users are, what they want or need to do, in which
preferred ways, and what are users' goals can guide UX research on this
matter. We argue that an AI-powered system could infer the user's goals
by observing his/her interactions with different systems and considering
its knowledge base – about the user, the group(s) s/he is part of, the applications' domains, the overall context, etc. Based on fieldwork executed for
a project where a knowledge-intensive process is analyzed and discussed
with support of an AI-Powered System, we propose the Cognitive Reasoning Interface (CoRgI) framework. This paper presents the fieldwork
observation that led to the development of the framework, how we conceptualize the framework, and our initial validation of the framework.

Keywords: Cognitive systems · AI-powered systems
Cognitive assistant · User experience · Fieldwork

1 Introduction

Cognitive systems are systems built with artificial intelligence (AI) resources
(thus, an AI-powered system) that learn at scale from their interaction with
humans and the environment. These systems evolve naturally from such learning, rather than being explicitly programmed. It allows people to harvest insights

© Springer International Publishing AG, part of Springer Nature 2018
M. Kurosu (Ed.): HCI 2018, LNCS 10902, pp. 398–409, 2018.
https://doi.org/10.1007/978-3-319-91244-8_32

from huge quantities of data to understand complex situations, make accurate predictions about the future, and anticipate the unintended consequences of actions [11,13]. In this approach, humans and computers work more interconnected to achieve unexpected insights.

In order to be useful, a cognitive system must be aware of its users' goals, so it can help him/her by bringing contextual information from multiple sources and guide him/her through the series of tasks associated with those goals. Recognize, structure, and represent user's goals, however, is not an easy or straightforward process. For example, users might need to perform more exploratory tasks, where goals might vary according to interaction results (*e.g.:* visual analytics systems [10]). Moreover, if a user is performing a knowledge-intensive task that requires access, production, and consumption of a large amount of knowledge, his/her goal might be too abstract to structure in a sequence of clear and defined steps. Taking a scientific paper writing process as an example, even if you have a document template to fill up, the content is defined by the combination of several knowledge sources: your previous knowledge, new reference papers that you have just looked up, inputs from discussions with colleagues, and so on.

The knowledge structuring (*i.e.:* creating a knowledge base) is a challenge by itself and it has been the focus of Knowledge Engineering research [22, pp. 33, 104][23]. Once the knowledge is structured, the challenge falls on UX researchers to investigate users and their goals with that structured knowledge. Questions like who the users are, what they want or need to do, in which preferred ways, and what are users' goals can guide UX research on this matter.

We argue that an AI-powered system could infer the user's goals by observing his/her interaction with different applications and considering its knowledge base – about the user, the group(s) s/he is part of, the applications' domains, the overall context, etc. With this information, this cognitive system is also able to support users on achieving those goals, since it has knowledge not only from previous times when that user performed a specific task, but also from multiple other users performing similar tasks. This system may tailor all this knowledge for a given user, creating a personal and unique dynamic with that user. Those abilities differentiate AI-powered systems from expert systems [8] – which focus on a particular domain of knowledge – and recommender systems [16] – which focus on the needs of a user.

With that in mind and focusing on the UX challenges for AI-powered systems, we present the Cognitive Reasoning Interface (CoRgI) framework. CoRgI's development has been guided by fieldwork studies performed on a project where a knowledge-intensive process is analyzed and discussed considering the support of a cognitive system.

We start by discussing previous works that we found related to the development of a cognitive system in Sect. 2. Following, in Sect. 3, we describe our fieldwork and discuss our initial findings on how a cognitive system could support knowledge-intensive tasks. These findings led us to decisions regarding CoRgI's architecture and preliminary user experience design, shown in Sects. 4 and 5 respectively. Section 6 discusses some user studies we plan to conduct to evaluate our solution. We conclude with Sect. 7, presenting some future directions of our work.

2   Related Work

Intelligent agents [22, 30–32] and cognitive assistants [14] have been a trending topic in AI research recently. They are not, however, a new subject on that field [6,7]. Early research in AI revolved around the study of high-level cognition, a feature that separated it from fields like pattern recognition and robotics. Its original research goal was to augment human intellect to address complex problems. However, AI research distanced itself from that goal and focused on a more specific issue – developing algorithms and technologies – without taking into account the context where those algorithms and technologies engaged with humans [12].

A cognitive agent is defined as a software tool that augments human intelligence [6]. Langley [12] says: "(...) intelligence is the capacity to engage in abstract thought that goes beyond immediate perceptions and actions. In humans, this includes the ability to carry out complex, multi-step reasoning, understand the meaning of natural language, design innovative artifacts, generate plans that achieve goals, and even reason about their own reasoning." There is no doubt that AI resources are powerful and innovative, but they need to be part of a bigger scene, part of a human motivated context where those resources can really augment human intelligence. Today's AI resources are fundamental for cognitive systems' infrastructure and development [12].

Intelligent agents have been used to support different tasks, like learning [15,17] and knowledge workers in general [14]. The idea of supporting a knowledge worker brings the context AI needs to get back to its original goal of research – augmenting human intelligence. The knowledge related to that worker will frame the space where the cognitive assistant needs to be aware of and learn from. That knowledge is dynamic, as any knowledge base that humans interact with needs to be.

The big technological companies have presented their assistants to the public (*e.g.*: Microsoft's Cortana[1], Apple's Siri[2], and Google Assistant[3]), even selling products based on such assistants (*e.g.*: Amazon's Alexa[4] and Google Home[5]). But a few glitches have been observed while interacting with those assistants, like adult content been offered to children[6] and unsolicited purchases[7]. Those cases brought up some important and relevant questions about how aware those devices need to be of users and their contexts. A lot has been done to avoid those glitches (*e.g.* user recognition and parental control settings), but that kind of system is becoming more omnipresent and omniscient in our everyday lives,

---

[1] https://www.microsoft.com/en-us/windows/cortana.

[2] https://www.apple.com/ios/siri/.

[3] https://assistant.google.com/.

[4] https://www.amazon.com/Alexa-Skills-Guide/b/ref=sv_a2s_4?ie=UTF8&node=15144553011.

[5] https://support.google.com/googlehome/.

[6] http://www.mirror.co.uk/news/weird-news/parents-panic-amazons-alexa-starts-9540023.

[7] http://fortune.com/2017/01/09/amazon-echo-alexa-dollhouse/.

bringing good and maybe bad impacts. The reality of cognitive assistants on our daily lives could be compared to personal computers made available to everyone in the 70's [1]. Every person in the world is a potential assistant's user, even if the person is not completely aware of it or its implications. Those social implications, however, are a theme for another work.

In this paper, we focus on the UX challenges of this new scenario where people and cognitive assistants (AI-powered systems) are interacting in a symbiotic way, collaborating and learning with each other and about each other [14]. Our research is motivated by a real problem scenario related to a knowledge-intensive process [5]. Those processes are human-centered, depends on people's experience (such as in decision-making scenarios [22]), normally evolve tacit tasks, and do not have a pre-established sequence of activities. Our work here considers the users and the interaction context of that user, the tasks performed, the related domain, and all the knowledge involved on that interaction. Focusing on a knowledge worker scenario, we have more pointers and domain knowledge bases to start the cognitive assistant development [14].

3   Fieldwork

Understanding a knowledge-intensive process requires an efficient and extensive fieldwork. Beyond that, investigating how and where an AI-powered system can be helpful in a knowledge-intensive process adds another layer of complexity on top of understanding the process itself. This work began with several face-to-face activities, precisely designed to comprehend the workflow of the target users and to detect UX improvement and research opportunities. Two researchers were responsible for conducting fieldwork activities and collecting data, that were later shared with the entire UX team working on this research project. The first activities were a series of semi-structured interviews and user observation in their work environment. We primarily focused on understanding their daily routine and all technologies supporting their work practices, including, but not limited to, software applications, auxiliary devices, and workstation configuration. Notes taken during the interviews and observations were classified in two main categories: "Tools" (applications currently being used) and "Work process." We then created clusters in a focused approach, defining additional semantic categories for a better analysis (box 1 and 2 of Fig. 1).

A more structured activity called "case presentation" was conducted to gather a few examples of different projects and possible applications of our future solution. To this end, we created a set of cards designed and organized in several categories. Each card represented a different set of specific domain information that experts use in their everyday work, as well as actions they might take to solve a problem (e.g.: search Google). As such, these cards represented the domain language utilized by experts when making decisions. The participants were then invited to present a scenario from a project in which they were currently working, using the cards to construct a narrative. The cards were placed on a board, creating a visual storyboard that combined data exposed on sticky notes with comments, drawings, and the cards. The interviews and card activities were captured using a tripod and a camera. We also collected videos and photos of the board where the activity was taking place. This information was later analyzed and five important use cases were considered, allowing us to extract decision moments, pain points, and common practices (box 3 of Fig. 1).

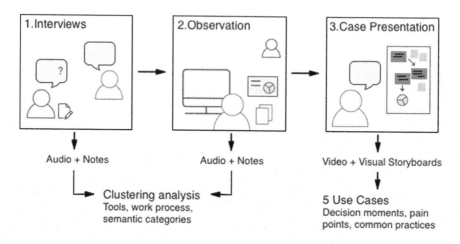

Fig. 1. Fieldwork activities

With all fieldwork data collected and analyzed, we gained a better understanding of user's activities and workflows, identifying opportunities for a cognitive assistant solution. Three main insights were the focus of our UX design:

1. **The importance of the paper notebook (from field observations):** We observed that users in the target context have a very strong connection with paper notebooks (usually small-sized), where they write meeting notes, to-do lists, hypothesis, and literature data. The paper notebooks support their everyday routine, revealing itself as an important instrument of their knowledge-intensive activities.
2. **The impact of exploring and reviewing the rationale behind each decision (from interviews):** Decision points were perceived as core moments that require strong grounded justification. Usually, users face strategic meetings and have to present their reasoning to stakeholders with diverse background. Thus, there is a clear need for reviewing and understanding the trail that led to each conclusion and decision.
3. **The complex and diverse search path to answering contextual questions (from card activity):** Answering contextual questions may not have a straightforward process in knowledge intensive practices. Cases described at the card activity shown that users frequently strive to discover the right source and even the right procedure to understand complex contextual questions.

In following design sessions, we devised a solution that included an annotation tool. We believe this could complement their paper notebooks, whilst allowing better semantic connections and quick information retrieval. Also, it included a history feature that aims to enable the user to articulate their rationale while making decisions, keeping track of the interaction events and the insights associated at each point. The approach for (3) is the dialog interface, where the user can use natural language to ask complex questions to the cognitive advisor, as an easy-to-access touchpoint.

4 CoRgI

From what we learned with fieldwork observation and data, we discussed and designed a technical solution for a cognitive assistant that aims to support knowledge-intensive and context-aware activities: Cognitive Reasoning Interface (CoRgI). It is a framework (seen in Fig. 2) comprised of three main components: advisor, brain, and cogs. The **advisor** acts as a hub where the applications can register interaction events and the user can interact with the cognitive system (as will be detailed in Sect. 5). The user may interact with different systems (*e.g:* use two different computers for the same goal), however, only a single advisor exists in each system.

The advisor in itself is just a front-end to the **brain** hosted in the cloud. The brain is responsible for storing information in the associate knowledge base regarding user preferences and events. The same brain may be connected to different advisors. Therefore, when the user is interacting with multiple systems, each advisor is connected to the same brain, creating a seamless integrated experience.

Symmetrically, the brain also acts as a hub, to which many **cogs** subscribe. Each cog is responsible for a single logic and, collectively, they are the "brain's intelligence." They subscribe to application-specific interaction events and provide insights considering the user's current context, the user's preferences, the application-specific databases, and the knowledge base.

Back to the example of writing a scientific paper, imagine that CoRgI is observing the user writing a survey paper for the 2018 edition of HCI International (HCII). With that input, the advisor could bring an insight about survey papers accepted on previous years at HCII, providing a *navigational link* to the 10 most recent ones. As an *actionable invitation*, the advisor could invite the user to see those papers similarities regarding their structure (*e.g:* half of the papers have a section with a comparative table which is explained along the paper text, while the other half just presents the survey topics, without comparison). Finally, for the *reasoning*, the advisor could show the perks of understanding what a survey is, presenting hints and insights related to the subject of the user survey and common survey structures in that given conference. Providing this visualization, CoRgI could help the user to improve his/her research agenda and writing strategies, adapting the content and style to the current target conference.

Inspired by Semiotic Engineering - an HCI theory that views human-computer interaction as a form of human communication between designers and

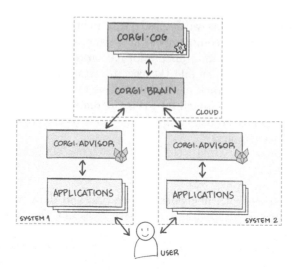

Fig. 2. CoRgI advisor basic architecture

users mediated by a computer system - we consider that the user's semiosis (*i.e.*: the process of sign interpretation that leads to the continuous production of meaning) while interacting with a computer system occurs in different abstraction levels [4]. It begins with the **strategic** level, in which the user establishes his/her goals. It is followed by the **tactical** level, when the user devises plans to achieve the goals considering the possibilities available in the system. Finally, at the **operational** level, the user performs a series of actions (operations) that are needed to execute his/her plans and, ultimately, achieve his/her goals.

Thus, the logging of interaction events should follow these three abstraction levels [9]. The **operational log level** deals with the low-level sequence of operations, typically local interactions (*e.g.*: user typed text "security incident"/user clicked in button "save"). These logs usually are domain-independent and can be extracted automatically, possibly using some sort of meta-data to increase its meaningfulness. The **tactical log level** adds a signification layer to the logged data, adding meaning spread over longer interactive paths (*i.e.*: considering many operational events). These logs are domain-dependant and specific to the system (*e.g.*: user saved new report containing message "security incident"). The system's designer can express this log level, since it is related to the features made available by the system (therefore planned by the designer) and closely related to its domain. Lastly, the **strategic log level** is related to a broader context of the user's plans. It adds even more signification to log data, relating to longer interactive paths and presenting knowledge about who the users are, what they want or need to do, how, and why [3] (*e.g.*: manager John reported security incident). The strategic level is closely related to the user's goal and can involve multiple systems, or even previous knowledge from the user. Therefore, it exists only in the user's mental model.

Only with the knowledge of the strategical level we can help users with insights that are contextualized and meaningful. The challenge of CoRgI is to infer the strategic level from the tactical and operational available data. To obtain the tactical log level, we rely on designers instrumenting their systems and providing the correct contextual information. Although the systems' instrumentation is not ideal, this was a conscious choice for the time being so we can focus on the other challenges, such as conceptualize the user experience of a cognitive advisor (as we discuss in the next section) and develop the intelligence behind the advisor.

5   CoRgI's Advisor Features

As previously mentioned, the advisor is the main interface for CoRgI. In the next sections we will go through some of the planned features of the advisor.

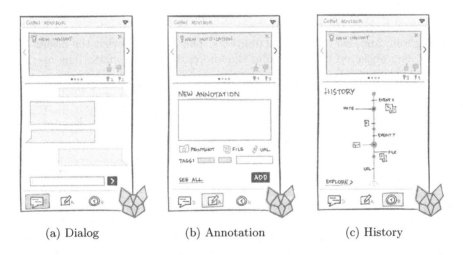

(a) Dialog   (b) Annotation   (c) History

Fig. 3. CoRgI advisor main features.

5.1   Dialog

Besides passive observation of interaction events, we plan to provide a dialog interface (shown in Fig. 3a) so the user can interact with the cogs using natural language. This feature may act as a shortcut and easy to access interface for the knowledge base. It will allow a rapid touchpoint between the user and the cognitive system, reinforcing interaction aspects. As similar assistants[8] we plan to offer besides text input, speech-to-text and text-to-speech functionalities.

---

[8] Google's Assistant, Microsoft's Cortana, Amazon's Alexa, Apple's Siri, and so on.

5.2 Annotations

Annotations (Fig. 3b) allow the user to create notes related to the current context. The user may add text, images, links, documents, and tags to an annotation. All the content of the annotation is then understood by the framework (using text/visual extraction/recognition techniques), associating concepts from the underlying knowledge base to the annotation. The annotation is then added to the knowledge base and may be considered in future insights.

Besides allowing the creation of new annotations, the advisor also allows the visualization of previously stored annotations associated with the current context. The advisor also offers a link to a separate environment to explore all the annotations, providing new ways to explore the annotations knowledge base. For example, the user could navigate through the knowledge base concept graph in order to search for annotations.

5.3 Events History

The events' history (shown in Fig. 3c) allows the user to check what CoRgI is learning from him/her and its contributions. The user can revisit the interaction events being observed by CoRgI and the annotations (s)he made. The user can also verify the insights and notifications triggered by CoRgI.

Inside the advisor, only a recent history will be shown along with a link to an external environment to explore the complete history. Inspired by previous research [19,20], in this visualization, we plan to highlight which interaction events were related to the insights and notifications.

5.4 Insights

Insights are the advisor's main feature and, as such, occupies a prominent space in the proposed UI (colored rectangles in the top of Figs. 3a and c). They appear according to the user's interaction, contextualized to the actions being performed. They are, therefore, dynamic, changing constantly to accompany the user's actions.

Each insight will have a feedback system, so the user can inform if the insight was useful or not. The user's feedback will be used to improve recommendation, personalizing the insights for the user, and improving the underlying knowledge base.

Each insight may also provide additional interaction rather than only the insight's conclusion. It may contain a *navigational link*, so the user can explore related information, even from other systems (*e.g.*: suggesting to read an academic paper from an external website). It may also contain an *actionable invitation*, inviting users to start a new interaction path related to the previous one (*e.g.*: asking if the user wants to notify co-authors when s/he finishes writing a paper).

Last, but not least, the insight may explicit its *reasoning*, explaining to users which interaction events and information were used to get to that insight. Exposing the rationale behind the insight will open the path to a new degree of feedback, since the user may provide input for each computational step, not only the final conclusion. This would also allow the user to "tweak" and personalize the cogs.

5.5   Notifications

Notifications share the same UI space as insights (as in Fig. 3b) and may share interaction patterns (feedback system, navigational links, actionable invitations). A major difference, although, set them apart: their temporal nature. While insights are dynamic, changing constantly due to the user interacting with systems, notifications are static – once they appear, only the user may dismiss them.

They should be used to alert users, usually due to some long-term processing. For example, consider a web application in which the user may run scientific algorithms that take some time to complete. The application may use the CoRgI framework to notify the user when the algorithm is complete, instead of relying on page-based or browser-based notifications, that depends on the web page being open on the browser.

6   Initial Validation

We are currently conducting a series of studies to investigate the usability and effectiveness of the designed solution. The same project that provided the field-work that guided CoRgI's development was an opportunity to validate our initial ideas. To help turn the idea more concrete and better communicate with users and stakeholders as well, we sketched several user interfaces (see examples on Fig. 3). Based on these drawings, we created a storyboard, illustrating the use of the envisioned system based on a real use-case presented by users, using the advisor to empower a knowledge-intense process. The storyboard was the foundation of a sketch based video that connected different features of the cognitive system through a consistent storyline. The video was shared with potential users with the intention of collecting feedback and validating the main concept of the designed system. Discussions with the clients and also the development team were rich and insightful for the UX team. The video worked very well as a material to reflect on the knowledge-intense tasks related to the client's domain [18] and also to experiment and discuss UX ideas of design interfaces and interaction flows. The positive feedback encouraged us to continue the design and development of the tool and to plan further testing activities (*e.g.* usability and communicability studies).

7 Discussion and Future Work

The fieldwork described in this paper allowed us to propose and discuss CoRgI. Evaluating it in a real context is essential for constructing a user-centered and context-aware cognitive solution, iterating the development considering the users' feedback. We still have the opportunity to execute other fieldwork studies with the same users, which will allow us to evolve our investigation around CoRgI and the related UX design.

As future usability studies, we plan to apply paper prototyping technique for rapidly testing design versions of the interface and simulating user interactions. Representative users will be asked to perform specific tasks using hand-drawn screens. One of us will facilitate the activity, manipulating the pages and playing the role of the computer, while the others observe and take notes. This low-fidelity prototype will be very useful for refining interaction issues and improving CoRgI's user experience [21].

We also envision to apply the Wizard of Oz methodology [2] in order to test and explore a more detailed user journey. In this technique, a human simulates the advisor's intelligence, reproducing an experience very similar to the one we are developing. It will help us evaluate and analyze interaction issues and also gather possible inputs for the dialog interface, facilitating the implementation of a more focused and context adapted natural language processing algorithm.

References

1. Carroll, J.M.: Human computer interaction-brief intro. The Encyclopedia of Human-Computer Interaction, 2nd edn. (2013)
2. Dahlbäck, N., Jönsson, A., Ahrenberg, L.: Wizard of oz studies: why and how. In: Proceedings of the 1st international conference on Intelligent User Interfaces, pp. 193–200. ACM (1993)
3. De Souza, C., Leitão, C.: Semiotic Engineering Methods for Scientific Research in HCI. Synthesis Lectures on Human-Centered Informatics. Morgan & Claypool, San Rafael (2009)
4. deSouza, C.S.: The Semiotic Engineering of Human-Computer Interaction (2005)
5. Di Ciccio, C., Marrella, A., Russo, A.: Knowledge-intensive processes: characteristics, requirements and analysis of contemporary approaches. J. Data Semant. 4(1), 29–57 (2015). https://doi.org/10.1007/s13740-014-0038-4
6. Engelbart, D.: A conceptual framework for augmenting human intellect [summary report, contract af49 (638)-1024]. SRI International, Menlo Park (1962)
7. Engelbart, D.C.: Toward augmenting the human intellect and boosting our collective IQ. Commun. ACM 38(8), 30–32 (1995)
8. Hildebrandt, T.T., Cattani, G.L.: Expert system. In: Jensen, K.B., Rothenbuhler, E.W., Pooley, J.D., Craig, R.T. (eds.) The International Encyclopedia of Communication Theory and Philosophy, pp. 1–4. Wiley, Hoboken, October 2016. https://doi.org/10.1002/9781118766804.wbiect244
9. Jansen Ferreira, J., Segura, V., Fucs, A., de Paula, R., Cerqueira, R.F.G.: Abstraction levels as support for UX design of user's interaction logs. In: Antona, M., Stephanidis, C. (eds.) UAHCI 2017. LNCS, vol. 10277, pp. 369–382. Springer, Cham (2017). https://doi.org/10.1007/978-3-319-58706-6_30

10. Keim, D.A., Mansmann, F., Oelke, D., Ziegler, H.: Visual analytics: combining automated discovery with interactive visualizations. In: Jean-Fran, J.-F., Berthold, M.R., Horváth, T. (eds.) DS 2008. LNCS (LNAI), vol. 5255, pp. 2–14. Springer, Heidelberg (2008). https://doi.org/10.1007/978-3-540-88411-8_2
11. Kelly III, J., Hamm, S.: Smart Machines: IBM's Watson and the Era of Cognitive Computing. Columbia University Press, New York (2013)
12. Langley, P.: The cognitive systems paradigm. Adv. Cognit. Syst. **1**, 3–13 (2012)
13. Moreno, M.F., Brandao, R., Cerqueira, R.: Challenges on multimedia for decision-making in the era of cognitive computing, San Jose, CA, USA (2016)
14. Nezhad, H.R.M.: Cognitive assistance at work. In: 2015 AAAI Fall Symposium Series (2015)
15. Reategui, E., Zattera, C.: Do learning styles influence the way students perceive interface agents? In: Proceedings of the VIII Brazilian Symposium on Human Factors in Computing Systems, IHC 2008, pp. 108–116. Sociedade Brasileira de Computação, Porto Alegre, Brazil (2008). http://dl.acm.org/citation.cfm?id=1497470.1497483
16. Ricci, F., Rokach, L., Shapira, B.: Introduction to Recommender Systems Handbook. In: Ricci, F., Rokach, L., Shapira, B., Kantor, P.B. (eds.) Recommender Systems Handbook, pp. 1–35. Springer, Boston (2011). https://doi.org/10.1007/978-0-387-85820-3_1
17. Schiaffino, S., Amandi, A., Gasparini, I., Pimenta, M.S.: Personalization in e-learning: the adaptive system vs. the intelligent agent approaches. In: Proceedings of the VIII Brazilian Symposium on Human Factors in Computing Systems, IHC 2008, pp. 186–195. Sociedade Brasileira de Computação, Porto Alegre, Brazil, Brazil (2008). http://dl.acm.org/citation.cfm?id=1497470.1497491
18. Schön, D., Bennett, J.: Reflective conversation with materials. In: Bringing Design to Software, pp. 171–189. ACM (1996)
19. Segura, V., Ferreira, J.J., Cerqueira, R., Barbosa, S.: Uma avaliação analítica de um sistema de visualização do histórico de interação do usuário usando CDN e PoN. In: Proceedings of the 15th Brazilian Symposium on Human Factors in Computing Systems (IHC 2016). Brazilian Computer Society, Porto Alegre (2016)
20. Segura, V.C.V.B., Barbosa, S.D.J.: History viewer: displaying user interaction history in visual analytics applications. In: Kurosu, M. (ed.) HCI 2016. LNCS, vol. 9733, pp. 223–233. Springer, Cham (2016). https://doi.org/10.1007/978-3-319-39513-5_21
21. Snyder, C.: Paper Prototyping: The Fast and Easy Way to Design and Refine User Interfaces. Morgan Kaufmann, San Francisco (2003)
22. Tecuci, G., Marcu, D., Boicu, M., Schum, D.A.: Knowledge Engineering: Building Cognitive Assistants for Evidence-Based Reasoning. Cambridge University Press, Cambridge (2016)
23. W3C: Semantic Web - W3c (2017). https://www.w3.org/standards/semanticweb/. Accessed 11 January 2017

Difficulties Implementing Big Data:
A Big Data Implementation Study

Kyle Spraker[✉]

Florida Gulf Coast University, Fort Myers, USA
krs.spraker@gmail.com

Abstract. The exponential increase in the volume of data, the velocity at which they are created and their vast and progressively expanding varieties can be derived from virtually all aspects of our everyday lives. This situation prompts the need for urgent change in the way data are stored, received, and analyzed. Today, organizations under appreciate the changes, growth and strategic development their Big Data are capable of providing. Organizations also overestimate their own ability to access and interrupt their data in order to derive benefit from it. Big Data problems in organizations have historically been approached with an isolated outlook, rather than viewing issues as co-dependent parts of one another. The purpose of this research is to identify and summarize the general challenges faced by an organizations ability to adequately utilize and capitalize on the opportunities presented by its Big Data. Through the research methods of data collection and multiple case study analysis, this paper proposes a three-step framework model, which focuses on definition, organization and value creation. The proposed framework serves to mitigate Big Data implementation challenges and their involved issues faced by an organization.

Keywords: Big data · Implementation · Difficulties

1 Introduction

Research from the International Data Corporation [1] shows that 1.8 ZB of data were created and replicated in 2011, and estimates that the figures will multiply 50 times by the year 2020. Currently, around 90% of the world's existing digital data were created over the past 2 years [2]. This exuberant amount of available data is widely referred to as "Big Data". The concepts and ideologies that support Big Data are rapidly evolving. The most frequently adopted definition of big data is one suggested from the 2001 research of Douglas Laney, in which he states that Big Data is based on its characteristics or the rule of 4 V: volume, variety, velocity, and value. However, more recent research suggests that veracity and visualization are also important characteristics when defining Big Data [3, 4].

Developing dimensions for what define big data is challenging due to the many existing definitions and lack of agreement as to what constitutes big data and how to recognize it [5]. Research that surveyed 400 companies from around the world identified that 77% of the companies surveyed did not have a clear vision or strategy for their enterprise Big data processes. Thus, organizations of all kinds are striving to build up their Big Data capabilities, leverage their data competitively and hurdle the inevitable challenges that Big Data presents [6].

Developments and investigations in Big Data have proven that organizations aren't ready to embrace and leverage big data to improve their organization's performance [3]. A number of new organizational challenges and barriers arise such as developing new employee skills, upgrading IT infrastructure and instating new management practices within an organization [3].

The article presents a focused overview of the characteristics that make up Big Data, their challenges and shared difficulties of implementations and compares them against existing research. The study proposes an enterprise framework as a holistic approach to overcoming the organizational challenges of Big Data.

2 Literature Review

2.1 Difficulties Implementing Big Data

Whether it's a government protecting its citizens, a cell phone sending a tweet, an airline offering a sale, or a farmer harvesting his crops mass amounts of data are being created and collected every second. The ability to use data in order to execute decisions as intended, to make a decision faster and to create competitive advantage, play a large role across many different types of organizations. An increasing reliance on technology, the growth of the global marketplace and an overabundance of data have increased the need for business units of all types to recognize, understand and deal with the challenges of interpreting and deriving value from mass quantities of data. The following review of literature confirms that big data collection and analysis present problems that go well beyond mass volume and variety of data, this review discusses specific and general solutions and concludes that enterprise-wide initiatives and a holistic view on big data are needed for gripping the challenges and difficulties that the implementation of big data present.

2.2 Identifying Potential Benefits

New technology and innovation in fields like big data are creating new and exciting application possibilities that have the potential to benefit many different industries. For example, the case study analysis research conducted by Huang [7] identifies multiple problems that big data can solve for health sciences. For example, healthcare recommendation systems, sensor-based health condition and food safety monitoring and internet-based epidemic surveillance [7]. Additionally, research performed by Wang [8] through a quantitative approach of multiple case analysis identified 179 potential benefits that big data analytics can derive for healthcare organizations. Most notably the immediate access to analyze clinical data and the ability to improve cross-functional communication and collaboration among administrative staffs [8]. The highly technical healthcare industry is not the only beneficiary of big data. Kamilaris's [9] research offers insights into big data opportunities and challenges in the agricultural field. The research was conducted via a bibliographic analysis beginning with 1330 papers and then narrowed down to 34 that were considered. Kamilaris's [9] research open by describing exciting potential areas of application for big data in the agricultural industry. A few of these applications being, remote sensing of land and crop mapping, self-operating agricultural robots and tools that help better predict harvest yields.

2.3 Defining the Problem

There are many potential benefits that can be derived from big data for all different types of industries, but prospective benefits don't come without their challenges. Kamilaris's [9] research goes on to suggest some of the current technical issues that the agricultural industry struggles with relating to big data, such as sensing systems that collect and deliver images in a timely manner, data accuracy, and other common issues like data reliability and variety of data. However, developing dimensions for what defines big data and data analytics are challenging due to the many existing definitions and lack of agreement as to what constitutes big data and how to recognize it [5]. Researched by Isitor and Stanier [5] through case study analysis they have identified big data in terms of data characteristics or the 3 V's which are velocity, variety, and volume. The speed at which data is received or processed, the format or structure in which the data is received and lastly, the mass volume of data that is received [5].

Each of the defining characteristics of big data come with their own unique challenges and implementation difficulties. For example, Friedberg [10] used surveys and voluntary data collection on health practices both large and small regarding their data which is required to participate in alternative payment models. The authors [10] reported that the data they received from external sources were not timely enough, therefore, limiting their usefulness towards the purpose of improving payment model performance. The authors [10] also found that performance data relating to one payer was continually begin corrected and coming in late, making hard for the operation to gauge its own performance and make corrections in a timely manner.

Products like cloud computing have paved the way for faster infrastructure set up and decreased pitfalls such as data delays [11]. However, cloud computing has also left security and privacy of user information in business-critical applications vulnerable [11]. Rastogi's [11] case study analysis research suggests that there are security and privacy concerns when the exchange of information occurs between a cloud server and a user. Unfortunately, the challenges don't end at the security and privacy of the data being collected. Porche [12] examined case studies and records to get a sense of the overwhelming amount of data being generated by the U.S. Navy. The Intelligence Science Board [13] said that the number of images and signal intercepts are far beyond the manpower and capacity available to the Navy. Huge backlogs for translators and image interpreters have amassed and most of what is collected has never been reviewed. The authors [12] present their view on big data as a data set so large that it passes the limits of traditional relational databases along the four parameters of volume, variety, velocity, and veracity. The authors [12] found that all of the information that the Navy collects is considered potentially useful, but processing and deriving value from the vast datasets is beyond the analytical capability of the Navy's human resources. As the Navy acquires new equipment and technology evolves the amount of data will only grow and so will the difficulty to process it [12].

Additional research into understanding the implementation challenges of big data in the search of a solution was done by Jin [3] through case study analysis of 21 different research studies present the grand challenges of big data. Jin [3] described that the traditional features of big data can be characterized by volume, velocity, variety, veracity, and value. However, other research conducted by Chen and Zhang [4] suggests that variability and visualization should be included in the characterization list as well. From research conducted by Huang [7], it is suggested that the best way to intuitively obtain meaning from data is through a graphical presentation, also known as "visualization." Ultimately, out of all of these characteristics presented, the main challenges of big data are suggested to be variety, velocity and veracity [3]. The authors [3] conclude by suggesting that the solution to solving these major big data challenges lie within an integrated data solution, rather than isolated successes of a few aspects of big data.

2.4   Finding Solutions

Ribarsky [14] conducted research about how value can be derived from the analysis of unstructured data, in this case, social media data, primarily focused on streaming Twitter data. The authors [14] collected a 1% random sample of these data for 1.75 years (approx. 20B Tweets). The authors [14] found that providing meaning and organization to unstructured data, with various technologies and naming strategies offers the ability to analyze competitor strategies and knowledge about the demographics of people that are generating messages during certain events. Another example of deriving value comes from a [15] study of sales data provided by a pharmaceutical distribution company. Other research methods included exploratory analysis, graph-based analysis, data sampling for model fitting and testing, model building or sales prediction and model evaluation. The authors [15] offered a suggested method for modeling and forecasting sales and how to control inventory levels in order to prevent costs of excessive inventory and to prevent losing customers due to a drug shortage.

Not all companies have answers to the hard-hitting questions of big data, Wang [8] points out research by Wegener and Sinha [16] who conducted a survey of 400 companies from around the world and found that 77% of companies surveyed did not have clear strategies for effectively utilizing their big data. Wegener and Sinha [16] also suggest that research is needed to formulate appropriate strategies that will enable organizations to leverage big data analytics efficiently and effectively. Additionally, Alharthi's [17] research through case study analysis and corporate benchmarks suggests that there are three main types of barriers to big data, which are, technological, human, and organizational. Under the barrier of organization, Alharthi [17] suggests that cultural barriers within an organization have a major impact on an organizations strategy, structure, and processes when it comes to their big data. In order to overcome these organizational barriers to big data, the authors [17] suggest that documenting, implementing and communicating a clear organizational vision in relation to big data is a step towards improving organizational performance.

2.5   Growing Smarter Before Data Grows Larger

The global marketplace will only continue to grow larger and data complexity and volume will grow alongside it. Research on difficulties in implementing big data are only just beginning to blossom and have much room to grow. In light of the adolescences of the topic, the literature review defines several issues involved in the characteristics of volume, velocity, variety, veracity, visualization, and value, which make up big data and states a few proposed solutions such as, defining a clear vision and strategy for big data. However, further research and innovation are going to be the fundamental factors in determining how companies and organizations choose to plan for and handle their big data operations.

3   Research Methodology

To reach the goals of this study we analyzed previous literature to gain a fundamental understanding of Big Data challenges and potential benefits.

3.1   Case Collection

Cases were collected from past Big Data research papers, articles, and reports from companies. Beginning with a keyword search from the scientific databases Science-Direct, ABI/Inform Collection, Academic Search Complete, ACM Digital Library and JSTOR (Ebsco). The following keywords were used in order to query the previously mentioned databases:

"Big Data" AND ["Enterprise" OR "Challenges" OR "Benefits" OR "Definition" OR "Opportunities" OR "Framework"]

Out of the large variety of Big Data research available, we initially identified 61 papers that were fitting to the research. Papers were then refined based on the case's presentation of Big Data implantation and categorized based on industry. The initial 61 papers were refined down to 32 that specifically met the themes and topics required for the study.

3.2   Research Approach and Process

A content analysis was then conducted on the reviewed research in order to extract topics and themes and understand the research on a more refined level. The process consisted of breaking down articles into relevant themes, organizing those themes based on their nature (problem, solution, challenges, and insight) and finally reporting on the research in a meaningful manner.

Themes were identified from the analysis in a structure that moved from potential benefits to challenges and difficulties and finally to potential solutions.

4   Proposed Framework

4.1   Research Themes

Three distinctive themes emerged from this study. One theme is that any contribution to Big Data analysis in an organization, mostly fall completely on an individual data analysis department. The second theme being that Big Data issues are being examined and researched as isolated challenges, rather than being examined as co-dependent events of the other Big Data characteristics. The last theme identified in this research is the lack of organizational structure and strategy in regards to Big Data.

Theme 1. One of the major barriers to successfully implementing and utilizing Big Data in an organization has to do with that organization's culture, specifically towards Big Data [17]. Alharthi [17] suggests that documenting and communicating a clear organizational vision in relation to Big Data is one of the methods in which to lift organizational barriers around Big Data. Successful Big Data operations require cross-functional communication and collaboration [8].

Theme 2. Developing dimensions that make up and define big data are challenging due to the many existing definitions and lack of agreeance on which is correct [5]. Big Data solutions lie within integrated solutions, rather than the isolated success of a few aspects of Big Data [3].

Theme 3. Organizing a controlled effort for implementation and utilization of Big Data methodologies can be difficult without a formal plan or order of operations. During a survey of 400 companies, 77% of companies self-reported that they did not have strategies for utilizing their Big Data effectively [8].

4.2   Open Issues in Implementing Big Data

Big Data is still largely an emerging field of study, therefore many risks and challenges still exist and have yet to be researched. However, from the literature review, we found a few of the outstanding problem areas in Big Data:

- Value creation
- Security and privacy
- Data format variety
- Organizational, technological and human barriers
- Clear vision and Big Data strategy [3, 11, 12, 17].

4.3   Enterprise Big Data Framework

According to prior studies, the following actions were typically done by organizations who were implementing Big Data:

- Relying solely on a Big Data team for all input, organization, and contribution to the organizations Big Data efforts. As opposed to a holistic organizational approach in which each business unit has some contribution, increasing the organizational overall chances of success with Big Data [17].
- Organizations are viewing big data issues as isolated events rather than viewing them as co-dependent challenges, which require an integrated solution [3].
- Large percentages of organizations have a lack of strategy and organizational structure when it comes to Big Data. The ability to express a clear vision of the organizations Big Data strategy can greatly improve its chances of success [8].

In light of these identified issues from the reviewed literature, we propose a framework which consists of three sections to consider when implementing Big Data processes in an organization, which are definition, organization and value creation (Table 1).

Table 1. Themes for Big Data implementation

Definition	Define the organizations Big Data vision • Vision: Define what the different characteristics of Big Data mean to your organization: • Volume • Velocity • Variety • Veracity
Organization	Identify a dedicated data owner for each business unit: • Sales: • Marketing: • Technology: • Engineering: • Human Resources: Establish single data sources to avoid overlapping/redundant data. Establish data standards: • Format • Timeliness/Time of delivery • Data Types • Data change procedures
Value creation	The last step is to interrupt and utilize your data to create value. • Visualization: • Implementation:

5   Conclusion

It is no secret that Big Data has become an aspect of everyday life and is gradually becoming more and more important in most business functions. Systems, data, and collection methods are becoming more complex and collecting more data than ever before. The IDC [1] reported that 1.8 ZB of data were created in 2011 and is expected to be 50 times that by the year 2020. As a result, Big Data opportunities and challenges are changing and expanding every single day. New technology will be needed to handle larger, more complex data, new organizational structures will be needed in order to develop company cultures conducive to a Big Data mindset, and new talent will be needed in order to keep up with the growing demand for data professionals [8, 17].

Successfully hurdling the challenges of implementing Big Data requires, not only technical abilities but structural and organizational abilities as well. The conclusion drawn from discussion and literature reviews suggests that Big Data developments are only as strong as the foundation and organization they're built on. In addition, multiple outstanding issues for future research have been identified and discussed. Finally, the challenges of Big Data implementation should be faced with a holistic ideology and framework, rather than a modular outlook that focuses on the isolated limitations to Big Data.

References

1. IDC. 2011 Digital universe study: extracting value from chaos (2011). http://www.emc.com/collateral/analyst-reports/idc-extracting-value-from-chaos-ar.pdf
2. Gobble, M.: Big Data: the next big thing in innovation. Res.-Technol. Manage. **56**(1), 64–67 (2013)
3. Jin, X., Wah, B., Cheng, X., Wang, Y.: Significance and challenges of big data research. Big Data Res. **2**(2), 59–64 (2015)
4. Philip Chen, C., Zhang, C.: Data-intensive applications, challenges, techniques and technologies: a survey on Big Data. Inf. Sci. **275**, 314–347 (2014)
5. Isitor, E., Stanier, C.: Defining Big Data (2016)
6. IDC: New IDC forecast sees worldwide big data technology and services market growing to $48.6 billion in 2019, driven by wide adoption across industries [Press Release] (2016). http://www.idc.com/getdoc.jsp?containerId=prUS40560115
7. Huang, T., Lan, L., Fang, X., An, P., Min, J., Wang, F.: Promises and challenges of big data computing in health sciences. Big Data Res. **2**(1), 2–11 (2015)
8. Wang, Y., Kung, L., Byrd, T.: Big data analytics: Understanding its capabilities and potential benefits for healthcare organizations. Technol. Forecast. Soc. Chang. **126**, 3–13 (2017)
9. Kamilaris, A., Kartakoullis, A., Prenafcta-Boldú, F.: A review on the practice of big data analysis in agriculture. Comput. Electron. Agric. **143**, 23–37 (2017)
10. Friedberg, M., Chen, P., White, C., Jung, O., Raaen, L., Hirshman, S., Lipinski, L.: Increased importance of data and data analysis. In: Effects of Health Care Payment Models on Physician Practice in the United States, pp. 53–62 (2015)
11. Rastogi, N., Gloria, M., Hendler, J.: Security and privacy of performing data analytics in the cloud: a three-way handshake of technology, policy, and management. J. Inf. Policy **5**, 129–154 (2015)
12. Porche, I., Wilson, B., Johnson, E., Tierney, S., Saltzman, E.: Big data: challenges and opportunities. In: Data Flood: Helping the Navy Address the Rising Tide of Sensor Information, pp. 1–6 (2014)

13. Intelligence Science Board, Integrating Sensor-Collected Intelligence. Office of the Under Secretary of Defense for Acquisition, Technology, and Logistics, Washington, D.C., November 2008
14. Ribarsky, W., Xiaoyu Wang, D., Dou, W.: Social media analytics for competitive advantage. Comput. Graph. **38**, 328–331 (2014)
15. Zadeh, N.K., Sepehri, M.M., Farvaresh, H.: Intelligent sales prediction for pharmaceutical distribution companies: a data mining based approach. Math. Prob. Eng., 1–15 (2014)
16. Wegener, R., Sinha, V.: The value of big data: how analytics differentiates winners
17. Alharthi, A., Krotov, V., Bowman, M.: Addressing barriers to big data. Bus. Horiz. **60**(3), 285–292 (2017). Bain and Company (2013)

Mobility as a Service (MaaS) Based on Intermodal Electronic Platforms in Public Transport

Ulrike Stopka[(⊠)], René Pessier, and Christian Günther

Technische Universität Dresden, Dresden, Germany
ulrike.stopka@tu-dresden.de

Abstract. Driven by megatrends such as globalization, urbanization, climate change and technological progress, the mobility sector is undergoing a strong process of change which is characterized in particular by the intermodal cross-linking of various public and private mobility services. The aim is to make transport as a whole more environmentally friendly. To meet this challenge "Mobility as a Service" (MaaS) concepts are introduced in the market which offer individualized one-stop access to several bundled travel services based on customer's needs. The supply of so-called mobility packages requires very close cooperation between the various players on the transport market who use electronic platforms for this purpose. First of all, the paper gives an overview about the research activities and the implementation status of MaaS concepts in different countries. In the following chapters, the general approach and methods for the development of mobility packages are discussed and first results of related research projects in Germany are presented.

Keywords: Urban mobility · Mobility as a Service · Intermodal transport
Mobility platform · Mobility packages · User requirements
Van Westendorp analysis · Conjoint analysis

1 Introduction

Mobility behavior in Germany is currently undergoing rapid changes. Especially in urban areas, people choose the means of transport much more pragmatically and flexibly then years before. As a result of the advancing technological development and the increasing demand of customers, more and more providers are entering the market and complete the network around public transport with a wide variety of mobility services such as car sharing, bike sharing, ride selling, ride pooling, rental cars, shuttle services, intermodal routing and ticketing apps and so on. This comprehensive approach to integrate the different forms of mobility and bundling various private and public transport services on an electronic platform is known as Mobility as a Service (MaaS). The core idea of MaaS is to offer individualized product packages for the integrated use of mobility services consistent with the current needs of the users.

First of all, the article considers the definition and general concept of MaaS and gives a short overview of the implementation status of such offers in different countries. After this, the scientific approach and first empirical research results from two research

© Springer International Publishing AG, part of Springer Nature 2018
M. Kurosu (Ed.): HCI 2018, LNCS 10902, pp. 419–439, 2018.
https://doi.org/10.1007/978-3-319-91244-8_34

projects are presented. Within the research projects "INTER-mobil" and "Regional Cooperation and Mobility Platform", both funded by the Federal Ministry of Transport and Digital Infrastructure, the prototypical provision of MaaS in Leipzig and in the area of the Rhine-Main Transport Association is investigated and tested in the period 2017/2018. In both projects, the Technical University of Dresden is responsible for the analysis of user requirements, the conceptual development of the intermodal product bundles (mobility packages) and during the implementation phase for the evaluation of usability, user experience and customer acceptance.

2   Definition and Concept of "Mobility as a Service" (MaaS)

Both the term and the concept "Mobility as a Service" are still quite new, but are becoming increasingly important. Therefore, the MaaS Alliance, formed by various companies, research institutions and state authorities, was founded during the ITS World Congress in 2015.

Until today, there has not been a common definition of the term "Mobility as a Service" (MaaS) in the literature. Many different opinions exist concerning the services which fall within the scope of MaaS and the extent of the integrated modes of transport.

For example, the transport service provider Uber itself is sometimes referred to as Mobility as a Service [1, p. 20]. Taken MaaS literally, this is certainly true, but it does not go far enough for the original idea of MaaS as a business model and mobility platform. According to this, MaaS is intended to bridge the gap between private and public transport, i.e. to link public transport with different sharing and hailing services, taxis as well as rental cars and integrate them in an organized way for the user [2, p. 2]. This understanding is also called "Combined Mobility Service" [1, p. 7].

Kamargianni et al. [3, p. 3294] underline "MaaS stands for buying mobility services based on consumer needs instead of buying the means of mobility".

In a paper from RailNewcastle 2016 [4], MaaS is defined as "a shift away from personally owned modes of transport and towards mobility solutions that are consumed as a service. This is enabled by combining transport services from public and private transport providers through a unified gateway that creates and manages the trip which users can pay for with a single account. Users can pay per trip or a monthly fee for a limited distance".

For this paper, the understanding of the term MaaS is the following: the customer makes a contract with a MaaS operator, also called "transport broker service", who then offers him or her different transport services bundled in a mobility package with a special price structure and makes them accessible via a single smartphone app. The requested transport service itself is provided by various transport companies. Billing and the communication with the customer are handled solely by the MaaS operator. The billing between the MaaS operator and the actual carrier or mobility service provider takes place in the background which is very convenient for the customer. This approach also enables a user-friendly roaming between various mobility service providers. The customer has access to an extensive mobility system from a single source. The mobility package includes quotas for public transport as well as car, bike, scooter and ride sharing, rental cars and taxis. The integration of further mobility services, such as long-distance buses and regional rail services, but also smart parking, charging of electro vehicles and usage of autonomous driving cars, could be considered in the future. Figure 1 shows the way in which MaaS will be implemented within the framework of the two above-mentioned research projects.

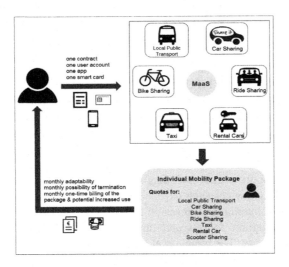

Fig. 1. Operating and using mode of MaaS [5, p. 21]

3 Brief Overview of International Research Activities and the Implementation Status of MaaS Concepts in Different Countries

MaaS research activities are mostly focused on supplier issues and the practical implementation of new mobility concepts. Business models between the individual transport companies and the MaaS operator, technical requirements as well as harmonized standards for data interfaces, access to data or infrastructure are of particular relevance for industry and science. Holmberg et al. [1] gives an overview of research activities in the Nordics and other European countries relating to MaaS until 2015/2016. The most research projects in this area have been conducted in Sweden and Finland, but also in the UK, USA and in Austria. For example, the "Mobility as a Service for Linking Europe" (MAASiFiE) project (2015–2017) was financed by the Conference of European Directors of Roads in its Transnational Road Research Program on Mobility and ITS. Objectives of the project included the future trends analysis of MaaS including multimodal traveler information services, ticketing/payment systems and sharing concepts, development of business and operator models as well as the evaluation of the social-economic and environmental impacts of MaaS. This MaaS Roadmap 2025 project was coordinated by the VTT Technical Research Centre of Finland Ltd. with the partners AustriaTech and the Chalmers University of Technology Sweden [6].

In 2017, Greater Manchester became one of the first regions in the UK to implement a business model around MaaS, delivered by Atkins Intelligent Mobility UK & Europe. As a part of Transport for Greater Manchester's vision to make travel easier for all residents, the project investigated smart technologies for planning and payment of door-to-door journeys – trams, buses, bike hire and ride sharing – in one transaction. The benefits for the region comprise a more comfortable travel experience for users and fewer cars on the region's busiest roads i.e. less congestion and pollution [7].

In Asia, a MaaS testbed and research was started in 2017 by the Nanyang Technological University (NTU) Singapore together with the Jurong Town Corporation (JTC) and the SMRT Corporation, one of the largest public-transport companies in Singapore. The testbed on the NTU campus and in the JTC CleanTech Park is focused on introducing new mobility services such as autonomous vehicles, shared personal mobility services, on-demand ride sharing, integration of MaaS mobile apps and developing parameters for data analytics, transport optimization and MaaS business models. The MaaS app "jalan" is the first of its kind in the region aimed at improving commuters' travel experience by seamlessly integrating train and bus networks with next generation transport modes, including self-driving vehicles, bike sharing systems and personal mobility devices such as e-scooters [8].

In the context of international research activities, the Maas4EU project within the EU's framework program for research and innovation, Horizon 2020, should be mentioned in particular. The main goal of MaaS4EU (2017–2020) is to provide quantifiable evidence, framework and tools to enable an interconnected EU transport market based on the MaaS concept by defining sustainable business models, supporting the cooperation between transport stakeholders, understanding user needs and choices, implementing the required infrastructure in the form of a MaaS mobility hub and identifying the adequate regulatory conditions. The project will quantify MaaS costs and benefits in three complementary real-life pilot cases by demonstrating the concept for urban, intercity and cross-border mobility services in three EU areas (UK, LU-DE, and HU). The project consortium consists of 17 partners from nine countries, among them leading industrial partners, research institutions and consultants, transport authorities, ministries and operators [9].

Although Helsinki with the Whim app may be the forerunner of the arising MaaS movement and introduction of pilots in practice, it is not alone. A lot of other cities around the world, such as Paris, Eindhoven, Gothenburg, Vienna, Hannover, Las Vegas, Los Angeles, Denver, Singapore or Barcelona, have launched local versions of MaaS in order to plan and pay for all modes of public, private and intermodal transportation (train, tram, taxi, bus, car-/bike sharing and ride hailing). Table 1 illustrates the implementation of selected MaaS pilots around the world. Some of them did not go beyond the test phase or are undergoing continuous further developments.

The research projects and the selected pilots in the different cities all over the world show very clearly that MaaS is still in an early stage with much experimentation underway. In general, they can be differentiated according to the integration level of various transport systems, the scope and type of payment systems, the offer of mobility packages and the level of ICT integration.

Table 1. Selected Maas pilots around the world

Project	Description	Operated by	Scope	Level of integration
Helsinki Model – Whim [10, p. 122]	Through its subscription-based integrated mobility app Whim, MaaS Global offers users access to a variety of transportation options, from taxis to rental cars, Helsinki public transport, and bike share. The users can choose between three mobility packages from "Whim to Go" (pay per ride) to "Whim Urban" (49 € per month) to "Whim Unlimited" (499 € per month). With the flat rate rules, customers can themselves assemble the above mentioned means of transport to varying proportions. The Whim app will be launched in Singapore in 2018	MaaS Global	Helsinki	Advanced with mobility packages
UbiGo [2, p. 2] [10, p. 122]	With this fully integrated mobility service, it is possible to use the regional public transport services as well as car and bike sharing, rental car and taxi services from a single source. Customers can combine household-based quotas for individual transport services within pre-paid packages. The booking of the contingents for rental cars, taxis, car and bike sharing is made on a time-based basis with variable additional costs if the contingent is exceeded or the unused contingents are credited for the next month. The service is accessible from the user's side via a smartphone app, in which, for example, the packages could be assembled and adapted,	Part of the project Go:Smart by Lindholmen Science Park, with partners from industry, academia, and government, co-funded by Vinnova	80 households; approx. 200 users in the city of Gothenburg	Advanced with mobility packages

(*continued*)

Table 1. (*continued*)

Project	Description	Operated by	Scope	Level of integration
	and a smart card that could be used to open the car sharing vehicles, for example			
Moovel [10, p. 122]	Enables users to search, book, and pay for rides with a single app - book and pay for car2go, mytaxi, and Deutsche Bahn in a single experience. Public transportation mobile payments are available in Stuttgart and Hamburg	Daimler	Germany; also testing in Boston, Portland, and Helsinki	Partial
EMMA [3, p. 3299]	EMMA is an integrated personal transport platform in Montpellier, France. Customers can purchase a monthly or a yearly mobility contract, including the usage of all services that TAM operates. These mobility contracts are tailored towards various user groups and differ in their payment structure. As the bike sharing service and the parking services include hourly rates, these can be paid after usage by cash or direct debit. TAM also cooperates with Montpellier's car sharing service "Modulauto" by offering users multimodal subscriptions. For a fixed annual or monthly fee, users have free access to the city's public transport network, car and bike parks and can also rent Velomagg bicycles and Modulauto cars	TAM public transport operator	Montpellier	Advanced with mobility packages
HannoverMobil [3, p. 3299]	Hannovermobil is the advanced integration of public transport, car sharing, and taxi and has a cooperative relationship with long distance rail and	Großraumverkehr Hannover Ltd. (GVH) – transport association of six transport companies and the region Hannover	Hannovermobil subscribers	Higher complexity

(*continued*)

Table 1. (*continued*)

Project	Description	Operated by	Scope	Level of integration
	car rental operators. Hannovermobil subscribers access Stadtmobil car sharing vehicles and get discounts for taxi services operated by Hallo Taxi, car rental by Hertz and long distance rail. Customers receive an integrated mobility bill at the end of each month that includes all basic cost as well as taxi and car sharing usage fees			
SMILE App [10, p. 122]	SMILE provides cooperation not only bet-ween urban public transport, rail, car sharing, bike sharing, car rental, and taxi but also between other interested partners such as software companies, engineers and environmental protection groups. It is an intermodal integrated solution delivering information, booking, and payment. A standardized interface enables all mobility partners to link their technical systems via specific adaptors to provide all their data, including ticketing	Wiener Stadtwerke in cooperation with Wiener Linien; Austrian Federal Railways; private car sharing, taxi, bike sharing, service providers	1,000 pilot participants in Vienna	Higher complexity
Communauto/ Brixi [10]	In Quebec, some municipal transport authorities have offered mobility packages that include bike sharing by BIXI and car sharing provided by Communauto. For example, a user can save on the regular price of a public transport pass and bike sharing by subscribing to the BIXI-AUTO-BUS package	Communauto	Cities in Quebec, Canada	Advanced with mobility packages

(*continued*)

Table 1. (*continued*)

Project	Description	Operated by	Scope	Level of integration
SHIFT [3, p. 3300]	SHIFT provides services including shuttle buses, bike sharing, car rental, car sharing as well as a valet service. It does this by owning all of the vehicles in its fleet and not by partnering with other service providers. The user chooses the destination in the journey planning tool and the SHIFT app will make a choice of transport modes for the user. One minute of travel time on bikes, cars or SHIFT's Valet + service equals one minute of trip time. As monthly trip time is determined for total usage, customers have the flexibility to divide up the time among the services in a way that best suits their lifestyle. These pre-paid monthly packages allow customers to pay for all their usage beforehand at once. If the customers run out of trip time, they can buy more à la carte	Las Vegas Transportation Startup SHIFT	Las Vegas	Advanced with mobility packages

4 Prerequisites and Stakeholders in the MaaS Ecosystem

MaaS needs a comprehensive cooperation between different players and components on the mobility market (see Fig. 2).

To the infrastructure aspect belong the customers' mobile devices (smartphones, tablets, phablets etc.), the needed 3G/4G/5G mobile phone networks and other radio technologies (WLAN, Bluetooth Low Energy, ZigBee etc.) assuring a high level of connectivity, secure real-time travel information, and cashless payment as well as different IT platforms from the various market players, application programming interfaces (APIs), apps and other software modules. Conditio sine qua non for sophisticated MaaS is a very thoughtful integration of both physical and virtual infrastructure components.

Data providers include a wide variety of public and private companies responsible for assembling, delivering and updating all the scheduled and real-time traffic data, navigation and whether data etc. users can access through a MaaS app or webpage.

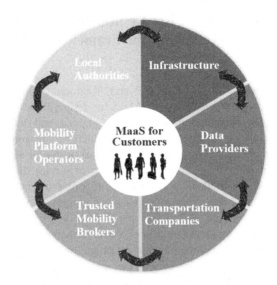

Fig. 2. MaaS ecosystem

The most important stakeholders in the MaaS ecosystem are the transport companies providing a broad range of travel modes – from public transport to a diverse spectrum of complementary services such as car sharing, bike sharing, shuttle services and on-demand bus rides. They are the owners of transportation assets.

Mobility platform operators perform the intermediary layer between the transport companies and users or amongst the transport users themselves. They collect data on customers' movement across the different transport networks in order to understand travel behavior and discover travel patterns. On this base, mobility platforms (e.g. CityMapper, Moovit, Ally, BlaBla Car, Flixbus or trainline.com) run on a fierce level of competition matching and calibrating mobility demand and supply.

Trusted mobility brokers are also a kind of intermediary. They manage the data exchange between the multiple mobility service providers, facilitate the APIs and gateways, link the offerings of the various private and public operators and arrange bookings and payments through a single point of sale. These third-party aggregators help to overcome the data sharing barriers amongst the heterogeneous mobility service providers and support their cooperation.

Whereas the transport companies and other business partners on the MaaS market search for profit, local public authorities create the framework conditions for Maas in their regions, seek the public benefits that stem e.g. from reduced congestion, less environmental pollution and reduced space for parking in order to improve the peoples' quality of life.

5   General Approach and First Results for the Creation of Mobility Packages Within the Framework of MaaS Concepts

Within the research projects "INTER-mobil" and "Regional Cooperation and Mobility Platform", the prototypical provision of MaaS in Leipzig and in the area of the Rhine-Main Transport Association will be investigated and tested in the period 2017/2018. In this context, the question arises in which way reasonable incentives for less private cars can be created through the conceptual design of MaaS, e.g. through a sophisticated price-performance structure and quality of service. In other words: What user requirements should a MaaS concept meet in order to ensure that people are willing to adjust their mobility behavior to such a multimodal mobility scheme in the long-term?

In the following sections, we would like to address a specific aspect connected to the above mentioned question, namely the investigation of the user acceptance for differently designed mobility packages. For that purpose, the results of a user survey are presented as a pretest for a more comprehensive mixed method approach in order to evaluate various product bundles.

5.1   Pretest: Focus Group Discussions

The first consideration was that the MaaS service provider take the position of a "virtual" broker combining the physically available mobility offers of the transport companies and bundles them, including a new price structure. This can facilitate the intermodal use of different means of transport for the customers considerably. The general approach for the focus group interviews is shown in Fig. 3.

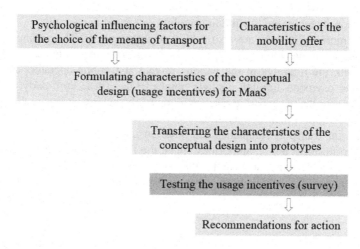

Fig. 3. Research design for the identification and testing of MaaS usage incentives

The guideline-based interviews were conducted in July 2017 with 15 subjects in Dresden and Frankfurt/Main. In accordance with psychological factors of influence on the users' mode of transport choice, such as control of mobility expenditure, situation-specific demands, emotional and affective attitudes, habits and personal norms, three MaaS concepts were presented to the subjects[1] for selection. A quantifying content analysis made it possible to transform the subjects' verbal answers into nominal scaled numerical data. Therefore, a four-categorical nominal scale $(-2, -1, 1, 2)$ with an additional score of "0" for indifferent statements was used. The scale is to be interpreted in the sense of "bad" (-2), "rather bad" (-1), "indifferent" (0), "rather good" (1) and "good" (2).

Light	Medium	Medium Extra	Premium
89 € / month	169 € / month	249 € / month	389 € / month
local public transport subscription (city rate until airport) + 1.000 mobility points	local public transport subscription (city rate until airport) + 3.250 mobility points	local public transport subscription (city rate until airport) + 5.500 mobility points	local public transport subscription (city rate until airport) + 10.000 mobility points
Use your mobility points just as you like!	Use your mobility points just as you like!	Use your mobility points just as you like!	Use your mobility points just as you like!
For example, for:	**For example, for:**	**For example, for:**	**For example, for:**
2 cab rides	4 cab rides + 1 day rental car	8 cab rides + 2 days rental car	10 cab rides + 5 days rental car
or	or	or	or
60 min car sharing + 100 min bike sharing	2 cab rides + 1 day rental car + 200 min car sharing or 300 min bike sharing	4 cab rides + 1 day rental car + 300 min car sharing or 400 min bike sharing	6 cab rides + 4 days rental car + 300 min car sharing + 400 min bike sharing

Fig. 4. MaaS prototype concept 1: mobility package according to Whim [5, p. 63]

Prototype 1: Mobility Packages (principle Whim – ideal concept)
Users can choose between different packages that contain a different contingent of "mobility points" in a prepaid scheme. Mobility points[2] are used to pay for mobility services. The scope of services includes taxi, rental car, public transport, car sharing and bike sharing. A monthly season ticket for public transport ticket is always

---

[1] In the sample were nine male and five female subjects in the age between 18 and 56 years, nine subjects employed, four in training and one unemployed, eleven subjects lived in urban areas and four in suburban areas. 40% of subjects were not intermodal and 33% showed a strong intermodal mobility behavior. 27% were car sharing users and 7% bike sharing users, 27% owned a car and 67% owned a public transport season ticket, i.e. they were regular public transport users.

[2] Since July 2017, the Whim concept has undergone changes. The packages are now "Pay per Ride", "Whim Basic" and "Whim to Go". Also, a price unlimited business package ("Whim Business") has been added. In addition, the Whim Points in the new system are worth one Euro. This means that the value of the Whim Points is better perceptible for the users.

integrated. One mobility point equals one Euro. The entire service chain (registration, booking, payment and billing) is bundled in one product. Four different mobility packages are available (Fig. 4).

Prototype 2: Pay-as-you-go (principle Leipzig mobil)
Basic fee of nine Euros per month including 300 min bike sharing contingent; the mobility services are individually bookable, no monthly package (Fig. 5).

Local Public Transport	Rental Car	Car sharing	Bike sharing
Monthly ticket (city rate until airport) 65 €	**Fixed price** *Small car* 25 € / day (incl. 400 km, then 0,21 € / km)	**Normal car** 0,29 € / min	**Fixed price** 300 minutes / month inclusive, then 0,50 € / minute
Seven-day ticket (city rate until airport) 20 €	*Mid-range car* 45 € / day (incl. 400 km, then 0,24 € / km)	**Deluxe car** 0,32 € / min	
Day ticket (city rate until airport) 6,50 €	*Luxury-class car* 80 € / day (incl. 400 km, then 0,29 € / km)		
Single ticket (city rate until airport) 2 €			

Fig. 5. MaaS prototype concept 2: basic fee and pay-as-you-go [5, p. 63]

Prototype 3: Reduced Mobility Packages (principle Whim simplified)
Like prototype 1 but less choice and less premium focus (no rental car) (Fig. 6).

Light	Medium	Medium Extra
89 € / month	**129 € / month**	**199 € / month**
local public transport subscription (city rate until airport) + 1.000 mobility points	local public transport subscription (city rate until airport) + 2.500 mobility points	local public transport subscription (city rate until airport) + 5.500 mobility points
Use your mobility points just as you like!	Use your mobility points just as you like!	Your carefree package!
For example, for:	**For example, for:**	**Including:**
100 min car sharing + 200 min bike sharing	250 min car sharing + 500 min bike sharing	600 min car sharing + unlimited bike sharing

Fig. 6. MaaS prototype concept 3: reduced mobility packages [5, p. 64]

The price calculation in the prototype concepts is based on the price structures of Whim in Helsinki with a discount between 6% und 20% depending on the package, the tariffs in the city of Leipzig and Frankfurt/Main as well as car rental and car sharing providers in Germany. In comparison to the former original price structure of Whim Helsinki (Light Package 89 €, Medium 249 € and Premium 389 €), an additional price level was introduced in the prototype concept 1 since a 2, 8-fold price jump between the first two price levels in Whim does not seem to be appropriate.

The evaluation of the guideline-supported interviews showed that all three concepts were evaluated clearly positively by the test persons on a scale of "−2" (poor, refusing, unfavorable) to "2" (good, favorable) (see Fig. 7).

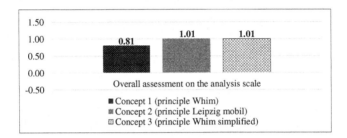

Fig. 7. Overall evaluation of the presented/proposed concepts (n = 15) [5, p. 73]

The basic idea behind MaaS was generally well accepted. The user can choose individually from a pool of mobility solutions at any time. It has been shown that the potential availability and the easy access to the most appropriate means of transport give the customer, in each case, a feeling of mobility insurance. Furthermore, it was evaluated positively that the services are all available via a smartphone app. Nevertheless, the ideal concept (concept 1), which guarantees the highest degree of flexibility, did not receive the best marks as to be seen in Figs. 7 and 8. On the one hand, this is partly due to the fact that the subjects were very price-conscious. In the interviews had to be emphasized again and again that the prices in the fictive packages should only give a better imagination for the subjects. On the other hand, 67% of the subjects owned public transport season tickets (semester ticket, student ticket, social ticket) so that the ideal concept 1 met their needs only to a limited extent.

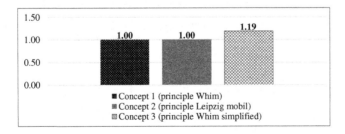

Fig. 8. Evaluation of the willingness to use the three presented concepts (n = 15) [5, p. 77]

In the context of price consciousness, the very different evaluation of the MaaS packages depending on the income of the subjects is very interesting (see Figs. 9 and 10).

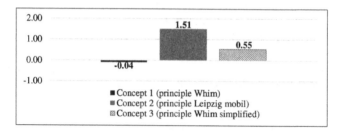

Fig. 9. Overall rating of the MaaS concepts among subjects without a fixed income (n = 5) [5, p. 79]

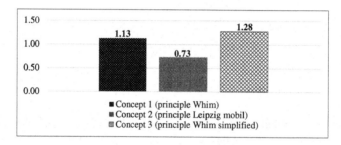

Fig. 10. Overall rating of the MaaS concepts among subjects with a fixed income (n = 10) [5, p. 79]

People without a fixed income prefer mobility services that are charged according to the pay-as-you-go principle. Persons with a fixed income see the plannable, pre-determined expenses as a significant advantage (flat rate character within the package budget).

These differences are also clearly reflected with regard to the willingness of use the MaaS concepts depending on income as shown in Table 2.

Table 2. Willingness to use MaaS concepts depending on income [5, p. 80]

	Without a fixed income (n = 5)	With a fixed income (n = 10)
Concept 1	0	1.38
Concept 2	1.5	0.71
Concept 3	1	1.4

What are the most important results and findings from the pretest for designing potential MaaS offerings in urban agglomerations in Germany?

The subjects consider the centralized access to a large number of bundled mobility services as an essential added value with regard to the ease of access, flexibility of choice and comparability. There is a willingness to pay a basic fee despite high price sensitivity, because it already offers access to a certain contingent of basic mobility (e.g. bike sharing minutes).

The concept of mobility points was misleading for a part of the subjects. The real value of the "point currency" was non-transparent in the direct comparison of mobility offers. The examples on how the mobility points could be used for a self-determined mix of various mobility services (see Figs. 4 and 6) were considered as being "set" or fix. On the contrary, subjects who correctly understood the mobility point concept appreciated the high level of flexibility.

The prepaid mobility packages were on the one hand considered as "cost airbags". On the other hand, they were regarded as a cost trap because the subjects were concerned about the expiry of points that have already been paid.

All in all, the customers could not sufficiently grasp the product in form of a mobility package and therefore, they had no idea of the price they are willing to pay for it. That means that the customers' imagination must be activated much more intensively with regard to the use of mobility packages and their pricing schemes. This can be achieved by testing real mobility packages (no dummies) in practice and possibly integrating them into existing mobility apps of a transport service provider.

5.2 Further Steps in the Research Work/Project

After basic theoretical considerations on flat rates, effects that promote flat rate bias and studies on special flat rates in the context of mobility, the following questions should be answered by further research work until the end of 2018:

- Is there a general acceptance of flat rate-based mobility packages among the population?
- How can the economic feasibility be achieved through restrictions on use?
- How is it possible to communicate the restrictions to the customer?
- Which characteristics of mobility packages should be addressed from both the customer's and the provider's point of view?

For that matter, the study design comprises a mixed method approach as shown in Fig. 11.

The mobility flat rate is a bundle of fixed service components including public transport, car sharing, bike sharing, taxi and rental car. Services that are relatively expensive (taxi, car sharing) must be restricted according to the package price (supply-side restrictions, time, quantity or price limits) or must be coupled with additional costs for the customer.

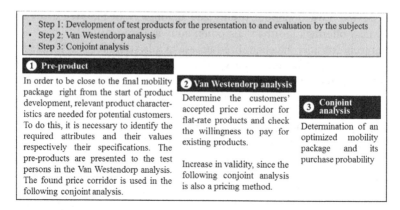

Fig. 11. Mixed method approach for determining optimized flat-rate based mobility packages

Systematics/Approach

In preparation of the Van Westendorp analysis, different user types were regarded in the form of personas. Personas are stereotypical users with different characteristics which make it easier to visualize the needs of customers for transport companies. The personas "professional beginners", "mother with small children", "working father" and "middle-aged workers" were used. School children and students were excluded due to lack of a driving license or low income. Furthermore, it is assumed that pensioners are less willing or able to handle innovative products and that their choice behavior does not change. On the basis of the objectives of the personas, the budget limits of the Leipzig Transport Services and estimated budget limits of the customers (see Fig. 12), full flat rate products will be developed and tested which should come as close as possible to the results of the future conjoint analysis.

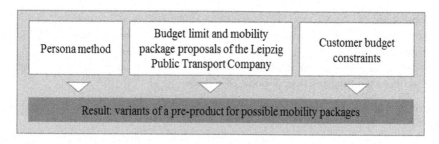

Fig. 12. General methodology of the Van Westendorp analysis

Within the framework of the Van Westendorp analysis, the subjects (n = 300) first will be divided into different mobility types. For this purpose, a questionnaire with the following contents has to be answered:

1. Is there a car available for private use? (always, occasionally, never)
2. Is there an own bicycle available in your household? (always, occasionally, never)

3. Do you have a public transport subscription?
4. Do you have a driving license?
5. How often do you use the following means of transport: private car, car with driver, private bicycle, free floating car sharing, station-based car sharing, bike sharing (daily, once a week, several times a week, once a month, several times a month, less, never)?

In addition, the subjects will be asked:

- to what extent they are interested in using car and bike sharing for doing their day-to-day tasks, leisure activities and professional purposes,
- how they basically assess the idea of getting access to different mobility services via a bundled product, and
- how important it is to them that public transport, free-floating and station-based car sharing, bike sharing, taxi and rental car services are components of a mobility package.

The following characteristic values of mobility packages have been developed according to the approach as to be seen in Fig. 12 and the use of the morphological box method. This method is generally applied for exploring all possible solutions to a multi-dimensional, non-quantified complex problem without prejudice (see Table 3).

Table 3. Types of limitation for mobility packages – morphological box – examples

	Supply			Time				Price
Local Public Passenger Transport	Only single tickets			–	Max. 10 tickets	8 am– 6 pm and 20 pm– 8 am	Ticket purchase only possible every 24 h	Subscription flat rate
Car sharing	Only vehicle category "Minis"	Only on mobility stations	Per booking only 5 free km	Lending time max. 2 h	Max. 10 bookings/month	Moil - Fri free and weekend free	Bookings only every 24 h free of charge	–
Bike sharing	–	Only on mobility stations	Only one bicycle	Lending time max. 1 h	Max. 10 bookings/month	20 pm – 8 am and weekend free	Bookings only every 24 h free of charge	–
Taxi	–	Places	Max. 5 km	Max. 20 min	Max. 3 rides/month	1–5 am	1 ride/week	–
Rental car	Classes	Stations	Free km	Lending time	Booking frequency	Limited hours	Cool down	–

For each of the following products (see Table 4), the subject will be asked for her or his willingness to pay with the following four questions:

1. At what price would you consider the product to be too expensive, i.e. not buying it at all?
2. At what price would you consider the product to be too cheap, i.e. you would have doubts about the quality of the product (dirty vehicles, broken bicycles)?

Table 4. Four characteristic values of a mobility package

	CV-1	CV-2	CV-3	CV-4
Free floating car sharing[a]	Flat rate, < 30 min	10 rides < 30 min	5 rides < 45 min	30 min
Station-based car sharing	48 h with 500 free km[b]	10 × 3 h incl. 30 km/ride	3 × 3 h incl. 15 km/ride	1 × 3 h incl. 15 km/ride
Bike sharing	12 h flat rate[c]	Flat rate, < 1 h	10 × 30 min	5 × 1 h
Taxi (within the city area)	Flat rate from 9 pm–5 am	50% discount on every ride	5 rides	1 ride
Public Transport	Subscription	50% discount on a single ticket	10 trips	4 trips

CV = *characteristic value.*
[a] Every additional minute 0, 30 €/min.
[b] Minimum lending time 1 h.
[c] 0–6 am will not count to the 12 h.

3. At what price would you evaluate the product to be expensive, but possibly buy it after careful consideration?
4. At what price would you consider the product to be cheap, in the sense of a very good offer (= bargain)?

The general approach of the Van Westendorp analysis is illustrated in Fig. 13. If the individual price requirements of the subjects are aggregated, four lines with four intersection points result as to be seen in Fig. 13. The Y-axis shows the cumulative frequency distribution while the X-axis shows the price to be chosen by the subjects. The interpretation of the results of the Van Westendorp price model is relatively simple because no hidden assumptions are made and all interesting information can be read directly from the distributions in the graphics.

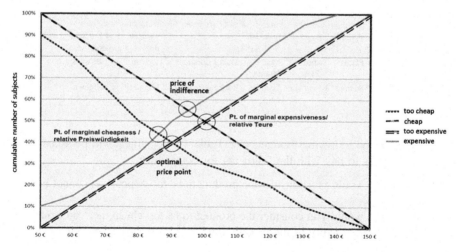

Fig. 13. Possible results of the Van Westendorp analysis

The accepted price corridor is between the points "Point of marginal cheapness" and "Point of marginal expensiveness". The best price results from the intersection of the straight lines "too expensive" and "too cheap". At this price, the smallest resistance should be expected and thus the greatest market penetration should be possible. The point of indifference lies at the intersection of "cheap" and "expensive".

As a result of the Van Westendorp analysis, which will be statistically handled with a software tool provided by the Sawtooth Company, arise acceptable price corridors for the various mobility packages used in the following conjoint analysis. The conjoint analysis is a decompositional method that estimates the structure of a consumer's preferences (i.e., estimates preference parameters such as part worth, importance weights and ideal points), given his or her overall evaluations of a set of alternative products that are specified in terms of different attributes [11]. Preferences and requirements of the customers are analyzed in order to design a product in line with the market and tailored to the customers' needs.

There are several theoretical approaches for conducting a conjoint analysis. The choice-based conjoint (CBC) analysis is currently the most widely used method. However, it is often connected with some disadvantages. For example, the subjects have to evaluate all displayed attributes of the products and evaluate them against each other. Answering many repetitive questions leads to signs of fatigue. There is often a "killer" property for the test person which the product absolutely has to have. Products that do not have this property are immediately excluded. In the choice-based conjoint analysis, however, all product combinations are displayed to the test person and must be evaluated. Therefore, a further type of conjoint analysis will be used in the research project which is known as adaptive choice-based conjoint analysis (ACA)[3]. This consists of four steps:

1. The subject creates his own ideal product. He or she chooses from a modular system and depending on the choice, the price increases.
2. Based on this, the subject is shown several products that are close to his or her ideal product. The subject scores these products. The answers are used to identify minimum requirements or exclusion criteria (the subject confirms this). The subject will then no longer be presented with any products that do not correspond to this. As a result, the survey can concentrate on products that are actually possible. The product combinations thus become more realistic.
3. The subject makes a product selection. However, he will only be shown the products he has considered as an option in the previous steps.
4. The purchase probability is determined by asking the customer the question directly: "Would you buy the presented product?" (very likely, probably, don't know, unlikely, very unlikely).

Overall, the adaptive choice-based conjoint analysis is more intuitive for the subject as he or she can make a pre-selection.

---

[3] The adaptive choice-based conjoint analysis can only be carried out by computer. This method is called adaptive because the subject's input is already processed by the computer during the interview and used to develop the next questionnaire page.

These studies will be conducted based on an electronic questionnaire in the spring of 2018 so that the results can be presented at HCII in July 2018.

6 Conclusion and Outlook

MaaS services, which are based on mobility packages, especially in urban regions, can have a very strong impact on people's choice of intermodal and multimodal transport. The decision to reduce or even eliminate the use of one's own car and to favor more environmentally friendly means of transport can be encouraged. Our investigations for the city regions of Leipzig and Frankfurt/Main have shown that flat rate-based mobility packages do not only mean potential benefits for customers (insurance, overestimation, taximeter and convenience effects) but are also evaluated critically. Price-sensitive users in particular often prefer pay-as-you-go concepts. Due to the contractual nature of mobility packages with mandatory payment in advance, they fear to lose money and flexibility. The planned Van Westendorp analysis and the adapted choice-based conjoint analysis will provide further insights in this area.

In addition, it would be of great interest to check the findings in long term real field tests since most of the assumptions could only be examined hypothetically in the survey. There could be offered test subscriptions for a few month to the customers or flat-rate mobility packages with a short-term contract. A further option is to integrate mobility packages and their use into already existing mobility providers' apps.

Besides the investigation of the customers' requirements it is also necessary to take a closer look at the economic efficiency of MaaS concepts for the mobility suppliers and their integration into mobility platforms of more and more complexity.

References

1. Holmberg, P.-E., Collado, M., Sarasini, S., Williander, M.: Mobility as a Service - MaaS, Describing the framework. Göteborg: Viktoria Swedish ICT AB (2016). https://www.viktoria.se/publications/mobility-as-a-service-maas-describing-the-framework. Accessed 08 Feb 2018
2. Sochor, J., Strömberg, H., Karlsson, M. A.: Travelers' motives for adopting a new, innovative travel service: insight from UbiGo field operational test in Gothenburg, Sweden. In: Detroit: 21st World Congress on Intelligent Transportation Systems, 7–11 September 2014
3. Kamargianni, M., Li, W., Matyas, M., Schäfer, A.: A critical review of new mobility services for urban transport. Elsevier Transp. Res. Procedia **14**, 3294–3303 (2016)
4. Nemtanu, F.C., Schlingensiepen, J.: New Technologies and ITS for Rail. In: Marinov, M. (ed.) Sustainable Rail Transport. LNM, pp. 225–247. Springer, Cham (2018). https://doi.org/10.1007/978-3-319-58643-4_13
5. Fleischer, T.: Mobility as a Service aus Nutzersicht: Untersuchung psychologischer Nutzungsreize in der Konzeptionierung von MaaS. Master Thesis, Technische Universität Dresden (2017)
6. VTT Technical Research Centre of Finland Ltd. (2018). http://www.vtt.fi/sites/maasifie.fi. Accessed 12 Feb 2018

7. Atkins: New releases 2017 – Greater Manchester signs up for Mobility as a Service (MaaS) research project with Atkins. 20 October 2017. http://www.atkinsglobal.com/en-gb/media-centre/news-releases/2017/oct/2017-10-20c. Accessed 12 Feb 2018
8. Nanyang Technological University Singapore: Mobility-as-a-Service (MaaS) Testbed and Research. 1st January 2018. http://ecocampus.ntu.edu.sg/Current-Projects/Pages/Mobility-as-a-Service%20-MaaS-Testbed-and-Research.aspx. Accessed 12 Feb 2018
9. MaaS4EU, Project ID: 723176, Horizon 2020. 3rd July 2017. https://cordis.europa.eu/project/rcn/210133_en.html. Accessed 12 Feb 2018
10. Goodall, W., Fishman, T. D., Bornstein, J., Bonthron, B.: The rise of mobility as a Service. Deloitte Rev. **20,** 112–129 (2017). https://www2.deloitte.com/content/dam/Deloitte/nl/Documents/consumer-business/deloitte-nl-cb-ths-rise-of-mobility-as-a-service.pdf. Accessed 12 Feb 2018
11. Green, P.E., Srinivasan, V.: Conjoint analysis in marketing: new developments with implications for research and practice. J. Mark. **54**, 3–19 (1990)

From HMI to HRI: Human-Vehicle Interaction Design for Smart Cockpit

Xiaohua Sun[✉], Honggao Chen, Jintian Shi, Weiwei Guo, and Jingcheng Li

College of Design and Innovation, Tongji University, Shanghai, China
{xsun,salor}@tongji.edu.cn, mollrechen@gmail.com,
shijintian1017@126.com, thinkheaven@gmail.com

Abstract. HMI is used to refer to human-vehicle interaction design from the perspective of taking car as a machine. However, with the quick increase of demand for smart cockpit, it would put strong constraints to the design of intelligent interactions and connected services if we still design from the perspective of control-oriented interface with a machine. By switching the concept from Human Machine Interaction (HMI) to Human Robot Interaction (HRI) can instead greatly open up the space of innovation for the development of natural interactions with the car as an intelligent system. This also make it possible to further focus on topics such as adaptive learning of the system through smart interaction. Designing from the perspective of human robot interaction is even more important for autonomous vehicles, which can provide to users a more consistent intelligent experience from driving control to in-vehicle functions and connected services. we introduce in this paper our approach in designing human-vehicle interaction from the HRI perspective, which is further composed of three parts: the intelligent sensing, predicting, and decision-making module, the adaptive user interface module, and the intelligent voice module.

Keywords: HRI · Human-vehicle interaction · Smart interaction
Smart cockpit

1 Introduction

The design of human-vehicle interaction has mainly gone through three stages [1]. In the first stage, the main mission is to design controls for the primary task of driving and introduce gauges to inform the driver about driving conditions and mechanical conditions of the vehicle. Some basic human factor design features were also considered, such as easy-to-operate steering equipment and switches, visible gauges, and reasonable driving positions. In the second stage, the main problem the industry faced is how information can be transferred effectively, and how drivers can operate and control the vehicles with less distraction and workload. In the third stage, as more new technologies and applications, such as in-vehicle applications, connected services, ADAS, and automatic driving, are added to the car, the main mission of human-vehicle interaction design changed to be supporting users better taking advantage of various types of functions and services. Recently, various techniques for reducing drivers' cognitive and operational

© Springer International Publishing AG, part of Springer Nature 2018
M. Kurosu (Ed.): HCI 2018, LNCS 10902, pp. 440–454, 2018.
https://doi.org/10.1007/978-3-319-91244-8_35

loads are used in vehicles, such as integrated digital assistant, voice interaction, augmented reality, etc. [2]. People's expectation for human-vehicle interaction also goes beyond the pursuit of safe, natural, comfortable experience, and has reached the level of expecting the whole cockpit to be the interface for smart interactions.

However, the concept of designing human-vehicle interaction from Human Machine Interaction perspective will tremendously limit the innovation in smart cockpit design. Switching from the perspective of Human Machine Interaction (HMI) to Human Robot Interaction (HRI) on the other hand, can greatly broaden the scope for design innovation and deepen the level of new technology application. While designing human-vehicle interaction as an interaction between human and intelligent system, it becomes natural to take advantage of latest research in AI and robotics and bring to users intelligent in-vehicle functions and connected services more compatible with the ever-increasing level of intelligence in driving control. Through autonomous learning, the intelligent system can also provide to users a more and more humanized and personalized experience.

This paper mainly introduces how the overall mechanism of a HRI system would be like, how it could predict function and service needs through intelligent sensing/predicting/decision-making module and interact with users through adaptive visual interface and intelligent voice. A use case is also presented to explain in detail to how the HRI system works.

2   Working Mechanism of HRI System

The working mechanism of the HRI system mainly includes the following four steps (see Fig. 1). Firstly, the intelligent system processes and analyzes data from various sources. Secondly, it predicts the functions that the user may need in the current context and decides the function constitution and their corresponding weights. Interface of different modalities will then be generated or triggered to interact with the users through appropriate forms. Finally, when user interact with the interfaces, the intelligent system will further collect their feedback and learn their behavior patterns to improve its ability of prediction and decision making.

Data collected by the intelligent the system is mainly included vehicle data, user data, environment data and data from connected services, such as speed, status of drivers, weather, and status of connected smart home, etc. The intelligent sensing, predicting and decision-making module is the brain of the HRI system which can sense what is happening now, predict what user needs, and decide what to display and which inter-action modality and interface to use. The interfaces between the user and the intelligent system mainly include the adaptive user interface module, the intelligent voice module and other natural interaction interfaces. Based on the prediction from the decision-making module, it can automatically generate an adaptive interface with functions meeting users' needs and with interface layout in line with their operating habit. The intelligent voice module is an intelligent interface which support multiple round dialogue, function context-based "wake" words setup and smart error-correcting. Also, the intelligent voice is an important way to expand the knowledge graph of the user through smart voice interactions. Other natural interactions, such as in-air gesture, steering wheel vibration and eye movements, can also be used in the suitable conditions.

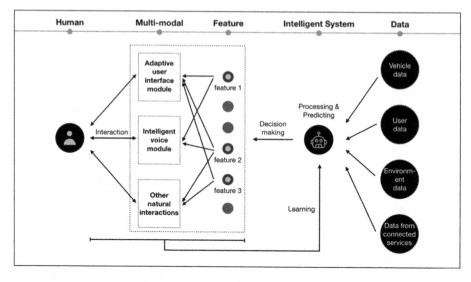

Fig. 1. Working mechanism of the HRI system.

3   Intelligent Sensing, Predicting, and Decision-Making Module

There are tree sub-components in the Intelligent Sensing, Prediction and Decision-Making module (ISPDM): (1) data acquisition; (2) knowledge inference and associating; (3) learning and knowledge graph construction [3]. With data captured from users, vehicles and the environment, this module carries out knowledge inference and association to predict user intent based on the knowledge graph and decides corresponding features to

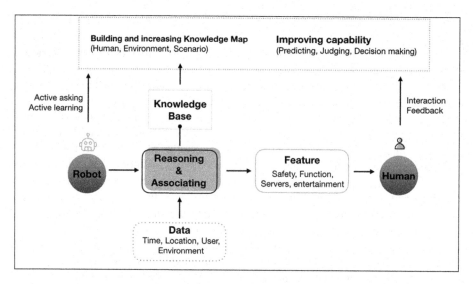

Fig. 2. Framework of the intelligent sensing, predicting, and decision-making module.

trigged. It is essential and necessary to build personalized knowledge graph and learn prediction models for intent prediction. However, the knowledge graphs and models need to be adaptive to the dynamic environment, which cannot be prebuilt perfectly. It should have the capability of life-long learning and evolve along with the interaction with users (see Fig. 2).

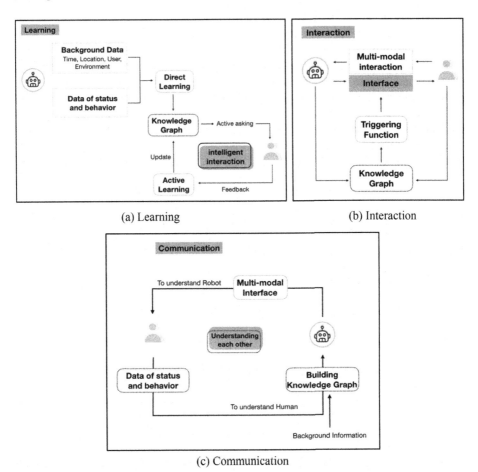

(a) Learning   (b) Interaction

(c) Communication

Fig. 3. Three aspects of the ISPDM module.

Learning is a core ability of ISPDM module [4]. As shown in Fig. 3(a), the initial knowledge graphs and prediction models are firstly learned directly from the collected training data. Due to the limited training data, these knowledge graphs and models are usually not very efficient in intent prediction. The module can actively acquire necessary information and feedbacks from users and then keep updating the knowledge graphs and models to improve their prediction performance [5–7]. With the intent prediction, it will trigger functional features and make adaptive interface to interact with users in multimodal ways [8], such as voice, visual and haptic (see Fig. 3(b)). Through the interactions, the module can get more data about the users, vehicles and environment, and then obtain more understanding about users and their context. As shown in Fig. 3(c) a closed loop supporting mutual understanding is formed between the user and the system.

4   Adaptive User Interface Module

Adaptive user interface module is the main visual interface in a HRI system. As shown in Fig. 4, it takes the function prediction input (function constitution and the weight of different functions) from the ISPDM module. Then decides the layout for these functions and their appropriate forms of display based the layout principles. Finally, following the requirements of the chosen form of display, the system will deploy suitable dynamic components to form the interface. Besides providing adaptive user interface supporting users' on-demand needs, this module can also serve as an interface to collect user's feedback or perform visual interface-based smart interaction. This could further help the HRI system better understand their users.

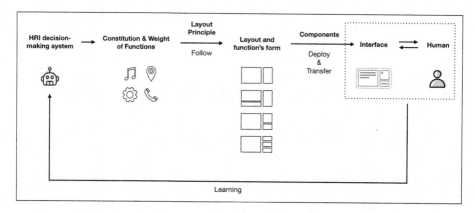

Fig. 4. Working mechanism of the adaptive user interface module.

Interface Composition.   Based on domain-specific knowledge of human-vehicle interaction design, contents in the interface mainly include: (1) functions which provide features and services, such as Navigation, Media, Phone, On Car Shopping, and so on; (2) information for presenting system status, such as Time and Cellular Connection; (3) components for controlling and displaying the status of the in-car environment and equipment. Functions can be displayed in two types of screen areas, the Primary and the Deck. Primary is where the user's main visual focus is, and where most of the interactions would happened. There is normally only one main function displayed in the Primary. Deck, on the other hand, is an area for supplementary functions and information. System status could be placed in the Status Bar. A Controller area can be used to control in-car equipment and display status information of the in-car environment.

Layout Principle. Based on general UI design principles and considering of the driving conditions, we proposed the following principles for adaptive user interface layout:

Place the Primary in the Area Nearest to the User. Since the Primary is where the most important functions or information is placed, to guarantee users to obtain information and carry out the operations in the most convenient and efficient way, the Primary is better to be placed in the area nearest to the user. For example, in a left-hand-drive vehicle, Primary is better to be placed in the left part of a horizontal screen and the upper part of a vertical screen (see Fig. 5).

Place the Deck to the Secondary Area. As an area that carries information and functions that the user does not need the most, the Deck is better to be placed to a secondary area, such as the lower part in a vertical screen and the right part in a horizontal screen in a left-hand-drive vehicle (see Fig. 5).

Place the Status Bar to the Area in Line with the Reading Habit. The Status Bar is an important area for displaying system information. According to the general UI layout principle and people's reading habit of from left to right and from top to bottom, the Status Bar is better to be placed the top of the vertical screen and the leftmost side of the horizontal screen in a left-hand-drive vehicle (see Fig. 5).

Place the Controller at the Bottom. The Controller works as a key area that users need to control in-car equipment and check their status. As a virtual replacement of the physical button or turn nobs controlling the in-car equipment, it is better to keep the Controller available for the users all the time. It is thus better to fix it to the bottom of the screen (see Fig. 5).

Provide a Menu for Users. Menu is an entrance for users to access all of the functions. When the main function that the system recommends can't match users' expectation, users should be able to select functions they want to use through the Menu, which will appear in the form of an overlay.

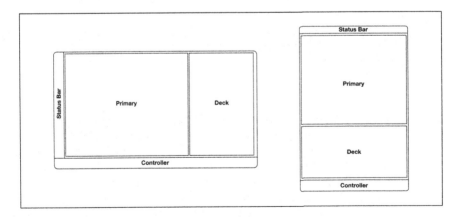

Fig. 5. Layout example of the adaptive user interface.

Development Phases. With the improvement in techniques and the availability of data and partner resources, the development of adaptive user interface and proposed functions can be realized step by step. Table 1 gives a summary of four major development phases.

Table 1. Development phases of the adaptive user interface.

Phase	Auto organize interface feature	Data	Technology requirement	Partner
0	• Provide common functions of using the interface	• Null	• Null	• Null
I	• Making certain judgments whether to present some traditional on-board functional modules • According to the principle of layout, module weight, etc. to auto organize and present the various functional modules	• Operating Data • Driving Data • Car Data • Driving Environment Data • Device Data • ……	• Technology of analyzing GPS data • Technology of analyzing car data • Technology of analyzing device data	• Map providers • Device providers
II	• Making certain judgments whether to present the interconnection service and car assistant service • According to the principle of layout, module weight, etc. to auto organize and present the various functional modules	• Interconnected Data • In-car intelligent hardware • Status and behavior of driver • ……	• Technology of analyzing interconnected data • Technology of analyzing hardware data	• App providers • Servers providers
III	• According to the user's knowledge map and intent prediction to accurately determines the function and information that the user needs at each moment exactly and organizes and presents these on the interface according to the layout principle	• All of above	• Technology of building Knowledge Map • Highly intelligent system	• All of above

(1) *Phase zero.* In this phase, the system will provide users with a default set of functions set in preset layout. It provides users with a complete set of functions when they use the adaptive user interface for the first time. Users could always switch and select a function module they want through the Menu and then place it to the Primary or the Deck. They could also delete those they don't need from the screen.

(2) *Phase one.* In this phase, the system will be able to accumulate and analyze data (including user's operational data, driving data, environment data, etc.) and is equipped with the ability of deciding whether and where to present a function or information based on the analysis result. For example, based on driving information

and car information, the system can decide to present over-speed info, low battery info; based on climate and environment information, the system can decide to give users warnings for careful driving; based on the driving scenario and layout principle, the system can decide to put Navigation function module in the Primary and place Media and Device Connection function modules in the Deck.

(3) *Phase two.* With more and more data and partnerships available and with the development of intelligent technologies, the system in this phase can provide more and more personalized functions and scenario-based services, such as POI-based recommendation. The strength of the adaptive user interface can be used to the most by generating ever-changing interfaces satisfying users' needs at every moment.

(4) *Phase three.* This is the most advanced phase, at which the system is highly intelligent and can use all the input data together with users' knowledge graph to accurately predict their on-demand needs at any time. Instead of placing the functions in the Primary or Deck as a whole, the system will be able to find the most attention-demanding operation steps or information of a function and present them in a most prominent area, the Hub, as shown in Fig. 6. For example, while the Media is playing, the system will display the control function of the Media in the Hub instead of having the whole Media function module placed in the Primary or Deck as in Phase two. The most relevant navigation related information such as turn-by-turn navigation are also displayed in the Hub, while the map and other low attention-demanding information or operations in the Navigation function module are displayed in the Main area which occupies the majority of the screen.

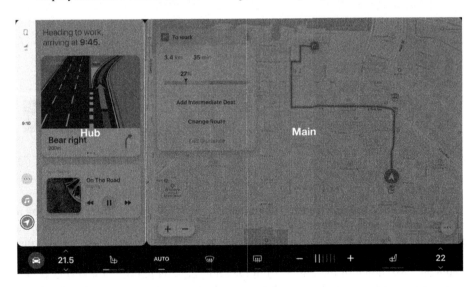

Fig. 6. Layout example of phase three of the adaptive user interface.

5   Intelligent Voice Module

As an interaction modality which frees up the hand and doesn't require visual attention to the user interface, voice interaction is a good candidate for human-vehicle interaction. However, with the current technology in natural language processing, it is hard to bring to users a natural voice-based interaction supporting complex tasks. We propose here four intelligent voice interaction features under the overall mechanism of the HRI system, which can help to improve user experience in the environment of a smart cockpit.

Function Context-Based "Wake" Words Mechanism. In most of the current voice interaction system,users have to speak out the "wake" words to wake up the voice system and then start the voice interaction [9]. However, it's not user-friendly to wake up the voice system and start from the root of the function every time when the user only needs to perform a specific task within the currently running functions. To solve this problem, we proposed a mechanism of setting function context-based "wake" words under each function, such as, setting "Play next" or "Next track" under the Media function. When users want to switch to the next song while the Media is running, instead of calling the root "wake" word and start from the beginning again, users can say "Play next", and the system will switch to the next song directly. Through this way, the voice interaction could become more natural and the process of interaction will become shorter (see Fig. 7).

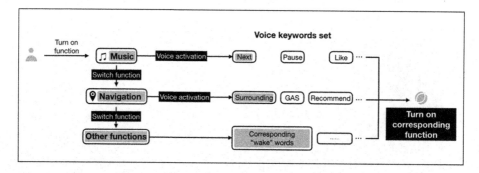

Fig. 7. Function context-based "wake" words mechanism.

Scenario-Based Multiple Round Dialogue. Constrained by the current technology in semantic analysis, it's difficult to build multiple rounds dialogues. In a HRI system, the knowledge graph of the user can help to construct a dialogue scenario, which can in turn contribute to semantic analysis of user input and support the generation of multiple round dialogues. As shown in the Fig. 8, from the knowledge graph of the user, the system knows his interest in NBA and establishes the NBA news scenario for the first round answer and later conversations.

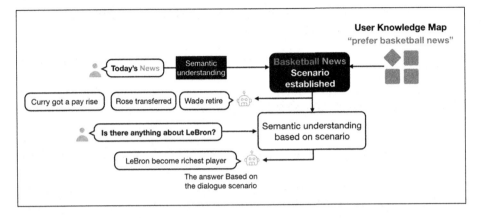

Fig. 8. Scenario-based multiple round dialogue.

Error-Correcting Mechanism. Unclear user expression and low prediction accuracy are two main reasons causing errors during the conversation with a voice system. The ISPDM module of the HRI system especially the user knowledge graph under continuous development can be of good help for increasing the prediction accuracy. We also propose here a mechanism to support users express their intensions more accurately. When the system made an error during a conversation, instead of going back to the very beginning and restart again like in most of the current systems, the user can use an error correction identifier, such as "Incorrect", to switch to the Error-Correcting mode, and correct the misunderstanding by speaking out the right intention using a predefined pattern for correction. For example, as showing in Fig. 9, a user inquires the news about James, the system gives back news about singer James Bay, which is not the "James" the user wants to follow. Now the user can say "Incorrect, NOT this James, BUT the NBA player LeBron James", then the system will switch to news about LeBron James.

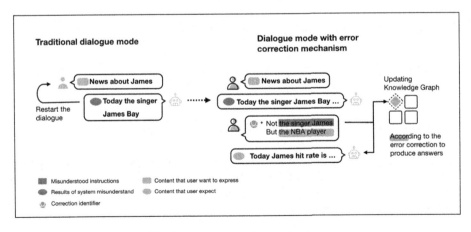

Fig. 9. Error-correcting mechanism.

At the same time, the HRI system will update the knowledge graph of this user with his interest in LeBron James, which will support more accurate prediction in the future.

Smart Voice Interaction. As an intelligent system like a robot, the HRI system should be able to proactively inquire necessary information supporting accomplishment different tasks. Besides getting information needed for the execution of the current task, gaining long term knowledge about the users is also crucial for an intelligent system. This is part of its autonomous learning process. For service robot, this could be achieved through Smart Interaction, which refers to interactions well designed to help the system acquire information they need to increase their capabilities. Smart Interaction can be carried out in various ways. In vehicle, voice would the most appropriate modality because of its less distraction characteristics. When the system detected some information missing in the knowledge graph of the user, it could initiate a smart voice interaction to acquire information and complete the missing part of the knowledge graph. As shown in Fig. 10, when holiday is approaching, the system is considering of reminding the user to do vehicle inspection at the 4S store if they are fans for self-drive touring. However, as a new car of the family, it has no information about their habits regarding self-drive touring. The system then initiates the query on this. Answer from the user will both be used to help the system decide its reaction and be added to the knowledge graph of the user.

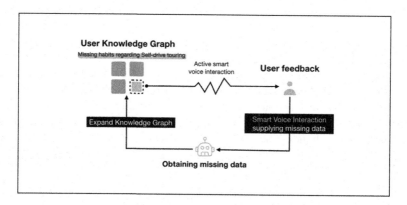

Fig. 10. Smart voice interaction.

6   Use Case

To better illustrate the HRI system introduced above, we present here a use case of a young man, Allen, on his way to gym after work and back home afterwards.

After using the HRI system for a period of time, a knowledge graph about Allen has been built with his personalized information, such as his habit of going to the gym on Fuxin Road every Friday after work and his habit of taking some beef and broccoli after exercising.

Today is Friday, Allen is driving on Fuxin Road after one day's work. Based on the date, time, location, driving direction, and personal schedule. The intelligent system predicts that he would go to the gym. Therefore, it initiates an intelligent voice interaction and asks Allen whether he would go to the gym or not.

After Allen confirms the query, the system starts to process the data including the gym's location, road condition, and occupancy rate of parking lots around the gym. It then books a parking space closest to the entrance of the gym and informs Allen both by voice and by displaying the parking lot on the map. A video with tips for today's exercise is then played on the Deck area of the screen (see Fig. 11).

Fig. 11. Adaptive user interface showing parking spaces and action tips on the screen.

After one hour of exercise, Allen goes back to the car. The system accesses the smart housing interconnected data and finds that Allen's favorite beef and broccoli are deficient at home. Therefor it informs Allen this fact vocally and asks him whether he prefers to order some food through Freshhema.com or prefers to buy some from a nearby market. The locations of the nearby markets are also displayed on the map for reference (see Fig. 12).

Allen answers that he would like to order some beef, broccoli and roasted meat from Freshhema.com. The system analyzes that roast meat is not suitable for eating after exercising and suggests Allen not to have greasing food like roasted meet (see Fig. 13).

Fig. 12. Adaptive user interface showing some shopping recommendations.

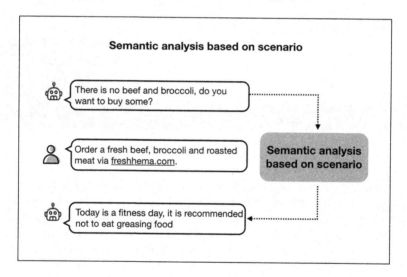

Fig. 13. Scenario-based multiple round dialogue.

Later on, based on related data of car speed, road condition and traffic light, the intelligent system realizes that Allen is stuck in a traffic jam. It then asks Allen whether he wants to listen to the news to kill time. Allen agrees. After entering to news function, the system recommends some news related to the snowstorm. Allen says "Next". Supported by the function context-based "wake" words mechanism, the system then continues to broadcast the news of today's weather. Allen then says "Change, James" to tells the system that he wants to hear the news about James. The system starts to broadcast news of James Bond immediately based on Allen's interest on James Bond stored in the knowledge graph. However, the "James" he wants to follow this time is the basketball player LeBron James at NBA. Allen says "Wrong" to enter the error-correcting mode and asks the system to change to news about the NBA James (see Fig. 14, 15).

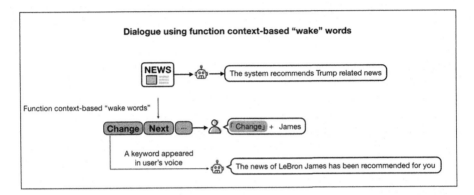

Fig. 14. Dialogue using function context-based "wake" words

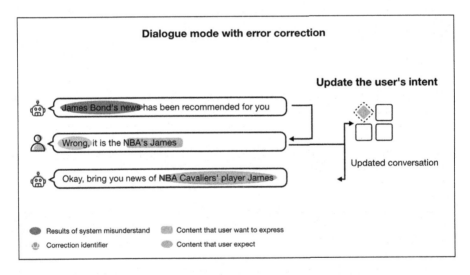

Fig. 15. Dialogue with error-correcting mechanism.

During the whole process, the system proactively initiates many rounds of intelligent voice-based interaction. The intelligent voice not only serves as the interface for helping Allen book the parking lot, check the food availability, get through the boring time of waiting for the traffic light, but also helps to acquire more information about Allen, such as his new interest in NBA Basketball player LeBron James. The system then has this information updated to Allen's knowledge graph, which will correspondingly enhance its understanding of Allen and help to make more accurate predictions in the future.

7 Conclusion

We present in this paper a human-vehicle interaction system designed from the perspective of Human Robot Interaction. It mainly includes three modules: the intelligent sensing, predicting and decision-making module, the adaptive user interface module, and the intelligent voice module. The adaptive user interface can organize and present on-demand functions based on user needs predicted by the intelligent system. The intelligent voice interaction with four innovative features can provide to users a natural experience towards dialogue-based communication. It can also help the system to obtain users' preferences through smart voice interactions, and eventually get better a understanding of the user. We intend to show through this paper that by switching the perspective from Human Machine Interaction to Human Robot Interaction can help open up the scope of innovation in smart cockpit design. This paper also exhibits a cross-disciplinary approach of expanding the boundaries of human-vehicle interaction design taking advantage of the latest advancement in AI and HRI technology. For the next step, we will carry out user evaluation of this system and further development of the component modules.

Acknowledgments. This paper was supported by the Funds Project of Shanghai High Peak IV Program (Grant DA17003).

References

1. Akamatsu, M., Green, P., Bengler, K.: Automotive technology and human factors research: past, present, and future. Int. J. Veh. Technol. **2013**(3), 1 (2013)
2. https://news.harman.com/releases/harman-demonstrates-advanced-connected-car-platform-for-industry-leading-intelligent-cockpit
3. Saxena, A., Jain, A., Sener, O., Jami, A., Misra, D.K., Koppula, H.S.: Robobrain: large-scale knowledge engine for robots. arXiv preprint arXiv:1412.0691 (2014)
4. Thrun, S., Mitchell, T.M.: Lifelong robot learning. Robot. Autonom. Syst. **15**(1–2), 25–46 (1995)
5. Senft, E., Lemaignan, S., Baxter, P.E., Belpaeme, T.: Leveraging human inputs in interactive machine learning for human robot interaction. In: Proceedings of the Companion of the 2017 ACM/IEEE International Conference on Human-Robot Interaction, pp. 281–282. ACM (2017)
6. Kober, J., Peters, J.: Reinforcement learning in robotics: a survey. In: Wierin, M., van Otterlo, M. (eds.) Reinforcement Learning, pp. 579–610. Springer, Heidelberg (2012). https://doi.org/10.1007/978-3-642-27645-3_18
7. Cakmak, M., Chao, C., Thomaz, A.L.: Designing interactions for robot active learners. IEEE Trans. Autonom. Ment. Dev. **2**(2), 108–118 (2010)
8. Turk, M.: Multimodal interaction: a review. Pattern Recogn. Lett. **36**, 189–195 (2014)
9. Pearl, C.: Designing Voice User Interfaces: Principles of Conversational Experiences. O'Reilly Media Inc., Sebastopol (2016)

Implementing Node-Link Interface into a Block-Based Visual Programming Language

Ryo Suzuki[✉], Takuto Takahashi, Kenta Masuda, and Ikuro Choh

Waseda University, 3-4-1 Ookubo, Shinjuku-Ku, Tokyo 169-8555, Japan
`reputeless@gmail.com`

Abstract. We developed a novel node-link style interface that can be introduced into a block-based visual programming language as an alternative representation of named variables. By using our new interface, the programmer no longer needs to decide the name of a variable. Tracking the data flow in the program can be easily achieved. Since keyboard typing is not required, the coding is expected to be more accessible to children and persons with disabilities, and it is also suitable for touch operations on mobile phones and tablets.

In our system, as the number of variables increases, the intersections of the links increase, which makes the appearance complicated. To avoid this problem, we implemented improvements in the design, such as emphasizing the focused link list, and making the curves of the links consistent.

Keywords: Visual programming language · Blocks-based programming
User interface

1 Introduction

1.1 Visual Programming Languages

A visual programming language is a programming language that expresses data, flow, and logic by correlation of visual elements such as graphics, icons, and texts. The visual programming language contrasts with text programming consisting of plain text. Many visual programming languages are developed for beginners of programming. In such languages, instead of typing the source code with a keyboard, code is edited by placing elements of the graphical user interface using a mouse or touch. By those design, the effort required for learning coding is made smaller than that of text programming. In programming education for young people, such as computer classes in elementary schools and events like Hour of Code [1], visual programming languages are widely used.

1.2 Block-Based Visual Programming Languages

Visual programming languages that express flows and scopes by aligned blocks are called block-based visual programming languages. A block expresses one unit of programming

© Springer International Publishing AG, part of Springer Nature 2018
M. Kurosu (Ed.): HCI 2018, LNCS 10902, pp. 455–465, 2018.
https://doi.org/10.1007/978-3-319-91244-8_36

elements such as variable definition and function call, and the execution order is defined by the direction in which the blocks are connected. Generally ordered from top to bottom, from left to right. The blocks are basically rectangular, and they often have irregularities like a piece of a puzzle, and they visually represent connectable blocks.

1.3 Representation of a Variable

Visual programming languages are often used as introductions to text programming languages. Structures such as loops and branches seen in Scratch [2] and Blockly [3] correspond to those of text programming languages such as C and Java. The concept of variables is also commonly used in these languages.

In this paper, we investigate existing methods for representing variables in visual programming languages and propose node-link interface as a new method.

2 Previous Approach

2.1 Block-Based Visual Programming Languages

Block-based visual programming languages such as Scratch (Fig. 1) and Blockly have been developed for programming education for novices, and they are widely used in introductory computer science classes [4]. This type of interface makes better productivity, makes less syntax errors, and provides better learnability compared to text programming. However, even in such visual programming languages, the concept of variables is still expressed in text form and the advantages of expressive visual programming languages are not utilized. The programmer always needs to read the code carefully to understand the name of the variable, where it is defined, where the value is modified, and where it is used as an argument of the function. Furthermore, naming variables takes time, and causes problems when the entire program is translated into a language of another country for localization.

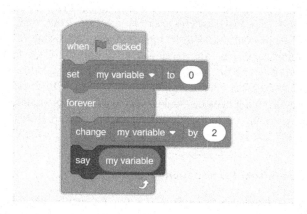

Fig. 1. An example of block-based visual programming language. (Scratch 3.0)

2.2   Node-Based Visual Programming Languages

Node-based interface is also famous option for visual programming languages. In the node-based interface as shown in Fig. 2, a program is created with the directed flow of data between operation and operation in a graph. The programmer connects the output node of the block corresponding to the return value of a function or a variable to an input node of the block to reuse the value. Since a programmer can place the blocks everywhere, space efficiency is poor compared to aligned blocks. In general, variables are not required to be named.

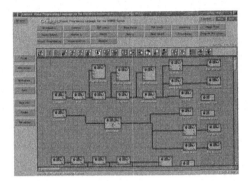

Fig. 2.   A classic node-based visual programming language.

3   Node-Link Interface Overview

We developed a new visual programming language "Enrect" [5] that introduces a node-based interface into a block-based visual programming language. In Enrect, flows and scopes are expressed by aligned blocks as well as a block-based visual programming language. Variables are represented by nodes and link curves as shown in Fig. 3.

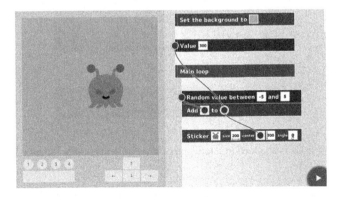

Fig. 3.   Node-link interface is used instead of named variables in our visual programming language.

The node is displayed at the left end of the block corresponding to a variable, and the user extends the curve of the link by dragging it and connects it to the parameter node (white box) of the argument on the function block. The connected box can be used as a new node that represents the same variable, and a new link can be created by dragging from the node. When a user drags outside the scope of a variable, it is displayed as an invalid operation. To remove the link from the argument box, the user grabs the node and releases it on the box. The order of the nodes and links to be visualized is updated each time when reconnection or block rearrangement event has occurred. The link always starts from the variable block, and the nodes are connected in the order in which they appear in the code. When a variable is statically typed, connectable boxes that accept the value are highlighted while dragging. This is one of the useful interface that cannot be achieved with a text-based IDE. Our code structure using the node-link instead of named variables is essentially the same as the ordinary block-based language, thus it can easily be converted to a text code as a traditional block-based language can.

The purpose of our node-link interface is to achieve the following usability during the coding with a visual programming language.

- Keyboard is not required
- Works on small mobile screen
- Can be operated with one finger
- Can translate source code into other languages (e.g. from English into Japanese).

3.1 Node

As shown in Fig. 4, a node is an element which is used as a starting point of a link that expresses a data flow. Colored circular or square nodes are attached to the left side of variable blocks or function blocks with return values, and white circular or square nodes are inside function blocks that accept arguments. Especially, we call the latter as a parameter node. By starting the drag operation with the mouse or touch from the node, the programmer can create a link and connect it to another node.

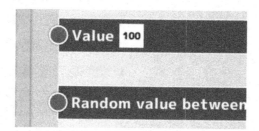

Fig. 4. Variable node is attached to a left side of a variable block or a function block that has a return value.

3.2   Parameter Node

The parameter node is an element expressing the argument of the function as a node. As shown in Fig. 5, a programmer can write a value directly instead of using a variable. The parameter node accepts a specific type of input, dependent on the value type. Programmer cannot connect a node when they don't match.

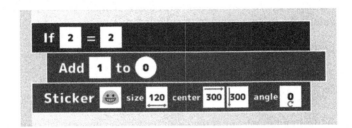

Fig. 5. A block usually has one or more parameter nodes. They are represented as a white box or circle inside the block.

3.3   Link Curve

The curve connecting the nodes is a link. As shown in Fig. 6, it is usually drawn as a cubic Bezier curve connecting the nodes. At the present Enrect specification, there are a maximum of two links connected to one node, but there is also a possibility that it will be increased due to implementation of branch representation in the future.

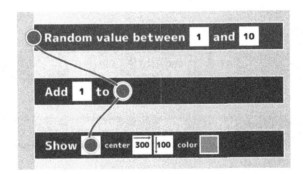

Fig. 6. Nodes are connected by a link curve.

4   Design Features

Enrect has several unique interface features for improving usability of programming. Large font size makes touch operation accurate. The input annotation provides additional information for the user to grasp the specification of the function. In-app software keyboard provides visual consistency and prevents source code from being covered. The shape of a parameter node changes depending on whether the argument may be modified or not. Allowing blank lines improves the expressiveness of source code.

4.1 Font Size

Enrect uses larger fonts compared to other visual programming languages (Table 1). It was designed to make it easier to operate with touch. This size is helpful for a teacher looking at the student's tablet screen in the classroom.

Table 1. Height of the minimum block in block-based visual programming languages.

Scratch 3.0	Blockly	Enrect
33px	24px	58px

It is planned to implement semantic zooming which supports adaptive scaling like online map service.

4.2 Input Annotation

As shown in Fig. 7, in some parameter nodes that receive numerical values, small symbols indicating the use of the numerical values are displayed as input annotations. In the parameter node corresponding to the width, arrows in both directions indicate that it is the thickness of the line. In the parameter node corresponding to the angle, the arrow rotating clockwise indicates the rotation and its direction visually to the programmer. Color and emoji are represented by image indexes and RGB values internally, but they are displayed visually in the source code.

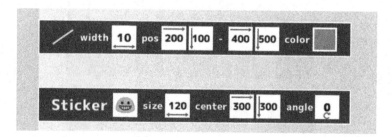

Fig. 7. Some parameter nodes have input annotations that represent their usages.

4.3 Anonymous Variable

By using our interface, variables in the source code are not required to be named by the programmer. Thus, programmer can save time and effort to devise the name of a variable and input it. The source code of Enrect can be translated into the language of each country by switching the system language setting. Since the variables in the source code do not have names, it is accessible for people who don't understand English. For example, a Japanese student and an American student can share their code with no barrier.

4.4 Software Keyboard

Although it is no longer necessary to input the name of a variable, the keyboard is still needed to input the numerical value and the text to be handled by the program. A general problem while coding a visual programming language on a tablet PC is that a software keyboard obscures the editor as shown in Fig. 8. We solved the problem partially by implementing an in-app input window in the editor (Fig. 9). Node link interface is used in the window for consistency.

Fig. 8. A text input window and a system software keyboard may hide the source code editor.

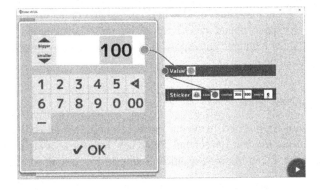

Fig. 9. In-app text input window connected to a parameter block with node-link interface.

4.5 Constant Value

Blocks that represent constants are implemented to make Enrect close to practical text programming languages. Constants cannot be connected to parameter nodes which perform destructive operation. To express it visually, the parameter node which modifies input has circular shape and an immutable variable block has a square node. Then a programmer can connect variable nodes (circle or square) to square parameter nodes, but only circle variable nodes can be connected to circle parameter nodes. This is a visualization of the lvalue/rvalue in C++ showed in the following code (Fig. 10).

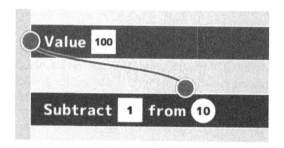

Fig. 10. A circle parameter node only accepts mutable variable.

```
void Add(int& x, int y);

Add(10, 5); // error. `10` is not a lvalue
```

4.6 Blank Line

When the link curve is complicated, and the readability drops, a programmer can eliminate complexity by inserting blank lines between blocks. This also has a secondary effect on the ease of programming. In text programming, a programmer can write blank lines in the code. A blank line is sometimes used to indicate that the contents of the function are not implemented or to express boundaries of processing units. Block-based visual languages generally do not allow elements corresponding to empty lines in consecutive blocks, but Enrect allows blank lines.

4.7 Creating a New Node

A new link cannot be inserted between connected nodes in an ordinary node-based language with one action, but Enrect can create new link for a variable from any nodes as shown in Fig. 11. It can improve usability while editing a long source code.

4.8 Avoiding Confliction

We found that link curves can be complicated when many variables are used in single source code. Then we improved the design of the link curves. The currently selected variable and its link curves are emphasized with bold and highlight visual effect. Each variable has unique color for its link curve. Random offset is added to the curve parameter to avoid overlapping. Curves are rendered consistently and smoothly through the all nodes instead of calculating the curve parameters on each link.

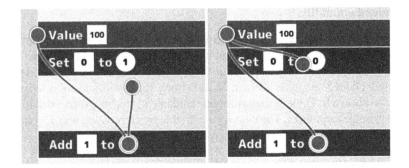

Fig. 11. A new link can be created from any active nodes.

5 Evaluation

5.1 Programming Effort

To investigate how much our programming language reduces the user's effort compared to the existing block-based visual programming language, we measure the minimum number of clicks and drags, and key touches required to implement the sample program. We used FizzBuzz [6] which is a famous programming practice as the sample program. The pseudocode is as follows.

```
int i = 1;

for(;;)
{
  if(i%3 == 0)
    Print("Fizz");
  if(i%5 == 0)
    Print("Buzz");
  if(i%3 != 0 && i%5 != 0)
    Print(i);
  ++i;
}
```

As shown in Table 2, Enrect user can implement the program with less actions.

Table 2. Action counts while coding FizzBuzz.

Language	Click	Drag	Key touch	Sum
Scratch 3.0	16	25	18	59
Blockly	24	24	22	70
Enrect	34	20	0	54

5.2 Understandability

To verify that our interface is comprehensible to beginners of programming, we conducted a experiment. The experiment was conducted for 10 students aged 11 to 12 years. They all use Enrect for the first time. In the experiment, we first presented guidance of Enrect for about 5 min, then let them develop freely for 40 min and collected operation log data. As shown in Table 3, except for one student, all students succeeded in creating multiple variables and links. The number of variable blocks created was 5.8 on average, and the link was created 23.3 times on average.

Table 3. The numbers of variables and links created during the test.

User ID	Variables created	Links created
#1	6	34
#2	4	16
#3	7	28
#4	12	29
#5	5	18
#6	4	21
#7	9	38
#8	4	12
#9	6	34
#10	1	3
Avg.	5.8	23.3

6 Future Work

6.1 Data Flow Animation

In complicated programs, it is difficult to infer the flow of data and the change in state from the source code. By visualizing data moving on link curves between nodes with animation, it is possible to implement a visual debugger that assists development.

6.2 Tagging

When using multiple variables, the meaning of each value is not explicit without its name. It can be improved by providing several types of variable blocks with roughly labeled as "count", "time", etc., or by allowing the user to attach pre-defined tags to variable blocks.

7 Conclusion

We showed our novel node-link style interface that can be introduced into a block-based visual programming language. By using our interface, variables are not required to be named, data flow in the program can be displayed clearly, and a programmer can make a simple program with less effort. Our experiment showed our system is almost comprehensible by novice programmers.

References

1. Hour of Code. https://code.org/learn. Accessed 1 Jan 2018
2. SCRATCH. https://scratch.mit.edu/. Accessed 1 Jan 2018
3. Blockly. https://developers.google.com/blockly/. Accessed 1 Jan 2018
4. Weintrop, D., Wilensky, U.: To block or not to block, that is the question: students' perceptions of blocks-based programming. In: Proceedings of the 14th International Conference on Interaction Design and Children. ACM (2015)
5. Enrect. https://enrect.org. Accessed 1 Jan 2018
6. Using FizzBuzz to Find Developers who Grok Coding. https://imranontech.com/2007/01/24/using-fizzbuzz-to-find-developers-who-grok-coding/. Accessed 1 Jan 2018

Development of Holographic Environment for Multi-user Virtual Robot Training System

Chaowwalit Thammatinno[(✉)] and Siam Charoenseang

Institute of Field Robotics (FIBO), King Mongkut's University
of Technology Thonburi, Bangmod, Thungkru, Bangkok, Thailand
chaowwalit.thammatinno@gmail.com,
siam@fibo.kmutt.ac.th

Abstract. This research presents the design and development of holographic environment for multi-user virtual robot training system. During On-the-Job Training (OJT), this proposed system assists the trainer to train the trainee for operating the virtual robot arm at the robot station. It is designed for multiple users to access the same augmented environment including the physics-based simulation at the same time. In the augmented environment, the trainer can demonstrate the operation of the robot through the hologram while the trainee can visualize and operate the virtual robot by interaction with the hologram. The result showed that the same augmented environment was interacted by the trainer and the trainee successfully. Hologram environment was accurately mapped to the real environment. In the future, the proposed system can send a set of commands to control the real robot as similar to the hologram version.

Keywords: Robot training · Simulation · Hologram · Augmented reality

1 Introduction

Training is the process involving with the trainees to learn and practice lead to gain knowledge and skill in their jobs. The presentation methods are the simple ways that deliver the information to the trainee. The simulation method is the method that helps the trainee to learn and practice in the virtual environment. The trainee can feel like operate in the real environment. On-the-Job Training is the method that the trainer directly instructs to the trainee. Also, the trainee can learn and practice at the actual workplace. This method generally is the most efficient [1–3].

Several research works presented the systems to improve the training process including avoiding the risk, reducing the cost of training, preparing the trainee in the specific task, assisting learning in the difficult task, and so on. Furthermore, the research works that implement the training method into are facilitating and improve the learning of the trainees as shown in Table 1.

Virtual Reality (VR) technology has been widely spread in various tasks. For the training task, the virtual reality especially augmented reality allowed the developer to create the virtual system for assisting the user in many roles such as virtual teacher, virtual environment, interactive information, and simulation. Teaching algorithm can also be integrated into the system as a virtual trainer. It responded to the user according

© Springer International Publishing AG, part of Springer Nature 2018
M. Kurosu (Ed.): HCI 2018, LNCS 10902, pp. 466–478, 2018.
https://doi.org/10.1007/978-3-319-91244-8_37

Table 1. Comparison of the training methods

Paper	Stereo-scopic	Multi user	Lecture	Simulation	Case study	OJT
4	*		*		*	*
5	*					*
6				*		
7				*		
8	*			*	*	
9				*		
10	*			*		
11	*			*		
12	*			*		
13					*	
Proposed system	*	*	*	*	*	*

to the environment and situation [4, 5]. During the training, some task was inconvenient for trainee to be trained in the actual workplace because of risk, cost, restriction, and time limit. The training system mostly aims to create the simulation for training that provided the interactive training environment [6–12]. Moreover, the virtual training allowed the trainee to practice the same situation many times for the specific scenario. Many case studies from the virtual training could help the trainee to find their suitable solutions for assigned tasks [4, 8, 13].

The above systems still have some problems related to the number of trainees at a time, unrealistic virtual training, distortion of the video camera, request of the marker, the difficulty of interaction, and limitation of point-of-view. The proposed system was designed to solve these problems by integration of networking system for multiple users and providing the holograms for natural interaction with the real environment and actual workplace.

2 System Overview

In general, most of the operational manuals, which are written in the document papers, are inconvenient [14]. Some previous research suggested that the Mobile Augmented Reality System (MARS) enhanced the capability of providing the graphics information to the user autonomously at anytime, in any place [15]. So, the MARS could be suitable for On-the-Job Training method which needs the direct instructions to perform the job in real-time. Moreover, MARS allows the users to use the natural interaction but it has to understand the details of environment at a workplace. Nowadays, the hardware device, which is suitable to the above requirements, is the Microsoft HoloLens.

During proposed On-the-Job Training, both trainer and trainee work at the same place and share some job's information in form of graphics information at the same time. So, the networking system could be good choice for sharing that kind of information. In addition, the Universal Robot 5 was chosen to be a manipulator in the proposed system because it is easy to be interfaced by sending an URScript via ethernet connection.

The main software platform chosen to development the proposed system is the Unity which is a game engine for developing the 3D application and supports various platforms including the Microsoft HoloLens [16]. In addition, Microsoft provided MixedRealityToolkit [17] that fully supports the development with the Unity.

Microsoft HoloLens was a primary hardware used to interact with the users. A desktop computer with system core was used to manage all user connections and deal with the augmented environment. The system core took care of the augmented environment which contained a lot of holograms such as virtual robot, script generator, script cube, script header, recycle bin, and general-purpose switch. The holograms were mapped and interacted by the user's gesture to the real environment accordingly to the spatial mapping [18, 19]. All users sent their information to each other via the system core. In addition, all users interacted the same augmented environment at the same actual workplace.

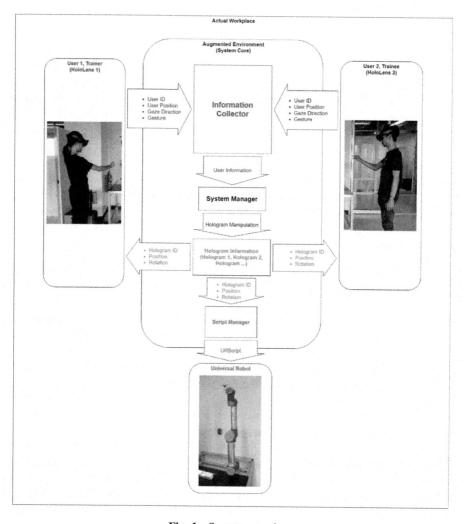

Fig. 1. System overview

During interaction with the augmented environment, all holograms were managed by the system core. So, the users had to sent the information consisted of user's position, gaze direction and gesture to the system core. Then, the processed holograms' information was broadcasted by the system core to all users. Finally, all users were able to visualize the same holograms at a the same time. In the system core, the users' information was utilized by the system manager to synchronize the interactions between users and holograms as shown in Fig. 1.

3 Holograms

In the proposed system, the holograms were the computer graphic display as the 3D object that responded to the gesture and real-world surface [20]. Moreover, it had the potential to mimic the behavior of real object including the industrial robot in the augmented environment.

3.1 Interaction

In the augmented environment, the holograms were interacted by Gaze, Air Tap, and Tap and Hold gestures. The holograms responded to Air Tap as clicking or selecting like a mouse click, Tap and Hold as selecting and dragging like a mouse click and drag. Both gestures were activated after targeting hologram with Gaze gesture.

3.2 Virtual Robot

The virtual robot was used to display the hologram and mimic behavior of the Universal Robot 5 including joint configuration, movement, size, and shape [21]. Multiple users could interact with each part of the virtual robot at the same time with gesture recognition. The virtual robot was constructed from many parts; base, shoulder, elbow, wrist 1, wrise 2, and wrise 3. Each part of a virtual robot was filled with different colors and labeled to help the users to identify each part easily. Moreover, each part was connected together by the configurable joint component and it allowed only one joint to be moved at a time. Each part of the virtual robot was also attached by the rigidbody component for physics simulation [22, 23]. Hence, the virtual robot performed similarly to the real robot as shown in Fig. 2.

3.3 Script Generator

The script generator consisted of two parts, which were a base and a gate. A base was a small gray cylinder with radius of 0.15 m to be snapped with a generated script cube. A gate was a blue ring spinning around itself over a base about 0.5 m. The main role of a script generator was to spawn a script cube when the user finished the manipulation of the virtual robot. During the spawning, a gate played an animation by moving itself down to a base and moving back to the previous position. Finally, a script cube was generate by a script generator then pushed to a base as shown in Fig. 3.

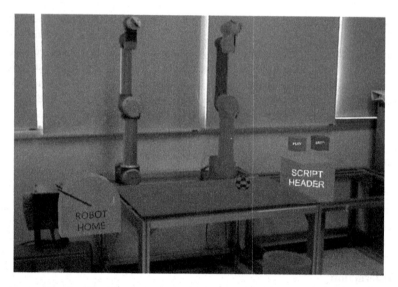

Fig. 2. Virtual robot superimposed on the right-sided real robot

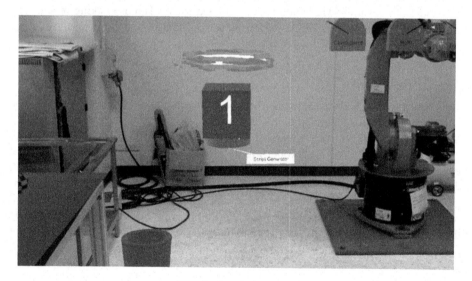

Fig. 3. Script generator

During the spawning, if the previous script cube was still at the base, that previous script cube was moved to the recycle bin automatically.

3.4   Script Cube

The script cube was displayed as a virtual cube sized of 0.3 cubic meter and carried the information of the virtual robot; joint rotation and gripper's action (active, deactive) during spawning of the script cube. Then, the script cube with the random color was labeled by the number accordingly to the order of spawning. The label was adjusted accordingly to the user's position. Hence, the user could read the label on every point-of-view as shown in. Moreover, a chain of script cube was made by the connections of several script cubes. Such a connection occurred when many script cubes were placed near each other. Finally, a chain connected to the script header displayed a line with gradient color of yellow and red as shown in Fig. 4. Furthermore, the users could rearrange the order of the script cube in a chain. The Air Tap gesture was used to activate the script cube for executing the virtual robot operations such as rotating and picking.

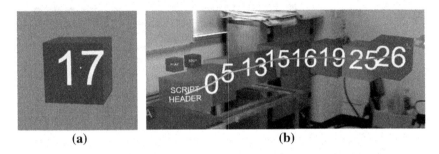

(a)   (b)

Fig. 4. (a) A script cube (b) A chain of script cube (Color figure online)

3.5   Script Header

The script header was an action executor for a chain of script cube. The users could simulate the virtual robot operation by using Air Tap gesture to a small green hologram of "PLAY" above the script header. Then, the virtual robot performed the operation accordingly to a chain of script cubes. The sequence of the operation began from a script cube which was connected next to the script header and it ran until the end of a chain as shown in Fig. 5.

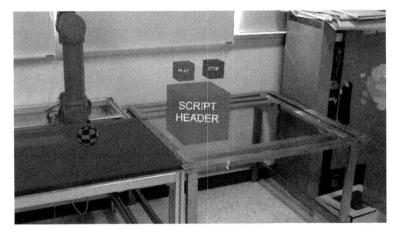

Fig. 5. Script header (Color figure online)

3.6   Recycle Bin

The recycle bin was used to destroy a script cube. During training, an unnecessary script cube could occur. The recycle bin was used to clean up an augmented environment by moving that unnecessary script cube into it as shown in Fig. 6.

Fig. 6. Recycle bin

3.7   General-Purpose Switch

The proposed system provided many functions that helped the users to clear many script cubes, show the tooltip, and execute a special script cube of driving the robot to the home position. To access those functions, the Air Tap gesture was used to turn the general-purpose switch composing of a label and a controlling handle to be on and off as shown in Fig. 7.

Fig. 7. Holograms of tooltip, clear script, and robot home

4   Coordinate Synchronization

The Unity engine supports the three dimensional coordinate system. The object in the Unity was described by the (x, y, z) position and the rotation about 3 axes. The HoloLens could track its position and rotation accordingly to the real world. Then, the Unity could read the HoloLens' position and rotation to update the user's head's position and rotation in the Unity coordinate or augmented environment coordinate.

In the proposed system, multiple users were able to join the same augmented environment and work place. So, each HoloLens had to synchronize its coordinate to the other one's coordinate. The augmented environment had its own coordinate system which started at the (0, 0, 0) position. To synchronize multiple HoloLenses, a simple solution was to put all HoloLenses at the same position and rotation during starting the proposed system as shown in Fig. 8. Hence, all HoloLenses' coordinates were mapped together and all users were able to interact with the same augmented environment accordingly to the same work place.

Fig. 8. Starting position

5   Experimental Results

To evaluate the proposed system's performance and usability, some experiments were conducted. The system performances such as frame rate was tested by the researcher. To check the usability, users were asked to participate with the proposed system as the trainees. First, the researcher, who was the trainer of this system, gave a brief about the proposed system's overview to the users. Then, the users were trained by the trainer using the Microsoft's Hologram application to operate the HoloLens using its recognized gestures, Air Tap, Tap and Hold, before starting the experiment. Next, experiments were conducted following the below topics. Finally, the feedback was given by the users via the USE Questionnaire [24].

5.1   Experimental Setup

In the experiments occured in the Human-Computer Interface (HCI) Lab, all participants, trainer and trainees, were students at the Institute of FIeld roBOtics, King Mongkut's University of Technology Thonburi. All devices consist of two HoloLens and a PC server connected to a dual-band WiFi router. The HoloLens was connected by 5.0 GHz wireless connection at 120 Mbps and a server was connected by ethernet connection at 100 Mbps. This configuration of the experimental setup was performed by the following below topics.

5.2   System Performance

Frame Rate

To display the holograms, the system had to make the user feel like the holograms were in the real world led to the fast graphics rendering. Normally, the rendering rate that gives the best experience for the user should be at least 60 fps [25]. In the proposed system, the script cube spawned by the script generator consumed the system resource and reduced the rendering performance. Hence, one experiment was set to measure the frame rate of rendering according to the number of the script cube. The frame rate was captured by the windows device portal over Wi-Fi [26] which covered 5 s before and after the spawning as shown in Fig. 9. The system spawned a script cube every 0.25 s while the position of script cube was randomized with radius of 1 m around the script header. The spawning ran until the number of script cube reaching to 30. The expected minimum frame rate was 24 FPS [27].

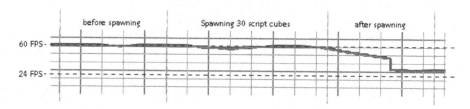

Fig. 9. Frame rates during spawning the script cubes

5.3   Usability

Gesture

In the proposed system, Tap and Hold gesture was mostly used by the user. So, one experiment was set to evaluate the capability of interaction with the holograms by Tap and Hold gesture. The number of user's interactions with the hologram was compared with the number of detected interactions by the system. Nine holograms were spawned in the form of 3 rows by 3 columns. The spawned hologram disappeared when it was moved far from the original position. The users were asked to move the spawned holograms until it disappeared. The number of Tap and Hold gesture was counted by the researcher. The number of Tap and Hold gesture performed by the users was expected to be 9 times according to the number of the spawned holograms (Table 2).

Table 2. Comparison of the Tap and Hold gesture counted by the reseacher and the system

Participant #	Number of interaction		Error (%)
	Counted by the researcher	Detected by the system	
1	14	9	55.56
2	11		22.22
3	10		11.11
4	12		33.33
5	9		0
6	10		11.11
7	10		11.11
8	12		33.33
Avg.	11.00	9	22.22

Basic Virtual Robot Operation

The virual robot operation was the core in this proposed system. One experiment was set to evaluate the ease of use, ease of learning, and satisfacation on the virtual robot operation. First, the trainer gave a brief about the proposed system. Secondly, the trainee was trained by the trainer to operate the virtual robot. Then, a specific task was given by the trainer to the trainee to operate the virtual robot to pick a virtual object from point A to point B as shown in Fig. 10. Finally, the feedback was given by the users via the USE Questionnaire (Tables 3, 4 and 5).

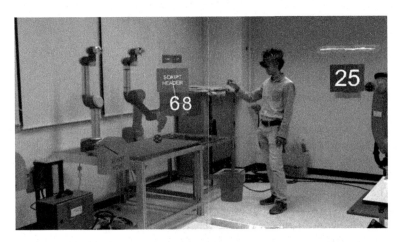

Fig. 10. Trainer's view during the virtual robot operation

Table 3. Result of the ease of use questionnaire (−3 = Strongly disagree, 3 = Strongly agree)

	Avg. score
It is easy to use	1.63
It is simple to use	2.25
It is user friendly	2.00
It requires the fewest steps possible to accomplish what I want to do with it	1.63
It is flexible	1.63
Using it is effortless	1.63
I can use it without written instructions	1.25
I don't notice any inconsistencies as I use it	1.25
Both occasional and regular users would like it	2.13
I can recover from mistakes quickly and easily	1.75
I can use it successfully every time	1.50

Table 4. Result of the ease of learning (−3 = Strongly disagree, 3 = Strongly agree)

	Avg. score
I learned to use it quickly	1.75
I easily remember how to use it	2.38
It is easy to learn to use it	2.63
I quickly became skillful with it	2.25

Table 5. Result of the satisfacation (−3 = Strongly disagree, 3 = Strongly agree)

	Avg. score
I am satisfied with it	1.75
I would recommend it to a friend	2.13
It is fun to use	2.25
It works the way I want it to work	1.75
It is wonderful	2.13
I feel I need to have it	1.75
It is pleasant to use	1.88

6   Conclusions and Future Work

This research proposed the utilization of augmented reality for robot training system. Several holograms were implemented to help multiple users to do On-the-Job Training related to virtual robot operation. Microsoft HoloLens was used to display the interactive holograms which mimiced the behaviors of the real objects, especially the UR5 robot. The system core, which covered chain of script cube, script generator, script header, recycle bin, general-purpose switch, coordinate synchronization, was developed at the Human-Computer Interface (HCI) Lab, Institute of FIeld roBOtics, King Mongkut's University of Technology Thonburi. The system performance and usability were tested. The result of the experiments showed that the frame rate was decreased from 60 to 30 fps after spawning because several script cubes began the connections among them. So, 30 script cubes still maintained the frame rate higher than the expected minimum frame rate. The error from Tap and Hold gesture was about 22.22% which was acceptable for the operation of the proposed system. Most of users joining the experiments had no experience with HoloLens and robot operation. The result of the virtual robot operation showed that the users strongly agreed that the proposed system was user friendly, easy to learn to use, and fun to use because its holograms provided the natural interaction for the users. In addition, the users slightly agreed that the proposed system was used without written instructions, learned to be used quickly, and users were satisfied with the system because most of users had no experience with holograms and robot operation and they suggested that some parts of user interface needed to be improved.

In the future work, some parts of user interface need improvement according to feedback from the users. In addition, the URScript could be integrated into the proposed system to control the real robot via socket connection and augmented reality. Hence, the real robot can operate accordingly to the virtual robot operation. Furthermore, the spatial mapping needs to be investigated to improve the coordinate synchronization of the proposed system.

References

1. Pike, R.W.: Creative Training Techniques Handbook (1989)
2. Saddler, K.: Developing HR Talent: Building a Strategic Partnership With the Business (2011)
3. Hersey, P.: Management of Organizational Behavior (1982)
4. Doswell, J.T., Mosley, P.H.: Robotics in mixed-reality training simulations: augmenting STEM learning. In: Sixth IEEE International Conference on Advanced Learning Technologies (ICALT 2006), pp. 864–868 (2006)
5. Syberfeldt, A., Danielsson, O., Holm, M., Wang, L.: Visual assembling guidance using augmented reality. Procedia Manufact. **1**, 98–109 (2015)
6. Cheng, I., Shen, R., Moreau, R., Brizzi, V., Rossol, N., Basu, A.: An augmented reality framework for optimization of computer assisted navigation in endovascular surgery. In: 2014 36th Annual International Conference of the IEEE Engineering in Medicine and Biology Society, pp. 5647–5650 (2014)
7. Xiaoling, W., Peng, Z., Zhifang, W., Yan, S., Bin, L., Yangchun, L.: Development an interactive VR training for CNC machining. In: Proceedings of the 2004 ACM SIGGRAPH International Conference on Virtual Reality Continuum and Its Applications in Industry, pp. 131–133. ACM, Singapore (2004)
8. Ghandorh, H., Mackenzie, J., Eagleson, R., Ribaupierre, S.D.: Development of augmented reality training simulator systems for neurosurgery using model-driven software engineering. In: 2017 IEEE 30th Canadian Conference on Electrical and Computer Engineering (CCECE), pp. 1–6 (2017)
9. Kwon, B., Kim, J., Lee, K., Lee, Y.K., Park, S., Lee, S.: Implementation of a virtual training simulator based on 360? Multi-view human action recognition. IEEE Access **5**, 12496–12511 (2017)

10. Boschmann, A., Dosen, S., Werner, A., Raies, A., Farina, D.: A novel immersive augmented reality system for prosthesis training and assessment. In: 2016 IEEE-EMBS International Conference on Biomedical and Health Informatics (BHI), pp. 280–283 (2016)

11. Santos, I., Dam, P., Arantes, P., Raposo, A., Soares, L.: Simulation training in oil platforms. In: 2016 XVIII Symposium on Virtual and Augmented Reality (SVR), pp. 47–53 (2016)

12. Jo, D., Kim, Y., Yang, U., Choi, J., Kim, K.-H., Lee, G.A., Park, Y.-D., Park, Y.W.: Welding representation for training under VR environments. In: Proceedings of the 10th International Conference on Virtual Reality Continuum and Its Applications in Industry, pp. 339–342. ACM, Hong Kong (2011)

13. Ordaz, N., Romero, D., Gorecky, D., Siller, H.R.: Serious games and virtual simulator for automotive manufacturing education & training. Procedia Comput. Sci. **75**, 267–274 (2015)

14. Cheryl, A.V.: Why switch from paper to electronic manuals. In: Proceedings of the ACM Conference on Document Processing Systems %@ 0-89791-291-8, pp. 111–116. ACM, Santa Fe (1988)

15. Doswell, J.T.: Context-aware mobile augmented reality architecture for lifelong learning. In: Sixth IEEE International Conference on Advanced Learning Technologies (ICALT 2006), pp. 372–374 (2006)

16. Unity. https://docs.unity3d.com/Manual

17. Microsoft. https://github.com/Microsoft/MixedRealityToolkit-Unity

18. Microsoft. https://developer.microsoft.com/en-us/windows/mixed-reality/spatial_mapping

19. Microsoft. https://developer.microsoft.com/en-us/windows/mixed-reality/gestures

20. Microsoft. https://developer.microsoft.com/en-us/windows/mixed-reality/hologram

21. https://github.com/qian256/ur5_unity

22. Unity. https://docs.unity3d.com/Manual/class-ConfigurableJoint.html

23. Unity. https://docs.unity3d.com/Manual/class-Rigidbody.html

24. Lund, A.: Measuring Usability with the USE Questionnaire (2001)

25. Microsoft. https://developer.microsoft.com/en-us/windows/mixed-reality/Hologram_stability. html

26. Microsoft. https://developer.microsoft.com/en-us/windows/mixed-reality/using_the_windows_ device_portal

27. How 24 FPS Became Standard. TWiT Netcast Network (2017)

Mobile and Wearable HCI

Investigating Users' Experiences and Attitudes Towards Mobile Apps' Reviews

Omar Asiri[(⊠)] and Carl K. Chang[(⊠)]

Iowa State University, Ames, IA 50010, USA
{oasiri, chang}@iastate.edu

Abstract. One of the daily routines of the smartphone users is using the mobile applications. Individuals explore the app stores and select a potential app. The selection procedure is affected by the information that the app stores display for each app. Reviews of the apps are an important factor in making decisions to select an app. Likewise, Users experiences and attitudes are affected by the information that they read and see on the interface of apps' reviews. In our study, we aim to investigate the users' experiences and attitudes towards mobile apps' reviews. To achieve our goal, we constructed a survey consists of statements divided into five categories to collect a variety of data about the users' experience and attitude. The questionnaire's categories were designed to generate data regarding users' experiences and attitudes when selecting apps. Likewise, to investigate the criteria that users set to evaluate the apps' quality. Moreover, participants were asked about their experiences with the comments section in the apps' reviews. Also, investigating if there are complaints regarding the reviews' comments. Furthermore, we investigated what users can know from the interface of the mobile apps reviews in the app stores. We had 102 participants in our survey. Our results showed that free apps, especially if there is a need for the app, have the most chance to be installed even with a lower rate. We also found that, besides the apps' rating and download statistics, users tend to adapt self-judgment for determining the apps' quality. Regarding the reviews' comments, users wish there is a way to limit the length of the reviews. Users like the reviews that are short and specific. We found that the current interface design of the review needs revisions to help users to be aware of critical apps-related issues such as apps' permissions.

Keywords: Apps' reviews · Users' experiences · Users' attitudes
Mobile apps · Reviews' interface

1 Introduction

Adam loves photography. Recently he bought a new smartphone that has a very powerful camera. Adam wanted to take pictures and post them on his Instagram account to show his talent to his followers. He needed to have a powerful app to do some photo editing before posting the images to his account. He searched for an app in the app store; he found multiple apps that look very useful. However, He was confused which app he should install. He found that the first five of them has a very high rating and so many positive comments, but still, he needs to decide and install one of the apps

© Springer International Publishing AG, part of Springer Nature 2018
M. Kurosu (Ed.): HCI 2018, LNCS 10902, pp. 481–499, 2018.
https://doi.org/10.1007/978-3-319-91244-8_38

he found. The problem is that he does not want to try them all. He wanted to find an easy way to know which app is better. He has concerns regarding the privacy, permissions required, and the battery consumption but he could not find a usable way to compare the apps and know which one is the best for his need. He tried to read the reviews, but there is a vast amount of reviews listed for each app. He could not find another way to read the reviews quickly and decide which one may help him. Adam ended up with installing the apps one after another until he found a mid-rated app that he liked the most.

A numerous portion of mobile apps' users has experienced Adam's experience at least once while they want to install an app. There is a huge increase in the apps developments. Every day we have new apps posted to the app stores. The number of apps that users can access on apps stores is very huge. As of March 2017, a recent statistical data shows that Google play has 2.8 million apps and Apple's App Store has 2.2 million apps [1]. In addition to that, many of the companies and developers try their best to have their apps ranked with a higher rating. Either by producing very good apps or by manipulating the reviews. In addition to that, there is a numerous number of reviews added every day. A study reported that the popular apps, like Facebook, receives on average more than 4000 reviews per day [2]. Thus, it is a hard job for users to read all reviews.

In our study, we aim to investigate the users' experiences and their attitudes towards mobile apps' review. When we mention mobile apps' reviews, we mean the whole interface design that illustrates information about an app. In another way, we mean all elements that app's info page contains such as the star rating, the comments, the number of downloads, versions history, permissions, etc.

In this paper, in order to get better understating, we investigate the users' experiences and their attitudes towards mobile apps' reviews in several dimensions. To achieve our goal we address the following research questions.

- RQ1: What are users' experiences and attitudes when selecting mobile apps?
- RQ2: What criteria do users set to evaluate apps' quality?
- RQ3: What are the users' experiences and attitudes towards the comments of mobile apps' reviews?
- RQ4: What are the users' complaints regarding the apps' reviews?
- RQ5: What can users know from the interface design of apps' reviews?

This paper is organized as follows. In Sect. 2, we illustrate the current and relevant research on mobile apps' reviews. In Sect. 3, we describe the methodology and how it was constructed. In Sect. 4, we report our research findings. In Sect. 5, we discuss our findings. Then we conclude this paper with our final thoughts and future directions.

2   Literature Review

2.1   The Importance of the Apps' Rating

Apps rating plays crucial roles to determine the apps successful in apps' stores [3, 4]. There is a strong correlation between apps rating and the number of downloads [5]. Moreover, the rating is a key role when users decide to purchase an app [6] or make an online purchase [7]. For many developers, the revenue will be tied with the star rating that their apps achieved [6]. Apps with better reviews will achieve better ranking which could result in better sales [8].

A research study found a relationship between the quantity of feedback that an app got and the app's overall rating and its price [9]. They reported that users tend to provide more feedback for lower rated apps. Moreover, reviews are 12 times more trusted than the description provided by the app's developer [9].

2.2 The Challenges in the Apps' Reviews

Increasing the number of reviews could limit the benefit for users because they will not be able to read all reviews. Iacob et al. [9] stated that the ability to read the reviews become limited when the app has a massive quantity of reviews. Moreover, quantity and length of reviews make spotting the weak points of product harder for people.

Reviews are very challenging and hard to be analyzed. On average, Apps receive 23 reviews per day, and the popular apps like Facebook receive on average more than 4000 reviews per day [2]. Since apps receive this huge amount of reviews, there are associated issues that make dealing with apps reviews difficult. Reviews are unstructured, vary in the quality, and hard to identify the useful ones [2, 10]. While users leave reviews in varying length, these reviews are not free of informal expression, using abbreviations, and misspelling [11]. Moreover, online reviews are not trusted every time. As stated in [12], the online products' reviews may provide misleading information and do not always revealing the products' real quality.

2.3 What Can We Get Out of Apps' Reviews?

Tian et al. [13] conducted a study to understand differences between high rated and low rated apps. They found that "high-rated apps have larger sizes, more complex code, more requirements on users, more marketing efforts, more dependence on libraries, and adopt higher quality Android APIs."

Reviews are not only beneficial for users but also developers can get valuable feedback. Apps' reviews could help developers with determining users' requirements, improvement suggestions, requesting desired features, expressing users experiences [2, 5, 14]. In addition to that, some users report issues related to the app's GUI, app's speed, or provide a comparative review with other apps [9].

One way to distinguish good apps from bad apps is their ratings. However, the rating is not always reflecting the reality of an app. Users might be unsatisfied with an app even if the app has a decent rating. A study suggested that app's trust should be built on several criteria not only on the app's rating. Apps' rating is not a reliable metric [15].

2.4 Users' Behavior with Exploring and Experiencing Apps

Apps' Selection
There are several ways for discovering a new app in the apps stores. Recommendations from known individuals, and browsing the apps' stores are the most discovery means

for apps installation [16, 17]. Approximately 25% of the reviews have recommendations for using the app to other users [9]. Moreover, Chin et al. [16] claimed that the price of an app and the app's popularity are considered aspects of app selection and installation.

Hoon et al. [18] analyzed 8.7 million reviews from 17,330 apps; their results showed users tend to leave short reviews for mobile apps. Additionally, the category of the app has an impact on the length of the review. The reviews are higher rated and longer in some apps categories than other. Moreover, as stated in [12], usually users provide a review when they are either extremely happy or extremely unhappy with the product.

Apps' Updates

In a study of the user's attitude and behavior towards applications' updates, about half of smartphone users set their phones to be automatically updated because they want their apps to be always up-to-date [19]. In addition, the study found that there are users who do not update apps due to privacy and permissions concerns. Another research found that users tend to install apps that are recently updated but not requesting frequent updates [20]. A recent study analyzed 10,713 mobile apps in 30 categories of apps found out that 14% of the mobile apps are frequently updated [21]. Moreover, they found that 45% of the frequently updated apps do not inform the users about the reasons behind the updates. As reported in [20], users have mixed feeling regarding apps update. Users often desire new updates for the apps. However, they are afraid of facing update-related issues. Nayebi et al. [20] found that both device and apps crashes are the frequently reported issues emerging after the updates. Trusting the app's developer, the type of the apps' reviews either negative or positive, and the type of permissions requested are factors that influence users' decision when they chose to update an app [16, 19].

Privacy and Permissions

To understand to what extent users value their information on their smartphones Chin et al. [16] found that users are more concerns about privacy in their phones than other devices like a laptop. Surprisingly, while users tend to see and read the permissions on the screen, research revealed that users have limited knowledge about privacy and security, and they do not understand permissions [22, 23]. Kelley et al. [22] found that people are unaware of the security risks associated with apps. Users believe that all apps on the app store are already tested and should be trusted. As claimed in [22], users are not prepared to make decisions regarding privacy and security. Moreover, not all users are unaware of privacy. There are users know that mobile apps violated their privacy unethically, but they still use these apps [24]. In fact, most users ignore permissions completely [25, 26].

Many of smartphone users are willing to share data with developers in the right way specifically when the data used for the agreed purpose. Research reported that users were surprised and felt violated when they found out that apps in their mobiles are accessing data without their knowledge [25, 27]. A recent study examined 10000 android apps and had found a relationship between permission popularity and the number of times it was misused [28].

One of unethical and misuse for the permissions is collecting users data. There are apps that are interested in collecting data from users phones [26].

Battery Consumption

An issue that might happen to some apps' users is when the app drains the cellphone's battery. Nagappan and Shihab [29] claimed that not all developers know how to program an energy efficient app. Thus, there is a need to make developers aware of the good habits to program an energy efficient apps. The apps may have access to multiple resources of the users' devices. Users might not be able to recognize which resource in the app is draining out their devices' batteries. Since resources vary in consuming the power of the device, Li et al. [30] studied 405 apps to investigate energy consumption. One of their findings is that networking is the component that consumes much energy.

Users' Complaints

In the body of literature, many studies have done text mining to investigate the complaints that users reported in the apps' reviews. Examples of the users' complaints were reported in [31, 32]. In [32] a categorization of 12 types of users' complaints have been identified. The identified complaints are

> *"App Crashing, Compatibility, Feature Removal, Feature Request, Functional Error, Hidden Cost, Interface Design, Network Problem, Privacy and Ethics, Resource Heavy, Uninteresting Content, and Unresponsive App (Pg.74)"*

To determine which complaint is reported the most, studies found that more than 50% of the users' complaints fall into three categories; reporting functional errors, requests for specific features, and reporting app crashes [31, 32]. From the 12 types of complaints, the most negatively perceived complaints were privacy and ethics, hidden cost, and feature removal [31]. Some apps got a low rating because the users have experienced some of these complaints. Although some apps are free to download, users need to pay monthly subscription fees to have the full membership privilege. Some users do not perceive that before installing the app. That led them to give a lower rating for the app. As reported in [31], more than half of low rating for Hulu plus was due to the hidden-cost, which is the monthly subscription fees. As claimed in [31], there is a correlation between users' complaints and the apps updates. They also found that users report their complaints after a recent update.

2.5   The Need to Redesign the Reviews' Interface

Users may have some issues with the design of the interface of the apps' reviews. A study showed that 13%–49% of the sentences of online reviews have feedback related to usability or user experience [33]. Some users may have difficulty to figure out why specific resource of their phone is being accessed. Liu et al. [34] suggested that app stores should design a simple interface especially when it comes to permissions and privacy information illustration. They claimed that simple interface would help users to make better decisions when it comes to granting permissions and control the resources of their devices. There should not be a trade where users give up the control for the sake of usability [34]. A Research claimed that users have limited knowledge about the security risks that are associated with app selection. Thus they suggested that apps stores should consider redesigning privacy communicating icons [23]. Also, they encourage apps' stores to display these icons at the beginning of the installation cycle so users can make decisions in the earlier stages. In [23], Rajivan and Camp recommended that privacy communication icons should fit the user mental models of security. Hence, users need visual cues that are simple, and easy to comprehend to reduce risks and concerns that are associated with app choices. In [23], Rajivan and Camp stated "privacy communicating icons should align with user mental models of security." As suggested in [27], users need to be informed about the reason of why each resource is being used because that could help to ease the users' privacy concerns. Due to the numerous amount of reviews in apps stores, users need a clear interface to be able to make decisions about apps quality [14].

It is worth to mention that none of the previous research has study the user experience with the interface of the apps' reviews, which is one of this research goals. We think that the users' experiences with the apps' reviews would be differ if the design is different. The number of the complaints would be reduced, and the users' awareness regarding some of the apps related technical issues would be increased.

3   Methodology

The goal of this study is to investigate users' experiences and their attitudes towards mobile apps reviews. Thus, we used an online questionnaire as a method for collecting our data. As stated in [35], it is appropriate to use questionnaires to explore people's attitudes and beliefs. In [36], Müller et al. stated that

> *"Surveys can gather insights about people's attitudes, perceptions, intents, habits, awarenesses, experiences, and characteristics, at significant moments both in time and over time."*

3.1   Subjects

The total number of completed responses is 102. Majority of the participants were students at Iowa State University and representing well-educated population. The primary recruitment method was via sending a mass email. We sent the link of the survey to the email list of the graduate students in computer science program and to the email list of Virtual Reality Application Center (VRAC). We also adopt snow bowling method in recruiting the participants by inquiring people who may participate to forward the study link to other people who might be interested in participating as well. While the snow bowling was helpful to recruit more respondents, it made the majority of the participants are individuals who are well educated.

Out of 102 respondents, 60 (58.82%) were male, and 42 (41.18%) were female. Regarding the operating system of participants' smartphones, 57 (55.88%) were using IOS, 43 (42.16%) were using Android, and 2 (1.96%) were using Windows phone system. Regarding the age range; 29 (28.43%) aged between (20–24), 30 (29.41%) participants aged between (25–29), 36 (35.29%) aged between (30–34), and 7 (6.86%) were older than 35 years of age. In term of the highest degree that the participants have received, 12 (11.76%) participants have high school, 3 (2.94%) have associate degree,

34 (33.33%) have Bachelor's degree, 45 (44.12%) have Master's degree and 8 (7.84%) participants have Doctorate degree.

3.2   Instrument

The questionnaire consists of six sections. The first one contains demographic data about the participants. The following five sections were divided to collect data regarding users' experiences attitudes towards mobile apps reviews. The statements in each group were designed as a 5 points Likert scale questions. Following each set of statements, there was an open-ended question to give the participants the opportunity to add additional thoughts. The statements were grouped according to their thematic similarities into five groups. The first group contains seven statements about the user experiences and attitudes regarding the mobile apps' selections. The second group has four statements to measure participants' attitudes regarding some of the criteria for evaluating the apps' quality. The third group has seven statements designed to reveal data about users' experiences and attitudes with the comment section on the apps reviews on the apps store. The fourth group contains six statements asking participants about their experiences and attitudes regarding frequent mobile apps issues. The fifth group consists of eight statements to determine participants' awareness regarding some of the app's issues as well as some elements of the reviews' interface.

A pilot study and review by three university professors helped the authors to modify the elements of the questionnaire. Modifications in the questionnaire included eliminating some of the statements as well as rephrasing other statements. For the internal consistency, the instrument's Cronbach's Alpha was $(\alpha = .765)$.

3.3   Procedure

To make the survey available online we used Qualtrics platform (www.qualtrics.com), a very well-known online platform for survey administration. The survey was made available for a month. Participants completed the survey on a duration ranged between 5 to 10 min. The survey questions were illustrated in separate pages. The first page had the demographic questions. The following pages were illustrated in groups of statements from group 1 to group 5. Each group has statements that are providing information regarding one aspect of the study. Following each group of statements, there was an open-ended question to give the participant the opportunity to provide the personal thought.

After completing the questionnaire, the participants were given a chance to enter a drawing to win a gift card. We had four gift cards each one valued $25. To ensure anonymity, and to separate the drawing data from the survey data, participants information and participants who wished to enroll in the drawing were required to click on a link that opens a new web page. Then they can add their email information.

To provide a degree of agreement for each statement, we have used five points Likert scale statements that were ranked 1–5, with 1 = "strongly disagree", 2 = "disagree", 3 = "neutral", 4 = "agree", and 5 = "strongly agree".

4   Results

This study has two types of data, quantitative and qualitative data. The quantitative data generated by analyzing the results of the Likert scale items. While the qualitative results generated by analyzing the open-ended questions that followed each group of statements in our scale. Following is our findings categorized according to our research elements.

4.1   Users' Experiences and Attitudes with Selecting Mobile Apps

The experience of picking an app differs from user to another. Table 1 summarizes results for participants' responses when they were asked to indicate their agreements regarding each statement in this part of our questionnaire. Results show that participants mostly tend to agree with all the statements. Preferring to install free apps was the highest among other statements in this group (M = 4.54, SD = .88). For installing applications with a lower rating, participants' answers tend to be, on average, "agree" (M = 3.45, SD = 1.03). Interestingly, when participants were asked about downloading trendy apps, the results were the lowest among other statements. The participants tend to answer, on average, "agree" (M = 3.04, SD = 1.07).

Table 1. Users' experiences and attitudes with selecting mobile apps

Statement	N	M	SD
1. I choose apps upon the ranking given to them	102	3.73	0.98
2. I prefer to install free apps more than paid apps	102	4.54	0.88
3. I do not install apps with lower rating	102	3.45	1.03
4. I install apps that I need even if they have a lower rating	101	3.49	0.99
5. I install apps that my friends suggested to me	102	3.80	0.82
6. I often install trendy apps	102	3.04	1.07
7. I trust apps reviews	102	3.68	0.75

As a part of investigating the users' attitudes and experience with selecting mobile apps. We had an open-ended question to ask participants to share their approaches of selecting apps to install. Results of this question revealed several patterns for the participants' experiences when they pick an app to install. The frequent words in most of the users' inputs for this question included star rating, number of downloads, need, and free app. One of the participants has described his experience with picking apps as "I start off reviewing the free apps, then I look within the free apps and look for the ones with the highest ratings." Another participant said, "I search for something I need, then read reviews. Both in the apps store and online to find the best app for me. If they are free, I might download a couple to try them out and see which I like best."

Some users reported that they only install important apps. Others identify their way for searching for an app is by using keywords. Some participants reported that they download apps, specifically the free ones, then they try it out. If the app met their desires, then they keep it. Otherwise, they try out a different app. Participants responses reveal several criteria to consider installing an app. Examples of these criteria include being rated above three stars, having positive comments, being a free app, having specific features, meet a specific need, specific brand, and having a nice interface design.

Installing an app is not always done purposefully, some participants reported that they install apps due to other factors. These factors include brand name, friends and relatives' suggestions, Advertisements, and social media.

Some users are not interested in installing apps unless they find themselves in situations that lead them to install the apps. On the other hand, some users like to browse the apps store from time to time to discover new apps. Also, they might browse the apps by their categories to compare the apps. We found participants who like to explore the apps by searching for a keyword. A participant in our study summarized his experience with exploring and choosing the apps as following

> "Search for a keyword. See the first 8–10 apps and compare them. if any of them were recommended by a close friend, then give them higher weightage. Second in line will be those recommended on the internet. One important point will be the app should have good review for the last few updates and negative comments mentioned should not be a big factor. If it is, then not go for the app. Else, do not worry. Also, one big factor is the specifications of my phone. If my phone could not handle the app even if it is best for the world I would not use it, e.g., Asphalt game for many users."

4.2 Users' Experiences and Attitudes with Perceiving and Evaluating Apps Quality

There are many ways to provide a judgment on apps quality. Our questionnaire focused on investigating three elements that are important factors to determine the attitudes towards the perception of apps' quality. These factors are number of downloads, number of the stars given to an app, and the amount of review comments in that the app page. Results showed that participants tended to answer, on average, "agree" for the all of the statements (M = 3.45, SD = 1.10; M = 4.09, SD = 0.78; M = 3.53, SD = 1.06) respectively. Results show that participants tended to answer, on average, "disagree" (M = 2.06, SD = 0.94) when they provided their responses to the statement there is no relationship between the app quality and its rating. Table 2 illustrates our findings in this category.

Table 2. Users' experiences and attitudes with perceiving and evaluating apps quality

Statement	N	M	SD
8. Number of downloads for an app is an indication of the app quality	102	3.45	1.10
9. Number of stars given to the app is an indication of the app quality	101	4.09	0.78
10. Number of reviews for an app is an indication of the app quality	102	3.53	1.06
11. I think there is no relationship between the app quality and the app rating	102	2.06	0.94

Participants were also asked to answer the open-ended question "Can you share how do you decide whether the app has good quality?" Answers to this question contained valuable thoughts. As a summary of the participants' thoughts; many participants think that the number of downloads and the stars rating are very important factors to determine the quality of an app. Other participants may have different criteria such as friend's advice or self-judgment to decide the apps' quality. A participant summarized his approach to determining the app quality by stating "By the following criteria: First, by downloading it and use it by myself. Second, friends' advice. Third, reviews. Fourth, app advantages." Moreover, the quality judgment may depend on the app technical features, and how it works without issues. A participant stated that "Whether it is buggy, slows the phone down, has too many in-app purchases…whether it is easy to use, fast response, fast load time, completes the task necessary." Other participants consider ease of use and beautiful interface as a part of the app quality.

4.3   Users' Attitudes and Experiences with Comments Section in the Apps' Reviews

The comments section on app reviews is very useful for many users. Results showed that participants tended to answer, on average, "agree" when they were asked about the usefulness of the comments in app reviews (M = 3.94, SD = 0.78). On the other hand, participants disagreed with the statements that claimed reading all the detailed comments is wasting their time (M = 2.94, SD = 1.19). We also found that participants tend to use the comments of apps' reviews as a supportive tool when they want to compare two apps (M = 3.85, SD = 0.91). Table 3 summarizes all findings related to statements of the apps' review comments.

Table 3. Users' attitudes and experiences with comments section in the apps' reviews

Statement	N	M	SD
12. The comments in the app review are useful	102	3.94	0.78
13. If the app has an excellent rating, it is a waste of time to read all of the detailed comments in the comment section	102	2.94	1.19
14. I tend to read the comments in the review when I want to compare two different apps	102	3.85	0.91
15. Comments associated with the rating may affect my decision regarding installing an app	102	3.97	0.78
16. I trust reviews that are associated with a lower rating	102	3.34	0.80
17. I trust negative comments more than positive ones	102	3.07	0.87
18. I extensively read comments in the review section associated with lower-rated apps	102	3.19	1.12

To give the participants more flexibility to deliver their thoughts regarding apps reviews comments, they were asked to answer an open-ended question "Can you share how do you read comments in the review section?" Analyzing the results of this question revealed the participants' behaviors when they interact with the reviews section. In general, participants reported that they do not read all of the reviews listed in the comments section specifically the long reviews. Participants reported several behaviors for reading apps reviews. Most users tend to scan reviews. When they need to read the reviews, they start with shorter, negative, and lower rating reviews. Some participants read both negative and positive reviews, which are associated with lower and higher rating to make a comparison when is needed. One of the participants described his behavior as following, "I tend to read comments when I want to compare two similar apps. If the apps are different, there is no need to compare apples to oranges." In addition, participants stated that they read the recent reviews because it reflects the current issues if there is any. One reason to read reviews was to investigate other users' experiences and make decisions according to what others have experienced with the app. While participants reported that apps reviews are fun to read, they also wish if there are a limited number of words for each review. Some participants claimed that they could distinguish fake reviews. They said those fake reviews usually consist of ridiculous qualities and many misspelling. A participant has shared his experience with the apps' review as following

> *"I know that just like news, product reviews, app reviews are also susceptible to being fake. The company can ask their acquaintances to write positive about them and their rivals can write negative too. It is hard to differentiate the genuine and fake ones, but I use the following observation for my sake. Do not go for one word, one-liner reviews (exception if the majority says the same thing). Do not go for super lengthy reviews, as they will be people criticizing the app like a bully. Go for reviews between the length of 2–6 lines or the ones that make sections of pros and cons.*
>
> *One more important thing is some people write comments just after a couple of days of use. We cannot verify this, but I prefer the ones that are written by users who used it for at least a month as sometimes system performance reduces with prolonged use of apps. Long ago we can view votes and comments from our friends but due to recent privacy changes it cannot be done now."*

4.4   Users' Experiences and Attitudes with the Common Complaints

Having complaints about any product is normal. For the apps users, they always complain about several common issues. We had several statements that measure the users' attitudes and experiences with frequent apps complaints. Surprisingly, participants tend to answer, on average, "strongly agree" for all statements. Results indicated that removing a favorite feature from an app was the highest average among other statements (M = 4.43, SD = 0.67). It is known that apps ask for some permission upon installing them. Participants tend to answer, on average, "strongly agree" with the statement that stated "apps should indicate specific reasons for using some permissions" (M = 4.30, SD = 0.76). Table 4 indicates all findings about statements on this section.

Participants were asked to answer the open-ended question "Do you have any complaints about mobile apps reviews? Would you like to share your thought?" we have found insightful thoughts in participants' responses for this question. Results regarding this question were not only including the complaints about the mobile apps' review, but also there were comments that would benefits the development of the apps. Some responses were commenting on the hidden cost of mobile apps. They reported that they hated when an app asks for small transactions for every single feature that they want to use. In addition, they said there is no trial period; consequently, they

Table 4. Users' experiences and attitudes with the common complaints

Statement	N	M	SD
19. It bothers me when an app asks for permission that I think is not related to the app purpose	102	4.22	0.93
20. Apps should indicate specific reasons for using some permissions	102	4.30	0.76
21. I am not comfortable with ads included in some apps	102	4.08	1.05
22. I do not like when an app asks me to pay money to use specific features	102	4.21	0.97
23. It bothers me when an app's developer removes a favorite feature from the app after updates	102	4.43	0.67
24. I feel disappointed when an app is not compatible with my smartphone	102	4.16	0.84

cannot undo their purchases. Moreover, participants prefer to pay one price upfront for the app and its features instead of paying separately for each feature specifically games. Participants agreed to the importance of paying some money for apps developments, but they wanted to be clear about what they will pay.

The participants in our study raised another issue which is the comments in apps review. Participants mentioned that there are reviews that are helpful but very long. They wish if there is a way to limit the review's words count and provide a specific structure for the review. A participant reported, "It is better to make them short, specific and helpful. Some comments might be helpful but long which makes me skip them." In addition to that, participants suggested that users should not be able to provide high app rating without writing a comment. Participants claimed that this process would limit fake and misleading reviews. One of our participants stated "it is easier to rate 5 starts rater than 3 and write why." Another issue about the apps' review is the lack of the reviews number. Usually, apps' stores do not display reviews for new apps until they reach a specific number of reviews. A participant reported that he hated when he found an app without published reviews. On the other hand, results indicated not all participants read the reviews. A participant mentioned that he downloads apps that he comes across and when they are not good, he uninstalled them.

Our results indicated several complaints regarding apps in general. Participants were not comfortable with the number of unnecessary permissions that they need to provide to the app upon the installing process. In addition, there were some complaints regarding the Ads. Participants reported that some apps contain many ads. Some users reported complaints regarding apps that have low-quality graphics and ugly avatars.

4.5   What Can Users Know from the Interface Design of Apps' Review?

The screen of apps reviews has many elements that users are not aware of. Moreover, there are other elements that are very important to be parts of the apps reviews, but unfortunately, most apps' stores do not provide it. For example, information about the battery consumption is important information that users should know. Our results indicated that users tend to answer, on average, "strongly disagree" ($M = 1.95$, $SD = 1.01$) when answering the statement regarding the ability to locate information about apps battery consumption on apps review screen. In addition to that users tend to answer, on average, "disagree" when they were asked to answer questions regarding the ability to find information about app's security, app's privacy, device compatibility, and app's ads. Table 5 summarizes our findings regarding the users' responses.

Table 5. What can users know from the interface design of apps' review?

Statement	N	M	SD
25. I think age rating is a necessary feature to classify apps	101	3.87	1.08
26. From the app review's screen, it is easy to determine if the app is suitable for my age	101	3.11	1.07
27. From the app review's screen, I can locate information about the app's battery consumption	101	1.95	1.01
28. From the app review's screen, I can tell whether the app is secure or not	101	2.04	1.02
29. From the app review's screen, I can find information about privacy	101	2.30	1.04
30. From the app review's screen, I can tell whether the app violates the privacy or not	100	2.15	1.02
31. From the app review's screen, I can tell if the app has ads or not	99	2.32	1.16
32. From the review's review screen, I can tell if the app is compatible with my smartphone	99	2.93	1.28

To give the participants more flexibility to deliver their thoughts regarding the interface of apps reviews, they were asked an open-ended question followed their responses for the statements in this section. The question was "Do you have any suggestion about the design of apps' reviews? Would you like to share your thought?" Responses to this question had valuable thoughts. We divided their answers into two categories. First complaints related to the interface design. Second, suggestions for a future design.

Participants reported that the current interface design for the mobile apps' reviews needs more simplicity in the design. The amount of information is very huge and bulky, which makes finding specific information sometimes a very hard task. Participants stated that the current design is not constant. There is information illustrated in the reviews of some apps while this information could not be found in other apps. In addition to that, users claimed that there were too many elements in the review info page. They needed more time to figure out relevant information to what they want to find.

Respondents have suggested some ideas for redesigning the interface of mobile apps' reviews. The suggestions included a specific request for some features like the apps battery consumption and illustration for the permissions required. A participant stated his ideas regarding redesigning the reviews interface as following "There should be a quick list where you can quickly see the most pertinent information about the app such as permissions, age range, ads or no, compatible OS, etc." Some participants suggested that reviews should contain some statistics about battery consumptions, and other technical factors. One of the participants suggested that there should be specific questions for the reviewers to be answered to enrich the reviews and to make them constant.

To conclude the study questionnaire, there was a final though question which asking the participants if they have any further input they would like to provide. There were very interesting responses that may improve the visualization and the interaction with the mobile apps reviews. A participant suggested that the reviewers should have credits for their reviews. He also suggested that apps store should consider gamification techniques to increase the interactivity with apps reviews. Many responses stated that apps should justify exactly why they use specific permission and how it would be used. There were suggestions to represent a portfolio for each developer and company to see all apps developed by them. Thus, users can have an idea about the quality of apps produced by those developers.

5 Discussion

The purpose of this study is to investigate the users' experiences and attitudes with the interface of mobile apps' reviews. Our results included rich data that could be helpful for both research and industry. In this part, we provide our rational towards the results that we got.

When we explored the users' attitudes and experiences with selecting an app, our results agree with what the previous research has done. Users have a variety of ways to select an app, and there are some factors affect his choices. In our study, we find that price of the app could be the most important factor in selecting an app. We think that because apps stores have free alternatives for most of the apps. Moreover, users consider uninstalling the app if they are not satisfied with it. In addition to that, developers might be interested in building apps that are similar to paid apps to gain quick revenue. Developers might get some income by using ads in their apps instead of selling their apps. However, this method is not comfortable for some of the users, who do not prefer ads in the selected apps. The problem is that installing an app then uninstall it does not go as what most users are expecting. If the app is malicious, during the period from installing the app until uninstalling it, the users' data might be at risk. So, we think there should be a way to represent the security level of the apps visually.

From our results, we infer that there is a portion of users who have the ability to set criteria for selecting an app. These criteria might not include the app rating specifically when the users are in need of using the app. Users might install an app even if they are not satisfied with its rating.

Regarding the apps' quality, our results indicated that participants tend to agree with all the statements there were asked. Participants consider the number of downloads, number of stars, and number of reviews as indications for the app quality. This is similar to what the previous studies have indicated [3–5, 9]. However, our findings infer that some users might consider self-judgment or friends' recommendations as factors in deciding the app quality. We think that is possible because one way to install an app is a referral from trusted people whom we know.

Our findings indicate that participants described the quality in another manner. The results indicate that there are participants who consider how the app works. Their perceived apps quality was not only limited to the visual communication icons that they see such as the number of stars or number of downloads but also they are seeking more easy to comprehend details. We think this kind of input from the users may help to figure out a way to have icons on the mobile apps info screen that reflects the technical aspect of the app. These icons may illustrate crashes, slowing down the device, freezing. Unexpectedly, the results indicate that there are users who consider the aesthetic of an app as a part of the quality.

Different from what other researchers have done, our study considers the users' experiences and their attitudes towards apps review. Our results indicate that, in general, users think that mobile apps reviews are helpful. However, users do not read all the comments in apps reviews. They scan the reviews and prefer to start with the reviews that are shorter, negative, and lower rating. We think this happens because users do not want to spend much of their time to read all the comments posted. Thus, they might look for the bad ones and then build their decision. While our findings infer that participants have multiple types of behavior reading the reviews, we think it is necessary to have a better design for the interface of the apps' reviews. Users do not want to spend numerous time reading 2000 reviews. Instead, it is advisable to have a better way to summarize and illustrate the reviews. Additionally, it might be useful to limit the words count for the reviews. As indicated in the results some of the reasons for reading the reviews are to help in making a comparison between apps and to support users decision-making process. Making reviews easy to read and comprehensive will ensure better user experience.

Prior research has investigated what the mobile apps users' complaints are. They have characterized number of the frequent complaints like hidden-cost, violate the users' privacy, frequent updates, removing a favorite feature from the app, and other complaints [31, 32]. Our results indicate similar results to what have been found in the previous research. However, there are some additions to the complaints list. Most of the previous research has adapted using text analysis for the reviews while we directly ask the users to provide their feedback regarding their complaints. Thus, we were able to have more information tied to the users' experiences. We found many of our participants were complaining about the length of the review. This complaint was reported in multiple parts of our study which indicates that is a real problem that needs to be solved. The findings also reported users concerns regarding ads in most of the free apps. The literature contains two dimensions for using the ads in mobile apps, which are the revenue and the power consumptions. Ads' content is an important topic and not getting much attention in the body of the literature. We think there should be some regulations for using ads by the developers specifically the contents of apps. We think that not all ads are suitable for all ages. Moreover, it is not justified when an app designed for kids having ads that are targeting adults.

The interface of the mobile apps reviews is a very important aspect that we considered in our study. Our results indicated that there is a need to rethink about the interface design of the apps' info page. While the current design seems to be simple, it is failing to help users to be aware of many issues and knowledge that are relevant to mobile apps. The prior research claimed that users do not read permissions and if they read they do not understand them [22, 23]. We agree with this and can add another reason. We notice that the app store and google play do not provide proper explanations for the permissions that apps ask users to grant. In addition to that, the apps information layout should be redesign in a way without misleading the users by the number of stars given to the app. We think that there should be an illustration for other necessary information in the top of the page. It is advisable to have information about the battery consumption, permissions, recent updates, security, and ads. Information like these should be illustrated on the top of the interface. That will help users to have easy access to these important aspects of the app.

Results of this study reveal the need of considering redesigning the interface of the mobile apps reviews. The new design should consider socializing the user experience with the apps and their selections. Moreover, considering techniques like gamification would increase the interaction between the users and the apps reviews. One important thing that users were not sure about was the developers' portfolio. Users reported that they do not have ideas about who made the apps. We think the most important thing to consider is making the interface as a tool to enhance the users' knowledge about apps related concerns. Examples of these concerns include an explanation for the required apps permissions, battery consumptions, ads, hidden cost, and any unique or specific features.

5.1 Limitations

One of the limitations of this study is that the majority of our participants were well-educated individuals. It is possible that results would contain additional output if there is a mixed of people who vary in their level of education. Moreover, it is possible that there would be additional points of view if the sample includes older adults and children.

6 Conclusion and Future Work

Previous research has done great work in extracting what users' complaints are. However, none of the previous research has investigated the users' attitudes and experience with the interface of the mobile apps review. We did a survey to measure the users' attitudes and reveal their experiences with the interface of the mobile apps reviews.

Our results indicated that users' complaints are not related only to how the apps work but also to the way that apps' stores illustrated the apps. In fact, users need to have awareness about the technical terms that are associated with reviewing an app. The way of illustrating the permissions and privacy-related issues should be considered when designing the interface. Information related to the ads, battery con-sumptions is also beneficial to be included in the interface of mobile apps' reviews. Our study found that users are frustrated from reading the reviews especially the lengthy reviews. There might be a way to summarize the reviews and help users to have better experience.

In the future, we would like to explore users' needs and desires for a suggested interface. An interview with apps' users could help to prioritize the elements of the visual design. Then we plan to have a suggested prototype that could enhance users' experiences and increase their awareness regarding apps- related issues. Users should be able to distinguish apps' risks and benefits easily.

Acknowledgment. Authors would like to thank all participants who spent their valuable time to participate in this study. In addition, we appreciate the University of Tabuk, Saudi Arabia for funding the first author.

References

1. App stores: number of apps in leading app stores 2017. In: Statista (2017). https://www.statista.com/statistics/276623/number-of-apps-available-in-leading-app-stores/. Accessed 5 Sept 2017
2. Pagano, D., Maalej, W.: User feedback in the appstore: an empirical study. In: 2013 21st IEEE International on Requirements Engineering Conference (RE), pp. 125–134. IEEE (2013)
3. Li, H., Zhang, L., Zhang, L., Shen, J.: A user satisfaction analysis approach for software evolution. In: 2010 IEEE International Conference on Progress in Informatics and Computing (PIC), pp. 1093–1097. IEEE (2010)
4. Palomba, F., Linares-Vasquez, M., Bavota, G., et al.: User reviews matter! Tracking crowdsourced reviews to support evolution of successful apps. In: 2015 IEEE International Conference on Software Maintenance and Evolution (ICSME), pp. 291–300. IEEE (2015)
5. Harman, M., Jia, Y., Zhang, Y.: App store mining and analysis: MSR for app stores. In: Proceedings of the 9th IEEE Working Conference on Mining Software Repositories, pp. 108–111. IEEE Press (2012)
6. Kim, H.-W., Lee, H.L., Son, J.E.: An exploratory study on the determinants of smartphone app purchase. In: The 11th International DSI and the 16th APDSI Joint Meeting, Taipei, Taiwan (2011)
7. Mudambi, S.M., Schuff, D.: What makes a helpful review? A study of customer reviews on Amazon.com. MIS Q. **34**, 185–200 (2010)
8. Finkelstein, A., Harman, M., Jia, Y., et al.: App store analysis: mining app stores for relationships between customer, business and technical characteristics. RN 14:10 (2014)
9. Iacob, C., Harrison, R., Veerappa, V.: What are you complaining about ?: A study of online reviews of mobile applications. In: Proceedings 27th International BCS Human Computer Interaction Conference, pp. 1–6 (2013)
10. Panichella, S., Di Sorbo, A., Guzman, E., et al.: How can i improve my app? Classifying user reviews for software maintenance and evolution. In: 2015 IEEE International Conference on Software Maintenance and Evolution (ICSME), pp. 281–290. IEEE (2015)
11. Platzer, E.: Opportunities of automated motive-based user review analysis in the context of mobile app acceptance. In: CECIIS-2011, pp. 309–316 (2011)
12. Hu, N., Pavlou, P., Zhang, J.: Can online reviews reveal a product's true quality?: Empirical findings and analytical modeling of online word-of-mouth communication. In: Proceedings 7th ACM Conference Electron Commerce, pp. 324–330 (2006). https://doi.org/10.1145/1134707.1134743
13. Tian, Y., Nagappan, M., Lo, D., Hassan, A.E.: What are the characteristics of high-rated apps? A case study on free android applications. In: 2015 IEEE 31st International Conference on Software Maintenance and Evolution, ICSME 2015 – Proceedings, pp. 301–310 (2015)
14. Guzman, E., Maalej, W.: How do users like this feature? A fine grained sentiment analysis of app reviews. In: 2014 IEEE 22nd International Requirements Engineering Conference (RE), pp. 153–162. IEEE (2014)

15. Kuehnhausen, M., Frost, V.S.: Trusting smartphone apps? To install or not to install, that is the question. In: 2013 IEEE International Multi-Disciplinary Conference on Cognitive Methods in Situation Awareness and Decision Support, CogSIMA 2013, pp. 30–37 (2013)

16. Chin, E., Felt, A.P., Sekar, V., Wagner, D.: Measuring user confidence in smartphone security and privacy. In: Proceedings of the Eighth Symposium on Usable Privacy and Security - SOUPS 2012, p. 1 (2012)

17. Matthews, T., Pierce, J., Tang, J.: No smart phone is an island: the impact of places, situations, and other devices on smart phone use. IBM RJ10452, pp. 1–10 (2009)

18. Hoon, L., Vasa, R., Schneider, J.-G., Mouzakis, K.: A preliminary analysis of vocabulary in mobile app user reviews. In: Proceedings of the 24th Australian Computer-Human Interaction Conference, pp. 245–248. ACM (2012)

19. Tian, Y., Liu, B., Dai, W., et al.: Study on user's attitude and behavior towards android application update notification. Usenix, Menlo Park, CA (2014)

20. Nayebi, M., Adams, B., Ruhe, G.: Release practices for mobile apps – what do users and developers think? In: 2016 IEEE 23rd International Conference on Software Analysis, Evolution, and Reengineering SANER, pp. 552–562 (2016)

21. McIlroy, S., Ali, N., Hassan, A.E.: Fresh apps: an empirical study of frequently-updated mobile apps in the Google play store. Empir. Softw. Eng. **21**, 1346–1370 (2016)

22. Kelley, P.G., Consolvo, S., Cranor, L.F., Jung, J., Sadeh, N., Wetherall, D.: A conundrum of permissions: installing applications on an android smartphone. In: Blyth, J., Dietrich, S., Camp, L.J. (eds.) FC 2012. LNCS, vol. 7398, pp. 68–79. Springer, Heidelberg (2012). https://doi.org/10.1007/978-3-642-34638-5_6

23. Rajivan, P., Camp, J.: Influence of privacy attitude and privacy cue framing on android app choices. In: Twelfth Symposium Usable Privacy and Security, pp. 1–7 (2016)

24. Shklovski, I., Mainwaring, S.D., Skúladóttir, H.H., Borgthorsson, H.: Leakiness and creepiness in app space. In: Proceedings of the 32nd Annual ACM Conference on Human Factors in Computing Systems - CHI 2014, pp. 2347–2356 (2014)

25. Felt, A.P., Ha, E., Egelman, S., et al.: Android permissions: user attention, comprehension, and behavior. In: Proceedings of the Eighth Symposium on Usable Privacy and Security, SOUPS 2012, pp. 1–14. ACM, Washington, D.C. (2012)

26. Felt, A.P., Egelman. S., Wagner, D.: I've got 99 problems, but vibration ain't one: a survey of smartphone users' concerns. In: Proceedings of the Second ACM Workshop on Security and Privacy in Smartphones and Mobile Devices, pp. 33–44. ACM (2012)

27. Lin, J., Amini, S., Hong, J.I., et al.: Expectation and purpose: understanding users' mental models of mobile app privacy through crowdsourcing. In: Proceedings of the 2012 ACM Conference on Ubiquitous Computing, pp. 501–510. ACM (2012)

28. Stevens, R., Ganz, J., Filkov, V., et al.: Asking for (and about) permissions used by android apps. In: Proceedings of the 10th Working Conference on Mining Software Repositories, pp. 31–40. IEEE Press (2013)

29. Nagappan, M., Shihab, E.: Future Trends in Software Engineering Research for Mobile Apps. In: 2016 IEEE 23rd International Conference on Software Analysis, Evolution, and Reengineering (SANER), pp. 21–32 (2016)

30. Li, D., Hao, S., Gui, J., Halfond, W.G.: An empirical study of the energy consumption of android applications. In: 2014 IEEE International Conference on Software Maintenance and Evolution (ICSME), pp. 121–130. IEEE (2014)

31. Khalid, H.: On identifying user complaints of iOS apps. In: International Conference on Software Engineering, pp. 1474–1476. IEEE Press, Piscataway (2013)

32. Khalid, H., Shihab, E., Nagappan, M., Hassan, A.E.: What do mobile app users complain about? IEEE Softw. **32**, 70–77 (2015). https://doi.org/10.1109/MS.2014.50

33. Hedegaard, S., Simonsen, J.G.: Extracting usability and user experience information from online user reviews. In: SIGCHI Conference on Human Factors in Computing Systems - CHI 2013, p. 2089 (2013)
34. Liu, B., Lin, J., Sadeh, N.: Reconciling mobile app privacy and usability on smartphones: could user privacy profiles help? In: Proceedings 23rd International Conference World Wide Web, pp. 201–212 (2014). https://doi.org/10.1145/2566486.2568035
35. Privitera, G.J.: Student Study Guide With IBM® SPSS® Workbook for Essential Statistics for the Behavioral Sciences. SAGE Publications, Thousand Oaks (2015)
36. Müller, H., Sedley, A., Ferrall-Nunge, E.: Survey research in HCI. In: Olson, J., Kellogg, W. (eds.) Ways of Knowing in HCI, pp. 229–266. Springer, New York (2014)

Are People Polite to Smartphones?

How Evaluations of Smartphones
Depend on Who Is Asking

Astrid Carolus[✉], Catharina Schmidt, Florian Schneider, Jule Mayr,
and Ricardo Muench

Julius-Maximilians University Würzburg, 97070 Würzburg, Germany
astrid.carolus@uni-wuerzburg.de

Abstract. Studies following the CASA paradigm showed that computers sending social cues elicited social reactions in their human users who e.g. adopted social norms (Reeves and Nass 1996). As these reactions were originally exclusive for human-human interactions, the derived paradigm stated that "computers are social actors" (CASA; Nass et al. 1994) referring to the theoretical concept of media equation, basically saying that "media equals real life" (Reeves and Nass 1996, p. 5). Nass et al. (1999) focused on the norm of politeness. In their experiment they showed that the evaluation of a computer was more positive if the computer itself asked for it compared to another computer asking. Our study adopts this experimental approach. However, as technology has evolved since the 1990's we replaced desktop PCs with smartphones transferring the CASA paradigm to modern devices. In a laboratory experiment, participants (n = 108) interacted with a smartphone which they evaluated afterwards. There were three different settings with (1) the target phone itself (2) another given smartphone or (3) the participants' own smartphone asking for the evaluation. Analysis of variance revealed significant differences between the first and third setting (F[2,105] = 3.35, p = .04, η^2 = .06) with evaluations being significantly better if the target phone itself asked for them. Homogeneous answers were interpreted as an indicator of dishonesty. Results revealed that evaluations on one's own smartphone were significantly less homogeneous than on the target phone (F[2,105] = 3.20, p = .05, η^2 = .06). Moreover, within experimental group 3, the participants' closeness to their own phone was shown to be significantly negatively associated with the evaluation of the target phone. In sum, results are interpreted as indicators of smartphones eliciting social norms of politeness. Hence, both the CASA paradigm and the integration of a psychological perspective constitute a heuristically fruitful approach for the analysis of users interacting with (modern) devices.

Keywords: CASA · Smartphones · Politeness · Media equation

1   Introduction

Have you ever been upset with your computer, blaming your device for not working properly? Although it was not the fault of the device but you who made a mistake? That

© Springer International Publishing AG, part of Springer Nature 2018
M. Kurosu (Ed.): HCI 2018, LNCS 10902, pp. 500–511, 2018.
https://doi.org/10.1007/978-3-319-91244-8_39

was not very polite of you. However, why should you be polite to a technological device? Social norms like politeness are relevant in human-human interactions but seem to be inappropriate for human-computer interactions. A series of experiments describing "computers as social actors" (CASA) challenged this obviously correct assumption. Coming from the concept of media equation and the idea of media equaling real life (Reeves and Nass 1996), CASA studies transfer sociopsychological rules and norms of human-human interactions to human-computer interactions. Following theoretical assumptions and methodological approaches known from social psychology, they focused on social norms of human-human interactions and replaced one interaction partner with a desktop PC (Johnson et al. 2004). Hence, they revealed computers to be able to elicit social responses in their human counterparts, e.g. gender stereotypes (Lee et al. 2000) or rules of politeness (Nass et al. 1999). However, since CASA research climaxed in the 1990's, desktop PCs were analyzed, which were largely distributed and used devices back then. Today, mobile devices and especially smartphones have overtaken regarding both distribution and usage frequency. Furthermore, smartphones might have overtaken regarding characteristics of an allegedly "social actor". They accompany their owners throughout the day, supporting them regarding a variety of daily challenges and their users are consequently confronted with a variety of social cues. Thus, smartphones constitute an appropriate research object for modern CASA studies. Furthermore, politeness has been shown to fundamentally affect the interaction with a computer, thus providing a promising focus for first modern CASA studies.

Technology has evolved rapidly since the CASA studies were conducted in the 1990's. Nevertheless, empirical research focusing on modern devices is rare. Our study aims to make a contribution in closing this research gap and asks if users adopt politeness norms when interacting with smartphones, thus following Nass and colleagues (1999). We therefore ask: Do users follow social norms of politeness when evaluating a phone they had interacted with before?

2   Theoretical Framework

2.1   CASA and Media Equation: Computers Are Social Actors Which Equal Real Life

The basic idea of this paper to conceptualize the device as an entity eliciting psychological reactions was established in studies on human-human interactions reaching back to the 1990's. Being confronted with a medium sending allegedly social cues the user instinctively reacts as if interacting with another human: rules originally exclusive for human-human interaction were adopted with technological devices. As "media equals real life" our media use is regarded as fundamentally social (Reeves and Nass 1996, p. 5). However, these processes operate automatically and are not consciously controlled. Furthermore, processes are universal and almost unavoidable as "media equation applies to everyone, it applies often, and is highly consequential"(Reeves and Nass 1996, p. 5). CASA research analyzing media equation transfers social dynamics known from human-human interactions to human-computer interaction (Nass and Brave 2005; Nass et al. 1994). Hence, rules and norms of human interactions, which are originally a subject of social psychology are transferred to settings of a user interacting with a computer (Johnson and Gardner 2007; Johnson et al. 2004). Basically, the human interaction partner is replaced by a media device which does not even need to send complex social cues to be regarded as a "social actor". On the contrary: research revealed that minimal social cues are sufficient to elicit social responses (Nass et al. 1994). Presenting text on the computer screen or giving the computer a name results in users attributing a personality to the computer. Moreover, computers appearing similar to the participant's personality were rated significantly better than computers with a dissimilar personality (Nass et al. 1995). In addition, simply telling participants that a certain computer belongs to their team (signified by a color) affected the evaluation of this computer. Both its performance and its friendliness were rated significantly better than a computer belonging to a different team (Nass et al. 1996).

Although reacting social, participants did not consciously regard computers as social beings. If asked directly, they would deny the computers' humanity. Reeves and Nass (1996) introduced an evolutionary explanation to solve this contradiction. From this perspective our human brain adapted to our early ancestors' environment. A world in which living creatures and mostly humans were the only origins of rich social behavior. Successful interactions with these other human beings sending a variety of social cues was essential for the individual's survival and reproduction. Consequently, psychological mechanisms evolved, which allowed automatic and therefore efficient processing of complex social situations resulting in the evolution of rapid, automatic reactions (Buss 2015). Today's human behavior is still affected by these adaptations. In fact, we are not adapted to the modern but to our ancestors' world, a world where no digital media were present. Thus, we are not adapted to the interaction with media devices and the cues these devices send. Consequently, if they send cues which are at least similar to social cues sent by humans, these cues will elicit the ancient mechanisms originally evolved to efficiently react to other human beings. Consequently, we automatically and unconsciously react to cues given by a computer.

In sum, social cues elicit psychological mechanisms originally evolved to navigate through our ancestors' world. Today's computers or virtual agents will trigger these mechanisms if they imitate human behavior by sending social cues – even if these social cues are rather minimal. Consequently, people will react to computers by e.g. adopting social rules originally established for interactions with other human beings.

2.2   Social Norms: Politeness and Groups

CASA research focused on social psychological factors constituting social interactions. Social norms are one of the essential factors guiding social behavior. A large amount of social psychological literature offers different perspectives and therefore definitions of social norms (Cialdini and Trost 1998). Essentially, norms refer to "folkways" (Sumner 1907) or rules which are negotiated on a group-level guiding and restricting social behavior (Sherif 1936; Triandas 1994). According to Stephan, Libermann and Trope (2010) politeness constitutes "an integral part in any human society" (p. 268). Violations of norms are carried out by the social network itself reflecting and regulating social distance, which results in both social control and group coherence (Blake and Davis

1964). Norms can be both interculturally different or universal. Brown and Levinson (1978) postulate the norm of politeness to be universal and to refer to all participants of a social interaction to feel validated and therefore happy. Politeness is a subject of research in many field calling for an interdisciplinary approach (Holtgraves 2005). However, this study concentrates on the basic principles relevant for the CASA paradigm thereby only broadly referring to Brown and Levinson (1978), who adopted the concept of the individual's "face". Goffman (1967) defined face as the public identity in terms of a public image which is shared by others. Consequently, as the face depends on others, two individuals are mutually interested in the maintenance of each other's face. Basically, this intention results in multi-faceted polite behavior. Social desirability as a fundamental challenge for social science research can be partly explained by politeness strategies. First, social desirability refers to the individual's tendency to conform with societal norms. Second, social desirability refers to the tendency to accommodate responses to the interviewer himself and his perceived preferences. Respondents follow politeness norms and avoid offending the interviewer (interviewer-based bias; Finkel et al. 1991).

2.3   CASA Studies Focusing on Social Norm of Politeness

How social norm of politeness affect users interacting with computers was described by Clifford Nass and his colleagues nearly twenty years ago. Users' evaluation of a desktop PC was affected by these users following social norms of politeness (Nass et al. 1994; Reeves and Nass 1996; Nass et al. 1999). Nass et al. (1999) conducted an experimental study. First, participants interacted with a desktop PC which "acted" as a tutor presenting facts on the topic of American culture. Second, participants were interviewed to evaluate the performance of that computer in one out of three settings: (a) they were interviewed by the target computer itself, (b) they switched to another computer, or (c) they answered a paper-and-pencil questionnaire. In line with the interviewer-based bias known from human interviewers (Finkel et al. 1991) Nass et al. (1999) demonstrated that participants would respond more positively when the computer itself asked for its evaluation compared to evaluations via paper-and-pencil and compared to evaluations at a different computer. Furthermore, they tested homogeneity of participants' evaluations with more homogeneous answers indicating dishonesty (Sproull 1986). Conforming their assumption, participants who were interviewed by the target computer itself evaluated this specific computer more homogeneously than participants evaluating via paper-pencil and via another computer. The authors concluded their findings to provide evidence that polite reactions can be elicited by a computer.

More current research on politeness strategies in human-computer interaction rather aims for optimizing the computer-based tutoring session (e.g. McLaren et al. 2011; Schneider et al. 2015). Although the session is presented by a computer, e.g. a virtual agent, this computer itself is not the main focus of interest. Instead, this research focuses on the effects of polite or impolite instructions and its effects on learning outcome, thereby deviating from CASA research. In contrast, studies on humanoid robots adopt the CASA perspective and analyze the effects of robots acting politely (e.g. Nomura and

Saeki 2009; Salem et al. 2013). However, they focus on technological devices rather emerging as part of everyday human-technology interactions.

2.4 CASA Studies Focusing on Today's Technology

Technological status quo has changed extensively since the CASA studies were conducted in the 1990's. Use of computers has become mobile with smartphones being one of the most popular devices (Pew Research Center 2018). In contrast to rather immobile desktop PCs, users carry their smartphone with them, using multiple applications for multiple reasons and independently of time and place. From a psychological perspective this pattern of usage might result in an emotional involvement with one's own phone (Walsh et al. 2011). Compared to desktop PCs, interacting with the phone integrates more variations and a larger amount of cues. Regarding the postulate that describes "computers as social actors", which referred to computers of the last century, smartphones seem to be predestined to act the part. However, CASA research on smartphones is rare. Goldstein, Alsiö and Werdenhoff (2002) analyzed personal digital assistants, but failed to replicate the results Reeves and Nass (1996) yielded. Kim (2014) showed that smartphones acting as a specialist in advertisement context were rated to be more trustworthy. Carolus et al. (2018) focused on smartphones eliciting gender stereotypes. They revealed that even minimal gender cues (pink or blue case) resulted in the ascription of gender to the phone and its performance was then evaluated gender-stereotypically.

In sum, CASA studies so far revealed computers to elicit social responses in their users, e.g. politeness effects regarding the evaluation of a computer participants had interacted with. The transfer of the CASA paradigm in general and the effects of politeness norms in particular are yet to come.

2.5 Hypotheses

In human-human interactions politeness has been found to be a social norm affecting conversational partners' behavior patterns (Brown and Levinson 1978). Nass et al. (1999) demonstrated these patterns to also occur when the conversational partner is a computer. Our study adopts the experimental design established by Nass et al. (1999) with two modifications: desktop PCs were replaced by smartphones and the paper-pencil-setting was replaced by the evaluation on the participants' own phone.

Referring to the interviewer-based bias and politeness norm, we postulate that the evaluations the target smartphone itself asks for will be more positive compared to evaluations a second smartphone asks for. If the participant's own smartphone asks for the evaluation, we hypothesize this evaluation will be even worse. Interacting with one's own phone should elicit interviewer-bias again. However, one's own phone is the interviewer now, a fact which results in users' attempts to maintain his face (Brown and Levinson 1978) and to accommodate to his perceived preferences. Following social norms in this setting corresponds to trying to avoid offending one's own phone, resulting in a more negative evaluation of the phone previously interacted with (Finkel et al. 1991).

H1: Participants will evaluate a smartphone significantly better if the phone itself asks for the evaluation compared to another phone asking.

H2: Participants will evaluate a smartphone significantly better if the phone itself asks for the evaluation compared to the participants' own phone asking.

Nass et al. (1999) also analyzed the homogeneity of responses which they postulated to be associated with the honesty of participants. According to the interviewer-based bias, we postulate that the evaluation will be more homogeneous if conducted on the target phone compared to the other phone and to one's own phone, as the latter two are regarded as being "more independent" resulting in more honest evaluations.

H3: Participants will evaluate a smartphone significantly more homogeneously if the phone itself asks for the evaluation compared to another phone asking.

H4: Participants will evaluate a smartphone significantly more homogeneously if the phone itself asks for the evaluation compared to the participants' own phone asking.

Smartphones exceed a desktop PC in frequency of usage resulting in users forming some kind of social relationship with their mobile devices. The intensity of this relationship might further influence the evaluation of the target phone, if one's own phone asked for it. Therefore, we hypothesize the closeness of participants to their own phone to be negatively associated with the evaluation of the target phone.

H5: Participants who feel closer to their phone evaluate the target phone significantly worse than participants who feel less close to their phone.

3   Method

3.1   Participants

108 volunteers participated in an experimental study at the University of Wuerzburg, Germany. They were recruited via flyers, social media postings and cold calls on the campus and were offered the chance to win a restaurant voucher. Participants' ages ranged from 18 to 52 (M 24.63 years; SD = 6.74). Gender was equally distributed (54 males). The majority of the sample was higher educated with 75.0% being qualified for university entrance and 21.3% having a university degree.

3.2   Procedure

Our study followed the approach established by Nass et al. (1999). However, we focused on smartphones instead of desktop PCs. Participants were instructed to interact with a smartphone which would guide them through their tasks. The experiment consisted of three parts: the tutoring, the testing and the evaluation session. During the tutoring session, the phone presented 20 facts, which participants were instructed to memorize. Previously, the experimenter had informed the participants, that the "tutor phone" would select these 20 facts from a pool of 1000 facts to best suit the participants' state of knowledge. Actually, all participants were presented the exact same 20 facts in the exact same order about Canada, e.g. "12.3% of Canada's total goods are imported from China" or "On average, a Canadian woman has 1.6 children". Canada was regarded to be an appropriate topic because preliminary analysis has revealed Canada to be both a subject of lower emotional involvement and lower prior knowledge (e.g. compared to the USA). Next, within the testing session, the phone asked 12 single-choice questions referring to the topic of the tutoring session. Six questions were derived from the facts participants had been presented with before, six questions were new. After the test, the smartphone gave some feedback on the participants' performance. However, this feedback was generic, the test score reported was independent of the actual performance by the partic-ipant: "You answered 8 out of 12 questions correctly – what a great result! The smart-phone provided you with helpful information and prepared you well for the test." In line with Nass et al. (1999), the self-praise of the smartphone was supposed to trigger a socially desirable and positive response. Finally, participants were randomly assigned to one out of three experimental settings to answer questions regarding the performance of the phone. The evaluation interview was either conducted by (1) the target phone itself, (2) by another foreign phone participants switched to or (3) by their own phone participants switched to. Thus, in contrast to the original study by Nass et al. (1999), we dropped the paper-pencil setting and focused on phones only. Furthermore, we took into account usage patterns of users primarily using their own phone, e.g. for the evaluation. Both the target phone as well as the second phone were Samsung Galaxy S5 models (operating system: Android). Hence, a between-subject design resulted in three exper-imental groups, which differed regarding the device that conducted the evaluation of the target phone. These devices asked four questions. Participants had to assess how well four adjectives described the tutoring skills of the target phone (analytical, helpful, useful, and informative). Answers were given on a 10-point Likert scale ranging from very poor to very well. The 21 items used by Nass et al. (1999) were content analytically reduced to only focus on the items which are relevant for the assessment of the compe-tence of the phone regarding its tutoring skills. The resulting index of the mean score of these four items exhibited high reliability (Cronbach's Alpha = .91). Furthermore, participants answered using an adaption of the "Inclusion of Other in Self (IOS) Scale", originally assessing closeness in relationships (Aron et al. 1992). In this pictorial scale we replaced the other person who the participant being assessed feels close to with their smartphone. Thus the participants indicated their closeness to the phone or their involve-ment with their own phone. Finally, participants were debriefed.

4   Results

Table 1 shows the descriptive results of the evaluations for all experimental groups revealing that the tutoring skills of the target phone would be evaluated best if partici-pants were asked by the phone itself. Evaluation would be slightly worse if another foreign phone asked for it and would be worst if participants switched to their own phones.

Table 1. Means and standard deviations regarding "tutoring skills" of the target phone

Target phone itself	Foreign phone	Own phone
M 7.86, *SD* 2.03	*M* 7.54, *SD* 2.09	*M* 6.56, *SD* 2.51

A one-way ANOVA between the three experimental groups revealed a significant effect of the different "evaluation devices" on the evaluated "tutoring skills" of the target phone, $F(2,105) = 3.35$, $p = .04$, $\eta^2 = .06$. Tukey HSD tests were conducted to compare mean ratings of each experimental group. Disproving hypothesis 1, evaluations on the phone itself did not differ significantly from evaluations on another foreign phone, with $p = .82$. Confirming hypothesis 2, the target phone itself asking resulted in significantly better evaluations compared to the participants' own phones asking, with $p = 0.4$. Furthermore, evaluations on a foreign phone and on one's own phone did not differ significantly ($p = .15$).

Following Nass et al. (1999) the homogeneity of participants' answers was regarded as an indicator of dishonesty. Thus, we analyzed the differences of the variances within the phone evaluation between the three experimental groups. For each of the three experimental settings separately, we computed the mean variance of every participant across the four evaluation items. This mean variance was treated as the unit of analysis in a one-way ANOVA between the three experimental groups. The analysis revealed a significant effect of the different "evaluation devices" on the mean variance of evaluations, $F(2,105) = 3.20$, $p = .05$, $\eta^2 = .06$. Once more, we conducted Tukey HSD tests to compare each experimental group. Hypothesis 3 was not confirmed, as the variance of evaluations at the same phone ($M = 1.73$, $SD = 1.15$) was not significantly smaller than the variance of evaluations at another foreign phone ($M = 1.88$, $SD = 1.15$), with $p = .84$. However, hypothesis 4 was confirmed. The variance of evaluations at one's own phone ($M = 2.39$, $SD = 1.12$) was significantly higher compared to evaluations at the "tutor phone", with $p = .05$.

Hypothesis 5 refers to the third experimental group (own phone) in particular. To control for effects of participants' closeness to their smartphone, this subgroup was divided in two separate groups by splitting them at the median ($Mdn = 3$). Of the 36 participants in the former third group, 19 people were part of the group feeling less close to their phone (group 3a) and 17 people reported feeling closer to their phone (group 3b). Afterwards we conducted an analysis of variance with the first experimental group (evaluation at target phone) and the two new groups evaluating at their own phone to test for differences in the evaluated "tutoring skill" of the target phone. The analysis revealed significant group differences, $F(2,69) = 6.19$, $p = .003$, $\eta^2 = .15$. Tukey HSD tests comparing each group were conducted. Participants in group 1 ($M = 7.86$, $SD = 2.03$) did not evaluate the target phone significantly different than group 3a ($M = 7.42$, $SD = 1.44$). However, group 1 evaluated the target phone significantly higher than group 3b ($M = 5.60$, $SD = 3.09$), with $p = .002$. Group 3a also evaluated the target phone significantly higher than group 3b, with $p = .04$. Hypothesis 5 was therefore confirmed.

5 Discussion

CASA research has revealed that social norms, e.g. politeness, originally established for human-human interactions are adopted by users interacting with a computer. The objective of this study was (1) to transfer the CASA paradigm to modern devices and (2) to examine effects on the evaluation of a phone as a consequence of which device asks for the evaluation. Therefore, this study followed the experimental design introduced by Nass et al. (1999) but focused on smartphones. Three evaluation settings were distinguished: evaluation took place on the target smartphone itself, on another phone or on the participants' own phone. The third setting particularly illustrates the differences between the use of desktop PCs and smartphones. While the former were primarily used in the office or at home, users of today's smartphones are constantly in touch with them throughout the day, which may potentially affect the evaluation. Results revealed that a smartphone was rated significantly differently depending on the evaluation setting. Results revealed only the difference between "own phone" and "target phone" to be significant with the target phone being evaluated worse on one's own phone. Thus, results confirmed hypothesis 2, but disproved hypothesis 1. Descriptive values of hypothesis 1 at least revealed that evaluations on the target phone itself were slightly, but not significantly, better compared to another phone. Analyses of the homogeneity of answers could be interpreted as one's own phone allowing participants to answer more honestly. One's own phone seems to appear as a more independent interviewer resulting in more honest answers. In addition, results point out the relevance of phone ownership associated with familiarity and a more emotional relationship. Accordingly, feeling close to one's own phone affected the evaluation of the foreign phone participants had interacted with before. Emotional aspects seem to be worth considering when it comes to users interacting with their devices.

According to the interviewer-based bias (Finkel et al. 1991) and the norm of politeness (Brown and Levinson 1978), participants seem to ingratiate themselves to a phone interviewing them. What seems to be counterintuitive has been shown by CASA studies before: electronic devices seem to elicit social responses which seem to differ depending on the individual's familiarity with the device. Consequently, it will make a difference, if the "other" phone is just another foreign phone or the participants' own phone. In addition to Nass et al. (1999), who refer to honesty as the reason for different evaluations, our results could be interpreted as an indicator for the "relationship" the participant has with the device to not only affect honesty but to trigger further social reactions. According to social identity theory (Tajfel 1978; Tajfel 1979) and group processes (Tajfel et al. 1971), interacting with one's own phone to evaluate another phone might elicit ingroup biases. As members of one's own group are favored and members of the out-group are rather derogated, the more negative evaluation of the target phone with participants' own phone asking the questions might trigger these processes.

The current study included several limitations. First, although we consequently referred to Nass et al. (1999) we modified some aspects due to the smartphone setting and due to the German population. We changed the topic of the tutoring session from US culture to Canadian culture. Preliminary studies revealed German participants to be less familiar with it as well as less emotionally involved. Thus, potential biases regarding tutoring session were avoided. However, the facts presented by the phone differed. Furthermore, due to the decreasing use of paper-and-pencil in general and in the context of smartphone interaction in particular, we dropped the paper-and-pencil setting. Hence, we are not able to compare different types of media. Moreover, we only used a small choice of four items compared to the original 21 items. However, we concentrated on the tutoring performance of the target phone, thus only using items directly referring to this competence. Analysis of reliability revealed our short scale to be reliable resulting in a less demanding way of performance assessment. However, measures need to be evaluated and developed further to assess the performance of a tutoring device (Carvalho et al. 2017). Finally, our sample lacks diversity as participants were mainly students of the local university. Besides common criticism regarding a sample of younger and more highly educated participants than average, the sample's familiarity with smartphones is crucial. Participants needed to interact with smartphones throughout the experiment resulting in the samples' habits of media use potentially affecting the results. Future samples will need to incorporate both older and less educated participants.

In sum, results confirm the idea of phones being able to elicit polite behavior and emphasize the importance of ownership and the emotional aspects associated with one's own device. Furthermore, the underlying question if the CASA paradigm can be transferred to modern technology can be approved. Transferring the CASA paradigm to smartphones seems to be a promising approach for analyzing social phenomena in users interacting with their own and with foreign devices.

6   Conclusion

To conclude, transferring the CASA paradigm to modern devices resulting in "smartphones as social agents" has been shown to be a heuristically fruitful approach for future analyses. Smartphones seem to elicit seemingly inappropriate social reactions in their users which are the result of psychological mechanisms deeply rooted in mankind. Future research will need to analyze these rather unconscious processes and the integration of a psychological perspective will be a promising approach. Moreover, this study provides indications exceeding scientific approaches. We interact with a variety of devices (e.g. phones, tablets, smart home assistants, and robots), which might trigger social reactions developers need to be aware of. At least when it comes to the evaluation of the device itself or services it provides, users' feedback might be biased by the device which is asking and by the (emotional) relationship users have with this device.

References

Aron, A., Aron, E.N., Smollan, D.: Inclusion of other in the self scale and the structure of interpersonal closeness. J. Pers. Soc. Psychol. **63**(4), 596–612 (1992)

Blake, J., Davis, K.: Norms, values, and sanctions. In: Handbook of Modern Sociology, 101, pp. 456–484 (1964)

Brown, P., Levinson, S.C.: Universals in language usage: Politeness phenomena. In: Questions and Politeness: Strategies in Social Interaction, pp. 56–311 (1978)

Buss, D.: Evolutionary Psychology: The New Science of the Mind, 5th edn. Routledge, New York (2015)

Carolus, A., Münch, R., Schmidt, C., Mayer, L., Schneider, F.: Pink stinks-at least for men. In: Kurosu, M. (ed.) HCI 2018. LNCS, vol. 10902, pp. 512–525. Springer, Las Vegas (2018)

Carvalho, R.M., de Castro Andrade, R.M., de Oliveira, K.M., Travassos, G.H.: Test case design for context-aware applications: are we there yet? Inf. Softw. Technol. **88**, 1–16 (2017)

Cialdini, R., Trost, M.: Social influence: social norms, conformity and compliance. In: Gilbert, D.T., Fiske, S.T., Lindzey, G. (eds.) The Handbook of Social Psychology, 4th edn., pp. 151–192. McGraw-Hill, Boston (1998)

Finkel, S.E., Guterbock, T.M., Borg, M.J.: Race-of-interviewer effects in a preelection poll Virginia 1989. Public Opin. Q. **55**(3), 313–330 (1991)

Goffman, E.: Interaction Ritual: Essays on Face-to-Face Behavior. Anchor Books, New York (1967)

Goldstein, M., Alsiö, G., Werdenhoff, J.: The media equation does not always apply: people are not polite towards small computers. Pers. Ubiquit. Comput. **6**(2), 87–96 (2002). https://doi.org/10.1007/s007790200008

Holtgraves, T.: Social psychology, cognitive psychology, and linguistic politeness. J. Politeness Res. Lang. Behav. Cult. **1**(1), 73–93 (2005). https://doi.org/10.1515/jplr.2005.1.1.73

Johnson, D., Gardner, J.: The media equation and team formation: further evidence for experience as a moderator. Int. J. Hum. Comput Stud. **65**(2), 111–124 (2007)

Johnson, D., Gardner, J., Wiles, J.: Experience as a moderator of the media equation: the impact of flattery and praise. Int. J. Hum. Comput. Stud. **61**, 237–258 (2004)

Kim, K.J.: Can smartphones be specialists? effects of specialization in mobile advertising. Telematics Inform. **31**(4), 640–647 (2014). https://doi.org/10.1016/j.tele.2013.12.003

Lee, E., Nass, C., Brave, S.: Can computer-generated speech have gender? an experimental test of gender stereotype. Paper presented at the Computer-Human Interaction (CHI) Conference, pp. 289–290 (2000)

McLaren, B.M., DeLeeuw, K.E., Mayer, R.E.: A politeness effect in learning with web-based intelligent tutors. Int. J. Hum. Comput. Stud. **69**(1–2), 70–79 (2011)

Nass, C., Brave, S.: Wired for Speech: How Voice Activates and Advances the Human-Computer Relationship. MIT Press, Cambridge (2005)

Nass, C., Fogg, B.J., Moon, Y.: Can computers be teammates? Int. J. Hum. Comput Stud. **45**, 669–678 (1996)

Nass, C., Moon, Y.M., Carney, P.: Are people polite to computers? responses to computer-based interviewing systems. J. Appl. Soc. Psychol. **29**(5), 1093–1110 (1999). https://doi.org/10.1111/j.1559-1816.1999.tb00142.x

Nass, C., Moon, Y., Fogg, B.J., Reeves, B., Dryer, D.C.: Can computer personalities be human personalities? Int. J. Hum. Comput Stud. **43**, 223–239 (1995)

Nass, C., Steuer, J., Tauber, E.R.: Computers are social actors. In: CHI 1994 Proceedings of the SIGCHI Conference on Human Factors in Computing, pp. 72–78 (1994)

Nomura, T., Saeki, K.: Effects of polite behaviors expressed by robots: a case study in Japan. In: Proceedings - 2009 IEEE/WIC/ACM International Joint Conference on Web Intelligence and Intelligent Agent Technology, vol. 2, pp. 108–114. IEEE Computer Society, Washington, DC (2009)

Pew Research Center: Mobile Fact Sheet. http://www.pewinternet.org/fact-sheet/mobile/

Reeves, B., Nass, C.: The Media Equation. How People Treat Computers, Television, and New Media Like Real People and Places. CSLI Publications and Cambridge University Press, New York (1996)

Salem, M., Ziadee, M., Sakr, M.: Effects of politeness and interaction context on perception and experience of HRI. In: Herrmann, G., Pearson, Martin J., Lenz, A., Bremner, P., Spiers, A., Leonards, U. (eds.) ICSR 2013. LNCS (LNAI), vol. 8239, pp. 531–541. Springer, Cham (2013). https://doi.org/10.1007/978-3-319-02675-6_53

Schneider, S., Nebel, S., Pradel, S., Rey, G.D.: Mind your Ps and Qs! How polite instructions affect learning with multimedia. Comput. Hum. Behav. **51**, 546–555 (2015)

Sherif, M.: The Psychology of Social Norms. Harper Torchbooks, Oxford (1936)

Sproull, L.: Using electronic mail for data collection in organizational research. Acad. Manag. J. **29**, 159–169 (1986)

Stephan, E., Liberman, N., Trope, Y.: Politeness and psychological distance: a construal level perspective. J. Pers. Soc. Psychol. **98**(2), 268–280 (2010). https://doi.org/10.1037/a0016960

Sumner, F.B.: Further studies of the physical and chemical relations between fishes and their surrounding medium. Am. J. Physiol.-Legacy Content **19**(1), 61–96 (1907)

Tajfel, H., Billig, M.G., Bundy, R.P., Flament, C.: Social categorization and intergroup behaviour. Eur. J. Soc. Psychol. **1**(2), 149–178 (1971)

Tajfel, H.: Differentiation Between Social Groups. Academic Press, London (1978)

Tajfel, H.: Individuals and groups in social psychology. Br. J. Soc. Clin. Psychol. **18**, 183–190 (1979)

Triandis, H.C.: McGraw-Hill Series in Social Psychology. Culture and Social Behavior. Mcgraw-Hill Book Company, New York (1994)

Walsh, S.P., White, K.M., Cox, S., Young, R.M.: Keeping in constant touch: the predictors of young Australians' mobile phone involvement. Comput. Hum. Behav. **27**(1), 333–342 (2011). https://doi.org/10.1016/j.chb.2010.08.011

Pink Stinks - at Least for Men

How Minimal Gender Cues Affect
the Evaluation of Smartphones

Astrid Carolus[✉], Catharina Schmidt, Ricardo Muench, Lena Mayer,
and Florian Schneider

Julius-Maximilians University Wuerzburg, 97070 Wuerzburg, Germany
`astrid.carolus@uni-wuerzburg.de`

Abstract. Based on the paradigm of "computers are social actors" (CASA) and the idea of media equation, this study aims to examine whether smartphones elicit social responses originally exclusive for human-human interaction. Referring to the stereotype of gender-specific colors, participants (n = 108) of a laboratory experiment interacted with a phone presented either in a blue (male) or a pink (female) sleeve to solve five social dilemmas with the phone always arguing for one of two options given. Afterwards, participants rated the femininity and the masculinity of the phone as well as its competence and trustworthiness. Furthermore, the participants' conformity with the choice recommendations the phone made was analyzed.

Consistent with gender stereotypes, participants ascribed significantly more masculine attributes to the blue sleeved smartphone and more female attributes to the pink phone. The blue phone was perceived as more competent and participants followed its advice significantly more often compared to the pink sleeved smartphone. Results on how trustworthiness was perceived were only found for male participants who perceived the blue phone to be more trustworthy. In sum, the study reveals both the CASA paradigm and the psychological perspective on users to be fruitful approaches for future research. Moreover, the results also reveal practical implications regarding the importance of gender sensitive development of digital devices.

Keywords: CASA · Smartphones · Gender stereotypes · Media equation

1 Introduction

Modern technology is female. At least when it comes to the "outward appearance" of the systems or the software we are interacting with. When we drive our car, the navigation device guiding us will talk with a female voice. When we address our iPhone, Siri will answer and when we activate our smart home assistant, Alexa will take over. Both systems come with a female name and a female voice. Are they consequently recognized as female entities? Or do they possibly trigger gender stereotypes? You might be vehemently opposed to this idea, pointing out that electronic devices do not have a gender, regardless of whether the hardware or the software is considered. Consequently,

© Springer International Publishing AG, part of Springer Nature 2018
M. Kurosu (Ed.): HCI 2018, LNCS 10902, pp. 512–525, 2018.
https://doi.org/10.1007/978-3-319-91244-8_40

they should not elicit gender ascriptions or stereotypes. In sum, these are objections that seem logically consistent. Everybody knows that Siri is not a girl, of course!

However, research on human-computer interaction has bidden defiance to common sense by challenging these rationally plausible assumptions. Back in the 1990ies, researchers analyzed users interacting with desktop computers by focusing on principles originally known from human-human interaction. They examined if, for example, social norms or stereotypes of human-human interactions will be adopted if the counterpart is not another human but a computer. Experiments revealed the users' tendency to automatically react in a way which is comparable to the reactions known from human counterparts. Consequently, Clifford Nass and his colleagues, who were early researchers in this field, conceptualized "computers as social actors" (e.g. Nass and Moon 2000; Nass et al. 1994). Their CASA paradigm basically assumes that computers are able to elicit social responses from their human users. Among these social responses is the utilization of gender stereotypes, resulting in, for example, a computer speaking with a male voice being evaluated as more knowledgeable when it comes to typical male topics such as technology, while a computer using a female voice was perceived to be more knowledgeable when it came to love and relationships (Nass et al. 1997). Male computers were also perceived to be more dominant and had an even greater influence on participants' decisions than female computers (Lee et al. 2000).

Research considering computers as social actors peaked in the (late) 1990ies resulting in experiments primarily focusing on desktop PCs at that time. Twenty years later, the technological status quo has changed fundamentally. Devices have become portable and their usage has become mobile. Particularly smartphones have become popular devices, which have overtaken stationary computers regarding distribution, frequency and variety of usage (Pew Research Center, 2018). Compared to the computers of the 1990ies, smartphones accompany us throughout the day, they provide support for a variety of issues and offer a number of different ways of both input and output which results in interactions integrating a variety of cues. Thus, referring to the idea of CASA with computers playing the part of the human counterpart, today's devices might meet the requirements of a "social actor" to an even greater extent than desktop PCs ever did. Coming from both (a) the questions asked at the beginning of ascribing gender attributes and corresponding stereotypes to "talking devices" and (b) the outlined pioneer research on desktop PCs, our study focuses on smartphones as potential social actors triggering gender stereotypes. Consequently we ask the following question: Will users ascribe gender attributes to smartphones if only minimal gender cues are available? And, furthermore, do these gender cues affect the evaluation of the phones?

2   Theoretical Framework

2.1   CASA Paradigm: Computers Are Social Actors

By conceptualizing "computers as social actors" a psychological perspective is introduced complementing the primarily technological approach in the field of human-computer interaction. Hence, following the psychological questions users are analyzed regarding their cognitions, emotions, motivations, and behavior while interacting with devices (Johnson and Gardner 2007). As outlined above, the guiding idea of this paper is not new but was established back in the 1990ies. Clifford Nass and his team revealed that computers can elicit responses in their human users which were originally regarded as being exclusive for human-human interactions. In a sequence of experiments they showed that sociopsychological concepts regarding social norms of human-human interaction are also adopted when interacting with a computer. Furthermore, they could show that these reactions are not limited to certain users who are e.g. not experienced in handling computers. It is rather an inevitable reaction which Reeves and Nass (1996, p. 8) identify as "fundamentally human" and rather unconscious. Hence, if asked directly users would deny that this behavior pattern applies (Nass and Moon 2000; Nass et al. 1994).

2.2   Media Equation: Media Equals Real Life

Reeves and Nass (1996) resolve this contradiction of conscious belief and unconscious behavior by arguing from an evolutionary psychological perspective. They introduce their concept of media equation which briefly says that if a medium "communicates" with us we unconsciously react as if it was a human resulting in their oft-cited core thesis: "media equals real life" (Reeves and Nass 1996, p. 5). Thus, users react to the output of an electronic device as if this device sends these cues intentionally. As a result, these reactions are similar to reactions to humans resulting in social rules and social norms established for human counterparts. From an evolutionary point of view this is the consequence of evolutionary adaptation. The human brain and the human body are products of evolution, which were designed by natural selection to serve survival and reproduction (Hagen 2002). However, this adaptation refers to our ancestors' world and not to today's world. Back then, interacting with other human beings was fundamental for survival resulting in a psychological mechanism evolved to automatically and therefore resource-efficiently detect them and react to them. To do so, the following heuristic equation was sufficient: everything that appeared as a person sure enough was a person. Today, defining these cues as a sufficient condition for humanity is not applicable anymore because modern media and technology send similar cues. Nevertheless, the old mechanisms still shape our behavior. Former exclusively human cues still automatically elicit (social) reactions regardless of the entity sending them (Buss 2015; Reeves and Nass 1996).

As these processes occur automatically and independent of conscious intention or control, users would deny equating media and humans if asked. Anyhow, they follow media equation principles on a behavioral level almost unavoidably. Consequently, research referring to media equation does not implement explicit surveys but experimental approaches. Social dynamics of human-human interaction are transferred to human-computer interaction with most studies following a similar approach: Replacing the human counterpart of human-human interaction by a media device to see if the same social rules apply (Johnson et al. 2004). The requirements of this replacement are low-threshold because research revealed that even minimal social cues are sufficient to trigger social responses (Nass and Moon 2000). Presenting a text on a screen or giving the computer a name resulted in users attributing personality traits to the computer. Moreover, a computer appearing similar to the participant's personality characteristics was rated significantly better by this specific user than a computer appearing dissimilar (Nass et al. 1995). Nass and his colleagues could also show that simply telling participants that a computer belongs to the same team as they do (signified by a color) resulted in significantly better evaluations of both performance and friendliness compared to a computer of the other team (Nass et al. 1996).

In sum, the paradigm of "computers as social actors" refers to research conceptualizing the computer as a "social" counterpart to whom social traits are ascribed and who elicits social responses in the human user (Nass and Brave 2005). The number of studies applying this paradigm peaked in the 1990ies. However, devices as well as user behavior have changed fundamentally since then, leaving the general question unanswered whether the paradigm and the resulting assumptions apply to modern technologies.

2.3 Social Categorization: Social Identity Theory and Stereotypes

Navigating through a social environment means navigating through complex social information. The social cognition approach refers to the processing of this information constituting the cognitive component of social psychological phenomena (Aronson et al. 2008). Organizing the complex social stimuli is central for a successful navigation because human information processing capacities are limited. Thus, we categorize objects to simplify information processing. Similarly, we categorize humans into groups with ourselves belonging to some of these groups. According the social identity theory, the individual's affiliation to certain groups is one aspect of the person's self-concept. Social identity is defined as a result of the individual's group "membership" and the value ascribed to them. The individual develops a variety of social identities, e.g. "we, the women" or "we, the men" or "we, the scientists" (Tajfel and Turner 1979). Hence, we show group behavior, e.g. the tendency to favor our own group (the in-group) and evaluate groups we do not belong to less favorably (the out-group). Consequently, a positive social identity is maintained resulting in self enhancement (Abrams and Hogg 1988).

Stereotypes refer to social categories which encompass beliefs about a certain social group in terms of associations between the social object and certain attributes (Fishbein and Ajzen 1975). These beliefs can be held by an individual or can be shared on a societal level reflecting a more general consensus (Eagly and Mladinic 1989). Meeting one representative of the category (e.g. scientist) triggers associations and guides both judgements and subsequent behavior without checking the accuracy of these conclusions. This tendency will be quite useful because the category provides us with more information (e.g. clever) than the single representative actually gives and with more than we are able or motivated to find out. However, regarding the scientist as a representative of a group and not as an individual might result in wrong attributions if the stereotype is wrong or the representative is not typical of the group. Furthermore, neglecting individuality raises ethical questions of prejudices and discrimination. Cunningham and Macrae (2011) even identify a "pernicious social problem" concluding that cultural stereotypes influencing "thoughts and behaviour are completely unacceptable" (p. 598).

2.4   Gender Stereotypes: Warm Women and Competent Men

Gender stereotypes can be defined as cognitive structures which encompass shared social knowledge about characteristics of men and women, e.g. physical features, personality traits, interests or job preferences (Ashmore and Del Boca 1979). In contrast to stereotypes regarding nationalities or age, gender stereotypes encompass descriptive as well as prescriptive parts. Both refer to traditional assumptions about male and female characteristics, on the one hand how men and women are, on the other hand how they should be. According to this, women are emotional and sympathetic while men are dominant and determined. Violations of descriptive aspects result in surprise but violations of the prescriptive parts result in rejection or punishment (Eckes 1994). According to Prentice and Carranza (2003), stereotypes are highly resistant to change and violations only rarely result in an adjustment. Only if the invested amount of mental effort is sufficiently high and the individual is aware of the stereotype as well as motivated to avoid stereotypical thinking, will he or she be able to avoid it (Bodenhausen and Macrae 1998).

Gender stereotypes are often associated with gender roles. Referring to social role theory, Eagly et al. (2000) assume gender stereotypes to be highly elaborated resulting in a "set of associations concerning men and women" as well as "a range of overall differences between these groups" (p. 124). Hence, social role theory argues that these beliefs result from observations of different behaviors shown by men and women as a consequence of their different social roles in society, which Eagly et al. (2000) summarize as "breadwinner and homemaker roles" (p. 125). Thus, shared expectations for appropriate behavior promote different behaviors for men and women. As sex roles are associated with different activities, they require different skills. Women and men who conform to their roles regarding e.g. house work vs. paid work, consequently acquire different abilities and competencies.

Research on the content of gender stereotypes reveals two fundamental dimensions: communion (interpersonal orientation: friendly, caring), which is associated with women and agency (action orientation: competitive, individualistic), which is associated with men (e.g. Diekman and Eagly 2000; Fiske et al. 2002). Furthermore, both dimensions are linked with social roles and different levels of social status. Fiske et al. (2002) established a model of stereotype content confirming that a higher degree of warmth is ascribed to women. However, they are rated to be less competent. On the contrary, men are regarded as more competent but less warm. Hence, contributions made by men are usually met with more attention and have a bigger impact on another person's decisions (Altemeyer and Jones 1974; Jacklin and Maccoby 1978; Propp 1995). Regarding social influence in terms of affecting another person's emotions, cognitions and behaviors (e.g. Deutsch and Gerard 1955), men exert more influence on others than women (e.g. Lockheed, 1985) resulting in effects of conformity. Basically, conformity is elicited in two ways: the individual is convinced by a valid source of information (informational social influence) or the individual complies with another person's expectations (normative social influence), which can be real or perceived (Deutsch and Gerard 1955; Kelman 1958; Kiesler and Kiesler 1969). Social influence is facilitated by the perceived trustworthiness of an information source thereby reflecting the reliability and expertise of the source (McCroskey et al. 1974; Fogg and Tseng 1999). Men's higher social influence goes along with higher credibility (Pearson 1982) resulting in a generally more significant impact on another person's decisions (Altemeyer and Jones 1974; Jacklin and Maccoby 1978; Propp 1995).

2.5 Colors and Gender Stereotypes: Blue Is for Boys, Pink Is for Girls

Gender stereotypes are deeply rooted within society resulting in gender specific sports, food, clothes or cars (Gal and Wilkie 2010). Gender-related color is another notable variation which Cunningham and Macrae (2011) trace back to the middle of the 20th century. So-called gender marketing causes a flood of products establishing the color scheme from childhood on. Children's rooms, clothes and toys seem to be colored following the color scheme. Pomerleau et al. (1990) examined the environment of 40 children and showed that girls have more pink and colorful clothes while boys wear mostly blue, red and white. Moreover, there were more blue objects in the boys' environments. According to Pomerleau et al. (1990), children are equipped conforming to gender before they can even express own preferences. Moreover, before they know about biological sex differences they learn that color is a sex-specific feature (Picariello et al. 1990). Thus, the association of gender and certain colors is regarded as a product of socialization that starts with birth and lasts an entire lifespan (Goddard and Meân 2009). Among other findings, Cunningham and Macrae (2011) demonstrated that associations between color and gender automatically trigger stereotypes: participants attributed more feminine features to men and women wearing pink clothes and more masculine features to men and women wearing blue clothes. Cunningham and Macrae (2011) concluded that associations between colors and gender are strong enough to create an associative pathway triggering stereotypical assumptions.

2.6 CASA Research Focusing on Gender Stereotypes

Two experiments following the CASA paradigm focused on the potential effects of gender ascribed to desktop computers. Nass et al. (1997) operationalized gender by implementing computers "talking" with either a female or a male voice. Participants interacted with a computer talking either with a female or a male voice and evaluated the performance of that particular computer afterwards. In accordance with gender stereotypes, results revealed that the male-voiced computer was perceived as more dominant and less likable than the female-voiced computer. Lee et al. (2000) received similar results. Their participants cooperated with a computer (again: male or female voice) to manage a social-dilemma situation. In line with gender stereotypes, the male-voiced computer had a greater impact on the participants' decision than the female-voiced computer. Furthermore, the male-voiced computer was perceived to be more socially attractive and trustworthy. Regarding social identification processes, female participants were found to rather conform to the female-voiced computer and male participants rather conform to the male-voiced computer.

Contemporary CASA research focusing on today's devices is rare with literature research revealing no studies focusing on both modern devices and potential gender stereotypes. However, e.g. Kim (2014) analyzed smartphones which acted as a specialist in an advertisement context and which were found to be rated more trustworthy. Carolus et al. (2018) showed that the evaluation of a smartphone depends on the device which is used for this evaluation afterwards. Evaluations were best when participants were asked directly by the phone which the evaluation refers to, evaluations were worse when the evaluation took place on another phone and worst if participants used their own phone to evaluate.

In summary, research regarding computers as social female or male actors is rather rare. Studies so far have focused on the effects of voices leaving open the question of effects of gender-stereotypic colors. In line with CASA research in general, participants of these first gender studies interacted with desktop PCs. Thus, the transfer to modern devices such as smartphones remains open.

2.7 Hypotheses

Based on the results of previous CASA research, computers sending gender cues should elicit gender stereotypes in their human users. These gender stereotypes were shown to affect both cognitions and behavior. Men and women are perceived differently, with men being e.g. more competent and trustworthy. Furthermore, colors seem to be gender-specific with tones of blue being associated with men and pink with women. Research also revealed these colors to trigger gender stereotypes in terms of gender-stereotypic ascriptions of characteristics. Our study brings together the experimental design implemented by Lee et al. (2000) and the idea of gender-specific colors. In contrast to the original study, we focused on smartphones instead of desktop computers. Furthermore, we replaced the male or female voice by either a pink or a blue sleeve as a minimal gender cue. In line with gender stereotypic colors, we postulate that these sleeves result in an ascription of gender to the phone. Hence, our first hypothesis is:

H1a: A phone presented in a blue case is rated to be significantly more masculine than a phone in a pink sleeve.
H1b: A phone presented in a pink case is rated to be significantly more feminine than a phone in a blue sleeve.

Lee et al. (2000) showed that "male" devices are perceived as more competent than "female" devices, which is in line with the stereotype regarding competence of men and women. Accordingly, we postulate differences regarding the evaluation of the smartphones' competence and trustworthiness as a consequence of their gender. Furthermore, and in line with both the results by Lee et al. (2000) and social identity theory (Tajfel and Turner 1979), we postulate the evaluation of the phones to be affected by the participants' gender.

H2: A male (blue) smartphone is evaluated to be significantly more competent than a female smartphone.
H2a: A male (blue) smartphone is evaluated to be significantly more competent by male participants.

H2b: A female (pink) smartphone is evaluated to be significantly more competent by female participants.

H3: A male (blue) smartphone is evaluated to be significantly more trustworthy than a female smartphone.

H3a: A male (blue) smartphone is evaluated to be significantly more trustworthy by male participants.

H3b: A female (pink) smartphone is evaluated to be significantly more trustworthy by female participants.

Research on gender differences revealed men to have greater social influence, while women's attempts to influence someone are more often ignored having a smaller impact on others (Lockheed 1985). In accordance, Lee et al. (2000) showed that participants more often complied with suggestions made by a computer speaking with a male voice. Therefore, our third hypothesis is as follows:

H4: Participants show significantly more conformity with a male (blue) smartphone compared to a female (pink) smartphone.

3   Method

3.1   Participants

A total of 108 volunteers (54 males; mean age 24.63 years; sd = 6.74 years) voluntarily participated in the study, with ages ranging from 18 to 52 years. 83 volunteers were mainly students (76.9%) or employees (13.9%). Volunteers were recruited through social media platforms and via flyers to participate in an experimental study conducted at the University of Wuerzburg, Germany. After completion of the experiment, participants were offered the opportunity to enter a prize draw to win restaurant vouchers.

3.2   Procedure

To analyze the idea of gender in human-smartphone interaction we adopted the CASA paradigm. Hence, our laboratory study followed the basic principles established by Lee et al. (2000) presented above. Participants who had interacted either with a female-voiced or a male-voiced computer to solve a social-dilemma situation were analyzed regarding their conformity with the computer's recommendation and their evaluations of competence and trustworthiness. In contrast to Lee et al. (2000), we used smartphones instead of desktop computers. Furthermore, we did not use voice output to manipulate the gender, but simply manipulated the color of the case the phone was presented with. The smartphones we used were Samsung Galaxy S5 models (operating system: Android) with either a blue (male) or a pink (female) sleeve.

In a 2 × 2 mixed factorial design participants were randomly assigned to either a "male" phone (blue case) or a "female" phone (pink case). A social dilemma was presented to them with the smartphone arguing for one of the two possible choices (e.g. "In my opinion Mr. D should think economically and take the risk to invest in the unknown shares. If his investment doubles, he will finally have enough money to buy the things he wants to. If the shares lose their value, he can still sell them and invest the rest in more secure blue-chip shares."). Then, participants had to make their decision. This process was repeated five times. Afterwards, participants were asked to evaluate the smartphones regarding competence and trustworthiness as well as masculinity and femininity. This evaluation concluded with demographic information and was conducted on a separate desktop PC. Finally, participants were debriefed. By using blue and pink smartphone-sleeves we asked whether these minimal gender cues are enough to trigger stereotypical responses from participants concerning their evaluation of the smartphones as well as their behavior when interacting with them.

3.3 Measures

Conformity to the smartphone was measured using five choice dilemma items. After the smartphone had argued for one of the two options, participants reported their decision on an eight-point scale (1 = absolutely option A, 8 = absolutely option B). Competence and trustworthiness were assessed using a 10-point Likert scale derived from Lee (2008). To evaluate competence participants rated the phone regarding three items (intelligent, competent and knowledgeable), to evaluate trustworthiness participants rated the phone regarding another three items (trustworthy, reliable and honest). Masculinity and femininity were measured using two four-items scales (masculine, dominant, competitive, ambitious and feminine, sensitive, understanding, sympathetic). Again, adjectives were rated on a 10-point Likert scale.

4   Results

Regarding hypothesis 1, we checked if the color of the sleeve affected ascription of gender to smartphones. Hence, we analyzed the participants' ratings of masculinity and femininity of the phone they interacted with. Results revealed that phones presented in a blue case were rated to be significantly more masculine than phones in pink cases, $t(106) = -1,94$, $p = .03$, $d = .37$, while phones with pink cases were rated to be significantly more feminine than the blue ones, $t(106) = 3.14$, $p < .001$, $d = .61$. Thus, hypothesis 1 can be confirmed.

Hypotheses 2 and 3 postulated effects of the colored sleeves on users' evaluation. We conducted analyses of variance (ANOVA) to check for the main effects of "phone gender" and the interaction between "participant gender" on the evaluation of the phone (H2: competence, H3: trustworthiness) and the tendency to follow its recommendation (H4: conformity). Regarding competence, the main effect of phone gender was significant, indicating that "male" phones were rated to be more competent than "female" phones $(F(1, 104) = 4.73$, $p = .03$, $\eta^2 = .043)$. Analyzing female and male users separately showed that men (but not women) rated "male" phones to be significantly more competent than "female" phones, $t(52) = -2.40$, $p = .01$, $d = .65$. Table 1 shows the descriptive values of all hypotheses tested.

Table 1. Means and standard deviations of smartphone evaluations: competence, trustworthiness and conformity

		Blue sleeve (n = 27)		Pink sleeve (n = 27)	
		M	SD	M	SD
Female participants	Competence[1]	19.96	6.34	19.19	5.63
	Trustworthiness[2]	18.81	6.48	19.56	4.91
	Conformity[3]	4.44	1.23	4.28	1.01
Male participants	Competence	21.30	7.38	16.37	7.70
	Trustworthiness	19.37	5.86	16.19	6.24
	Conformity	4.55	1.50	3.89	1.21
		(n = 54)		(n = 54)	
		M	SD	M	SD
All participants	Competence	20.63	6.85	17.78	6.83
	Trustworthiness	19.09	6.12	17.87	5.81
	Conformity	4.50	1.36	4.09	1.13

Note. [1] Competence scale ranges from 1 to 30.

[2] Trustworthiness scale ranges from 1 to 30.

[3] Conformity scale ranges from 1 (absolutely option A) to 8 (absolutely option B).

Contradicting hypothesis 3, ANOVA did not reveal significant results for trustworthiness, $F(1, 104) = 1.16$, $p = .28$. However, focusing on men and women separately, again male (not female) participants favored "male" phones and rated "male" phones to be more trustworthy than "female" phones ($t(52) = -1,93$, $p = .03$, $d = .53$).

Finally hypothesis 4 is corroborated with conformity ratings of "male" phones being significantly higher. Both female and male participants followed the recommendations of a "male" phone ($M = 4.50$, $SD = 1.36$) significantly more often than those of a "female" phone ($M = 4.09$, $SD = 1.13$), $t(106) = -1.71$, $p = .04$, $d = .33$.

5   Discussion

Smartphones are ubiquitous in modern society. Coming from the CASA paradigm, which postulates computers to be social actors, smartphones might to be some kind of digital companion fulfilling a variety of needs. Compared to the desktop PCs of the 1990ies, which CASA studies focused on and which were shown to play the part of a "social actor", it stands to argue that today's phones might meet the requirements of a "social actor" even more. However, research is rare. This study aims to reveal first insights by transferring the CASA paradigm to smartphones. Hence we adopted an experimental setting Lee et al. (2000) established for desktop PCs. In contrast to the original study, we focused on smartphones. Furthermore, we referred to gender-stereotypes. However, we did not manipulate the gender of the voice the device was talking with but focused on the color of the sleeve. Following gender-stereotypic ascriptions to colors, participants of our study interacted either with a phone in a blue or a pink sleeve and we subsequently analyzed if users would ascribe gender attributes to the phone and, furthermore, if the evaluation of the phone as well as the participants' conformity is affected by these minimal gender cues.

Confirming our hypotheses, blue phones were rated to be significantly more male than pink phones and pink phones significantly more female, although both types of phones did not differ in terms of the content they presented. Thus, ascriptions of gender were triggered only by the pink or the blue phone case revealing the strong link between these two colors and gender. Furthermore, we could show that the color and the ascriptions they caused affected the evaluation of the phone.

In line with our second hypothesis, blue phones were rated to be significantly more competent than pink phones, thus confirming that not only colors trigger the ascription of gender but also gender stereotypes do, like men being more competent, even though the interaction was exactly the same for both smartphones. A more detailed analysis revealed specifically men to rather favor "male" smartphones, as they rated blue phones to be significantly more competent as well as trustworthy while women did not. Men seemed to be more prone to reject pink phones while the evaluation of blue and pink phones barely differed with women.

Data analysis also supports hypothesis 4. Both male and female participants followed the recommendations of a blue phone significantly more often thus showing more conformity to it. This is a clear indication for "male" smartphones having a greater social influence compared to "female" smartphones which is in line with findings from social psychology regarding gender stereotypes (Tajfel and Turner 1979).

In sum, our study could show that gender does matter, even for smartphones and even if "gender" was nothing more than the color of a phone case. Recognizing a gender seems to trigger stereotypes and deeply rooted beliefs about how men and women "are".

While this study provides first insights into the idea of conceptualizing smartphones as social actors, there are some limitations as well as questions remaining unanswered regarding both methodological as well as theoretical considerations. Starting with methodology, the part of the experiment in which participant interacted with the phone needs to be reconsidered. The smartphone participants interacted with was not their own but rather a foreign one, which is highly uncommon as we usually only interact with our own smartphone. However, previous research could show that interacting with one's own smartphone vs. a foreign smartphone did not make any difference regarding its evaluation (Carolus, Schmidt, Muench, & Schneider, submitted).

For further research a broader perspective regarding underlying social psychological phenomena should be considered: for this study we transferred the ascription of gender stereotypes to human-smartphone interaction, however there are many more aspects of human-human interaction that have already been transferred to human-computer interaction that warrant further research. More specifically, widening the perspective regarding other devices has to be considered as for example the concept of smart homes increases, opening a new research area.

6 Conclusion

The focus of this study was to offer first insights into the transfer of the CASA paradigm to smartphones. Conceptualizing "smartphones as social agents" indicates a heuristically fruitful approach for future analyses of human-smartphone interaction. Smartphones seem to elicit social norms in users interacting with them. The findings are considered as important for both theory and practice. The study offers multiple starting points for further research in the field of human-computer interaction thereby pointing out the importance to integrate a psychological perspective. The interaction with a device might be affected by psychological processes that appear rather illogical at first glance. Taking into account the concepts of media equation and its perspective on humans, who are a product of evolution and therefore not adapted to the use of media (devices), results in a theoretical framework which is highly relevant for the analysis of user experience. At the latest when the evaluation of the device itself is regarded, the relevance for a commercial perspective becomes obvious. Intelligent assistants (Siri) as well as smart home assistants (Alexa) are evidently designed to appear female. With regard to our findings the question arises if this should be reconsidered at least for certain areas where performance in terms of competence or trustworthiness and persuasive power are more important than the gender-stereotypic "female" interpersonal orientation associated with triggering warmth and communion.

References

Abrams, D., Hogg, M.A.: Comments on the motivational status of self-esteem in social identity and intergroup discrimination. Eur. J. Soc. Psychol. **18**, 317–334 (1988)

Altemeyer, R.A., Jones, K.: Sexual identity, physical attractiveness and seating position as determinants of influence in discussion groups. Can. J. Behav. Sci. **6**, 357–375 (1974)

Aronson, E., Wilson, T.D., Akert, R.M.: Social Psychology, 6th edn. Pearson Studium, München (2008)

Ashmore, R.D., Del Boca, F.K.: Sex stereotypes and implicit personality theory: toward a cognitive-social psychological conceptualization. Sex Roles **5**, 219–248 (1979)

Bodenhausen, G.V., Macrae, C.N.: Stereotype activation and inhibition. Stereotype Activation Inhib. Adv. Soc. Cogn. **11**, 1–52 (1998)

Buss, D.: Evolutionary Psychology: The New Science of the Mind, 5th edn. Routledge, New York, NY (2015)

Carolus, A., Schmidt, C., Muench, R., Schneider, F.: Impertinent mobiles- Effects of polite and impolite feedback on the evaluation of smartphones. Manuscript submitted for publication (2018)

Carolus, A., Schmidt, C., Schneider, F., Mayr, J., Muench, R.: Are people polite to smartphones? How evaluations of smartphones depend on who is asking. In: Proceedings from the HCI International 2018. Las Vegas: Springer (in press)

Cunningham, S.J., Macrae, C.N.: The color of gender stereotyping. Br. J. Psychol. **102**, 598–614 (2011)

Deutsch, M., Gerard, H.B.: A Study of normative and informational social influences upon individual judgment. J. Abnorm. Soc. Psychol. **51**, 629–636 (1955)

Diekman, A.B., Eagly, A.H.: Stereotypes as dynamic constructs: women and men of the past, present, and future. Pers. Soc. Psychol. Bull. **26**(10), 1171–1188 (2000)

Eagly, A.H., Mladinic, A.: Gender stereotypes and attitudes toward women and men. Pers. Soc. Psychol. Bull. **15**(4), 543–558 (1989)

Eagly, A.H., Wood, W., Diekman, A.B.: Social role theory of sex differences and similarities: a current appraisal. In: Eckes, T., Trautner, H.M. (eds.) The Developmental Social Psychology of Gender, pp. 123–174. Erlbaum, Mahwah (2000)

Eckes, T.: Features of men, features of women: assessing stereotypic beliefs about gender subtypes. Br. J. Soc. Psychol. **33**(1), 107–123 (1994)

Fishbein, M., Ajzen, I.: Belief, Attitude, Intention and Behavior: An Introduction to Theory and Research (1975)

Fiske, S.T., Cuddy, A.J., Glick, P., Xu, J.: A model of (often mixed) stereotype content: competence and warmth respectively follow from perceived status and competition. J. Pers. Soc. Psychol. **6**, 878–902 (2002)

Fogg, B.J., Tseng, H.: The elements of computer credibility. In: CHI Proceedings of the SIGCHI Conference on Human Factors in Computing Systems, pp. 80–87 (1999)

Gal, D., Wilkie, J.: Real men don't eat quiche: regulation of gender-expressive choices by men. Soc. Psychol. Pers. Sci. **1**, 291–301 (2010)

Goddard, A., Meân, L.: Language & Gender, 2nd edn. Routledge, New York (2009)

Hagen, E.: The evolutionary psychology (2002). http://www.anth.ucsb.edu/projects/human/epfaq/ep.htm

Jacklin, C.N., Maccoby, E.E.: Social behavior at thirty-three months in same-sex and mixed-sex dyads. Child Dev. **49**, 557–569 (1978)

Johnson, D., Gardner, J., Wiles, J.: Experience as a moderator of the media equation: the impact of flattery and praise. Int. J. Hum Comput Stud. **61**, 237–258 (2004)

Johnson, D., Gardner, J.: The media equation and team formation: further evidence for experience as a moderator. Int. J. Hum Comput Stud. **65**(2), 111–124 (2007). https://doi.org/10.1016/j.ijhcs.2006.08.007c

Kelman, H.: Compliance, identification, and internalization: three processes of attitude change. J. Conflict Resolut. **2**(1), 51–60 (1958). https://doi.org/10.1177/002200275800200106

Kiesler, C.A., Kiesler, S.B.: Conformity. Addison Wesley Publishing Company (1969)

Kim, K.J.: Can smartphones be specialists? Effects of specialization in mobile advertising. Telematics Inform. **31**(4), 640–647 (2014). https://doi.org/10.1016/j.tele.2013.12.003

Lee, E.: Gender stereotyping of computers: resource depletion or reduced attention? J. Commun. **58**, 301–320 (2008)

Lee, E., Nass, C., Brave, S.: Can computer-generated speech have gender? an experimental test of gender stereotype. Paper presented at the Computer-Human Interaction (CHI) Conference, pp. 289–290 (2000)

Lockheed, M.E.: Sex and social influence: a meta-analysis guided by theory. In: Berger, J., Zelditch, Jr. M., (eds.), Status, Rewards, and Influence: How Expectations Organize Behavior, pp. 406–429. Jossey-Bass, San Francisco (1985)

McCroskey, J.C., Weiner, A.N., Hamilton, P.R.: The effect of interaction behavior on source credibility, homophily, and interpersonal attraction. Hum. Commun. Res. **1**, 42–52 (1974)

Nass, C., Fogg, B.J., Moon, Y.: Can computers be teammates? Int. J. Hum Comput Stud. **45**, 669–678 (1996)

Nass, C., Brave, S.: Wired for Speech: How Voice Activates and Advances the Human-computer Relationship. MIT press, Cambridge, MA (2005)

Nass, C., Moon, Y.: Machines and mindlessness: social responses to computers. J. Soc. Issues **56**, 81–103 (2000)

Nass, C., Moon, Y., Green, N.: Are machines gender neutral? Gender-stereotypic responses to computers with voices. J. Appl. Soc. Psychol. **27**, 864–876 (1997)

Nass, C., Moon, Y., Fogg, B.J., Reeves, B., Dryer, D.C.: Can computer personalities be human personalities? Int. J. Hum Comput Stud. **43**, 223–239 (1995)

Nass, C., Steuer, J., Tauber, E.R.: Computers are social actors. In: CHI 1994, Proceedings of the SIGCHI Conference on Human Factors in Computing, pp. 72–78 (1994)

Pearson, J.C.: The role of gender in source credibility. Paper presented at the Annual Meeting of the Speech Communication Association, Louisville, KY (1982)

Pew Research Center: Mobile Fact Sheet (2018). http://www.pewinternet.org/fact-sheet/mobile/

Picariello, M.L., Greenberg, D.N., Pillemer, D.B.: Children's sex-related stereotyping of colors. Child Dev. **61**, 1453–1460 (1990)

Pomerleau, A., Bolduc, D., Malcuit, G., Cosette, L.: Pink or blue: environmental gender stereotypes in the first two years of life. Sex Roles **22**, 359–367 (1990)

Prentice, D.A., Carranza, E.: Sustaining Cultural Beliefs in the Face of Their Violation: The Case of Gender Stereotypes. In: Schaller, M., Crandall, C.S. (eds.) The Psychological Foundations of Culture, pp. 259–280. Erlbaum, Mahwah (2003)

Propp, K.M.: An experimental examination of biological sex as a status cue in decision-making groups and its influence on information use. Small Group Res. **26**, 451–474 (1995)

Reeves, B., Nass, C.: The Media Equation: How People Treat Computers, Television, and New Media like Real People and Places. Cambridge University Press, New York (1996)

Tajfel, H., Turner, J.: An integrative theory of intergroup conflict. In: Austin, W.G., Worchel, S. (eds.) The Social Psychology of Intergroup Relations, pp. 33–37. Brooks/Cole, Monterey (1979)

Investigating the Behavior of Sequence Typing on the Mobile Devices

Hsi-Jen Chen$^{(\boxtimes)}$, Chia-Ming Kuo, and Yung-Chueh Cheng

National Cheng Kung University, Tainan, Taiwan
Hsijen_chen@mail.ncku.edu.tw

Abstract. Text entry on any small mobile devices, such as a smartphone remains challenging and inconvenient. The "lack of realistic tactile feedback" on the touch screens and "the screen sizes wuld limit the key sizes" have not been fully overcome yet. In addition, when entering text, the fingers have to move constantly and quickly to locate letters in a limited area. Therefore, this research aims at "the relationships between finger movement speeds, distances, directions and accuracies while making continuous data entry inside the keyboard areas of the mobile devices". We developed an App for data entry testing to analyze how the finger movement directions, speeds, distances would affect the falling points of the data entry. The results showed that the directions of the finger movements would affect the touch point positions. It's more significant along the vertical axis than the horizontal axis. Moreover, only the fingers' moving speeds and movement distances would affect the taping accuracy, and the fingers' moving directions would not have influence on the taping accuracy.

Keywords: User interfaces · Interaction styles · Mobile device
Text entry · Touchscreen

1 Introduction

Small mobile devices have been integrated into the lives of most people. Undoubtedly they have become a kind of necessities, and among them the smart phones are the most obvious examples. According to the surveys, the global penetration rate of smart phones has exceeded 62% in 2015. The most commonly used features for surfing the internet with smartphones are "social network visits" (71%), "search engine uses" (64%), "map functions" (60%) [1]. The above-mentioned functions all require text entry, thus it stands for a fact that "text entry" plays an important role in the uses of mobile devices. However, the "lack of realistic tactile feedback" on the touch screens and "the screen sizes would limit the key sizes" have not been fully overcome yet.

Owing to the maturity achieved in the developments of mobile devices and the various hardware and software, their functions and applications are being enhanced day after day, therefore the mobile devices with large screen sizes are increasingly favored by consumers and have gradually become the trend [2, 3]. The larger the screens of the devices, the more information can be displayed, and that would enlarge the virtual keyboards'sizes and make text entry even more comfortable. However, even if it is a 5.5-inch screen, the key sizes of the virtual keyboard is still subject to great restrictions.

© Springer International Publishing AG, part of Springer Nature 2018
M. Kurosu (Ed.): HCI 2018, LNCS 10902, pp. 526–541, 2018.
https://doi.org/10.1007/978-3-319-91244-8_41

For instance, the iPhone 6 s Plus's virtual keyboard key size is about 5.8 × 7.5 mm only. Those figures are still below the recommendations made in the iOS Human Interface Guidelines [4]; that is, the key sizes for App designs should not be less than 6.74 x 6.74 mm. Thus so far it still deserves our efforts for discussing and studies about the operation habits of the keyboards and how to improve the efficiency of text entry through the virtual keyboards.

Therefore, this research aims at "the relationships between finger movement speeds, distances, directions and accuracies while making continuous data entry inside the keyboard areas of the mobile devices". The users' operation behaviors are different when they tap on the mobile devices to perform "text entry" and "non-text entry". When a "non-text entry" is performed, the user moves his finger to the targeted key (icon) and taps, and the task is completed after repeating several times of such behaviors. If we take taking a picture for example, we tap the camera key firstly, tap on the function keys we want to use (for example: taking picture, video recording, special effects...), and then we press on the shutter key to complete the task. As for "text entry", although we tap on the targeted keys similarly, we have to quickly, repeatedly and continually move our fingers to tap and select the targets. Such behavior differences would affect the design specifications and research contents of the ordinary buttons and keyboard keys.

The importance of text entry on small mobile devices goes without saying owing to the mobile devices' becoming popular, but the efficiency of text entry is not as good as traditional physical keyboards [5]. The screen space constraint which makes the keys too small is one of the important reasons lowering down the entry efficiency [6]. Therefore, this research intends to discuss in depth on the behaviors, that is, the finger movement speeds, distances, directions, and accuracies of text entry on mobile devices when we continuously and rapidly make inputs into the panel area of a small mobile device. We anticipate to find out the problems through the understanding of the entry behaviors, so as to improve the efficiency of text entry.

2 Related Work

2.1 Fitts's Law

Fitts's [7] law has provided a very useful norm for tapping targets by using pointing devices on traditional screens. Fitts's law states that the smaller the selection target and the farther it moves, the longer time it would take to reach the target point. In addition, in the case of speed-accuracy tradeoff, the faster the moving speeds, the smaller the target sizes, and the higher the error rates would be. Concerning the study of Fitts's law [7] and finger touch, Lee and Zhai [8] have studied the use of virtual keys and provided specifications for the use of touch screens, and their researches have also shown that Fitts's Law is not fully applicable on small mobile devices. Later on, some researchers also modified and extended it based on Fitts's law and proposed the FFitts Law model [9].

Although the guidelines which the Fitts's Law has provided are not entirely in line with the relations between target and selection of the current small mobile devices, the theory and core, in other words the corresponding relationships between target sizes, moving distances, speeds and accuracies if there exist any behavior differences between ways of text entry and ordinary icon taping are very valuable for reference that they worth applications and in-depth researches.

2.2 Target Size

There have been extensive discussions on the sizes of touch targets, and there exist absolute correlations on the entry error rate values if the target is too small [6]. Too-small keys would increase the entry time and entry error rate [10]. Different scholars have different opinions on the sizes of the touch screen keys. The traditional key size is 22 mm [8], but there are other studies which claim that the keys can be smaller, for example 11.5 mm [11], 10.5 mm [12], 9 mm [13], and iOS Human Interface Guidelines 2010 [4] has suggested that the keys or target sizes should not be smaller than 6.74 × 6.74 mm while designing an App. At present the keyboard keys on the screen of a small mobile devices are too small. For example, the English keyboard keys of the iPhone 5 are only about 6 mm × 3.9 mm in size, thereby increasing the entry difficulty and reducing the accuracy. But the typing performance on a very small device could be also very well [14].

2.3 Text Entry Performance

Both the indicators of entry speed and error rate have been used to benchmark an input device often [15]. The entry speed measurements can be expressed in characters per second (CPS) or words per minute (WPM), and among them the WPM has been more commonly used. In the WPM calculation rules, a "word" has been defined as "five keystrokes," meaning that it would be calculated as a "word" as long as the keyboard has been tapped five times rather than denoting a meaningful word. These five strokes may contain all letters, numbers, blank keys, punctuation, backspace keys, etc. [15, 16]. However, scholars of both Arif and Stuerzlinger [17] have further argued that the calculation formula of WPM should be slightly adjusted. They think that the correct total number of keystrokes is the total number of keystrokes minus one, as timing usually begins after the first key is tapped. Currently the entry speeds on small mobile devices range from about 35 to 50 WPM, depending on the mode of operation [18, 19].

Comparing with the measurements of entry speeds, the measurement error rates at data entry are comparatively complicated, because the causes of the occurrences and the calculation measures are very diverse. The entry errors can be divided into four categories according to their attributes: substitution, omission, insertion, and transposition, and the numbers of corrective actions required for different situations are also different [20]. The method which is more commonly known for measurement error rates is to calculate the ratio between number of keystrokes and characters (Key Strokes per Character, KSPC), i.e. actual strokes/expected strokes [17, 21].

Offsets for touch points.

Henze and others have designed a target selection game to collect a large number of touch-point data. They found that when a user selects a target on a mobile device, the occurrence of wrong selections may be affected by the positions and sizes of the keys, and the preference of the touch points also has a tendency of concentration. When taping on the touch screen target, offset conditions have happened quite often. The point which the user gazes at is not consistent with the actual touch point detected on the touch screen [12]. Vogel and Baudisch both argued that the offset can be ascribed to: firstly, the target is obscured by the finger, and secondly, which portion of the finger is to be used for touching the screen is vague and difficult to control [12]. Holz and Baudisch [22, 23] have further explored the ways the fingers touch the screens and pointed out that different users, tilt angles of the fingers, and the rotation angles of the fingers all may cause certain offsets between the gazing points and the touch points, and they stressed that the offsets are the main reasons why the touch screen entry measure is not accurate enough. In addition, when the data entry is made with one thumb, the offset issue would be more serious when the user taps the left and right keys [24, 25].

On the touch screen keyboards, both Azenkot and Zhai [18] have tangibly summarized the offset conditions of each key, and the results are as follows: 1. The actual touch points in most of the cases would be located on the lower portion of the center position 2. The vertical offsets are obvious if the users only use right index fingers to operate 3. Only use right index fingers or right thumbs to operate would result in offsets to the right side 4. The blank key has obvious offset to the right side. The study has showed that even if the keyboard keys have been shifted, the touch-points still could distribute throughout all the positions of the keys.

Based on the above literature about data entry performance, we believe that text entry is of very fast and continuous actions which is different from the non-text data entry. This study would consider the Fitts's law, key sizes, input offsets and other factors to discuss about the relationships between movement distances, speeds and accuracies while quickly and continually taping on the targets inside the panel areas in order to understand the text entry behaviors and thereby enhance efficiency.

3   Method

3.1   App Design for Usability Test

This research has designed a taping-purpose App to observe, record and analyze the various data and behaviors of the subjects while they taped on the touch panels. We got to know from the literature that the general test methods for text entry efficiency are to have the subjects to input some series of sentences and then calculate the entry speeds and error rates. Under such experimental methods the subjects must look at the title articles first, look at the keyboards to find the correct key positions, and finally watch the entry fields to make sure correct data inputs are made. Hence, the subjects must constantly switch their viewpoints between the subjects, input fields and keyboard fields. Such method not only increases the workloads of the subjects while making data entry, may increase error rates, and on the other hand such measure does not correspond to the real circumstances when the users are making data entry. Because under normal circumstances for data entry the users know what they want to input that their viewpoints do not need to have much switching between input fields, titles and keyboards, and they just need to concentrate on the keyboards searching for the target keys instead. The purpose of the experimental tests is to find out whether the speeds, distances, and directions of the finger movements would affect the taping points. To achieve this purpose, there is no need to test with meaningful texts or sentences, therefore the keyboards used in the experiments would rid off letter symbols and only the blank keys are left for the testing (Fig. 1).

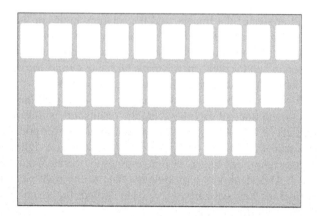

Fig. 1. Experimental keyboard

The App operation is very simple, the keys on the keyboard would be lit randomly, and the subjects must tap sequentially. However, in the real text entry scenario the users know the positions of the next keys beforehand; for example, when a user wants to input "key", he already knows that the next key is the "e" key when he touches the first letter "k", and then the "y" key that he could be psychologically and motionally prepared. In order to simulate the actual text entry scenario, three keys would be lit randomly, and the numbers "1", "2" and "3" are respectively displayed in red. The subjects tap according to the numerical sequence, and then another 3 keys individually displaying "A", "B", "C" would be lit randomly in blue color after the 2nd key has been taped. The subjects must tap on the numbers in sequence and then tap on the English letters, and the targeted numbers or letters taped would disappear. They would repeat in the same way until the end of the experiment (Fig. 2). In this way, a subject can know the next key and its position to be taped by using peripheral vision or screen scanning, and to proceed with the test process smoother. Such practice is more similar to the typical way of text entry operation.

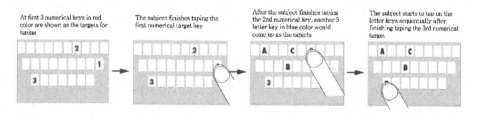

Fig. 2. Descriptions of entry test keys (color figure online)

3.2 Participants

The personal characteristics of the subjects, such as age, gender, dominant hand, familiarity with the operations of the touch devices, etc. may affect the data entry efficiency. Therefore, some constraints must be imposed on the subjects for participating the experiments.

According to the surveys, in Taiwan, the smart phones have a penetration rate of 96% between the ages of 25 and 30, and as high as 95% under the age of 25 (Google, 2015). Therefore, we have chosen 20–30-year-old smart phone users as the experiment subjects. In order to avoid impact from being unfamiliar with the touch screen operations, the subjects must have more than six months of experiences using smart phones. In addition, in order to simplify the experiments, the right-handed users would be invited as the main exploring objects of this study, and they must be able to make text entry by using their right thumbs. Thirty subjects have finally been invited to participate in the experiments, male half and female half for conducting the experiments.

3.3 Collecting Data

The related taping data were recorded via the experimental App, and the data would be stored in the back-end database. The stored data have included: keys taped, taping sequence, touch point coordinates of each taping, each moving distance, each moving speed, each moving direction, distances of touch points to the key centers/offset key centers, entry speeds (WPM), error rates, etc. For moving directions, the top/down and left/right displacements are recorded respectively. As to the center points, the "key center" and "offset key center" data have been recorded at the same time. The term "key center" refers to the center of a key that its position remains unchanged. As for the "offset key center" positions, they could only be obtained after we finished the experiments of each individual subject, figuring out the average position coordinates statistically. Therefore, the "offset key center" of each key varied from person to person, but the offset key center could be regarded as the relative center of all touch points.

The key design of this experiment App has included both visual target (48.48 × 31.03 pixel) and actual target (72.72 × 46.55 pixel), so as to eliminate the condition that any subject mis-identifies or touches the target key by mistake unreasonably. For example, if the target key is the leftmost Q key while the L key which is the rightmost on the screen has been touched by mistake somehow. This type of mistaken entry has nothing to do with the research project, would cause big deviation to seriously affect the experimental results, and thus such data must be deleted before proceeding with the analysis.

3.4 Experiment

This study uses the usability test as the primary research method. The subjects have been placed in a quiet lab to proceed with the experiments, and the entire process has been recorded by video. The iPhone 6S mobile phones have been used as experimental devices with screen resolution of 1334 × 750 pixels, 326 ppi, while the App used for the experiments has configured the screen coordinates to 375 pixels along the horizontal length and 667 pixels along the vertical length, with the upper left corner of the screen as the origin.

In the experiments the right-hand thumbs were used for data entry. The subjects were allowed to practice for two sessions to get familiar with the experimental App prior to the experiments, and there followed with one session of testing as the experiments.

4 Results

This research has collected experimental data of 30 subjects with a total of 3194 valid taping data, average entry speed (WPM) of 22.54 and an error rate of 0.92%. Figure 3 shows the distribution of all the touch points and their 95% confidence ellipse. The data have been used by descriptive statistics, analysis of variance, regression analysis for post analysis, and to proceed with the discussions about the data entry impacts from the directions, distances and speeds of the finger movements.

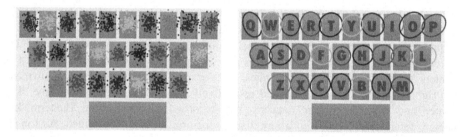

Fig. 3. Touch points distribution status (left) and 95% confidence ellipse (right)

4.1 Data Entry Impacts from the Fingers' Moving Directions

As shown in Table 1 for the overall movement directions, the proportions of left-movement/right movement, upward movement/downward movements were pretty much the same. At this stage the analyses have been made mainly focusing on the "possibilities which the touch points fall into the key center/offset key center's corresponding side (Top/Down, Left/Right)" and "the relative positions of the touch points in related to the key centers/offset key centers" when the fingers were moving in different directions.

Table 1. The overall number and proportion of the fingers' moving directions

Horizontal move			Vertical move		
	Frequency	Percent		Frequency	Percent
Left	1583	49.6	Top	1580	49.5
Right	1611	50.4	Down	1614	50.5
Total	3194	100.0	Total	3194	100.0

Possibilities: Touch Points Fall into the Corresponding Side of Key Center/Offset Key Center

In the "possibilities which the touch points fall into the key center/offset key center's corresponding side" analysis, the touch points' falling onto the two sides of the center point was regarded as a factor, the appearance percentages of both sides were used as dependent variables for one-way ANOVA analysis, and the finger directions were divided into four directions for discussions; for instance, whether there existed differences on the opportunities if the touch points would fall above or below the key center/offset key center when a finger was moving upwards. When we took the key center as the basis, the Levene's test results indicated significant, so we did not continue on the analysis. When we took offset key center as the basis, it indicated significant when the finger moved upward ($F(1.58) = 136.243$, $p < .001$), so that there existed significant difference in the probability when the touch points fell on the corresponding side of the offset key center. The results were also significant when the fingers moved down ($F(1.58) = 210.825$, $p < .001$), the results of fingers' left-movement ($F(1,58) = 6.646$, $p < .001$) and right-movement ($F(1.58) = 36.485$, $p < .001$) were similarly significant too.

Table 2 shows the four fingers' moving directions' percentage means of the occurrences of touch points' falling on the corresponding sides. When the fingers moved upward, the touch points appeared above the offset key center with a probability of 56.83%, which was above the bottom possibility of 43.17%. When the fingers moved downwards, the touch points appeared below the offset key centers with a possibility of 59.31%, which was above the top portion of 40.69%, and the horizontal results were similar. Therefore, it could be concluded that when an offset key center was taken as basis, the touch points would have a higher chances of falling on one side of the finger's moving direction.

Table 2. Fingers' moving directions and location ratios of the falling points

Location of touch point	N	Mean	Location of touch point	N	Mean
Top move			*Left move*		
Down	30	43.17	Right	30	48.42
Top	30	56.83	Left	30	51.57
Down move			*Right move*		
Top	30	40.69	Left	30	45.58
Down	30	59.31	Right	30	54.41

Relative Positions of the Touch Points to the Key Center/Offset Key Center

In the "relative positions of the touch points to the key center/offset key center" analysis, the fingers' horizontal movements and vertical movements have been analyzed respectively by using one-way ANOVA. The fingers' moving directions (Top/Down, Left/Right) were the factors, and the touch points in related to the key center/offset key center coordinate values were the dependent variables. In this analysis, each touch point's relative coordinate values in related to the center of each key has been calculated by the App; for example, if the center point coordinate of the A key was (10, 10) and the touch point coordinate was (5, 15), the relative coordinate of the touch point to the center point was (−5, 5).

When we took the key centers as the basis and the fingers moved horizontally, the results have indicated significant (F (1.3192) = 21.219, p < .001). Therefore, there existed significant differences in the relative coordinates of the touch keys in related to the key centers when the fingers made left/right movements. Likewise, significant results (F (1.3192) = 232.7, p < .001) could be obtained when the fingers moved vertically. When we took an offset key center as the basis, since we have obtained significant results from both horizontal axis (F(1.3192) = 13.86, p < .001) and vertical axis (F(1.3192) = 106.163, p < .001), we thus concluded that the fingers' moving directions would affect the touch point positions.

Table 3. Coordinate means of the touch points in related to the central point v.s. differ finger moving directions

	N	Mean	SD	Minimum	Maximum
Key center					
Right move	1611	1.6234	7.84342	−32.13	32.33
Left move	1583	0.3597	7.65770	−25.78	27.86
Total	3194	0.9971	7.77643	−32.13	32.33
Down move	1614	1.1346	7.63402	−22.68	27.32
Top move	1580	5.3557	8.00317	−26.59	31.87
Total	3194	3.2227	8.09753	−26.59	31.87
Offset key center					
Right move	1611	0.3754	5.96923	−23.00	23.00
Left move	1583	−0.4110	5.96787	−21.00	29.67
Total	3194	−0.0144	5.98057	−23.00	29.67
Down moving	1614	−1.0170	5.50759	−24.00	22.00
Top moving	1580	0.9847	5.47080	−16.40	19.83
Total	3194	−0.0268	5.57909	−24.00	22.00

Table 3 displays the relative coordinate positions' average values of the finger movement directions and touch points in relation to the key centers/offset key centers. For instance, when we took a key center as the basis, the touch point was 1.6234 pixel from touch center on the X-axis when the finger made right movement, the touch point would be 0.3579 pixel from the key center when left-movement was made; if we took offset key center as the basis, the touch point would be 0.3754 pixel from offset key center on the X-axis when the finger made right movement, the touch point would be −0.411 pixel from the offset key center when left-movement was made, a negative sign means that the touch point is on the offset key center's left side.

4.2 Analyses of Finger Movement Speeds, Distances and Directions in Relation to Accuracy

This analysis focuses on the data entry accuracy. In this research the data entry accuracy does not refer to whether the subjects have correctly taped the target keys that it is referring to the distance between a touch point and the center point. The smaller the distance, the more accurate; and on the contrary, the larger the distance, the less accurate. Therefore, the accuracy value is referring to the absolute value of each individual touch point in related to the touch key's central coordinate values. In addition, this analysis has solely taken offset key center as the basis because habitual shift happens on every subject while doing the taping, and such habitual shift conditions differ from one to the others. Therefore, it should make more sense to take the distance between the touch point and the offset key center as the basis of accuracy.

The correlation analysis between fingers' moving speeds, movement distances in relation to accuracy is performed by regression analysis with the moving speeds and movement distances as the independent variable, and the distances between touch points and offset key centers as the dependent variable. The analysis results show that the fingers' moving speeds on the horizontal axis are significantly related to accuracy (Table 4). The regression equation is:

$$Y = 3.781 + 2.824\,(X1) \tag{1}$$

while the results are also significant on the vertical axis (Table 5) with the regression equation to be:

$$Y = 3.805 + 0.004\,(X2) + 1.357\,(X1). \tag{2}$$

Table 4. Result of regression analysis on the horizontal axis

Model		Unstandardized coefficients		Standardized coefficients	t	Sig.
		B	Std. error	Beta		
1	(Constant)	3.781	0.158		23.853	0.000
	Distance of finger move on X-axis (X2)	0.000	0.001	0.008	0.309	0.758
	Speed (X1)	2.824	0.785	0.095	3.599	0.000

Dependent variable: distance between touch point and offset key center (Y)

Based on the above results, we have learned that accuracy is affected by fingers' moving speeds and movement distances no matter in vertical or horizontal directions. When the fingers move faster or when the distances get longer, the touch points would get away from offset key centers farther too, and that indicates that the accuracy would be reduced accordingly.

Table 5. Result of regression analysis on the vertical axis

Model		Unstandardized coefficients		Standardized coefficients	t	Sig.
		B	Std. error	Beta		
1	(Constant)	3.805	0.152		25.031	0.000
	Distance of finger move on Y-axis (X2)	0.004	0.002	0.046	2.499	0.013
	Speed (X1)	1.357	0.490	0.050	2.769	0.006

Dependent variable: distance between touch point and offset key center (YD)

Finally, the finger movement directions and accuracy analyses have been performed by One-way ANOVA with the moving directions as a factor and the distances between touch points and offset key centers are of a dependent variable. As a result, it indicated non-significant both on horizontal axis and vertical axis, therefore finger movement directions do not affect the accuracy.

5   Discussion

Although the last analysis in Sect. 4.2 has shown that the directions of finger movements had no obvious effects on the data entry accuracy, the analysis of Sect. 4.1 clearly has shown that the directions of finger movements do affect the touch point positions. Figures 4 and 5 have presented the probabilities of four kinds of falling points in related to vertical and horizontal movement respectively, and from that we could see the consistent tendency of touch point position deviation. When the offset key centers were used as the basis, the touch points tended to fall on the same side of the fingers' moving directions. When the fingers moved upwards, the probabilities for the falling points' appearing above the offset key centers were significantly higher than that of below. For down-move, the probabilities of falling points' on the lower side were higher than that of on the upper side; for left move, the probabilities of falling points' on the left side were higher than that of on the right side; as for right move, the probabilities of falling points' on the right side were higher than that of on the left side. Such tendency was even more obvious along the vertical axis, especially when the fingers moved downwards that the probabilities of the touch points' falling below the offset key centers were significantly higher than the probabilities of falling above the offset key centers by nearly 20% (Fig. 4).

The analysis results of the "relative positions of the touch points in related to the key centers/offset key centers" have also shown that the fingers' moving directions would affect the touch point positions. Figures 6 and 7 have shown the average values of the coordinates of the touch points in related to the key centers/offset key centers along the horizontal and vertical axes. Regardless of whether the fingers were moving horizontally or vertically, the touch points were biased towards the directions of fingers' moving directions. When we took offset key centers as the basis, the average falling points even coincidently distributed on both sides of the center points. When the fingers made left moves the mean of the falling points was −0.41 pixel which was

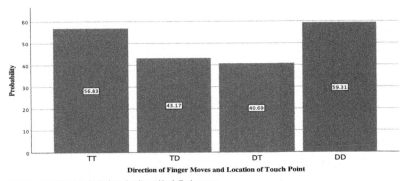

TT=finger moved top and touch point located on the top side of offset key center
TD=finger moved top and touch point located on the down side of offset key center
DT=finger moved down and touch point located on the top side of offset key center
DD=finger moved down and touch point located on the down side of offset key center

Fig. 4. Appearance possibilities of touch points' positions when fingers moved vertically

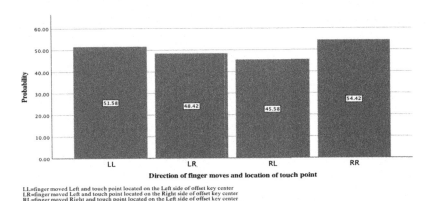

LL=finger moved Left and touch point located on the Left side of offset key center
LR=finger moved Left and touch point located on the Right side of offset key center
RL=finger moved Right and touch point located on the Left side of offset key center
RR=finger moved Right and touch point located on the Right side of offset key center

Fig. 5. Appearance possibilities of touch points' positions when fingers

located on the left side of the offset key centers. As for right moves, it was 0.38 pixel, located on the right side. There was a gap of 0.79 pixel between both, and it was similar for vertical movement cases. The mean value of the falling points was 0.98 pixel for up-moves, located at the upper position, and the mean value of the falling points was −1.02 pixel for down-moves, located at the lower position. The difference of falling point ranges on both sides was as large as 2 pixels. In the Sect. 4.1 analyses, "the probabilities for the touch points' falling on the corresponding side of the key centers/offset key centers" and "the relative positions of the touch points in related to the key centers/offset key centers" have shown very consistent results.

When we configured the touch points' four directions movements to analyze as 95% confidence ellipse setting, we could see the four directions' distribution status of the finger movements on the keyboards (Fig. 8). Under horizontal movement circumstances, the keys which near the left and right edges of the keyboards, such as the L, O, P, Q, do not have enough data samples due to the effects from finger moving

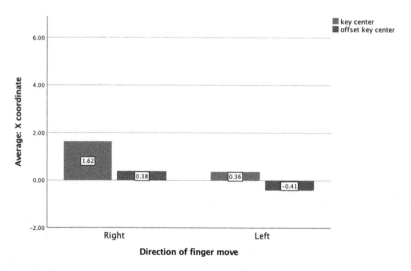

Fig. 6. Fingers' horizontal movements and means of touch points' location coordinates

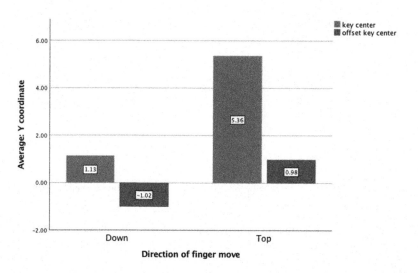

Fig. 7. Fingers' vertical movements and means of touch points' location coordinates

directions, therefore such inappropriate ellipses must be skipped off, for example, unless the P key has been taped twice in succession, the fingers won't have a chance to make a left-move to P. Under the horizontal movement circumstances, on most of the keys the number of right-biased ellipses are slightly more on the right side than the left-biased ellipses, and under vertical movement circumstances we could tell that there existed significant differences in the positions of the upward and downward ellipses.

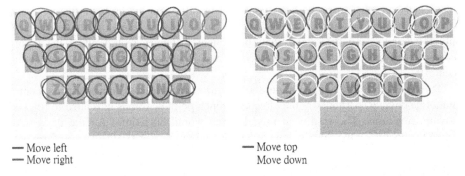

— Move left   — Move top
— Move right   Move down

Fig. 8. Appearance possibilities of touch points' positions when fingers moved horizontally

Based on the above mentioned, the touch point positions have higher probabilities of shifting towards the directions of finger movements. To speculate the causes, it could be because under the continuous data entry circumstances the movements were rather fast that the fingers could not accurately touch on the keys timely, and thus have taped in the moving directions at convenience. Such results were even more obvious on the fingers' vertical movement behaviors, and perhaps that was because the vertical lengths of the keys were larger than the horizontal widths which made the subjects to have relatively more spaces for movements in the vertical direction, and thereby made the difference more significant.

In terms of accuracy, the analyses showed that speeds and distances also affected data entry precision. This result was similar to Fitts's Law except that the results of this research could only show that the touch points would have a higher chances of getting away from the offset key centers when the fingers moved faster or when the fingers were farther away from the targets.

6   Conclusion

This research has designed an App for data entry testing to analyze how the finger movement directions, speeds, distances would affect the falling points of the text entry, and the research has had some findings. First of all, the directions of the finger movements would affect the touch point positions regardless of whether vertical or horizontal finger movements have been made. They all made the touch points to move towards the directions of the finger movements. From the offset key centers' point of view the falling points would have higher chances of following the fingers' moving directions to fall on the offset key centers' corresponding sides. For example, if the fingers moved upwards and then the falling points would have higher chances to fall above the offset key centers, and at the same time the average position of the falling points would distribute on the offset key centers' corresponding sides according to the fingers' moving directions; and when the fingers moved upwards the average position of the falling points would be right above the offset key centers. Secondly, according to the above phenomenon mentioned the results along the vertical axis were more significant than what from the horizontal axis despite what the probabilities were and where the average position of falling points was. Thirdly, in terms of taping accuracy, only the fingers' moving speeds and movement distances would affect the taping accuracy, and the fingers' moving directions would not have influence on the taping accuracy.

This research has discussed about the operation behaviors of continuous data entry on mobile devices, particularly the effects on touch point positions in related to fingers' moving directions. The results of this research would be helpful for the designs of virtual keyboards on the mobile devices, and would upgrade the data entry performance accordingly. In addition, further in-depth studies can be made in the future on such research; for example, analyses can be made on the status of every specific key, or to inspect the differences of keys according to different block divisions.

References

1. Consumer Barometer with Google. Google (2015)
2. Worldwide Smartphone Growth Expected to Slow to 10.4% in 2015, Down From 27.5% Growth in 2014, According to IDC. IDC (2015)
3. (2017) Smartphone Screen Size Trend. In: ScientiaMobile. https://www.scientiamobile.com/page/smartphone-screen-size-trend. Accessed 25 Jan 2018
4. iOS Human Interface Guidelines. Apple Inc. (2010)
5. Hoggan, E., Brewster, S.A, Johnston, J.: Investigating the effectiveness of tactile feedback for mobile touchscreens. In: Proceedings of the SIGCHI Conference on Human Factors in Computing Systems, pp. 1573–1582. ACM, New York (2008)
6. Henze, N., Rukzio, E., Boll, S.: 100,000,000 taps: analysis and improvement of touch performance in the large. In: Proceedings of the 13th International Conference on Human Computer Interaction with Mobile Devices and Services, pp. 133–142. ACM, New York (2011)
7. Fitts, P.M.: The information capacity of the human motor system in controlling the amplitude of movement. J. Exp. Psychol. **47**, 381–391 (1954). https://doi.org/10.1037/h0055392
8. Lee, S., Zhai, S.: The performance of touch screen soft buttons. In: Proceedings of the SIGCHI Conference on Human Factors in Computing Systems, pp. 309–318. ACM, New York (2009)
9. Bi, X., Li, Y., Zhai, S.: FFitts law: modeling finger touch with fitts' law. In: Proceedings of the SIGCHI Conference on Human Factors in Computing Systems. pp. 1363–1372. ACM, New York (2013)
10. Colle, H.A., Hiszem, K.J.: Standing at a kiosk: effects of key size and spacing on touch screen numeric keypad performance and user preference. Ergonomics **47**, 1406–1423 (2004). https://doi.org/10.1080/00140130410001724228
11. Wang, F., Ren, X.: Empirical evaluation for finger input properties in multi-touch interaction. In: Proceedings of the SIGCHI Conference on Human Factors in Computing Systems, pp. 1063–1072. ACM, New York (2009)
12. Vogel, D., Baudisch, P.: Shift: a technique for operating pen-based interfaces using touch. In: Proceedings of the SIGCHI Conference on Human Factors in Computing Systems, pp. 657–666. ACM, New York (2007)
13. Targeting - UWP app developer. In: Microsoft. https://docs.microsoft.com/en-us/windows/uwp/design/input/guidelines-for-targeting. Accessed 11 Jan 2018

14. Yi, X., Yu, C., Shi, W., Shi, Y.: Is it too small?: investigating the performances and preferences of users when typing on tiny QWERTY keyboards. Int. J. Hum.-Comput. Stud. **106**, 44–62 (2017). https://doi.org/10.1016/j.ijhcs.2017.05.001
15. MacKenzie, I.S., Soukoreff, R.W.: Text entry for mobile computing: models and methods, theory and practice. Hum.-Comput. Interact. **17**, 147–198 (2002). https://doi.org/10.1080/07370024.2002.9667313
16. Gentner, D.R., Grudin, J.T., Larochelle, S., et al.: A glossary of terms including a classification of typing errors. In: Cooper, W.E. (ed.) Cognitive Aspects of Skilled Typewriting, pp. 39–43. Springer, New York (1983). https://doi.org/10.1007/978-1-4612-5470-6_2
17. Arif, A.S., Stuerzlinger, W.: Analysis of text entry performance metrics. In: Proceedings of IEEE TIC-STH, pp. 100–105. IEEE (2009)
18. Azenkot, S., Zhai, S.: Touch behavior with different postures on soft smartphone keyboards. In: Proceedings of the 14th International Conference on Human-computer Interaction with Mobile Devices and Services. pp, 251–260. ACM, New York (2012)
19. Rudchenko, D., Paek, T., Badger, E.: Text text revolution: a game that improves text entry on mobile touchscreen keyboards. In: Lyons, K., Hightower, J., Huang, E.M. (eds.) Pervasive 2011. LNCS, vol. 6696, pp. 206–213. Springer, Heidelberg (2011). https://doi.org/10.1007/978-3-642-21726-5_13
20. Suhm, B., Myers, B., Waibel, A.: Model-based and empirical evaluation of multimodal interactive error correction. In: Proceedings of the SIGCHI Conference on Human Factors in Computing Systems, pp. 584–591. ACM, New York (1999)
21. Soukoreff, R.W., MacKenzie, I.S.: Metrics for text entry research: an evaluation of MSD and KSPC, and a new unified error metric. In: Proceedings of the SIGCHI Conference on Human Factors in Computing Systems, pp. 113–120. ACM, New York (2003)
22. Holz, C., Baudisch, P.: The generalized perceived input point model and how to double touch accuracy by extracting fingerprints. In: Proceedings of the SIGCHI Conference on Human Factors in Computing Systems, pp. 581–590. ACM, New York (2010)
23. Holz, C., Baudisch, P.: Understanding touch. In: Proceedings of the SIGCHI Conference on Human Factors in Computing Systems, pp. 2501–2510. ACM, New York (2011)
24. Park, Y.S., Han, S.H.: One-handed thumb interaction of mobile devices from the input accuracy perspective. Int. J. Ind. Ergon. **40**, 746–756 (2010). https://doi.org/10.1016/j.ergon.2010.08.001
25. Park, Y.S., Han, S.H.: Touch key design for one-handed thumb interaction with a mobile phone: effects of touch key size and touch key location. Int. J. Ind. Ergon. **40**, 68–76 (2010). https://doi.org/10.1016/j.ergon.2009.08.002

Interactive Public Displays for Paperless Mobility Stations

Cindy Mayas[✉], Tobias Steinert, and Heidi Krömker

Technische Universität Ilmenau, Postfach 10 05 65, 98684 Ilmenau, Germany
{cindy.mayas,tobias.steinert,heidi.kroemker}@tu-ilmenau.de

Abstract. A current development in public transport is the transition of paper-based mobility information into public displays at mobility stations. Mobility providers and users can benefit equally from this progress. This paper describes the evaluation of eight interactive public displays at a completely paperless test station in Stuttgart, Germany. The evaluation is based on analytical and empirical methods and covers data of the first year of operation.

Keywords: Public displays · Usability · Mobility information
Public transport

1 Introduction

The future of mobility is characterized by digitalization and flexibilization [1]. Firstly, the transfer of information within mobility providers and between mobility providers and travelers is mostly based on digital communication. Secondly, more public, shared, and individual mobility modalities are offered, for instance on-call busses, car and bike sharing, or taxi offerings, and enable more individual and flexible routing of travelers. Within these developments, stations are the hubs of mobility and mobility information and have to face new challenges:

- Increasing amount of information about departures and arrivals,
- Increasing amount of information about terms of use, and
- Increasing demands on actuality of information about delays and disturbances.

Today, the majority of information (about timetables, network plans, terms of use, construction zones and so on) is provided on paper, which has to be changed manually in case of modifications, at German stations. Thus, the introduction of paperless mobility information systems at stations does not only support the mentioned challenges, but also enables more efficient organization structures for mobility providers. The public mobility provider of Stuttgart introduced interactive displays [2] at one test station, in order to replace completely paper-based mobility information. This paper presents the user-oriented evaluation of the first year of use of eight interactive displays at the test station.

© Springer International Publishing AG, part of Springer Nature 2018
M. Kurosu (Ed.): HCI 2018, LNCS 10902, pp. 542–551, 2018.
https://doi.org/10.1007/978-3-319-91244-8_42

2   Objective and Test Subject

The interactive displays comprise the same collective information as the hardcopies at the same place before. The interactive application is controlled via a 46'' touchscreen (see Fig. 1) and includes the following information:

- Timetable,
- Route map,
- Ticket information,
- Station map, and
- Information on disturbances and deviations from timetable.

Fig. 1. Example of an interactive public display at the paperless test station [3]

Some supportive functions, as zooming and searching, are implemented next to the navigation functions, which were tested in an usability study according to the established criteria of usability und user experience of DIN EN ISO 9241-110 [4, 5]. The results of the usability study were included in the subsequent final development of the interactive public displays. Therefore, the field evaluation focuses on the following three aspects of use, next to the detection of further usability issues:

- Extent of use,
- Context of use, and
- Degree of acceptance.

3   Method

3.1   Overview

According to these objectives, a method mix (see Fig. 2) is applied, considering data on different levels. In a first step, system logfiles are analyzed from six months in order to find out general information about the extent of use. In a second step, an online survey is conducted in order to reveal the different aspects of acceptance and some factors of the context of use. Finally, users of the interactive displays are observed and interviewed in the field in order to gather specific data about the context of use and the usability.

Fig. 2. Evaluation methods

3.2   Logfile Analysis

The logfile analysis includes data from eight interactive public displays from October 2016 to March 2017. The data of the first month after the introduction of the new technology at the station was neglected due to many aimless uses for exploration or for fun. Therefore, the data from October 2016 was excluded from the analysis and the evaluation is based on the datasets from November 2016 to March 2017. In addition, data sets of three to four days per device are missing for technical reasons. After this data cleansing a total of 252 948 user interactions were analyzed on 151 days.

3.3   Passenger Inquiry

Questionnaire. The passenger inquiry was conducted with a standardized online questionnaire. The questionnaire includes questions about the previous uses of the interactive public display, the acceptance, further opinions about the displays, and personal information. The acceptance was analyzed according to the dimensions for the acceptance of media technologies by Quiring [6]:

- Relative Advantage - the degree to which an innovation is considered better than its predecessor technology,
- Compatibility - the degree to which an innovation is considered consistent with existing experiences, values and needs,
- Conceivableness of Complexity - the degree of difficulty to understand and use the technology,
- Observability - the degree of noticeability of the benefits of the technology.

Participants. A total of 219 persons took part in the survey. 57 persons cancelled the survey after few questions. The data shows that the majority of these participants either have never visited the test station or have never used the interactive public display and were therefore not interested in finishing the questionnaire. A total of 162 completed questionnaires remained for the analysis.

Due to the self-selection process of the participants through an online acquisition, the sample of the survey is not representative for all travelers. Especially, male travelers in the ages between 18 and 34 years are over-represented with a total share of 38% of the participants. In contrast, women and persons in the age over 65 years are underrepresented in the survey (see Table 1). This mismatch will be compensated in the final user field observation and interviews.

Table 1. Participants of the passenger inquiry (n = 162)

Gender	Percentage	Age	Percentage	Public transport usage [6]	Percentage
Male	70%	<18 years	9%	Power user	60%
Female	26%	18–34 years	49%	Commuter	8%
Not specified	4%	35–49 years	22%	Daily user	11%
		50–65 years	11%	Occasional user	17%
		>65 years	5%	Not specified	4%
		Not specified	4%		

46 participants did not receive further questions about the use of the interactive display, because they either haven't visited the test station before or haven't used the interactive public display at their visits of the paperless station.

3.4   User Field Observation and Interview

Observation. The observation of the users in the real context at the test station was conducted at three days. For this purpose, a weekday with average intensity of use (Thursday) and two days with above-average intensity of use were selected (Friday and Saturday) in several weeks in August 2017. The observations were conducted each day at different times of day. Overall, 55 use session of the interactive public displays could be observed. The aim was to cover the under-represented group of occasional passengers, female passengers and passengers, who are especially older than 65 years. The observation was documented in a semi-standardized observation protocol.

Post-observation-Interview. Due to the fact, that travelers often use the interactive public display shortly before or even while the expected train enters, only 25 persons could be interviewed directly after the observed use. 30 people entered a streetcar immediately after use or left the station on direct route. The interview covered questions about the actual information need, the context of the travel and the assessment of usability criteria.

Participants. Table 2 shows that the share of participants of the user observation are well suited to compensate for the under-representativeness of some groups in the user survey. The observation includes 30 observed female persons and 32 observed persons, who were older than 50 years, respectively 65 years. In addition, 75% of the users were on their way for errands or leisure activities and covers mainly the group of daily and occasional users. In that way, the data of the observation and interview complements the data of the passenger inquiry.

Table 2. Participants of the user field observation ([1]n = 55; [2]n = 25)

Gender[1]	Percentage	Age[1]	Percentage	Public transport usage[2] [6]	Percentage
Male	40%	<18 years	4%	Power user	20%
Female	55%	18–34 years	24%	Commuter	5%
Group	5%	35–49 years	14%	Daily user	30%
		50–65 years	25%	Occasional user	45%
		>65 years	33%		

Half of the interviewees had never used the interactive public display before. The results of this group are therefore a good indicator of the intuitive usability of displays. One quarter of the interviewees have already used displays in a few cases (one up to five times). Another quarter of interviewees uses the displays regularly.

4   Results

4.1   Extend of Use

Dwell time. The dwell time of a user session was analyzed as the time from the first interaction (click) of the user up to the moment he or she leaves the interactive display. The time before the first click, while the user is standing in front of the display without interaction, was neglected because the first click is required in order to activate the display from the standby mode and the majority of users activates the display immediately. The median dwell time of all 57984 users session of the logfile analysis takes 18 s with 3 interaction clicks. The dwell time of the majority of users is even much shorter. Figure 3 shows, that 32.6% of the users remains less than 10 s at the interactive display. Most of them aim to check the planned departure time of the next streetcar and tap two times at the most.

The dwell times were computed in the following way:

$$t_{kn} - t_{k1} + 5\,s = \text{dwell time}$$

$t_{kn} =$ time of the last click of a session
$t_{k1} =$ time of the first click of a session
$5\,s =$ median time of all differences between two clicks as estimated dwell time after the last click.

This very efficient use might be supported by the developed 2-click-navigation and the station-based information concept, which should enable travelers to fulfill the basical information needs as fast as possible. The short dwell times of the users are very important for the success of the interactive public displays instead of paper-based information.

While static, large paper-based information is available for more than one user at the same time, the interactive public displays provides information for only one user at the same time. Therefore, some more frequented waiting points are equipped with two interactive public displays, in order to guarantee each traveler the possibility to get the required passenger information by the interactive displays.

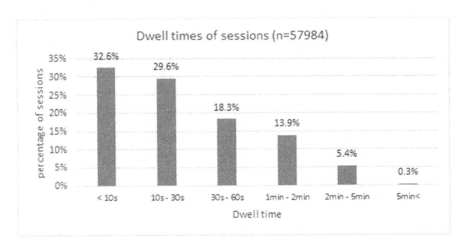

Fig. 3. Dwell times of use sessions

Clicks. The analysis of the overall amount of clicks of all interactive public displays shows, that displays in waiting areas are used more than three times more than displays in passage areas. Figure 4 displays the mean amount of overall clicks of the five interactive displays in waiting areas of streetcars and of the three interactive displays in passage areas at the entrance of the station.

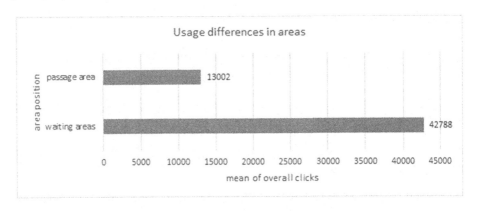

Fig. 4. Differences in the use between passage and waiting areas

The displays in the entrance area are especially important for tourists or occasional users, in order to orientate at the station and find the correct waiting point. In contrast, the majority of the passengers, for instance commuters and further daily users, already knows their waiting point and can orientate at the station without further information.

4.2   Context of Use

Next to the context of the travel, the travelers' information needs as the basic motivation of use are most relevant for the content decisions. The results of the data from the inquiry and the post-observation-interview indicate a similar share of information needs, see Fig. 5. The predominant information need is the information about the next departure time of the required streetcar or bus. Although the real-time departures of the next arriving vehicles are displayed separately on dynamic displays, most users check the timetables for their travel plan. Therefore, the route of a line as well as information about disturbances are the next important information needs. All the other available information, for instance about tickets or station maps, are specialized information, which are required for several user group, for instance tourists or occasional users.

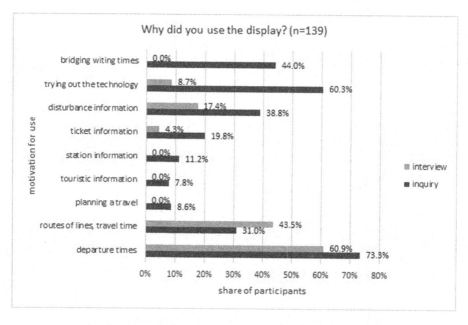

Fig. 5. Motivations for use of the interactive public display

4.3   Degree of Acceptance

The general acceptance of the new information technology at the station is evaluated on a 0 to 4 scale, which corresponds with a very low to a very high fulfillment of the dimensions of technology acceptance, as described in 3.3.

Corresponding to the good usability results of the interactive public display, the compatibility to users' expectations was assessed positively by more than three quarters of the users. The highest rates for observability (see Fig. 6) can be explained by the receivable benefit of the increased up-to-dateness of information for passengers, which is perceived positively by 83% of the participants of the inquiry. Nevertheless, every third respondent would still prefer the paper-based information instead of interactive public displays, which causes the lowest assessments for the dimensions of the relative advantage.

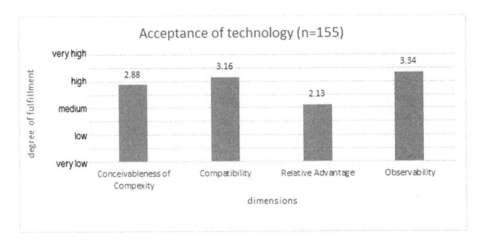

Fig. 6. Assessment of the acceptance of the interactive displays

The conceivableness of the complexity also offers chances for improvement. On the one hand, 69% of participants agree with the statement that the interactive public display facilitates the search of passenger information. On the other hand, 13% of the participants disagree with this statement and 18% are undecided. Thus, nearly every third participant assesses the interactive displays as not up to only partially controllable. This uncertainty should be reduced by certain action, presented in Sect. 5.

5   Recommendations

The results reveal the following general fields of action for interactive public displays:

- Communicate the benefits of the interactive public displays: Especially the user groups, which are more critical towards the interactive public displays, should be sensitized by focusing the communication on aspects that increase the value for the passengers. Especially, the aspects of information variety, actuality, and accessibility should be addressed in communication.
- Use interactivity to increase information quality: Some static content, such as a tariff zone plan, is not self-explanatory. Capacities in the utilization of public displays could be used for the communication of more detailed and assisting information. Further improvements of information quality could be achieved through detailed disturbance information or real-time information.

- Ensure short dwelling times: An intuitive navigation concept, which makes the main content available with two clicks at the maximum, guarantees a fast satisfaction of the travelers' information needs and the vacancy of the interactive public display for further travelers. A clear collective information concept, which focuses on the most important collective information needs, such as timetables, route of lines, travel times and disturbance information prevents long-term uses by single users delving into detailed individual information.
- Integrate the interactive public displays in the overall passenger information concept: Interactive public displays are a concept to replace static paper-based information by more dynamic information. The public displays are not suitable to completely replace individual and personal information via personal devices, such as smart phones. The public displays add the existing broad information service, including dynamic real-time-departure displays, passenger information applications for personal devices, service staff and so on.

6 Discussion

The selected method mix for the study design provides advantages and disadvantages. The major advantage is the positive cost-benefit ratio. The combination of the three methods logfile analysis, passenger questionnaire and field observation enables a fast overview of the key criteria extend and content of use as well as the acceptance. The study design is easy to repeat, in order to gather comparison data in other test stations or other cities, for other concepts of interactive public displays, and at a later point of time. These comparison of data is planned for subsequent studies and might reveal additional insights in effects of environmental factors on the use of the interactive public displays.

The disadvantage of the shown application of the methods is the varying representativity of the participants. Although the study covers data about all user groups and especially all representative courses of interactions with the interactive public display, it would be desirable to reach representative data according to the average of the population in each method. To reach this aim it is recommended to support the self-selective online questionnaire by a paper-based questionnaire and personal interviews, which are conducted based on defined selection criteria in the field. In addition, the presented three-day-observation should be extended to a seven-day-observation covering an artificial week over two or three months.

In summary, the study revealed very positive results regarding the degree of acceptance and matching the information needs of the travelers. Nevertheless, the field interviews and the acceptance data detected also some reluctance of the use of the interactive displays, especially of elder travelers and first-time users. Therefore, a regular sensitization for the benefits of paperless mobility information at stations and the continuous optimization of the information quality and usability is required.

References

1. Schade, W., Krail, M., Kühn, A.: New mobility concepts: myth or emerging reality? In: Transport Research Arena (TRA) 5th Conference: Transport Solutions from Research to Deployment, Paris (2014)
2. Hörold, S., Mayas, C., Krömker, H.: Interactive displays in public transport – challenges and expectations. Proced. Manuf. **3**, 2808–2815 (2015). https://doi.org/10.1016/j.promfg.2015.07.932
3. Pictures by ST-VITRINEN Trautmann GmbH & Co. KG
4. DIN EN ISO 9241-210:2010: Ergonomics of human-system interaction – part 210: human-centered design for interactive systems (2010)
5. VDV-Report 7036: User Interface Design für die elektronische Aushanginformation. VDV, Cologne (2014)
6. Quiring, O.: Methodische Aspekte der Akzeptanzforschung bei interaktiven Medientechnologien. Elektronische Publikationen der Universität München. Kommunikations- und Medienforschung. Münchener Beiträge zur Kommunikationswissen-schaft Nr. 6, Dezember (2006). https://epub.ub.uni-muenchen.de/1348/1/mbk_6.pdf. Accessed 19 Apr 2018

Sencogi Spatio-Temporal Saliency: A New Metric for Predicting Subjective Video Quality on Mobile Devices

Maria Laura Mele[1,2,3(✉)], Damon Millar[1], and Christiaan Erik Rijnders[1]

[1] COGISEN Engineering Company, Rome, Italy
{marialaura,damon,chris}@cogisen.com
[2] Department of Philosophy, Social and Human Sciences and Education,
University of Perugia, Perugia, Italy
[3] ECONA, Interuniversity Centre for Research on Cognitive Processing in Natural
and Artificial Systems, Sapienza University of Rome, Rome, Italy

Abstract. Objective Video Quality Assessment (VQA) is often used to predict users visual perception of video quality. In the literature, the performance evaluation of objective measures is based on benchmark subjective scores of perceived quality. This paper shows the evaluation of an algorithmic measure on videos presented on mobile devices. The VQA measure is called Sencogi Spatio-Temporal Saliency Metric (Sencogi-STSM), and it uses a spatio-temporal saliency to model subjective perception of video quality. Since STSM was previously validated with a subjective test conducted on laptop computers, the goal of this work was to verify whether the measure is able to significantly predict users' perception of video quality also on mobile devices. Results show that, compared to the standard VQA metrics, only Sencogi-STSM is able to significantly predict subjective DMOS. This paper describes Sencogi-STSM's biologically plausible model, its performance evaluation and the comparison with the most commonly used objective VQA metrics.

Keywords: Video quality perception · Computer vision
Spatio-temporal saliency · Objective video quality assessment

1 Quality Assessment Today

1.1 Introduction

Subjective testing with human participants is still the most reliable method to assess the perceived quality of an image or a video, even though it requires high cost and time effort. In order to measure participants' opinion scores of quality, standard recommendations are currently used, but the whole evaluation procedure often results in time-consumption and requires high costs. To avoid the cost and delay of subjective quality evaluation, objective quality assessment methodologies that do not involve participants are proposed in the literature to be used instead of subjective tests.

© Springer International Publishing AG, part of Springer Nature 2018
M. Kurosu (Ed.): HCI 2018, LNCS 10902, pp. 552–564, 2018.
https://doi.org/10.1007/978-3-319-91244-8_43

As Chikkerur and colleague highlights in 2011 [1], "the fidelity of an objective quality assessment metric to the subjective assessment is considered high if the Pearson and Spearman correlation coefficients are close to 1 and the outlier ratio is low. Some studies use the Root Mean Square Error (RMSE) to measure the degree of accuracy of the predicted objective scores. For the 95% confidence interval, it is desirable that the RMSE be less than 7.24". Following the methodology recommended by the ITU Tele-communication Standardization Sector [2], this study uses the aforementioned four analyses to compare objective and human video quality scores. None of the most used objective measurements seems to be able to adequately model human vision in the range of conditions used in typical subjective tests [3].

There are three types of objective video quality assessment methods: full-reference, wherein a an undistorted image or video is fully used for comparisons with distorted videos, reduced-reference, which use only some features of the undistorted quality reference image or video, and no-reference methods, wherein the reference video is not available at all [2]. This paper considers only full-reference methods.

1.2   Image and Video-Frame Quality Assessment

The next two paragraphs briefly show the state of the art of both image and video quality assessment. They also describe some of the most used image quality assessment metrics because they are often used to predict subjective video quality too.

Image Quality Assessment (IQA) metrics aim to measure the quality of a single static image. IQA metrics can also be used to measure video quality by treating the video stream as a collection of images, and calculating an aggregate score. In the literature, there is a wide choice of IQA metrics, such as Peak Signal to Noise Ratio (PSNR), Structural Similarity index (SSIM), Mean Structural Similarity (MSSIM), Universal Quality Index (UQI), Information Content Weighted Peak Signal to Noise Ratio (IWPSNR), Visual Information Fidelity (VIF), Feature Similarity Index (FSIM), Gener-alized Block-edge Impairment Metric (GBIM), NR Blocking Artifact Measure (NBAM), NR Perceptual Blur Metric (NPBM), Just Noticeable Blur Metric (JNBM). These IQA metrics include full reference and no reference metrics, and range from the purely pixel-based IQMs without the characteristics of the human visual system (HVS) to IQA metrics that contain complex HVS modeling. The ITU recommendations suggest using full reference measure in order to directly compare objective estimates of subjec-tive quality and human quality evaluations. For this reason, and since video encoders have access to full reference, in this paper we only focus on full reference measures.

Among the above listed measures, the full reference measures are Peak Signal to Noise Ratio (PSNR), Structural Similarity Index (SSIM), Multiscale Structural Similarity (MSSIM), and Universal Quality Index (UQI). PSNR calculates pixel-by-pixel the mean squared error between a distorted image and its high quality copy. PSNR is widely used since it returns a measure of distortion and noise that is easy to calculate. PSNR has also been extended with a pooling strategy of the locally calculated distortions, in order to incorporate some of the temporal features of human vision into PSNR. However, PSNR does not account for human visual perception, since its model treats pixels as being of equal importance and is unaware of any relationship between pixels. For this reason, PSNR is increasingly becoming inadequate for newer video codecs that apply visual perception models to remove data that falls beyond the threshold of visual perception.

SSIM aims to calculate how much an image or a video frame is "structurally similar" to the way the human visual system perceives quality. When an image or a video-frame is compressed, there is a change in structural information. SSIM has been also extended with a pooling strategy (i.e., the information content weighting) of the locally calculated distortions. Compared to PSNR, SSIM also considers pixels interdependency, which conveys important information about the structure of visual scene. Three visual components of an image are considered to calculate an SSIM value: luminance (high values are weighed more) contrast (locally unique values for pixels are weighed more) and structure (the more pixel values change together with their neighbors, the more they are weighed). The structure of each point is the covariance of x and y over the product of the variance x and y [4].

The perception of static images, such as video frames, is different than the perception of an entire moving video. Compared to static images, the continually changing visual stimuli of video-frames require more visual attentional from a viewer to process salient information. For this reason, the most-used image and video quality assessment metrics are not able to fully account for the HVS observing video. In a large-scale subjective study conducted by Seshadrinathan and colleagues to evaluate different video quality assessment algorithms [5], the authors found low correlation values for both PSNR (Spearman rho = 0.36; Pearson r = 0.40) and SSIM (Spearman rho = 0.52; Pearson r = 0.54) when compared to subjective values. The traditional video quality metrics, such as speak-signal-to-noise ratio (PSNR) or signal-to-noise ratio (SNR), are known to neglect the characteristics and the viewing conditions of human visual perception [6].

PSNR and SSIM are the most used measures to estimate image and video-frame quality, even though their model is not able to account for some aspects of the HVS, such as saliency processing. Therefore, new objective VQA models are still needed that are able to calculate the salient parts of video information.

1.3 Saliency Perception Models

One of the most important attention processes guiding visual perception is saliency. Saliency works like a filter that directs cognitive resources toward a subgroup of elements that may be significant for a certain visual context, allowing the HVS to process only partial amounts of information from a wide amount of information. Without the saliency regulation of attentional processes, large amount of information could overload the cognitive system [7] by accessing higher level processing systems in the brain.

In the literature, saliency perception models are based on either a bottom-up or a top-down main theoretical approach. The bottom-up approach is based on the visual saliency hypothesis, which describes visual attention as a data-driven answer to visual information [8], whereas the top-down approach is based on the cognitive control hypothesis [8, 9]. The bottom-up approach is the most studied one, and describes the process of selecting an area to fixate as a feature-guided process. On the other hand, according the top-down approach, visual attention is guided by context, task-related demands, and perceivers' needs. In the top-down approach, visual stimuli are still relevant as for the bottom-up one, but they are strictly related to cognitive information rather than on the saliency of visual data in itself [7].

Saliency is the primary process involved in subjective quality perception [10]. Many image quality assessment approaches attempt to use visual saliency to predict visual quality [11], and some efforts combine saliency with traditional measures of quality to produce saliency-weighted SSIM and PSNR performance [12].

1.4 Video Quality Assessment Based on Saliency Models

In order to determine salient areas, some spatial saliency algorithms [13] use frequency domain methods [14–20] reacting to patterns in the image. The algorithms that are based on frequency domain spatial saliency are biologically plausible and in line with the features of the human visual cortex [21] and are able to deal with most of the issues that usually arise in spatial salience calculation methods [9, 22], such as, for example, low resolution salience maps, and distorted object borders.

Calculating saliency of videos is more complicated than analysing still images because the regions of consecutive frames have a spatio-temporal correlation. Spatio-temporal correlation among video-frames changes the importance of each image in a scene, thus leading to different saliencies [23]. Some VQA methods deal with the changing salience of videos by incorporating spatial measures of salience, thus performing significantly better than traditional VQA methods [11]. However, these models only consider within-frame spatial saliency, neglecting to calculate between-frames spatio-temporal saliency. The primary reason why spatio-temporal saliency is rarely used for video compression is that it is difficult to discriminate salient motion from the noise produced by compression codecs or camera sensors [23, 24]. New measures are able to overcome noise related issues are still needed.

2 Spatio-Temporal Saliency for Video Quality Assessment

2.1 Cogisen's Video Compression Algorithm

This paper describes a saliency VQA metric called Sencogi Spatio-Temporal Saliency Metric (Sencogi-STSM), which looks at change in saliency as a measure of distortion and calculates video quality by applying spatio-temporal saliency principles. The Sencogi VQA metric is able to predict subjective quality of videos compressed by saliency-based codecs. The metric is based on a video compression spatio-temporal saliency algorithm developed by Cogisen [25].

Lossy image and video compression algorithms are closely related to quality assessment metrics because a successful compression algorithm must remove the maximum amount of information with minimal effect on quality. To achieve this trade-off, image and video compression algorithms include a tuned model of the human visual system. A compression algorithm generally calculates which parts of a video frame would influence the human perceived quality, and uses this information to compress data more heavily in the parts that are less visually salient, in order not to affect perceived image quality [9] (Fig. 1).

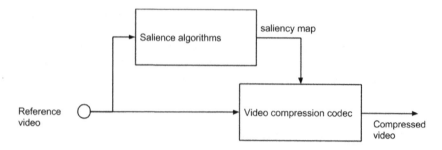

Fig. 1. Cogisen's saliency algorithms used to differentially compress video.

2.2 Cogisen's Saliency Algorithm

The VQA metric developed by Cogisen is based on saliency algorithms for video compression. Cogisen developed a very fast frequency-domain transformation algorithm called Sencogi, and used it to calculate frequency-domain saliency for a saliency-based image compression algorithm [26, 27]. Cogisen's saliency algorithm differs from most other saliency algorithms because it also predicts whether compression artifacts will cause a change in saliency. This is particularly important when saliency is used as a driver for varying compression levels, because perceptible image quality degradation can lead to perceptible changes in an image's low-level features on which bottom-up saliency models are based [11].

When working with low resolutions, the number of pixels to calculate edges and contrasts may be not enough, so video encoders may find it difficult to estimate saliency. However, due to the pervasive use of devices such as smartphones and tablets, video compression algorithms that are able to compress low resolution video recordings or live videos streamed with devices with limited processing capacity and bandwidth are needed.

As described in [27], Cogisen's algorithm uses four saliency drivers so that information removal in one domain does not introduce salient artifacts in another domain. In Cogisen's algorithm, "four different types of saliency algorithms are simultaneously run on a real-time video stream and combined to drive the codec's variable macro-block compression" [27]. In order to create Sencogi- STSM, Cogisen's saliency-based compression algorithms were used. The four types of saliency computed are:

- Pixel noise detection. Pixel noise detection is developed to discern between motion and pixel noise because video codec's cannot discern genuine scene motion from sensor pixel noise.
- Static image saliency. The static image saliency algorithms calculate saliency within each video frame.
- Spatio-temporal saliency. The spatio-temporal saliency algorithms calculate saliency between video frames.
- Delta-quality saliency. The delta-quality algorithm calculates whether the quality changes of a video can affect the scene saliency [28] by introducing artifacts that are subjectively perceived by viewers.

The combination of all four saliency algorithms are used to make a saliency map that drives the codec's variable macroblock compression. The use of four simultaneous saliency algorithms on a real-time video stream is possible because of the very fast Sencogi frequency-domain conversion. The four saliency drivers ensure that information removal in one domain does not introduce salient artifacts in another domain. The four algorithms are weighted by tunable thresholds, and then added to form a global saliency map (Fig. 2).

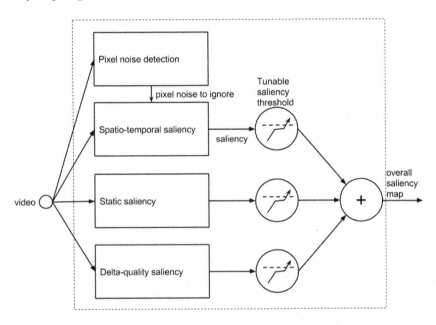

Fig. 2. Figure shows Cogisen's saliency algorithms combined to form an overall saliency map.

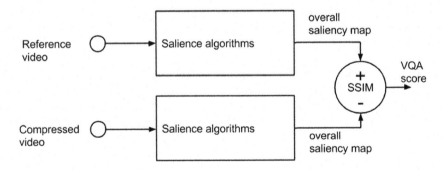

Fig. 3. The Sencogi-STSM VQA is measured as a change in saliency map.

2.3 Sencogi Spatio-Temporal Saliency Metric

The Sencogi Spatio-Temporal Saliency Metric is a VQA score calculated by comparing the saliency maps of the compressed video to the saliency map of the reference video. The comparison of saliency maps is performed using SSIM (Fig. 3).

3 Performance of Sencogi Spatio-Temporal Saliency Metric

3.1 Methodology

In a previous paper [27], the performance evaluation of Sencogi-STSM with laptop computers was described. The aim of this paper is to verify whether Sencogi-STSM is able to significantly predict users' perception of video quality also on mobile devices, in a way that is significantly more accurate than the most commonly used VQA metrics, i.e., PSNR and SSIM.

The evaluation of the performance of the Sencogi-STSM followed the same methodology as in the previous work [27]. We used a subjective a benchmark database to compare with objective measures calculated with PSNR, SSIM, and Sencogi-STSM. Finally, the performance of all objective models was tested by the Spearman Rank Order and the Pearson Linear correlation measures, the Outlier Ratio, and the Root Mean Square error, between subjective and objective scores.

3.2 Subjective Evaluation

Method. A benchmark subjective video quality database was created by using five video clips compressed at two different Constant Rate Factor values (CRF 21 and CRF 27), and by two different compression methods, i.e. X264 and a saliency based compression model. We used a saliency-based model to create a version of reference videos that keeps similar subjective perception of quality but uses higher compression levels [26, 27]. Finally, the subjective quality of five reference videos compressed by two compression methods at two compression levels (CRF) was evaluated in order to create a video quality assessment database.

Material. The subjective test used five high technical-complexity benchmark videos, lasting less than 10 s. Videos were in the uncompressed YUV4MPEG 4:2:0 format, in 426 × 224 landscape resolution. Reference videos were compressed with a visually lossless CRF value of 10, and then compressed to CRF 21 and CRF 27 by both the H264 model and the saliency based model.

Procedure. The procedure used for the subjective test was the Single Stimulus Continuous Quality Scale (SSCQS) method with hidden reference removal [3], which shows only one video at a time. The test was administered to mobile devices users only, by means of a web-based survey software tool called SurveyGizmo [29] with a methodology that has been previously validated by the authors [26, 27].

At the beginning of the subjective test, an example of a high quality video is shown, then reference high quality videos and compressed videos are randomly presented for each participant, in order to make sure that each video is presented only once in the succession. For each video, viewers are asked to rate the quality by using a slider marked from 1 to 100. The scale was divided into 5 equal parts labeled with the adjectives "Bad", "Poor", "Fair", "Good", and "Excellent".

Pre-screening conditions were set. Before beginning the test, users were asked to: plug their smartphone to a power connector, set the smartphone display to its maximum brightness; use only the Wi-Fi connection and disable any other type of internet connection mode; set the display orientation in the vertical (landscape) mode. Download speeds were tested and those with less than 40 megabits per second were excluded from the test. Users were also asked to report the lighting conditions under which they were performing the test, their position of use (e.g. seated on a chair, standing up), and the model of the smartphone they were using, its display size and resolution.

Subjects. Thirty-six participants completed the subjective test in a single session on June, 2017 (mean age 31.9 years old, 36.1% male, 13.8% expert viewers, 22.3% indoor with artificial lights, 77.7% indoor with natural lights, 100% sitting position, smartphone brands: 38.8% Apple iPhone 5/6/7, 36.1% Samsung Galaxy S6/S7, 25.1% other brands and models, smartphone screen-size: 41.7% 4.7/4.87 in., 58.33% 5.1/5.5/5.7 in.). Twelve outliers were removed.

Results. The internal consistency of the scale was validated by using Cronbach's alpha (alpha = 0.968) and Spearman Brown split-half value (rho = 0.942) (Cronbach's Alpha = 0.944 for the first half and alpha = 0.941 for the second half).

For each subject, the Mean Opinion Scores assigned to the reference videos were used to calculate the Difference Mean Opinion Scores (DMOS) (CRF 21: H264 = 63, Saliency based compression DMOS = 63.87, CRF 27: H264 = 56.9, Saliency based compression DMOS = 54.35) (Table 1) between reference videos and the related compressed videos using the formula explained in the previous work [27].

Table 1. Values of DMOS (range 1–100), PSNR (range 33–37), SSIM (range 0–1) and Sencogi-STSM (range 3.0–3.4) for videos compressed with the H264 compression model or the saliency based compression model at CRF 21 and CRF 27.

Compression	CRF	DMOS	PSNR	SSIM	Sencogi SMST
H264	All CRFs	3.529	37.996	0.972	3.319
H264	CRF 21	3.966	38.195	0.972	3.333
H264	CRF 27	3.097	37.798	0.971	3.306
Saliency based compression	All CRFs	11.337	33.799	0.931	3.060
Saliency based compression	CRF 21	10.067	33.977	0.932	3.062
Saliency based compression	CRF 27	12.608	33.622	0.930	3.058
All compressions	All CRFs	7.470	35.898	0.951	3.190
All compressions	CRF 21	3.604	37.996	0.972	3.319
All compressions	CRF 27	11.337	33.799	0.931	3.06

3.3 Objective VQA Prediction of Subjective Scores

Three objective VQA metrics were used to evaluate the same videos used during the subjective evaluation: (1) PSNR; (2) SSIM; (3) Sencogi-STSM (means: PSNR = 35.898; SSIM = 0.951; Sencogi-STSM = 3.190). Detailed results are reported in Tab. 1.

3.4 Prediction Performance: Comparative Analyses

Method. Four analyses comparing objective and subjective scores were performed by following the methodology recommended by the ITU Telecommunication Standardization Sector [2]: (1) Spearman Rank Order Correlation Coefficient (SROC); (2) Pearson Linear Correlation Coefficient (PLCC) (calculated after a nonlinear regression with a logistic function, as recommended by the ITU standards [3]); (3) Root Mean Square Error (RMSE); all calculating how much the VQA metric predicts subjective scores; (4) Outlier Ratio (OR), which calculates percentage of the predictions number that falls outside plus/minus 2 times the standard deviation of subjective DMOS.

Results

(1) Spearman Rank Order Correlation calculated on all types of compression combined show a significantly positive correlation between all objective measures and subjective scores: Sencogi-STSM values and DMOS values (rho = 0.655, p < 0.01), SSIM and DMOS values (rho = 0.627, p < 0.01), and PSNR and DMOS values (rho = 0.464, p < 0.05). Results on highly compressed videos (CRF 27), show that both Sencogi-STSM (rho = 0.503, p < 0.05) and SSIM (rho = 0.539, p < 0.01) are able to significantly predict subjective DMOS, whereas PSNR (rho = 0.248, p > 0.05) shows no significant correlation with DMOS values.

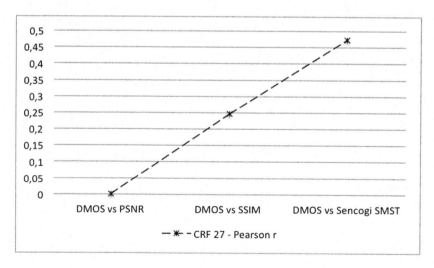

Fig. 4. Pearson Linear Correlation Coefficient between subjective and objective scores assigned to videos compressed at a CRF 27 value.

(2) Pearson Linear Correlation Coefficient on all videos and all types of compression CRF show a significant correlation between Sencogi-STSM and DMOS (r = 0.625, p < 0.01), between SSIM and DMOS (r = 0.632, p < 0.01), and between PSNR and DMOS (r = 0.451, p < 0.05). Results on highly compressed videos (CRF 27) show that only Sencogi-STSM (r = 0.472, p < 0.05) is able to significantly predict subjective DMOS. No significant correlation between PSNR and DMOS (r = 0.001, p > 0.05) and SSIM and DMOS (r = 0.246, p > 0.05) was found (Fig. 4).

(3) Paired t test of the Root Mean Square Error scores shows a significant difference between Sencogi-STSM scores and PSNR scores (t(10) = 7.757, p = 0.000), and SSIM (t(10) = 4.667, p = 0.001), meaning that Sencogi STMS has RMSE values significantly lower than both traditional objective measures (Sencogi-STSM RMSE = 7.049; SSIM RMSE = 8.508; PSNR RMSE = 29.652). Results on highly compressed videos (CRF 27), show a significant difference between both PSNR (RMSE = 23.153) and SSIM (RMSE = 11.207), and Sencogi-STSM (RMSE = 9.290), which has significantly lower prediction scores compared to the other objective measures (Sencogi-STSM vs PSNR: (t(4) = −3.506, p < 0.01; Sencogi-STSM vs SSIM: (t(4) = −15.403, p < 0.01) (Fig. 5).

(4) Results on the Outlier Ratio analysis show that only 7.75% of the values predicted by both SSIM (OR = 0.8) and Sencogi-SMST (OR = 0.75) fall outside ±2 of the standard deviation (SD) of subjective DMOS, whereas all PSNR values (OR = 1) fall outside ±2 of the SD of subjective DMOS.

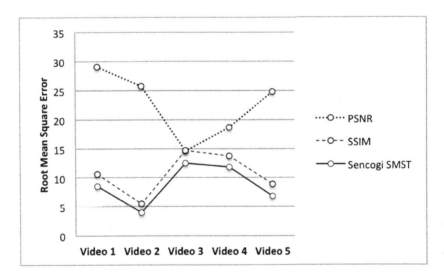

Fig. 5. Figure shows the Root Mean Square Error value of PSNR, SSIM, and Sencogi-STSM. The lower the RMSE value, the higher the degree of accuracy of the predicted objective scores is. Results on paired comparisons showed that Sencogi-STSM has significantly better prediction scores than PSNR and SSIM.

3.5 Discussion

The perception quality of videos compressed at two different constant rate factor values, and displayed on smartphone devices, has been calculated with three different objective measures: two traditional VQA measures called PSNR and SSIM, and one new VQA saliency based measure, called Sencogi-STSM. A previous study [27] proved the efficacy of the new Sencogi-STSM metric for predicting subjective quality scores of videos displayed on laptop computers, finding an overall better prediction performance by Sencogi-STSM than SSIM and PSNR metrics.

Results obtained in this study confirm the efficacy of Sencogi-STSM in predicting subjective scores for mobile phone screens. Globally, all the compared objective VQA metrics are able to significantly predict subjective scores of compressed videos displayed on smartphone devices, but only Sencogi-STSM and SSIM accurately predict subjective scores for highly compressed video (CRF 27), and only Sencogi-STSM is able to significantly predict subjective scores with low error. Moreover, Sencogi-STSM has lower RMSE values than PSNR and SSIM, especially for videos compressed at CRF 27. Sencogi-STSM obtained better prediction performance over the classic SSIM and PSNR metrics especially for highly distorted videos. For non-salience-compressed videos at CRF 27, STSM is 6.8% more accurate than SSIM. For salience compressed videos at CRF 27, STSM is 14.44% more accurate than SSIM. Results show that, at high compression levels, the logic behind Sencogi-STSM (which uses perceptual quality features) ensures that high saliency areas are given more significance than low saliency.

4 Conclusion

The performance of Sencogi Spatio-Temporal Saliency Metric (Sencogi-STSM) with mobile devices was compared to the most used objective Video Quality Assessment metrics, i.e. Peak Signal to Noise Ratio (PSNR) and Structural Similarity index (SSIM). Sencogi-STSM model uses spatio-temporal saliency to predict subjective perception of video quality. Sencogi-STSM uses four visual complexity algorithms, which calculate saliency within a video-frame, motion saliency between video-frames, delta-quality saliency showing where a quality change may be subjectively noticed, and noise detection. The performance evaluation with mobile devices showed that Sencogi-STSM is significantly more accurate in predicting subjective scores of videos compressed at high Constant Rate Factor (CRF) values than the other objective VQA metrics.

References

1. Chikkerur, S., Sundaram, V., Reisslein, M., Karam, L.J.: Objective video quality assessment methods: a classification, review, and performance comparison. IEEE Trans. Broadcast. **57**, 165–182 (2011)
2. BT.500: Methodology for the subjective assessment of the quality of television pictures (n.d.). http://www.itu.int/rec/R-REC-BT.500-7-199510-S/en. Accessed 9 Oct 2017

3. Brunnstrom, K., Hands, D., Speranza, F., Webster, A.: VQEG validation and ITU standardization of objective perceptual video quality metrics [Standards in a Nutshell]. IEEE Sign. Process. Mag. **26**, 96–101 (2009)

4. Staelens, N., Moens, S., Van den Broeck, W., Marien, I., Vermeulen, B., Lambert, P., Van de Walle, R., Demeester, P.: Assessing quality of experience of IPTV and video on demand services in real-life environments. IEEE Trans. Broadcast. **56**(4), 458–466 (2010)

5. Seshadrinathan, K., Soundararajan, R., Bovik, A.C., Cormack, L.K.: A subjective study to evaluate video quality assessment algorithms. In: Human Vision and Electronic Imaging, vol. 7527, p. 75270 (2010)

6. Wang, Z., Bovik, A.C.: Modern image quality assessment. Synth. Lect. Image Video Multimedia Process. **2**, 1–156 (2006)

7. Duchowski, A.: Eye Tracking Methodology, Theory and Practice, vol. 373. Springer Science & Business Media, New York (2007). https://doi.org/10.1007/978-1-4471-3750-4

8. Itti, L., Koch, C.: A saliency-based search mechanism for overt and covert shifts of visual attention. Vis. Res. **40**, 1489–1506 (2000)

9. Wolfe, J.M.: Visual search in continuous, naturalistic stimuli. Vis. Res. **34**, 1187–1195 (1994)

10. Mitchell, R.K., Agle, B.R., Wood, D.J.: Toward a theory of stakeholder identification and salience: defining the principle of who and what really counts. Acad. Manag. Rev. **22**(4), 853–886 (1997)

11. Zhang, L., Shen, Y., Li, H.: VSI: a visual saliency-induced index for perceptual image quality assessment. IEEE Trans. Image Process. **23**, 4270–4281 (2014)

12. Larson, E.C., Chandler, D.M.: Unveiling relationships between regions of interest and image fidelity metrics. In: Visual Communications and Image Processing 2008 (2008). https://doi.org/10.1117/12.769248

13. Zhang, W., Borji, A., Wang, Z., Le Callet, P., Liu, H.: The application of visual saliency models in objective image quality assessment: a statistical evaluation. IEEE Trans. Neural Netw. Learn. Syst. **27**, 1266–1278 (2016)

14. Achanta, R., Estrada, F., Wils, P., Süsstrunk, S.: Salient region detection and segmentation. In: Gasteratos, A., Vincze, M., Tsotsos, John K. (eds.) ICVS 2008. LNCS, vol. 5008, pp. 66–75. Springer, Heidelberg (2008). https://doi.org/10.1007/978-3-540-79547-6_7

15. Hou, X., Zhang, L.: Saliency detection: a spectral residual approach. In: 2007 IEEE Conference on Computer Vision and Pattern Recognition (2007). https://doi.org/10.1109/cvpr.2007.383267

16. Harel, J., Koch, C., Perona, P.: Graph-based visual saliency. In: Advances in Neural Information Processing Systems, pp. 545–552 (2007)

17. Itti, L., Koch, C.: A saliency-based search mechanism for overt and covert shifts of visual attention. Vis. Res. **40**, 1489–1506 (2000)

18. Itti, L., Koch, C., Niebur, E.: A model of saliency-based visual attention for rapid scene analysis. IEEE Trans. Pattern Anal. Mach. Intell. **20**(11), 1254–1259 (1998)

19. Li, J., Levine, M., An, X., He, H.: Saliency detection based on frequency and spatial domain analyses. In: Proceedings of the British Machine Vision Conference 2011 (2011). https://doi.org/10.5244/c.25.86

20. Ma, Y.-F., Zhang, H.-J.: Contrast-based image attention analysis by using fuzzy growing. In: Proceedings of the Eleventh ACM International Conference on Multimedia, MULTIMEDIA 2003 (2003). https://doi.org/10.1145/957092.957094

21. Bian, P., Zhang, L.: Biological plausibility of spectral domain approach for spatiotemporal visual saliency. In: Köppen, M., Kasabov, N., Coghill, G. (eds.) ICONIP 2008. LNCS, vol. 5506, pp. 251–258. Springer, Heidelberg (2009). https://doi.org/10.1007/978-3-642-02490-0_31

22. Achanta, R., Hemami, S., Estrada, F., Susstrunk, S.: Frequency-tuned salient region detection. In: 2009 IEEE Conference on Computer Vision and Pattern Recognition (2009)
23. Yubing, T., Cheikh, F.A., Guraya, F.F.E., Konik, H., Trémeau, A.: A spatiotemporal saliency model for video surveillance. Cogn. Comput. **3**, 241–263 (2011)
24. Arvanitidou, M.G., Sikora, T.: Motion saliency for spatial pooling of objective video quality metrics (2012)
25. Cogisen Homepage. http://www.cogisen.com. Accessed 22 Jan 2018
26. Mele, M.L., Millar, D., Rijnders, C.E.: The web-based subjective quality assessment of an adaptive image compression plug-in. In: 1st International Conference on Human Computer Interaction Theory and Applications, HUCAPP, Porto, Portugal (2017)
27. Mele, M.L., Millar, D., Rijnders, C.E.: Using spatio-temporal saliency to predict subjective video quality: a new high-speed objective assessment metric. In: Kurosu, M. (ed.) HCI 2017. LNCS, vol. 10271, pp. 353–368. Springer, Cham (2017). https://doi.org/10.1007/978-3-319-58071-5_27
28. Redi, J., Liu, H., Zunino, R., Heynderickx, I.: Interactions of visual attention and quality perception. In: Human Vision and Electronic Imaging XVI (2011). https://doi.org/10.1117/12.876712
29. SurveyGizmo Homepage. http://www.surveygizmo.com. Accessed 22 Jan 2018

Improving Mobile User Experience of New Features Through Remote Tests and Evaluation

Lúcia Satiko Nomiso[(✉)], Eduardo Hideki Tanaka, and Raquel Pignatelli Silva

Eldorado Research Institute, Campinas, SP, Brazil
{lucia.nomiso,eduardo.tanaka,raquel.silva}@eldorado.org.br

Abstract. This paper presents a process to evaluate a new feature which allowed users to do gestures in a fingerprint sensor located at the bottom of smartphones. The idea was, with these gestures in the fingerprint sensor, users could perform all functions available on a typical Android navigation bar (go back, go to home screen and open the recent apps), so that the navigation bar could be hidden from all screens, allowing the users to enjoy a larger screen in all apps. The whole evaluation process was remotely performed at the end of the development process, with 115 participants receiving a smartphone containing not only the new feature to be evaluated but also a few embedded apps to collect logs, let users raise any issues they found and answer user satisfaction surveys after some time using the feature. The findings from this evaluation process were useful to refine the feature, enhance the user experience and make all stakeholders more confident about the user's acceptance before releasing it to market.

Keywords: User trial · User experience · Remote evaluation

1   Introduction

A mobile phone is a must-have consumer product for most of the population. Over the years, mobile phones became much more than just ordinary voice communicating devices to deliver a variety of rich experiences, allowing people to be always connected to friends and family, play games, listen to music, be up-to-date with any kind of news of the whole world, and others.

Given that any people in the world could be a smartphone user nowadays, deliver a great user experience is a high priority requirement for all the top smartphone manufacturers. In fact, ease of use is something that people seeks in a smartphone. Also, even customization of mobile phones is mostly done by users because they wanted to use a mobile phone easily [1].

Knowing about the relevance of the user experience for mobile phones, this paper presents a process that evaluated the user experience of a new feature called "One Button Nav" added to Lenovo Motorola mobile phones before they hit the market. The process involved a remote evaluation through log collection and pre-installed apps to let users to describe any issues they found as well as to answer surveys applied after users effectively utilized the new feature for a while.

M. Kurosu (Ed.): HCI 2018, LNCS 10902, pp. 565–575, 2018.
https://doi.org/10.1007/978-3-319-91244-8_44

The collected information about users, their expectations and experiences allowed designers to continuously enhance the user experience. Moreover, it helped product managers to decide whether this new feature should have been effectively included in a mobile phone, given that it measures the user satisfaction and adoption - and, as stated by [2], the value of a new feature is realized only by the users adopting it or not.

The next sections will describe the One Button Nav feature, the process applied to evaluate the feature and the major findings.

2   One Button Nav

The One Button Nav is a new feature introduced by Lenovo Motorola in their smartphones, delivered first on Moto G family in 2017 [3]. Previous models from Lenovo Motorola have already been shipped with a fingerprint sensor, but that sensor was only utilized to authenticate the user as an alternative for passwords, PINs and drawn patterns to authenticate the user and unlock the device. Figure 1 shows pictures of Moto G4 Plus and Moto G5 Plus, highlighting the fingerprint sensor at the bottom of them.

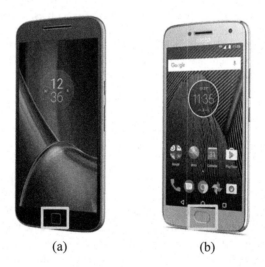

(a)   (b)

Fig. 1.   (a) Moto G4 Plus and (b) Moto G5 Plus. Fingerprint sensor in both devices is highlighted.

The One Button Nav takes advantage of the fingerprint sensor built at the bottom of the latest Lenovo Motorola smartphones to enhance it and give the ability to make gestures on the sensor itself. Thus, the idea is to have specific gestures available on the fingerprint sensor to completely replace the typical Android navigation bar and its icons (back, home and recent apps, shown in Fig. 2), increasing the useful area of the display. Although the concept of this feature is very simple, all users need to learn new gestures to use existing functionalities in a different way [4]. And, as highlighted by Nayebi et al. [5], easy to learn is a characteristic that users appreciate in mobile apps and was, in fact, one of the major objectives of the One Button Nav development.

Fig. 2. Typical navigation bar from Android [6].

A few screenshots of the One Button Nav tutorial are presented in Fig. 3.

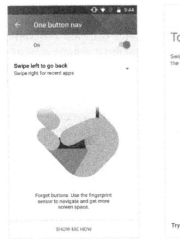

Fig. 3. One Button Nav screenshots.

Table 1 summarizes all the available One Button Nav gestures.

Table 1. One Button Nav gestures.

Gesture	Function
Tap on the sensor	Go to home screen
Swipe from right to left on the sensor	Go back
Swipe from left to right on the sensor	Open recent apps
Touch and hold the sensor until a short buzz	Turn the screen off (lock the device)
Touch and hold the sensor until a long buzz	Launch Google assistant

One of the greatest advantages of One Button Nav is that it can completely replace the Android navigation bar, so that this bar can be hidden, giving to the users some more useful space on the screen – and, according to the findings from Liu and Liang [7], screen size is a key factor that people adopt to decide to buy a new smartphone.

3   User Experience Evaluation

Considering the concerns mentioned in the previous sections about the user experience, 115 participants from all over the world were recruited to test a new mobile phone containing the One Button Nav for three months. By default, One Button Nav was disabled, but participants were invited to enable it and use it as much as possible. The test devices were configured to automatically collect logs (especially errors and bugs) as well as to trigger some user satisfaction surveys if the user activated the feature and used it for a while. Participants could also manually report issues they faced through a bug report app pre-installed in their devices. Additionally, an online forum was created to let participants freely express and share with the others their opinions about the One Button Nav.

Some weeks after each survey was applied and its results analyzed, users were invited to change their devices for a newer, improved hardware and software containing enhancements based on their feedbacks. To sum up, during those three months, 62 issues related to One Button Nav were manually raised. After the development team analyzed these issues, this number decreased to 22 valid – from all issues, 41.9% were duplicated, 8.1% unreproducible, 8.1% considered invalid, 6.5% cancelled by the development team, 6.5% decided not to fix, 22.6% unresolved and 6.5% corrected for the new versions. Figures 4 and 5 shows some charts summarizing how the issues were handled.

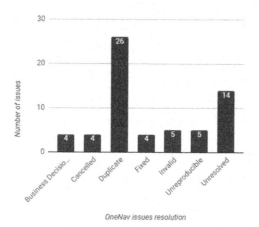

Fig. 4.   One Button Nav issues resolution (number of issues per resolution).

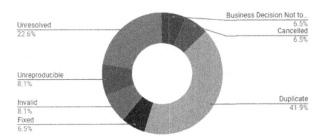

Fig. 5. One Button Nav issues resolution (distribution).

Issues classified as "unreproducible" and "invalid" were mostly related to performance due to the mobile phones used in this study had some apps listening to events and collecting logs all the time. As end user devices don't have these apps, these performance issues won't be faced by them.

"Business decision not to fix" issues were related to incorrect gestures performed in the fingerprint sensor. For example, when the user tried to open all apps by swipping from left to right but the finger was a little far from the sensor or not totally touching it, so that the One Button Nav was not able to effectively identify the performed gesture.

Cancelled issues were related to some misunderstanding of how the fingerprint sensor works or the usage behavior. For example, when setting up the authentication methods of the device, users can select a combination of fingerprint and password to unlock the device after restarting it. However, some users forgot about this behavior and raised an issue because the device did not unlock only with fingerprint when restarted.

Unresolved issues do not mean exactly that nothing was done. During this study, 14 issues were marked as unresolved, although 10 of 14 (72.4%) were related to expected behavior of initial design of the feature. For example, a user had the impression that the gesture was being interpreted incorrectly, but after development team analysis it was possible to conclude that the user could be right just as gesture was incorrect and sensor couldn't interpret. The other 4 unresolved issues were raised after the release of the final user build. As it wouldn't be possible to fix them before the release of the device, they were moved to be analyzed in the next build updates and eventually users would receive fixes through an upcoming Play Store update.

The number of fixed issues was only four to this product. But it doesn't mean that only four issues found were effectively fixed for it, as some of the duplicated issues were also found in similar products before, so that these problems were fixed for the other products first and then the same solution was applied to this product. Therefore, the number of fixed issues presented in the previous chart was actually the number of issues firstly found on this product (not in others) and fixed for it during the development cycle.

Some other interesting data about the usage of the fingerprint sensor and One Button Nav gestures were also collected during this study. Based on them, it was found out that, although all participants were invited to use the fingerprint sensor to unlock the device (which was the simplest gesture and not really related to One Button Nav gestures), less than 24% were effectively using it at the end of the study, as seen in Fig. 6. Additionally, Fig. 7 shows the One Button Nav gesture usage.

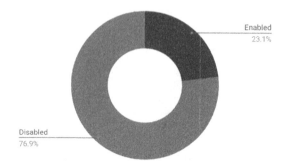

Fig. 6. Adoption of fingerprint sensor to unlock the device at the end of the study.

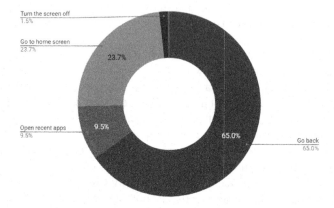

Fig. 7. One Button Nav gestures usage.

From Fig. 7, it is noticeable that the most common gesture performed in One Button Nav was the "Go back" to the previous screen (65.0%), followed by the "Go to home screen" (23.7%). On the other hand, the least used gesture was "Launch Google assistant (0.3%). Other interesting data about the usage of One Button Nav gestures can be viewed in Table 2. Based on these data, it is interesting to notice that, on average, users performed the "Go back" gesture about 205 times daily. In fact, the top 3 gestures most used were the ones that really replaced the ordinary Android navigation bar (go back, go to home screen and open recent apps). The small frequency of usage of turn the screen off and launch the Google assistant gestures may not be really related to users not using them, but, as there are other methods to turn the screen off (through the power button, for instance) and launch the Google assistant (saying "Ok, Google", for instance), users may prefer them instead of One Button Nav. A deeper investigation to understand the actual usage of Google assistant and how users turn the screen off is required.

In addition to the raised issues and the data automatically collected about the users interacting with One Button Nav, four user satisfaction surveys were applied during the research period, as mentioned before. The surveys were composed by Likert Scale [8] questions to rate agreement/disagreement with some statements about the One Button Nav experience. The first survey collected 53 responses from distinct participants whereas in the last one 115 participants answered. The surveys were applied when the users changed their devices to newer ones containing hardware changes and when a new software version containing One Button Nav improvements was available to the users. Figure 8 shows the number of participants in each survey.

Table 2. Daily usage of One Button Nav gestures.

Gesture	Number of occurrences	Average per user
Go to home screen	2018	74.74
Go back	5533	204.93
Open recent apps	813	30.11
Turn the screen off	130	4.81
Launch Google assistant	23	0.85

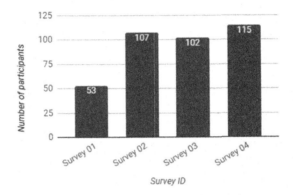

Fig. 8. Number of participants per survey.

The survey contained questions to assess the overall satisfaction of the users with the fingerprint sensor and with the One Button Nav, as well as let users identify whether they experienced issues when using One Buton Nav gestures. Figure 9 shows the responses, among all the surveys, for the question about the overall satisfaction with the One Button Nav feature. Clearly, the positive responses were increasing over the time – in the first survey, 78% of the responses were positive whereas, in the last one, it became 83%. Additionally, the unfavorable responses decreased from 10% to 5% between the first and last surveys.

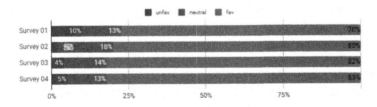

Fig. 9. Overall satisfaction with the One Button Nav among all surveys.

Table 3 summarizes the responses for each questions, comparing the results from the first and the last survey. Among all One Button Nav gestures, it is possible to verify an increase of the user satisfaction for "Go home", "Open recent apps" and "Launch Google assistant". For the "Go back" gesture, there was a slightly decrease of the favorable responses, but the neutral responses were raised and the unfavorable responses were hugely decreased, possibly because users started to learn how to do this gesture.

Table 3. One Button Nav survey responses for Survey 01 (first) to Survey 04 (last).

	Survey 01 (first)			Survey 04 (last)		
Questions	fav	neutral	unfav	fav	neutral	unfav
Overall how satisfied are you with the One Nav feature on your device?	78%	13%	10%	83%	13%	5%
Q1. I experience issues authenticating with FPS.	90%	9%	1%	93%	4%	3%
Q2. I experience issues navigating to home using the FPS Sensor.	84%	8%	8%	91%	4%	5%
Q3. I experience issues navigating back using the FPS Sensor.	72%	9%	19%	71%	21%	8%
Q4. How satisfied are you with turning the screen off via the FPS?	89%	4%	7%	81%	7%	12%
Q5. I experience issues turning the screen off via the FPS.	85%	7%	8%	77%	11%	12%
Q6. How satisfied are you with launching Google Now via the FPS?	76%	15%	9%	90%	5%	4%
Q7. I experience issues launching Google Now via the FPS.	82%	9%	9%	89%	5%	5%

The only gesture that the negative responses increased and the positive responses decreased from the first survey to the last survey was the "turn the screen off". In fact, some users complained that it was because they unintentionally performed the gesture: they were holding the fingerprint button without noticing that and then got the device locked by mistake.

Figures 10 and 11 show bar charts containing the responses in the first and the last surveys, respectively, for the specific questions related to the One Button Nav gestures.

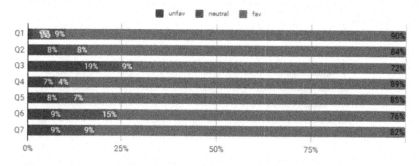

Fig. 10. User satisfaction responses for One Button Nav gestures (first survey).

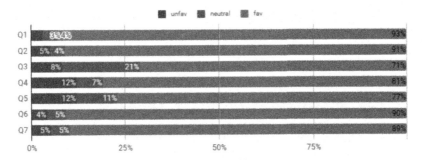

Fig. 11. User satisfaction responses for One Button Nav gestures (last survey).

Checking all the One Button Nav gestures, all of them got value considered satisfactory.

4 Consumer Analysis

The One Button Nav was first available on the Lenovo Motorola Moto G5 family of devices, launched worldwide on August 2017. After some months of usage, a few data about how consumers (end users) have been utilizing the device became available. As seen in the chart of Fig. 12, "Go back" (66.7%) is the most frequent gesture of One Button Nav used by consumers, followed by "Go home" (17.8%) and "Open recent apps" (11.0%). For this chart, 1329003 end users were considered.

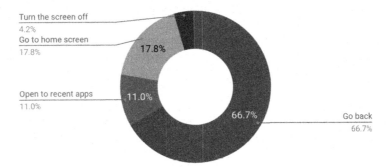

Fig. 12. One Button Nav gestures usage (consumers).

Comparing with the pre-release study performed, data about the usage of One Button Nav gestures were similar, as shown in the chart of Fig. 13. However, the percentage of end users that are really using One Button Nav was not the same as in the study: during the user experience evaluation, One Button Nav was adopted by 23% of participants whereas, for consumers, this number was only 9.2%. A few hypotheses could explain this difference: participants of the study were more tech-savvy than end users and were invited several times to try the feature, while end users didn't receive any advertisement about One Button Nav during the initial set up of the device. A further investigation is still required, though.

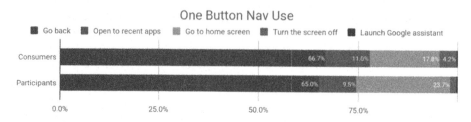

Fig. 13. Usage of One Button Nav gestures (consumers vs. participants).

A deeper analysis of the consumer needs, expectations and satisfaction could also help to understand the lower adoption of One Button Nav. Yet, informal feedbacks from consumers that have been using One Button Nav gestures highlight the major benefit of the feature: more screen space.

5   Concluding Remarks

This paper presented a remote user experience evaluation performed to assess a new feature added to recent smartphones that let users make gestures in a fingerprint sensor to replace the default Android navigation bar, giving to the users more screen space. The conducted evaluation was helpful to identify issues and possible enhancements during the development stage, as well as brought some insights about the most common interactions (go back, go to home screen and open recent apps).

As future work, authors would like to apply a survey to consumers to measure the user satisfaction with One Button Nav and compare the numbers with the ones from the remote user experience evaluation.

Acknowledgements. The authors would like to thank all participants of the user trial program who contributed with valuable feedbacks about their experiences with the One Button Nav. The authors also thank Motorola and Eldorado Research Institute, which allowed us to conduct this research.

References

1. Choe, P., Liao, C., Sun, W.: Providing customisation guidelines of mobile phones for manufacturers. Behav. Inf. Technol. **31**(10), 983–994 (2012)
2. Revang, M.: How to Reduce Functionality to Improve User Experience. Gartner, Inc. https://www.gartner.com/document/3410730?ref=solrResearch&refval=192919994&qid=ID:G0027 6825. Accessed 17 Aug 2016
3. Motorola Moto G 5 Plus. https://www.motorola.com/us/products/moto-g-plus#experiences. Accessed 05 Feb 2018

4. Motorola Moto G 5 Plus Fingerprint Reader. https://www.motorola.com/us/products/moto-g-plus-gen-5-special-edition#fingerprint-reader. Accessed 05 Feb 2018
5. Nayebi, F., Desharnais, J.M., Abran, A.: The state of the art of mobile application usability evaluation. In: 25th IEEE Canadian Conference on Electrical and Computer Engineering (CCECE), Montreal, QC, pp. 1–4 (2012)
6. Material Design – Android Navigation Bar. https://material.io/guidelines/layout/structure.html#structure-system-bars. Accessed 05 Feb 2018
7. Liu, C., Liang, H.: The deep impression of smartphone brand on the customers' decision making. Proc. Soc. Behav. Sci. **109**, 338–343 (2014)
8. Wuensch, K.L.: What is a Likert Scale? and How Do You Pronounce 'Likert?'. East Carolina University. Accessed 27 Oct 2017

What Drives the Perceived Credibility of Mobile Websites: Classical or Expressive Aesthetics?

Kiemute Oyibo[1]([✉]), Ifeoma Adaji[1], Rita Orji[2], and Julita Vassileva[1]

[1] University of Saskatchewan, Saskatoon, Canada
{kiemute.oyibo,ifeoma.adaji}@usask.ca, jiv@cs.usask.ca
[2] Dalhousie University, Halifax, Canada
rita.orji@dal.ca

Abstract. Credibility is considered one of the most important Human-Computer Interaction design attributes that are responsible for the success of e-commerce websites. In web design, research has shown that *visual aesthetics* is one of the strongest determinants of the *perceived credibility* of websites. However, there is a dearth of knowledge regarding which of the two main dimensions of *visual aesthetics* (*classical aesthetics* and *expressive aesthetics*) is the stronger determinant of *perceived credibility*. To bridge this gap, we conducted an empirical study of 526 subjects from five continents to investigate which of the two dimensions of *visual aesthetics* has a stronger influence on *perceived credibility* using a utilitarian mobile website as a case study. Our results show that *classical aesthetics* significantly influences *perceived credibility* more strongly than *expressive aesthetics* does. The findings generalize across age and gender and different levels of user interface aesthetics. Our findings underscore the need for website designers to pay special attention to *classical aesthetics* features (e.g., simplicity, clarity, orderliness, cleanness and pleasantness) rather than *expressive aesthetics* features (complexity, richness, novelty and special effects) when designing utilitarian systems. A *classically pleasing* website is more likely to be perceived *credible* than an *expressively arousing* website.

Keywords: Aesthetics · Classical aesthetics · Expressive aesthetics · Credibility
Mobile website · Utilitarian website · Age · Gender · Path model

1 Introduction

Credibility has been found to be a very important attribute not only in the field of human-to-human interaction but also in Human-Computer Interaction (HCI) as well. In online business, for example, it has been attributed to the success of several e-commerce websites [24]. Research [5] has shown that the *perceived credibility* of a given website has the power to change user attitudes towards the website and their behaviors. For example, with respect to user attitude, a website perceived as highly credible can make a user: (1) think positively about the site owner; (2) feel at ease interacting with the site; and (3) embrace the site owner's viewpoint [5]. Moreover, with respect to user behavior, such a website can encourage the user to: (1) register with the website by willingly

© Springer International Publishing AG, part of Springer Nature 2018
M. Kurosu (Ed.): HCI 2018, LNCS 10902, pp. 576–594, 2018.
https://doi.org/10.1007/978-3-319-91244-8_45

providing required personal information; (2) complete a financial transaction on the website; and (3) use the website more often [5].

Research has shown that *visual aesthetics* is one of the strongest determinants of the *perceived credibility* of websites, especially during users' first contact with or visit to a website [13, 24]. However, hitherto, there is a lack of knowledge on which of the two theoretical dimensions of *visual aesthetics* (*classical aesthetics* and *expressive aesthetics*) [12] is the stronger determinant of the *perceived credibility* of a website. Answering this research question will help HCI designers creating certain types of website—hedonic or utilitarian—to understand which of the two dimensions of *visual aesthetics* resonate more with users when evaluating the *credibility* of a website. Hedonic websites are websites aimed at providing pleasure and enjoyment to their users (e.g., game-based websites [26]), while utilitarian websites are websites focused at providing instrumental or productive value to their users (e.g., search engines) [10, 30]. We hypothesize that the question whether *classical aesthetics* or *expressive aesthetics* is stronger in determining *perceived credibility* may depend on the type or function of a website. Hence, uncovering which of the two distinct dimensions of *visual aesthetics* —which have virtually opposing design objectives [12]—has a stronger impact on *credibility* will enable website designers at a finer-grain level to know which of the *aesthetics* dimensions to pay more attention to when designing hedonic or utilitarian websites.

We conducted an empirical study among participants from five different continents to investigate: (1) whether *classical aesthetics* or *expressive aesthetics* has a stronger influence on the *perceived credibility* of a website; and (2) how age and gender of the user moderate the interrelationships among the three design attributes. As a case study, we implemented the homepage of a utilitarian mobile website with four user interface (UI) versions, characterized by different levels of aesthetics, and evaluated them with 526 subjects from five continents. The data collected was analyzed using Structural Equation Modeling (SEM) [8]. The results of our SEM analysis show that, regardless of the levels of aesthetics of the mobile website, *classical aesthetics* influences *perceived credibility* more strongly than *expressive aesthetics* does. Moreover, our multigroup analysis shows that the finding generalizes across age, gender and different levels of UI aesthetics. Our finding underscores the need for designers of utilitarian websites who want to increase the *perceived credibility* of their websites to focus more on *classical aesthetics* (simplicity, clarity, orderliness, cleanness, etc. [12]) than *expressive aesthetics* (complexity, novelty, richness, sophistication, etc. [16]).

The paper is organized as follows: Sect. 2 defines the main concepts used in this work; Sect. 3 presents related work; Sect. 4 presents the research method and hypotheses of the study; Sect. 5 presents the results; and Sect. 6 discusses the results, their implications and limitations. Finally, Sect. 7 concludes the paper.

2   Background

In this section, we provide an overview of *credibility, aesthetics, classical aesthetics* and *expressive aesthetics*. For brevity, we will, in some cases, as we have done here, omit the qualifier "*perceived*" when referring to the design constructs.

2.1   Credibility

Credibility refers to the believability of a system, e.g., a website. It is viewed as a user-perceived quality and not a property that is resident in the system under evaluation. In HCI, Fogg and Tseng [7] theorize that *perceived credibility* is composed of two distinct dimensions: *perceived expertise* and *perceived trustworthiness*. *Perceived expertise* is defined as the degree to which a user perceives the designer of a given website to be competent, knowledgeable and experienced. Thus, it captures the perceived knowledge and skill of the source (i.e., the designer of the website). Moreover, *perceived trustworthiness* is defined as the degree to which a user perceives a website to be well-intentioned, truthful and free of bias [6]. It mainly captures the perceived goodness or morality of the source (i.e., the owner of the website). Fogg [4] asserts that, in the evaluation of the *credibility* of a website, both dimensions are perceived and judged simultaneously. As such, to judge a website as *credible*, the user must perceive it to be high in both *trustworthiness* and *expertise* [6].

2.2   Aesthetics

The concept of "*aesthetics*" is closely related to the concept of "*beauty*," which plays an important role in many aspects of human existence, including nature, art, culture, architecture, etc. Historically, *aesthetics* is defined as the branch of philosophy which deals with "*the nature and appreciation of art, beauty and good taste*" [15]. In the eighteen century, it was redefined by Baumgarten, a German philosopher, as the sensory pleasure or delight derived from the visual perception of an object. In other words, it refers to the gratification of the senses as a result of the visual experience of an object [11]. There are three schools of thought, which view *aesthetics* in three different ways. The first school of thought views *aesthetics* as an objective concept (a property resident in the object). The second school of thought views it as a subjective concept (resident in the eye of the beholder). Finally, the last school of thought (the interactionist position) adopts the middle ground: *aesthetics* being objective as well as subjective [12, 16]. While we may not disagree that *aesthetics* could be both objective (depending on the object or stimulus) and subjective (depending on the characteristics of the observer) as most current theories (such as the interactionist theory) hold, in our empirical study, we adopt the view of the second school of thought. In other words, our measurement of *aesthetics* is based on the subjective perception of the observer, regardless of the aesthetic property of the object from the designer's perspective.

In human-computer interaction design, *aesthetics* (often known as "*visual aesthetics*") refers to the visual appeal or pleasing appearance of a HCI artifact [29]. Research has shown that users are able to make stable aesthetic judgment within the first 50 ms of encountering the UI of a website [14]. Moreover, Lavie and Tractinsky [12], in a factorial analysis study, found that *visual aesthetics* is composed of two main dimensions: *classical aesthetics* and *expressive aesthetics*.

Classical Aesthetics. *Classical aesthetics* reflects the traditional notion of *aesthetics*: orderliness, symmetry, proportion, clarity, harmony, etc. Its ultimate goal is to increase the understanding of UIs and reduce ambiguity in users' interaction with them. Besides reflecting the objective notion of *aesthetics*, *classical aesthetics* has been found to be highly correlated with *perceived usability* [12, 22]. According to Lavie and Tractinsky [12], *"the classical aesthetic dimension may serve as a linkage between usability and aesthetics, being both an aesthetic concept and a usability principle"* (p. 290). Moreover, given that *classical aesthetics* induces pleasure, it is theorized *"to have a calming effect on the senses"* (p. 148) [23].

Expressive Aesthetics. *Expressive aesthetics* reflects the expressive power of the designers, which borders on creativity, originality and novelty. Its expression in UI design is often described by words such as "creative," "original," "sophisticated," "fascinating," "uses special effect," etc. The ultimate goal of *expressive aesthetics* is to increase arousal and user involvement [12]. Hassenzahl and Monk [9] have argued that *expressive aesthetics* is strongly associated with *hedonic quality*.

3   Related Work

Given the importance of *credibility* in the internet space, a great body of work has been dedicated to uncovering its determinants. Fogg et al. [3] conducted a study among 2,684 participants to investigate the design attributes that influence the judgment of *web credibility* the most. They found that *design look* (related to *visual aesthetics*) is the strongest determinant of the *perceived credibility* of a website, followed by *information design/structure*. Robins and Holmes [24] investigated users' evaluation of the *credibility* of websites with high and low levels of aesthetic treatment. They found that the high-aesthetic websites were judged higher in *credibility* than the low-aesthetic websites. Alsudani and Casey [1] also found that the *perceived aesthetics* of a website influences users' judgment of its *credibility*. In the mobile domain, Oyibo et al. [18–21] found that, irrespective of culture or gender, the *perceived aesthetics* of mobile websites influences their *perceived credibility* more strongly than *perceived usability* does. In general, most of the studies that have been conducted so far in the desktop and mobile domains have only examined *visual aesthetics* at a high level, i.e., as a composite construct predicting *perceived credibility*. However, in recent years, Lavie and Tractinsky [12] have found that *visual aesthetics* is composed of two main dimensions: *classical aesthetics* and *expressive aesthetics*. This makes it pertinent for researchers to investigate which of these two dimensions has a stronger influence on *perceived credibility*, especially with respect to the different types of websites. Answering this research question will help designers of HCI systems know which of the *aesthetics* dimensions they should focus more on when designing hedonic and utilitarian websites. Our study aims to bridge this gap in the extant literature using a utilitarian website as a case study.

4   Method

This section presents our research objective and design, research hypotheses, measurement instruments and the demographics of participants.

4.1   Research Objective and Design

In this study on the relationship between *aesthetics* and *credibility* at a finer-grain level, we set out to answer the following research questions:

1. *Which of the two dimensions of visual aesthetics (classical or expressive) has a stronger influence on perceived credibility in mobile website design?*
2. *Are the mutual relationships between classical aesthetics, expressive aesthetics and perceived credibility moderated by age and gender?*
3. *Are the relationships replicable across different levels of UI aesthetics?*

To answer the above research questions, we came up with a hypothetical mobile website[1] (named "G-Ranch") in the tourism domain. Figure 1 shows all four versions of the UI at different levels of aesthetics, which were systematically arrived at using a "UI transformation framework," we called Artifact-Action framework [17].

The artifacts are the UIs themselves (in the quadrants) and the actions are the aesthetic manipulations (on the axes) carried out on them to arrive at a new UI different from the previous one. For example, to transform version WA to WB, we apply the action *"make gray and add icons."* Based on all four UIs, we designed a questionnaire and asked participants from five different continents in an online survey to respond to questions on *classical aesthetics*, *expressive aesthetics* and *perceived credibility*. We also requested participants to provide comments on the visual design. The study was based on a within-subject design in which each participant had to evaluate all four UIs and respond to the respective questions based on them. With respect to color scheme, we have three levels: (1) minimalist (WA); (2) moderate (WC and WD); and (3) multi-color (WA). With respect to content presentation, we have two layouts: (1) list layout (WA, WB and WC); and (2) grid layout (WD). We combined a color scheme with a layout to arrive at each of the four configurations (versions) shown in Fig. 1. However, to limit the experiment duration and to prevent participant fatigue, we could not investigate all of the possible UI configurations in our survey. Each of the four UI versions represents different levels of aesthetic treatment of the mobile website.

---

[1] The UIs are basic homepages of a four mobile websites adapted from actual websites (m.wakanow.com, mobile.united.com, mobile.utah.com and tourismwinnipeg.com) on the market in 2014. They are basically used to search for tourism-based services such as places, hotels, etc. As of the time of writing this paper, most of the sites have been redesigned [17].

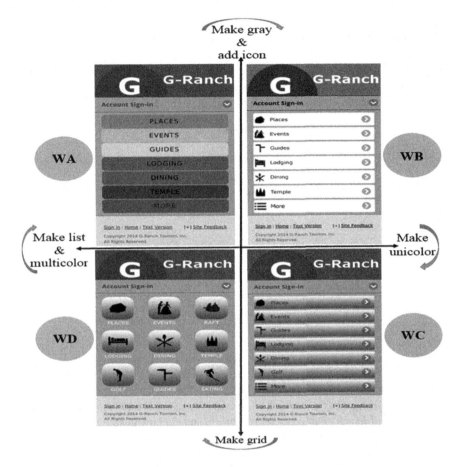

Fig. 1. Systematically designed mobile websites using a UI transformation framework

4.2   Research Hypotheses

Based on prior findings and theories in the literature [12, 13, 21, 23, 24, 28], we formulated three hypotheses as represented in Fig. 2. The hypotheses are stated as follows:

H1: The *classical aesthetics* of a website user interface will significantly influence its *perceived credibility*.

H2: The *expressive aesthetics* of a website user interface will significantly influence its *perceived credibility*.

H3: The *classical aesthetics* of a website user interface will significantly influence its *expressive aesthetics*.

The first and second hypotheses (H1 and H2) are based on a prior finding in the desktop [6, 24] and mobile [20, 21] domains, in which *visual aesthetics*—as a composite construct—significantly influences the *perceived credibility* of the websites evaluated by users. Thus, we hypothesize that, as separate constructs, *classical aesthetics* (H1) and *expressive aesthetics* (H2) will significantly influence *perceived credibility*. The third hypothesis (H3) is based on the findings from previous studies by Lavie and Tractinsky [12] in the desktop domain and Oyibo and Vassileva [22] in the mobile domain. Both studies found that there is a significant relationship between both dimensions of *visual aesthetics*. Thus, in our study, we hypothesize that *classical aesthetics* will significantly influence *expressive aesthetics* (H3).

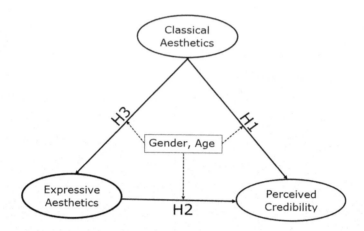

Fig. 2. Hypothesized research model (dashed arrows indicate explored moderated paths)

However, due to the paucity of research in this topic area, we adopted an exploratory approach in investigating: (1) which of *classical aesthetics* and *expressive aesthetics* has a stronger influence on *perceived credibility*; and (2) how gender and age moderate the interrelationships among all three design constructs. As a working rule, we pre-stated that, for any of our hypotheses to be fully validated, it has to be replicated across, at least, two of the UI designs characterized by different levels of aesthetics. Otherwise, if a relationship is validated with respect to one UI only, we conclude it is partially validated and requires further research.

4.3   Measurement Instruments

To measure the three HCI design constructs in our research model, we used validated instruments from prior literature. They are shown in Table 1. *Classical aesthetics* and *expressive aesthetics* are based on the 3-item scales developed by [12] as adapted by [26]. The measurement of *perceived credibility* is based on a single-item scale, which, previous research [2, 27] has shown, is equally reliable as a multi-item scale. All of the scales have been validated in previous studies (e.g., [27]); they ranged from "Strongly Disagree (1)" to "Strongly Agree (7)."

Table 1. Scales measuring all three mobile design constructs

Scale	Items in each scale
Classical aesthetics	1. Visual
	2. Clean
	3. Pleasant
Expressive aesthetics	1. Fascinating
	2. Sophisticated
	3. Creative
Perceived credibility	1. Credible

In the online questionnaire, prior to presenting the snapshot of each UI version to each study participant (in the order—WC, WA, WB and WD), the following opening statement (1) was presented, after which the question (2), which preceded all of the items shown in Table 1, was asked. Specifically, all six items in the *classical aesthetics* and *expressive aesthetics* scales were combined and randomized in a block. Finally, the questions (3 and 4) on *perceived credibility* and UI appeal, respectively, were asked.

1. *Assume you were looking for a website on travels and tourism on your mobile phone, and you happened to open this webpage by clicking on one of the links returned by a search engine.*
2. *Please rate the website [label of website] on the following criteria based on your first impression.*
3. *Based on your first impression of the mobile webpage [label of website], please rate its credibility level.*
4. *Please kindly comment on the things that appeal to or interest, or annoy, you regarding the above mobile web page [label of website], if any.*

4.4   Participants

The survey was submitted to and approved by the first author's university's Research Ethics Board. Thereafter, participants were recruited on social media, via email and on the first author's university website to participate in the study. Over 540 participants took part in the study. After cleaning the data, a total of 526 were retained for the data analysis. Participants are spread across five continents (Africa, Asia, Europe, North America and South America). Table 2 shows the demographics of participants. Overall 53.6% of them were males, while 44.5% were females. Age-wise, 50.2% of the participants were between 18 and 24 years old, while 48.5% were above 24 years old.

Table 2. Participants' demographics (adapted from [20])

Variable	Group	NG	GH	BR	CH	CA	OTH	ALL	PER
Gender	Male	115	37	34	46	25	25	282	53.6%
	Female	40	13	16	63	71	31	234	44.5%
	Unidentified	1	0	0	6	2	1	10	1.9%
Age	18–24	118	6	16	51	55	18	264	50.2%
	25–34	32	40	21	59	31	31	214	40.7%
	>34	2	3	13	5	12	6	41	7.8%
	Unidentified	4	1	0	0	0	2	7	1.3%
Years on Internet	<10	116	12	8	82	13	9	230	43.7%
	>= 10	50	38	42	33	85	48	296	56.3%
Education	Technical/Trade	8	0	1	12	4	1	26	4.9%
	High School	108	2	8	9	40	10	177	33.7%
	Bachelor	21	36	13	67	42	13	192	36.5%
	Postgraduate	11	9	28	25	11	31	115	21.9%
	Unidentified	8	3	0	2	1	2	16	3.0%
	Subtotal	156	50	50	115	98	57	526	100%
	National %	**29.7**	**9.5**	**9.5**	**21.9**	**18.6**	**10.8**	**100%**	

NG = Nigeria, GH = Ghana, Br = Brazil, CH = China, CA = Canada, OTH = Other countries, PER = %

4.5 Data Analysis

Upon the completion of data gathering, we proceeded to data analysis. We carried out SEM analysis [8]. Specifically, we used the Partial Least Square Path Modeling (PLSPM) package ("plspm" [25]) in the R programming language to build and analyze our path models. All three design constructs were specified as reflective in our models. Two multigroup analyses were carried out. They were based on gender (male vs. female) and age (18–24 vs. above 24). The bootstrap test for statistical significance of the path coefficients (the strength of the relationship between two constructs) was based on 5000 samples as recommended by Hair et al. [8].

5   Result

In this section, we present the results of our SEM analysis, including the assessment of the measurement models, analysis of the structural models and the multigroup analyses.

5.1   Evaluation of Measurement Model

Prior to analyzing the structural models, we evaluated the respective measurement models to ensure the required preconditions are meant, both for the global and subgroup models. We report the respective criteria in the measurement models that were assessed.

Indicator Reliability. All of the indicators in the respective measurement models have an outer loading greater than 0.7. Thus, the indicator reliability criterion is met, as the communality values for each indicator in the respective models are greater than 0.5 [8].

Internal Consistency. We used the composite reliability criterion, DG.rho (ρ), to assess the internal consistency reliability of each multi-item construct in the respective models. The respective values for both *aesthetics* constructs are greater than 0.7 [8].

Convergent Validity. The Average Variance Extracted (AVE) was used to assess convergent validity of each multi-item construct in the respective models. The AVE for each construct in the respective models is greater than the threshold value of 0.5 [8].

Discriminant Validity. This criterion was assessed using the crossloading of each construct on the other. No indicator of a given construct loaded higher on any other construct than the one it was meant to measure [8].

5.2 Analysis of Structural Model

Figure 3 shows the global models of the four UIs for the general population. The global models characterize the following parameters: (1) path coefficients (β), which indicates the strength of the direct effect exerted by an exogenous construct (e.g., *classical aesthetics*) on an endogenous construct (e.g., *perceived credibility*); (2) the coefficients of determination (R^2), which indicates the amount of variance of an endogenous construct explained by its exogenous constructs; and (3) the goodness of fit (GOF), which indicates the predictive power of the model, i.e., how well the model fits its data [25].

Overall, the path models for all four webpages have a moderate to high GOF. A moderate GOF ranges between 60% and 70%, while a high GOF is 70% and above. Thus, the WA model has a high GOF, while the rest three models (WB, WC and WD) have a moderate GOF, which are nearly high and considered acceptable [25]. Furthermore, *classical aesthetics* explains between 63% and 69% of the variance of *expressive aesthetics*. Based on the 60% benchmark [25], R^2 values greater than 60% indicates high predictive accuracy. Thus, *expressive aesthetics* is well explained or predicted by *classical aesthetics* for all four webpages given that all of the R^2 values are greater than 60%. Moreover, *perceived credibility* is highly well-explained or predicted by *classical aesthetics* and *expressive aesthetics* in the WA model (69%) and WB model (64%), while it is moderately well-explained or predicted in the WC model (50%) and WD model (59%).

Finally, all of the interrelationships among the three design constructs are statistically significant at p < 0.0001, with *classical aesthetics* having the strongest effect on *expressive aesthetics* (β = 0.79 to 0.83, p < 0.0001), followed by *classical aesthetics* on *perceived credibility* (β = 0.50 to 0.64, p < 0.0001), and *expressive aesthetics* on *perceived credibility* (β = 0.19 to 0.25, p < 0.0001). Overall, *classical aesthetics* has a stronger effect on *perceived credibility* than *expressive aesthetics* does. For example, in the WB and WC models, the direct effects of *classical aesthetics* on *perceived credibility* are (β = 0.64 and 0.50, respectively) at p < 0.0001, while the corresponding direct effects of *expressive aesthetics* on *perceived credibility* in both models are (β = 0.19 and 0.24, respectively) at p < 0.0001.

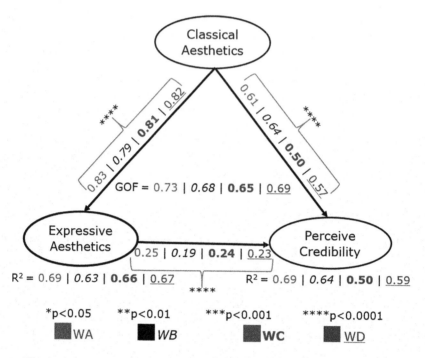

Fig. 3. Data-driven global models for all of the mobile website user interfaces

5.3 Subgroup Models Based on Multigroup Analysis

Figure 4 shows two pairs of submodels based on the gender-based and age-based multigroup analyses. Overall, the significant interrelationships among all three design constructs in each pair of submodels replicate those in the global model. However, the multigroup analyses show that the two subgroups in each pair of submodels significantly differ at p < 0.05.

The gender-based multigroup analysis (see Fig. 4a) shows that males and females significantly differ at p < 0.05 with respect to the influence of *classical aesthetics* on *expressive aesthetics* and the influence of *classical aesthetics* on *perceived credibility*. In the WC model, the direct effect of *classical aesthetics* on *expressive aesthetics* is stronger for males (β = 0.83, p < 0.0001) than for females (β = 0.78, p < 0.0001). Similarly, in the WA model, the direct effect of *classical aesthetics* on *perceived credibility* is stronger for males (β = 0.66, p < 0.0001) than for females (β = 0.52, p < 0.0001).

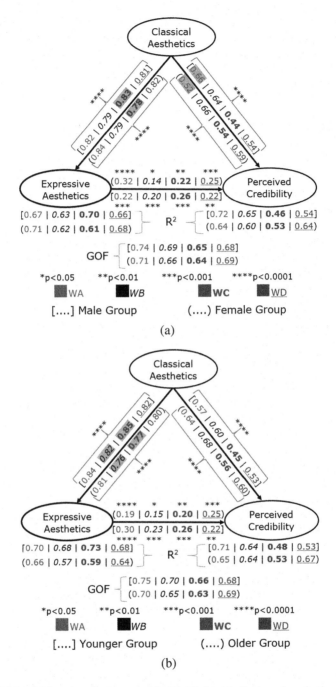

Fig. 4. (a) Male and female subgroup models (highlighted indicates where both groups differ). (b) Younger and older subgroup models (highlighted indicates where both groups differ)

Moreover, the age-based multigroup analysis (see Fig. 4b) shows that younger and older people significantly differ at $p < 0.05$ with respect to the influence of *classical aesthetics* on *expressive aesthetics*. In the WB and WC submodels, the direct effect between both constructs is stronger for younger people ($\beta = 0.82$ and 0.85, $p < 0.0001$, respectively) than for older people ($\beta = 0.76$ and 0.77, $p < 0.0001$, respectively).

6 Discussion

The *perceived credibility* of the UI design of an e-commerce website is critical to its success, so is the *perceived aesthetics*—a strong determinant of *perceived credibility*. In this paper, we have presented a path model based on four UI versions of a hypothetical mobile website to uncover which of the two dimensions of *visual aesthetics* (*classical* and *expressive*) has a stronger influence on the *perceived credibility* of a utilitarian website. We have also presented the results of multigroup analyses to uncover how age and gender moderate the interrelationships among all three design constructs. In the subsequent subsections, we discuss the validation of our hypotheses and the summary of our findings vis-à-vis our research questions.

6.1 Validation of Hypotheses

Our SEM analysis shows that, irrespective of age and gender, all of the three hypothesized relationships in our research model are significant at different levels of UI aesthetics, with *classical aesthetics* having a stronger influence on *perceived credibility* than *expressive aesthetics* does. Table 3 shows the summary of our main findings in respect of our hypotheses and exploratory analysis.

Our SEM analysis shows that our first hypothesis (H1: *the classical aesthetics of a website user interface will significantly influence its perceived credibility*) is supported and replicated across all four UI designs. This suggests that a *classically aesthetic* utilitarian website is more likely to be perceived *credible* than a less *classically aesthetic* website. This is evident in some of the participants' comments. For example, participant 283 comments on webpage WC thus: "*credible[,] information are obtain[ed] eas[i]ly.*" For this participant, webpage WC is credible because information can be easily accessed. This suggests that this participant must have based his/her judgment of the *credibility* of WC on the perceived *classical aesthetics* features, such as clarity and orderliness of the webpage, which generally facilitate access to sought information on the web.

Secondly, our SEM analysis shows that our second hypothesis (H2: *the expressive aesthetics of a website user interface will significantly influence the perceived credibility*) is supported and replicated across all four UI designs. This suggests that an *expressively aesthetic* website is more likely to be perceived *credible* than a less *expressively aesthetic* website. This is evident in some of the comments from participants. For example, participant 236 comments on webpage WD thus: "*looks clearer and more professional with the grid layout and better colour coordination.*" The participant seems to have made his/her *credibility-related judgment* on the site's professionalism partly based on the perceived "*colour coordination*" of webpage WD, which hints at *expressive aesthetics.* On the flip side, unfavorable *expressive aesthetics perception* can harm *credibility perception* as well as evident in participant 119's comment on webpage WA: "*too many different colours to seem credible.*" This suggests that the multicolor scheme in webpage WA may have taken away from its *perceived credibility.* This clearly demonstrates how an unfavorable perception of *expressive aesthetics* can negatively influence the perception of *credibility.*

Table 3. Summary of supported hypotheses

No.	Hypothesis	Remark
H1	The *classical aesthetics* of a website user interface will significantly influence the *perceived credibility*	Supported and replicated
H2	The *expressive aesthetics* of a website user interface will significantly influence the *perceived credibility*	Supported and replicated
H3	The *classical aesthetics* of a website user interface will significantly influence the *expressive aesthetics*	Supported and replicated
H4*	The influence of *classical aesthetics* on *perceived credibility* is stronger than the influence of *expressive aesthetics* on *perceived credibility*	Supported and replicated
H5*	The influence of *classical aesthetics* on *expressive aesthetics* is stronger for male than for female	Supported but not replicated
H6*	The influence of *classical aesthetics* on *perceived credibility* is stronger for male than for female	Supported but not replicated
H7*	The influence of *classical aesthetics* on *expressive aesthetics* is stronger for younger people than for older people	Supported and replicated

*Hypotheses that were not pre-stated but found to be true by the SEM analysis

Moreover, by replicating the validation of H1 and H2 across all four different UI versions, we have particularly demonstrated that, irrespective of the level of UI aesthetics, characterized by layout (a *classical aesthetics* feature) and color (an *expressive aesthetics* feature), the perceptions of both dimensions of *visual aesthetics* significantly influence the perception of *web credibility.* However, our results reveal that the influence of *classical aesthetics* on *perceived credibility* is stronger than the influence of *expressive aesthetics* on *perceived credibility.* One possible reason why *classical aesthetics* influences *perceived credibility* more than *expressive aesthetics* does is that the website we investigated is a utilitarian system aimed at accomplishing a productive task: search and retrieval of information. According to [30], a utilitarian system addresses a productive task. As such, users' motivation in using a utilitarian system is driven by the expectation of a reward or benefit that is external to the user interaction with the system. In our case, the hypothetical G-Ranch website helps the user to find a desired place, hotel, event, etc., for tourism purpose. Thus, being able to get the right information as quickly and easily as possible becomes the user's reward or benefit. Our utilitarian website contrasts hedonic systems (e.g., games), which sole aim is to provide users with entertainment by satisfying their intrinsic need. Consequently, in our model, we see *classical aesthetics* (operationalized by "clean," "clear," "orderly," etc. [12])— which is closely linked to *perceived usability* (operationalized by "easy to navigate," "easy to use," etc.) [22]—having a stronger influence on *perceived credibility* than *expressive aesthetics* (operationalized by arousal-based items such as "fascinating," "sophisticated," "creative," etc.) does. This finding is consistent with Lavie and Tractinsky's [12] submission that "*the classical aesthetic dimension may serve as a linkage between usability and aesthetics, being both an aesthetic concept and a usability principle*" (p. 290), as confirmed by Oyibo and Vassileva [22]. Based on this finding, summarized in our fourth hypothesis (H4: *the influence of classical aesthetics on perceived credibility is stronger than the influence of expressive aesthetics on perceived credibility*), we make the following recommendation to website designers:

> When designing websites with utilitarian value or benefit, such as a tourism website aimed at finding tourist attractions via search, designers should focus on enhancing classical aesthetics features (cleanness, orderliness, clarity and simplicity) more than expressive aesthetics features (richness, novelty and sophistication) to increase the chances of their sites being perceived credible and eventually used by first-time users.

Finally, given that both *classical aesthetics* and *expressive aesthetics* influence *perceived credibility*, this suggests, by extension, that both dimensions of *visual aesthetics* have a significant relationship between them. This is validated by our third hypothesis (H3: *the classical aesthetics of a website user interface will significantly influence the expressive aesthetics*), which holds true irrespective of the level of aesthetic treatment of the UI, age and gender of the user. This suggests that a *classically aesthetic* website is more likely to be perceived as *expressively aesthetic* by users than a less *classically aesthetic* website. The strong relationship between *classical aesthetics* and *expressive aesthetics* can be likened to the *aesthetic-usability* halo effect, where the *perceived aesthetics* of a UI spills to influencing its *perceived usability* [12, 21]. Specifically, in our case, the relationship between *classical aesthetics* and *expressive aesthetics* could be regarded as the "*classical-expressive aesthetic*" halo effect, in which the perception of *classical aesthetics* of the UI spills to influencing the *expressive aesthetics* dimension.

6.2   Gender and Age Differences in the Evaluation of Website UIs

Our multigroup analysis shows that there are gender and age differences in the interrelationship between *classical aesthetics* and the other two design constructs in the path model. With respect to gender, the result of the multigroup analysis shows that the influence of *classical aesthetics* on *expressive aesthetics* (for version WC) is stronger for males than for females (see H5 in Table 3). This finding suggests that males are more likely to judge a website as *expressively aesthetic* based on the perception of *classical aesthetics*. However, given the non-replication of this finding for the other website versions (WA, WB and WD), it requires further investigation. The same applies to the sixth hypothesis (H6: *the influence of classical aesthetics on perceived credibility is stronger for male than for female*), which only holds true for version WA.

The result of the age-based multigroup analysis shows that younger people are more likely than older people to base the evaluation of the *expressive aesthetics* of a website on the perception of *classical aesthetics* (see H7 in Table 3). Specifically, this finding holds true in participants' evaluation of version WB and WC (see Fig. 4b). This suggests that, in web design, younger people are less likely to differentiate between the traditional notion of *visual aesthetics* (orderliness, clarity and pleasantness) and the expressive power (creativity, originality and novelty) of the designer. Put differently, younger people are more likely than older people to judge a *classically aesthetic* (minimalist) design, such as WB, as *expressively aesthetic*. To verify this assertion, we analyzed the participants' ratings of versions WB and WC, where both age groups differ, in terms of *classical aesthetics* and *expressive aesthetics*. Aesthetically, both WB and WC differ in terms of color scheme. While version WB (relative to WC and the other UI versions) is *classically aesthetic* given its minimalist (gray) color scheme, version WC (relative to WB) is *expressively aesthetic* given its blue color scheme.

Our one-way analysis of variance on the overall mean values of *classical aesthetics* and *expressive aesthetics* for WC shows that there is no significant difference between younger people's ratings (4.75 and 4.06, respectively) and older people (4.72 and 3.90, respectively) ratings. Similarly, with respect to the overall mean values of *classical aesthetics* for WB (the minimalist webpage), there is no significant difference between younger people's rating (4.74) and older people's rating (4.64). However, with respect to the overall mean values of *expressive aesthetics* for WB, younger people's rating (4.15) is significantly higher than older people's rating (3.85) at $p < 0.05$. This shows that the perception of *classical aesthetics* (virtually the same for both age groups) resulted in higher perception of *expressive aesthetics* for younger people (4.15) than it does for older people (3.85). This confirms the SEM-based multigroup analysis finding that *classical aesthetics* is more likely to influence *expressive aesthetics* for younger people than for older people (H7). The design implication of this finding is as follows:

> When designing websites, for example, to entertain people, the designer will have to be more creative to implement designs that older users will perceive novel, fascinating, sophisticated, creative, etc. The reason is that older people are less likely to be subject to the "classical-expressive aesthetic" halo effect than younger people. Moreover, older people are more likely to be critical in their judgment of expressive aesthetics than younger people.

6.3 Summary of Findings and Contributions

In this paper, we presented a path model of the interrelationships between the two dimensions of *visual aesthetics* and the *perceived credibility* of a utilitarian website. Our main findings vis-à-vis our three research questions can be summarized as follows:

1. *Classical aesthetics* influences *perceived credibility* more strongly than *expressive aesthetics* does.
2. Irrespective of the age and gender of the user, the interrelationships among *classical aesthetics*, *expressive aesthetics* and *perceived credibility* hold true.
3. Irrespective of the level of UI aesthetics, the interrelationships among *classical aesthetics*, *expressive aesthetics* and *perceived credibility* hold true.

Our main contribution to the body of knowledge in the field of HCI is that we have shown at a finer-grain level that, with respect to utilitarian websites, the *classical aesthetics* dimension contributes more strongly than the *expressive aesthetics* dimension in the *aesthetics-credibility* relationship. We specifically showed that this finding holds true, irrespective of the level of aesthetic treatment of the target website, age and gender of the user. Furthermore, as a second contribution, we have shown in a replicated fashion that the influence of *classical aesthetics* on *expressive aesthetics* is stronger for younger people than for older people. Our work, to the best of our knowledge, is the first in HCI research to uncover the relationship between *perceived aesthetics* and *perceived credibility* at a finer-grain level in a replicated fashion.

6.4 Limitations and Future Work

Our study has a number of limitations. The first and foremost limitation is that our findings are based on users' (subjective) perception and evaluation of a hypothetical website interface (with four versions) and not on the outcome of an actual interaction with a live or experimental website. Consequently, our findings may not generalize to a real-life application setting. The second limitation of our study is that we did not investigate the moderating effect of other user characteristics than age and gender. User characteristics, such as culture, education level, internet experience, etc., could also moderate the strengths of the various interrelationships among the three design constructs we investigated in our path model. Consequently, we recommend that, in future research efforts, researchers can address these limitations. Moreover, with respect to our research question on which of the two dimensions of *aesthetics* has a stronger influence on *perceived credibility*, future work can investigate hedonic systems.

7 Conclusion

In this paper, we presented the results of an empirical study among 526 participants, which investigated, at a finer-grain level, which of the two dimensions of *visual aesthetics* (*classical* and *expressive*) has a stronger influence on *perceived credibility* in the evaluation of websites. Using a mobile website as a case study, we showed that, for utilitarian websites aimed at providing instrumental values to users, *classical aesthetics* influences *perceived credibility* more strongly than *expressive aesthetics* does. This finding holds true irrespective of the level of aesthetic treatment of the target website, the age and gender of the user. Moreover, we showed that the relationship between *classical aesthetics* and *expressive aesthetics* is stronger for younger people than for older people. The broad implication of our findings is that designers of utilitarian websites should focus on designing user interfaces which possess *classical aesthetics* features (e.g., clarity, cleanness, orderliness, pleasantness, etc. [12]) rather than *expressive aesthetics* features (e.g., novelty, richness, special effects, etc.) to increase the overall *perceived credibility* of their websites. A *classically pleasing* website is more likely to be perceived *credible* than an *expressively arousing* website.

References

1. Alsudani, F., Casey, M.: The effect of aesthetics on web credibility. In: 23rd British HCI Group Annual Conference on People and Computers: Celebrating People and Technology, pp. 512–519 (2009)
2. Bergkvist, L., Rossiter, J.R.: The predictive validity of multiple-item versus single-item measures of the same constructs. J. Mark. Res. **44**(2), 175–184 (2007)
3. Fogg, B.J., et al.: How do users evaluate the credibility of Web sites?: a study with over 2,500 participants. In: Proceedings of the 2003 Conference on Designing for User Experiences, pp. 1–15 (2003)
4. Fogg, B.J.: Persuasive Technology: Using Computers to Change What We Think and Do. Morgan Kaufmann, San Francisco (2003)
5. Fogg, B.J.: What Makes a Website Credible? http://static.lukew.com/web_credibility_lecture.pdf
6. Fogg, B.J., et al.: What makes web sites credible? a report on a large quantitative study. In: CHI 2001, pp. 61–68 (2001)
7. Fogg, B.J., Tseng, H.: The elements of computer credibility. In: Proceedings of the SIGCHI Conference on Human Factors in Computing Systems the CHI is the Limit, CHI 1999, pp. 80–87 (1999)
8. Hair, J.F., et al.: A primer on partial least squares structural equation modeling (PLS-SEM). Sage Publications Inc., Washington, DC (2014)
9. Hassenzahl, M., Monk, A.: The inference of perceived usability from beauty. Hum.-Comput. Interact. **24**, 37–41 (2010)
10. Van Der Heijden, H.: User acceptance of hedonic information systems. MIS Q. **28**(4), 695–704 (2004)
11. Hekkert, P.: Design aesthetics: principles of pleasure in design. Psychol. Sci. **48**(2), 157 (2006)
12. Lavie, T., Tractinsky, N.: Assessing dimensions of perceived visual aesthetics of web sites. Int. J. Hum. Comput. Stud. **60**(3), 269–298 (2004)
13. Lindgaard, G., et al.: An exploration of relations between visual appeal, trustworthiness and perceived usability of homepages. ACM Trans. Comput.-Hum. Interact. **18**(1), 1–30 (2011)
14. Lindgaard, G., et al.: Attention web designers: you have 50 milliseconds to make a good first impression! Behav. Inf. Technol. **25**(2), 115–126 (2006)
15. Mastin, L.: The Basics of Philosophy, http://www.philosophybasics.com/branch_aesthetics.html
16. Moshagen, M., Thielsch, M.T.: Facets of visual aesthetics. Int. J. Hum. Comput. Stud. **68**(10), 689–709 (2010)
17. Oyibo, K., et al.: An empirical analysis of the perception of mobile website interfaces and the influence of culture. In: CEUR Workshop Proceedings, Salzburg, Austria, pp. 44–56 (2016)
18. Oyibo, K., et al.: Gender difference in the credibility perception of mobile websites: a mixed method approach. In: Proceedings of the 2016 Conference on User Modeling Adaptation and Personalization, UMAP 2016, pp. 75–84 (2016)
19. Oyibo, K., et al.: The influence of personality on mobile web credibility. In: Adjunct Proceedings of User Modeling, Adaptation and Personalization (UMAP 2017), Slovakia (2017)
20. Oyibo, K., Vassileva, J.: The interplay of aesthetics, usability and credibility in mobile website design and the moderation effect of gender. SBC J. Interact. Syst. **8**(2), 4–19 (2017)

21. Oyibo, K., Vassileva, J.: The interplay of aesthetics, usability and credibility in mobile websites and the moderation by culture. In: Proceedings of the 15th Brazilian Symposium on Human Factors in Computer Systems, IHC 2016, pp. 1–10 (2016)

22. Oyibo, K., Vassileva, J.: What drives perceived usability in mobile web design : classical or expressive aesthetics? In: 19th International Conference on Human-Computer Interaction. pp. 445–462, Vancouver (2017)

23. Porat, T., Tractinsky, N.: Affect as a mediator between web-store design and consumers' attitudes toward the store. In: Affect and Emotion in Human-Computer Interaction, pp. 142–153 (2008)

24. Robins, D., Holmes, J.: Aesthetics and credibility in web site design. Inf. Process. Manage. **44**(1), 386–399 (2008)

25. Sanchez, G.: PLS Path Modeling with R. Trowchez Editions, Berkley (2013)

26. van Schaik, P., Ling, J.: The role of context in perceptions of the aesthetics of web pages over time. Int. J. Hum. Comput. Stud. **67**(1), 79–89 (2009)

27. Setterstrom, S.: Assessing credibility and aesthetic perception across different exposure times on a health care information website. Iowa State University (2010)

28. Sonderegger, A., et al.: Expressive and classical aesthetics: two distinct concepts with highly similar effect patterns in user–artefact interaction. Behav. Inf. Technol. **33**(11), 1180–1191 (2014)

29. Tractinsky, N.: Visual Aesthetics. Interaction-Design, pp. 1–71 (2002)

30. Wigelius, H., Väätäjä, H.: Dimensions of context affecting user experience in mobile work. In: Gross, T., Gulliksen, J., Kotzé, P., Oestreicher, L., Palanque, P., Prates, R.O., Winckler, M. (eds.) INTERACT 2009. LNCS, vol. 5727, pp. 604–617. Springer, Heidelberg (2009). https://doi.org/10.1007/978-3-642-03658-3_65

A Study of Applying Slow Technology on Wearable Devices

Meng-Dar Shieh[1][✉], Shu-hui Meng[1], Tzu Yu Chuang[1],
Fang-Chen Hsu[2], and Chih-Chieh Yang[2]

[1] Industrial Design Department, National Cheng Kung University,
Tainan, Taiwan
mdshieh@mail.ncku.edu.tw
[2] Department of Multimedia and Entertainment Science,
No.1, Nantai Street, Yongkang City, Tainan, Taiwan

Abstract. This study proposes two conceptual products using wearable devices (smartwatches) for the purpose of emotional management. One is designed with Slow Technology, and the other is designed with Personal Informatics. Questionnaire survey method was used in this study. The questionnaire consists of two types, AttrakDiff and INTUI. Subjects filled out the questionnaires after watching two videos of conceptual products. The questionnaire data were analyzed by the independent sample and paired sample t-test in order to find the differences of ideas and user experience (pragmatic quality, hedonic quality, attractiveness, and intuition) about these two kinds of products. It is important to find out that the Slow Technology products are inferior to Personal Informatics products in pragmatic quality and intuition, but superior in hedonic quality and attractiveness.

This study suggests that the wearable devices can be integrated with furniture and appliances to provide a material basis of intelligent decoration transformation for users with the help of recorded information and data. Before the emotion identification technology gets mature, this study can be a pilot study for future product design strategy, preparing for Slow Technology products' going to the public to improve user's emotions.

Keywords: Slow Technology · Calm Technology · Affective computing
Wearable device · Personal Informatics · Design for reflection

1 Introduction

The wearable device is an important topic in the field of Ubiquitous Computing; people can record their own physiological data through sensors. The data can be used to further understand themselves and reflect on themselves. Quantified Self Movement is meant to record physiological data to understand all aspects of people's movements by wearable devices, which are very popular in the market in recent years. The sales of wearable devices are depended on the features and usability of the devices. The eMarketer survey found that young people are the most important users of wearable devices. The main reason for young adults interested in wearable devices is the fitness tracker curiosity.

© Springer International Publishing AG, part of Springer Nature 2018
M. Kurosu (Ed.): HCI 2018, LNCS 10902, pp. 595–614, 2018.
https://doi.org/10.1007/978-3-319-91244-8_46

It has the significance and values for this group because of the reasonable price and clear product orientation. Another exciting survey found that the initial users of wearable devices are males basically, but with the fitness bracelets and trackers releasing regularly, females are becoming the primary consumer groups because women are willing to lose weight and keep fit. Therefore, the use of wearable devices as a tool for quantified self is still a trend. The explicit purposes and the right target consumer segmentation will be the critical factors for the success of wearable devices in the market.

Slow Technology, proposed by Hallnäs and Redström, is also a topic of discussion in Ubiquitous Computing. They believed that the digital data in daily lives could be treated as interactive design information, which can be presented in some forms to allow users to absorb the information and get the aesthetic experiences in the process of interaction in order to have further reflections on the technology. Science and technology products tend to give people a quick and accurate experience, while there are few products that provide vague information, which makes people feel that it is a lousy product. However, it is rarely discussed whether the Slow Technology products have their marketability. Therefore, this study wants to discuss the ideas of users whether we can apply the concept of Slow Technology on wearable devices, smart bracelets or watches.

According to the study of science and technology development, there are two concepts of products design related to the wearable devices. The first one is the combination of the wearable device and Slow Technology concept with the support of affective computing. The concept product shown in this paper is called "Atmosphere Light." The second one is the wearable device itself supported with affective computing. The concept product shown in this paper is called "Mood Diary." This study examines the current ideas and acceptance of two conceptual products, as well as the possibilities of designing the wearable devices and home appliances, and exploring potential customers.

There are four goals of this paper.

1. To explore the ideas and acceptance of users with the two conceptual products.
2. To discuss the possibility of designing the wearable devices with furniture collocation, and studying the potential customers.
3. To explore the possibility of applying Slow Technology in Quantified Self products.
4. To investigate the obstacles and design opportunities for the wearable products using a multi modal.

2   Background Review

2.1   How Can Technology Support Reflection?

People can get insight through reflection. These reflections could help people grow in a better state in return. Reflection is encouraged to help people get more benefits in the field of education, design, and health care [1, 2]. These digital technologies could not only provide people with the opportunity to reflect but also enhance their own professional skills and improve people's quality of life. An increasing number of researchers began to study the issue in the field of human-computer interaction. However, reflections usually do not happen naturally. Therefore, people tend to need some reasons or are encouraged to behave in a reflective way. Technology products have the ability to sense by drawing, showing and presenting exciting information to users. Technology also could give users the opportunity to experience the confusion, suspicion, and surprise, which could be used as a mechanism to trigger reflection [4]. In the field of human-computer interaction, the equipment or system is designed for meditation. Based on the degree of the process of the reflection created by designers, Baumer divided it into three kinds: Personal Informatics, Reflective Design, and Slow Technology (Table 1).

Table 1. Three types of designing for reflection

Personal Informatics	Personal Informatics is driven by data and often focuses the reflection by the user on the user himself/herself and his/her behavior
Reflective Design	Explore the use of a variety of design methods by the user and the designer to make each interactive part of an interactive system designed, which could prevent the interaction process from experiencing the possibility of unintentional or even harmful experience
Slow Technology	Slow Technology explores how technology products can be designed to allow users to be tempted to reflect when interacting with a product or system

2.2 Personal Informatics

Since the wearable device is becoming popular, people could record a lot of information about their own through a variety of sensors, such as acceleration sensors, gyroscopes, magnetic sensors and temperature sensors. For example, the physiological data includes body temperature, breathing, heart rate and blood pressure. State of mind comprises thinking pattern and mood. Location information includes environment and travel. Time information includes time intervals, performance time. People information contains people interaction. Different types of applications are generated and could be classified into the following three methods to obtain information, direct measurement (wearable device, environmental sensor), inference (semantic reasoning and algorithms, some information can be directed to other meanings), self-reporting (manual date entry) [10].

The purpose of collecting this information is nothing more than self-monitoring and self-reflection to improve ourselves, such as enhancing behavior, improving mental state or medical condition, and so on [12]. The whole movement is called the Quantified Self Movement, which is used to understand the various aspects of the various mental data recorded by the wearable device. Quantified Self could help people achieve goals in health, fitness, mood, goals, and time management. However, at present, the areas of success in Quantified self are healthy, emotional, and athletic. Depending on different focuses, Quantified Self also has different terms, such as Personal Informatics, Personal analytics, Self-Tracking, Living by Numbers, and so on. Personal Informatics, as literally, focuses on how to present the optimal visualization to users, ensuring that they do absorb information and move towards the goal.

Personal Informatics in Mood Regulation: Affection is considered the most extensive mental state, including the evaluation of feelings, for example, people feeling good or bad, like or do not like what happened today. Emotion is at the top of the psychological structure. Emotion, mood, and feeling are under this structure. The mood is considered to be a broader concept than emotions. Emotions are short, quick and direct to some external stimuli. Moods last longer than emotions, which do not need for external stimuli [5].

Today, mood tracking has received much attention in this area of research. Many applications or services related to tracking moods are trying to help users increase their awareness and understanding of factors that affect emotions. It may be useful to collect emotional information for the following reasons: The therapist usually asks the patient to keep track of their emotional state (along with daily life at all levels) to ensure that they could help them with depression or fitness. Doctors and patients are able to understand the causes of symptoms and effectiveness of the treatment through the data record.

The general public may also desire to collect their own emotional information to more easily understand themselves. People could find relevance between some things and emotion and more opportunities to find a specific way to change their habits and behavior through the data [3]. Many applications use different visual methods to present the results of the data, allowing users to understand how their mental state is affected by the surrounding or social factors and reflect the mood changes and the relationship between varieties of factors.

2.3   Slow Technology

Hallnäs and Redström proposed the concept of Slow Technology of human-computer interaction design. They believed that people living in a particular environment and the impact of the environment on people would make people respond to the situation. Hallnäs and Redström thought that we had to create a technology that allowed people to live in changing daily life. That is, the computer's needs should make changes from "purely to improve the efficiency of the tool" to "the technology products helping us engaged in any daily life" [6–8].

Hallnäs and Redström proposed three aspects of Slow Technology.

1. Reflective technology: Reflective technology is technology which "in its elementary expression opens up for reflection and ask questions about its being as a piece of technology."
2. Time technology: Time technology is technology "that through its expression amplifies the presence–not the absence–of time." It stretches time and slow things down.
3. Amplified environment: the Amplified environment is technology that amplifies "the expression of a given environment in such a way that it, in practice, is enlarged in space or time" and thus enhances the expressions and functionality of existing artifacts. Hallnäs, Redström, and others researchers further proposed eight Slow Technology examples in 2001. Not discussing the premise of the function, they enlarged the way of beauty and introduced us how to deliver the information that is filled with our life to the people [6–8].

Table 2. The expressions of Slow Technology [6–8]

Works' photo	Expressions
 **Fan House (display)**	Equipped with three by three matrix of the cabinet. The cabinet is equipped with a fan. Each row of wooden cabinets is also linked by cloth with different colors and materials. **Reading**: The movement of the cloth **Writing**: Control the degree of fan rotation with a certain amount of information.
 **Fabric Door (sensor)**	The cloth with numbers of sensors is installed in the ceiling of the room at the entrance. When people go through the door and enter the room, the information was recorded by the accelerated sensor due to the cloth disturbed by the wind. It was sent to a computer in the form of data. **Reading**: The movement of the cloth **Writing**: When people go through the cloth, the fabric could pull the sensor due to the wind disturbance.
 **Tray (display)**	There is a quadrilateral tray from the ceiling. The motor installed in the ceiling controls the line on the four sides of the tray. The ball on the plate will also show different graphics with the changing length of the line. **Reading**: The pattern of beads on the tray. **Writing**: Some information controls four stepper motors in the ceiling.

Hallnäs and Redström et al., record a variety of physical signals with a digital way by sensors, and then send this digital signal to other actuators through two computer functions. One is reading (what type of people to read), the other is writing (what information type to write to the computer). Descendants could use different materials into this form. When the user receives and starts to analyze these signals, it takes time to understand and digest [6–8] (Table 2).

Table 3. The integration of Slow Technology: The presentation film of the Atmosphere Light

Work's photo	Description
 The movement crafter [11]	**Material**: The sensor records the shaking of the needle and thread. **Form**: Put shaking the data as the animation and display it on the screen of the other side. Install the sensor to the braid. The two woven boxes could link each other in a long distance. When you are in the woven scarf, you could increase the length of the cotton thread by looking at the screen. Even if you are not in the weaving, you could feel the existence the through the screen.
 A Sound Mirror [6,7,8]	**Material**: Recording audio. **Form**: Every other time, play recorded sound by video at the different time. Installing multiple recording devices in the corridor of the office to record different moments of the sound. The recorded sound is played when people walk through the hallway. This device could create a "slow echo effect" to make people spend more time to listen patiently.
 Fading Photo [9]	**Material**: Digital photo. **Form**: After 24 hours, the color photos gradually become black and white. Digital photo frame connected to a device. This digital photo in 24 hours will turn from the bright color to dark black. The user must turn the device on the knob to restore the original photo glory.

Take the Tray as an example. The four stepper motors could be connected with the information of home appliances, such as the volume of the sound, the TV information, temperature measurement information (indoor, outdoor). When the Tray beads concentrated on one side, it represents the amount of information on the appliance is higher than the other three devices.

The core concept of Slow Technology is that Material and Form. The material is any information that people are familiar with, for example, e-mail, digital photos, music, data transfer rate, etc., Form is to convey the information to the people. When the material is translated by form, its expression will often have ambiguity. Therefore, people could not instantly understand the information to convey the real meaning (Table 3).

3 Methodology

3.1 Independent Sample T-Test

Independent Sample T-Test is that independent samples were randomly assigned to different groups and the subjects did not have any relationship with each group, also known as completely randomized design. The t-test is used to test whether the average difference between two independent samples reaches a significant level, which means the two independent samples can be achieved by grouping. When calculating t-test numbers, two variables are needed. Variable x is divided into two groups, the average of the two independent samples should be tested whether there is a significant difference. Two maternal random samples are considered after calculating all the average number of differences in the situation. Depending on whether the number of samples in the two groups is equal and whether the variance is same, there are several algorithms:

Equal sample sizes, equal variance:

Given two groups (1, 2), this test is only applicable when:

The two sample sizes (that is, the number, n, of participants of each group) are equal; it can be assumed that the two distributions have the same variance; Violations of these assumptions are discussed below.

The t statistic to test whether the means are different can be calculated as follows:

$$t = \frac{\overline{X_1} - \overline{X_2}}{s_p\sqrt{2/n}}, \text{ where } s_p = \sqrt{\frac{s_{X1}^2 + s_{X2}^2}{2}}$$

Here s_p is the pooled standard deviation for $n = n_1 = n_2$ and s_{x1}^2 and s_{X2}^2 are the unbiased estimators of the variances of the two samples. The denominator of t is the standard error of the difference between two means. For significance testing, the degree of freedom for this test is $2n - 2$ where n is the number of participants in each group.

Equal or unequal sample sizes, equal variance:

This test is used only when it can be assumed that the two distributions have the same variance. (When this assumption is violated, see below.) Note that the previous formulae are a particular case valid when both samples have equal sizes: $n = n_1 = n_2$. The t statistic to test whether the means are different can be calculated as follows:

$t = \frac{\overline{X_1} - \overline{X_2}}{s_p \sqrt{\frac{1}{n_1} + \frac{1}{n_2}}}$, where $s_p = \sqrt{\frac{(n_1-1)s_{X_1}^2 + (n_2-1)s_{X_2}^2}{n_1 + n_2 - 2}}$ is an estimator of the pooled standard

deviation of the two samples. It is defined in this way so that its square is an unbiased estimator of the common variance whether or not the population means are the same. In these formulae, $n_i - 1$ is the number of degrees of freedom for each group, and the total sample size minus two (that is, $n_1 + n_2 - 2$) is the total number of degrees of freedom, which is used in significance testing.

Equal or unequal sample sizes, unequal variances:

This test, also known as Welch's T-test, is used only when the two population variances are not assumed to be equal (the two sample sizes may or may not be identical) and hence must be estimated separately. The t statistic to test whether the population means are different is calculated as:

$$t = \frac{\overline{X_1} - \overline{X_2}}{S_{\bar{\Delta}}}, \text{ where } S_{\bar{\Delta}} = \sqrt{\frac{s_1^2}{n_1} + \frac{s_2^2}{n_2}}$$

Here s_i^2 is the unbiased estimator of the variance of each of the two samples with n_i = number of participants in group, $i = 1$ or 2. Note that in this case $S_{\bar{\Delta}}$ is not a pooled variance. For use in significance testing, the distribution of the test statistic is approximated as an ordinary Student's t distribution with the degrees of freedom calculated using

$$\text{d.f.} = \frac{\left(s_1^2/n_1 + s_2^2/n_2\right)^2}{\left(s_1^2/n_1\right)^2/(n_1 - 1) + \left(s_2^2/n_2\right)^2/(n_2 - 1)}$$

This is known as the Welch–Satterthwaite equation. The exact distribution of the test statistic actually depends (slightly) on the two unknown population variances.

In this study, independent samples t-test was used in the analysis of the subjects in accordance with the "gender," "whether to buy furniture," is divided into two groups to test significant surgery.

3.2   Paired Sample T-Test

Paired Sample T-Test usually has two kinds of methods. One is the "repeat number," which means measuring before and after the test, just like measuring weight before and after losing weight. Therefore, every paired data are from the same subject, and this is the most common paired samples. The other one is called "pair group method." Although each paired data from two subjects, we identify a trait they (concerned researchers) are the same intelligence of male and female students. This is not a standard comparison of paired samples. However, regardless of the first case or the second, we would think that the two data are relevant, so we should use the paired sample t-test instead of independent sample t-test.

$$t = \frac{\bar{X}_D - \mu_0}{\frac{s_D}{\sqrt{n}}}.$$

For this equation, the differences between all pairs must be calculated. The pairs are either one person's pre-test and post-test scores or between pairs of persons matched into meaningful groups (for instance drawn from the same family or age group). The average $(\bar{X}_D)$ and standard deviation (s_D) of those differences are used in the equation. The constant μ_0 is non-zero if you want to test whether the average of the difference is significantly different from μ_0. The degree of freedom used is $n - 1$, where n represents the number of pairs. In this research, the paired sample t-test was used to analyze whether there is a significant difference between "Atmosphere Light" and "Mood Dairy."

4 Research Procedure

4.1 Research Framework

In this study, the conceptual design factors are derived from Calm Technology, Slow Technology, and Personal Informatics. Two conceptual products are proposed in the study. One is Atmosphere Light designed with Slow Technology, and the other is Mood Diary designed with Personal Informatics. Questionnaire survey method is used in this study. The questionnaire is based on two types of inquiries, AttrakDiff and INTUI, and then the subjects will fill out the questionnaires after appreciating the two product videos. The questionnaire data will be tested by the paired sample t-test and independent sample t-test in order to test the different qualities (pragmatic quality, hedonic quality, attractiveness, and intuition) of the two kinds of products. The differences and acceptability of the user experience of Personal Informatics and Slow Technology, the possibility of applying Slow Technology on quantified-self products, and the obstacles of developing quantified-self products with a multi modal will be discussed.

4.2 Conceptual Design

On the basis of science and technology of affective computing development, two conceptual products are put forward to track the user's emotional state. In the future, the Ubiquitous Computing and affective computing technology will be more and more mature. The differences of pragmatic quality, hedonic quality, attractiveness and intuition between the two conceptual products designed with Slow Technology and Personal Informatics concept respectively are studied in the research. These two conceptual products are presented in the way of photos in series and appreciated by the subjects. After the appreciation, two AttrakDiff and INTUI questionnaires and some essential data are filled out.

The two conceptual designs use smartwatches to record the user's emotions and identify the user's emotions through heart rate measuring and emotional speech processing. When the user's emotions and the heartbeat speeds change, the recording function starts to identify more accurate users' emotions. If the heart rate changes at the moment, the users don't speak, they will only be measured by heart rate to infer the users' emotions. These recorded data are divided into two products with different presentation methods. The one is presented in the Slow Technology design concept, and the other is shown in Personal Informatics.

Atmosphere Light: It is a situation table lamp with projection function, after receiving the emotional data from the affective computing system, the lamp will judge the current emotional state, choose a proper picture projecting on the lampshade from past emotional data storages to adjust users' emotion and guide users to reflect.

Mood Dairy: It is an application which has a function of data visualization, and data is recorded by a smartwatch. The smartwatch can record users' voices of speaking and turn them into wordings as diaries. By the viewing of the recorded data, users can compare their emotional data month on month and reflect upon emotional management.

4.3   Product Represented in Films

See Tables 4 and 5.

4.4   Descriptive Statistics

In descriptive statistics, 119 questionnaires were retrieved, and 16 surveys were invalid. One hundred and three valid questionnaires were used for statistical analysis of SPSS software. The method used was the paired sample t-test. The questionnaire was conducted with subjects ranging in age from 13 to 55 years. There are 3 people under the age of 18, 91 people aged between 19 and 35 years old, and 9 people over the age of 36. The male to female ratio was close to 1 to 1, with 52 males and 51 females. Among them, there are 29 people, who have industrial design, art design, interactive design related backgrounds. The remaining 74 people did not have the relevant background. There are 15 people usually use a wearable device to record their habits, and 88 people do not have the practice. There are 64 people will add some atmosphere for their home and buy furniture, while 39 people won't.

Paired Sample T-Test of Two Conceptual Products

Having "*" means that the product has a higher quality of evaluation. "**" means that the two have a completely opposite direction, which is a strong difference.

Table 4. The presentation film of the Atmosphere Light

Usage situation	Scenario description
I'm wearing a smartwatch. It starts recording when it senses my emotional changes and records both emotion recognition and recording.	The user is wearing a smartwatch, and the watch will activate the recording function when it senses that the user's heart rate changes due to emotional changes, and the system combines the heartbeat and voice information to identify the emotion.
As usual, I finished my day trip and went back home.	The user finished his day's trip and returned home.
This is my desk lamp. It has a projection function, also has the capability of data processing.	This is the table lamp of the users'. It has a projection function, and can receive data from a smartwatch and calculate.
Whenever I return home, it receives the watch's recorded emotions and audio messages, and stores and calculates them.	Whenever the user comes home, it will receive emotional and recording information recorded by the watch, and stores and calculates it.
(There is no description of this picture.)	According to the information recorded by the user's past smartwatch, the system will guess what kind of pictures can adjust the user's emotion, search the appropriate picture from the network database and project it on the lamp.

(*continued*)

Table 4. (*continued*)

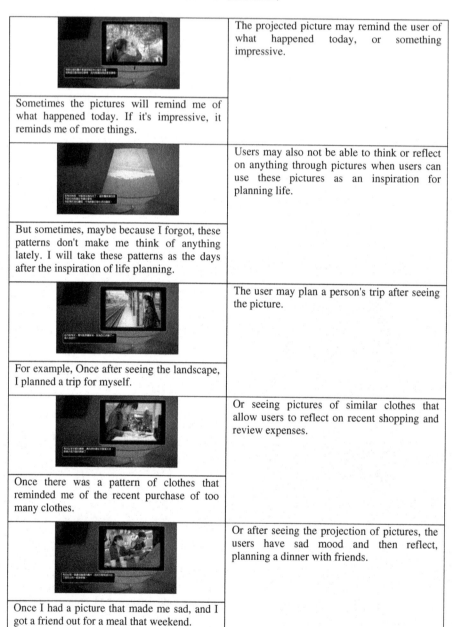

	The projected picture may remind the user of what happened today, or something impressive.
Sometimes the pictures will remind me of what happened today. If it's impressive, it reminds me of more things.	
	Users may also not be able to think or reflect on anything through pictures when users can use these pictures as an inspiration for planning life.
But sometimes, maybe because I forgot, these patterns don't make me think of anything lately. I will take these patterns as the days after the inspiration of life planning.	
	The user may plan a person's trip after seeing the picture.
For example, Once after seeing the landscape, I planned a trip for myself.	
	Or seeing pictures of similar clothes that allow users to reflect on recent shopping and review expenses.
Once there was a pattern of clothes that reminded me of the recent purchase of too many clothes.	
	Or after seeing the projection of pictures, the users have sad mood and then reflect, planning a dinner with friends.
Once I had a picture that made me sad, and I got a friend out for a meal that weekend.	

(*continued*)

Table 4. (*continued*)

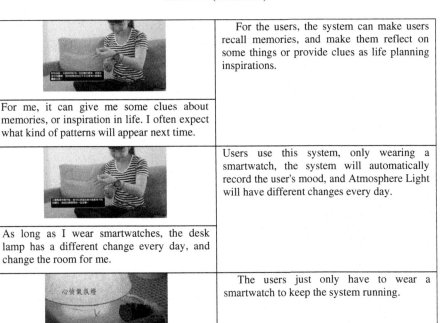

	For the users, the system can make users recall memories, and make them reflect on some things or provide clues as life planning inspirations.
For me, it can give me some clues about memories, or inspiration in life. I often expect what kind of patterns will appear next time.	
	Users use this system, only wearing a smartwatch, the system will automatically record the user's mood, and Atmosphere Light will have different changes every day.
As long as I wear smartwatches, the desk lamp has a different change every day, and change the room for me.	
	The users just only have to wear a smartwatch to keep the system running.
(There is no description of this picture.)	

It can be found that in the evaluation of practical items, the Mood Diary makes the subjects feel more "Practical," "Clear," "Manageable." However, in the ratings of hedonic quality and attractiveness, none of the rating terms of Mood Diary is higher than the Atmosphere Light (Table 6). In the Atmosphere Light, PQ5 (unpredictable vs. predictable), is tested by linear regression analysis with HQI3, HQI7, HQS1, HQS2, ATT1, ATT2, ATT4, and ATT6 respectively. It can't prove that PQ5 has the correlation with the above items, so we can't explain that the property of "Unpredictable" can directly lead to the properties of HQI3 HQI7, HQS1, HQS2, ATT1, ATT2, ATT4, and ATT6.

Having "*" means that the product has a higher quality of evaluation. Through the "E_02", it can show that the Atmosphere Light has the characteristic of making the users "feel lost," and "G_03" is "feeling guided." However, in the "V_01", "V_02", "V_03", the evaluation of the Atmosphere Light is lower than the Mood Dairy (Table 7).

Table 5. The presentation film of the Mood Diary

Usage situation	Scenario description
I'm wearing a smartwatch. It starts recording when it senses my emotional changes and records both emotion recognition and recording.	The user is wearing a smartwatch, and the watch will activate the recording function when it senses that the user's heart rate changes due to emotional changes, and the system combines the heartbeat and voice information to identify the emotion.
As usual, I finished my day trip and went back home.	The user finished his day's trip and returned home.
(There is no description of this picture.)	Users use smartphones to open apps - Mood Dairy.
Through the mood diary, I can know that I have experienced those emotions that day, and each emotion has a story to explain, because the watch is brilliant to help me record each of the current voice, after identification into a text.	By using the Mood Diary, users can know what emotions they have experienced that day. Every user who experiences the moment, if he speaks, the system will identify and then turn it into text, which helps the user to review the current experience through the application.

(*continued*)

Table 5. (*continued*)

 I almost forgot that I lost the train ticket at 8:00 in the morning, but some warm heart people picked up and handed it to me, I hope next time I can do a good thing every day.	For example, the user forgot that he lost his train ticket at 8:00 in the morning, but some warm heart people picked up and handed it to him, so he hopes he can do a good thing every day.
 After 5 minutes, almost no sleep friends finally appeared, he looks really funny, next time I'll remind him to sleep well......	For example: the user meets with his friend, the mood change and the words which say to the friend are recorded down.
 At 11:20, I encountered unfriendly waiter, at that moment I really angry, but later I think about it, perhaps he had a bad day today, and something makes him unhappy.	For example, the user can check the anger and the recorded text through the application. The user is able to reflect on the event and review whether there is a better way to deal with it.
 The mood journal not only lets me know all sorts of mood that day. I can also know what percentage of mood I had last month and which mood accounts for the majority.	The Mood Dairy lets users know the emotions of the day, and also lets users know which emotions are in the majority each month.
 Make a comparison between each month and examine my mood.	Users can compare themselves by month and check their percentage of moods.

(*continued*)

Table 5. (*continued*)

	Users can reflect on how to adjust their views and attitudes towards events if they make up the majority of happiness in the coming month.
I recalled many unhappy things that happened last month, starting this month. I'll adjust my views and attitudes about things and be happier next month.	
	The Mood Dairy uses smartwatches to record users' emotions, helps users understand their emotional changes and alert users to emotional management.
For me, this app, the Mood Diary can analyze emotions in my smartwatch and help me understand my short and long-term moods, and remind me to do emotional management every day.	
	This application can clearly and coherently record users every emotion by the smart phone or tablet computer to check out the information, and then reflect the mood and other related things.
(There is no description of this picture.)	

5   Discussion

From the analysis results of an AttrakDiff questionnaire, while the Mood Diary is higher than the Atmosphere Light in pragmatic quality, however in hedonic quality and attractiveness aspects, the Mood Diary is lower than those of the Atmosphere Light. The Atmosphere Light has more qualities of "Stylish," "Original," "Creative," "Pleasant," "Pretty," "Inviting" and "Pleasing." From the analysis of INTUI questionnaire, it was found that the scores of the two conceptual products have the same quality under the "Gut Feeling," "Magical Experience" and "Effortlessness". The differences are items of "E_02", "G_03", and "X_03". The difference between the average number of "E_02" item is significant, indicating that the Atmosphere Light has more nature of "…I felt lost" than the Mood Dairy, the subjects need to spend time and energy to use the Atmosphere Light to reach the desired target. The average difference in the "G_03" item is significant. Compared to the Mood Diary, the Atmosphere Light has more nature of "I was guided by feelings." The furniture and furnishings with "I was guided by feelings…" than "I was guided by reason…" characteristics, will be much proper. The average difference of the "X_03" item is significant, which means

Table 6. The comparison of the qualities of the two conceptual products (AttrakDiff)

		Pragmatic		Hedonic(identity)		Hedonic(stimulation)		Attractiveness
Atmosph– ere Light	PQ1	Human	HQI1	Connective	HQS1	**Inventive***	ATT1	**Pleasant***
	PQ2	Simple	HQI2	Professional	HQS2	**Creative***	ATT2	**Attractive***
	PQ3	Practical	HQI3	**Stylish***	HQS3	Bold	ATT3	Likable
	PQ4	Straightforward	HQI4	Premium	HQS4	Innovative	ATT4	**Inviting***
	PQ5	**Unpredictable****	HQI5	Integrating	HQS5	Captivating	ATT5	Good
	PQ6	Clearly structured	HQI6		HQS6	Challenging	ATT6	**Appealing***
	PQ7	Manageable	HQI7	**Presentable***	HQS7	Novel	ATT7	Motivating
Mood Diary	PQ1	Human	HQI1	Connective	HQS1	Inventive	ATT1	Pleasant
	PQ2	Simple	HQI2	Professional	HQS2	Creative	ATT2	Attractive
	PQ3	**Practical***	HQI3	Stylish	HQS3	Bold	ATT3	Likable
	PQ4	**Straightforward***	HQI4	Premium	HQS4	Innovative	ATT4	Inviting
	PQ5	**Predictable****	HQI5	Integrating	HQS5	Captivating	ATT5	Good
	PQ6	**Clearly structured***	HQI6	Brings me closer	HQS6	Challenging	ATT6	Appealing
	PQ7	**Manageable***	HQI7	Presentable	HQS7	Novel	ATT7	Motivating

that the Mood Diary brings the users more Magical Experience ("…carried me away.") than Atmosphere Light. In the items of "Verbalizability," the differences of averages in the two products are all significant, indicating that subjects may think using a smartphone is more familiar with the usage and relatively more comfortable than interacting with the Atmosphere Light.

In the "E_02" item, the Mood Light has the property of "I felt lost," which means that more efforts are needed to achieve the goal of the operation. It means Atmosphere Light can give users the opportunity to experience the confusion, so it can be inferred that Atmosphere Light has the opportunity to guide users to reflect. The further study found that females had significantly different grades of two concept products than males, and females were more likely to be exposed to these types of products than males. For those willing to add atmosphere to the house, they give more positive rating rather than those don't want to buy it. People, who choose "buying," think the Atmosphere Light has more properties of "High quality", "…was inspiring" and "… was a magical experience" than "not buying." People who choose "buying" love this information recording method, and more expect the next time interacting with the product than those who choose "not buying."

According to the open questions, some respondents believe that if people want to do emotional management, the use of APP will be more appropriate. If using Atmosphere Light to do emotional management, people need to discuss with the doctor, and the product needs further redesigning. The respondents also replied, "Modern life has been quite boring, the use of this (lamps) will feel more boring, but if you do not attach importance to the Mood Dairy, just as decoration to change the mood will be good.", "I

Table 7. The comparison of the qualities of the two conceptual products (INTUI)

	Gut Feeling		Effortlessness		Magical Experience		Verbalizability	
Atmosphere Light	G_01	...I acted on impulse	E_01	...I reached my goal effortlessly	X_01	...was inspiring	V_01	...I have no problem describing the individual operating steps
	G_02	...I performed unconsciously, without reflecting on the individual steps	E_02	...I easily knew what to do	X_02	...was a magical experience		
	G_03	**...I was guided by feelings***	E_03	...ran smoothly	X_03	...carried me away	V_02	...I can easily recall the operating steps
	G_04	...I acted without thinking	E_04	...was easy	X_04	...was fascinating		
			E_05	...came naturally	Intuitive		V_03	...I can say exactly in which way I used the product
					INT_01	...was very intuitive		
Mood diary	G_01	...I acted on impulse	E_01	...I reached my goal effortlessly	X_01	...was inspiring	V_01	**...I have no problem describing the individual operating steps ***
	G_02	...I performed unconsciously, without reflecting on the individual steps	E_02	**...I easily knew what to do***	X_02	...was a magical experience		
	G_03	...I was guided by feelings	E_03	...ran smoothly	X_03	**...carried me away***	V_02	**...I can easily recall the operating steps***
	G_04	...I acted without thinking	E_04	...was easy	X_04	...was fascinating		
			E_05	...came naturally	Intuitive		V_03	**...I can say exactly in which way I used the product***
					INT_01	...was very intuitive		

feel the Atmosphere Light is good. While its problem maybe not to perceive one's feelings, but the need for new or positive energy into our body." The Atmosphere Light, as decorations for the primary function with emotional management, will give participants living pressure. If transformed the purpose of the product into conditioning life sentiment rather than management, the concept of products will be more suitable.

6 Conclusion

In the field of Personal Informatics, data is recorded and presented by clear visualization for users, and in the Slow Technology, data is recorded and presented in a fuzzy way for users to guide users to reflect. Both of them need users to spend time on reflection. In the study, the two kinds of conceptual products designed with Personal Informatics and Slow Technology respectively are proposed. The one designed with Personal Informatics is named Mood Diary, the other designed with Slow Technology is named Atmosphere Light. These two conceptual products are presented in the way of photos in series and appreciated by the subjects. After the appreciation, two AttrakDiff and INTUI questionnaires and some basic data are filled out. According to eMarketing analysis, one of the reasons for the decline in the number of sales of smart bracelets and smartwatches is that users don't know the exact cause and what the way the devices are used. If the change of the decorations is based on information derived from the wearable device, the Atmosphere Light has the opportunity to attract people who are willing to buy decorations to purchase the wearable device.

References

1. Baumer, E.P.S., Khovanskaya, V., Matthews, M., Reynolds, L., Schwanda Sosik, V., Gay, G.: Reviewing reflection, pp. 93–102 (2014). https://doi.org/10.1145/2598510.2598598
2. Baumer, E.P.S.: Reflective informatics: conceptual dimensions for designing technologies of reflection. In: The Proceedings of the 33rd Annual ACM Conference on Human Factors in Computing Systems, Seoul, Republic of Korea, pp. 585–594 (2015)
3. Cena, F., Lombardi, I., Rapp, A., Sarzotti, F.: Self-monitoring of emotions: a novel personal informatics solution for an enhanced self-reporting. In: The Proceedings of the 2nd Workshop Emotions and Personality in Personalized Services (EMPIRE 2014) at Conference on User Modeling, Adaptation and Personalization (UMAP14), Aalborg, Denmark (2014)
4. Chetty, M., Banks, R., Harper, R., Regan, T., Sellen, A., Gkantsidis, C., Key, P.: Who's hogging the bandwidth: the consequences of revealing the invisible in the home. In: The Proceedings of the SIGCHI Conference on Human Factors in Computing Systems, Atlanta, Georgia, USA, pp. 659–668 (2010)
5. Gray, E.K., Watson, D.: Assessing positive and negative affect via self-report. In: Handbook of Emotion Elicitation and Assessment, pp. 171–183 (2007)
6. Hallnäs, L., Redström, J.: Slow technology – designing for reflection. Pers. Ubiquitous Comput. 5, 201–212 (2001)

7. Hallnäs, L., Jaksetic, P., Ljungstrand, P., Redström, J., Skog, T.: Expressions: towards a design practice of slow technology. In: The Proceedings of Interact 2001, IFIP TC.13 Conference on Human-Computer Interaction, 9–13 July 2001, Tokyo, Japan, pp. 447–454 (2001)

8. Hallnäs, L., Redström, J.: From use to presence_ on the expressions. Comput.-Hum. Interact. **9**, 106–124 (2002)

9. Krogh, M.: Exploring slow technology in the home. (Master), K3 Malmö University (2015)

10. Marcengo, A., Rapp, A.: Visualization of human behavior data, pp. 236–265 (2014). https://doi.org/10.4018/978-1-4666-4309-3.ch012

11. Pschetz, L., Banks, R., Molloy, M.: Movement crafter. In: The Proceedings of the 7th International Conference on Tangible, Embedded and Embodied Interaction, Barcelona, Spain, 393–394 (2013)

12. Rapp, A., Cena, F.: Self-monitoring and technology: challenges and open issues in personal informatics. In: Stephanidis, C., Antona, M. (eds.) UAHCI 2014. LNCS, vol. 8516, pp. 613–622. Springer, Cham (2014). https://doi.org/10.1007/978-3-319-07509-9_58

13. Sengers, P., Boehner, K., David, S., Kaye, J.J.: Reflective design. In: The Proceedings of the 4th Decennial Conference on Critical Computing: Between Sense and Sensibility, Aarhus, Denmark, pp. 49–58 (2005)

Experience Maps for Mobility

Tobias Wienken[(⊠)] and Heidi Krömker

Ilmenau University of Technology, Ilmenau, Germany
tobias.wienken@tu-ilmenau.de

Abstract. Intermodal mobility services are enabled by the complex orchestrations of different service providers and resources. Looking at users, service providers aim to offer users a great holistic experience across the entire journey. For designing the holistic mobility experience, methods and tools must be provided that address the emerging challenges. This article examines the method *experience map* to apply it to the field of mobility. The goal is to create assistance for the design activities: Understanding existing experience, exploring service ideas and communicating service concepts. Based on a best practice analysis, the article investigates the structure of currently used *experience maps*. Building on these results, a two-stage expert study is conducted in order to provide a framework for the creation and analysis of a *mobility experience map*. Finally, the article discusses the implications for the analysis of the holistic experience using the *mobility experience map*.

Keywords: Experience map · Mobility experience · Service design

1 Introduction

Thinking and offering services in the terms of systems generate a new competitive advantage, this is how Kalbach defines the yardstick for future services [1]. The mobility sector is also facing up to this challenge. Mobility providers cooperate with each other to provide customers a seamless intermodal travel chain. In contrast to traditional services, users can individually determine their journey across multiple means of transport and thus the user experience arises over the entire travel, from travel planning to arrival at the destination. In order to systematically design this holistic experience, the concept of the mobility experience was introduced. The mobility experience covers all the passenger's perceptions and responses resulting from any direct or indirect contact and anticipated contact with the service providers along the journey [2].

For designing new mobility services, methods and tools are required that can describe and visualise the holistic nature of the mobility experience in order to understand the design space, make design decisions and assess their impact in advance. For example, it is crucial to design each touchpoint, without losing sight of the user's overall experience [3]. Yet despite the recognition of the importance, there are hardly any scientific discussions on this subject [3], especially in mobility sector. By contrast, in design practice the method *experience mapping* is partly used to face these challenges. Building on findings from practical work, the present research is investigating

© Springer International Publishing AG, part of Springer Nature 2018
M. Kurosu (Ed.): HCI 2018, LNCS 10902, pp. 615–627, 2018.
https://doi.org/10.1007/978-3-319-91244-8_47

whether the mobility experience of users can be conceptually expressed in the form of an *experience map*. In doing so, the investigation is guided by the research question: How can the mobility experience be described and visualized in a generic way in order to build a framework for a *mobility experience map*?

Answering the issue, this article discusses at the beginning different approaches for *experience mapping* in the theoretical basics. Afterwards, the study identifies the essential elements and interrelations that constitute the mobility experience and thus builds the framework for the experience visualisation in the form of an *experience map*. Finally, the implications for the analysis of the holistic mobility experience and the specific limitations of the presented framework will be discussed.

2 Background on Experience Mapping

The literature in service science and user-centered design historically has not considered *experience maps* as a separate research topic. However, efforts have already been made with other methods to illustrate the experience of users. All methods visualise the experience to support the designers in their design activities: Understanding experience, exploring the experience of new design ideas and communicating users' experience. The methods provide different insights, depending on the described factors influencing the user's experience and the described responses of a user. The influencing factors show which elements affect the experience during a user journey. The latter shows physical and psychological responses of users to the provided services. In order to distinguish the *experience map* from the other methods, different approaches are discussed with each other.

The *service blueprint* is an applied process diagram that subdivides the service delivery process from the customer's perspective [e.g. 4]. The process covers the physical activities of a customer that lead to interactions with the service provider. The *mental model diagram*, on the other hand, provides deeper insights into a user's cognitive perspective. Young transferred the concept of mental models into simplified affinity diagrams of behaviours [cf. 5]. The goal is to contrast the behaviour of the users with the potential solutions of an organization. In contrast, the *empathy map* uses a more comprehensive approach to understand the user's behaviour. Therefore the *empathy map* integrates the elements what users think and feel, hear, see, say and do, as well as the pain and gain of the users [e.g. 6]. The method tries to uncover why users are functioning the way they are and investigates cognitive, affective, sensorial, and physical responses of a user. Thereby the focus is on the description of the responses, the influencing factors as well as the interactions with a service providers are not considered. This combination of the user responses and the influencing factors depicts the *customer journey map*. The customer journey involves all activities and events related to the delivery of a service from the customer's perspective [7]. But the displayed spectrum of the experience varies in the different *customer journey maps*. In summary, the goal of the *customer journey map* is to illustrate how customers behave across a journey, what they are feeling, and what their motivation and attitude is across that journey [7].

Building on these insights, recent definitions point out that *"experience maps focus on a general human activity within a given domain"* [1]. In contrast to the *customer journey map*, the *experience map* separates a user's experience from the concrete solutions of a provider [1]. In doing so, it illustrates the user's journey, in which a user interacts with a variety of different touchpoints and providers. Adding to the above, the *experience map* represents an archetypal user journey through a certain domain and considers all activities and events that are relevant to the user's experience. In order to give a comprehensive picture of the holistic experience, the *experience map* should contain the cognitive, affective, and physical responses of a user.

3   Research Design

In this research, the method *experience map* is investigated and adapted to the field of mobility. The aim is to develop a framework for the *mobility experience map* that enables the analysis and communication of holistic mobility experience. To achieve this goal, the research procedure is divided into four phases and is oriented on the design science research framework [8] (Table 1). In the phase I, a basic construct for the *mobility experience map* is determined. The subject of this investigation is the disclosure of a uniform structure for *experience maps*. In detail, it is examined which elements are used to describe the experience, by the authors of *experience maps*. For this purpose, 40 practical *experience maps* from the sector of entertainment, finance, healthcare, mobility, and retail are investigated. All used elements from the 40 practical examples are documented and then evaluated according to their frequency of use. Building on these results, the basic elements of a *mobility experience map* can be determined.

The phase II covers the evaluation of the developed construct. Ten experts are provided with the construct and use it to develop an *experience map* for mobility. In the following interviews, the experts assess the construct in terms of completeness, simplicity, elegance, understandability, and ease of use [cf. 8]. The results are then evaluated and combined in the model for a *mobility experience map* (Phase III).

Finally, the application and evaluation of the *mobility experience map* follow in two case studies (Phase IV). The case studies are carried out as part of two research projects by the *Federal Ministry of Education and Research* and *Federal Ministry of Transport and Digital Infrastructure* in Germany. Depending on the focus of the projects, a map for electric mobility and a map for public transport are developed. To validate the developed framework, the two experience maps are examined using the member checking method. Experts interviewed in Phase II assess the two *mobility experience maps* and the underlying model, giving their approval or rejection of the results. The *mobility experience maps* are evaluated in terms of their fidelity with real world phenomena, completeness, and level of detail [cf. 8].

Table 1. Research procedure

Phase I	Phase II
Objective: Identification of used elements in experience maps from different sectors and modelling of the construct	**Objective:** Evaluation whether construct is suitable for the mobility sector
	Method: Expert interview
Method: Best practice analysis and conceptual modelling	**Evaluation criteria:** Completeness, simplicity, elegance, understandability, and ease of use
Criterion for analysis: Frequency of the elements occurring	**Study size:** Ten experts in mobility and user experience domain
Study size: 40 Experience maps	
Sector considered: Entertainment, finance, healthcare, mobility, and retail	
Phase III	**Phase IV**
Objective: Definition of the framework for mobility experience maps	**Objective:** Evaluation of the framework for mobility experience maps
Method: Conceptual modelling	**Method:** Case study and member checking
	Evaluation criteria: Fidelity with real world phenomena, completeness, level of detail
	Study size: Two projects are reviewed by the experts

(margin labels: Research output - Construct · Research output - Model · Research activity - Build · Research activity - Evaluate)

4   Results

As explained in the beginning, the main goal of this research is to provide a framework for an *experience map* that allows the designers to accurately describe and visualize the mobility experience of a user. The underlying structure of the framework consists of basic elements that describe the content of a *mobility experience map*. Furthermore, the interrelations within the *mobility experience map* are investigated in order to reveal general perspectives that can support the designers to understand the holistic experience and to carry out a systematic analysis and design.

4.1   Basic Elements of Mobility Experience Maps

Looking for an appropriate basic structure for the *mobility experience map*, the initial question arises: Which elements are necessary in an *experience map* in order to adequately represent the mobility experience? The search for the basic structure of the *mobility experience map* is accompanied by two contradictory objectives. The experience map intends to both provide the designers with a comprehensive understanding of the mobility experience, and at the same time to ensure that the experience map is

Table 2. Comparison of experience maps from practice

Column headers (Elements of experience maps):

1. Content of use
2. Guiding principles for providers
3. Influencing factors on user experience
4. Key moments for user experience
5. Provider activities
6. Provider aims
7. Provider description
8. Provider opportunities
9. Provider strengths
10. Scenarios
11. Statistical data on usage behaviour
12. Timeline
13. Touchpoints
14. Usage process
15. User activities
16. User aims
17. User barriers
18. User description
19. User needs
20. User emotions
21. User decision point in usage process
22. User expectations
23. User experience
24. User thinking

Number of elements used in all experience maps:
1, 4, 5, 6, 4, 3, 1, 20, 2, 13, 6, 4, 31, 40, 33, 8, 4, 23, 6, 32, 4, 4, 5, 23

Experience maps of the entertainment sector

1. Playing online games
2. Playing online games
3. Playing social online games
4. Visiting festivals
5. Visiting museums
6. Visiting museums
7. Visiting museums
8. Visiting restaurants

Total: 0, 1, 1, 1, 2, 0, 0, 4, 0, 1, 0, 1, 7, 8, 7, 2, 0, 4, 1, 6, 0, 0, 1, 5

Experience maps of the finance sector

9. Applying for loans
10. Applying for loans
11. Applying for mortgages
12. Dealing with financial affairs
13. Dealing with financial affairs
14. Dealing with loans
15. Registering and identifying for online banking
16. Using internet banking

Total: 0, 0, 1, 2, 1, 2, 1, 4, 0, 2, 2, 0, 6, 8, 7, 1, 2, 6, 1, 7, 2, 1, 1, 5

Experience maps of the healthcare sector

17. Consuming healthy and organic food
18. Consuming healthy and sustainable food
19. Dealing with cancerous diseases
20. Dealing with cancerous diseases
21. Dealing with cholesterol diseases
22. Managing therapy
23. Seeking medical support
24. Selecting health insurance

Total: 1, 2, 2, 1, 0, 0, 0, 4, 1, 6, 2, 3, 7, 8, 7, 3, 1, 5, 2, 5, 1, 1, 2, 5

Experience maps of the mobility sector

25. Planning a journey
26. Planning and doing holiday trips
27. Planning and doing a trip by airplane
28. Planning and doing a trip by airplane
29. Planning and doing a trip by train
30. Using autonomous vehicles
31. Using breakdown services
32. Using breakdown services

Total: 0, 1, 1, 1, 0, 0, 0, 7, 0, 2, 0, 0, 4, 8, 7, 1, 0, 5, 1, 7, 0, 2, 1, 5

Experience maps of the retail sector

33. Ordering grocery online
34. Ordering grocery online
35. Purchase decision-making process
36. Purchase decision for mobile telecommunications
37. Purchase decision for telecommunications
38. Purchase decision for telecommunications
39. Using vouchers
40. Visiting shopping centres

Total: 0, 0, 0, 1, 1, 1, 0, 1, 1, 2, 2, 0, 7, 8, 5, 1, 1, 3, 1, 7, 1, 0, 0, 3

easy to use. Therefore, a trade-off must be sought between the completeness and simplicity of a *mobility experience map*.

Due to the lack of scientific discussions and the limited practical use of *experience maps* in the field of mobility, a step-by-step approach is conducted to answer this question. The best practice analysis conducted in Phase I examines 40 *experience map* examples covering the sectors of entertainment, finance, healthcare, mobility, and retail. As the result, the synthesis reveals that seven elements are used most often in an *experience map*: Descriptive user model, provider opportunities, touchpoints, usage process, user activities, user emotions, and user thinking (Table 2).

However, the comparison of the results of the best practice analysis (Phase I) with the results of the expert study (Phase II) shows that the elements of an *experience map* used in practice must be adapted to meet the characteristics of the mobility sector. The experts express the need to extend the *mobility experience map* by the element context. According to experts, context influences the effectiveness and efficiency of an executed user activity. In addition, the perception of a mobility service is also influenced by the environment (so-called service scape) in which the usage process takes place. The element context is particularly relevant for the area of public mobility services. For example, a long queue at the ticket machine or insufficiently air-conditioned vehicles can have a negative impact on the experience of a passenger. But also in the case of individual transport, the context, such as traffic density or road conditions, influences a user's mobility experience.

According to the experts, there is a need for further changes with regard to the element provider opportunities. The opportunities illustrate how providers can influence and improve the user experience. The experts are of the opinion that provider opportunities should not be part of a *mobility experience map*. This element does not

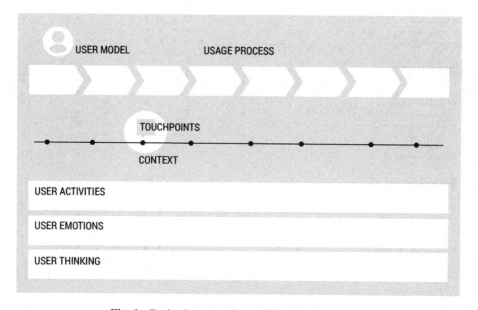

Fig. 1. Basic elements of a mobility experience map

provide any further information about the users and their behaviour. The experts see the provider opportunities as a further analysis that can be carried out on the basis of the *mobility experience map*. The results of the analysis have a special relevance in deciding and prioritizing future measures.

In summary, the studies carried out (Phase I + II) reveal that the mobility experience can best be described using seven basic elements (Fig. 1) (Table 3).

Table 3. Description of the basic elements of a mobility experience map

Element	Description
Usage process and its phases	A usage process is any purposeful activity or group of activities that result in an outcome [cf. 9]. In general the usage process of services follows a tripartite division, the pre-service phase (getting in touch), the actual usage phase, and the post-service phase [cf. 10]. By dividing the usage process further into domain related phases, each phase is implicitly assigned a goal which the users are supposed to achieve
	For the mobility sector, this division can be further concretized by archetypal process independent of the means of transport: Planning a journey – Starting a journey – Entering a stopping point – Boarding a means of transport – Travelling on means of transport – Alighting a means of transport – Leaving a stopping point – Arriving at destination. (Stopping point corresponds e.g. to car park or bus stop.)
Descriptive user model	User descriptions contain stereotypical users and embody their motivations, expectations, attitudes, and skills that are relevant to the use of the services [cf. 11]
	For the mobility sector, the experts emphasise the enrichment of the mobility experience map with a user model. The described user type acts as a sort of filter and concretizes the findings of a mobility experience map. In order to divide the users into different user types, the criteria like the choice of means of transport and the availability of the means of transport are used, for example [cf. 12]
User activities	The user activities contain all the actions that users actually perform to achieve a goal during the mobility service [cf. 13]
User emotions	User emotions generally involve the physiological response of the brain and body to threats and opportunities [15]. Emotions have a prominent cause, occur and decrease rapidly and thus are relatively intense and clear cognitive contents [15] (e.g. Anger over train failure)
User thinking	User thinking indicates which actions a user thinks through before deciding to execute them
	For the mobility sector, user thinking provide insights into a user's mental model what is defined as a rich and elaborate structure, reflecting the user's understanding of what a mobility service contains, how it works, and why it works that way [cf. 14]

(continued)

Table 3. (*continued*)

Element	Description
Touchpoints	A touchpoint is defined as any possible contact point between users and providers. These interactions take place human-human, and human-machine, but also occur indirectly via third parties, such as reviews from other users [cf. 10] For the mobility sector, the touchpoints are characterised by the means of transport used. For public transport, the mobile passenger information application or the timetable at the bus stop can be mentioned as examples
Context	The term of context can be used to characterize the situation of an interaction between users and service providers In the sector of mobility, touchpoints are closely interwoven with the context, which shows to what extent a prevailing situation influences the perception and interaction of the users. In order to precisely identify and analyse these situational influences, the context for mobility can be defined in five categories: Spatial, temporal, environmental, social, and informational context [16]

4.2   Three Perspectives for Understanding Mobility Experience Maps

The perspectives serve as an instrument for the analysis of a *mobility experience map*. The goal is to illustrate the interrelations within the *experience map* for designers in order to increase their understanding of the mobility experience. These perspectives are the result of the investigations in the phases II + IV. In the discussions with the experts, the interrelations within a *mobility experience map* could be extracted and subsequently generalized in the terms of the three perspectives (Fig. 2). The perspectives *sequence* and *interaction-response* reveal findings on the internal structure of the *experience map*. Whereas the perspective *experience cycle* describes how the users perceive a service and shows how the mobility experience occurs and alters.

Sequence Perspective (Chronological Order – Workload – Rhythm). Mobility services are dynamic processes that take place over a certain period of time [cf. 10] and therefore the chronological order is crucial for the understanding of mobility experience. This chronological order arranges the elements of the mobility experience in terms of content (horizontal axis) and indicates which sequence of the usage process appears plausible to the user. In addition to that, the chronological order also makes it possible to divide the usage process into individual phases. In this way, the single phases, such as planning a journey, can be considered separately, which allows a detailed analysis of the mobility experience.

This sequence of the individual phases is usually depicted in the *experience map* as a linear process. Contrary to this linear and at the same time seemingly ideal-typical process, experts estimate that in reality the use of a mobility service is often not linear. The planning of a journey is usually cited as an example. Passengers of public transport services perform identical activities several times in order to compare different mobility providers and their travel connections. Due to the non-linear usage process, the

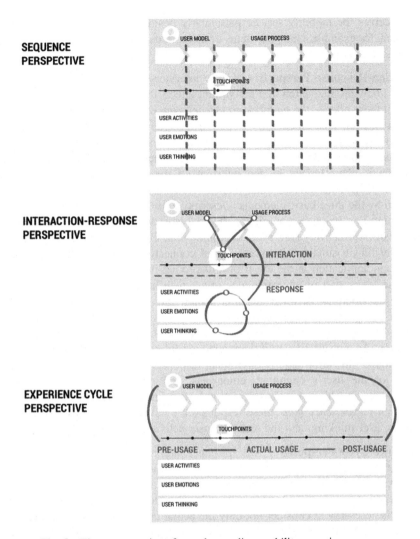

Fig. 2. Three perspectives for understanding mobility experience maps

workload for the users increases. This workload is reflected in a large number of cognitive and physical activities for the users and possibly through increased resource input. Both can influence the mobility experience.

Analog to the workload in the usage process, the rhythm of a mobility service also becomes visible when the touchpoints in a *mobility experience map* are related to each other. The rhythm shows the user involvement per period in usage process. A decisive factor for mobility experience is thereby the intensity of interaction, which can be described by the frequency and the extent of the interactions between users and mobility providers. According to the experts, the timing of the interaction also plays an important role. During the usage process, so-called key moments arise, in which the user perceives the mobility service particularly positively or negatively. The experts have cited, for example, changing trains or disruptions in the public transport as critical moments.

Interaction-Response Perspective. In the interviews with the experts, it was often discussed how an interaction at a touchpoint affects the mobility experience of a user. To reveal these effects, the *mobility experience map* can be divided vertically into two areas: Interaction area and response area. This contrast compares the relevant components for an interaction (upper part of the *experience map*) with the user's responses to an interaction (lower part). From the human-machine-interaction perspective, an interaction is characterized by the interplay of the three factors: Human – task – technique [17]. Transferred to the *mobility experience map*, an interaction can be described by the three basic elements: Descriptive user model – Goal of usage phase – Touchpoint. For the service providers, the goal is to design an optimal interplay of the three factors within every single interaction. So that, for example, even occasional users can easily find a suitable alternative travel connection with their mobile passenger information application in the event of a disruption in public transport.

In the lower part of an *experience map*, there arises the question of how users perceive the interplay between the three factors and how they response to it. If, for example, occasional users do not find current information about the disruption, they wonder (cognitive response) whether they are looking in the wrong place in the application. As a result, they quit the interaction (physical response) frustrated without having found the information (emotional response). The example shows that the analysis of the user's cognitive, emotional, and physical responses provides an understanding in which way the interaction has an impact on the mobility experience. In a *mobility experience map*, these responses are covered by the basic elements user emotions, user thinking, and the resulting user activities.

Experience Cycle Perspective. An *experience map* tends to focus on the depiction of the usage phase of an user journey. However, the usage phase is only one part of the user's experience perception and processing. Rather, the user's experience perception and processing can be interpreted as a cycle. In order to understand this experience cycle, it is necessary to consider not only the actual use of a mobility service, but also the assumptions and expectations prior to use as well as the reflection after the actual use [cf. 18]. In relation to the *mobility experience map*, it is therefore advisable to divide the process into the phases: *Pre-usage – Actual usage – Post-usage*.

The experience cycle closes when analysing how the mobility experience after the usage affects a user and may influence his or her expectations, beliefs, and future behaviour. In the context of the experience map, this means that the perceived and processed experience may lead to the reshaping of the user description created at the beginning. As a result, the user description in the *mobility experience map* is both the starting point and the end point of the experience cycle.

5   Discussion - Contributions to Designing for Mobility Experience

The *mobility experience map* enables the user-centered visualization of complex intermodal mobility services. Thus the visualization represents the mobility experience that is formed through interactions with multiple services from multiple organizations that go beyond the provider's offerings [cf. 19]. In doing so, the method helps to consider service concepts and touchpoints in the holistic context of the mobility experience and contribute a crucial support for design activities, such as understanding existing experience, exploring service ideas and communicating service concepts.

The *mobility experience map* contributes to a change in the way of thinking and thus promotes holistic design decisions. From now on, a design solution will not be evaluated on the basis of its performance at a single touchpoint, but on the basis of its contribution to the holistic mobility experience along the entire intermodal journey. In addition, the *experience map* can also serve as a source of inspiration and provide valuable insights for the identification of new service ideas and further developments. The experience map reveals during which phase of a journey barriers and problems arise for the user. At the same time, it also becomes apparent to what extent users are supported by the existing touchpoints, or whether these user barriers have not been addressed at all so far. This systematic decomposition based on the travel chain also helps to determine and prioritize user needs during requirements engineering for new services. Beyond the understanding and exploring of the mobility experience, the method also contributes to the communication. The method creates a common ground and understanding for the user's perspective in complex mobility systems in terms of a visual language. The visualization provides a rapid introduction to complex mobility systems so that different members of multidisciplinary teams can use the *experience map* to comprehend and communicate design issues in every stage of the development process.

In additional to the contributions to the design, the expert study also reveals the limitations of the framework. According to the experts, adapting the *mobility experience map* to the intended use can be beneficial. For example, when communicating with external stakeholders, information must be focused on the essentials. For this purpose, a kind of experience indicator could be introduced in the framework. The objective of these indicators is to describe the experience in a compressed form with the help of a certain scale.

When creating a *mobility experience map*, experts also see a challenge in how to show the insights in the visual layout. This question was not explicitly addressed in this study. In practice, the layouts vary widely. For the visualization of the user emotions, for example, the authors use bar charts, plane diagrams, and curve representations or descriptions of the experience through phrases. Further investigations are required to identify visual presentations that can highlight the essential features of the mobility experience and their interrelationships and de-emphasize less important details.

6   Conclusion

Creating a holistic mobility experience has been gaining increasing attention from mobility providers. However, there has been a dearth of adequate methods for analysing and communicating the holistic mobility experience.

Therefore, the article investigates the method of the *experience map* in order to use it in the field of mobility. In the best practice analysis conducted at the beginning, the article examines currently used *experience maps*. Based on these findings, the two-stage expert study reveals the basic elements of the *mobility experience map*. The expert study also shows which perspectives are suitable for analysing an experience map in order to increase the understanding of the holistic mobility experience. As the result of this research, the seven basic elements together with the three perspectives build a framework for *mobility experience maps*. Subsequently, the article discusses the implications for the analysis of the holistic experience and the limitations of the presented framework, highlighting those that are especially in need of further research.

Acknowledgements. Part of this work was funded by the German *Federal Ministry of Education and Research* (BMBF) grant number 02K12A175 within the project *Move@ÖV* and the German *Federal Ministry of Transport and Digital Infrastructure* (BMVI) grant number 19E16007F within the project *Digitalisierte Mobilität – die offene Mobilitätsplattform*.

References

1. Kalbach, J.: Mapping Experiences: A Complete Guide to Creating Value Through Journeys, Blueprints, and Diagrams. O'Reilly Media, Sebastopol (2016)
2. Wienken, T., Krömker, H.: Designing for mobility experience - towards an understanding. In: Stopka, U. (ed.) Mobilität & Kommunikation, edition winterwork, Borsdorf (2018)
3. Sangiorgi, D., Prendiville, A., Ricketts, A.: Mapping and Developing Service Design Research, SDR Service Design Research UK Network, Lancaster (2014)
4. Shostack, G.L.: Designing services that deliver. Harvard Bus. Rev. **62**(1), 133–139 (1984)
5. Young, I.: Mental Models: Aligning Design Strategy with Human Behaviour. Rosenfeld Media, New York (2008)
6. Osterwalder, A., Pigneur, Y.: Business Model Generation: Ein Handbuch für Visionäre, Spielveränderer und Herausforderer. Campus Verlag, Frankfurt am Main (2011)
7. Zomerdijk, L.G., Voss, C.A.: Service design for experience-centric services. J. Serv. Res. **13**(1), 67–82 (2010)
8. March, S.T., Smith, G.F.: Design and natural science research on information technology. Decis. Support Syst. **15**(4), 251–266 (1995)
9. Haksever, C., Render, B.: Service Management: An Integrated Approach to Supply Chain Management and Operations. FT Press, New Jersey (2013)
10. Stickdorn, M., Schneider, J.: This Is Service Design Thinking. BIS Publishers, Amsterdam (2012)
11. Cooper, A., Reimann, R., Cronin, D.: About Face 3: The Essentials of Interaction Design. Wiley, Indianapolis (2007)
12. Follmer, R., Gruschwitz, D., Jesske, B., Quandt, S.: Mobilität in Deutschland 2008: MiD 2008 - Struktur, Aufkommen, Emissionen, Trends-Ergebnisbericht (2010)

13. ISO 9241-210:2010: Ergonomics of human-system interaction – Part 210: Human-centered design for interactive systems (2010)
14. Carroll, J.M., Olson, J.R.: Mental models in human-computer interaction. In: Helander, M. (ed.) Handbook of Human-Computer Interaction. Elsevier Science Publishers, Amsterdam (1988)
15. Jeon, M.: Emotions and affect in human factors and human-computer interaction: taxonomy, theories, approaches, and methods. In: Jeon, M. (ed.) Emotions and Affect in Human Factors and Human-Computer Interaction. Academic Press, London (2017)
16. Krömker, H., Wienken, T.: Context elicitation for user-centered context-aware systems in public transport. In: Kurosu, M. (ed.) HCI 2015. LNCS, vol. 9170, pp. 429–439. Springer, Cham (2015). https://doi.org/10.1007/978-3-319-20916-6_40
17. Winograd, T., Flores, F.: Understanding Computers and Cognition: A New Foundation for Design, 5th edn. Ablex Publishing, New Jersey (1986)
18. Sarodnick, F., Brau, H.: Methoden der Usability Evaluation: Wissenschaftliche Grundlagen und praktische Anwendung, 2nd edn. Hans Huber, Bern (2006)
19. Patrício, L., Fisk, R.P., Falcão e Cunha, J., Constantine, L.: Multilevel service design: from customer value constellation to service experience blueprinting. J. Serv. Res. **14**(2), 180–200 (2011)

Analyzing Impact Factors for Smartphone Sharing Decisions Using Decision Tree

Tao Xu[1,2(✉)], Yun Zhou[3], Alexander Raake[4], and Xuyun Zhang[5]

[1] School of Software and Microelectronics, Northwestern Polytechnical University,
Xi'an 710072, Shaanxi, People's Republic of China
xutao@nwpu.edu.cn
[2] State Key Laboratory for Manufacturing Systems Engineering,
Xi'an Jiaotong University, Xi'an 710054, Shaanxi, People's Republic of China
[3] School of Education, Shaanxi Normal University,
Xi'an 710062, Shaanxi, People's Republic of China
zhouyun@snnu.edu.cn
[4] Audiovisual Technology Group, Institute for Media Technology,
University of Technology Ilmenau, 98693 Ilmenau, Germany
alexander.raake@tu-ilmenau.de
[5] Department of Electrical and Computer Engineering, University of Auckland,
Auckland 1010, New Zealand
xuyun.zhang@auckland.ac.nz

Abstract. The sharing activities of smart devices have been proved to occur commonly among users and discussed by many studies. In contrast to sharing behaviors of personal computer, smartphone sharing is impromptu. It occurs pervasively like on the street between strangers or at home between family members. The variety of sharing behaviors requires the investigation of the most impact factors for smartphone sharing, which underlies the design of usable privacy user interface. This work investigates and analyzes the influencing factors of smartphone users sharing decisions based on CART algorithm of Decision Tree. The data for analyzing is based on a survey involving 165 participants' responses. Results indicated the features belonging to the sharing attitudes and behaviors impacted users' sharing decisions mostly.

Keywords: User study · Sharing · Smartphone · Decision tree

1 Introduction

Smart devices sharing [4,10] has been proved to occur commonly among users and discussed by many studies, even though smartphones are personal objects. Compared with sharing behaviors of personal computer, smartphone sharing is impromptu. It occurs pervasively like on the street between strangers or at home between family members. The impromptu behaviors and various sharing decisions require the investigation of impact factors for smartphone sharing, which

© Springer International Publishing AG, part of Springer Nature 2018
M. Kurosu (Ed.): HCI 2018, LNCS 10902, pp. 628–637, 2018.
https://doi.org/10.1007/978-3-319-91244-8_48

underlies the design of usable privacy user interface. Due to the missing studies, this work investigates and analyzes the influencing factors of smartphone users sharing decisions using the CART algorithm of Decision Tree. First we collect data from a survey with 165 pieces of responses, obtaining users' attitudes towards tablet and smartphone sharing respectively. Next, we present the Decision Tree induction, CART algorithm and Gini index. The Gini index was used for analyzing and three users' sharing decisions were explored, including: the willingness to use multiple user accounts as the owner, the willingness to use multiple user accounts as the guest, and whether the individual taking actions to delete the trace history as the guest. Finally, results and a discussion were presented.

2   Related Work

2.1   Sharing Practices

Sharing practices analysis is the first step to investigate the sharing behaviors. In the work [4], Karlson et al. interviewed 12 smartphone users to explore the diversity of guest user categorizations and associated security constraints expressed by the participants. Hang et al. [1] conducted a focus group and a user study to analyze which data people are concerned of, which data people are willing to share and with whom people would share their device. The study [5] examined the privacy expectations of smartphone users by exploring participants' concerns with other people accessing the personal information and applications accessing this information via platform APIs.

Most of the time, it is daunting to identify the likely number of types and categorize behaviors into distinct types. Prior studies obtained sharing types by collecting data and analyzing distinct patterns from the observation. For example, Zhou et al. analyzed the relationship of sharer and sharee, sharing activities could be categorized as stranger, acquaintance, close people and kids [12]. Matthews et al. [6] organized sharing practices into a taxonomy of six sharing types, including borrowing, mutual use, setup, helping, broadcasting and accidental. This work involved a survey of 99 participants, a 21 days diary study with 25 participants and interviews with 24 participants. Behaviors are under the influence of multiple factors. In the work [11], the authors investigated the correlations between basic information, general privacy attitudes and sharing behaviors. However, with regard to sharing decisions, the analysis of the sharing types as well as the correlation and association is inadequate; it requires figuring out the influencing factors.

2.2   Solutions to Protect Privacy

Previous studies showed than users had concerns and negative emotions on the privacy leakage. Both their attitudes and behaviors implied that all-or-nothing mechanisms of privacy interfaces [2,7] on protecting privacy have not been useful to assist individuals to control their personal information protection adequately. To bridge the gap between people's requirements and all-or-nothing mechanisms, new access control of exposing more options for users has been obtained the focus of researchers, the usability of which have been tested and investigated. The numbers of researches that revolve around exploring usability of new access control mechanisms and interfaces, as well as users' perception and feedbacks on the complex terminologies and interfaces, are increasing. For example, in the work [2], questions were designed and the usability of both all-or-nothing control and new access control mechanisms have been tested and the results showed that the new flexible access control gained more interests of participants.

Although the fine-grained access control is beneficial for users, there are still some problems requiring be considering and solving. Achieving new access control of exposing more options for users requires increased effort of users [9], and a heavy burden to understand terminologies and options would be on users when the number of apps increasing [10]. With regard to sharing activities, smartphone OSs have started to consider multiple user account or guest mode important since 2014, and integrated this feature into OSs. Android users can access multiple-user settings and employ a Guest/Profile/User account to share their smartphone in a safe way. Users of iOS, could define and block several interactive areas in Settings under the category of accessibility for the individual who is shared to use the phone. In this way, the owner of the phone could explicitly switch to this feature and disable user interface items that were not wanted to be used by a guest. Even though multiple user account or guest mode is beneficial for users, the burden of interactivity and understanding terminologies confuses the users. Therefore, to investigate the usability and finding out the issues existing in the usability has been considered essential. Among exploring the issues of usability, figuring out impacting factors of sharing decisions could provide the implications for the design of usable privacy interface, especially for informing the specific interface for sharing phone with the kid, the acquaintance, the close person and the stranger.

3   The Architecture of Analysis

Decision Tree (DT) induction [3] constructs a tree-like flowchart model where each nonleaf node denotes a test on a feature, each branch refers to an outcome of the test, and each leaf node corresponds to a class prediction. At each node, the algorithm selects the assumed "best" feature to partition the data into individual classes. Quinlan [8] developed a decision tree algorithm known as ID3 (Iterative Dichotomiser). Then Quinlan presented a successor of ID3 later, that is, C4.5. CART tree is also an algorithm used commonly. Decision Tree algorithms (e.g., ID3, C4.5, and CART) were originally used for classification. It is the learning of decision trees from class-labeled training tuples. The construction of decision tree classifiers does not require any prior knowledge or parameter setting. Therefore, it is appropriate for exploratory knowledge discovery. Besides, DT has the ability to handle multidimensional data and the acquired knowledge represented in tree form is intuitive and easy to interpret. Usually, the training steps and classification speed are fast and the performance is good. DT induction has been widely used in many research and industry areas.

Commonly, the data sets used for analysis contain hundreds of features (also referred as attributes or dimensions). Many of these features may be redundant or irrelevant to the classification tasks. Keeping irrelevant or redundant features for analysis may be detrimental for the algorithm to analyze the data, as well as consume resources and slow down the processing speed. Therefore, rejecting these features is an essential step for further analysis. Feature subset selection (also known as attribute subset selection in data mining) could reduce the size of the dataset through removing irrelevant or redundant features. One of the feature subset selection methods is decision tree induction. When the decision tree induction method is employed for feature subset selection, a tree is constructed without the irrelevant features based on the given data. In this way, the set of features appearing in the tree form a reduced subset of features.

During tree construction, feature selection measures (or attribute selection measures, known as splitting rules) are used to select the feature that best partitions the tuples into distinct classes. A feature selection measure is a heuristic process which is for selection splitting criterion that "best" divides a given partition. Information gain, gain ration and Gini index are three most popular feature selection measures.

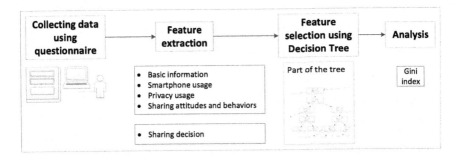

Fig. 1. The architecture of analysis

In this exploratory and preliminary work, we use the CART algorithm to test and find the most relevant features, which impact users' sharing decisions. Therefore, the Gini index will be discussed in the section of Results and Discussion. The architecture of analysis is as shown in Fig. 1, containing four steps: collecting data using questionnaire, extracting features, selecting features as the impacting factors using decision tree, and analyzing the impacting factors. First, we propose a questionnaire to obtain users' attitudes towards phone sharing and their sharing decisions. Then, the features are extracted and the values of features are collected based on participants' responses. Next, we employ the data to construct DT induction and measure Gini index. Finally, we analyze the impacting factors through the Gini index of each category of the feature.

4   Survey Participants and Data Collecting

In our previous work [12], we conducted a fine-grained survey with 165 participants, including German and Chinese to study users' attitudes towards smartphone sharing as the owner and the guest, and their behaviors on such control mechanism. To go a step further, to know at which level the factors influencing on sharing activities, in this latest work, we use the decision tree algorithm to process the data.

4.1   Participants

165 participants' responses were collected and made into a dataset. In this dataset, we had 69.1% males and 30.9% females. Their ages were distributed and covered almost all age groups. However, 66.7% were in the range of 18 to 24. There was a bias towards higher education levels and 94.0% of participants were under a higher education.

4.2   Data Collecting

The dataset were divided into five following parts:

(a) Basic information including (1) age, (2) gender, (3) nationality, (4) educational level
(b) Smartphone usage including (1) budget for smartphone, (2) price of owned phone, (3) numbers of years' experience using smartphone, (4) smartphone OS, (5) numbers of apps installed, and (6) the time spent on smartphone daily
(c) Privacy usage including (1) importance and (2) sensitivity of personal information stored on smartphone
(d) Sharing attitudes and behaviors, including (1) frequency of sharing behaviors, (2) concern levels when lending the phone, (3) the time let others use the phone, and (4) necessity of using multiple user accounts as the owner
(e) Sharing Decision, including (1) the willingness to use multiple user accounts as the owner, (2) the willingness to use multiple user accounts as the guest, and (3) whether taking actions to delete the trace history as the guest.

The features (or could be also called as variables in this paper) and the scales of measurement that are used for analyzing are listed as below:

(a) age, ordinal
(b) gender, categorical
(c) nationality, categorical
(d) education level, ordinal
(e) budget for smartphone, ordinal
(f) price of owned phone, ordinal
(g) numbers of years' experience using smartphone, ordinal
(h) smartphone OS (Operating System), categorical

(i) numbers of apps installed, ordinal
(j) the time spent on smartphone daily, ordinal
(k) the importance of personal information stored on smartphone, interval
(l) the sensitivity of personal information, interval
(m) frequency of sharing behaviors, interval
(n) concern levels when lending the phone, interval
(o) the time let others use the phone, ordinal
(p) necessity of using multiple user accounts as the owner, interval.

We listed the following the classes and the scales of measurement that are used for analyzing:

(a) the willingness to use multiple user accounts as the owner, interval
(b) the willingness to use multiple user accounts as the guest, interval
(c) whether taking actions to delete the trace history as the guest, categorical.

The former sixteen items are selected as features, that is, the impacting factors. The last three items are treated as the classes.

5 Results and Discussion

In this work, we construct the decision trees that are built using basic information, smartphone usage, privacy usage and sharing attitudes as features and three sharing decisions as three classes. The decision tree has been built using basic information, smartphone usage, privacy usage and sharing attitudes as features and the first sharing decision as the class, which is a multi-class decision tree. As shown in Fig. 2, with regard to feature ranking, we plot a tree-like structure based on the first four layers of this decision tree and present the Gini index. The X[number] refers to a feature, which has been listed as shown on the right. The features that were selected and ranked by the tree induction had a higher weight, which means these features determined the users' sharing decisions. Figure 2 indicated the features as shown on the right impacted the willingness to use multiple user accounts as the owner, the answer of which were organized with the Likert items based on seven-point scale with anchor points of "1-weak/7-strong".

Figure 3 indicated the features as shown on the right impacted the willingness to use multiple user accounts as the guest, the answer of which were organized with the Likert items based on seven-point scale with anchor points of "1-weak/7-strong".

Figure 4 indicated the features as shown on the right impacted whether users were taking actions to delete the trace history as the guest, the answer of which were organized with four options of "Yes, I tried to go something, like logging out, deleting the number I dialed", "No, I did nothing, because I thought I don't need to take actions", "No, I did nothing, but I thought I need to take actions", and "No, I did nothing because I didn't become aware of privacy issues".

Figure 5 indicated the features as shown on the right impacted the three classes as stated above. Among these features, the following three features were mostly impacting users' sharing decisions:

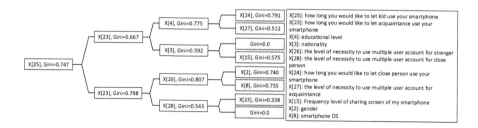

Fig. 2. Part of the tree for the class 1.

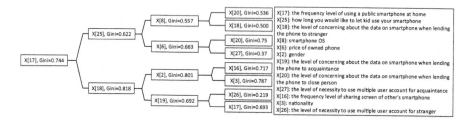

Fig. 3. Part of the tree for the class 2.

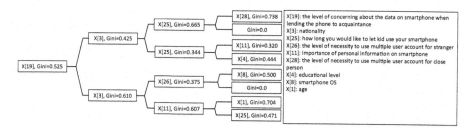

Fig. 4. Part of the tree for the class 3.

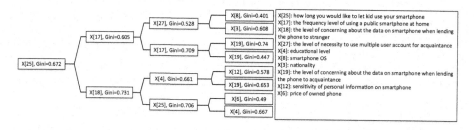

Fig. 5. Part of the tree for all classes.

(a) how long the individual would like to let kid use the smartphone
(b) the frequency level of using a public smartphone at home
(c) the level of concerning about the data on smartphone when lending the phone to stranger.

6 Conclusion

This work investigates and analyzes the influencing factors of smartphone users sharing decisions using the CART algorithm of Decision Tree. The data for analyzing is based on a survey involving 165 participants' responses. The Gini index was used for analyzing and three users' sharing decisions were explored, including: the willingness to use multiple user accounts as the owner, the willingness to use multiple user accounts as the guest, and whether the individual taking actions to delete the trace history as the guest. Results sharing decisions indicated the following features impacted these sharing decisions mostly: "how long the individual would like to let kid use the smartphone", "the frequency level of using a public smartphone at home" and "the level of concerning about the data on smartphone when lending the phone to stranger".

Acknowledgements. This work was supported by the National Natural Science Foundation of China (61702417, 61703259), the Shaanxi Natural Science Foundation (2017JM6097, 2017JQ6077), and the Opening Project of State Key Laboratory for Manufacturing Systems Engineering (sklm s2016001).

Appendix

Basic information

1. Which of the following group best describes your age?
2. What is your gender?
3. Which of the following best describes the highest level of your education?

Smartphone usage

1. Which of the following best describes your budget to buy a smartphone?
2. Which of the following best describes the price of your smartphone?
3. How long have you been using a smartphone generally?
4. Which smart device operating system (OS) are you using?
5. How many apps do you install by yourself on your phone?
6. How much time on average do you spend on using apps (free or paid) and internet on your smart devices per week?

Privacy usage

1. Please rate the importance of personal information on your smartphone.
2. Please rate the sensitivity of personal information on your smartphone.

Sharing attitudes and behaviors

1. Please select which best describes the frequency of your sharing behaviors (lending my smartphone, borrowing other's smartphone, sharing screen of my smartphone, sharing screen of other's smartphone, using a public smartphone at home).

2. Please describe how much you are concerned about your data on your smart phone when you lending your phone to stranger, someone you know but not close (neighbor, coworker, etc.), closed people (like good friend, brother, wife, etc.), kid (kid of yours, friend's, relative's, etc.).
3. Please indicate how long you would like to let the people use your smart phone (stranger, someone you know but not close, closed people, kid).
4. How necessary do you think it's to use multiple user account/guest mode for each person (stranger, someone you know but not close, closed people, kid).

Sharing Decision

1. Please indicate how much for each device you would like to use the one-button function to clear the guests' trace histories (to protect guest's privacy), instead that the guests clear and delete their traces manually.
2. Please indicate how much for each device you would like to use the one-button function to clear your trace histories as the guest to protect your privacy, in case you may forget to log out or delete browser histories.
3. Did you take actions to delete/erase your trace history before you return smartphone?

References

1. Hang, A., Von Zezschwitz, E., De Luca, A., Hussmann, H.: Too much information! User attitudes towards smartphone sharing. In: Nordic Conference on Human-Computer Interaction: Making Sense Through Design, pp. 284–287 (2012)
2. Hayashi, E., Riva, O., Strauss, K., Bernheim Brush, A.J., Schechter, S.: Goldilocks and the two mobile devices: going beyond all-or-nothing access to a device's applications. In: Eighth Symposium on Usable Privacy and Security, p. 2 (2012)
3. Karimi, K., Hamilton, H.J.: Generation and interpretation of temporal decision rules. Int. J. Comput. Inf. Syst. Ind. Manag. Appl. **3**(1), 314–323 (2010)
4. Karlson, A.K., Bernheim Brush, A.J., Schechter, S.: Can i borrow your phone? Understanding concerns when sharing mobile phones. In: SIGCHI Conference on Human Factors in Computing Systems, pp. 1647–1650 (2009)
5. King, J.: How come i'm allowing strangers to go through my phone? Smartphones and privacy expectations. SSRN Electron. J. (2014)
6. Matthews, T., Liao, K., Turner, A., Berkovich, M., Reeder, R., Consolvo, S.: "She'll just grab any device that's closer": a study of everyday device & account sharing in households. In: CHI Conference on Human Factors in Computing Systems, pp. 5921–5932 (2016)
7. Mazurek, M.L., Arsenault, J.P., Bresee, J., Gupta, N., Ion, I., Johns, C., Lee, D., Liang, Y., Olsen, J., Salmon, B.: Access control for home data sharing: attitudes, needs and practices. In: SIGCHI Conference on Human Factors in Computing Systems, pp. 645–654 (2010)
8. Quinlan, J.R.: Simplifying Decision Trees. Academic Press Ltd., London (1987)
9. Smetters, D.K., Good, N.: How users use access control. In: Symposium on Usable Privacy and Security, SOUPS 2009, Mountain View, California, USA, July 2009, pp. 1–12 (2009)

10. Zhou, Y., Piekarska, M., Raake, A., Tao, X., Xiaojun, W., Dong, B.: Control yourself: on user control of privacy settings using personalization and privacy panel on smartphones. Procedia Comput. Sci. **109**, 100–107 (2017)
11. Zhou, Y., Raake, A., Xu, T., Zhang, X.: Users' perceived control, trust and expectation on privacy settings of smartphone. In: Wen, S., Wu, W., Castiglione, A. (eds.) CSS 2017. LNCS, vol. 10581, pp. 427–441. Springer, Cham (2017). https://doi.org/10.1007/978-3-319-69471-9_31
12. Zhou, Y., Xu, T., Raake, A., Cai, Y.: Access control is not enough: how owner and guest set limits to protect privacy when sharing smartphone. In: Stephanidis, C. (ed.) HCI 2016. CCIS, vol. 617, pp. 494–499. Springer, Cham (2016). https://doi.org/10.1007/978-3-319-40548-3_82

A Lifelog Viewer System Supporting Multiple Memory Cues

Jiaming Zhang[(✉)], Jie Liang[(✉)], and Jiro Tanaka[(✉)]

Graduate School of IPS, Waseda University, Fukuoka, Japan
zhangjiaming777@toki.waseda.jp, liangjie@fuji.waseda.jp,
jiro@aoni.waseda.jp

Abstract. Lifelog means using wearable devices to record human's life automatically which can help users recall. More and more lifelog cameras with multiple sensors become available to the public. To view the vast amount of lifelog photos captured by the devices, the manufacturers provide supporting viewer systems. However, current systems only enable users to view the photos in time order by installing the specialized software. Previous research stated that memories can be recalled by memory cues, such as where the event happened, who was involved. In this research, we intend to find out the most important memory cues that help people recall and create a new lifelog viewer system to help users recall past more efficiently without increase the burden on users. To find out which cues appear more in events remembered by people, we conducted several experiments. The proposed new lifelog viewer system can recognize object, location, face and time information in lifelog photos automatically and show photos according to these memory cues information instead of in time order. With the system, users can retrieve photos of past events via these multiple memory cues. We also conducted a preliminary user study to evaluate, the results show the validity of the proposed system.

Keywords: Lifelog · Autographer · Memory recall · Memory cues combination · Computer vision

1 Introduction

The term "lifelogging" appeared in the 1980s. Steve Mann did experiments with a wearable personal imaging system designed and built by himself to capture continuous physiological data [1]. Since then, more and more work has been conducted in this field. Progressive miniaturization by the computer industry has enabled wearable devices to become less obtrusive. In the 2000s, lifelog cameras with multiple sensors entered the market and became available to the public such as SenseCam, Vicon Revue and Autographer [2]. These cameras can be used for memory aids by capturing digital record of wearer's life, including photos and other sensor data. Manufacturers also provide supporting viewer systems for reviewing this information. For example, SenseCam provides a PC-based viewer application that can manage and replay image sequences and sensor data captured by the device [3]. The application allows users play an image

© Springer International Publishing AG, part of Springer Nature 2018
M. Kurosu (Ed.): HCI 2018, LNCS 10902, pp. 638–649, 2018.
https://doi.org/10.1007/978-3-319-91244-8_49

sequence at different speed. Users can delete individual images from the sequence if they are badly framed or of inferior quality. Also, users can create bookmarks with certain images which can be used to navigate the image in a long image sequence. Autographer also provide a desktop software for users to view photos and select photos to share [5]. Each photo is along with a GPS coordinate, and the additional captured metadata, such as ambient light, temperature, etc.

However, these systems only enable users to view the photos in time order. Some previous research state that people usually think of several elements in the event when they recall past moments [7]. For example, who was involved, what they used or saw, when and where the event happened. Time is not the only cue helps people recall. We call these elements that can help people recall as memory cues.

With embedded sensors and GPS unit in lifelog devices, we can get information like the positions where the photos were taken. Moreover, there are many available computer vision services [11, 12] which make it possible to extract useful information from lifelog photos automatically without users' effort. This potential information could be used as memory cues to help users recall past.

In this paper, we propose a new lifelog viewer system to help user recall past more efficiently without increase the burden on users. The system can extract memory cues information automatically by integrating with several services. With the viewer system, users can retrieve related photos of past events via multiple memory cues.

2   Goal and Approach

In this paper, we present a new lifelog viewer system to help users recall past more efficiently. Before designing the system, we should verify whether lifelog can help users recall more events and find out the most important memory cues in helping people recall.

To achieve these goals, we conduct experiments which consist of record part and recall part. Based on the experiment results, we develop the new lifelog viewer system. The system can recognize important memory cues information in lifelog photos automatically and enable users to retrieve related photos of past events via specific memory cues.

2.1   Experiment Setup

Device. We use a wearable lifelog camera called Autographer as our experiment record device. Autographer is a hands-free, wearable device which can take photos automatically every 30 s.

Autographer has 6 built-in sensors, including GPS positioning, accelerator, light sensor, magnetometer, motion detector and thermometer to help determine when to shoot [5]. For example, when the wearer runs through the bus, the camera's accelerator will automatically sense the movement and take a photo or when the wearer goes from a warm bar to the snowy street to greet friends, the camera will also take a photo automatically by sensing the change of temperature. There's an official desktop software of Autographer for users viewing photos in time order.

Experiment Sheet Design. Each sheet represents an event. Participants should write down each event with a brief description and four memory cues including *who*, *what*, *when* and *where*. *Who* means the subjects related to this event, if the participant is the only person in this event, he/she can write "myself". *What* means the specific objects participant interacts with. *When* means the occurred time of the event, which is accurate to hour. *Where* means the specific place where the event happens. At last, participants should write down the memory cues which he/she thinks are most important to help him/her recall this event.

2.2 Procedure

We invited 12 participants (6 males and 6 females) ranging in age from 22 to 28. We gave participants a brief explanation about the experiment and told them how to use Autographer, then let participants wear Autographer to collect their one-day life for continuous 6 h between 9am to 7pm. And participants can switch off the device during their private time.

Experiment 1. The first experiment is the record part. Immediately after 6-h recording, all lifelog photos were imported into the Autographer viewer system. We divided all participants into two groups. Participants in Group 1 wrote down the events they can remember by themselves not using any reference (Type A) at first, and then viewed the lifelog photos in Autographer viewer system to write down some additional events (Type B). Participants in Group 2 viewed lifelog photos with Autographer viewer system directly and wrote down all the events (Type C).

Experiment 2. The second experiment is the recall part. We gathered all participants and asked them to recall events again after a month. The division of group and event types are the same with the first experiment. For example, participants in Group 1 first recalled what happened one month ago by themselves and viewed the previous recorded photos to write down more events.

2.3 Results

We collected 196 (63 (Type A) +34 (Type B) +99 (Type C)) sheets in the first experiment and 158 (27 (Type A) +47 (Type B) +84 (Type C)) sheets in the second experiment. The sum of Type A and B was almost the same with the number of Type C, which means that independent thinking before using lifelog doesn't make sense. The total average number of recalled events decreased because some memories of what happened one month ago were missing. The events recalled by independent thinking decreased a lot (Type A), from 10.5 to 4.5. However, participants could recall more events with the help of lifelog (Type B and Type C), the total average amount only dropped from 16.5 to 14 (see Fig. 1). It indicated that lifelog is indeed useful in helping people recall past.

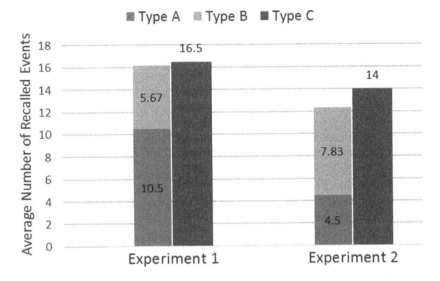

Fig. 1. Comparison of the average number of recalled events between experiment 1 and experiment 2.

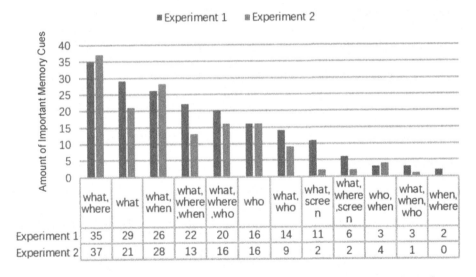

	what, where	what	what, when	what, where ,when	what, where ,who	who	what, who	what, scree n	what, where ,scree n	who, when	what, when, who	when, where
Experiment 1	35	29	26	22	20	16	14	11	6	3	3	2
Experiment 2	37	21	28	13	16	16	9	2	2	4	1	0

Fig. 2. Comparison of memory cues result between experiment 1 and experiment 2.

We also counted the important memory cues written by participants. Unexpectedly, *when* and *who* were not as important as we imagined. Instead, *what* was the most important as a single cue, followed by *who*. The result showed that participants preferred to write down multiple memory cues. And despite the results slightly changed, the rankings had no significant difference between these two experiments: the combination of *what* and *where* ranked first. Although it turned out that *when* was almost useless as a single cue, but it could be useful when combined with other memory cues, such as *what* and *when* (see Fig. 2).

In summary, we can say that current viewer systems only enable users to view lifelog photos in time order are not good enough in helping users recall.

3 Lifelog Viewer System

We propose a web-based lifelog viewer system that can extract object, location, face and time information from lifelog photos automatically by integrating with Microsoft cognitive services [12, 13] and Google Maps API [14]. These kinds of information are corresponding to the important memory cues we found through our experiments, including *what*, *where*, *who* and *when*. Our proposed system enables users to retrieve photos of events via these multiple memory cues, instead of only viewing photos in time order, which helps users recall past events more efficiently.

3.1 Scenarios

The user met one of his/her friends and wanted to recall what happened with this friend in the past. He/she could view the photos he imported to our system and double click the avatar image of this friend to view the related photos contains the face of this friend. Or the user remembered he/she went to a convenient store but forgot what he/she bought. He/she could double click the location image of the store to view the related photos.

Another suitable scenario is, the user remembered he/she read some books at a bookstore, but he/she forgot what the title of a book was and wanted to recall the scene. He/she could click cue images of book and the bookstore to query related photos. Then the system would show the result photos captured at the bookstore, which contain books after user clicked the query button.

3.2 System Design

The system mainly provides users the following four functions to enable users to import lifelog photos captured by Autographer, view the photos in categories of memory cues that we found important through the experiments and retrieve photos via cues to recall past events.

The lifelog photos import function, which requires user to import photos captured by Autographer to the system.

The memory cues extraction function, which will automatically recognize the memory cues information in lifelog photos, including object, location, face, and time. Then the system will show the cue images in these four categories (see Fig. 3).

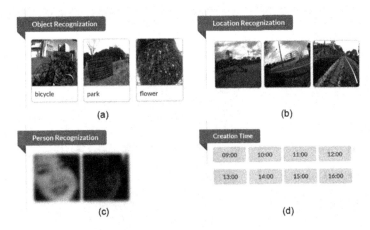

Fig. 3. Cue images in four categories. Object (a), Location (b), Person (c), Time (d).

The view photos via single memory cue function, which enables user to view related photos with one specific cue by double clicking the cue image. Because the results of experiments indicated *when* is useless as a single cue, so time cannot be used independently.

The view photos via cues combination function, which enables user to retrieve photos via multiple memory cues. If there are no photos satisfied the query, the system will send a feedback and inform user to choose another cue.

Process of Recalling Events with Proposed System. User needs to plug the Autographer into his/her computer and select lifelog photos to import to the system by accessing the website of the system at first (see Fig. 4). After system extract memory cues information, user can view and retrieve photos via cues.

Fig. 4. Import lifelog photos.

View Photos via Single Cue. User double clicks the object cue image. The retrieved photo sequence is organized in time order. Each photo retrieved is tagged with the date it was taken and the location. User can view these photos by clicking next or previous button (see Fig. 5).

Fig. 5. View photos sequence retrieved by single memory cue.

View Photos via Multiple Cues. User can click cue image to select it as a query cue, all the chosen ones will be shown on the right of the page, user also can deselect a query cue by clicking it. After determining the cues to be selected, user can click the query button to view related photos (see Fig. 6).

Fig. 6. View photos sequence retrieved via multiple cues.

3.3 Implementation

The system is implemented based on Browser/Server pattern and mainly uses the combination of the Spring Boot [13] and the Hibernate [11]. The system design follows the principles of the MVC. View is responsible for rendering output results in webpages, which are coded using HTML, CSS and JavaScript. Controller is for handling requests, which is coded in Java. Model is responsible for managing the data [10]. We make use of a MySQL database to store data. The database mainly contains picture, avatar, object, location entities, which are used to store photos in byte arrays and related memory cues information.

User uses our system by accessing the website via browser, each manipulation will send a request to our server, the request will achieve to the Spring Dispatcher Servlet and the Spring Boot will dispatch the request to related services. There are four services in our system, including object service, location service, avatar service and time service, which are integrated with the services from Microsoft and Google to handle the object, location, face and time information in photos. The integrated services include Computer Vision API, Face Recognize API, and Google Maps API. The services will connect with database and deal with data via Hibernate Framework and return the retrieved data to the browser. A MySQL database is used to store the data of memory cues information extracted from the photos (see Fig. 7).

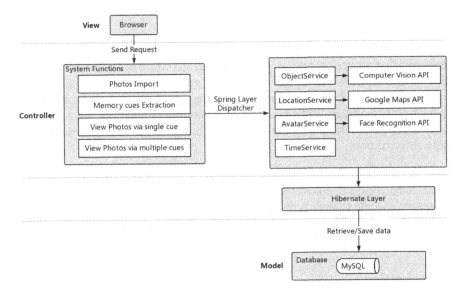

Fig. 7. System architecture.

Object Service. This service handles all requests related to objects, including recognize objects from photos, store object information into database, show object cue images and query photos via objects.

Microsoft Computer Vision API [12] is used to recognize objects in photos. This API can return a list of object tags by uploading the image bytes of the photo and sending the request to http://westus.api.cognitive.microsoft.com/vision/1.0/analyze, each object in the returned list has its name and confidence. The system will only store objects with confidence over 0.8. This threshold of confidence is set to filter unreliable results.

Location Service. This service is responsible for all requests related to location, including extract location information from photos, store location information into database, show location cue image and query photos via location.

Google Maps API [14] is used to deal with the location information in photos. The system uses this API as a dependency with Maven. For each photo, the system will load latitude and longitude from image bytes and get address information by calling the function GeocodingApi.reverseGeocode().

Avatar Service. This service handles all requests related to face, including recognize faces from photos, store face avatar into database, show avatar cue images and query photos via the face of person. Microsoft Face API [13] is used to detect faces in photos.

To detect faces and store the avatar for each person's face, the system will create a face list with a specified ID at first to store the faces recognized from photos by sending request to http://westus.api.cognitive.microsoft.com/face/v1.0/facelists. Then, the system will process each imported photo to detect faces by uploading the image bytes of the photo and sending request to https://westus.api.cognitive.microsoft.com/face/v1.0/detect. Each detected face has a unique ID and the rectangle area of the face in the photo.

The detected faces will be added into the face list the system maintains by sending request to http://westus.api.cognitive.microsoft.com/face/v1.0/facelists/persistedfaces. The required parameters contain the ID of the face list which is created before and the rectangle area of the face in the lifelog photo. Then the system will find similar faces with the new detected face in the face list by sending request to https://westus.api.cognitive.microsoft.com/face/v1.0/findsimilars. If the returned similarity confidence is over 0.6, the face will be considered as a new, unique face. An avatar will be created for each unique detected face.

Time Service. This service handles request related to time information, including extract capture time of photos and query photos via time. Photos captured by Autographer have a specific naming format, the system extract the time information from the filename of photos and store it in a specific format. The hour of the captured time is also stored in units of half an hour.

4   Evaluation

We conducted a preliminary user study to verify whether our proposed system is more efficient to help users recall than current viewer system.

Procedure. We invited 4 participants (1 males and 3 females) ranging in age from 22 to 25. All participants were asked to capture photos with Autographer for 3 h. After 3 days, we gathered all participants and divided them into two groups. Participants were asked to import photos to the lifelog viewer system. Specifically, participants in Group 1 used Autographer viewer system, and participants in Group 2 used our proposed system. Then we let participants finish several tasks (see Table 1).

Table 1. Tasks description

Task	Description
1	Given a single cue, like *what*, retrieve related photos and recall the event
2	Given multiple cues, like *what* and *where*, retrieve related photos and recall the event
3	Recall all events as much as possible

Results. We collected a total of 1535 lifelog photos from 4 participants, average photos for per participant is 383.7.

Task 1 is used to investigate whether using single memory cue like *what*, *where* or *who* to retrieve photos is more efficient than viewing photos in time order. Task 2 is used to investigate whether using multiple memory cues like *what* and *where*, or *who* and *where* to retrieve photos is more efficient than viewing photos in time order. Participants in Group 1 took 12.5 s for completing Task 1 and 21.5 s for Task2 on average. Participants in Group 2 took 7.5 s for completing Task 1 and 9 s for Task2 on average. The results show that users can retrieve photos of past events in a shorter time with our proposed system. In particularly, when given multiple memory cues, using our proposed system is much more efficient (see Fig. 8).

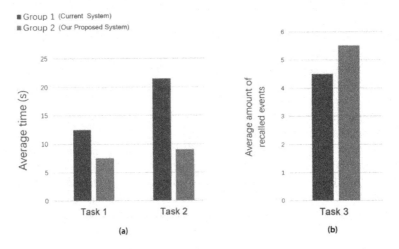

Fig. 8. Tasks results. Comparison of average time of completing Task 1 and Task 2 (a). Comparison of average amount of recalled events in Task 3 (b).

Task 3 is used to verify whether our system can help users recall. The average amount of recalled events of participants in Group 1 is 4.5 and participants in Group 2 recalled 5.5 events on average. The result shows that our proposed system can help users recall past events as current Autographer system does (see Fig. 8).

5   Related Work

5.1   Memory Cue

Episodic memory [6] enables individuals to remember their personally experienced past. This kind of memory can be recalled by memory cues. Wagenaar spent 6 years on his study of his autobiographical memory from 1978 [7]. He recorded all events by means of four aspects, what the event was, who was involved, and where and when it happened. In the recall phase he cued himself with one or more of these four aspects to recall the other aspects. He found *what* as a single cue was very powerful, and *when* was almost useless. He also stated combination of cues was more effective than single cues.

5.2   Lifelog System

With lifelogging technology, we can capture everything we experienced. Sellen et al. found evidence that SenseCam images do facilitate people's ability to recollect past events [4]. With the vast number of lifelog photos, how to extract valid information and retrieve events more conveniently are nowadays researchers focusing on.

Memon developed a prototype system using an Android smart phone that can recognize the present situation and search for relevant past episodes [9]. In his research, there are three key elements: people in sight, objects of interaction and present location. With the system, lifelog related to current location or the specific location which users defined can be accessed directly. Likewise, lifelogs can be retrieved based on people and objects currently present near the user.

Matsuoka designed a system by linking lifelog photos with tags [8]. In her system, users need to manually select photos and edit tags of cues information one by one at first. Users can enter keywords to retrieve events and the system will show related photos and suggest related tags as feedback. This series of operations increase the burden on the users and not friendly enough.

Comparing with above mentioned systems, our work has several advantages. First, our system can automatically recognize object, location and face information from lifelog photos by integrating with services like Microsoft Computer Vision API and Google Maps API, which relieves users' burden. While Matsuoka's system requires users to manually select photos and enter tag information. Second, we make use of Autographer, which can capture photos automatically and unobtrusively. The prototype device in Memon's system requires users to capture manually and needs several other alternatives, like RFID sensors for individuals' identification.

6   Conclusion and Future Work

In this paper, we present a new lifelog viewer system for helping users recall past events more efficiently. By integrating with services like Computer Vision API and Google Maps API, the system can extract object, location, face and time information automatically. These kinds of information are corresponding to the important memory cues we found through the experiments, including *what*, *where*, *who* and *when*. Users can retrieve photos via multiple cues to recollect the past events. The results of the preliminary user study indicate that user can retrieve lifelog photos and recall past events more efficiently with our proposed system.

In the future work, we will improve the system further. For example, the processing time of the vast amounts of photos is a problem, which affects the user experience. And Matsuoka [8] stated that *screen* could be a potential memory cue because people spend considerable time on computing devices. *Screen* means the display of computing devices users interact with. Our system may support *screen* cue by collecting computer and smartphone usage data of users in the future studies.

References

1. Mann, S.: Wearable computing: a first step toward personal imaging. Computer **30**(2), 25–32 (1997)
2. Zhou, L.M., Gurrin, C.: A survey on life logging data capturing. In: SenseCam Symposium (2012)
3. Hodges, S., et al.: SenseCam: a retrospective memory aid. In: Dourish, P., Friday, A. (eds.) UbiComp 2006. LNCS, vol. 4206, pp. 177–193. Springer, Heidelberg (2006). https://doi.org/10.1007/11853565_11
4. Sellen, A., Fogg, A., Aitken, M., Hodges, S., Rother, C., Wood, K.: Do life-logging technologies support memory for the past? An experimental study using SenseCam. In: CHI 2007 Proceedings of the SIGCHI Conference on Human Factors in Computing Systems, pp. 81–90. ACM, California (2007)
5. Thoring, K.C., Mueller, R. M., Badke-Schaub, P.: Ethnographic design research with wearable cameras. In: CHI EA 2015 Proceedings of the 33rd Annual ACM Conference Extended Abstracts on Human Factors in Computing Systems, pp. 2049–2054. ACM (2015)
6. Tulving, E., Donaldson, W.: Organization of Memory. Academic Press, New York (1972)
7. Wagenaar, W.A.: My memory: a study of autobiographical memory over six years. Cogn. Psychol. **18**, 225–252 (1986)
8. Matsuoka, R.: Understanding how cues in lifelog affect memory recalls. University of Tsukuba (2016)
9. Memon, M., Mahoto, N., Khuhawar, F., Tanaka, J.: Retrieval of life logs based on users context. Sindh Univ. Res. J. (Sci. Ser.) **47**(4), 851–860 (2015)
10. Gupta, P., Govil, M.C.: Spring Web MVC Framework for rapid open source J2EE application development: a case study. Int. J. Eng. Sci. Technol. **2**, 1684–1689 (2010)
11. Xia, C.-L., Yu, G.-C., Tang, M.: Efficient implement of ORM (Object/Relational Mapping) use in J2EE framework: hibernate. In: International Conference on Computational Intelligence and Software Engineering, pp. 1–3 (2009)
12. Cognitive services Computer Vision API reference. https://azure.microsoft.com/en-gb/services/cognitive-services/computer-vision/. Accessed 26 Jan 2018
13. Cognitive services Face API reference. https://azure.microsoft.com/en-gb/services/cogntive-services/face/. Accessed 26 Jan 2018
14. Google Maps API reference. https://developers.google.com/maps/. Accessed 26 Jan 2018

Defining a Model for Development of Tactile Interfaces on Smartphones

Fan Zhang, Shaowei Chu[✉], Naye Ji, and Ruifang Pan

Zhejiang University of Media and Communications, Hangzhou, China
chu@zjicm.edu.cn

Abstract. Tactile interaction on smartphones is becoming increasingly important in assistive technologies and special purpose applications. Although various tactile techniques exist, the development of effective and user-friendly tactile applications lacks design guidance. This work describes a distinct model that guides designers and developers in developing tactile interfaces on smartphones. The model has three distinct parts, namely, quantifying tactile stimuli, clustering, and tactile application experiment. We review existing techniques for processing each part and discuss their advantages and disadvantages. And we implement a tactile application on a TPad (Tactile Pattern display) phone on the basis of the design procedure of the model to demonstrate its usage. Results show that the workflow of the model can guide developers in implementing efficient tactile applications.

Keywords: Tactile interface · Design model
Empirical studies in interaction design · Usability · Tactile reading

1 Introduction

Developing effective tactile interfaces for mobile devices is challenging not because of the complexity of development and usability evaluation but because of the lack of guidelines with distinct design models for developers, such as the development of graphical user interface (GUI) and window/icon/menu/pointer (WIMP) interfaces.

The present development procedure of tactile interfaces is as follows: designing the prototype, which significantly depends on experiences; implementing the prototype; and inviting participants to use the prototype and evaluate its usability [1–3]. Though this method can result in a distinct usability result of the designed tactile interface, no existing guideline requires developers to follow up in the next development stage of new tactile interfaces in other fields with partially or completely identical usability results.

In this work, we aim to define a distinct model for use in developing tactile interfaces, specifically for mobile devices (i.e., smartphones), with available vibrotactile or frictional surface feedback. We summarize and review the exact procedure of designing and implementing a tactile interface. In each design step, we provide multiple choices for developers along with detailed advantages and disadvantages of methods and discuss the appropriate techniques that must be adopted in different contexts.

© Springer International Publishing AG, part of Springer Nature 2018
M. Kurosu (Ed.): HCI 2018, LNCS 10902, pp. 650–658, 2018.
https://doi.org/10.1007/978-3-319-91244-8_50

Finally, we develop a tactile number reading system that uses the designed procedure model to demonstrate the usage of the model.

2 Related Works

Previous works [4–6] introduced the working ISO (International Organization for Standardization) TC159/SC4 (WG9 Tactile and Haptic Interactions) standards for haptic and tactile hardware and software interactions, including standards related to the design and evaluation of hardware and software. These standards summarize the physical attributes of haptic devices, including force, shape, size, friction, texture, mass, hardness, temperature, orientation, location, vibration, duration, motion, and deformation. The ISO 9241-920 working draft also provides application development guidance, including applicability consideration, tactile/haptic inputs/outputs, attributes of encoding information, content-specific encoding, layout of tactile/haptic objects, and interaction. Although these standards cover all the aspects of haptic development, they are still under development, and their implementation is not yet scheduled.

Previous works [1, 7–9] by the same authors developed a usability evaluation framework for haptic systems. The researchers defined the evaluation in three stages: literature review and structured interview, card sorting to shortlist the usability sub-factors, and identification of relevant measures. The authors presented various factors used to measure the usability of haptic systems. Usefulness, efficiency, effectiveness, satisfaction, user preference, acceptability, and learnability were listed for discussion. These factors may be suitable for evaluating the usability of different haptic devices, such as Phantom, Haptic Master, Falcon Haptic, Force Dimension Omega, and Barrett Hand. Similarly, previous work [2] proposed a standard in three aspects for evaluating tactile/haptic system: validation of system requirements, the verification that system meets the requirements, and the usability of the system.

The focus of the current work is on vibration or programmable friction techniques for smartphones, which are available for practical use. Therefore, we not only need to enhance the usability evaluation factors and find the appropriate factors for tactile interfaces on smartphones, but also need to define workflow of the model that can guide developers in implementing efficient tactile applications.

3 Model

The tactile interface design model has three distinct parts.

- Quantification. Providing tactile stimuli a magnitude with quantified values in a user experiment
- Clustering. Classifying different tactile stimuli into various groups using the obtained quantified values
- Application experiment. Applying the design using the clustered group stimuli to map different tactile information or codes and conducting a user experiment to evaluate the usability of the application.

The design model is shown in Fig. 1.

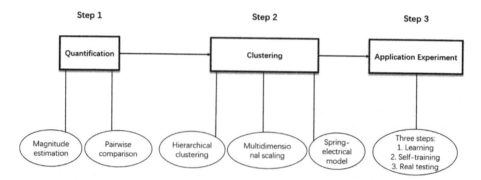

Fig. 1. Model for development of tactile interfaces.

3.1 Quantification

The first step in the model involves quantifying various tactile stimuli into values in the user experiment. Two classical methods can be used for quantification.

- Magnitude estimation. Users estimate the strength of individual stimuli by assigning them numbers [10, 11]. The novelty of this method lies in its capability to provide stimuli with a distinct subjective value, which can be used to cluster many stimuli into groups.
- Pairwise comparison. This method divides candidate stimuli into different pairs, thereby allowing users to discriminate their differences. The test trails are generally substantially large because this method must compare every single stimulus with all other stimuli. The typical examples of this method are spatial period [12] and affective subjective evaluation [13].

3.2 Clustering

After the tactile stimuli are quantified, they are clustered into groups to allow users to discriminate them as different stimuli. Many clustering algorithms can be used, such as hierarchical clustering, multidimensional scaling, and spring-electrical. Hierarchical clustering is recommended for clustering ordinal data, such as data obtained from magnitude estimation [14]. Multidimensional scaling is appropriate for measuring dissimilarity to derive a perceptual space [15]. The spring-electrical method works well for sparse incidence matrices [16].

3.3 Application Experiment

In the last step, the clustered groups of tactile stimuli are adopted to design tactile codes and enhance feedback with GUI or tactile notification applications. After the application is implemented, the final usability of the design must be evaluated in user experiments.

A typical procedure can generally be followed in tactile interface evaluation [16, 17]. First, the tactile interface is introduced to the users, who are then allowed to learn how to use the interface. Second, users are allowed to self-train with the design test trials. Third, an actual test session is conducted to assess the usability of the interface in terms of effectiveness, efficiency, and subjective evaluation [2].

- Effectiveness is measured using two factors: the capability to perform the task and the number of errors.
- Efficiency is the number of seconds consumed by participants to complete the task.
- Subjective satisfaction is measured through the answers to a questionnaire, which covers efficiency, ease of use, and preferences.

4   Model Usage Example

We implemented a tactile application on a TPad (Tactile Pattern display [18]) phone to demonstrate the usage of the model. The application is an eyes-free tactile number reading system. To implement the application, we followed the procedure of the proposed model.

The application adopts tactile patterns to convey number information. The design must first select a group of appropriate tactile stimuli that can easily be discriminated and then assign specific meanings to these stimuli. Finally, after the application was developed, the user experiment was conducted to evaluate the design. The tactile application development usually met the procedure of the proposed model.

4.1   Quantification

First, we must find several tactile stimuli for conveying code interface. These stimuli must be easily discriminated and memorized. As described in the model, two methods can be utilized for such task: magnitude estimation and pairwise comparison methods. Our previous work [14] applied the pairwise comparison method, which resulted in considerably large test trails. Thus, in this simple example, we adopted the AME (Abstract Magnitude Estimation) method to quantify the stimuli.

Twelve undergraduate students (six male, six female) were recruited from the university to participate in the experiment. The mean age of the participants was 21.1 years (SD = 1.52; range 20–23).

Experiment Procedure: Participants were asked to sit and use their right index fingers to perform the experiment task. On the testing application interface (left side of Fig. 2), the bottom-left area displayed the 40-40 pattern, and the bottom-right area displayed the 1-1 pattern as the reference. The main area of the screen displayed the random patterns for testing. The pattern graphic was not shown during the experiment to avoid providing any visual cue that would affect the perception of patterns. In each test task, the user perceived the pattern and reported his/her estimation magnitude of the roughness strength to the experimenter for recording.

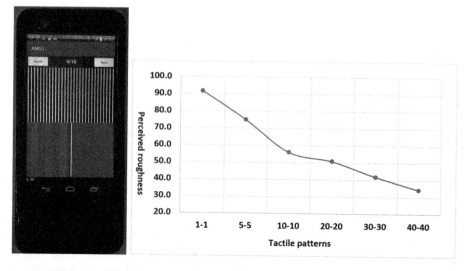

Fig. 2. Left: TPad phone with AME test application. Right: Experiment result.

Result: The roughness of the strengths of the patterns is shown in Fig. 2(right). The roughness strengths decreased as the stripe width value increased. We obtained each stimulus strength from the AME experiment, where 1-1:91, 5-5:75, 10-10:56, 20-20:51, 30-30:42, 40-40:34.

4.2   Clustering

The subjectively quantified data from the experiment must then be clustered to convey different code information. Hierarchical clustering was used to cluster the obtained data because it is recommended for clustering ordinal data. Table 1 shows the various clustering results, which can be used in further studying the distinguishability of different patterns and the conveyed code information.

Table 1.   Classification of six tactile patterns into various clusters.

2 Clusters	3 Clusters	4 Clusters
1-1	1-1	1-1
Others	5-5	5-5
	Others	10-10, 20-20
		Others

4.3   Application Experiment

As shown in Table 1, pattern 1-1 was the most distinguishable and isolated in all the clusters. In the pilot study, if we presented three or more patterns to users, then they felt difficult in remembering and identifying exact patterns. Thus, we adopted only adopt two patterns, 1-1 and 40-40, to design a tactile interface and thus improve the reliability of the tactile code perception application.

The implemented application is a tactile number reading system. The interaction scheme for tactile code perception was designed as follows:

- Touch and slide the finger to left/right to sense the first tactile pattern presented on the device and count the sliding gesture as the number 1 action.
- Then, move the finger to the opposite direction to sense whether a tactile pattern is still presented on the device while sliding. If a texture is presented, then count the sliding gesture as the number 2 action.
- The left/right sliding must be continued until no tactile pattern is presented on the device. When sliding in a direction without a tactile pattern presented, the perception of a tactile code is completed. The number of sliding gestures performed with tactile texture presented is the perceived tactile code.

One example of perception procedure of Code 2 is shown in Fig. 3. On the basis of the preceding interaction paradigm and by additionally combining two tactile texture patterns (dense pattern 1-1 as D and sparse pattern 40-40 as S), numerous tactile codes could be implemented. In the present study, we adopted 10 tactile codes: D1, D2, D3, D4, D5, S1, S2, S3, S4, and S5.

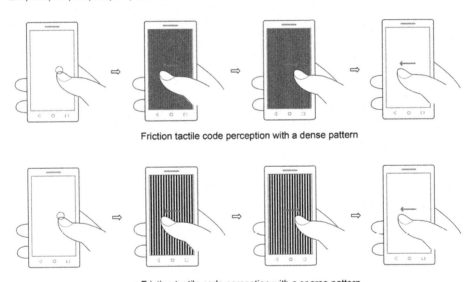

Friction tactile code perception with a dense pattern

Friction tactile code perception with a sparse pattern

Fig. 3. Tactile code perception procedure with two types of friction patterns: (a) dense pattern, (b) sparse pattern.

On the basis of the preceding system, we then conducted a user experiment with 12 university student participants to evaluate the tactile code perception. The mean age of the participants was 20.6 (SD = 1.1).

Experiment Procedure: As described in the application experiment model, the evaluation experiment comprised three steps: learning, self-training, and actual testing. Therefore, in the experiment, we first introduced the tactile number reading interface to the users and allowed them to learn how to use such interface. Second, we allowed users to self-train with the designed test trials. Third, we conducted the actual test session to assess the usability of the interface.

The tasks of the experiment were designed such that the participants were asked to perceive the tactile code on the TPad by using sliding gestures and report it to the experimenter. Each participant went through 30 random tactile codes and filled out a questionnaire after the test. The overall experiment last about 30 min, and each participant was paid 50 yuan for participating in the experiment.

Results: The usability evaluation was measured in three aspects: effectiveness, efficiency, and satisfaction.

– Effectiveness: all the participants completed the tasks (100% completeness), and the errors that participants reported were 9.72% (SD = 6.22).
– Efficiency: the times for each tactile code perception are shown in Table 2.

Table 2. Mean (and SD) of times (seconds) for perception of tactile codes.

D1	D2	D3	D4	D5	Sum
0.873 (0.403)	1.723 (0.572)	2.388 (0.646)	3.226 (0.894)	4.434 (1024)	12.644 (1.227)
S1	S2	S3	S4	S5	Sum
0.885 (0.344)	1.959 (0.726)	2.661 (0.758)	3.651 (1.057)	4.545 (1.045)	13.701 (1.276)

– The subjective satisfaction: user satisfaction of the system is shown in Fig. 4.

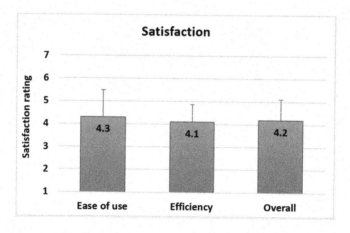

Fig. 4. Subjective satisfaction of system.

5   Conclusion

The model is described and defined by summarizing and reviewing the exact procedure of tactile interface. Three distinct parts compose the model: quantifying tactile stimuli, clustering, and tactile application experiment. An example of designing a tactile code reading application is provided to demonstrate the usage of the model. Results show that the workflow of the model can guide developers in designing tactile interfaces efficiently. In the future, additional techniques will be reviewed and integrated into each model part to make it suitable for many types of tactile application development.

Acknowledgments. This research was supported by National Natural Science Foundation of China (NSFC) (No. 61502415) and Public Projects of Zhejiang Province (No. 2016C31 G2240012).

References

1. Khan, M., Sulaiman, S., Said, A.M., Tahir, M.: Empirical validation of usability evaluation framework for haptic systems. In: 2012 International Conference on Computer and Information Science (ICCIS), pp. 1058–1061 (2012). http://dx.doi.org/10.1109/ISVRI. 2011.5759670
2. Sinclair, I., Carter, J., Kassner, S., Van Erp, J., Weber, G., Elliott, L., Andrew, I.: Towards a standard on evaluation of tactile/haptic interactions. In: International Conference on Human Haptic Sensing and Touch Enabled Computer Applications, pp. 528–539 (2012)
3. Grussenmeyer, W., Folmer, E.: Accessible touchscreen technology for people with visual impairments: a survey. ACM Trans. Accessible Comput. **9**(2), 1–31 (2017). http://dx.doi.org/ 10.1145/3022701
4. van Erp, J.B., Carter, J., Andrew, I.: ISO's work on tactile and haptic interaction guidelines. In: Proceedings of Eurohaptics, pp. 467–470 (2006)
5. van Erp, J.B.F., Kern, T.A.: ISO's work on guidance for haptic and tactile interactions. In: Ferre, M. (ed.) EuroHaptics 2008. LNCS, vol. 5024, pp. 936–940. Springer, Heidelberg (2008). https://doi.org/10.1007/978-3-540-69057-3_118
6. van Erp, J.B.F., Kyung, K.-U., Kassner, S., Carter, J., Brewster, S., Weber, G., Andrew, I.: Setting the standards for haptic and tactile interactions: ISO's work. In: Kappers, A.M.L., van Erp, J.B.F., Bergmann Tiest, W.M., van der Helm, F.C.T. (eds.) EuroHaptics 2010. LNCS, vol. 6192, pp. 353–358. Springer, Heidelberg (2010). https://doi.org/ 10.1007/978-3-642-14075-4_52
7. Khan, M., Sulaiman, S., Said, A.M., Tahir, M.: Classification of usability issues for haptic systems. In: 2011 7th International Conference on Emerging Technologies, pp. 1–4 (2011). http://dx.doi.org/10.1109/ICET.2011.6048455
8. Khan, M., Sulaiman, S., Said, A.M., Tahir, M.: Usability studies in haptic systems. In: 2011 International Conference on Information and Communication Technologies, pp. 1–5 (2011). http://dx.doi.org/10.1109/ICICT.2011.5983569
9. Khan, M., Sulaiman, S., Said, A.M., Tahir, M.: Research approach to develop usability evaluation framework for haptic systems. In: 2011 National Postgraduate Conference, pp. 1–4 (2011). http://dx.doi.org/10.1109/NatPC.2011.6136325
10. Lederman, S.J.: Tactile roughness of grooved surfaces: the touching process and effects of macro- and microsurface structure. Atten. Percept. Psychophys. **16**(2), 385–395 (1974)

11. Strohmeier, P., Hornbak, K.: Generating haptic textures with a vibrotactile actuator. In: Proceedings of the 2017 CHI Conference on Human Factors in Computing Systems, pp. 4994–5005 (2017). http://dx.doi.org/10.1145/3025453.3025812

12. Biet, M., Casiez, G., Giraud, F., Lemaire-Semail, B.: Discrimination of virtual square gratings by dynamic touch on friction based tactile displays. In: 2008 Symposium on Haptic Interfaces for Virtual Environment and Teleoperator Systems, pp. 41–48 (2008). http://dx.doi.org/10.1109/HAPTICS.2008.4479912

13. Salminen, K., Surakka, V., Lylykangas, J., Raisamo, J., Saarinen, R., Raisamo, R., Rantala, J., Evreinov, G.: Emotional and behavioral responses to haptic stimulation. In: Proceedings of the SIGCHI Conference on Human Factors in Computing Systems, pp. 1555–1562 (2008). http://dx.doi.org/10.1145/1357054.1357298

14. Chu, S., Zhang, F., Ji, N., Zhang, F., Pan, R.: Experimental evaluation of tactile patterns over frictional surface on mobile phones. In: Proceedings of the Fifth International Symposium of Chinese CHI, pp. 47–52 (2017). http://dx.doi.org/10.1145/3080631.3080639

15. Lee, J., Han, J., Lee, G.: Investigating the information transfer efficiency of a 3 × 3 watch-back tactile display. In: Proceedings of the 33rd Annual ACM Conference on Human Factors in Computing Systems, pp. 1229–1232 (2015). http://dx.doi.org/10.1145/2702123.2702530

16. Prasad, M., Russell, M., Hammond, T.A.: Designing vibrotactile codes to communicate verb phrases. ACM Trans. Multimedia Comput. Commun. Appl. 11(1s), 1–21 (2014). http://dx.doi.org/10.1145/2637289

17. María Galdón, P., Ignacio Madrid, R., De La Rubia-Cuestas, E.J., Diaz-Estrella, A., Gonzalez, L.: Enhancing mobile phones for people with visual impairments through haptic icons: the effect of learning processes. Assistive Technol. 25(2), 80–87 (2013). http://dx.doi.org/10.1080/10400435.2012.715112

18. Mullenbach, J., Shultz, C., Colgate, J.E., Piper, A.M.: Exploring affective communication through variable-friction surface haptics. In: Proceedings of the SIGCHI Conference on Human Factors in Computing Systems, pp. 3963–3972 (2014). http://dx.doi.org/10.1145/2556288.2557343

Author Index

Printed in the United States
By Bookmasters